SHAKESPEARE'S WORLD

GARLAND REFERENCE LIBRARY
OF THE HUMANITIES
(VOL. 83)

SHAKESPEARE'S WORLD
Renaissance Intellectual Contexts
A Selective, Annotated Guide, 1966–1971

W. R. Elton
with the assistance of Giselle Schlesinger

GARLAND PUBLISHING, INC. • NEW YORK & LONDON
1979

Library of Congress Cataloging in Publication Data

Elton, William R   1921–
  Shakespeare's world.

  (Garland reference library of the humanities ; v. 83)
  Includes index.
  1. Shakespeare, William, 1564–1616—Bibliography.
2. Shakespeare, William, 1564–1616—Contemporary Europe
—Bibliography.   3. Renaissance—Bibliography.
4. Great Britain—Civilization—16th century—
Bibliography.   5. Great Britain—Civilization—17th
century—Bibliography.   I. Schlesinger, Giselle, joint
author.   II. Title.
Z8813.E38   [PR2910]   016.94105'5   76-52681
ISBN 0-8240-9890-0

Printed on acid-free, 250-year-life paper
Manufactured in the United States of America

for Paul Oskar Kristeller
and Harry Levin
maestri di color che sanno

CONTENTS

PREFACE

This is, uniquely, a *non*-literary bibliography for Shakespeareans—as well as a selective compilation for Renaissance
students generally. Examining Shakespeare's world of ideas, it
provides a conspectus of those Renaissance forms through
which his theatrical intelligence expressed itself. In a field of
self-duplicating *literary* bibliographies—unconcerned to dis-
courage the notion of Shakespeare as a *virtuoso in vacuo*—its
purpose is to reemphasize contextual significances in Shakespearean interpretation.

Secondly, it aims to make a necessary clearing within the
thickening *selva oscura* of scholarly publications. It does this by
selecting out of the over 40,000 items for the years covered,
1966–1971 (cf. the unselective and unannotated annual *Bibliographie internationale de l'Humanisme et de la Renaissance)*, fewer
than one-tenth that number. In addition to classifying these
items, it cites reviews and provides annotations. Further, it includes dissertations as well as books and articles. Of special utility
is the dictionary listing (in over 100 pages) of themes, *topoi*,
emblems, and related *Stoffgeschichte*. Following this is a list of
research tools useful to Renaissance scholars.

Thirdly, although selection is made within a broad range of
possible Shakespearean concern, the list encourages interdisci-
plinary uses by Renaissance specialists in those other fields by
which it is classified. Since these encompass almost every major
area of Renaissance interest, the compilation forms a multi-
disciplinary research aid for students of the Renaissance.

In scope, the compilation for the most part favors works and
journals not usually considered by Shakespeareans. With some
exceptions, it excludes editions, reprints, revisions, and translations. While American dissertations are listed with universities

according to date of abstract-publication, rather than date of completion, foreign theses are cited with date of completion, along with directors. References that fall into more than one class may be found in alternative categories, e.g., political or historical. Where possible, thematic materials are placed under alphabetical headings in the penultimate section. Abbreviations follow, to a large extent, those listed in the *MLA International Bibliography*, while some have been expanded for clarity.

At the publisher's suggestion, this list, which originally appeared in numbers of *Shakespearean Research and Opportunities*, is issued, revised and enlarged, in book form. Since this is a selective compilation, omissions, owing to space restrictions and personal judgment, will inevitably be noted. In a few cases, items inadvertently omitted from the original numbered list are appended at the end of the appropriate sections. In contrast to the present instance, such compilations are usually the product of international scholarly committees. An illustrious predecessor, covering but one year (1931; volume II covers 1932–33), is the Warburg Library's *Kulturwissenschaftliche Bibliographie zum Nachleben der Antike* (1934, 1938; repr. 1968), which lists over fifty collaborators; the current annual *Bibliographie internationale de l'Humanisme et de la Renaissance* is produced by committees in over twenty countries. It is hoped that the present, relatively individual effort will encourage further improved and collaborative compilations; a selective bibliography for the decade would be desirable.

The compiler is indebted to Ralph Carlson, who proposed the book's publication, and who patiently encouraged its completion; to the staff of Garland Publishing, particularly Barbara Bergeron; to Provost Hans J. Hillerbrand; to the Faculty Research Award Program of the City University of New York; to S.F. Johnson, Paul O. Kristeller, Allen Mandelbaum, and Marlene Spiegler; and to student assistants through the years, including Jerome William Hogan, and Giselle Schlesinger, specifically for her assiduous consolidation of the original *Shakespearean Research* entries and preparation of a preliminary index.

Evidently, the utility of many of the following references will depend on the breadth of knowledge and imagination brought to them. In response to objections that Shakespeare was "only" an actor and playwright, or that he wrote for "all time," the present work's premise is that he wrote in the language of his time, for the diverse awarenesses of his own anticipated audiences. This he did, with a knowledge and profundity theatrically unrivaled. Shakespearean meanings, throughout the canon, and especially in his seventeenth-century plays, still require further contextual elucidation. To literary commentators dissatisfied with taking in and refurbishing each other's critical *aperçus*, this compilation on *Shakespeare's World* is intended to suggest (with *Coriolanus*), "There is a world elsewhere."

W.R.E.
The Graduate School and University Center,
City University of New York

SHAKESPEARE'S WORLD

I. ECONOMIC-SOCIAL CONTEXTS

1. Alberti, Leone Battista, *The Family in Renaissance Florence*, trans. R. N. Watkins. Columbia, S.C.: Univ. of South Carolina Pr., 1969. Rev. *RenQ*, 24 (1971), 53-55.

   Trans. of Alberti's *I libri della Famiglia*. Deals with personal value system of Florentine bourgeois class.

2. Alford, B.W.E., and T.C. Baker, *A History of the Carpenters Company*. London: Allen and Unwin, 1968.

   Rev. *TLS*, June 26, 1969, 712.

   Focuses especially upon "domestic life" of the company from its beginning in 1497. Early centuries were concerned with the company's attempt to control the craft of carpentry.

3. Allmand, C.T., "The Lancastrian Land Settlement in Normandy, 1417-1450," *Econ.H.R.*, 2nd ser., 21 (1968), 461-479.

   Makes use of hitherto unexploited primary sources to show that land served as incentive, payment, and reward in Englishmen's decisions to follow Henry V into Normandy during 1417-1450.

4. Anderson, Mark A., "Jonson's Criticism of Society: Development in the Major Comedies," *DA*, 29 (1969), 4443-A (Univ. of Wisc.).

   Argues that the society Jonson depicted on stage grew to be more illustrative of his England as the plays progressed; detects a similar progress in Jonson's characterizations.

5. Andrews, K.R., *Drake's Voyages: A Reassessment of Their Place in Elizabethan Maritime Expansion*. London: Weidenfeld and Nicolson, 1967.

   Rev. *Econ.H.R.*, 2nd ser., 21 (1968), 391-392; *History*, 53 (1968), 107-108.

   Characteristic form of Elizabethan maritime warfare was privateering; Drake pointed the way to plundering.

6. Arbour, Roméo and Jean-Claude Dubé, "Pierre Charron et ses idées sociales," *Rev. de l'Univ. d'Ottawa*, 40 (1970), 386-417.

   Charron believed in three basic social principles: obedience, the inequality of men, and the primacy of the state.

7. Ashton, Robert, "The Aristocracy in Transition," *Econ. H.R.*, 2nd ser., 22 (1969), 311-325.

Review article on Lawrence Stone's book, *The Crisis of the Aristocracy 1558-1641* (Oxford, 1965).

8.   ———, "Jacobean Free Trade Again," *Past and Present*, 43 (1969), 151-157.

Response to Rabb's reply (*Past and Pres.*, 1968, 155-173) to Ashton's original article, which appeared in *Past and Pres.* (1967, pp. 40-55). Parliamentary attitude toward free trade was determined by their interests as landowners, not as merchants.

9.   ———, "The Parliamentary Agitation for Free Trade in the Opening Years of the Reign of James I," *Past and Present*, No. 38 (1967), 40-55.

Examines views of Friis and Rabb, and concludes that Rabb's argument about the purposes of the reformers is wrong; rather, restrictive membership regulations in the mercantile companies and provincial antagonism to London were profoundly influential factors. (See Rabb below.)

10.   Baron, Salo W., *A Social and Religious History of the Jews: Late Middle Ages and Era of European Expansion (1200-1650)*; Vol. XIII: Inquisition, Renaissance, and Reformation; Vol. XIV: Catholic Restoration and Wars of Religion, New York: Columbia University Press, 1969. Rev. *NYTBR*, Mar. 15, 1970, 20.

Vol. XIII begins with analysis of Spanish and Portuguese Inquisitions. Discusses the vast Marrano dispersion in Western Europe, Italy, and the burgeoning European settlements in the New World, and shows deep effects upon the culture and economy of the host peoples. Vol. XIV: effects of Counter-Reformation and Wars of Religion on destinies of European Jewry.

11.   Bean, John Malcolm William, *The Decline of English Feudalism, 1215-1540*. Manchester U.P.; N.Y.: Barnes & Noble, 1968.

Rev. *AHR*, 74 (1969), 967; *EHR*, 85 (1970), 354-355.

Traces changes in legal and financial consequences of feudal tenure, emphasizing development of feudal lord's fiscal rights in relation to concept of English landowning.

12.   Bec, Christian, *Les Marchands écrivains. Affaires et humanisme à Florence: 1375-1434*. Paris, La Haye: Mouton, 1967.

Rev. A. Tenenti, "Les marchands et la culture à Florence (1375-1434)," *Annales: Ec., soc., civil.*, 23 (1968), 1319-1329.

Treats usury and faith; *fortuna, ragione, prudenza, libertas*. Bibl., pp. 449-473.

13.   Beecham, H.A., R.S. Craig, and R.C. Floud, "List of Publications on the Economic History of Great Britain and Ireland published in 1965," *Econ.H.R.*, 2nd ser., 20 (1967), 365-384.

Publications listed alphabetically: original documents, books and pamphlets, articles. Annual.

14. Beier, Augustus Leon, IV, "Studies in Poverty and Poor Relief in Warwickshire, 1540-1680," *DA*, 31 (1970), 2831-A (Princeton Univ. diss.).

Causes of poverty and methods of relief implemented by state in Elizabethan and later times.

15. Berry, Lloyd E., and Robert O. Crummey, eds., *Rude & Barbarous Kingdom: Russia in the Accounts of Sixteenth-Century English Voyagers*. Madison: Univ. of Wisconsin Press, 1968.

Accounts, modernized and annotated, of six English travellers who visited Russia in late 16th cent.

16. Bird, George Leonard, "The Earl of Essex: Patron of Letters," *DA*, 30 (1970), 3935-A (Univ. of Utah diss.).

Examines literary and political importance of patronage system under Elizabeth I, with Robert Devereux as case study.

17. Bitton, Davis, *The French Nobility in Crisis, 1560-1640*. Stanford Univ. Press, 1969.

Rev. *Choice*, 6 (Feb., 1970), 1818.

Examines contemporary comments by and about the French nobility as expressed in hundreds of treatises, memoirs, and pamphlets of the period. Chapters on anti-noble sentiment, military service, public office, and general ambiguity of noble status.

18. Blanchard, Ian, "Population Change, Enclosure, and the Early Tudor Economy," *Econ.H.R.*, 2nd ser., 23 (1970), 427-445.

Using price, wage, and arable rent indexes, author verifies population decline until 1510-1520 and then a recovery. Population pressure after 1520 led to anger at tenants and at enclosure; land-demand produced prosperous landlords.

19. Blitz, R.C. "Mercantilist Policies and the Pattern of World Trade, 1500-1750," *Journal of Economic History*, XXVII (1967), 39-55.

Discusses the simple specie flow model, bimetallic systems, demand for Oriental imports, and foreign investment.

20. Bossy, John, "The Counter-Reformation and the People," *Past and Pres.*, 47 (1970), 51-70.

Control of individual religious life in Catholic Europe of Counter-Reformation. In absence of new codes, traditional observances were better enforced.

21. Brailsford, Dennis, *Sport and Society, Elizabeth to Anne*. Toronto: Univ. of Toronto Press, 1969.

Rev. *AHR*, 76 (1971), 1542.

Challenges idea that English sports were the glory of the Renaissance but extinguished by the Puritans.

22. Braudel, Fernand, *Civilisation Matérielle et Capitalisme (XV-XVIIIe siècles)* Paris: Armand Colin, 1967.

    Rev. *AHR*, 73 (1968), 766-767; *EHR*, 84 (1969), 168-169.

    Vol. I, dealing with economic-social daily life, through *Annales* approaches. Vol. II to deal complementarily with capitalism. Ren. a time of transition between old limited productivity and new technological improvements in production and wider prosperity.

23. Breen, Timothy Hall, "The Non-Existent Controversy: Puritan and Anglican Attitudes on Work and Wealth, 1600-1640," *Church History*, XXXV (1966), 273-287.

    Anglicans and Puritans, contrary to popular belief, were not opposed in their attitude toward work. Both believed that each man had his calling, that work was the expression of human goodness, and that it was man's duty to work for the glorification of God and the welfare of other men. They did differ slightly in their attitudes toward the accumulation of wealth. The Anglicans viewed ambition and covetousness less seriously than the Puritans did.

24. Brewster, Paul G., "Games and Sports in Shakespeare," in Elliott M. Avedon and Brian Sutton-Smith, *The Study of Games*. N.Y.: Wiley, 1971, pp. 27-47.

    Detailed classification of games and sports, also with references to other Elizabethan and Stuart drama (repr. from *FF Communications*, 72 [177], 1959, pp. 3-26).

25. Bridenbaugh, Carl, *Vexed and Troubled Englishmen, 1590-1642*. New York: Oxford Univ. Press, 1968.

    Rev. *AHR*, 74 (1968), 164; *N.Y. Rev. of Books*, 10 (9 May 1968), 38-40.

    Social, economic, and cultural backgrounds in 16th cent. of Englishmen who in 17th cent. left for America.

26. Brown, R., "The Achievement Norm and Economic Growth: The Case of Elizabethan England," *Rev. Soc. Econ.*, 27 (2) (1969), 181-201.

    Examination of Englishmen's cosmology, psychology, marriage and family life, and child socialization and formal education between 1540 and 1640. Aims to establish causal relationship between concept of "achievement norm," a force encouraging behavioral characteristics conducive to economic growth, and Elizabethan rapid industrial expansion.

27. Burnett, John, *A History of the Cost of Living*. London: Penguin Books, 1969. Rev. *EHR*, 86 (1971), 426.

    Middle Ages and period 1500-1700 receive chapters filled with facts, particularly significant about landed households.

28. Carlton, Charles Hope, "The Court of Orphans: A Study in the
    History of Urban Institutions with Special Reference to London,
    Bristol, and Exeter in the 16th and 17th Centuries," *DA*, 31
    (1970), 1721-A (Univ. of Calif., Los Angeles).

    On governmental dealings re: orphans through Court of Orphans.
    Court as financial institution which formed the orphan fund, and
    as social organization which supervised the orphan's future.

29. Cederberg, Herbert Renando, Jr., "An Economic Analysis of English
    Settlement in North America, 1583 to 1635," *DA*, XXX (1969),
    1102-A - 1103-A (Univ. of Calif., Berkeley).

    Aims to measure extent to which economic factors influenced out-
    come of English attempts at settlement during this period--to
    determine why some attempts were favored by success while others
    floundered.

30. Charles, B.G., ed., *Calendar of the Records of the Borough of
    Haverfordwest, 1539-1660.* Cardiff: Univ. of Wales Press, 1967.

    Rev. *AHR*, 74 (1968), 978; *Econ.H.R.*, 2nd ser., 21 (1968), 385;
    History, 53 (1968), 433.

    Records considered probably best of their kind in Wales; appen-
    dix has financial records for most of Elizabeth's reign.

31. Charlton, K., "The Professions in Sixteenth-Century England,"
    Univ. of Birmingham History Journal, 12 (1969), 20-41.

    Treats medical, legal, and teaching professions in the 16th cent.
    Concludes that the cent. saw both a growing division of labor
    and a growing secularization of the professions.

32. Christensen, Thorkild Lyby, "Scots in Denmark in the Sixteenth
    Century," *Scott. Hist. Rev.*, 49 (1970), 125-145.

    Biographical and bibliographical information on individuals; on
    Scots in general as an element of Danish population.

33. Christian, Roy, *Old English Customs*. N.Y.: Hastings House,
    1966 (also: *The Country Life Book of Old English Customs*,
    London: Country Life, 1966). Rev. *TLS*, 9 Mar. 1969, 205.

    Deals with such Elizabethan pastimes as the Morris dance, folk
    drama, May Day, etc.

34. Cipolla, Carlo M., *Literacy and Development in the West*. London:
    Penguin Books, 1969.

    Rev. *TLS*, June 5, 1969, 605.

    Concerned primarily with how literacy has come about, much less
    with its effects. Includes 30 tables. Accepts Lawrence Stone's
    theory that there was a decline in literacy in England for the
    100 years following middle of 17th cent.

35. Clarkson, L.A., "The Leather Crafts in Tudor and Stuart England,"
     Agr. Hist. Rev., 14 (1966), 25-44.

     On the economy of a craft with which Shakespeare's father was
     connected.

36. Cliffe, J.T., *The Yorkshire Gentry: From the Reformation to the
     Civil War.* (Univ. of London Historical Studies, no. 25.) Lon-
     don: Athlone Press, 1969.

     Rev. *AHR*, 76 (1971), 775-776; *TLS*, 14 May 1970, 534.

     Studies 1,000 dominant families in Yorkshire, 1588-1642. Analy-
     sis of economic fortunes of various subgroups which composed
     Yorkshire's gentry class on the eve of the Civil War. Chapters
     on development of puritanism and Catholicism, 1570-1642.

37. Coleman, D.C., "The 'Gentry' Controversy and the Aristrocracy
     in Crisis, 1558-1641," *History*, LI (June 1967), 165-178.

     Deals with Lawrence Stone's *The Crisis of the Aristocracy, 1558-
     1641*, and other opinions on the subject, and questions validity
     of statistical studies in relation to the problem.

38. Cooper, J.P., "The Social Distribution of Land and Men in Eng-
     land, 1436-1700," *Econ.H.R.*, 2nd ser., 20 (1967), 419-440.

     Response to F.M.L. Thompson, "The Social Distribution of Landed
     Property in England since the Sixteenth Century," *ibid.*, 2nd
     ser., XIX (1966), 505-517. Reviews work of Thompson, Wilson,
     King, Stone, and others in some detail, and presents approxima-
     tions and estimates in table form. Variety of evidence for
     determining distribution of landownership and men.

39. Cornwall, Julian, "English Population in the Early Sixteenth
     Century," *Econ.H.R.*, 2nd ser., 23 (1970), 32-44.

     Using such tools as military survey of 1522 and lay subsidy rolls
     of 1524, author approximates population for England: 1545--2.8
     million; 1603--3.75 million.

40. Crofts, J., *Packhorse, Waggon, and Post: Land Carriage and
     Communications under the Tudors and Stuarts* (Studies in Social
     History). Toronto: Univ. of Toronto Press; London: Routledge
     & Kegan Paul, 1967.

     Rev. *AHR*, 74 (1968), 591-592; *TLS*, 25 January 1968, p. 94.

     On work of carriers, posts, etc., as means of communication of
     information, oral and written, from one place to another. Bad
     roads, delays, dangers.

41. Cross, Claire, "Supervising the Finances of the Third Earl of
     Huntingdon, 1580-1595," *Bulletin of the Institute of Historical
     Research*, XL (1967), 34-49.

     Examines the financial difficulties which confronted the 3rd Earl
     of Huntingdon and demonstrates the enormous difference between an

estimated income and the actual amount a nobleman could rely upon in the latter half of the 16th cent.

42. Cunnington, Phillis, and Catherine Lucas, *Occupational Costume in England: from the Eleventh Century to 1914.* N.Y.: Barnes and Noble, 1967.

    Rev. *AHR*, 74 (1969), 975; *QJS*, LIV (1968), 303-304.

    Documents dress of English working classes.

43. Davies, D.W., *Elizabethans Errant: The strange fortunes of Sir Thomas Sherley and his three sons, as well in the Dutch Wars as in Muscovy, Morocco, Persia, Spain, and the Indies.* Ithaca: Cornell Univ. Press, 1967.

    Rev. *AHR*, 74 (1968), 162; *Historian*, XXX (1968), 663.

    Adventurous careers of Elizabethan gentry and their penetration of exotic lands at close of Elizabeth's reign.

44. Davis, Natalie Zemon, "Gregory Nazianzen in the Service of Humanist Social Reform," *RenQ*, XX (1967), 455-464.

    Apparent 16th-cent. paradox: belief that giving to poor is either sign of election or meritorious act, while trying to eliminate poverty at same time.

45. Devine, T.M., and S.G.E. Lythe, "The Economics of Scotland under James VI: A Revision Article," *Scott. Hist. Rev.*, 50 (1971), 91-106.

    Expansion and prosperity. Negative revaluation of Weber-Tawney thesis (on Calvinism and work ethic). Yet Scottish Reformation had economic impact. Plagues of 1580's and early 1600's slowed population growth. Gap in historical literature noted.

46. Dorson, Richard M., *The British Folklorists: A History.* Chicago: Univ. of Chicago Press, 1969. Rev. *VS*, 13 (1969), 237-238.

    Intellectual history of British folklore movement from 16th cent. to World War I; extension of movement's influence into areas such as literature, history, anthropology.

47. Dow, James, "Scottish Trade with Sweden, 1512-80," *Scott. Hist. Rev.*, 68 (1969), 64-79.

    In early part of 16th cent., Scottish trade with Sweden was a complete novelty, yet by 1580 a trade unknown to Scottish and Swedish people in Middle Ages had become very firmly established.

48. ――――, "Scottish Trade with Sweden, 1580-1622," *Scott. Hist. Rev.*, 68 (1969), 124-150.

    Concludes that while Scotland was not very important to Sweden, Swedish trade did have a certain significance for Scotland.

49.   Draper, John W., "Shakespeare's Antonio and the Queen's Finance,"
      Neophilologus, LI (1967), 178-185.

      Suggests that Antonio is a portrayal of Orazio (Horace) Palla-
      vicino who succeeded Sir Thomas Gresham as the Queen's financier.

50.   Du Boulay, F.R., *An Age of Ambition: English Society in the
      Late Middle Ages*. London: Nelson, 1970.

      Rev. *TLS*, 11 June 1970, 634.

      14th and 15th-cent. attitudes toward class, marriage, sex,
      authority, and religion. Time of change, protest, and criticism.

51.   Elliott, J.H., *The Old World and the New, 1492-1650*. The Wiles
      Lectures given at the Queen's University of Belfast. Cambridge:
      Univ. Press, 1970.

      Rev. *LJ*, 96 (February 1971), 476; *TLS*, 6 August 1971, 936.

      Intellectual, economic, and political facets of European dis-
      covery of America, and the new self-discovery of European
      civilization.

52.   Entner, Heinz, and Werner Lenk, "Literatur und Revolution im 16.
      Jahrhundert. Zu einigen Aspekten der Renaissancekultur," *Wei-
      marer Beiträge*, 16, No. 5 (1970), 139-162.

      Revolutionary nature of humanism.

53.   Everitt, Alan. "Social Mobility in Early Modern England," *Past
      and Present*, No. 33 (1966), 56-73.

      Discusses a period of rapid social development, 1560-1700.
      Shows how the pattern of social mobility varied between dif-
      ferent districts, classes, and communities. Social change was
      not as rapid as many seem to believe; much of the old order and
      a degree of continuity were maintained. (Notes differences in
      Stuart inns from our own types of taverns or alehouses. For-
      mer were combination hotel, warehouse, bank, exchange, auction-
      room, scrivener's office, coach and wagon park, etc.)

54.   Ferguson, A.B., *Articulate Citizen and the English Renaissance*.
      Durham, N.C.: Duke University Press, 1966.

      Rev. *Spec.*, 41 (1966), 323-324.

      Discusses English social and economic criticism from the begin-
      ning of the 15th cent. to Elizabeth's accession. Treats major
      social critics including Fortescue, More, Starkey, Latimer,
      Crowley.

55.   Fleming, David A., S.M., "John Barclay: Neo-Latinist at the
      Jacobean Court," *Renaissance News*, XIX, 3 (Autumn, 1966), 228-
      236.

      Elucidates custom of patronage in King James's court.

56. Forbes, Thomas R., "Life and Death in Shakespeare's London," *Amer. Scientist*, 58 (1970), 511-520.

    Parish records of St. Botolph--without Aldgate (1558-1625 and beyond); detailed records about burials, births, disease, lawsuits, etc.

57. Gair, W.R., "Literary societies in England from Parker to Falkland, *c.* 1572-1640." (Director, L.G. Salingar.) Cambridge Ph.D., 1969.

58. Gibbons, Brian, *Jacobean City Comedy*. London: Hart-Davis, 1968. Rev. *Genre*, 3 (1970), 173-175.

    Jacobean social turbulence and life, reflected in dramatic satire.

59. Gilbert, Creighton, "When Did a Man in the Renaissance Grow Old?" *Studies in the Renaissance*, XIV (1967), 7-32.

    Suggests a lack of concern about precision on age. Renaissance views conceived of the beginning of old age as a point five to ten years less than the modal age of death, i.e., at forty.

60. Goldthwaite, Richard A., *Private Wealth in Renaissance Florence: A Study of Four Families*. Princeton Univ. Press, 1968.

    Rev. *AHR*, 75 (1969), 155-156; *Choice*, 6 (October 1969), 1068; *Spec.*, 45 (1970), 132-134; *VaQR*, 45 (1969), 110.

    Importance of Strozzi, Guicciardini, Gondi, and Capponi families in the economic and social life of 15th- and 16th-cent. Florence; pattern of investment, drawing from material in account books of the Archivio di Stato.

61. Gough, J.W., *The Rise of the Entrepreneur*. London: B.T. Batsford, 1969. Rev. *AHR*, 75 (1970), 1717; *TLS*, 26 March 1970, 345.

    History of activities of businessmen in manufacturing and extractive industries in late 16th and 17th cents.

62. Gould, J.D., "F.J. Fisher on Influenza and Inflation in Tudor England," *Econ.H.R.*, 2nd ser., 21 (1968), 361-368. Cf. rejoinder by F.J. Fisher, pp. 368-370.

    Opposes Fisher's essay, "Influenza and Inflation in Tudor England," *ibid.*, 2nd ser., VIII (1965), 120-129. Fisher had suggested that earlier demographic setback might explain puzzling features of mid-16th-cent. economic history; his reply agrees that it is still an open question.

63. ————, *The Great Debasement: Currency and the Economy in Mid-Tudor England*. Oxford: Clarendon Press, 1970.

    Rev. *AHR*, 77 (1972), 784-785; *History*, 56 (1971), 98-100; *Hist. Jour.*, 14 (1971), 440-441; *TLS* (19 July 1970), 846.

Determinants of mint supply and behavior of foreign exchanges in 1540's and 1550's; study reconstructs mint output during the Great Debasement and influence of the debasement on power of English monarchy. Attempts to determine whether exports were stimulated in 1520's and 1540's by exchange depreciation.

64. Graham, W. Fred, *The Constructive Revolutionary: John Calvin and his Socio-Economic Impact.* Richmond, Va.: John Knox Press, 1971.

     Rev. *AHR*, 77 (1972), 772; *Ren. and Ref.*, 9 (1973), 70-71.

     Deals with social ethics of Calvin as revolutionary thinker. Confirms view of Calvinism as a major European revolutionary ideology.

65. Grass, Milton and Anna, *Stockings for a Queen: The Life of the Rev. William Lee, the Elizabethan Inventor.* London: Heinemann, 1967.

     Inventor of framework knitting machine.

66. Grimm, Harold J., "Luther's Contributions to Sixteenth Century Organization of Poor Relief," *ARG*, 61 (1970), 222-234.

     Social and religious aspects of his statements in terms of motivations and influence.

67. Grussby, Richard, "The Personal Wealth of the Business Community in Seventeenth Century England," *Econ.H.R.*, 2nd ser., 23 (1970), 220-234.

     Using records of the Court of Orphans of London, author examines wealth of businessmen in London; compares it with business wealth in provinces and studies changes of wealth throughout 17th cent.

68. Guarini, E. Fasano, "L'europa del cinquecento," *Studi Storici*, 3 (July/September 1970), 572-583.

     Criticism of *L'europa del cinquecento* by Koenigsberger and Mosse (cf. below). History of religion; history of states' formation and structure not properly connected with history of social-economic processes.

69. Hankinson, Margie Mae, "William Thomas: Italianate Englishman," *DA*, XXVIII (1968), 4175-4176-A (Columbia Univ. diss.).

     On author of *Historie of Italie* (1549); though he was a Protestant, his work reveals longing for Italian-created art of life he feels rest of world might share and he shows interest in Machiavellian reason of state. (Cf. *RLI*, LXXI [1967], 260-261.)

70. Harris, G.G., *The Trinity House of Deptford, 1514-1660.* Oxford Univ. Press, 1969.

     On Deptford Trinity House, corporation which is now main lighthouse and pilotage authority of U.K. Traces its development under Tudors and early Stuarts.

71. Hartwell, Richard M., "Economic Growth in England Before the
     Industrial Revolution: Some Methodological Issues," *Journal of
     Econ. Hist.*, XXIX (1969), 13-31.

     On type of economic system existing in England in centuries be-
     tween the Norman Conquest and industrial revolution; type of
     change which occurred; trends compounded by such change.

72. ———, and Wilson, Charles, "Social Distribution of Landed
     Property in England Since the Sixteenth Century," *Econ.H.R.*,
     2nd ser., 19 (December 1966), 5-18.

     Concerned with three classifications of landowners: nobility,
     gentry, and freeholders. From 1559 to 1602 the great landowners
     were increasing, while from 1602 to 1641 there was a decline in
     land owned by the nobility or peers.

73. Hawkyard, A.D.K., "Some late medieval fortified manor-houses:
     a study of the building works of Sir John Fastolf, Ralph, Lord
     Cromwell, and Edward Stafford, 3rd duke of Buckingham." (Direc-
     tor, C.F. Richmond.) Keele M.A. 1969.

74. Hay, Bryan Scott, "William Dunbar's Vision of Disorder," *DA*, 30
     (1970), 3429-30-A (Univ. of Rochester diss.).

     Yearning for a source of hierarchical order and abhorrence of
     disorder is the thematic unity of Dunbar's work, from his satiric
     petitions to his ceremonial poems.

75. Hembry, Phyllis M., *The Bishops of Bath and Wells, 1540-1640:
     Social and Economic Problems.* Univ. of London Historical Stud-
     ies, No. 20. London: Athlone Press; N.Y.: Oxford Univ. Press,
     1967.

     Rev. *AHR*, 73 (1967), 472-473; *Church History*, 37 (1968), 116-
     117; *Econ.H.R.*, 2nd ser., 21 (1968), 388; *EHR*, 83 (1968), 598;
     History, 53 (1968), 104; *Journal of Modern Hist.*, 40 (1968),
     592-593; *RenQ*, 20 (1967), 492-493; *SCN*, 26 (1968), 14.

     Socio-economic effects of English Reformation with its attack
     upon ecclesiastical wealth.

76. Herlihy, David, "Family Solidarity in Medieval Italian History,"
     Explor. in Econ. Hist., 7 (1969-1970), 173-184.

     Traces tight family structure in Italy up to 15th cent. claiming
     its applicability to family situations in all Europe. Criticizes
     the notion of progressive nuclearization of family structure in
     late Middle Ages as hard to document. Consortial family, i.e.,
     large household with common ownership of property. In late
     medieval times, property bonds decreased, moral bonds increased.

77. Hexter, J.H., "The English Aristocracy, Its Crises, and the
     English Revolution, 1558-1660," *JBS*, VIII (1968), 22-78. Re-
     joinder by Stone, pp. 79-82.

Aims to redress injustice done to Lawrence Stone's *Crisis of the Aristocracy, 1558-1641,* but includes his own reservations. Insisting that the English Revolution had much deeper social causes than Hexter will admit, Stone objects that Hexter places too much emphasis on Puritanism alone as the "sufficient cause" of the English Revolution.

78.   ————, "Postscript to an Awfully Long Review," *JBS,* 9 (1969), 45-48.

On exchange between author and Lawrence Stone concerning Stone's major *Crisis of the Aristocracy.*

79.   Hill, Christopher, *Reformation to Industrial Revolution, a Social and Economic History of Britain, 1530-1780.* London: Weidenfeld and Nicolson; N.Y.: Pantheon, 1967.

Rev. *AHR,* 74 (1968), 595-596; *International Rev. of Social Hist.,* XII (1967), 511; *N.Y. Rev. of Books,* 13 February 1969, pp. 29-30; *Science and Society,* XXXII (1968), 328-330; *Spec.,* CCXIX (1967), 361-362; *TLS,* 30 November 1967, 1169.

Marxist view of "17th-cent. revolution" that gave rise to industrial English state.

80.   Hodgen, Margaret T., "Ethnology in 1500: Polydore Vergil's Collection of Customs," *Isis,* LVII (Fall 1966), 315-324.

As part of *De inventoribus rerum,* Polydore Vergil made one of earliest Renaissance efforts to assemble a collection of human customs, seeing need for attention to the social or ethnological activities of man in separation from his role in the theological, cosmological, and biological world.

81.   Holmes, Martin R., *Elizabethan London.* London: Cassell; N.Y.: Frederick Praeger, 1969.

Rev. *Hist. Today,* 19 (August 1969), 584.

Deals with people and topography of the period, drawing from primary sources, chroniclers, pamphleteers, and mapmakers. Present-day plans set alongside of Elizabethan ones for comparison.

82.   Holsinger, John Calvin, "A Survey of the Major Arguments Used by English Promoters to Encourage Colonization and Interest in America in the Early Colonial Era," *DA,* XXIX (1968), 1192-1193-A (Temple Univ.).

English propaganda promoting colonization as solution for many domestic problems, economic and religious.

83.   Horwich, Richard David, "Marriage and Money in English City Comedy, 1597-1625," *DA,* XXVIII (1967), 2209-A (Columbia Univ. diss.).

Primary concerns of comedies (including Shakespeare's) of London
life in first quarter of 17th-cent., marriage and money; reflections of socio-economic revolution. Relations to Aristophanic
comedy.

84. Howells, B.E., ed., *A Calendar of Letters Relating to North
Wales, 1553-ca. 1700.* Cardiff: Univ. of Wales Press, 1967.

Rev. *AHR*, 74 (1968), 978; *Econ.H.R.*, 2nd ser., 21 (1968), 385;
History, 53 (1968), 433.

Miscellany of four sets of family letters, mostly from 17th cent.
and from three North Wales counties.

85. Huizinga, Johan, *Dutch Civilization in the Seventeenth Century
and other Essays*, ed. P. Geyl and F.W. Hugenholtz, tr. by A.J.
Pomerans. N.Y.: Ungar, 1968.

Rev. *Choice*, 7 (1970), 286.

Includes discussion of Dutch civilization in 17th cent.; and
"The Netherlands as Mediator between Western and Central Europe."

86. Hurstfield, Joel, *The Elizabethan Nation.* N.Y.: Harper Torchbooks, Harper and Row, 1967.

Social, political, and economic account of the nation as a
whole.

87. *Individu et société à la Renaissance. Colloque international
tenu en avril 1965 sous les auspices de la Fédération Internationale des Instituts et Sociétés pour l'étude de la Renaissance et du Ministère de l'Education Nationale de la Culture de
Belgique.* (Université Libre de Bruxelles. Travaux de l'Institut pour l'étude de la Renaissance et de l'Humanisme, III.)
Brussels: Presses Universitaires de Bruxelles; Paris: Presses
Universitaires de France, 1967.

Rev. *AHR*, LXXIV (1968), 147-148; *BHR*, XXX (1968), 628-629;
Janus, LV (1968), 77-78; *Moreana: Bulletin Thomas More*, XVIII
(1968), 81-86.

Essays on individualism and society in such areas as letter-
writing (P. Mesnard); law (J. Gilissen); Reformation (H. Meylan);
tolerance (G. Kisch); iconography, Dürer (J.-C. Margolin); medicine and venereal disease (H. Brabant).

88. Irwin, Larry Wayne, "A Critical Edition of Thomas Middleton's
Micro-Cynicon, Father Hubburds Tales, and *The Blacke Booke*," *DA*,
30 (1969), 1137-A (Univ. of Wisc. diss.).

The three satires of interest for realistic portrayal of English
life and for links with Middleton's city comedies.

89. Ives, E.W., "Andrew Dymmock and the Papers of Antony, Earl
Rivers, 1482-1483," *BIHR*, 41 (1968), 216-229.

Earl's papers contain instructions to his business agent and
lawyer, Andrew Dymmock, thus revealing relationship between the
two men and shedding light on the Earl's business interests,
political maneuvers of 1482-1483, and Edward's accession crisis.

90. Jones, Whitney R.D., *The Tudor Commonwealth. A Study of the Im-
     pact of the Social and Economic Developments 1529-1559 in Mid-
     Tudor England upon Contemporary Concepts of the Nature and
     Duties of the Commonwealth.* Univ. of London: Athlone Press;
     N.Y.: Oxford Univ. Press, 1970.

     Rev. *AHR*, 76 (1971), 497; *History*, 55 (1970), 458-459; *RenQ*, 24
     (1971), 270-272; *TLS*, 31 July 1970, 846.

     Impact of mid-Tudor social, economic, and religious crises on
     reformist ideas of the nature and duties of the commonwealth.
     Thinkers such as More, Elyot, Starkey, and Morison stressed
     general good transcended consideration of private gain. Pro-
     blems of poverty, crimes, inflation, and economic conflict of in-
     terests; these crises in social values gave power once held by
     Church to civil government.

91. Kamen, Henry, "Galley Service and Crime in Sixteenth-Century
     Spain," *Econ.H.R.*, 2nd ser., 22 (1969), 304-305.

     Questions equation (by I.A.A. Thompson in "A Map of Crime in
     Sixteenth-Century Spain," *EHR*, 21 [1968]), of galley service
     with criminality. Points out that Moriscos, gypsies, and vaga-
     bonds were sent to the galleys.

92. Kerridge, E., *Agrarian Problems in the Sixteenth Century and
     After.* London: Allen and Unwin, 1969.

     Half of vol. includes introductory essay on manor; tenures and
     estates; enclosures, depopulation; and half, documents from
     period.

93. Kew, John, "The disposal of Crown Lands and the Devon Land Mar-
     ket, 1536-1558," *Agr. Hist. Rev.*, 18 (1970), 93-105.

     Total land market in a single county following dissolution of
     monasteries. Influence of property market on changing social
     structure of Tudor and Stuart ages.

94. Kitch, M.J., ed., *Capitalism and the Reformation.* London:
     Longmans, 1967; N.Y.: Barnes & Noble, 1968.

     Weber thesis as subject of interdisciplinary debate; original
     sources in selections.

95. Kochan, Lionel, "The History of Chess, II: From the Renaissance
     to the Twentieth Century," *Hist. Today*, 19 (1969), 190-196.

     Traces history of chess from end of 15th cent., when the queen
     and bishop received increased power and the game thus assumed
     the modern form.

96. Kuczyński, Jürgen, "Shakespeare und die Englische Agrarge-
     schichtsschreibung," *Jahrbuch für Wirtschaftsgeschichte* (1970,
     Teil I), 249-254.

     Agricultural condition in England, 1500-1640, crucial to know-
     ledge of over-all social circumstances, and to understanding
     of Shakespeare as middle-class dramatist. (Rev. of Thirsk,
     below.)

97. Larner, John, "The Artist and the Intellectuals in Fourteenth
     Century Italy," *History*, 54 (1969), 13-30.

     On relation of the artist and of art to the intellectual world
     and the changing status of the artists as seen by writers of
     the time.

98. Laslett, Peter, *The World We Have Lost*. N.Y.: Scribner's, 1966.

     Rev. *AHR*, 72 (1967), 972-973.

     From Cambridge Group for the History of Population and Social
     Structure; on pre-industrial vs. industrial worlds. Family or
     household as unifying center of Stuart England. Demographic
     and sociological approach.

99. Le Guin, Charles A., "Sea Life in Seventeenth-Century England,"
     Amer. Neptune, XXVII (1967), 111-134.

     Detailed account of daily life at sea, crew, food, disease and
     illness, crime and punishment, land and liberty.

100. LeMoine, Roger, "La découverte de l'Amérique et la hausse de la
     monnaie de change, selon Jean Bodin," *RUO*, 40 (1970), 62-68.

     Bodin was first to attribute French economic inflation to the
     Spanish colonization of New World.

101. Lewis, Allan, "Shakespeare and the Morality of Money," *Social
     Research*, 36 (1969), 373-389.

     Implications of the multiple meanings of the word *commodity*
     in Faulconbridge's speech, *Jn.*, II, i, 523-561. (Cf. 2324.)

102. Liebel, Helen P., "Inflation: Its History and Policy, 1500-
     1968," *Dalhousie Rev.*, 49 (1969), 5-19.

     Brief survey (pp. 5-10) of 16th-cent. "Price Revolution."

103. Litchfield, R. Burr, "Demographic Characteristics of Florentine
     Patrician Families, Sixteenth to Nineteenth Centuries," *Jour.
     Econ. Hist.*, 29 (1969), 191-205.

     Study of the surviving families shows that decline was due to a
     demographic crisis and to a change in structure of the families.

104. Lloyd, Howell A., "Camden, Carmaden, and the Customs," *EHR*, 85
     (1970), 776-787.

Elizabethan customs houses and revenues, organization, corruption, and need for revenue in late years of the reign. Camden's history of Elizabeth and Carmaden's *Caveat for the Queen* considered.

105. ———, *The Gentry of South-West Wales, 1540-1640.* Cardiff: Univ. of Wales Press, 1968.

Rev. *EHR*, 85 (1970), 412-413.

Gentry of Pembrokeshire, Cardiganshire, and Carmarthenshire, and their gradual rise by process of accumulation; stresses regional variations within British gentry.

106. Loschky, D.J., "The Usefulness of England's Parish Register," *Rev. of Econ. and Statistics*, XLIX (1967), 471-477.

On sources for population theory; method for detecting relative reliability of registers, etc. Though data are taken from 18th-cent. registers, this is useful check.

107. Maczak, A., "Produzione e commercio della lana nell'europa centro orientale dal 14 al 17 secolo," *Studi Storici*, 1 (January-March 1970), 1-25.

How wool production and trade affected Ren. society of middle-eastern Europe and its economic structure.

108. Magalhães-Godinho, Vitorino, *L'Economie de l'empire portugais aux XVe et XVIe siècles.* Paris: S.E.V.P.E.N. (Distributed by Parkers of Oxford, 1969.) (Also *s.v.* Godinho.)

Rev. *TLS*, 18 December 1969, 1444.

French version of Portuguese edition. On currency and foreign-exchange problems; offers new information about the gold trade; disentangles complexities of 16th-cent. world trade.

109. Malament, Barbara, "The 'Economic Liberalism' of Sir Edward Coke," *Yale Law Jour.*, LXXVI (1967), 1321-1358.

Examining the career of Sir Edward Coke, this article denies usual view that he was forerunner to *laissez-faire* economics.

110. Martin, Henri-Jean, *Livre, pouvoirs et société à Paris au XVIIe siècle (1598-1701).* 2 vols. Genève: Droz, 1969.

Rev. *AHR*, 75 (1970), 1458-1459; *BHR*, 33 (1970), 495-497.

On literature of Catholic Renaissance; humanities, philosophy, science, and literature; book production and circulation.

111. Mason, Alexandra, "The Social Status of Theatrical People." *SQ*, XVIII (1967), 429-430.

Theater proprietor Cuthbert Burbage, brother of Richard, apparently refused to take up a knighthood in 1630; social implications drawn.

112. Mauro, Frédéric, *Le XVIe Siècle Européen: Aspects économiques.*
      Paris: Presses Univ. de France, 1966.

      Rev. *AHR*, 73 (1968), 798-799.

      Detailed economic study of 16 cent. Includes Chap. III, "Les
      jeux de l'offre et de la demande" (supply and demand). Biblio-
      graphy of 1739 items.

113. McGovern, John F., "The Rise of New Economic Attitudes--Economic
      Humanism, Economic Nationalism--during the later Middle Ages
      and the Renaissance, A.D. 1200-1550," *Trad.*, 26 (1970), 217-
      253.

      Beginnings of Europe's capitalistic outlook traced. Origins in
      Renaissance and later Middle Ages. Budgetary poverty in pri-
      vate households and fiscal deficits in government treasuries
      resulted in economic humanism for individuals and economic
      nationalist policies for governments.

114. McKinley, R.A., *Norfolk Surnames in the Sixteenth Century.*
      Leicester Univ. Press, 1970.

      Rev. *TLS*, 13 November 1970, 1337.

      Study of distribution of surnames in Norfolk during Henry VIII's
      reign.

115. McPeek, James A.S., *The Black Book of Knaves and Unthrifts, in
      Shakespeare and Other Renaissance Authors.* Storrs: Univ. of
      Conn. Press, 1969. Rev. *ShSt*, 6 (1972), 358-360.

      Studies the response of citizens, statesmen, and authors to the
      increase in knavery in Renaissance England. Examines drama and
      the pamphlet literature.

116. Minchinton, W.E., ed., *The Growth of English Overseas Trade in
      the Seventeenth and Eighteenth Centuries.* London: Methuen,
      1969.

      Rev. *TLS*, 21 May 1970, 558.

      Articles reprinted focus on some aspect of English overseas
      trade between 1600 and 1770 and all (except the editor's newly
      published essay) are well known. Descriptive, analytical, and
      statistical material on role of overseas trade in English de-
      velopment leading to Industrial Revolution.

117. Miskimin, Harry A., *The Economy of Early Renaissance Europe.
      1300-1460.* Prentice-Hall, 1969. Rev. *JEH*, 30 (1970), 465.

      Survey of European economic developments in 14th and 15th cents.;
      chapters on "The Agrarian Economy," "Town and Industry," and
      "The International Economy."

118. Mitchell, Robert M., "The Weber Thesis as Tested by the Writings
      of John Calvin and the English Puritans of the Sixteenth and
      Seventeenth Centuries," *DA*, 30 (1969), 2465-A (Mich. State
      Univ. diss.).

To test Weber's thesis by attempting to find proto-capitalistic
views in the writings of John Calvin and the English Puritans.
Results negative, but much ignorance on the part of Weber concerning views of Calvin and English Puritans, misrepresentation,
and quoting out of context were found.

119.   Molho, Anthony, ed., *Social and Economic Foundations of the
       Italian Renaissance.* ("Major Issues in History" series)   N.Y.:
       Wiley, 1969. Rev. *Social St.*, 62 (1971), 42.

       Collection of essays on: "The City," "Sources of Wealth and
       Techniques of Business," "The Crisis of the 14th Century (the
       Plague)," "The Economy 1350-1500," "The Commune," "A New Aris-
       tocracy," "The Merchant and His World," and "The Court and the
       Courtier."

120.   Monckton, H.A., "English Ale and Beer in Shakespeare's Time,"
       Hist. Today, XVII (1967), 828-834.

       Beer was national drink, neither tea nor coffee having been im-
       ported; average consumption was 21 pints a week. It was dark
       and probably sweet; "ale-tasters," of whom Shakespeare's father
       had been one, required beer to pass purity test. Includes
       Shakespearean references to ale and beer.

121.   Morton, A.L., "Utopia Yesterday and Today," *The Matter of Bri-
       tain: Essays in a Living Culture.* London: Lawrence & Wishart,
       1966, pp. 59-72.

       Utopian theories and dreams could only exist with rise of a
       bourgeoisie--which occurred in the 15th and 16th cents. A
       feudal society made such conceptions impossible because it was
       fixed and regarded change with suspicion. Beginning with the
       humanistic view that man has the ability to control his environ-
       ment and the basic confidence in human progress, coupled with a
       rise of a bourgeoisie, Utopian ideas became important.

122.   Muchmore, Lynn Roy, "An Analysis of English Mercantile Litera-
       ture, 1600-1642," *DA*, 29 (1969), 4170-4171-A (Univ. of Wisc.
       diss.).

       Extended testing of hypothesis that this mercantile literature
       was formulated in response to immediate economic events, and
       that it is devoid of consistency which would qualify it as a
       doctrinal unit. The writers responded to short-run crises and
       specific controversies. They did not concur with state power
       in the wisdom of wide-scale government intervention.

123.   Murray, J.K.R., "Some Notes on the Small Silver Money of James I
       (of England) and VI (of Scotland)," *Numismatic Chron.*, 7th ser.,
       8 (1968), 169-172.

       Critique of description of James's rose and thistle silver money
       given by E. Burns in *The Coinage of Scotland* (1887), who erred
       in some of his descriptions of this type of money because he
       did not have a comprehensive collection of English coins.

124. Nelson, Benjamin, "Conscience and the Making of Early Modern Culture: *The Protestant Ethic* beyond Max Weber," *Social Research*, 36 (1969), 5-21.

   Focuses on 16th and 17th cents. Opposes viewing Weber's purposes in *The Protestant Ethic* in terms of a local historical proposition about the relations of economics and religion in 16th cent. Examines early modern cultures from point of view of revolutions in rational systems in the sphere of conscience. Sees limitation imposed when focus is restricted to purely political and social-economic perspectives.

125. Nicolaisen, W.F.H., Margaret Gelling and Melville Richards, eds., *The Names of Towns and Cities in Britain*. London: Batsford, 1970.

   Rev. *ScS*, 15 (1971), 82-83.

   Scholars from England, Wales, and Scotland contributing information on derivation of place-names. Stress is on extra-linguistic factors.

126. O'Brien, George A.T., *An Essay on the Economic Effects of the Reformation*. N.Y.: Kelley, 1970. Rev. *Church Hist.*, 40 (1971), 225.

   Protestant reformers upset the balance of the Middle Ages by introducing social ills, including capitalism. (Repr. 1923 book.)

127. Outhwaite, R.B., *Inflation in Tudor and Early Stuart England*. London: Macmillan, 1969.

   Rev. *EHR*, 85 (1970), 415.

   Compresses into 50 pages much basic research of recent years; divided into four sections: a) chronology and proportions of the inflation, b) outline of the awareness of contemporary opinion, c) claims of monetary theorists, focusing on potential weaknesses of the Irving Fisher equation of exchange, and d) the role of "real" factors, notably the growth of population and pressures of excess demand. Agrees with revisionists of 1950's in minimizing monetary causes of price rises; yet emphasizes role of mid-16th cent. English currency debasements.

128. ———, "The Price of Crown Land at the Turn of the Sixteenth Century," *Econ.H.R.*, 2nd ser., 20 (1967), 229-240.

   Investigates effect of large sales of land which Crown had confiscated from the Church on the land market, 1599-1601. It touches on the reasons the Crown was anxious to obtain great sums of money and its degree of success in the land market.

129. Paffard, Michael, "A Sixteenth-Century Farmer's Year," *Hist. Today*, 20 (1970), 397-403.

   Thomas Tusser's (b. 1524?) books on husbandry: *A Hundreth Good Pointes of Husbandrie* (1557), expanded in 1573 to *Five Hundred*

Pointes; added *Pointes of Huswiferie* later; all were pithy verses dealing with practical virtues of thrift, emphasizing self-
sufficiency of farmer and his household.

130. Parry, J.H., ed., *The European Reconnaissance: Selected Docu-
      ments*. London: Macmillan, 1968.

      Rev. *EHR*, 85 (1970), 404; *TLS*, 7 November 1968, 1242.

      Accounts by explorers or by their contemporaries on achievements
      of their voyages, mainly from 15th and 16th cents.; with intro-
      duction and commentaries.

131. Pearlman, E., "Historical Demography for Shakespeareans: An
      Introduction," *Shakespearean Research and Opportunities*, nos.
      7-8 (1972/74), 69-74.

      Towards statistical outline of social structure of Elizabethan
      England: life expectancy, age at marriage, family size, infant
      mortality, through computerized study of parish registers.
      Useful bibliography, pp. 72-74.

      Accounts by explorers or by their contemporaries on achieve-
      ments of their voyages, mainly from 15th and 16th cents.; with
      introduction and commentaries.

132. Perini, L., "Gli eretici Italiani del'500 e Machiavelli," *Studi
      Storici*, 10 (1969), 877-918.

      Opposes H.R. Trevor-Roper's claim in *Protestantism and Social
      Transformation* that emigration of Italian artisans of an Eras-
      mian point of view spurred growth of Protestantism and capital-
      ism in Europe. Finds little evidence for this influence.

133. Petersen, E. Ladewig, "La crise de la noblesse danoise entre
      1580 et 1660," *Annales E.S.E.*, 23 (1968), 1237-1261.

      Defines and explains symptoms of economic crisis of Danish
      nobility 1580-1660.

134. ———, "The Elizabethan Aristocracy Anatomized, Atomized and
      Re-Assessed," *Scand. Econ. Hist. Rev.*, 16 (1968), 176-194.

      Critical review essay on Lawrence Stone, *The Crisis of the
      Aristocracy, 1558-1641*, Oxford, 1965.

135. Phillips, William, "Elizabeth I and Her Subjects," *Brit. Tax
      Rev.*, November-December 1967, 404-410.

      Refutes view of M. St. Clair Byrne (in *Elizabethan Life in Town
      and Country*, 1925, many times reprinted and rev.) that increas-
      ing devotion of her people to Elizabeth is shown by supposed
      increasing warmth of the preambles to the 12 revenue statues of
      her age (1559-1601).

136. Pigafetta, Antonio, *Magellan's Voyage, a Narrative Account of
      the First Circumnavigation*, trans. and ed. R.A. Skelton. New
      Haven: Yale Univ. Press, 1969.

      Rev. *TLS* (1970), 167-168.

Manuscript of the great era of world discovery, reproduced in
color. Critical summary of eye-witness evidence concerning
Magellan's voyage around the world as editor's supplement to
account of the voyage written by Magellan's colleague Pigafetta from his detailed log of the journey.

137. Pinchbeck, Ivy, and Margaret Hewitt, *Children in English
      Society. Vol. 1: From Tudor Times to the Eighteenth Century*.
      Univ. of Toronto Press, 1969.

      First of two volumes dealing with changing social attitudes
      toward children in English society and resulting influences on
      social policy and legislation. Present volume treats early
      Tudor idealistic policies and their ultimate failure, and sub-
      sequent alternating patterns of enthusiasm and neglect during
      17th and 18th cents.

138. Pollard, Sidney, and David W. Crossley, *The Wealth of Britain,
      1085-1966*. N.Y.: Schocken Books, 1969.

      Rev. *Historian*, XXXII (1970), 280-281.

      An examination of economic levels the British people have
      achieved. The "pre-statistical" chapters (1-5) on the 1085-
      1760 era provide over three-fifths of the text.

139. Ponko, Vincent, Jr., *The Privy Council and the Spirit of Eliza-
      bethan Economic Management, 1558-1603*. Transactions of the
      American Philosophical Society, N.S., LVIII, Pt. 4; Philadelphia:
      American Philosophical Society, 1968.

      Rev. *AHR*, 77 (1972), 507-508.

      Monograph showing that planned economic program was not integral
      to economic attitude of Privy Council, which administered
      England for Elizabeth.

140. Porter, Enid, *Cambridgeshire Customs and Folklore*. N.Y.:
      Barnes and Noble, 1969. Rev. *TLS*, 14 Aug. 1969, 902.

      Subjects range from folklore of courtship, marriage, birth, and
      death, of trees and plants and world of nature to traditional
      Cambridgeshire food and drink; from ghosts and witchcraft and
      cure of disease to charity and land-letting customs. Describes
      traditional occupations of the county; its sports and pastimes;
      section on university customs.

141. Pound, John, *Poverty and Vagrancy in Tudor England*. London:
      Longman, 1971. Rev. *TLS*, 1 Oct. 1971, 1185.

      Condensed vol.: Part I. Background: causes of poverty; extent
      of the problem. Part II. Descriptive Analyses: early Tudor
      legislation; Elizabethan poor laws; urban experiments in sup-
      pression of vagrancy and the relief of the poor; contributions
      of the individual (philanthropy, etc.). Part III. Assessments.
      Part IV. Documents. Bibliography of secondary sources: 77
      items.

142. Quinn, David B., "Thomas Hariot and the Virginia Voyages of
      1602," *WMQ*, 27 (1970), 268-281.

      Based on notes of Hariot about Mace's preparation for 1602 voy-
      age. Ralegh's attempt to deal with glut of sassafras on market
      as consequence of Mace's return cargo.

143. Rabb, Theodore K., *Enterprise & Empire: Merchant and Gentry
      Investment in the Expansion of England, 1575-1630*. Cambridge,
      Mass.: Harvard Univ. Press, 1967.

      Rev. *AHR*, 74 (1968), 163-164; *History*, 53 (1968), 425-426;
      Jour. of Econ. Hist., 28 (1968), 724-725.

      Studies social origins, etc., of investors who financed early
      English overseas expansion from mid-Elizabethan times to ca.
      1630. Transformation of England from economically backward
      nation to one with foundations of overseas empire. (Book said
      to be first major attempt to apply computer techniques in early
      modern European history.)

144. ———, "Free Trade and the Gentry in the Parliament of 1604,"
      Past and Present, No. 40 (1968), 165-173; rejoinder to Robert
      Ashton, "The Parliamentary Agitation for Free Trade in the Open-
      ing Years of the Reign of James I," *ibid.*, no. 38 (1967), 40-55.

      Attempts to modify approach of Astrid Friis (1927) in Rabb's
      "Sir Edwin Sandys and the Parliament of 1604," *AHR*, 69 (1963-
      1964), 646-670; Ashton grants Rabb's contention that Friis's
      analysis was incomplete because the motivation of the gentry in
      events of 1604 cannot be reduced to outport jealousy of London.
      Defining point at issue as, "what prompted gentry's actions?"
      Rabb opposes Ashton's view that aim of free traders in Parlia-
      ment was to prevent creation of national chartered companies
      for trades not yet under control of such bodies. This was ir-
      relevant, Rabb holds, to the gentry, who flocked to companies
      of this sort in the next few years; he emphasizes role of free
      trade in the founding of the British empire. (See Ashton
      above.)

145. ———, "Investment in English Overseas Enterprise, 1575-1630,"
      Econ.H.R., 2nd ser., 19 (1966), 70-81.

      Attempts, with use of computer techniques, to investigate whole
      of Elizabethan and Jacobean investment in overseas enterprises.
      Magnitude of popular involvement, even among the non-merchant
      classes. Outlines fluctuations of interest in new ventures,
      which show a definite pattern--the Elizabethan period was in-
      active compared to Jacobean.

146. Ramsey, Peter H., ed., *The Price Revolution in Sixteenth-Century
      England*. London: Methuen; N.Y.: Barnes and Noble, 1971.

      Includes essays by J.D. Gould, "The Price Revolution Recon-
      sidered"; C.E. Challis, "The Circulating Medium and the Movement
      of Prices in Mid-Tudor England." Selected bibliography.

147. Reddaway, T.F., "The Livery Companies of Tudor London," *History*, 51 (October 1966), 287-299.

    Examines the 12 great gilds or companies of Tudor London. The gilds were, at once, capitalist employers, Friendly Societies, social clubs, contributors to charity, trainers of craftsmen, and instruments of the central and civic government. By end of Elizabeth's reign, gilds were on a high peak of splendor. Their leading men were knighted; daughters were rich matches for sons of nobility. By end of 16th cent. gilds were dominated by merchants rather than craftsmen. Decline of gilds begins under Stuarts--a slow decline from greatness. Shakespeare's father was a gildsman--a glover--in Stratford.

148. Rich, E.E., and C.H. Wilson, eds., *The Cambridge Economic History of Europe*, Vol. IV: *The Economy of Expanding Europe in the Sixteenth and Seventeenth Centuries*. Cambridge/N.Y.: Cambridge Univ. Press, 1967.

    Rev. *AHR*, 74 (1968), 145-147; *Historian*, 30 (1968), 256-257; *Historical Journal*, 2 (1968), 583-586; *History*, 53 (1968), 420-423; *Journal of Modern History*, 40 (1968), 535-537; *Listener*, 78 (1967), 88.

    Chapters on demographic history; science and technology, transport and trade routes; European economic institutions, especially chartered companies; introduction from New World of crops, live-stocks, etc.; colonial settlements; survey of price history, 1450-1750; trade, society, and the state.

149. Roberts, B.K., "A Study of Medieval Colonization in the Forest of Arden, Warwickshire," *Agric. Hist. Rev.*, 16 (1968), 101-113.

    Study of the colonization which shaped medieval landscape, focusing on causes, processes, and effects. Documented by large collection of private land charters. (Cf. [ARDEN] in *Topoi*.)

150. Rudolph, Günter, "Das sozialökonomische Denken des Erasmus von Rotterdam," *Deutsche Zeitschrift f. Philosophie*, 17 (1969), 1076-1092.

    On one hand, Erasmus' *Institutio Principis Christiani* supports growing power of new mercantile class; on the other hand, it looks toward an ideal, classless society.

151. Scammell, G.V., "Manning the English Merchant Service in the Sixteenth Century," *Mariner's Mirror*, 60 (1970), 131-154.

    Labor force in 16th cent. England, as seen in crews of merchant ships. Source for authentic idiom and oaths of seamen.

152. Scaperlanda, A., "Thomas Mun and the Export Balance: A Note of Re-valuation," *Nebraska Journal of Economics and Business*, 7 (1968), 57-62.

    Analysis of mercantilism, based on *Englands Treasure of Forraign Trade*, by Thomas Mun (1571-1641), an English merchant.

153. Seymour, William, "The Company that Founded an Empire," *History Today*, 29 (1969), 642-650.

Survey of activities of East India Company during its first hundred years.

154. Sills, David L., ed., *International Encyclopedia of the Social Sciences*, 17 vols. N.Y.: Macmillan, Free Press, 1968.

Rev. *Choice*, 5 (1968), 603-605.

Important revision of the major social science encyclopedia.

155. Smith, R.B., *Land and Politics in the England of Henry VIII: the West Riding of Yorkshire 1530-1546*. Oxford: Clarendon Press, 1970.

Rev. *AHR*, 76 (1971), 1540-1541; *Hist. Jour.*, 14 (1971); 221-223.

Link between possession of land and exercise of political power. Analyzes the Pilgrimage of Grace and argues rebellion was deliberately organized by disaffected nobility and gentry.

156. Smith, Richard S., "Sir Francis Willoughby's Ironworks, 1570-1610," *RMS*, 11 (1967), 90-140.

Significant example of Elizabethan member of aristocracy or gentry with industrial interests, documenting his great expenditure and profits.

157. Steensgaard, Niels, "European Shipping to Asia, 1497-1700," *Scand. Econ. Hist. Rev.*, 18 (1970), 1-11.

Divides 16th and 17th cent. fluctuations in European shipping to Asia into six periods. Periods of growth: 1) before 1510, 2) 1591-1620, 3) 1651-1670. Periods of decline or stasis: 1) 1511-1590, 2) 1621-1650, 3) 1671-1700. Overall European figures throw doubt on concept of "17 cent. economic crisis."

158. Stephens, W.B., "The Cloth Exports of the Provincial Ports, 1600-1640," *Econ.H.R.*, 2nd ser., 22 (August 1969), 228-248.

Studies volume of overseas trade in woolen cloth from provincial ports as a preliminary step to filling in the general picture of 17th-cent. English commerce.

159. Stone, Lawrence, Review articles on his *Crisis of the Aristocracy, 1558-1641*, Oxford, 1965, cited elsewhere in this section.

An important review of this major book appears in *TLS* [7 April 1966], 285-288. While it points to the work's significance, it raises serious questions concerning statistical evidence.

160. ———, "Social Mobility in England 1500-1700," *Past and Present*, 33 (1966), 16-55.

Cites the period between 1540-1640 as one of exceptional social
mobility which eventually caused great instability politically
and a "crisis of the aristocracy." He claims that the mobility
was due to a shift in ownership of the lands from the titled
nobility to the rising middle classes, and also to the sudden
growth in population in these upper classes. This rise in
power of the middle-class merchant and "lower gentry" brought
alarmed reactions from the aristocracy.

161. Tate, William Edward, *The English Village Community and the En-
     closure Movements*. London: Gollancz, 1967.

     Rev. *Archives: Journal of the British Record Association*, 8
     (1968), 165; *N & Q*, n.s., 15 (1968), 400.

     Includes chapter on enclosure movement in Tudor times and in
     17th cent., pp. 63-79, and "Glossary of Technical Terms Used,"
     pp. 185-192.

162. Taylor, Harland, "Price Revolution or Price Revision? The Eng-
     lish and Spanish Trade after 1604," *Ren. and Mod. Stud.*, 12
     (1968), 5-32.

     Traditional view on bullion as basis of English-Spanish trade
     questioned. New perspectives on "price revolution" following
     work of Vicens Vives; questions E.J. Hamilton's *American
     Treasure and the Price Revolution in Spain, 1501-1650* (1934)
     on effect of American precious metals imported into Europe.
     Spain, like the rest of Europe, had a severe economic disloca-
     tion during last decade of 16 cent. and early years of the 17th
     cent.--but in Spain, it began earlier, went deeper, lasted
     longer.

163. Thirsk, Joan, ed., *The Agrarian History of England and Wales*.
     Vol. IV: *1500-1640*. Cambridge/N.Y.: Cambridge Univ. Press,
     1967.

     Rev. *AHR*, 73 (1968), 805-807; *Econ.H.R.*, 2nd ser., 21 (1968), 614-
     619; *Heythrop Journal*, 9 (1968), 98-99; *Historical Journal*, 2 (1968),
     583-586; *History*, 53 (1968), 95-97; *Journal of Economic His-
     tory*, 28 (1968), 742-745; *Listener*, 78 (1967), 88; *Northern
     History*, 3 (1968), 231-232.

     First of seven vols. to be published of complete social and eco-
     nomic history of rural England and Wales (gen. ed., H.P.R. Fin-
     berg); analysis of farming regions, climate, tools, etc.; in-
     fluence of types of land on social organization; landlords
     (crown, noblemen, gentlemen, yeomen) and farm laborers; enclo-
     sures; housing, marketing, prices, profits, rents; market town
     and private trader.

164. ———, ed., *Land, Church, and People: Essays Presented to
     Professor H.P.R. Finberg*. Reading: British Agricultural His-
     tory Society, 1970.

     Rev. *Econ.H.R.*, 2nd ser., 24 (1971), 703-704.

Festschrift published as supplement to *Agric. Hist. Rev.*, Vol.
28. Articles by Joan Thirsk, "Seventeenth-Century Agriculture
and Social Change"; by V.H.T. Skipp, "Economic and Social
Change in the Forest of Arden, 1530-1649"; by Claire Cross,
"The Economic Problems of the See of York: Decline and Recovery
in the Sixteenth Century"; and by Margaret Spufford, "The
Schooling of the Peasantry in Cambridgeshire, 1575-1700."

165. ———, "Younger Sons in the Seventeenth Century," *History*, 54
(1969), 358-377.

Argues that gentry of 16th and 17th cents. rose at expense of
their younger brothers; illustrates point through contemporary
literature of protest by and for younger sons.

166. Thompson, F.M.L., "The Social Distribution of Landed Property
in England Since the Sixteenth Century," *Econ.H.R.*, 2nd ser.,
19 (1966), 505-517.

The major purposes of this study are to warn economic historians of errors in their methodology which lead to mistaken conclusions, and to reevaluate statistics provided in following
works (among others): Lawrence Stone, *The Crisis of the Aristocracy, 1558-1641*; E. Kerridge, "The Movement of Rent, 1540-
1640," *EHR*, 6 (1953); Thomas Wilson, *The State of England,
1600*. Article pertinent to consideration of property holdings
between 1550 and Civil War.

167. Thompson, I.A.A., "A Map of Crime in Sixteenth-Century Spain,"
Econ.H.R., 2nd ser., 21 (1968), 244-267.

Quantitative study of incidence and distribution of crime in
16th-cent. Spain.

168. Trevor-Roper, H.R., "The Bishopric of Durham and the Capitalist
Reformation," *Durham Research Review*, 5 (1967) 103-116.

Discusses Thomas Sutton, said to have been model for Ben Jonson's *Volpone*, and John Dudley, and their economic manipulations
during late 16th and early 17th cents.

169. Tucker, G.S.L., review of D.V. Glass and D.E.C. Eversley, eds.,
Population in History: Essays in Historical Demography (London,
1965), in *Econ.H.R.*, 2nd ser., 20, 1 (1967), 131-140.

An extensive critical review of this compendium of 27 essays
(some are reprints) by several authors. More than third of the
essays are on English demographic history, although France is
also well represented, with others on Ireland, Scandinavia,
Italy, Flanders, and North America.

170. Tucker, M.J., "Life at Henry VII's Court," *Hist. Today*, 19
(1969), 325-331.

Examines Henry's cultural and athletic pursuits, circle of edu-
cated men at court, education of his children, and his reputation as a builder.

171. Van Dorsten, J.A., "Mr. Secretary Cecil, Patron of Letters,"
      ES, 50 (1969), 545-553.

      Cecil's literary relations with English and foreign writers.

172. Vesce, Thomas E., "Chivalric Virtue and the *Histoire du Seig-
      neur de Bayart*," *Rom. N.*, 12 (1970/71), 192-197.

      Document on nobility, illustrating destruction of chivalry by
      rise of modern statecraft.

173. Vives, Jaime Vicens and Jorge Nadal Oller, *An Economic History
      of Spain*, trans. F.M. Lopez-Morillas. Princeton Univ. Press,
      1969.

      Rev. *Choice*, 6 (1969), 424.

      Spanish economy from early times through the 19th cent., with
      chapters on 16th and 17th cents.

174. Wagner, Sir Anthony, *Heralds of England: A History of the
      Office and College of Arms*. London: H.M.S.O.; distributed by
      British Information Service, 1967.

      Rev. *AHR*, 74 (1968), 590-591; *Hist. Today*, 18 (1968), 504-505.

      Central to national pageantry, Office and College of Arms was
      also office of visitation, and approved and registered claims
      to arms, pedigrees, and gentility. Illus. study of its chang-
      ing role in English society.

175. Warner, Oliver, "Elsinore and the Danish Sound Dues," *Hist.
      Today*, 17 (September 1967), 619-626.

      Importance of Elsinore as a source of raw materials in shipping
      as well as the Baltic products; illustrates how Elsinore was
      topical in England during Shakespeare's time and its signifi-
      cance in *Hamlet*.

176. Welch, Edwin, ed., *Plymouth Building Accounts of the Sixteenth
      and Seventeenth Centuries*. Devon and Cornwall Record Society,
      N.S., Vol. 12. Torquay: Devonshire Press, 1967.

      Rev. *Econ.H.R.*, 2nd ser., 2, 21 (1968), 388-389.

      Three sets of accounts on erection of public buildings at Ply-
      mouth in later 16th and early 17th cents. (1564-65; 1606-07;
      1614-20).

177. Wernham, R.B., *The Counter-Reformation and the Price Revolution*,
      Vol. III of *New Cambridge Modern History*. Cambridge, Eng.:
      Cambridge Univ. Press, 1968.

      Rev. *AHR*, 75 (1969), 478-481.

      Studies period between end of Lutheran Reformation and first
      warnings of Thirty Years' War.

178. Wolffe, B.P., *The Crown Lands, 1461 to 1536. An Aspect of
      Yorkist and Early Tudor Government.* London: Allen and Unwin;
      N.Y.: Barnes and Noble, 1970.

      Rev. *AHR*, 76 (1971), 759-760; *Econ.H.R.*, 2nd ser., 25 (1972),
      359-360.

      On administration of royal lands under Yorkists and Henry VII,
      and on administration and finance under Henry VII and Henry
      VIII. Illustrated documents.

179. Woolf, Stuart, "The Aristocracy in Transition: A Continental
      Comparison," *Econ.H.R.*, 2nd ser., 23 (1970), 520-531.

      Responds to Stone's *The Crisis of the Aristocracy, 1558-1641*,
      and his claim that crisis of nobility was one of three main
      causes of English revolution. By comparing the English with
      continental aristocratic crisis where there were no political
      upheavals, author finds that existence of large non-aristocratic
      group with economic and administrative power in England accounts
      for different outcomes. Cites this "tax-payer" opposition to
      church and crown as more important in producing revolution than
      crisis of aristocracy.

180. Wrigley, E.A., "Family Limitations in Pre-Industrial England,"
      Econ.H.R., 2nd ser., 19 (1966), 82-109.

      Family control in England 1560-1837, based on English parish
      registers. Figures for 16th and 17th cents. are revealing.
      Notes especially high fertility rates during reigns of Eliza-
      beth and James I. (Rev. by M. Flinn, in *Econ.H.R.*, 2nd ser.,
      20, 1, 1967, 140-144.)

II. EDUCATIONAL CONTEXTS

181. Ascham, Roger, *The Schoolmaster (1570)*, ed. Lawrence V. Ryan. Ithaca, N.Y.: Cornell Univ. Press for Folger Shakespeare Library, 1967.

Rev. *BHR*, 30 (1968), 424–426.

Modernized text of humanist advice on education.

182. Benrath, Gustav Adolf, "Die Universität der Reformationszeit," *Archiv für Reformationsgeschichte*, 57 (1966), 32–51.

Distinguishes three periods of history of German Protestant universities: Humanism (1460–1520), Reformation (1527–1560), Confessionalism (1560–1648).

183. Bierlaire, F., "Un manuel scolaire: les *Familiarium colloquiorum formulae* d'Erasme," *Et. class.*, 36 (1968), 125–139.

Erasmus addresses himself, as pedagogue, to young people, instructing them to speak Latin with proper grammar and vocabulary. Suggests works in which they will find not only models, but wisdom.

184. Booty, J.E., "The Expulsion of John Sanderson: Trouble in an Elizabethan University," *Historical Magazine of the Protestant Episcopal Church*, 36 (1967), 233–247.

Expulsion of young don of Trinity College, Cambridge, 1562, for alleged papist statements; points of 16th- cent. relationship of university to nation, influence of Puritanism, and extent of intellectual freedom.

185. Borckman, William W., "Education of the Poor in Historical and International Perspective until 1800," *Rev. de l'Univ. d'Ottawa*, 40 (1970), 531–560.

Survey from Biblical times. Includes Luther's *Ordnung eines germanen Kasten* (1523), in which procedures for fighting vagrancy and poverty are recommended. Short discussion of Elizabethan provisions for poor.

186. Bullough, Vern L., "Educational Conflict and the Development of Science in the Renaissance," *BuR*, 15 (1967), 35–45.

Scientific invasion of religion, philosophy, and curriculum, aided by availability of printed books.

187.   Cobban, Alan B., *The King's Hall within the University of Cam-*
       bridge in the Later Middle Ages. Cambridge Studies in Medieval
       Life and Thought, 3d ser., vol. I. Cambridge Univ. Press, 1969.
       Rev. *History*, 54 (1969), 418-419.

       On growth of early tutorial and lecture systems; relations with
       university and ecclesiastical authorities; chapter on the war-
       dens and some notable scholars illuminates history of humanism
       and learning in 15th and early 16th cents.

188.   Cordeaux, Edward H., and D.H. Merry, *A Bibliography of Printed*
       Works Relating to the University of Oxford. Oxford: Clarendon
       Press, 1968. Rev. *SCN*, 27 (1969), 34.

       8,868 items, with limiting date 1965-66. Classification: his-
       tory, government, benefactions, reform, teaching, extension,
       religion, social history, almanacs, periodicals, buildings,
       and institutions. Bodleian shelf-marks throughout.

189.   Fletcher, A.J., "The Expansion of Education in Berkshire and
       Oxfordshire, 1500-1670," *Brit. Journal of Educational Studies*,
       15, i (1967), 51-59.

       Examines increase in number of grammar schools in counties of
       Berkshire and Oxfordshire over 170 years. New importance edu-
       cation came to have during this period and benefit to illiterate
       of the area. Concludes that the expansion was aided by a "suc-
       cessful gentry."

190.   Fletcher, John M., "The Teaching of Arts at Oxford, 1400-1520,"
       Paedagogia Historica, 7 (1967), 418-454.

       On what was demanded by Faculty of Arts from its students and
       what changes took place during 15th cent. in methods of instruc-
       tion; 16th-cent. implications.

191.   Fussell, G.E., "The Classical Tradition in West European Farm-
       ing: The Sixteenth Century," *Econ.H.R.*, 2nd ser., 22 (1969),
       538-551.

       Invention of printing in 15th cent. put surviving Latin text-
       books on farming more freely at disposal of anyone who was in-
       terested. Whether these printed editions were read as guides
       to farming or as representative of ancient learning is a dif-
       ficult question, but these sources were used by writers of new
       Latin and vernacular handbooks produced in increasing numbers
       as 16th cent. advanced.

192.   Garin, Eugenio, *L'Educazione in Europa, 1400-1600: Problemi e*
       Programmi. Bari: Laterza, 1966. 2nd ed. (1957. Rev. *BHR*,
       19 [1957], 541-543).

193.   Gibbons, Sister Marina, ". . . English Renaissance Handbooks,
       1477-1550," *DA*, 27 (1967), 3046-A - 3047-A (St. Louis Univ.).

Publications issuing from Caxton press and other early printers
included manuals for self-education in a variety of fields.
Diss. examines them for what they reveal about literacy and attitudes of the period, for instruction they provided a social
class neglected in Renaissance educational system, and for contribution to understanding of ordinary person's state of knowledge in early Tudor England.

194. Greaves, Richard L., *The Puritan Revolution and Educational
      Thought: Background for Reform.* New Brunswick, N.J.: Rutgers
      Univ. Press [1969].

      Rev. *Choice*, 7 (1970), 605.

      Follows debate over education in England from 1640 to 1660,
      focusing on differences between the liberal Puritans and the
      Sectaries.

195. Grendler, Paul F., "The Rejection of Learning in Mid-*Cinque-
      cento* Italy," *Studies in the Renaissance*, 13 (1966), 230-249.

      A small group of mid-16th-cent. Italians known as *Poligrafi*
      protested against Renaissance humanistic insistence upon exten-
      sive classical education. They held that man's surest path to
      happiness was a pastoral life and simple ignorance.

196. Hart, William Robert, "*The English Schoole-Maister* (1596) by
      Edmund Coote: An Edition of the Text with Critical Notes and
      Introductions," *DA*, 28 (1967), 1397-A (Univ. of Michigan).

      Relates the work to Petty School instruction in Elizabethan
      England. Considers its utility as evidence for standard London
      speech and usage in the 1590's.

197. Hattaway, Michael, "Paradoxes of Solomon: Learning in the Eng-
      lish Renaissance," *JHI*, 29 (1968), 499-530.

      Attitudes to Solomon as indications of ambivalent attitudes to
      learning in late 16th cent.: learning as related to divine
      wisdom, but marked by human limitations. Opposition symbolized
      by Pope Innocent III and F. Bacon.

198. Henson, Edwin, and A.J. Loomie, "A Register of the Students at
      St. Gregory's College at Seville, 1591-1605," *Recusant History*,
      9 (1967), 163-170.

      Lists English students and priests.

199. Herding, Otto. "Ambiguity in Writings on Humanistic Education:
      Text Criticism and the Concept of Man: Supplementary Remarks,"
      Studies in the Renaissance, 13 (1966), 220-229.

      Concerned mostly with the Continent. Connects "form interpre-
      tation and the history of ideas," especially in the case of
      Erasmus. Article supplements Herding's "Zur Problematik human-
      istischer Erziehungschriften: Textforschung und Menschenbild,"

Rapports of the XIIe Congrès International des Sciences Historiques (Wien, 1965), III, 87-93.

200. Jenzer, Carlo, *Lebensnähe, Lebensferne und Realismus, in den pädagogischen Ansichten von Michel de Montaigne*. Berne: H. Lang, 1969.

    Rev. *BHR*, 32 (1970), 509-512.

    First part is study of concept of *Lebensnähe* (proximity or attachment to life) in work of Montaigne. Second part contains analysis of Montaigne's attitude regarding pedagogical realism. Third part insists on opposition between Montaignian trust in nature and the realistic attitude, consisting of intervening actively to modify nature according to human utility.

201. Kearney, Hugh, *Scholars and Gentlemen: Universities and Society in Pre-Industrial Britain, 1500-1700*. Ithaca, N.Y.: Cornell Univ. Press, 1970.

    Rev. *AHR*, 76 (1971), 1161-1162; *Choice*, 8 (1971), 1554; *History*, 56 (1971), 95-96; *Studies: An Irish Quarterly*, 59 (1970), 429-432.

    Connects universities (Oxford and Cambridge) with Tudor social pressures, both humanist and ecclesiastical-administrative. Notes Ramist influence in Elizabethan periods as a potential revolutionary force.

202. Kessler, John David, "Leonhard Culmann and the German-Language School Drama in Nürnberg in the Sixteenth Century," *DA*, 31 (1970), 1762-63-A (Univ. of Texas at Austin).

    Development of these plays from school programs written and directed by Culmann. Content is didactic, staging unsophisticated.

203. La Fontaine, Sister Mary Joan, "A Critical Translation of Philip Melanchthon's *Elementorum Rhetorices Libri Duo*," *DA*, 30 (1969), 852-A (Univ. of Mich.).

    Modes of thought prevalent in Renaissance educational theories. Provides the first translation of *Elementorum Rhetorices libri duo* (1542).

204. Lawson, John, *Medieval Education and the Reformation*. Student's Library of Education; N.Y.: Humanities Press, 1967.

    Rev. *Historian*, 30 (1968), 461-462.

    English educational institutions through 16th cent. Depends on A.F. Leach's compilation, *Educational Charters and Documents*.

205. Margolin, J.-C., ed., *Erasme. Declamatio de Pueris Statim ac Liberaliter Instituendis*. Translated into French, with introd. and commentary. Geneva: Droz, 1966. Rev. *YWML*, 28 (1966), 56-57.

    Introduction has chapter on Erasmus' educational views: on the education of the child.

206. McLuhan, Marshall, "Cicero and the Renaissance Training for Prince and Poet," *Ren. and Ref.*, 6 (1970), 38-42.

Tradition of stateman's manuals, with Ciceronian-Augustine concept of the *doctus orator*. (Machiavelli outside this tradition, knowing it and rejecting it; opposing Circeronian civic eloquence, and favoring a curt style. He shares with Luther and Calvin a split between reason and grace, which is also Christian. He is opposed to eloquence as he distrusts reason.) Hal and Hamlet are in Castiglione-Elyot tradition of fashioning of king and orator.

207. Meyer, Carl S., "Melanchthon's Influence on English Thought in the Sixteenth Century," in *Miscellanea Historiae Ecclestiasticae II* (Bibliothèque de la Revue d'Histoire Ecclésiastique, fasc. 44.) Congress, 1965. Louvain: Publications Universitaires, 1967, pp. 163-185.

Detailed essay on Melanchthon's English impact in diverse areas: religious, moral, educational, rhetorical. Develops from T.W. Baldwin's view that Melanchthon the educator was widely used in English grammar schools and at times plagiarized by English writers. Essay aims to go further, to show by preliminary effort how *praeceptor Germaniae* was also *praeceptor Angliae*. Basic article intended to stimulate further work on other 16th-cent. reformers.

208. Mulder, John R., *The Temple of the Mind: Education and Literary Taste in Seventeenth-Century England*. N.Y.: Pegasus, 1969.

Rev. *SCN*, 28 (1970), 6-7; *Milton Quarterly*, 3 (1969), 73-74.

Describes 17th-cent. educational methods and ideals. Second half of the book is devoted to relations between religion and literature. Description of traditional exegesis of types and anti-types in Old and New Testaments.

209. Müller, Gregor, *Bildung und Erziehung im Humanismus der Italienischen Renaissance*. Wiesbaden: Franz Steiner Verlag, 1969.

Detailed 627-page study. Bibliography, pp. 504-600; Stichwortregister, pp. 601-612, including major relevant topics, e.g., Stoizimus, Epikureismus, etc.; Christian education, humanistic ideals, moral-civil aims. Deals with "Die Grundkonzeption der *studia humanitatis.*"

210. Neuville, H. Richmond, Jr., "The Scepter and the Soul: the Nature and Education of a Prince in Renaissance Literature," *DA*, 30 (1969), 692-A (New York Univ.).

Renaissance theoretical and literary writing evidence two attitudes: that of ideal Christian prince and that of politically astute prince whose *virtù* is not necessarily moral. Problem of ruling well is treated idealistically by More, Erasmus, Elyot, and Castiglione; and realistically by Machiavelli.

211. Oakeshott, Walter, "Sir Walter Raleigh's Library," *The Library*,
      5th ser., 23 (1968), 285-327.

      Studies Raleigh's library to determine extent of its relation
      to the *History* and its value as mirror of Raleigh's mind.
      Prints list of 515 books from list in Raleigh's hand in common-
      place book once in Phillipps Library (MS 6339).

212. Pace, Richard, *De Fructu qui ex doctrina percipitur, The bene-
      fit of a liberal education*, ed. and trans. Frank Manley and
      Richard S. Sylvester. Publ. of the Renaissance Society of
      America: Renaissance Text Series, 2; N.Y.: Ungar, 1967.

      Rev. *SCN*, 26 (1968), 47-48.

      Pace (1483-1536) in *De Fructu* (1517) provides a defense of
      learning and liberal arts against those favoring mere common
      sense (*prudentia*), which he holds is nothing.

213. Pérouse, Gabriel-A., "Le Dr. Huarte de San Juan: Pédagogie et
      politique sous Philippe II," *BHR*, 32 (1970), 81-93.

      Huarte's *Examen de Ingenios para las Sciencias* proposes that
      education ought to be suited to the natural preferences of the
      individual, and envisions a mobile society based on natural
      ability, not birth.

214. Petrarch, F. *Four Dialogues for Scholars*, ed. and trans. Con-
      rad H. Rawski. Cleveland, Ohio: Press of Western Reserve
      Univ., 1967. Rev. *MLR*, 63 (1968), 987; *Spec.*, 43 (1968), 534.

      Dialogues: "On the Abundance of Books," "On the Fame of Wri-
      ters," "On the Master's Degree," and "On Various Academic
      Titles"; from *De remediis utriusque fortunae*. Reflections on
      problems of human existence, intellectual, emotional, moral.

215. Prest, W.R., "The Learning Exercises at the Inns of Court 1590-
      1640," *Journal of the Society of Public Teachers of Law*, 9
      (1967), 301-313.

      Though causes of eventual collapse of legal instruction system
      (by aural "learning exercises") at Inns of Court were present
      before the Civil War, they had little effect on the performance
      of learning exercises. Refutation of Holdsworth's thesis re-
      garding beginning of decline in later 16th cent., and mainten-
      ance only with "immense difficulty" during first half of 17th
      cent. During 50 years prior to Civil War, aural learning exer-
      cises, despite partial obsolescence, continued to be performed
      conscientiously and successfully. For (1), they were practical
      complement to book learning, allowing training "on feet," and
      (2) they were one of the means by which students qualified for
      call to bar.

216. ————, "Legal Education of the Gentry, 1560-1640," *Past and
      Present*, No. 38 (1967), 20-39.

Inns of Court in that period closely rivaled Oxford and Cambridge in status, serving both as law schools and as fashionable academies with urban diversions.

217. Purvis, J.S., "The Literacy of the Later Tudor Clergy in Yorkshire," *Studies in Church History*, vol. 5, ed. G.J. Cuming. Leiden: Brill, 1969.

At least half of parochial clergy did not show a high level of Latin learning, but after 1560 there was a rise in literacy owing to policy and efforts of episcopate.

218. Rebhorn, Wayne A., "Renaissance Optimism and the Limits of Freedom: Educational Theory in the Quattrocento, Erasmus, Castiglione, and Rabelais," *DA*, 30 (1969), 735-A (Yale Univ.).

Optimistic faith of Renaissance was qualified by limits education placed on human freedom.

219. Reif, Sister Patricia, "The Textbook Tradition in Natural Philosophy, 1600-1650," *JHI*, 30 (1969), 17-32.

Argues that the manualists, despite their assertions about the primacy of reason and experience over authority, were enslaved by the written word. Their procedure consisted in a perusal of authors rather than a direct investigation, and reflective analysis, of sense experience. Textbook natural philosophy was involved with "pouring continually upon a few paper Idols" and was dominated by textual controversies. (Based on her diss., St. Louis Univ., 1962, "Natural Philosophy in Some Early Seventeenth Century Scholastic Textbooks.")

220. Simon, Joan, *Education and Society in Tudor England*. Cambridge Univ. Press, 1966.

Rev. *AHR*, 72 (1966), 178-179; J.E. Neale, *English Historical Rev.*, 82 (1967), 384; Kenneth Charlton, *Brit. Journal of Educational Studies*, 14 (1966), 84-87.

Book divided into three parts: 15th cent. background and humanist innovations; effects of Reformation on education; place of education in Elizabethan age, including expansion of vernacular education fostered by Protestant ethic and pressure of practical needs. Discusses influence of Colet, Erasmus, and Vives.

221. Stelling-Michaud, Sven, ed., *Les Universités Européennes du XIVe au XVIIIe Siècles. Aspects et Problèmes. Actes du Colloque International à l'Occasion du VIe Centenaire de l'Université Jagellonne de Cracovie, 6-8 mai 1964*. (Commission Internationale pour l'histoire des Universités, Etudes et travaux, 1). Geneva: Droz, 1967.

Rev. *AHR*, 73 (1968), 1506.

Includes W.A. Pantin, "The Conception of the Universities in England in the Period of the Renaissance," pp. 101-113.

222. Warkentin, Germaine, "Some Renaissance Schoolbooks in the Os-
      borne Collection," *Renaissance and Reformation* (Univ. of Toron-
      to), 5 (1969), 2-10.

      Many kinds of early young people's books represented in Renais-
      sance holdings of the collection, ranging from a black-letter
      grammar (Strasbourg, 1505), through *Valentine and Orson*, etc.

223. Watson, Foster, ed., *English Writers on Education, 1480-1603:
      A Source Book*, ed. Robert D. Pepper. Gainesville, Fla.:
      Scholars' Facsimiles, 1967 (orig. ed. 1902-1906).

      Bibliographical descriptions, content-analyses, and extracts
      from writings published in England on education, in facsimile
      reproduction from reports.

224. White, Eugene R., "Master Holdsworth and 'A Knowledge Very Use-
      ful and Necessary,'" *QJS*, 53 (1967), 1-16.

      Regarding "Directions for a Student in the Universitie," con-
      temporary account of education at Cambridge college during
      first half of 17th cent.

225. Wood, Anthony A., *Athenae Oxonienses*. Hildesheim: Olms, 1969.

      History of writers and others who had their education in the
      University of Oxford, from 1500 to 1690: to which are added
      the *Fasti*, or *Annals* of the university. New edition with
      additions and a continuation by Philip Bliss to the edition of
      London, 1813-1820. Bibliographic note by Bernhard Fabian.

III. ETHICAL

226. Allen, Richard Ottaway, "Jacobean Drama and the Literature of
Decay: A Study of Conservative Reaction in Literature," *DA*,
30 (1970), 3899-A - 3900-A (Univ. of Mich.).

Literature of decay as a reaction to social change, from 1596
to 1616.

227. Archambault, Paul, "Commynes' *Saigesse* and the Renaissance Idea
of Wisdom," *Bibliothèque d'Humanisme et Renaissance*, 29 (1967),
613-632.

Renaissance ideas of wisdom tended to be ethically oriented,
based on traditional Christian morality, and to follow precepts
of medieval theologians and classical philosophers. Some exceptional figures, experienced in political life, disregarded
textbook admonitions and based their recommendations on empirical awareness. The latter group included Machiavelli and Commynes, and their political wisdom had a ring of moral neu-
trality.

228. Aulotte, Robert, *Amyot et Plutarque. La tradition des "Moralia" au XVI siècle* (Geneva: Droz, 1965), summarized in *Annales
de l'Université de Paris*, 36 année (1966), no. 2, 212-214.

Less known than the *Parallel Lives*, Plutarch's *Moralia* had great
success in second half of 15th cent. and through all of the
16th cent.

229. Babut, Daniel, *Plutarque et la Vertu Éthique*. Paris: Société
d'Edition "Les Belles Lettres," [1969?].

Introduction, text, translation, commentary; long introduction
and notes, pp. 1-88.

230. Baldwin, William, *A Treatise of Morall Philosophie*, enlarged by
Thomas Palfreyman, ed. Robert H. Bowers. Gainesville, Fla.:
Scholars' Facsimiles, 1967.

Oft-reprinted Renaissance collection of philosophical sentences
and sayings. Baldwin's 1547 work expanded by Palfreyman, reproduced from 1620 edition.

231. Baraz, Michäel, *L'Être et la Connaissance selon Montaigne*.
Paris: Jose Corti, 1968.

Rev. *BHR*, 32 (1970), 707-710.

Clarification of Montaigne's ideas about being in relation to
constant flux and the core of human nature. Purpose of

intellectual activity is proper use of reason, which forms personality and culminates in friendship. Includes section on
Montaigne's imagery.

232.   Bennett, John W., "Comments on 'The Renaissance Foundations of
       Anthropology,'" *Amer. Anthropologist*, 68 (1966), 215-220. This
       is reply to John H. Rowe's article in that journal, 67 (1965),
       1-20. Rejoinder by Rowe, 68 (1966), 220-222.

       On Rowe's article, which Bennett considers to add important
       supplement to book by Margaret Hodgen, *Early Anthropology in
       the Sixteenth and Seventeenth Centuries* (1964). Bennett ques-
       tions, among other points, Rowe's views on Renaissance-medieval
       relationships and his frank "Burckhardtian" bias.

233.   Bercovitch, Sacvan, "Shakespeare's Sonnet CXXIV," *Expl.*, 27,
       no. 3 (1968), 22.

       Apparent parallel to Montaigne's "Of the Inconsistencie of our
       Actions."

234.   Berlin, Normand, *The Base String: The Underworld in Elizabe-
       than Drama*. Rutherford, N.J.: Fairleigh Dickinson Univ.
       Press, 1968. Rev. *Studia Neoph.*, 42 (1970), 469-471.

       Chapters on climate of opinion regarding the underworld; the
       morality tradition. Dekker, Jonson, Shakespeare.

235.   Boon, Jean-Pierre, "Filiation entre religion et morale dans
       les *Essais* de Montaigne," *RR*, 58 (1967), 12-22.

       Attempts to show connection between Montaigne's professed
       Catholicism and the moral ideas of the *Essais*, notably that man
       lives best in conformity with the "human condition." Finds
       that though Montaigne's morality is highly individualistic, it
       is better understood against a background of Catholic thought
       on sin, repentance, original sin, the Creator, Purgatory,
       grace, and the will.

236.   ————, "L'idéal de l'honneste homme' est-il compatible avec la
       théorie évolutive des *Essais* de Montaigne?" *PMLA*, 83 (1968),
       298-304.

       Montaigne's ideas on the "honnête homme" evidence, more than
       any others, his role as precursor in the history of French and
       European thought. Elucidation of Montaigne's *Essais* by certain
       aspects of the ideal of the "honnête homme."

237.   ————, "Montaigne et Epicure: Aspects de l'hédonisme dans les
       Essais," *CL*, 20 (1968), 64-68.

       Influence of Epicurus on Montaigne, especially regarding death.

238.   ————, "Montaigne et ses 'grands hommes,'" *French Rev.*, 43
       (1969/70), 34-41.

       Montaigne's ancient models and his changing relations to them.

239. Bradford, Arnold May, "The Moral Vision in Mid-Tudor Lyric Poetry," *DA*, 28 (1968), 2642-2643-A (Univ. of Virginia).

   On English poetry, 1530-1579, more fully understood when even amatory and apparently hedonistic verse is related to an intrinsic moral vision and broader moral perspective.

240. Brock, Dewey H., "Poet and Society: A Critical Study of Ben Jonson's Concept of Society in Light of Classical and Christian Ideals," *DA*, 30 (1969), 5440-A (Univ. of Kansas).

   Although influenced by Aristotle, Jonson's social ideals are essentially English and Christian; man is by nature a social and rational creature.

241. Burns, Sister Josephine, "The Early Theory of Human Choice in the Philosophy of Francisco Suárez," *DA*, 29 (1969), 4046-A (Marquette Univ.).

   Early Suarezian position on the theory of causality, focusing on pertinent sections of works formulated as early as 1571: *De Anima V* and *Metaphysical Disputations*.

242. Cameron, K., "Montaigne and the Mask," *ECr*, 8, no. 3 (1968), 198-207.

   Importance of mask theme in Montaigne's attitude towards life is indicated by his use of it in a wide range of thought: love, philosophy, avarice, language, etc.

243. Chassang, A., and Ch. Senninger, *XVIe siècle, tome II, Points de vue et références*. Paris: Hachette, 1969.

   Rev. *BSAM*, no. 19 (1969), 54-55.

   Senninger devotes part of this volume to aspects of Montaigne and his works.

244. *Cicero on Moral Obligation*. New translation of Cicero's *De Officiis*, introduction and notes by John Higginbotham. London: Faber & Faber, 1967.

   Rev. *Heythrop Journal*, 9 (1968), 196-197.

   Indicates location of manuscript of Cicero's *De Officiis* with Petrarch's annotations. Introduction deals with Renaissance, natural law, Petrarch, and Cicero; Cicero's preference for active life.

245. Clark, Carol E., "Seneca's Letters to Lucilius as a Source of Some of Montaigne's Imagery," *BHR*, 30 (1968), 249-266.

   Opposes widely held view that the mature Montaigne evolved away from Seneca's influence, rejecting Stoicism. Montaigne shows strong Senecan influence indirectly in use of images and metaphors; Seneca changes from his master to personal friend.

246. Crawley, D., "Decision and Character in Chapman's *The Tragedy of Caesar and Pompey*," *SEL*, 7 (1967), 277-297.

    Moral value in play based on Stoic doctrine.

247. Dassonville, M., "De Quelques Préjugés de Montaigne," *Esprit Créateur*, 8, no. 3 (1968), 175-184.

    Selection from among the *Essais* of a certain number of affirmations or definitions which attest to prejudices of a middle-class gentleman of old France.

248. Delany, Paul, *British Autobiography in the Seventeenth Century*. London: Routledge and Kegan Paul, 1969.

    Rev. *ELN*, 8 (1971), 321-325; *History*, 55 (1970), 119-120.

    Origins of modern autobiographical writing set in the Renaissance; the book questions generalizations on rise of individual self-consciousness. Divides material into religious and secular; then subdivides former according to denomination.

249. Diekstra, F.N.M., ed., *A Dialogue between Reason and Adversity: A Late Middle English Version of Petrarch's "De Remediis."* Ed. from manuscript Ii.VI.39 in the University Library, Cambridge, with an introduction, notes and glossary, and the original Latin text. N.Y.: Humanities Press; Assen, The Netherlands: Van Gorcum, 1968.

    Rev. *Spec.*, 47 (1972), 113-116.

    Apart from Chaucer's use of Petrarch, this is said to be the first adaptation of any of Petrarch's works in England; antedates Tudor translation by Thomas Twyne. Petrarch's earliest reputation in England was as moralist. Senecan influence on Petrarch, Boethian borrowings in English text, pointed out. Relation of work to dialogue, *contemptus mundi, consolatio*. Work provides Latin and English parallel versions.

250. Doherty, Dennis, O.S.B., *The Sexual Doctrine of Cardinal Cajetan*. Regensburg: Verlag F. Pustet, 1966.

    How Tommaso De Vio, Cardinal Caetano or Cajetan (1469?-1534?) enlarges and departs from St. Thomas on issues of sexuality. Part I. Life of Cajetan; II. Sexual Order. III. Marriage. Chap. 8 deals with Sexual Order Abused, including adultery, etc.

251. Eisenstadt, S.N., ed., *The Protestant Ethic and Modernization: A Comparative View*. N.Y./London: Basic Books, 1968.

    On Max Weber thesis: 18 essays by various hands on "Protestantism and Capitalism in Pre-Revolutionary England," "Once Again: Calvinism and Capitalism," etc. Book divided into the Protestant Ethic thesis in the framework of sociological theory of Weber's work; the application of the Protestant Ethic thesis in Europe and America; the application outside of Europe.

252.   ————, "The Protestant Ethic Thesis in Analytical and Compara-
        tive Context," *Diogenes*, 59 (1967), 25-46.

        Surveys controversy over Weber thesis and subsequent tendency
        to emphasize the "transformative" capacities of religion, i.e.,
        those impulses beyond the original direct *Wirtschaftsethik*
        which lead to the transformation of social reality.

253.   Erasmus, D., *Julius Exclusus*, trans. Paul Pascal; introduction
        and notes by J. Kelly Sowards. Bloomington: Indiana Univ.
        Press, 1968.

        Rev. *Church History*, 39 (1970), 272-273; *History*, 54 (1969),
        421.

        Accepts attribution to Erasmus and relates the *Julius* to *Praise
        of Folly*, presenting the former as important document in moral
        and intellectual biography of Erasmus.

254.   Fleisher, Martin, "Trust and Deceit in Machiavelli's Comedies,"
        JHI, 27 (1966), 365-380.

        Machiavelli did not divorce public and private life. The
        themes he uses in his *Discourses* he applies in his comedies,
        e.g., *Clizia* and *Mandragola*. Article refers to disorder in
        the family and use of wit and deceit to achieve a *new* order.
        Shows a changing attitude to family life and changing values,
        with an application to all levels of life.

255.   Fothergill-Payne, Louise W., "*La Celestina* como esbozo de una
        lección Maquiavelica," *RF*, 81 (1969), 158-174.

        La Celestina anticipates attitudes expressed in Machiavelli's
        Principe, especially individual's responsibility for his own
        actions, one's need to make the most of his own ingenuity, and
        to profit from his adversary's weakness.

256.   Frame, Donald M., *Montaigne's Essais: A Study*. Englewood
        Cliffs, N.J.: Prentice-Hall, 1969.

        Rev. *French Rev.*, 43 (1969), 354-355.

        Compendium of past and recent criticism in an introduction to
        the *Essais*; Montaigne's thought, style, humanism, evolution.

257.   Fraser, Russell, *The War against Poetry*. Princeton, N.J.:
        Princeton Univ. Press, 1970.

        Rev. *JEGP*, 70 (1971), 645-655; *SJ (West)*, (1971), 212-213.

        Traces, from Plato, history of war against art. Claims Protes-
        tant attackers of English stage after 1570 were motivated by a
        sense of utility, not piety. The new men of science and theo-
        logy wanted to refine and rationalize truth; they saw drama as
        a useless ceremony and poets as sycophants toward aristocracy.

258. Gagneux, Marcel, "Nature et condition humaines selon François
      Guichardin," *REI*, 16 (1970), 231-263.

      Man is the moving force of history but he confronts a hostile
      reality in which reason and past examples are poor guides and
      the future is always uncertain.

259. Gutwirth, Marcel, "Montaigne pour et contre Sebond," *Revue des
      Sciences Humaines*, 34 (1969), 175-188.

      Montaigne's apology as reflecting a moral and intellectual--as
      well as oedipal--crisis; its ambivalence; his secret misprizing
      of the views of Sebond, as well as of his beloved, protecting
      father, for whom he translated Sebond.

260. Hall, H.B., "Segismundo and the Rebel Soldier," *Bull. Hisp.
      Stud.*, 45, no. 3 (1968), 189-200.

      In *La Vida es Sueño* of Calderón, justice (poetic or otherwise)
      is sacrificed to the reestablishment of order, one which even
      from a political point of view seems extremely fragile.

261. Holyoake, S. John, "Montaigne and the Concept of 'Bien Né,'"
      BHR, 30 (1968), 483-498.

      Montaigne distinguishes between those who were "bien nés" and
      pedants--the former are closer to the more favorable sugges-
      tions of the term "nature."

262. Howells, Anne Blackman, "Bravery and the Observation of the In-
      evitable: A Study of Beaumont and Fletcher, Ford and Middle-
      ton," *DA*, 29 (1968), 871-872-A (Univ. of Wash.).

      In Middleton's and Beaumont and Fletcher's era, c. 1610-1625,
      a less active "bravery" is admired which accepts and endures
      pain and chaos. In Middleton vice pervades and is inevitable,
      erasing distinctions.

263. Isler, Alan David, "Moral Philosophy and the Family in Sidney's
      Arcadia," *HLQ*, 31 (1968), 359-371.

      Theme of household in *Arcadia*; harmony in each of three levels
      of responsibility--individual, household, state--depends on
      each of the others; concern in *Arcadia* with ethics as well as
      politics.

264. ———, "The Moral Philosophy of Sidney's Two *Arcadias*: A Study
      of Some Principal Themes," *DA*, 30 (1969), 1567-A (Columbia
      Univ.).

      The old *Arcadia* cannot be dismissed as a "mere romance." A
      principal theme of both *Arcadias* is the interrelationship of
      the body natural and the body politic.

265. Lablénie, E., ed., *Montaigne, auteur de maximes*. Paris: Société d'édit. d'enseignement supérieur, 1968.

   A repertory of Montaigne's maxims with indexes.

266. Ladner, Gerhart B., *"Homo Viator*: Mediaeval Ideas on Alienation and Order," *Speculum*, 42 (1967), 233-259.

   Intellectual survey of Middle Ages touching on Renaissance. Man as stranger and wayfarer between two worlds; he may assume role of pilgrim, alienated rebel, or fool. Pilgrim as "personnage régnant" of Middle Ages; fool as "personnage régnant" of Renaissance.

267. Legouis, Pierre, "La Leçon Morale du XVIIe Siècle," *EA*, 22 (1969), 113-117.

   On the interior life of 17th-cent. man.

268. Levine, Gerald M., "Violence and Sensationalism in Elizabethan England," *DA*, 30 (1970), 5413-A (New York Univ.).

   Violence in the environment and literature of Elizabethan England as milieu of dramatic writers.

269. Lewis, Clive Staples, *Spenser's Images of Life*, ed. Alastair Fowler. Cambridge U. P., 1967. Rev. *SCN*, 26 (1968), 35.

   Discusses the "False Cupid," Antitypes to the False Cupid, Images of Evil and Good, etc.

270. Lewis, Marjorie Dunlavy, "Shakespeare's Uses of the Duelling Code for Comic and Satiric Effect," *DA*, 18 (1968), 3190-A (Univ. of Kansas).

   Historical background of duelling and the "duello" code against which satirical treatments of pretentious characters are examined. Ideals against which pretenders are contrasted are elaborated in Ruth Kelso's *Doctrine of the English Gentleman in the Sixteenth Century*.

271. Lievsay, John L., "Politic and Moral Maxims in Tassoni's *Annali*," *RenP.* (1967), 11-17.

   Tassoni's compendium of Cardinal Baronius' *Ecclesiastical Annals* (1619-1621) contains over 500 maxims concerning the Church, clergy, state, and prince.

272. Loche, J.B. De, Jr., "Judgment Here: the Homiletic Art of Cyril Tourneur," *DA*, 28 (1968), 2678-9-A (Univ. of Pittsburgh).

   Deals with complexity and aesthetic sophistication of Tourneur's homiletic art, which makes it more than moralizing.

273. Long, A.A., "The Stoic Concept of Evil," *PhQ*, 18 (1968), 329-343.

Stoic evil, *kakia*, set in human sphere, independent of God's actions and intentions, caused by men's misunderstandings of their
own nature and that of the universe. Since almost all men are
guilty of this, *kakos* (morally bad) being, in effect, a description of normal men, the concept itself provides little to guide
moral action.

274. Macquarrie, John, ed., *Dictionary of Christian Ethics*. London:
     S.C.M. Press; Philadelphia: Westminster Press, 1967.

     Contributions by 80 scholars and theologians on ethical topics
     in philosophy, psychology, and theology, with brief biblio-
     graphies; the work is ecumenical. Biblical and Christian ethics
     are of special relevance.

275. Michel, Pierre, "Initiation à une bibliographie pratique de
     Montaigne," *BSAM*, Quatrième série, no. 14 (1968), 47-60.

     Useful primary and secondary bibliography. Records editions,
     followed by lists of materials, e.g., on "Montaigne, la maladie
     et les médecins," "Montaigne homme public . . .," "Montaigne et
     les *Essais*," "Le problème religieux," "Philosophie morale et
     Humanisme," "Montaigne et le 'bon Sauvage.'"

276. Montaigne, M. de, *Essais*. Réproduction photographique de la
     deuxième édition (Bordeaux, 1582). Naples: Liguori, 1969.

     Rev. *BHR*, 32 (1970), 486-487.

     Concise history of editions of *Essais* and an explanation of
     differences between first and second editions; most of 1582
     additions stem from Montaigne's personal and literary experience
     during his trip to Italy.

277. Moore, W.G., "Lucretius and Montaigne," *YFS*, 38 (1967), 109-114.

     Influence of Lucretius on Montaigne, seen as less cerebral than
     physical, a savoring of mystery and human instability, and an
     antipathy to final causes, as well as to large affirmations.

278. Neuse, Richard, "Atheism and Some Functions of Myth in Marlowe's
     Hero and Leander," *MLQ*, 31 (1970), 424-439.

     Hero and Leander explores ethical implication of a godless
     universe.

279. Ochman, Jerzy, "Człowiek i świat dzieł ludzkich w filozfii
     Cardana" [Man and the Work of Mankind in the Philosophy of
     Jerome Cardan (1501-1576)], *Acta Universitatis Wratislāviensis,
     Prace Filozoficzne*, 6, no. 120 (1970), 3-36.

     Presents Cardan's theory that the structure of humanity is
     analogous to that of nature and that man's worth is measured
     by his work and struggles.

280. Orsten, Elisabeth M., "'Patientia' in the B-Text of *Piers
     Plowman*," *Medieval Studies*, 31 (1969), 317-333.

Orthodox Christian teaching in Langland's thinking; on Will's dream-visions, through which he gains understanding and grows in patience.

281. Parfitt, G.A.E., "Ethical Thought and Ben Jonson's Poetry," *SEL*, 9 (1969), 123-134.

Jonson's ethical views embody traditional Renaissance attitudes, but are distinctive in their social rather than religious bias.

282. Pisk, George Michael, "Rogues and Vagabonds in Tudor England: A Study in Fact and Fiction," *DA*, 29 (1968), 576-A (Univ. of Texas).

Pt. I deals with pre-Elizabethan backgrounds; chap. IV treats rogue literature and jest books in England and on the Continent, 1485-1558. Pt. II parallels I, but covers 1558-1603, discusses laws and punishments, social conditions or disruptions conducive to roguery, and offers biographies of some famous criminals, as well as a survey of Elizabethan rogue literature.

283. Pouilloux, Jean-Yves, *Lire les "Essais" de Montaigne*. Paris: Maspero, 1969.

Rev. *BSAM*, no. 20 (1970), 66-69; *TLS*, 7 May 1970, 503.

Opposes critics who extract maxims and eternal truths from *Essais*, or impose order on their willed disorder. Disorder is whole object of the book, which reflects the multiple levels of Montaigne's enterprise. Like Montaigne, reader must abandon quest for essence of things and concentrate on how they appear at different moments, and look at himself looking at his own opinions.

284. Pozzo, G.M., "L'umanesimo morale della persona nel platonismo italiano del Quattrocento," *G. Metafis.*, 23, no. 4 (1968), 463-485.

On moral humanism of Nicholas of Cusa and the origins of the Platonic Academy of Florence; Ficino's moral humanism of the individual; Pico's syncretism and the problem of human dignity.

285. Redding, J.A.Z., "François de la Mothe le Vayer and Morality," *MLR*, 63 (1968), 47-53.

In *La Vertu des Payens*, the moralist uses, for polemic ends, his knowledge of geography and anthropology; virtue is not reserved for Christians and can be attained by practice of natural morality. From this study La Mothe (1588-1672) emerges as neither a thorough-going skeptic nor a rationalist nor a fideist. His moral code is one based on experience and his approach to the problem of morality is an empirical one.

286. Santoro, Mario, *I Concetto dell' uomo nella letteratura del Cinquecento*. Naples: Liguori, 1967.

Contains essays: "La 'fortuna' nella coscienza guicciardiniana
del reale," "Il *Dialogo di Fortuna* di Antonio Phileremo Frego-
so," "L'irrazionale nel territorio dell' umano: Bandello,"
"L'esclusione della 'fortuna' dal destino dell 'uomo': L'Utopia
di Anton F. Doni," "La 'discrezione' nel Galateo di Giovanni
della Casa."

287. Seward, James Hodson, "*Romeo and Juliet*: A Study of Shakespeare's Tragic Vision," *DA*, 29 (1969), 2684-2685-A (Univ. of
Mich.).

Argues that Renaissance possessed a commonly accepted psychology; once this is understood, love between Romeo and Juliet
emerges as a destructive passion. Basic assumptions which
Renaissance made about the nature of man derived from thought
of Aquinas.

288. Soudek, Josef, "Leonardo Bruni and his Public: A Statistical
and Interpretative Study of his Annotated Latin Version of the
(Pseudo-) Aristotelian *Economics*," *Studies in Medieval and Ren.
History*, 5 (1968), 49-136.

Bruni's annotated Latin translation of this work was the most
widely read Renaissance translation of this ancient Greek work
on moral philosophy; editions studied in universities.

289. Sprott, S.E., "The Damned Crew," *PMLA*, 84 (1969), 492-500.

The Damned Crew was a class of roisterers in London from the
1590's to the late 1620's who were represented in literature as
perjurers, assassins, and revellers and who were thought to be
reprobate with the damned crews of devils in hell. Such an interpretation explains view taken by theological controversial-
ists, e.g., Dove, Kellison, and Sutcliffe, and playwrights,
e.g., Chapman.

290. Starobinski, Jean, "Montaigne: Des Morts Exemplaires à la vie
sans Exemple," *Critique*, 24 (1968), 923-935.

Rev. article on Montaigne studies (Michel Butor, *Essai sur les
Essais*, Paris: Gallimard, 1968; Eva Marcu, *Répertoire des
Idées de Montaigne*, Geneva: Droz, 1965; Hugo Friedrich, *Montaigne*, trans., Paris: Gallimard, 1968). Discusses Montaigne's
grief on death of friend, La Boétie.

291. Staub, Hans, *Le Curieux Désir: Scève et Peletier du Mans,
poètes de la connaissance*. Travaux d'Humanisme et Renaissance,
94. Geneva: Droz, 1967.

Rev. *Archiv für das Studium der neueren Sprachen*, 205 (1968),
324-326; *SFr*, 12 (1968), 343.

New desire for knowledge as Renaissance motif; epistemological
preoccupation of a group of poets.

292. Stavig, Mark, *John Ford and the Traditional Moral Order*. Madison: Univ. of Wisconsin Press, 1968.

Rev. *Criticism*, 11 (1969), 102-103; *JEGP*, 67 (1968), 699-702; *SCN*, 26 (1968), 43.

Opposes romantic view that we admire Ford's sinners as great rebels against society. Vice is destroyed in Ford through its own excess. His morality has it both ways, pleasing a sophisticated audience, outraging yet placating at the same time.

293. Stempel, Daniel, "The Silence of Iago," *PMLA*, 84 (1969), 252-263.

In his speech on "vertue" (I.iii) Iago defends absolute power of of the individual to will freely. Iago's subtle twisting of moral values falls into pattern of malign casuistry and cynical self-aggrandizement associated with Jesuit image in England. Iago is the Jesuitical Machiavel who employs language of piety.

294. Thompson, Craig R., "Better Teacher than Scotus or Aquinas," in John L. Lievsay, ed., *Medieval and Renaissance Studies*. (Proceedings of the Southeastern Institute of Medieval and Renaissance Studies, 1966. Medieval and Renaissance Ser., 2;) Durham, N.C.: Duke Univ. Press, 1968, pp. 114-145.

Deals with Erasmus' *The Godly Feast (Convivium Religiosum)*, dialogue of 1522, as significant for 16th-cent. ideas--commonplaces on social, ethical, and religious topics. Effect of Christian humanism on later English religious thought.

295. Trinquet, Roger, "Les deux sources de la morale et de la religion chez Montaigne," *BSAM*, Quatrième série, no. 13 (1968), 24-33.

Despite demonstrations of Montaigne's faith, the impression remains of a man absorbed with pagan values, trained in the pagan classics, incompatible with Christian thought. Faith subsists in Montaigne in dialectical form.

296. Walsh, James J., "Buridan and Seneca," *JHI*, 27, i (1966), 23-40.

Discusses Buridan's commentary on the *Nicomachean Ethics* and its role in preparing the way for the enthusiasms of the Renaissance, since Buridan was used as a textbook during the transition from medieval thought. Treats Buridan's use of Seneca as an authority in the discussion of the *Ethics*.

IV. HISTORICAL

297. Adamson, Jack H., and Harold F. Folland, *The Shepherd of the Ocean; an Account of Sir Walter Raleigh and His Times.* Boston: Gambit; London: Bodley Head, 1969. Rev. *WHR*, 24 (1970), 88-89.

Literary portrait against historical background of Elizabethan England during Raleigh's lifetime, 1552-1618. Based on sources in contemporary literature and government documents.

298. Akrigg, G.P.V., *Shakespeare and the Earl of Southampton.* Harvard U.P.; Toronto: Saunders, 1968. Rev. *TLS*, 19 Sept. 1968, p. 1049.

Begins with biography of Southampton and then considers the connection with Shakespeare.

299. Archambault, Paul, "Sallust in France: Thomas Basin's Idea of History and of the Human Condition," *PLL*, 4 (1968), 227-257.

Views Basin's chronicle as the work of a 15th-cent. humanist and man of letters, rather than that of an historiographer. His writings include a paradoxical conception of the human condition.

300. Asher, R.E., "Myth, Legend and History in Renaissance France," *SF*, 13 (1969), 409-419.

Refers to historical and semi-historical works by French 16th-cent. writers to give support to certain commonplaces related to the French Renaissance. Slow disappearance of faith in the Trojan legend is one reminder that the Renaissance does not re-present a complete break with Middle Ages. At the same time there is consciousness of rebirth of culture and intellectual activity.

301. Ashley, Maurice, *The Golden Century, Europe 1598-1715.* London: Weidenfeld and Nicolson, 1969.

Rev. *History*, 54 (1969), 426; *Hist. Today*, 19 (1969), 288-289.

Deals with the period between the deaths of Philip II and Louis XIV. Analysis of social structure of Europe; Thirty Years' War given critical attention.

302. Ashton, Robert, ed., *James I by his Contemporaries: An Account of His Career and Character as Seen by Some of His Contemporaries.* London: Hutchinson, 1969.

Rev. *Spectator*, 221 (31 Jan. 1969), 140.

Contemporary extracts which comment on James's career and character: his qualities as philosopher and diplomat; his dealings with Anglicans, Catholics, and Puritans; and his relations with favorites, family, court, and subjects.

303. Aston, Margaret, *The Fifteenth Century: the Prospect of Europe*. London: Thames and Hudson, 1968.

Rev. *Choice*, 5 (1968), 852; *LibJ*, 93 (1968), 2494.

Citing examples from contemporary writers and observers, author describes emergence of Europe as an entity; impact of plague, capture of Constantinople, invention of printing press, world exploration, and revival of classical studies, as well as challenge to authority culminating in Reformation.

304. Aston, Trevor H., ed., *Crisis in Europe 1560-1660*. Introduction by Christopher Hill. N.Y.: Doubleday, 1967.

Rev. *SCN*, 26 (1968), 62.

Includes 14 articles reprinted from *Past and Present*. The "crisis" is suggested to be the last phase in the transition from feudal to capitalist economy.

305. Aveling, Hugh, O.S.B., *Northern Catholics: The Catholic Recusants of the North Riding of Yorkshire, 1558-1790*. London, Dublin, Melbourne: Chapman, 1966. Rev. *TLS*, 20 Apr. 1967, 337.

Detailed work, from manuscript sources. Includes: I. Years of Confusion and Depression, 1558-1582; II. Heroic Years of the Catholic Recusancy, 1583-1603; III. Recusants of the Early 17th Cent.

306. Bacquet, Paul, *Un Contemporain d'Elisabeth I: Thomas Sackville. L'Homme et l'oeuvre*. (C.R.N.S.; Travaux d'humanisme et renaissance 76.) Geneva: Droz, 1966. Rev. *TLS*, 14 July 1966, 614.

On *Gorboduc* collaborator (1536?-1608).

307. Baker, Herschel C., *The Race of Time; three lectures on Renaissance historiography*. University of Toronto Press, 1967.

Rev. *AHR*, 73 (1968), 808-809.

Treats Renaissance historians, their individual approaches, and the main themes of current historiography. The search for truth, the limited view of time, periodic and apocalyptic concepts, history as instruction in moral action, reliance on the Bible as supreme unchallenged source, the criticism by Bacon.

308. Becker, Marvin B., "Some Common Features of Italian Urban Experience (c. 1200-1500), *Medievalia et Humanistica*, new ser., no. 1 (1970), 175-201.

Forceful political rule of northern Italy in 14th and 15th cents.; expansion of public credit; status of military.

309. Beckett, J.C., ed., *Historical Studies VII: Papers Read before the Irish Conference of Historians*. N.Y.: Barnes and Noble, 1969. Rev. *EHR*, 86 (1971), 220.

Includes papers on Ireland and Anglo-Irish relations, medieval Scotland, social legislation in Britain.

310. Beckingsale, B.W., "The Characteristics of the Tudor North," *Northern Hist.*, 4 (1969), 67-83.

Questions stock characterization of the North as feudal, Catholic, violent, and backward; stress on impressive military organization; Tudor attempts to maintain control.

311. Bingham, Caroline, *The Making of a King: The Early Years of James VI and I.* N.Y.: Doubleday; London: Collins, 1968.

Rev. *Economist*, 226 (1968), 43; *LibJ*, 94 (1969), 2917; *Observer* 28 Jan. 1968, 30; *TLS*, 25 April 1968, 416.

Study of James's childhood and adolescent years, explaining his development into a complex and neurotic king.

312. Burke, Peter, *The Renaissance Sense of the Past.* (Documents of Modern History, ed. A.G. Dickens and A. Davies.) London: Edward Arnold, 1969; N.Y.: St. Martin's Press, 1970.

Rev. *BHR*, 32 (1970), 688-689; *Ren. and Ref.*, 7 (1970), 13-14.

Quotations exemplifying Renaissance historiography. Holds that Renaissance effected new sense of historical perspective; stresses sociological interpretation.

313. ————, "The Sense of Historical Perspective in Renaissance Italy," *JWH*, 11 (1969), 615-632.

Equates sense of perspective with development of a sense of change; medieval minds less aware of the past as being different from the present.

314. ————, "A Survey of the Popularity of Ancient Historians, 1450-1700," *History and Theory*, 5 (1966), 135-152.

Charts of ancient historians and the editions and languages of their works in the era between invention of the printing press and advent of "modern" historians. Reveals a trend from history as morality to history as relevant to contemporary problems.

315. Christensen, Thorkild L., "Scots-Danish Relations in the Sixteenth Century," *Scott. Hist. Rev.*, 48, no. 1 (1969), 80-97.

Survey of material on 16th-cent. Scots-Danish relations. Indicates fields open to historiographic research in the period. Concentrates on Danish literature; selective annotated bibliography.

316. Christie, Ian R., ed., *Essays in Modern History Selected from the Transactions of the Royal Historical Society on the Occasion of its Centenary.* London: Macmillan; N.Y.: St. Martin's Press, 1968. Rev. *Choice*, 6 (1969), 420.

Includes Sir John Neale's "The Commons' Journals of the Tudor Period" and F.J. Fisher's "The Development of London as a Centre of Conspicuous Consumption in the Sixteenth and Seventeenth Centuries."

317. Cooper, J.P., ed., *New Cambridge Modern History. Vol. IV: The
      Decline of Spain and the Thirty Years War, 1609-48/59.* Cam-
      bridge Univ. Press, 1970.

      Rev. *AHR*, 76 (1971), 1535-1536; *Choice*, 8 (1971), 133.

      Chapters include: "European Economy 1609-50," "The Scientific
      Movement and Its Influence 1610-50," "Drama and Society,"
      "Spain and Europe 1598-1621," "The State of Germany (to 1618),"
      "The Thirty Years War," "The Fall of the Stuart Monarchy."

318. Cross, Claire, ed., *The Letters of Sir Francis Hastings, 1574-
      1609.* (Somerset Record Society, Vol. 69.) Yeovil: The Socie-
      ty, 1969.

      Rev. *AHR*, 76 (1970), 147.

      Introduction on Hastings, Puritan manager of affairs in the
      West Country of the Earl of Huntingdon; during this time, Hunt-
      ingdon was president of the Council of the North. Volume in-
      cludes 88 items relating to Hastings. Nearly half of the manu-
      scripts are among the Hastings papers at the Huntington Library.

319. Cumming, Robert Denoon, *Human Nature and History: A Study of
      the Development of Liberal Political Thought*, 2 vols. Chicago:
      Univ. of Chicao Press, 1969.

      Rev. *AHR*, 75 (1970), 1405-1407.

      Sections on historicism, humanism, individualism.

320. Curtis, David Edward, *Progress and Eternal Recurrence in the
      Work of Gabriel Naudé 1600-1650.* Hull Univ. Occasional Papers
      in Modern Languages, no. 4; Hull: Univ. of Hull Press, 1967.

      Pamphlet on humanism and the idea of progress; Naudé and the
      cyclic theory of history.

321. Donaldson, Gordon, *The First Trial of Mary, Queen of Scots.*
      N.Y.: Stein and Day, 1970.

      Rev. *Choice*, 7 (1970), 604.

      On enquiry conducted by Elizabeth's government into charges
      made against Mary by those who had driven her into exile, as
      well as into Mary's countercharges.

322. ————, *Scotland: James V to James VII.* N.Y.: Praeger, 1966;
      Edinburgh and London: Oliver and Boyd, 1965.

      Rev. *AHR*, 72 (1966), 576-577.

      This is volume 3 of *Edinburgh History of Scotland*, gen. ed.
      Gordon Donaldson. Covers period from 1513, when James V became
      King of Scots, to Scotland in later 17th cent. Detailed bib-
      liography, pp. 402-421.

323. ————, "Scotland's Conservative North in the Sixteenth and
      Seventeenth Centuries," *Transactions of the Royal Historical
      Society*, 5th series, 16 (1966), 65-79.

Sixteenth- and seventeenth-cent.-Scotland was strongly conservative as far as ecclesiastical or political change was concerned.
The people strongly supported the cause of Queen Mary as long
as she lived.

324. ———, *Scottish Historical Documents*. London: Scottish Academic Press, distributed by Chatto and Windus, 1970.

Rev. *TLS*, 1 Jan. 1971, 11.

Texts of most principal documents of Scottish history up to
1707. Treaties, charters, Acts of Parliament, Privy Council
and General Assembly, records, extracts from books, important
correspondences.

325. Edwards, R. Dudley and David B. Quinn, "Sixteenth-Century Ireland, 1485-1603," *Irish Historical Studies*, 16 (1968), 15-32.

Useful survey of past generation in Irish historical studies:
bibliography, sources, general surveys; political history,
foreign relations, ecclesiastical history, military history,
maritime history, colonies and plantation, constitutional, and
institutional history, etc.

326. Eisenstein, Elizabeth L., "The Advent of Printing in Current
Historical Literature: Notes and Comments on an Elusive Transformation," *AHR*, 75 (1970), 727-743.

Far-reaching effects of invention of printing press.

327. ———, "Clio and Chronos: Some Aspects of History-Book Time,"
History and Theory, Beiheft, 6 (1966), 36-64.

Capsule account of the course of historiography, stressing differences between knowing about an event through printed word
and hearing by word of mouth. Importance placed upon invention
of printing press in changing study of historiography as well
as history itself. Discusses Renaissance as transitional period
which saw blending of many myths into history, myths that are
still being uncovered.

328. ———, "Some Conjectures About the Impact of Printing on Western Society and Thought: A Preliminary Report," *Journal of
Modern History*, 40 (1968), 1-56.

Theories to account for the consequences of the invention of
printing.

329. Elliott, J.H., *Europe Divided, 1559-1598*. London: Collins,
1968.

Rev. *EHR*, 85 (1970), 406-407.

Condensed survey which includes current research on aspects of
the second half of the 16th cent. Stresses 1560's as an "age
of general crisis." Balanced treatment of European history,
carefully relating contemporary events to each other; considered among best short textbooks on the period.

330. *El tránsito de la Edad Media al Renacimiento en la historia de*
      España (*Cuadernos de Historia, Annexos* to *Hispania*, vol. 1).
      Madrid: Consejo superior de Instituto J. Zurita, 1967.
      Rev. *Bull. of Hisp. Studies*, 47 (1970), 143-144.

      Twelve studies on 15th- and 16th-cent. Spain, including A.
      Rumeu de Armas on Christian Spanish attitudes to pagans.

331. Elton, Geoffrey R., *England, 1200-1640*. Ithaca, N.Y.: Cornell
      Univ. Press, 1969. Rev. *Spec.*, 223 (27 Sept. 1969), 410.

      Sees unifying theme of this "era of the public record" in the
      nature of its historical evidence; provides an analysis of the
      problem of historical writing in this period.

332. ———, "Literaturbericht über die Englische Geschichte der Neu-
      zeit 1485-1945," *Hist. Zeit.*, 3 (1969), 1-132.

      An account of recent work on Renaissance and modern English
      history.

333. ———, *Modern Historians on British History, 1485-1945: A*
      Critical Bibliography, 1945-1969. London: Methuen, 1970.

      Covers post-war scholarship concerning British history. Running
      commentary with bibliographic footnotes. Chap. 11 covers His-
      tory of Ideas. Rev. *LJ*, 96 (1971), 1597.

334. Epperson, James Allen, III, "English Historiography in the Six-
      teenth and Seventeenth Centuries," *DA*, 27 (1967), 3425-A -
      3426-A (Univ. of Calif., Berkeley).

      Before 1600 writers regarded history as repetitive and non-
      evolutionary. Under Providence, past and present were analo-
      gous. Thus history could offer examples which taught men how
      to act in the present. Given this moral stress, objectivity and
      facts were easily disregarded. There are strong correlations
      between many poetic "histories" of the period and contemporary
      prose histories. In the later decades of the 16th cent. in-
      terest in empirical historiography increased. James I sup-
      pressed the political use of such history in 1614. After the
      Civil War, historians clearly relied more exclusively on fact
      than on theory. History-writing became more dialectical and
      critical, without the earlier providential ontological ideas.

335. Esplin, Ross S., "The Emerging Legend of Sir Philip Sidney,
      1586-1652," *DA*, 31 (1970), 2341-A (Univ. of Utah).

      How a Sidney legend was created by poets and writers for 60
      years after his death.

336. Farmer, Norman, Jr., "Fulke Greville and Sir John Coke: An
      Exchange of Letters on a History Lecture and Certain Latin Ver-
      ses on Sir Philip Sidney," *HLQ*, 33 (1969/1970), 217-236.

      Greville's idea of progress and how it affected his thinking
      about history, which helped establish first professorship of
      history at Cambridge.

337. Fenn, E.A.H., "The Writing on the Wall," *Hist. Today*, 19 (1969), 419-423.

    Prisoners' graffiti on the walls of the Tower of London. Short description of 16th-cent. individuals, reasons for their imprisonment, and their writing, mostly of a religious or philosophic nature.

338. Ferguson, Arthur, "The Historical Thought of Samuel Daniel: A Study in Renaissance Ambivalence," *JHI*, 32 (1971), 185-202.

    Daniel and the new sense of history.

339. ———, "Reginald Pecock and the Renaissance Sense of History," *Studies in the Renaissance*, 13 (1966), 147-166.

    Historical significance of Reginald Pecock, a pre-Renaissance English bishop, in development of Renaissance intellectual attitudes. His writings as a contributor to the growth of a new sense of history, independent of subsequent introduction of European humanism to England. Development of humanism from a background of medieval scholasticism.

340. Fiehler, Rudolph, "Sir John Oldcastle, the Original of Shakespeare's Falstaff," *DA*, 31 (1970), 2341-2342-A (Univ. of Texas).

    Life of Oldcastle, his 15th-cent. role as folk-hero, and his stage history, beginning with *The Famous Victories of Henry the Fifth*. (Diss., 1950, now available as book from author.)

341. Fraser, Antonia, *Mary Queen of Scots*. London: Weidenfeld & Nicolson, 1969.

    Rev. *Hist. Today*, 19 (1969), 579; *TLS*, 3 July 1969, 729-730.

    Presents Mary as a heroine and a martyr and Queen Elizabeth as something of a villainess. James I, Mary's only child to survive her, also portrayed as heartless. Authenticity of the "casket letters" is questioned. The letters are ignored as evidence for Mary's character.

342. French, A.L., "Joan of Arc and Henry VI," *ES*, 49 (1968), 425-429.

    Attacks Tillyard's reading of first tetralogy, in order to question his whole interpretation. Tillyard's notion of Joan of Arc as "scourge" or instrument of Divine Vengeance in *1 Henry VI* or as a witch is dubious. If this is so, doubt exists whether Vengeance is operating in *Henry VI* at all and whether England is, in fact, shown as having crime to be avenged, or as laboring under guilt of deposition and murder of Richard II.

343. Furber, Elizabeth Chapin, ed., *Changing Views on British History. Essays on Historical Writing since 1939*. Ed. for Conf. on Brit. Studies. Harvard Univ. Press, 1966.

    Rev. *AHR*, 72 (1976), 966.

    Fourteen essays, in chronological order, scanning work in each period. Reprinted are esp. useful ones by Lacy B. Smith, "The Taste for Tudors since 1940," pp. 101-118; and Perez Zagorin, "English History, 1558-1640: A Bibliographical Survey," pp. 119-140.

344. Fussner, F. Smith, *Tudor History and the Historians*. N.Y. and
      London: Basic Books, 1970.

      Rev. *Choice*, 7 (1971), 743; *History and Theory*, 10 (1971),
      253-258.

      Historiographical problems that have affected the development
      of 16th-cent. history; role of intellectual, historical revi-
      sionism, significance of the appearance of printed sources in
      19th cent., and increased reliance upon archival research in
      the 20th cent.; influences of new methods and growth of his-
      torical consciousness in Tudor England.

345. Gaeta, Franco, ed., *Relations des Ambassadeurs Vénitiens*.
      Trans. J. Chuzeville and P. de Montera. (Collection Unesco
      d'Oeuvres Représentatives. Série Européenne.) Paris: Klinck-
      sieck, 1969.

      Rev. *Revue des études italiennes*, n.s., 16 (1970), 305.

      Texts of 16th- and 17th-cent. accounts of Venetian ambassadors
      to European states: 1507, 1535, 1557, 1651, 1691. Thirty-page
      index.

346. George, C.H., "Puritanism as History and Historiography," *Past
      and Present*, 41 (1968), 77-104.

      Treats history of English Puritanism since its origins and
      analyzes works of historiographers, particularly of the 19th
      cent. Aims to "exorcise the Weberian incubus."

347. Gilbert, Felix, "The Renaissance Interest in History," in
      Charles S. Singleton, ed., *Art, Science, and History in the
      Renaissance* (Baltimore: Johns Hopkins Press, 1968), pp. 373-
      387.

      Renaissance man's expanded historical perspective accompanying
      his concern with politics and the ancient world.

348. Goodman, Anthony, "The Countess (Joan of Essex) and the Rebels:
      Essex and a Crisis in English Society (1400)," *Essex Archaeo-
      logical Soc., Trans.*, 3rd ser., 2 (1970), 267-279.

      Events subsequent to planned uprising of friends of Richard II
      to capture Windsor and Henry of Lancaster.

349. Green, Louis, "Historical Interpretations in Fourteenth-Century
      Florentine Chronicles," *Journal of the History of Ideas*, 28
      (1967), 161-178.

      Medieval Florentine chronicles show an ambivalence between a
      secular and a religious attitude primarily because the chroni-
      clers are trying to adapt old attitudes to new conditions and
      flux of events.

350. Grendler, Paul F., "Francesco Sansovino and Italian Popular
      History 1560-1600," *StRen*, 16 (1969), 139-180.

      Study proposes to discuss and analyze examples of Italian
      popular history in last 40 years of 16th cent. Sansovino emer-
      ges as central figure.

351. Grierson, Edward, *The Fatal Inheritance*. London: Gollancz, 1969.

    Rev. *TLS*, 19 February 1970, 198.

    In his study of this "fatal inheritance"--the Burgundian lands which Philip II inherited from Emperor Charles V--Grierson tells again the story of the Dutch revolt against Spain. Covers years of Philip's reign: 1555-1598.

352. Griffiths, R.A., "The Glyndwr Rebellion in North Wales through the Eyes of an Englishman," *Bull. Board of Celtic Studies*, 22 (1967). (As listed in *EHR*, 83 [1968], 661.)

    On Thomas Barnely, North Wales Yorkshireman, a protégé of Harry Hotspur, Chamberlain of North Wales, 1406-1414; stresses Henry V's efforts to pursue reconciliation with Wales.

353. Gutkind, E.A., *International History of City Development*, vol. 4, *Urban Development in Southern Europe: Italy and Greece*. N.Y.: Free Press, 1969.

    Rev. *AHR*, 75 (1970), 1407-1408.

    Treats classical and Christian Italy (to the 19th cent.) and classical Greece. Renaissance section contains survey and summary of various Renaissance plans for new, remodeled, and ideal cities.

354. Hale, John R., ed., *The Evolution of British Historiography*. London: Macmillan, 1967.

    Rev. *New Statesman*, 73 (1967), 440-441.

    Contains extracts from British historians, Raleigh to Namier. Introduction touches on issues in historiography.

355. Hamilton, Albert J., "Ireland and Spanish Intervention, 1569-1603," *Duquesne Review*, 13 (1968), 96-104.

    Irish appeals for Spanish aid and constant contact between Spain and Irish rebels, both the Celtic chiefs and the Anglo-Irish who feared inroads being made in Ireland by new Tudor gentry.

356. Hanrahan, R., "History in the 'Española Inglesa,'" *MLN*, 83 (1968), 267-271.

    The English embassy in Spain (1605) furnished Cervantes with traits which he introduced into his story to provide an impression of reality.

357. Hardacre, P.H., "Seventeenth-Century Materials in the Public Record Office," *SCN*, 25 (1967), 29-30.

    P.R.O. 17th-cent. documents, obtained by gift, purchase, etc., usefully listed.

358. Harris, G.L., "Cardinal Beaufort, Patriot or Usurer?" *Trans. of the Royal Historical Society*, 20 (1970), 129-140.

    Monetary loans made by the Cardinal to Henry V and Henry VI reveal that his motives stemmed from political ambition rather than usurious purposes.

359. Harrison, William, *Description of England*, ed. Georges Edelen.
      Folger Documents of Tudor and Stuart Civilization.   Ithaca,
      N.Y.: Cornell U. P., 1968. Rev. *TLS*, 12 June 1969, 645.

      Introduction to Holinshed provides view of mid-Elizabethen Eng-
      land. Index and annotations.

360. Hearnshaw, F.J.C., *English History in Contemporary Poetry. No.
      IV, Court and Parliament, 1588-1688*. Teaching of History Series,
      no. 29. London: G. Bell & Sons, 1969.

      On extent to which struggle for sovereignty between monarch and
      Parliament, the Puritans' attempts at a second Church reforma-
      tion and foundation of England's overseas colonial and commer-
      cial empire, are reflected in poetry between 1588 and 1688.

361. Heitmann, Klaus, "Das Verhältnis von Dichtung und Geschichts-
      schreibung in älterer Theorie," *AKG*, 52 (1970), 244-279.

      On humanist history and 15th- and 16th-cent. theories.

362. Helm, P.J., *England Under the Yorkists and Tudors, 1471-1603*.
      N.Y.: Humanities Press, 1969. Rev. *AHR*, 74 (1969), 975.

      Survey of Tudor England covering all aspects of the period,
      without losing sight of Continental affairs and their influence
      upon England.

363. Henderson, John Patrick, "Sir William Paulet, Marquess of Win-
      chester, a Tudor Time-Server," *DA*, 31 (1970), 2284-85-A (St.
      Louis Univ.).

      Based mainly on published state papers from beginning of reign
      of Henry VIII to end of Mary's first year of reign. Shows how
      Paulet's caution and prudence as a time-server par excellence
      allowed him one of most fruitful careers of Tudor era.

364. Hess, Andrew C., "The Evolution of the Ottoman Seaborne Empire
      in the Age of the Oceanic Discoveries, 1453-1525," *AHR*, 75
      (1970), 1892-1919.

      Development of Ottoman navy and its discoveries. Shows Muslim
      influence on, and stimulation of, Western imperialism and events
      of European history.

365. Hexter, J.H., "The Rhetoric of History," *History and Theory*, 6
      (1967), 3-13.

      Suggests that science-oriented notions of meaning and truth and
      of the access to them are inappropriate to historical discourse;
      discusses inadequacies of usual ways of setting forth historical
      data.

366. Hibbard, G.R., "George Chapman: Tragedy and the Providential
      View of History," *ShS*, 20 (1967), 27-31.

      Chapman transcends limitations that his use of the providential
      idea of history would otherwise have set his tragedies.

367. *"History Today,"* Conflicts in Tudor and Stuart England: A Selection of Articles from "History Today," ed. I.A. Roots. Edinburgh: Oliver & Boyd, 1967. Rev. *TLS*, 18 Jan. 1968, 70.

368. Holmes, Martin, "Richard Grafton and his Chronicle," *History
Today*, 19 (1969), 634-641.

Biographical sketch of Grafton and an evaluation of his history
of England.

369. Hosley, Richard, ed., *Shakespeare's Holinshed*. N.Y.: G.P. Putnam's Sons, 1968. Rev. *NQ*, n.s. 16 (1969), 122.

Modern edition of Holinshed's *Chronicles* (1587); includes sources of Shakespeare's history plays, *Lear*, *Cymbeline*, and
Macbeth.

370. Howell, Roger, *Sir Philip Sidney: The Shepherd Knight*. London:
Hutchinson, 1968.

Rev. *AHR*, 74 (1969), 1624-1625; *TLS*, 25 April 1968, 416.

Historian's, rather than literary student's, approach; political
context.

371. Humphreys, Arthur R., "Shakespeare and the Tudor Perception of
History," *Shakespeare Celebrated*, ed. Louis B. Wright. Ithaca:
Cornell Univ. Press, 1966, pp. 89-112.

Evaluates the Elizabethan concern for history, reasons for this
concern, and means by which Shakespeare gratified the interest
in his plays. History's change from a mere recording of events
to a dramatic source during the Tudor administration.

372. Huppert, George, *The Idea of Perfect History: Historical Erudition and Historical Philosophy in Renaissance France*. Urbana:
Univ. of Ill. Press, 1970.

Rev. *AHR*, 76 (1971), 511-512; *Catholic Hist. Rev.*, 62 (1971),
61-63.

Sixteenth-cent. French historical movement in context of growth
of historiography. Dominance of philosophy, history, and scientific use of historical data.

373. ————, "The Renaissance Background of Historicism," *History
and Theory*, 5 (1966), 48-60.

Explores origins of modern historicism and finds it in works of
French historians of 16th cent., especially in La Popelinière,
who in writing of France's national history employed means and
theories applicable to study of more general history. Innovation was watchword of the Renaissance, in La Popelinière's
"pure" history of France and Shakespeare's dramatic histories
of England.

374. Hutchison, Harold F., *King Henry V*. N.Y.: John Day Co., 1967.

Research in early 15th-cent. archives provides very different
view from Shakespeare's. Rev. *Obs.*, 24 Sept. 1967, 26.

375.   ————, "Shakespeare and Henry V," *Hist. Today*, 17 (1967),
       510-517.

       Ways in which Shakespeare's version of history varies from
       facts.

376.   Jeannin, Pierre, *L'Europe du Nord-Ouest et du Nord aux XVIIe et
       XVIIIe siècles*. Paris: Presses Universitaires de France,
       1969.

       Rev. *History*, 55 (1970), 120-121.

       Begins with a systematic survey of sources; bibliography of 685
       titles. Second part contains comparative chapters, dealing
       with factors common to all countries concerned: British Isles,
       the Low Countries, and Scandinavia.

377.   Jexlev, Thelma, "Scottish History in the Light of Records in the
       Danish National Archives," *Scot. Hist. Rev.*, 48 (1969), 98-106.

       Surveys material on three principal problems: relations between
       the ruling houses, political relations between the two coun-
       tries, commercial intercourse.

378.   Johnson, Jerah and William A. Percy, *The Age of Recovery: The
       Fifteenth Century*. Ithaca and London: Cornell Univ. Press,
       1970.

       Rev. *BHR*, 33 (1971), 448-450.

       On artistic, intellectual, and geographic advances in 15th cent.

379.   Jordan, W.K., *Edward VI, the Young King: The Protectorship of
       the Duke of Somerset*. London: Allen & Unwin; Cambridge, Mass.:
       Harvard Univ. Press, 1968.

       Rev. *AHR*, 75 (1970), 1449-1450; *Church Hist.*, 39 (1970), 555-
       556; *Choice*, 6 (1969), 1288; *EHR*, 85 (1970), 796-799; *JMH*, 42
       (1970), 393-395; *Spectator*, 221 (1969), 140.

       First of a two-volume work covering reign of Edward VI; focuses
       on early reign during which the Duke of Somerset acted as ad-
       ministrator, and deals with foreign affairs, power struggles,
       military history, and socioeconomic developments in a narrative-
       historical mode.

380.   ————, *Edward VI: The Threshold of Power. The Dominance of
       the Duke of Northumberland*. London: Allen & Unwin; Cambridge,
       Mass.: Harvard Univ. Press, 1970.

       Rev. *AHR*, 77 (1972), 132-133.

       Vol. 2 of two-volume history of reign of Edward VI. Revises
       Froude's and Pollard's accounts of the reign of this least
       known of the Tudors, here given more serious inspection than
       ever before. Excurses: on dismantling of Roman Catholic re-
       ligion; and on secularism, in relation to changing views of
       charity.

381. Joseph, B.L., *Shakespeare's Eden: The Commonwealth of Eng-
      land, 1558-1629*. N.Y.: Barnes and Noble; London: Blandford,
      1971.

      Rev. *RenQ*, 26 (1973), 363-364.

      Popular background on such subjects as "The Royal Government,"
      "Man, the Cosmos, and Providence Divine," "Degree, High and
      Base"; applications to Shakespeare and Renaissance literature.

382. Kabat, Lillian Trena Gonan, "*The History of the World*: Reason
      in Historiography of Sir Walter Raleigh," *DA*, 29 (1968), 901-A
      (Univ. of Southern Calif.).

      The *History* reflects Raleigh's contemporary values, especially
      a strong attachment to reason in the Baconian sense. Discusses
      close relation of the *History* to its age in Raleigh's argument
      from probability. Finds a skeptical element in Raleigh's think-
      ing in his sensitivity to complexity of forces that determine
      events.

383. Kasprzak, Jan, "A Riddle of History: Queen Elizabeth I and the
      Albertus Laski Affair," *Polish Review*, 14 (Winter 1969), 53-67;
      (Spring 1969), 63-88.

      Evidence on the Laski affair; insight into both Machiavellian
      methods of handling English foreign affairs at time of Elizabeth
      I and relations of England with Central and Eastern Europe.

384. Keeler, Mary Frear, ed., *Bibliography of British History:
      Stuart Period, 1603-1714*, 2nd ed. of Godfrey Davies' standard
      (1928) work. Oxford: Clarendon, 1970. Rev. *PBSA*, 65 (1971), 434.

      Sponsored by American Historical Assoc. and Royal Historical
      Soc. of Great Britain. Annotated. Standard Stuart biblio-
      graphy includes social history and cultural history.

385. Keen, Benjamin, "The Black Legend Revisited: Assumptions and
      Realities," *Hisp. Amer. Hist. Rev.*, 49 (1969), 703-719.

      Historical accuracy of the "Black Legend" examined through
      study of influence of Bartolomé de las Casas' *Very Brief Account
      of the Destruction of the Indies*, which severely criticized
      Spanish policies towards Indians in America.

386. Kelly, Henry Ansgar, *Divine Providence in the England of
      Shakespeare's Histories*. Cambridge, Mass.: Harvard Univ.
      Press, 1970. Rev. *ELN*, 9 (1971), 139-141.

      Supernatural references in historical accounts of period of
      Shakespeare's double tetralogy (1398-1485). Evaluates use made
      of historical writings, in particular, mention of divine provi-
      dence in lives of kings. Examines Lancaster, York, and Tudor
      myths of 15th-cent. writings and 16th-cent. chronicles of Ver-
      gil, Hall, Holinshed, and Fleming. Views of Elizabethan poets
      also considered.

387. Kenny, Robert W., "Peace with Spain, 1605," *Hist. Today*, 20
      (1970), 198-208.

      On stay of Lord High Admiral (Charles Howard) in Spain to ob-
      tain ratification of peace treaty. Describes his fall into
      disfavor upon returning to England.

388. Koenigsberger, H.G. and G.L. Mosse, *Europe in the Sixteenth
      Century*. N.Y.: Holt, Rinehart and Winston, 1968.

      Rev. *Church Hist.*, 39 (1970), 402-403.

      Political-economic history of century considered as a whole;
      political-economic context of Reformation stressed.

389. Kraus, Hans P., *Sir Francis Drake: A Pictorial Biography*.
      Amsterdam: N. Israel, 1970.

      Rev. *TLS*, 5 July 1970, 520.

      Documents, maps, drawings, etc., with historical introduction
      to life and times of Drake.

390. LaBranche, Anthony, "Poetry, History, and Oratory: The Renais-
      sance Historical Poem," *SEL*, 9 (1969), 1-20.

      In examining passages of *Barons Warres*, author attempts to
      demonstrate the "poetic" uses of source material and of rhetor-
      ical amplification. Aims at new understanding of what unifica-
      tion of history and rhetoric meant to Renaissance poet.

391. Lacey, Robert, *Robert, Earl of Essex*. N.Y.::Athenaeum;
      London: Weidenfeld and Nicolson, 1971.

      Rev. *AHR*, 77 (1972), 509-510.

      Popular biography.

392. Lach, Donald Frederick, *China in the Eyes of Europe: The Six-
      teenth Century*. 2 vols. Chicago: Univ. of Chicago Press,
      1968.

393. ————, *India in the Eyes of Europe: The Sixteenth Century*.
      Chicago: Univ. of Chicago Press, 1968.

394. ————, *Japan in the Eyes of Europe: The Sixteenth Century*.
      Chicago: Univ. of Chicago Press, 1968.

      Rev. *Journal of Modern History* (September 1967), 306.

      Examines the trend of European exploration of Asia; focuses on
      effects on Europe, as knowledge grew from confused folklore to
      geographical enlightenment.

395. Lancashire, Anne B., "*Look About You* as a History Play," *SEL*,
      9 (1969), 321-334.

      Study of sources of *Look About You* reveals that play is based
      on chronicle history. It is also concerned with political
      parallels and didacticism, dealing with problems of succession,
      rebellion, and royal favoritism, and in particular with faction-
      alism at court of Elizabeth I and with Queen's relationship to
      Earl of Essex.

396. Lander, J.R., *Conflict and Stability in Fifteenth-Century England*. London: Hutchinson Univ. Library, 1969.

 Rev. *AHR*, 75 (1970), 1438-1439; *History*, 55 (1970), 107.

 Surveys problems and achievements of Lancastrian, Yorkist, and early Tudor government; assesses the country's economic vitality, religious life, and cultural attainment; and discusses how aristocracy and monarchy discharged their common obligation to provide stable government.

397. Leech, Clifford, "Shakespeare and the Idea of the Future," *Univ. of Toronto Quarterly*, 35 (1966), 213-228.

 Shakespeare, especially in his histories, projects the listener's mind into the future. He also makes use of the audience's knowledge of historical events. The impact of a play may be partly dependent on something that is not in the play at all.

398. Leff, Gordon, *History and Social Theory*. University, Ala.: Univ. of Alabama Press, 1969. Rev. *TLS*, 21 Aug. 1969, 934.

 Nature of historical thinking; its place among other fields. Part I: Historical knowledge, includes sections on contingency, value, objectivity, periodization. Part II: Ideology, with sections on class, ideology, and knowledge.

399. Lefranc, Pierre, *Sir Walter Ralegh écrivain: l'oeuvre et les idées*. Paris: A. Colin, 1968.

 Rev. *J. Hist. Phil.*, 8 (1970), 212-215; *TLS*, 12 September 1968, 97.

 Monumental study, first to offer such detailed analysis of Raleigh, including historical writing, political and philosophical views.

400. Levine, John M., "Tudor Antiquaries," *Hist. Today*, 20 (1970), 278-285.

 Tudor antiquarianism originated with John Leland's desire to preserve the monastic libraries during reign of Henry VIII. His methods of collecting and arranging. Work of Bale, Parker, Cotton, Coke, Selden, Ley, and Dodderidge also considered.

401. Levine, Joseph M., ed., *Elizabeth I*. Englewood Cliffs, N.J.: Prentice-Hall, 1969. Rev. *LJ*, 94 (1969), 2599.

 First two sections consist of primary sources by and about Elizabeth; last section includes sketches of the Queen by several writers and historians including Neale, Lingard, Froude, and Strachey.

402. ————, "From Caxton to Camden: The Quest for Historical Truth in Sixteenth-Century England," *DA*, 29 (1968), 200-201-A (Columbia Univ.).

 Effects of new currents of thought (Renaissance humanism, Protestantism, Tudor patriotism) on 16th-cent. English historical writing and theorizing. Trend to more critical historiography and to more precise distinction between historical fiction and history.

403. Levine, Mortimer, "Henry VIII's Use of His Spiritual and Tempo-
      ral Jurisdictions in His Great Causes of Matrimony, Legitimacy
      and Succession," *Historical Journal*, 10 (1967), 3-10.

      Henry VIII's power politics; increase of power of Henry VIII
      over that of Richard III in similar situation.

404. ————, *Tudor England, 1485-1603*. Conference on British Studies
      Bibliographical Handbooks, 1; Cambridge, Eng./N.Y.: Cambridge
      Univ. Press, 1968.

      Rev. *TLS*, 7 November 1968, 1252.

      To September 1966. Over 2,350 entries, full annotations. Sup-
      plements Conyers Read's Tudor bibliography, ending 1956.

405. Levy, Fred J., *Tudor Historical Thought*. San Marino, Calif.:
      Huntington Library Press, 1967.

      Rev. *AHR*, 73 (1968), 1520-1521; F. Smith Fussner, *History and
      Theory*, 3 (1969), 371-387.

      Explores humanism, theology, antiquarianism, Machiavellianism,
      as effecting changes in historical thinking, from the age of
      Caxton to that of Bacon, Raleigh, and Camden.

406. Linkletter, Eric, *The Royal House of Scotland*. London: Mac-
      millan, 1970.

      Rev. *TLS*, 21 May 1970, 603.

      History of the Stuarts from 15th through 18th cents.

407. Lloyd, Rachel, *Dorset Elizabethans, At Home and Abroad*. London:
      John Murray, 1967.

      Rev. *AHR*, 74 (1968), 979.

      Documented and illustrated scenes from lives of Dorset Elizabe-
      thans; includes the Howards of Bindon, the Turberviles, chief
      Catholic families, pirates, etc.

408. Lobel, M.D., "The Value of Early Maps as Evidence for the Topo-
      graphy of English Towns," *Imago Mundi* (Amsterdam), 22 (1968),
      50-61.

      Tendency to underrate value of Elizabethan town maps, which ac-
      tually give much useful historical information: street pat-
      terns, fortifications, suburban development; large-scale maps
      also may depict house structures and provide other important
      details.

409. Lynch, John, *Spain Under the Hapsburgs*. Vol. 2: *Spain and
      America, 1598-1700*. Oxford: Blackwell, 1969.

      Rev. *AHR*, 75 (1970), 1467-1468; *TLS*, 18 September 1969, 1028;
      VQR, 45 (Winter 1970), 24.

      Second volume of author's history of 17th-cent. Hispanic world,
      in which he discusses the later Hapsburgs, the regime of Philip
      III, imperial policies of Philip IV, and Olivares, the mid-
      century revolution, and the crisis under Charles II.

410. MacCaffrey, Wallace T., *The Shaping of the Elizabethan Regime*. Princeton, N.J.: Princeton Univ. Press, 1968.

Rev. *AHR*, 74 (1969), 1623-1624; *Choice*, 6 (1969), 126; *Economist*, 233 (1969), 52; *TLS*, 19 March 1970, 305.

On period between 1558 and 1572 as bridging the crisis of the Tudor century, and as a turning point between the Middle Ages and modern England; new interpretation of roles of Elizabeth and Earl of Leicester in diplomatic and political events.

411. MacGillivray, Royce, "The Use of Predictions in Seventeenth Century Historians," *Cithara*, 8 (1968), 54-63.

Examines assumption that persons could sometimes foretell or that portents sometimes indicate the future course of history, among 17th-cent. historians of the English Civil War.

412. MacQueen, John, "Some Aspects of the Early Renaissance in Scotland," *Forum for Modern Language Studies*, 3 (1967), 201-222.

Description of changes in Scottish literature which the author terms "Renaissance," and discussion of the part the Scottish Renaissance played in the Northern Renaissance; for example, the Council of Basle. Documents Scottish contacts with the Continent and shows some literary reflections of those contacts, that is, of the humanistic influence. Dates the Scottish Renaissance as extending from the late 15th through the 16th cent. generally.

413. Mandrou, Robert, *Magistrats et sorciers en France au 17e siècle*. Paris: Plon, 1970.

Rev. *TLS*, 30 October 1970, 1237-1239.

Attitude of French lawyers and clergy regarding witchcraft. Little connection is found with religious conflict of period.

414. Manning, John Joseph, Jr., "John Hayward's *The First Part of the Life and Raigne of King Henrie the IIII*," *DA*, 29 (1968), 1210-1211-A (Univ. of Mich.).

Traces the book's history, the development of Tudor interest in Richard II, the tendency of Elizabeth's enemies to see in Richard II's actions a source of unflattering analogies to her, the appearance of Essex as a latter-day Bolingbroke, political suppression and forbidden printing, burning of books in 1599.

415. Mathew, David, *James I*. University, Ala.: Univ. of Alabama Press, 1968.

Rev. *TLS*, 25 April 1968, 416.

Biographical study.

416. Mathew, Gervase, *Court of Richard II*. London: John Murray, 1968. Rev. *Obs.*, 12 May 1968, 29.

Based on manuscripts, many at Bodleian; covers 1380-1425 and interweaves political history, changes in social structure and ideals, developments in literature and art forms.

417. McCue, Robert J., "The Ambassadorial Career of Sir Edward Staf-
      ford, Elizabethan Ambassador to France 1583-1590," *DA*, 30
      (1970), 715-A (Brigham Young Univ.).

      Analysis of motives for the English ambassador's treason.

418. McHugh, Kathleen, "The New Heroes of Renaissance Historical
      Drama on Religious Themes," *DA*, 27 (1966), 750-A (New York
      Univ.).

      In 16th-cent. as part of effort to express new, often national,
      self-consciousness, playwrights turned to past and recent his-
      tory for material. As well as introducing new heroes, the play-
      wrights created a form to contain them—historical tragedy.

419. McInnes, Ian, *Arabella: The Life and Times of Lady Arabella
      Seymour 1575-1615*. London: W.H. Allen, 1968.

      Rev. *Bks. & Bkmn.*, 13 (1968), 55.

      Biography of Arabella Stuart which focuses on her significance
      as a political pawn; relation to Elizabeth I; political and
      social setting.

420. Merrifield, Ralph, *Roman London*. N.Y.: Praeger, 1969.

      Author demonstrates how London as Roman town was laid out and
      the advantage it took of the Thames; its own stream, the Wal-
      brook; and the great road system in and beyond it. Temple of
      Mithras examined. Rev. *CW*, 61 (1968), 256.

421. Merriman, M.H., "The Assured Scots: Scottish Collaborators with
      England during the Rough Wooing," *Scott. Hist. Rev.*, 47 (1968),
      10-34.

      Assurance, a formal agreement between contracting parties not
      to molest each other during a specified period, was mid-16th-
      cent. procedure. In the Rough Wooing (1543-1550), it meant
      English effort to create body of collaborators among the more
      insecure border Scots.

422. Miller, Helen, "L'Angleterre au XVIe siècle," *Revue Historique*,
      241 (1969), 381-408.

      Review of work on 16th-cent. English mostly written between
      1964-1967. Sections on political and religious history, social
      and economic history, and biography.

423. Milne, Alexander Taylor, *A Centenary Guide to the Publications
      of the Royal Historical Society, 1868-1968, and of the Former
      Camden Society, 1838-1897*. London: Offices of the Royal His-
      torical Society, 1968. Rev. *EHR*, 86 (1971), 221.

      Lists volumes and contents, with general index.

424. Mitchison, Rosalind, *A History of Scotland*. London: Methuen,
      1970.

      Rev. *ScS*, 15 (1971), 72-75; *Scott. Hist. Rev.*, 50 (1971), 72-73.

      Stresses post-Reformation Scotland (1550-1707), central insti-
      tutions of society and culture. Annotated reading list.

425. Mousnier, Roland, *Ein Königsmord in Frankreich.* *Die Ermordung Heinrichs IV.* (Propyläen Bibliothek der Geschichte.) Berlin: Propyläen Verlag, 1970.

 Rev. *Archiv für das Studium der neueren Sprachen,* 208 (1971), 74-76.

 New edition of work originally part of *Trente journées qui ont fait la France* (Gallimard, 1964). Description of the event followed by analysis in light of Renaissance-Reformation ideas of "Tyrannenmord."

426. Mullins, E.L.C., *A Guide to the Historical and Archaeological Publications of Societies, in England and Wales, 1901-1933.* Institute of Historical Research. Univ. of London: Athlone Press, 1968. Rev. *Choice,* 6 (1970), 1558.

 Indexes titles and authors of books and articles bearing upon the history and archaeology of England and Wales, issued 1901-1933. Complements *Writings on British History, 1901-1933* (5 vols. in 7, Jonathan Cape, Royal Historical Soc.) and is continued by *Writings on British History,* 1934, comp. A.T. Milne. Contains 6,560 items. Useful general index includes subjects, pp. 491-788.

427. Myers, A.R., ed., *English Historical Documents,* vol. 4, *1327-1485.* London: Eyre and Spottiswoode, 1969.

 Rev. *Hist. Journal,* 13 (1970), 343-345; *TLS,* 19 February 1970, 193.

 Division into four parts: political framework, government of the realm, Church and education, and economic and social development. Bibliography for each.

428. ———, "Richard III and Historical Tradition," *History,* 53 (1968), 181-202.

 Shows that historians have been influenced by their own particular climates in writing about Richard III. Shakespeare's portrait picks up a tradition which appeared soon after Richard's death. Thomas More first gave consistent picture of Richard's villainy--here he first becomes "croke-backed Richard."

429. Nadel, George H., "History as Psychology in Francis Bacon's Theory of History," *History and Theory,* 5 (1966), 275-287.

 Assembles Bacon's stated historical principles and specific recommendations, examines the relationship between them. Bacon's theory of history as beginning of the behavioral sciences: it judges actions as representative of social pressures and as expression of Renaissance moral philosophy.

430. Negri, Antonio, "Problemi di Storia dello Stato Moderno Francia: 1610-1650," *RCSF,* 22 (1967), 182-220.

 On power of the state in early 17th-cent. France; useful bibliographic survey with footnote references to Renaissance works; sections, e.g., on historiographical tradition.

431. Parry, J.H., *The Age of Reconnaissance: Discovery, Explora-
     tion, and Settlement, 1450 to 1650*. N.Y.: Praeger, 1969 (1963).

     European geographical exploration, trade, and settlement out-
     side France in 15th, 16th, and 17th cents. Factors which stimu-
     lated expansion and consequences.

432. ————, *Europe and a Wider World, 1415-1715*. London: Hutchin-
     son Univ. Library, 1969 (1949).

     Influence of Europeans outside of Europe in terms of religion,
     economics, and politics.

433. Pellegrini, Giuliano, *Un fiorentino alla corte d'Inghilterra
     nel Cinquecento: Petruccio Ubaldini*. Torino: Bottega d'Eras-
     mo, 1967.

     Rev. *RLI*, 72 (1968), 152.

     Ubaldini, born probably in first quarter of 16th cent., died
     ca. 1600; interesting figure of the Italian intellectual, who
     had long sojourns at English court in second half of 16th cent.;
     wrote report from England (1552), which reflected its times.

434. Preston, Joseph Harold, "English Ecclesiastical Historiography:
     From Foxe to Lingard," *DA*, 27 (1966), 1009-A (Univ. of Missouri).

     Discusses growing sophistication and concern for objectivity in
     ecclesiastical history. "As result of cosmographical revolution
     of late sixteenth and early seventeenth centuries, Providence
     seemed less immanent...." Historians "gave more emphasis to
     secular value of history, while ... clinging to its moral
     utility." (Cf. Preston, "English Ecclesiastical Historians and
     the Problem of Bias, 1559-1742," *JHI*, 32 [1971], 203-220.)

435. Queller, Donald E., *Early Venetian Legislation on Ambassadors*.
     Geneva: Droz, 1966. Rev. *EHR*, 84 (1969), 164.

     One hundred and eleven Italian and Latin documents comprise over
     half the volume.

436. ————, *The Office of Ambassador in the Middle Ages*. Princeton,
     N.J.: Princeton U.P., 1967. Rev. *Spec.*, 44 (1969), 489.

     Chapters on the functions of ambassador, his immunities and
     ceremonials. Bibliography, pp. 229-247.

437. Quinn, David B., *The Elizabethans and the Irish*. Ithaca, N.Y.:
     Cornell Univ. Press, 1966. Rev. *AHR*, 72 (1967), 986.

     What some Englishmen thought about some Irishmen, their society,
     and modes of life during the 16th cent. By extensive contempo-
     rary quotations, the book reveals as much about the English ob-
     servers as it does about the Irish themselves.

438. Rae, Thomas I., "A List of Articles on Scottish History Pub-
     lished During the Year 1966," *Scott. Hist. Rev.*, 46 (1967),
     177-184.

439. ————, "A List of Articles on Scottish History Published During the Year 1968," *Scott. Hist. Rev.*, 48 (1969), 213-219.

Arranged chronologically with a section on "General and Auxiliary Studies."

440. Reed, Richard B., "Richard Eden: An Early English Imperialist,"
Serif, 4 (1967), 3-11.

Eden (1522-1576), translator of scientific, geographic, and
travel works, condemned the English for failing to advance exploration of the New World, while praising Spanish and Portuguese initiative. His *The Decades of the New World or West
India* (1555), a translation of various works on discovery by
Spanish and Portuguese authors, gave English readers access to
the successes of these foreign explorers.

441. Rees, Joan, *Fulke Greville, Lord Brooke, 1554-1628: A Critical
Biography*. London: Routledge and Kegan Paul; Berkeley: Univ.
of Calif. Press, 1971.

Rev. *Choice*, 8 (1971), 677; *Hist. Today*, 21 (1971), 524.

Life and works examined; influence of his political and Protestant beliefs and his pragmatic skepticism on his poetry and
plays. Friend and biographer of Sir Philip Sidney, he may have
befriended Shakespeare.

442. Reinmuth, Howard S., ed., *Early Stuart Studies: Essays in
Honor of David Harris Willson*. Minneapolis: Univ. of
Minn. Press, 1970.

Rev. *AHR*, 77 (1972), 133-134; *TLS*, 25 February 1972, 230.

Includes essays on the Gunpowder Plot by Joel Hurstfield, office-
seekers in light of Dudley Carleton's correspondence by J. Bar-
croft, Lord Chancellor Ellesmere by W.J. Jones, Robert Cecil as
minister by Thomas Coakley. (Cf. [GUNPOWDER PLOT] under *Topoi*.)

443. Rice, Eugene Franklin, *The Foundation of Early Modern Europe,
1460-1559*. N.Y.: W.W. Norton, 1970. Rev. *Choice*, 8 (1971), 897.

Chronicle of shift from medieval to early modern period, and
necessary gradual shift of modes of perception; includes chapters on science, politics, economics, culture, and church.

444. Richardson, Walter Cyril, *Mary Tudor: The White Queen*. Seat-
tle: Univ. of Wash. Press, 1970.

Rev. *AHR*, 76 (1971), 145-146; *Choice*, 8 (1970), 1426-1428;
Hist. Mag. of the Prot. Episcopal Church, 40 (1971), 246.

Biography of sister of Henry VIII; marriage to Louis XII of
France, her widowhood and unauthorized marriage to Duke of
Suffolk stressed because more primary information available.
Richardson provides material on clothing, court ceremonies,
Field of Cloth of Gold, and Renaissance views of feminine
beauty.

445. Ridley, Jasper, *John Knox*. Oxford: Clarendon Press, 1968.

Rev. *EHR*, 85 (1970), 579-581.

Biographical detail concerning Scottish reformer. Commentary
on Knox's views on resistance to authority, different from Calvin's. Questionable assumptions regarding Knox's opposition to
episcopacy.

446. Ridley, Nancy, *A Northumbrian Remembers*. London: Robert Hale,
1970.

Rev. *TLS*, 4 December 1970, 1412.

Short biographies of Northumbrians, including Harry Percy.
Also topographical description of area.

447. Roach, John, *A Bibliography of Modern History*. Cambridge:
Cambridge Univ. Press, 1968.

Rev. *SCN*, Autumn 1968, 60-61.

Concise bibliography based on plan of the *New Cambridge Modern
History*. Emphasizes books in English.

448. Roberts, Michael, *The Early Vasas: A History of Sweden 1523-
1611*. N.Y.: Cambridge Univ. Press, 1968.

Rev. *AHR*, 74 (1968), 638.

Background investigation to Roberts' earlier volume, *Gustavus
Adolphus*, beginning with Gustav Vasa's coup in 1523 through
the dynasty's development of the remote Swedish provinces into
a European power.

449. Rogers, Alan, "Henry IV and the Revolt of the Earls, 1400,"
Hist. Today, 18 (1968), 277-283.

On plot to kill Henry IV and restore the dethroned Richard II.

450. Rott, Jean, and Faerber, Robert, "Un anglais à Strasbourg au
Milieu de XVIe Siècle: John Hales, Roger Ascham, et Jean
Sturm," *EtA*, 21 (1968), 381-394.

Strasbourg sojourn of John Hales is example of level on which
relations between Strasbourg and England occurred in 16th cent.
Meetings, friendships, favors, mutual hospitality, and spiritual communion mark history of this period.

451. Rowse, A.L., "Lord Burghley: The Relevance of a Great Elizabethan Today," *Contemp. Rev.*, 217 (1970), 231-235.

Burghley's contributions to England's economic health and realistic approach to contemporary problems; ability to direct
economic policy; position of "incomparable servant of state."

452. Royal Historical Society, *Writings on British History, 1901-
1933: A Bibliography of Books and Articles on the History of
Great Britain from about 400 A.D. to 1914. Published during
the Years 1901-1933 Inclusive, with an Appendix Containing a
Select List of Publications in These Years on British History
since 1914*. N.Y.: Barnes and Noble; London: J. Cape, 1968.

Rev. *AHR*, 74 (1968), 589-590.

Vol. I: Auxiliary Sciences and General Works; Vol. II: The
Middle Ages, 450-1485; Vol. III: The Tudor and Stuart Periods,
1485-1714. The volumes contain 19,523 entries; a major reference tool, each volume well indexed. Extending the coverage of
Writings on British History, volumes provide a single bibliographic guide for a period which previously required the con-
sultation of numerous indexes.

453. Rubinstein, Stanley Jack, *Historians of London: An Account of
the Many Surveys, Histories, Perambulations, Maps and Engravings made about the City and its Environs, and of the Dedicated
Londoners Who Made Them.* Hamden, Conn.: Archon; London:
Owen, 1968. Rev. *Pub. Wkly.*, 194 (1 July 1968), 51.

Includes an appendix up to the period 1890, a glossary of terms,
a bibliography, and indexes of statues, names, and subjects.

454. Russell, Joycelyne G., *The Field of Cloth of Gold: Men and
Manners in 1520.* N.Y.: Barnes and Noble, 1969.

Rev. *AHR*, 75 (1970), 838-839; *Historian*, 32 (1970), 280; *HT*,
19 (1969), 285-286; *RenQ*, 22 (1970), 192-194; *TLS*, 12 February
1970, 158.

Meticulous description of the event, although the author fails
to clarify its significance in the Anglo-French political
reforms.

455. Scarisbrick, J.J., *Henry VIII.* Berkeley: Univ. of Calif.
Press; London: Eyre & Spottiswoode, 1968.

Rev. *AHR*, 74 (1968), 592-594; *History*, 54 (1969), 31-48; *Hist.
Journal*, 12 (1969), 158-163; *Hist. Today*, 18 (1968), 585-587;
UTQ, 38 (1968), 101-103.

Most important study since Pollard over 60 years ago; book begins with the subject as man and works out from royal person
to his historical environment. King's incompetence and frivol-
ity behind the façade of greatness. Reconsiders such important
problems as the canon law of the Divorce, Henry's theology,
the Reformation, the establishment of the Royal Supremacy, and
foreign policy.

456. Senning, Calvin Franklin, "The Gondomar Embassy: Religious Aspects, 1613-1614," *DA*, 29 (1968), 1502-1503-A (Univ. of Alabama).

Study concerns Gondomar, Spanish ambassador in England (1613-
1618, 1620-1622). It examines tradition concerning his personal
ascendancy over the mind of James, supposed to have reduced
monarch to total subservience to Spanish interests. In contrast, James emerges as stronger and more responsible than he
is usually portrayed.

457. Setton, Kenneth M., "Pope Leo X and the Turkish Peril," *Proc.
Amer. Phil. Soc.*, 113 (1969), 367-424.

Turkish problem forced popes to take all Europe into account in
formulating their major policies, broadened their outlook at
every critical juncture, and helped them maintain universal
character of the papacy.

458. Silke, John J., *Kinsale, the Spanish Intervention in Ireland at the End of the Elizabethan Wars.* N.Y.: Fordham Univ. Press, 1970.

      Rev. *AHR*, 76 (1971), 1554-1555; *Choice*, 8 (1971), 726; *Thought*, 46 (1971), 312-313.

      Spain's attempt to aid Irish rebels against their English over-lords. Insight into structure of government and of policy-making at court of Philip III.

459. Simons, Eric N., *Henry VII: The First Tudor King.* N.Y.: Barnes and Noble, 1968.

      Rev. *AHR*, 74 (1968), 158-159.

      Romantic characterization of first Tudor king.

460. Smith, J. Beverely, "The Last Phase of the Glyndwr Rebellion," *BBCS*, 22 (1967). (As listed in *EHR*, 83 [1968], 661, citing *ibid.*, other Hotspur materials.)

      Prints and redates 1410-1417 and 1417, five documents previously assigned to the beginning of the rebellion in 1400.

461. Smith, Lacy Baldwin, *The Elizabethan World.* N.Y./Boston: Houghton Mifflin, 1967.

      Rev. *AHR*, 73 (1968), 1521-1522; *QJS*, 54 (1968), 183-184.

      Originally published as *The Horizon Book of the Elizabethan World* (N.Y.: American Heritage, 1967--rev. *N.Y. Times Book Review*, 5 November 1967, pp. 6-7), with better illustrations.

      Popular survey of 16th-cent. history, including a chapter on the Armada, political and religious controversies, with chapters on France and Spain.

462. Smith, R.B., *Land and Politics in England of Henry VIII: The West Riding of Yorkshire, 1530-1546.* Oxford: Clarendon Press, 1970.

      Rev. *Econ.H.R.*, 2nd ser., 25 (1972), 161.

      Tawney-inspired economic and political analysis of Tudor York-shire on eve of Reformation. Appendixes provide excellent reference work for last years of monasteries and monastic estates.

463. Smout, T.C., *The History of the Scottish People 1560-1830.* N.Y.: Scribner's, 1970.

      Rev. *TLS*, 9 April 1970, 376.

      First of two parts: the Age of Reformation (1560-1690), traces impact of reform in the church and in government on the insti-tutions and pattern of life in Scotland.

464. Stalnaker, Robert C., "Events, Periods, and Institutions in Historians' Language," *History and Theory*, 6 (1967), 159-179.

Exposes various ways of viewing the Renaissance and the various
historical concepts one can use as a framework in discussing
this period. Discusses arguments of Huizinga, Chabod, Panofsky,
and Kristeller. Concludes that "holistic terms" and general
"age-concepts" are subject to interpretative judgments and that
flexibility is justified because historians are uncertain about
what exactly happened in relevant periods of history.

465. Starr, Chester G., "Historical and Philosophical Time," *History
and Theory, Beiheft*, 6 (1966), 24-35.

Comments on the concept of Time throughout the ages, shedding
light on its value metaphorically and historically in the
Renaissance.

466. Stone, Donald, Jr., *France in the Sixteenth Century: A Medieval Society Transformed*. Englewood Cliffs, N.J.: Prentice-
Hall, 1969.

Rev. *Choice*, 6 (1969), 1095; *MLJ*, 54 (1970), 134; *RenQ*, 22
(1969), 383-384.

Chapters corresponding to reigns and milieu of political,
social, and artistic events; subsequent chapters on events or
literary works which transcend these bounds.

467. Storey, R.L., *The Reign of Henry VII*. N.Y.: Walker, 1968.

Arrangement is topical, with discussion of the central government, diplomacy and sedition, law and order, population, industry, economy, church, education, and the arts. Genealogical
tables, documentation. Rev. *TLS*, 18 Apr. 1968, 406.

468. Sutherland, N.M., "The Nunciatures de France, 1546-1604,"
Journal of Ecclesiastical History, 20 (1969), 299-308.

Review article of three volumes in the series of *Acta Nuntia-
turae Gallicae*--records of papal nuncios as ambassadors.

469. Tenenti, Alberto, *Florence à l'Epoque des Médicis: De la Cité
à l'Etat. Questions d'Histoire*. Paris: Flammarion, 1968.

From democracy to oligarchy, 1370-1400; on culture and society
which emerged in secular aspects in 15th cent. to make Florence
center of arts, politics, sciences, and philosophy. Second
part contains documentation and analysis of problems in fore-
going description.

470. Trevor-Roper, Hugh, ed., *The Age of Expansion: Europe and the
World, 1559-1660*. N.Y.: McGraw-Hill, 1968.

Rev. *LibJ*, 94 (1969), 191; *New Statesman*, 76 (1968), 320; *TLS*,
29 August 1968, 924.

Accounts by political historians which emphasize the intellectual and artistic unity of the period despite its political
divisiveness; includes Spain, Netherlands, Central Europe,
Thirty Years' War, Poland and Russia, Turkey, Persia and India,
China and Japan.

471. ————, *Religion, the Reformation and Social Change, and other Essays*. London: Macmillan, 1967. (Published in U.S. as *The Crisis of the Seventeenth Century: Religion, the Reformation and Social Change*. N.Y.: Harper and Row, 1968.)

Rev. *Spectator*, 29 September 1967, 361-363.

Chapters include Religion, the Reformation and Social Change; General Crisis of the 17th Century; European Witch-craze of the 16th and 17th centuries; Union of Britain in the 17th century. All the essays focus on the crisis of government, society, and ideas in Europe and England between the Reformation and the mid-17th cent.

472. Tuck, J.A., "Richard II and the Border Magnates," *Northern History*, 3 (1968), 27-52.

In Richard II's reign, the crown played off one border group against another while trying to regulate border politics. Article deals with Richard II's relations with the Percy family.

473. Tyler, Philip, "The Significance of the Ecclesiastical Commission at York," *Northern History*, 2 (1967), 27-44.

Ecclesiastical Commission at York was second most important conciliar court in the north from the earliest years of Elizabeth to 1641. Bulk of Ecclesiastical Commission proceedings survive (Borthwick Institute, York). Intended to be private, they are relatively important source for northern history. (Two Act Books, however, missing, covering April 1603 to January 1607 and October 1634 to June 1638.)

474. Vale, Malcolm Graham Allan, *English Gascony, 1399-1453: A Study of War, Government and Politics during the Later Stages of the Hundred Years' War*. London: Oxford Univ. Press, 1970.

Rev. *Choice*, 8 (1971), 1728.

Emphasizes the area's importance in general context of Anglo-French relations, and especially of English war aims.

475. Vander Molen, Ronald Jay, "Richard Cox (1499-1581), Bishop of Ely: An Intellectual Biography of a Renaissance and Reformation Administrator," *DA*, 30 (1970), 5396-97-A (Mich. State Univ.).

Cox adjusted his Erasmian humanism and Swiss Protestantism to needs of Englishmen. Consequently, he played an important practical role in formulation and institutionalizing of Anglicanism.

476. Van Eerde, Katherine S., "The Spanish Match through an English Protestant's Eyes," *HLQ*, 32 (1968), 59-75.

Documents changing position of Parliamentary leader Sir Robert Phelips on proposal of marriage between England's heir and a Spanish Infanta (1613-1623).

477. Vaughan, Richard, *Phillip the Good: The Apogee of Burgundy.*
      N.Y.: Barnes and Noble, 1970.

      Rev. *Choice*, 4 (1970), 747.

      Political narrative, but also includes analytical chapters on
      economics, administration, intellectual life, and religion.

478. Vernadsky, George, *The Tsardom of Moscow, 1547-1682: A His-
      tory of Russia*, vol. 5. New Haven, Conn.: Yale Univ. Press,
      1969. Rev. *Choice*, 6 (1969), 1467.

      Examines ideological foundations of the Tsardom and establish-
      ment of Romanov dynasty in 1613, concluding with discussion of
      Russian culture in this period and a consideration of the im-
      pact and spread of Western influences.

479. Voisé, Waldemar, "Machiavel et Guichardin ou la naissance de
      l'historisme moderne," *Organon*, 7 (1970), 147-176.

      Machiavelli and Guicciardini were caught in the conflict be-
      tween the old concept of a static universe and the new one of
      a historical process at work.

480. Wernham, R.B., ed., *List and Analysis of the State Papers,
      Foreign Series, Volume II: July 1590-May 1591.* London:
      H.M.S.O., 1969.

      Rev. *Hist.*, 55 (1970), 117.

      Struggle with Spain remains central in this volume. Main prob-
      lems of the English government concern appraisal of operations
      in the United Provinces and France; Parma and Henry IV were
      anxiously watched.

481. Wheeler, Thomas V., "Sir Francis Bacon's Historical Imagina-
      tion," *Tennessee Stud. Lit.*, 14 (1969), 111-118.

      Though Bacon associated history with memory, poetry with imagi-
      nation, his *History of the Reign of King Henry VII* shows strik-
      ing uses of imagination.

482. Whitfield, Christopher, "The Stratford Riots of 1619 and Richard
      Dover of Evesham: Robert Dover and Sir Baptist Hicks," *N&Q*,
      212 (1967), 92-93.

      Newly discovered historical links concerning brothers Richard
      and Robert Dover. Both were of Gray's Inn; Richard defended
      William Reynolds, indicating possibly that Shakespeare knew
      them both.

483. Wilcox, Donald J., *The Development of Florentine Humanist His-
      toriography in the Fifteenth Century.* Cambridge, Mass.: Har-
      vard Univ. Press, 1969. Rev. *YWML*, 31 (1969), 383.

      Historical perspective of Leonardo Bruni, Poggio Bracciolini,
      and Bartolommeo della Scala. Illustrates methodology and value
      of studying historians by determining object of their loyalty
      and intellectual commitment, and their understanding of nature
      of historical reality.

484. Wilkinson, B., "Fact and Fancy in Fifteenth-Century English
      History," *Speculum*, 42 (1967), 673-692.

      Fifteenth-cent. historical data are highly colored by propa-
      ganda. Suggests area of investigation, especially in consti-
      tutional history; calls for new appraisal of 15th cent.

485. ————, *The Later Middle Ages in England*. London: Longmans,
      1969.

      Rev. *EHR*, 86 (1971), 122-125.

      Constitutional history of birth of sovereign national state;
      effect of politics on ideologies. Holds that Yorkists rather
      than Lancastrians favored alliance of Crown with people; Lan-
      castrians in 1399 favored alliance with aristocracy.

486. Williams, C.H., ed., *English Historical Documents*, vol. 5:
      1485-1558. London: Eyre and Spottiswoode; N.Y.: Oxford, 1967.

      Rev. *AHR*, 73 (1968), 805; *Moreana*, no. 18 (1968), 89-90.

      Source book on early Tudor period: 1) the writing of history;
      2) the land; 3) the commonweal; 4) government and administra-
      tion; 5) religion; 6) daily life in town and country.

487. Williams, Neville, *Elizabeth Queen of England*. London: Weiden-
      feld and Nicolson, 1967. (Published in U.S. as *Elizabeth the
      First, Queen of England*. N.Y.: E.P. Dutton, 1968.)

      Rev. *AHR*, 74 (1968), 596-597.

      Based on P.R.O. material said not to have been available to
      other biographers. Court history with full documentation.

488. Winkler, Frances Huntington, "The Making of King's Knights in
      England, 1399-1461," *DA*, 29 (1968), 1185-A (Yale Univ.).

      Studies class origins and social roles of "king's knights"
      under the Lancaster kings; concludes that the lord-retainer
      relationship showed vitality under stresses experienced during
      Wars of the Roses, in which majority of his "king's knights"
      remained loyal to Henry VI.

489. Wolper, Roy S., "The Rhetoric of Gunpowder and the Idea of
      Progress," *JHI*, 31 (1970), 589-598.

      Gunpowder as not within realm of progress, in same sense as
      were compass and the printing press.

490. Wood, Neal, "Frontinus as a Possible Source for Machiavelli's
      Method," *JHI*, 28 (1967), 243-248.

      Machiavelli's main innovation--not using history as a guide for
      present action, but his method of applying examples and comment-
      ing on them. Influenced by the ancient writer Frontinus, from
      whom he also probably borrowed the method of accumulating many
      examples to prove a number of theses; using both contemporary
      and ancient examples, with negative examples to determine dif-
      fering circumstances; and treating moral actions as expedient.

491. Woodward, D.M., "Short Guides to Records No. 22 Port Books," *History*, 55 (1970), 207-210.

      One in a series of such guides. Nature and use of customs records (1564 on) kept in the ports of England and Wales.

492. Wray, Frank Junior, "History in the Eyes of the Sixteenth Century Anabaptists," *DA*, 28 (1967), 1521-A (Yale Univ.).

      On 16th-cent. Anabaptists' thought concerning history, its nature, course, and final consummation. Within the limits of divine sovereignty, they perceived the working of a limited human free will, permitting man at least to choose between obedience and disobedience. Their views were reflected in Anabaptist social behavior; withdrawal from the world; and rejection of war, the oath, civil magistracy, and infant baptism.

493. Yarrow, Philip John, *The Seventeenth Century, 1600-1715*. N.Y.: Barnes and Noble, 1967.

      Rev. *Choice*, 5 (1968), 632.

      Second volume in five-part series, *Literary History of France*; divides period into four parts, each preceded by an introduction relating literary developments to political, social, scientific, and philosophical changes.

V. HUMANIST-CLASSICAL

494. Baron, Hans, *From Petrarch to Leonardo Bruni: Studies in Humanistic and Political Literature*. Chicago/London: Univ. of Chicago Press, 1968. Rev. *YWML*, 30 (1968), 378.

Chapters on Evolution of Petrarch's Thought; Petrarch's *Secretum*; Bruni's *Laudatio* and *Dialogue*; Florentine Historiography; Imitation, Rhetoric, and Quatrocento Thought in Bruni's *Laudatio*; Aulus Gellius in the Renaissance, etc.

495. Beardsley, Theodore S., *Hispanico-Classical Translations printed between 1482 and 1699*. Pittsburgh: Duquesne Univ. Press, 1970.

Rev. *BH*, 73 (1971), 486-488; *Ren. and Ref.*, 8 (1971), 87-88; *RenQ*, 24 (1971), 260-265.

Analysis and overview of all but a few of the known texts of translations of classics. Bibliographical study with annotations: problems of authorship, deletions, and emendations in translation.

496. Bec, C., "Recherches sur la culture à Florence au XVe siècle," *Rev. Ét. ital.*, 14, no. 3 (1968), 211-245.

In first half of 15th cent. humanists were known only by a restricted elite. In the second half of that cent., Latin classical authors advanced to first place, at expense of Latin Christian authors, and humanists experienced considerable progress; also, Greek authors were better known.

497. Bellorini, Maria Grazia, "Tracce di cultura italiana nella formazione di Thomas North," *Aevum*, 41 (1967), 333-338.

Italian influences in the family of the translator (via Amyot) of Shakespeare's Plutarch.

498. Béné, Charles, *Erasme et saint Augustin, ou l'Influence de saint Augustin sur l'humanisme d'Erasme*. Geneva: Droz, 1969.

Rev. *BHR*, 32 (1970), 710-714.

On Erasmus' borrowings from Augustine's *De doctrina christiana* in relation to his humanism.

499. Bergel, Lienhard, "The Horatians and the Curiatians in the Dramatic and Political-Moralist Literature before Corneille," *RenD*, n.s., 3 (1970), 215-238.

Livy's history of the duels between the Horatian brothers and the Curiatians as treated by Augustine, Dante, Petrarch, Machiavelli, Pietro Aretino, Lope de Vega. Shows that the choices of plots of Renaissance dramatists were not accidental, since they were familiar with the various interpretations before them.

500.   Betts, John H., "Classical Allusions in Shakespeare's *Henry V*,
       with Special Reference to Virgil," *Greece and Rome*, 2nd ser.,
       15 (1968), 147-163.

       Opposed to notion of Shakespeare's "small Latine"; Virgilian-
       epic use in *Henry V*.

501.   Black, M.W., "Aristotle's Mythos and the Tragedies of Shakes-
       peare," *SJ (West)* (1968), 43-55.

       Correspondences between rules of tragedy in Aristotle's
       Poetics and non-historical tragedies of Shakespeare.

502.   Boggess, William F., "Aristotle's *Poetics* in the Fourteenth
       Century," *SP*, 67 (1970), 278.

       To establish which English translation was used in 14th cent.;
       eventually led to Renaissance concept of the *Poetics*.

503.   Bolgar, R.R., "Humanism as a Value System with Reference to
       Budé and Vivès," *Humanism in France* ..., ed. A.H.T. Levi.
       Manchester and N.Y.: Harper and Row, 1970, pp. 199-215.

       Humanism as intellectual framework, complex of ideas and values
       which give shape to experience; humanist compromises as unre-
       solved contradiction--uneasy tight-rope on which men walked
       out of Middle Ages.

504.   Bonicatti, Maurizio, *Studi sull' Umanesimo. Secoli XIV-XVI*.
       Firenze: La Nuova Italia, 1969.

       Includes "La crisi dell' Umanesimo 'eroico,' ed il concetto di
       Rinascimento nella cultura dei Paesi Bassi," pp. 141-175; "La
       concezione Saturnina," on melancholy, pp. 255-291, plus illus-
       trations. Also discusses phases of Italian and North European
       humanism, including use of myth as reflected in painting and
       literature of the time.

505.   Breen, Quirinus, *Christianity and Humanism: Studies in the
       History of Ideas*. Collected and published in his honor. Fore-
       word by Paul Oskar Kristeller, Preface by Heiko A. Oberman,
       and edited by Nelson Peter Ross. Grand Rapids, Mich.: William
       B. Eerdmans, 1968.

       Rev. *AHR*, 74 (1968), 542-544; *Church History*, 37 (1968), 466-
       467.

       "Three Renaissance Humanists on the Relation of Philosophy and
       Rhetoric" (Giovanni Pico della Mirandola, Ermolao Barbaro, and
       Philipp Melanchthon); "The Twofold Truth Theory in Melanchthon";
       "The Terms 'Loci Communes' and 'loci' in Melanchthon"; "John
       Calvin and the Rhetorical Tradition"; "Twelfth Century Revival
       of Roman Law"; "Renaissance Humanism and Roman Law." Final
       section on "The Church as the Mother of Learning."

506.   Brown, Peter M., "A Significant Sixteenth-Century Use of the
       Word 'Umanista,'" *MLR*, 64 (1969), 565-575.

       Salviati employs the word "umanista" in his funeral oration for
       Varchi, who deserves this consummate praise on account of his
       competence in Florentine, the most "noble" of all the languages.

Humanist-Classical   83

507. Buck, August, *Die Humanistische Tradition in der Romania*. Bad
      Hamburg V.d.H.: Verlag Gehlen, 1968.

      Collection of 19 essays under headings "Das antike Erbe," "Hu-
      manismus und Wissenschaften," "Humanismus und Kunst," "Humanis-
      mus und Politik."

508. ———, "Italienischer Humanismus: Forschungsbericht," *AKG*, 52
      (1970), 121-140.

      Report on works published in the last decade; discussion of
      major problems and positions.

509. ———, "Der Rückgriff des Renaissance-Humanismus auf die
      Patristik," *Festgabe für W. v. Wartburg zum 80. Geburtstag*, ed.
      K. Baldinger. Tübingen: Niemeyer, 1968, pp. 153-175.

      Extent to which, as spiritual vehicle on the Renaissance, human-
      ism interpreted patristic writings.

510. Bush, Douglas, "Tudor Humanism and Henry VIII" in *Engaged and
      Disengaged*. Harvard U.P., 1966. Rev. *SQ*, 18 (1967), 183-184.

      Discusses the Tudor policy toward education and religion, par-
      ticularly the abolition and reorganization of religious insti-
      tutions in relation to new educational policies. Death of
      classical humanism, rise of more practical humanism as guide to
      the active Christian.

511. *Colloquium Erasmianum*. Actes du Colloque International réuni
      à Mons du 26 au 29 octobre 1967 à l'occasion du cinquième cen-
      tenaire de la naissance d'Érasme. Mons: Centre Universitaire
      de l'Etat, 1968.

      Rev. *Church Hist.*, 39 (1970), 115-116.

      Contains 18 papers on: 1) philology and theology; 2) Erasmus
      as thinker and moralist; 3) his influence; 4) Erasmus, the man.
      Contains summaries of discussions. Second group: essay on
      Christian Epicureanism in Valla's *De voluptate*, More's *Utopia*,
      and Erasmus's colloquy *Epicurus*; another essay on Erasmus's
      idea of truth, the freedom it implies, and tie between *fides*
      and *ratio*.

512. Coppens, Joseph, ed., *Scrinium Erasmianum*. *Mélanges histo-
      riques publiés sous le patronage de l'Université de Louvain à
      l'occasion du cinquième centenaire de la naissance d'Erasme*.
      2 vols. Leiden: Brill, 1969.

      Rev. *BHR*, 32 (1970), 460-461.

      Vol. 1: three main groups: *Érasme, son milieu, ses relations;
      les oeuvres d'Erasme--genèse et diffusion; l'humanisme d'Erasme
      et son influence aux Pays-Bas*. Vol. 2 also deals with his
      ideas.

513. Cosenza, Mario Emilio, comp., *Biographical and Bibliographical
      Dictionary of the Italian Humanists and the World of Classical
      Scholarship in Italy, 1300-1800*. Boston: G.K. Hall, 1962;
      Supplementary vol. VI, 1967.

      Includes Renaissance writers of Italian birth and others iden-
      tified with Italy, who studied phases of Greek and Roman civili-

zation. Helps locate individuals with multiplicity of names.
67,900 entries plus synopsis and bibliography, reproduced in
five volumes; supplementary Vol. VI with 5,000 entries.

514. Cotton, Julia Hill, "Politian, Humanist Poet," *Italica*, 46
(1969), 176-190.

Discussion of Sorbonne doctoral thesis by Ida Maier on Politian
(1454-1494). Vol. 1: a catalogue of manuscripts related to
Politian. Vol. 2: *Ange Politien, La Formation d'un poète
humaniste (1469-1480)*.

515. Davis, Natalie Zemon, "Poor Relief, Humanism and Heresy,"
Studies in Medieval and Renaissance History. Vol. 5 (ed.
William M. Bowsky. Lincoln, Neb.: Univ. of Nebraska Press,
1968), pp. 215-275.

Lyons' religious and intellectual heterogeneity in 1530's is
helpful in isolating religious variables involved in creating
and supporting its Aumône-Générale. This information is used
to inquire into change in European religious sensibility regarding begging and charity, and role of secular as well as Christian humanists; Erasmian as well as Protestant views of education, order, and charity, in reforming poor relief on the
Continent.

516. De Gaetano, Armand L., "The Florentine Academy and the Advance-
ment of Learning through the Vernacular: the Orti Oricellari
and the Sacra Accademia," *BHR*, 30 (1968), 19-52.

Renaissance phase of the Academy in its campaign for vernacular
to replace Latin in all fields of knowledge--the Academy as an
expression of cultural force leading to nationalism. Bembo's
role in showing that Italian was the language for any field of
knowledge. Relationship of the Academy to plays and other theatrical forms, e.g., *canti carnascialeschi* and *cicalate* (p. 28).
List of topics discussed in lectures (p. 44).

517. Devereux, E.J., *Checklist of English Translations of
Erasmus to 1700*. Oxford: Oxford Bibliog. Soc., 1968.

518. Dorey, T.A., ed., *Erasmus*. London: Routledge and Kegan Paul.
1970.

Rev. *TLS*, 18 December 1970, 1494.

Essays by M.M. Phillips on "Erasmus and the Classics"; J.W.
Binns on Erasmus's letters and theory of letter writing; D.F.S.
Thompson on Erasmus's Latinity; B. Hall on "Erasmus, Biblical
Scholar and Reformer"; A.E. Douglas, "Erasmus as a Satirist."

519. Elorza, Antonio, "El Humanismo de Maquiavelo y Guicciardini,"
Cuadernos Hispanoamericanos, 73, no. 218 (1968), 359-368.

Commentary on Moravia's essay, "Maquiavelo" and Gilbert's
study, *Machiavelli and Guicciardini: Politics and History in
Sixteenth-Century Florence*, both of which treat the humanist
foundations of these personalities, the former, however, from a
moral viewpoint and the latter in a socio-cultural context.

520. Erasmus, *Opera Omnia*. Vol. 1. Amsterdam: North-Holland Pub. Co., 1969.

     Rev. *BHR*, 32 (1970), 461-463.

     To mark the 500th anniversary of the birth of Erasmus, the first volume of a newly edited and annotated edition of the Latin text of his complete works has been published. P.S. Allen's edition of the *Opus Epistolarum* (1906-1958) has provided a completely new basis for research.

521. *Etudes Rabelaisiennes*. Tome VIII. (Travaux d'Humanisme et Renaissance, XCIX). Geneva: Droz, 1969.

     Rev. *Fr. Studies*, 25 (1971), 66-67.

     Includes articles by J. Bichon, "Sagesse Humaine et Sagesse Canine," on use of *sagesse* in Rabelais; and by M.A. Screech, on Renaissance views of 11-month pregnancies. M. Masters deals with Rabelais and emblems.

522. Ferguson, Arthur B., "John Twyne: A Tudor Humanist and the Problem of Legend," *Jour. of Brit. Studies*, 9 (1969), 24-44.

     Twyne represents typical English humanist of Renaissance England, eager to apply classical learning to some problem of more general concern to the commonwealth--in this case, national mythology.

523. Françon, Marcel, "Humanisme," *BHR*, 30 (1968), 300-303.

     On 16th-cent. use of the term. Agrees with Kristeller that the Italian humanists were not professional philosophers. "Humanists" as distinguished from "specialists."

524. ————, "Humanisme, Renaissance, Réforme," *Rev. de l'Univ. d'Ottawa*, 38, no. 1 (1968), 35-39.

     A brief discussion of the use of these terms: Renaissance, Reform, reformism, humanism; conflicts represented by the opposition of abstractions such as the Middle Ages against the Renaissance or humanism against reformism.

525. ————, "Montaigne et l'Humanisme," *Bulletin de la Société des Amis de Montaigne*, no. 17 (1969), 34.

     On the creation of the term *Humanismus* by F.J. Niethammer in 1808. In French, *humanisme* was first used by Th. Gerold in 1874.

526. Freeman, John Francis, "French Humanists and Politics under Francis I," *DA*, 30 (1969), 1945-1946-A (Univ. of Mich.).

     French humanists participated through deeds and words in the politics of France between 1515 and 1547. Some lived around the royal court and discussed how politics ought to be conducted; others were actively engaged in diplomatic negotiations.

527.   Garin, Eugenio, *Italian Humanism: Philosophy and Civic Life
       in the Renaissance*, tr. Peter Munz. N.Y.: Harper, 1966 (1965).

       Provides a useful, comprehensive account of Italian Renaissance
       philosophy; 14th-cent. humanism. Rev. *AHR*, 72 (1967), 631-633.

528.   ————, "Quel 'humanisme'? Variations historiques," trans.
       Pierre van Bever, *Rev. intern. de Philos.*, 22, no. 3-4 (1968),
       263-275.

       Traces changing connotations of the term "humanism" from 14th
       cent. through Heidegger and Sartre.

529.   ————, *Ritratti di umanisti*. Firenze: Sansoni, 1967.

       Includes Enea Silvio Piccolomini, Paolo dal Pozzo Toscanelli,
       Guarino Guarini, Filippo Beroaldo il Vecchio, Angelo Poliziano,
       Girolamo Savonarola, Giovanni Pico della Mirandola.

530.   ————, *Science and Civic Life in the Italian Renaissance*. Tr.
       Peter Munz. N.Y.: Doubleday, 1969. Rev. *LJ*, 94 (1969), 545.

       Ethical and political ideas and ideals of Italian cities of
       15th cent.; science of the Renaissance and its connection to
       the rebirth of humanistic studies. How cultural development,
       tied to life of 14th- and 15th-cent. cities, came to be one of
       preconditions of modern science.

531.   Gerlo, A., and Frans De Raeve, *Répertoire des Lettres Traduites
       d'Erasme*. Brussels: Presses Universitaires de Bruxelles,
       1969.

       Rev. *BHR*, 32 (1970), 199; *Moreana*, no. 24 (1969), 116; *Revue
       Belge de Philologie et d'Hist.*, 48 (1970), 175-176; *Rev. Hist.
       Eccl.*, 64 (1969), 869-870.

       Index of translations into all major European vernaculars of
       the separate epistles of Erasmus has been prepared.

532.   Green, Otis H., *The Literary Mind of Medieval and Renaissance
       Spain*. Introduction, John E. Keller. (Studies in Romance
       Languages 1.) Lexington, Ky.: Univ. of Kentucky Press, 1970.

       Contains 12 essays, plus three excerpts from *Spain and the
       Western Tradition*. Rev. *Choice*, 8 (1971), 72.

533.   ————, *Spain and the Western Tradition: The Castilian Mind in
       Literature from "El Cid" to Calderón*. Vol. 4. Madison, Wisc.:
       Univ. of Wisconsin Press, 1966. (Vol. 1, 1963; II, 1964;
       III, 1965.) Rev. *Choice*, 4 (1967), 842.

       Final volume in series. Chapters include: I. "From *Universi-
       tas Christiana* to Balance of Power"; II. Optimism-Pessimism in
       the Baroque; III. *Desengaño*; IV. Death; V. Religion. Contains
       bibliography and cumulative index.

534.   Grendler, Paul F., "Five Italian Occurrences of *Umanista*, 1540-
       1574," *RenQ*, 20 (1967), 317-325.

       Uses such occurrences to speculate on the true meaning of the
       term for the Renaissance.

535. Gundersheimer, Werner L., ed., *French Humanism, 1470-1600*. N.Y.: Macmillan, 1969.

Rev. *TLS*, 12 February 1970, 158.

Articles in this collection include reprints of Raymond Lebègue on the Christian interpretation of pagan authors, Eugene Rice on Lefèvre d'Etaples and his circle, Lucien Romier on the importance of Lyon, Henry Hornik on three interpretations of the French Renaissance, N.M. Sutherland on Parisian life. H.-J. Martin on what Parisians read in the 16th cent., an excerpt from Otto Benesch's *The Art of the Renaissance in Northern Europe*, and Rudolf Hirsch on printing in France from 1470 to 1480.

536. ————, *The Life and Works of Louis Le Roy*. Geneva: Droz, 1966. Rev. *NYRB*, 24 Aug. 1967, 24.

Study of the intellectual development of the 16th-cent. French humanist who ended his career as Royal Professor of Greek. Follows history of ideas approach and compares Le Roy to Machiavelli and Bodin. Analyzes Le Roy's important work, the *Vicissitude ou variété des choses en l'univers*.

537. Gutmann, Elsbeth, *Die Colloquia Familiaria des Erasmus von Rotterdam*. (Basler Beiträge zur Geschichtswissenschaft, hrsg. Edgar Bonjour et al., Bd. 111.) Basel/Stuttgart: Verlag von Helbing & Lichtenheim, 1968.

Useful study of the *Colloquia*. 1) Die Entstehung der *Colloquia*; 2) Die Ideen der *Colloquia*. Bibliography.

538. Halkin, Léon-E., *Erasme* (Classiques du XXme siècle, no. 116). Paris: Editions universitaires, 1969.

Rev. *BHR*, 32 (1970), 699-701.

Numerous quotations translated from Erasmus by author, specialist in humanist studies, in book intended for general public. Portrait of Erasmus as prince of humanists.

539. Hillerbrand, Hans J., ed., *Erasmus and His Age. Selected Letters*. Trans. M.A. Haworth. N.Y.: Harper and Row, 1970.

I. Youth and Apprenticeship: 1486-1495; II. Further Studies and First Travels: 1495-1509; III. Mature Scholar and Humanist: 1510-1517; IV. Challenge of Luther and the Reformation: 1517-1529; V. Twilight Years: 1529-1536.

540. Hogrefe, Pearl, *The Life and Times of Sir Thomas Elyot*. Ames, Iowa: Iowa State Univ. Press, 1967.

Rev. *Manuscripta*, 12 (1968), 40-41; *QJS*, 53 (1967), 298; *RenQ*, 21 (1968), 216-219.

Elyot's relationship to major events of the period; emphasizes English elements in his life and writings. Appendix I: list of 16th- and 17th-cent. works with a possible relation to the *Governour*; Appendix II: alleged influences of Elyot on other writers.

541. Hommages à Marie Delcourt (Collection Latomus, vol. 114),
      Brussells, 1970.

      Rev. BHR, 33, no. 3 (1971), 752-753.

      Articles on problems of Erasmus's works and on other lesser
      humanists: Torrentius, Jacques Grévin. Also on the Cymbalum
      mundi and "La Cité du Soleil" of Campanella.

542. Humanistica lovaniensia. Post H. De Vocht, edenda curavit J.
      Ijsewijn. Vol. 18. Louvain: Vander, 1969.

      Rev. BHR, 32 (1970), 502.

      Contains editions of neo-Latin poems and deals especially with
      topics pertinent to 16th cent.

543. Hunter, G.K., "Seneca and the Elizabethans: A Case Study in
      'Influence,'" ShS, 20 (1967), 17-26.

      Questions Cunliffe's thesis (1893) of Senecan "influence" on
      Elizabethan theater. Stresses Ovid and Terence; Seneca known
      as moralist. Discusses vernacular elements and questions no-
      tion of tragedy as "watertight" genre, immune to other than
      "tragic" influences.

544. Jodogne, Pierre, "Les rhétoriqueurs et l'humanisme: problème
      d'histoire littéraire," Humanism in France ..., ed., A.H.T.
      Levi. Manchester and N.Y.: Harper & Row, 1970, pp. 150-173.

      "Rhétoriqueurs" originally had pejorative connotation; but
      without them, the Pléiade could neither have conceived nor
      achieved its aims.

545. Kaufmann, R.J., "The Seneca Perspective and the Shakespearean
      Poetic," CompD, 1 (1967), 182-198.

      Seneca significantly anticipates the structural and thematic
      elements in Shakespearean tragic drama.

546. King, Ethel, Doctor Linacre: 1460-1524. Brooklyn, N.Y.:
      Theodore Gaus, 1968.

      On writer of the Latin grammar; his contributions as a medical
      man, priest, teacher, and exemplary humanist.

547. Kranz, Walther, "Shakespeare und die Antike: Drei Beiträge,"
      Studien zur antiken Literatur und ihrem Fortwirken. Kleine
      Schriften, ed. Ernst Vogt. Bibliothek der klassischen Alter-
      tumswissenschaften, Bd. 3 (Heidelberg: Winter, 1967), pp.
      447-451.

      On MV and Pythagoras; JC I.ii and Tro. III.iii, and Alcibiades in
      Plato; Lr. and gods as judges.

548. Kristeller, Paul Oskar, Der italienische Humanismus und seine
      Bedeutung (Vorträge der Aeneas-Silvius-Stiftung an der Univer-
      sität Basel, 10.) Basel, Stuttgart: Helbing und Lichtenhahn,
      1969.

Relation of humanism to seven liberal arts; influence of Italian humanism outside Italy; within Italy, on literature, music, and musical theory, political theory, mathematics, medicine, law, religious and philosophical thought.

549. La Rosa, Frank Edward, "A Critical Edition of John Heywood's *A Play of Love*," *DA*, 29 (1969), 2218-A (Univ. of Illinois).

Glossary of those words in the play which carry special theological and Christian humanistic meaning relevant to Heywood's humanistic intent. Included in Introduction is discussion of Renaissance humanism.

550. Mann, Nicholas, "Petrarch's Role as Moralist in Fifteenth-Century France," *Humanism in France* ..., ed. A.H.T. Levi. Manchester and N.Y.: Harper & Row, 1970, pp. 6-28.

Petrarch's *De remediis*; history of interpretation and popularity suggests that Stoic and humanist originality of work was sometimes correctly perceived in France, while in northern Europe it was regarded as product of devout Christian moralist.

551. Margolin, Jean-Claude, *Quatorze Années de Bibliographie Erasmienne, 1936-1949*. (De Pétrarque à Descartes, 21.) Paris: Vrin, 1969.

Rev. *BHR*, 32 (1970), 200-201; *Moreana*, no. 24 (1969), 19-20.

On works and texts of Erasmus, and books, articles, and communications devoted to Erasmus or Erasmism. Annotated; critical reviews frequently cited. Indexes: periodical, author, general, works of Erasmus, and translations of works.

552. ———, *Recherches érasmiennes*. Geneva: Droz, 1969.

Rev. *BHR*, 32 (1970), 202-204; *Moreana*, no. 24 (1969), 20.

Seven studies on thought of Erasmus; internal approach based on critical examination of texts, and external one, which considers editors', translators', critics', etc. views of Erasmus, as well as contemporary studies affecting the thought of Erasmus himself. Erasmus' idea of nature; Erasmus and truth; and Mnemosyne; and music; and the "savage woman."

553. Markowski, M., "Nauki Wyzwolone i Filozofia na Uniwersytecie Krakowskim w XV wieku" [Liberal Arts and Philosophy at the University of Krakow in the 15th Cent.], *Studia Mediewistyczne*, 9 (1968), 91-115.

Describes how under influence of humanism the traditional classifications of quadrivium and trivium were broadened to comprise more subjects, including philosophy of science, providing atmosphere in which Copernicus was led to make his discoveries.

554. Masek, Rosemary, "The Humanistic Interests of the Early Tudor Episcopate," *Church Hist.*, 39 (1970), 5-17.

Members of Tudor episcopate who pursued interests in education and learning between 1447 and 1488 and into next cent. Richard Fox, Richard Nykke, Robert Sherborne, William Warham, John Fisher among those discussed.

555. McFarlane, I.D., "George Buchanan and French Humanism,"
      Humanism in France ..., ed. A.H.T. Levi. Manchester and N.Y.:
      Harper & Row, 1970, pp. 295-319.

      Influence of French Renaissance humanism; difficulties in in-
      terpreting Buchanan's career and attitudes; international im-
      portance of French Renaissance humanism.

556. Mesnard, Pierre, *Érasme: La philosophie Chrétienne.* (Philo-
      sophes de tous les temps, no. 22.) Paris: Vrin, 1969.

      Rev. *Moreana*, no. 24 (1969), 11-12.

      Introduction, notes, and translation of: *Praise of Folly,
      Letter from Erasmus to Dorpius, Essay on Free Will, Ciceronian,*
      and *Refutation of Clichtove.*

557. ———, *Érasme ou le Christianisme critique* . (Philosophes de
      tous les temps, no. 52.) Paris: Vrin, 1969.

      Rev. *BHR*, 32 (1970), 456; *Moreana*, no. 24 (1969), 113.

      Thought of Erasmus as "critical Christianity"; pocket
      edition.

558. Montano, Rocco, "From Italian Humanism to Shakespeare: The
      Fight with the Angel," *Umanesimo*, 1 (1967), 24-45.

      Shakespeare as Christian humanist, antinaturalist; chapter of
      book in progress, *From Italian Humanism to Shakespeare.*

559. ———, "Humanistic Positions," *IQ*, 13 (1969), 3-31.

      View of 15th- and 16th-cent. humanism which links study of
      classical literature to advent of naturalism and secularism as
      without historical justification. It results from Protestant
      Reformers' rejection of humanist ideas that Grace perfects,
      that the divine is immanent in man, and that nature has the
      power to commune with God.

560. Mulryan, John James, "Natalis Comes' *Mythologiae*: Its Place in
      the Renaissance Mythological Tradition and Its Impact upon
      English Renaissance Literature," *DA*, 31 (1970), 2350-2351-A
      (Univ. of Minn.).

      Published in 1568, the *Mythologiae* compiles and interprets the
      classical myths; study aims to place the work in the Renaissance
      mythological tradition and to describe its impact on English
      Renaissance literature.

561. Nurse, Peter H., "Érasme et Des Périers," *BHR*, 30 (1968), 53-64.

      Sees the *Cymbalum mundi* as a revised and extended version of
      Praise of Folly, adapted to the circumstances created by Luthe-
      ran reform; both basically dominated by the idea of Charité,"
      and both attack a too superficial, too literal, and too super-
      stitious attitude to Christianity.

562. Oppermann, Hans, ed., *Humanismus; Weg der Forschung, XVII.* Darmstadt: Wissenschaftliche Buch Gesellschaft, 1970.

    Rev. *Revue des Études Anciennes*, 73, no. 1-2 (1971), 299-300.

    Collection of articles on humanism, primarily in Germany, from 16th cent. to present.

563. Partee, Morriss Henry, "Sir Philip Sidney and the Renaissance Knowledge of Plato," *ES*, 51 (1970), 411-424.

    Discusses Sidney's references to Plato to discover which parts of the dialogues were common property for Renaissance critics.

564. Peters, Robert, "John Colet's Knowledge and Use of Patristics," *Moreana*, no. 22 (1969), 45-58.

    Colet's quotations are in their original context; he is qualified as Christian humanist by his concentration on exegetical works of Fathers and those influenced by Christian neo-Platonism.

565. Phillips, Margaret Mann, *Erasmus on his Times: A Shortened Version of the "Adages" of Erasmus.* Cambridge/N.Y.: Cambridge Univ. Press, 1967. Rev. *Hist. Today*, 18 (1968), 207.

    Erasmus' *Adagia* translated and condensed.

566. Pinckert, Robert Carl, "Sir Thomas Elyot's *The Image of Governance* (1541): A Critical Edition," *DA*, 28 (1968), 2653-2654-A (Columbia Univ.).

    Complement to Elyot's *The Boke Named the Governour* (1531); the earlier work is a treatise on ethics, the present one a study of politics--in guise of biography of Roman emperor Alexander Severus. Contains description of utopian community as formed by Alexander, compared by Pinckert with More's *Utopia*; also studies Elyot's *Image* as a *speculum principum*.

567. Pineas, Rainer, *Thomas More and Tudor Polemics.* Bloomington: Indiana Univ. Press, 1968.

    Rev. *Manuscripta*, 12 (1968), 112-113.

    More's penultimate period (1528-1533), devoted to religious controversy. Analyzes polemical technique of More and his opponents, Luther, Tyndale, Barnes, Fish, Frith, Saint-Germain. The polemical dialogue as form influencing later Tudor drama.

568. Platnauer, M., ed., *Fifty Years and Twelve of Classical Scholarship.* 2nd ed., rev.; Oxford: Basil Blackwell, 1968.

    Useful surveys of authors, with substantial additions.

569. Prete, Sesto, "Humanism in Fifteenth-Century Ferrara," *Thought*, 43 (1968), 573-585.

    Ferrara as primary source of humanist thought and important center of Italian culture.

570. Prévost, André, *Thomas More, 1477-1535, et la crise de la pensée européenne.* Paris: Mame, 1969.

Rev. *Moreana*, no. 25 (1970), 89-90.

More's thought placed in Renaissance context. Influence of Erasmus. Controversies involving Luther and Tyndale. Political, social, and economic thought of More's *Utopia*.

571. Reedijk, C., "Erasmus in 1970," *BHR*, 32 (1970), 449-466.

Account of Erasmus studies during the last several years, providing news on events and activities in recent years.

572. Reynolds, L.D., and N.G. Wilson, *Scribes and Scholars. A Guide to the Transmission of Greek and Latin Literature.* Oxford Univ. Press, 1968.

Rev. *Latomus*, 30 (1971), 196-199.

Translation into Italian makes the Renaissance reference more specific: *Copisti e filologi. La tradizione dei classici dall' Antichità al Rinascimento*, trans. M. Ferrari, Padova: Antenore, 1969. Authors trace descent of works from the source to texts as these emerge at start of 16th cent.

573. Rice, Eugene F., Jr., "Humanist Aristotelianism in France: Jacques Lefèvre d'Etaples and His Circle," *Humanism in France* ..., ed. A.H.T. Levi. Manchester and N.Y.: Harper & Row, 1970, pp. 132-149.

Relationship between French and Italian humanism; Lefèvre's debt to Italian humanism, and his relationship with central humanist traditions of his age.

574. Romano, John Rigoletto, "The Scholarly Archer: A Study of the Humanism of Ascham's *Toxophilus*," *DA*, 29 (1968), 578-A (Columbia Univ.).

Relationship between humanism and physical exercise; *Toxophilus* and other humanistic treatises on sport. The work as humanistic imitation of ancient dialogue.

575. Rossi, Sergio, *Ricerche sull' umanesimo e sul rinascimento in Inghilterra.* (Pubbl. dell' Univ. Cattolica del Sacro Cuore, ser. 3, scienze filol. e lett., 19.) Milan: Società Editrice: Vita e Pensiero, 1969.

Includes chapters on *Henry V*: "dalla cronaca alla poesia"; Henrician humanism; Erasmus and More; "Esuli italiani in Inghilterra. Controversia religiosa e teatro riformato (1548-1553)"; Florio.

576. Rothschild, Herbert B., "Blind and Purblind: A Reading of the *Praise of Folly*," *Neophil.*, 54 (1970), 223-243.

Maintains that the book was not an exception to, but rather a more artistic presentation of, Erasmus' humanist ideals.

577. Santinello, Giovanni, *Studi sull'umanesimo europeo (Cusa e Petrarca/Lefèvre/Erasmo/Colet/Moro)*. (Università di Padova, Pubbl. dell'Ist. di Storia della Filosofia e del Centro per ricerche di filosofia medievale, n.s., no. 7). Padova: Antenore, 1969.

Rev. *BHR*, 32 (1970), 736-738.

Traces European diffusion of Petrarchanism and of Cusa's "learned ignorance." Compares Petrarchan and Cusan views of man and the universe, without being able to establish a conceptual dependence between the writers.

578. Santoro, Mario, *Note umanistiche*. Napoli: Liguori, 1970.

Includes "Pace e guerra nel pensiero di Erasmo"; "L'umanesimo e il volgare."

579. Schäfer, Eckart, "Erasmus und Horaz," *Antike und Abendland*, 16 (1970), 54-67.

Classical influence on thought of Erasmus, especially that of Horace.

580. Schmidt, Albert-Marie, *Études sur le XVIe siècle*. Paris: Albin Michel, 1967.

Rev. *EP*, 23 (1968), 189-190.

Miscellaneous essays of 16th-cent. interest; e.g., "Traducteurs français de Platon (1536-1550)," pp. 17-44; "Calvinisme et poésie au XVIe siècle en France," pp. 55-66; cf. pp. 67-78.

581. Schottenloher, Otto, "Erasmus und die Respublica Christiana," *Hist. Zeit.*, 210 (1970), 295-323.

Political character of Erasmian Humanism and its influence on desire to spread knowledge of Bible and classical literature.

582. Schwencke, Olaf, "Zur Ovid-Rezeption im Mittelalter," *ZDP*, 89 (1970), 336-346.

Examples from *Metamorphoses* in traditional biblical-exegetical folk literature of 14th and 15th cents.

583. Screech, Michael A., *Aspects of Rabelais's Christian Comedy*. (An inaugural lecture ... at University College. London, 2 February 1967.) London: H.K. Lewis, 1968.

Rev. *MLR*, 64 (1969), 422; *TLS*, 15 February 1968, 163.

Argues for a reading of Rabelais as a critical Christian, whose comic vision of the world fulfilled an artistic function and was based on a sense of judgment in keeping with his essentially Christian spirit.

584. Seigel, Jerrold E., *Rhetoric and Philosophy in Renaissance Humanism: The Union of Eloquence and Wisdom, Petrarch to Valla*. Princeton, N.J.: Princeton Univ. Press, 1968.

Rev. *QJS*, 55 (1969), 78-82.

Analyzes the ideas of four humanists, Petrarch, Salutati, Bruni, Valla, to show that they were primarily professional rhetoricians, believing fully in the relationship between philosophy and rhetoric.

585.   Sellin, Paul R., *Daniel Heinsius and Stuart England, with a Short-Title Checklist of the Works of Danial Heinsius.* Publications of the Sir Thomas Browne Institute. Leiden, General Series, 3; Oxford Univ. Press, 1968.

State historiographer of Holland and his English intellectual connections under the early Stuarts.

586.   Silver, Isidore, *The Intellectual Evolution of Ronsard.* I. "The Formative Influences." St. Louis: Washington Univ. Press, 1969.

Rev. *BHR*, 32 (1970), 729-731.

Emphasis on humanism as forming element of Ronsard; his links with the great humanists: Baïf, Dorat, Turnèbe, Muret, H. Estienne; with Peletier du Mans and their conceptions of love poetry.

587.   Simone, Franco, "Une Entreprise Oubliée des Humanistes Français ...," *Humanism in France* ..., ed. A.H.T. Levi. Manchester and N.Y.: Harper & Row, 1970, pp. 106-131.

Renaissance sense of historical distance; changing historical contexts in which French Renaissance humanists saw their work, reflecting growing self-confidence.

588.   ————, "Per una storia dell'umanesimo francese: i tempo e i modi di un periodo storico," *RR*, 59, no. 3 (1968), 174-184.

Independent historical development of French humanism is as important in European culture as the corresponding Italian movement, but not recognized owing to organization of French literary history.

589.   ————, *Umanesimo, Rinascimento, Barocco in Francia.* Milan: Mursia, 1968.

Rev. *MLR*, 66 (1971), 183-184; *TLS*, 2 February 1969, 162.

Collection of essays written 1947-1965, many focusing on historiographical problems; other topics include Florentine and Venetian influences on French culture. Tries to show evolution in France of progressivist notions of history and culture--symbolized by the topos *veritas filia temporis*--as opposed to the cyclical view of many Italian humanists. Traces dialectic of the two historical views in the emergence of a modern historical sense.

590.   Slavin, Arthur Joseph, "Profitable Studies: Humanists and Government in Early Tudor England," *Viator*, 1 (1970), 307-325.

Sociology of Tudor humanism: humanist participation in, or alienation from, civic activity.

591. Sozzi, Lionello, "La *dignitas hominis* dans la littérature française de la Renaissance," *Humanism in France* ..., ed. A.H.T. Levi. Manchester and N.Y.: Harper & Row, 1970, pp. 176-198.

 Values of French humanism; attitudes to human existence and conditions necessary for its fulfillment.

592. Spitz, Lewis W., "Reports on Scholarship in the Renaissance: German Humanism," *RenQ*, 21 (1968), 125-131.

 Rev. article.

593. Stachniw, Joann., "A Sixteenth-Century Latin Teacher Talks on the Value of a Classical Education," *CJ*, 65 (1969/1970), 258-260.

 Lecture given by classical scholar, Marc-Antoine Muret, to his students. Latin and Greek seen as foundations of education, the liberal arts.

594. Stäuble, Antonio, *La commedia umanistica del quattrocento*. Firenze: Istituto Nazionale di Studi sul Rinascimento, 1968.

 Rev. *MP*, 68 (1970), 93-96.

 Distinguishes three influences: classical, medieval, contemporary; holds that these comedies are "predictive of the spirit of theater to come." Bibliography.

595. Stearns, Raymond P., "Hugh Peter was a Wit," *Proc. of the Amer. Antiq. Soc.*, 77, Pt. I (1967), 13-34.

 Ancient theories of wit and comedy revived by Renaissance scholars. Sixteenth- and 17th-cent. views of humor; 17th-cent. Hugh Peter's sermons and wit.

596. Swanson, Donald C., *The Names in Roman Verse: Lexicon and Reverse Index of All Proper Names of History, Mythology, and Geography found in the Classical Roman Poets*. Madison, Wisc.: Univ. of Wisconsin Press, 1967.

 Rev. *CHum*, 3 (1968), 119-122.

 A computer-produced lexicon.

597. Tateo, Francesco, *Tradizione e realtà nell' Umanesimo italiano*. Bari: Dedalo Libri, 1967.

 Rev. *BHR*, 30 (1967) 643-644.

 Deals, *inter alia*, with humanists' moralistic dialogues; Poggio Bracciolini; "La disputa della nobilità."

598. Thompson, David, "Pico della Mirandola's Praise of Lorenzo (and critique of Dante and Petrarch)," *Neophil.*, 54 (1970), 123-126.

 Pico's comparison of the three contemporaries with one another rather than with the classics, as evidence of growing historical sense in Italian literature.

599. Thompson, Lawrence Sidney, A *Bibliography of American Doctoral
      Dissertations in Classical Studies and Related Fields.* Hamden,
      Conn.:   Shoe String Pr., 1968. Rev. *CRL*, 30 (1969), 77.

600. Thomson, D.F.S., "The Quincentenary of Erasmus and Some Recent
      Books," *UTQ*, 39 (1969/1970), 181-185.

      Recent books on Erasmus, including some translations from him.

601. Tracy, James Donald, "Erasmus: The Growth of a Mind," *DA*, 28
      (1967), 608-A (Princeton Univ.).

      Evaluates Erasmus' ideal of *libertas* and opposition to strict
      discipline, his emphasis on native spontaneity. He favored
      Christian *libertas* against compulsory monastic ceremonies and
      welcomed Luther as likely defender of *libertas*. Role of alle-
      gory in his views discussed, as well as ideal of Christian
      simplicitas.

602. Trinkaus, Charles, *In Our Image and Likeness: Humanity and
      Divinity in Italian Humanist Thought.* 2 vols. London: Con-
      stable; Chicago: Univ. of Chicago Press, 1970.

      Rev. *AHR*, 76 (1971), 1147-1149; *EHR*, 86 (1971), 356-358; *TLS*,
      19 February 1970, 207.

      To define humanist attitudes toward Christian religion and
      their influence on religious thought by examining the view of
      human nature held by early Renaissance Italian scholars. Pe-
      trarch, Salutati, Valla, Manetti, and Ficino emphasized.

603. Vallese, Giuilio, *Studi di Umanesimo.* Naples: Libreria Edi-
      trice Ferraro, 1971.

      Chapters include: "La filosofia dell'amore, dal Ficino al Bem-
      bo, de Leone Ebreo al minori"; "Erasmo e Cicerone ..."; "Erasmo
      e il *De duplici copia verborum ac rerum.*"

604. Vasoli, Cesare, *Umanesimo e Rinascimento.* Palermo: Palumbo,
      1969.

      Includes Dilthey, Burckhardt, Cassirer, Gentile, Croce; contains
      anthology of critics from Renaissance to 20th cent.

605. Weber, Henri, "La facétie et le bon mot du Pogge à Des Periers,"
      Humanism in France ..., ed. A.H.T. Levi. Manchester and N.Y.:
      Harper & Row, 1970, pp. 82-105.

      Renaissance *facétie*; change in linguistic power during different
      epochs; tradition leading up to Erasmus' *Praise of Folly.*

606. Weiler, Anton, "The Christian Humanism of the Renaissance and
      Scholasticism," *Concilium* (Paulist Press, N.Y.), 27 (1967),
      29-46.

      Renaissance humanism as expression of new freedom, on way to
      emancipation, requires dialogue with Christianity.

607.   Weiss, Roberto, "The Dawn of Humanism in Italy," *Bull. Inst.
       Hist. Research*, 42 (1969), 1-16.

       Italian humanism was already in existence before Petrarch and
       Boccaccio and was a spontaneous and natural development of
       classical studies as pursued during the later Middle Ages,
       rather than a reaction against some philosophical aspect or a
       desire for a "renovatio studiorum" and hopes of a new golden
       age. Bibliographic appendix.

608.   ———, *The Renaissance Discovery of Classical Antiquity*. Ox-
       ford: Blackwell, 1969; N.Y.: Humanities, 1970.

       Rev. *TLS*, 23 April 1970, 447.

       Covers 1300-1527; includes index of manuscripts. Developments
       in classical archaeology, epigraphy, numismatics, and anti-
       quarianism in the Renaissance; impact of classical antiquity in
       less studied areas.

609.   Westfall, Carroll W., "Painting and the Liberal Arts: Alberti's
       View," *JHI*, 30 (1969), 487-506.

       Alberti wrote as a humanist, not as an art theorist; it is
       therefore essential to interpret his theory of art in its pro-
       per place in humanist thought from about 1400 to 1435.

610.   Winegrad, Dilys Veronica, "Expression and Being and the *Essais*
       of Montaigne," *DA*, 31 (1970), 2894-A (Univ. of Pa.).

       Montaigne saw man's dilemmas as result of language--social and
       philosophical as well as literary.

611.   Yost, John K., "German Protestant Humanism and the Early English
       Reformation: Richard Taverner and Official Translation," *BHR*,
       32, no. 3 (1970), 613-625.

       Taverner, leading religious writer in Cromwell's administration,
       demonstrates the link between English and German Reformations,
       giving evidence that in England the Reformers received govern-
       ment support for *both* Humanist *and* Protestant aspects of their
       work.

612.   ———, "Taverner's Use of Erasmus and the Protestantization of
       English Humanism," *RenQ*, 23 (1970), 266-276.

       Claims Richard Taverner's (1505-1575) versions of Erasmus' edu-
       cational works were turning point for the Erasmian humanism
       that followed. Dates the transition from late 1530's.

613.   ———, "Tyndale's Use of the Fathers: A Note on his Connection
       to Northern Humanism," *Moreana*, no. 21 (1969), 5-13.

       Tyndale appealed to patristic authority in delineating his pro-
       gram of ecclesiastical reform. He depended to a large extent
       on the works of such leading northern humanists as Erasmus,
       Oecolampadius, and the author of *The Union of Doctors*, for his
       knowledge of Christian antiquity.

614. Zambelli, Paola, "Agrippa von Nettesheim in den neueren kritischen Studien und in den Handschriften," *AKG*, 51 (1969), 264–295.

Importance of recent studies in consideration of Agrippa (1486–1535) as humanist; Renaissance magic and skepticism.

ADDENDA

614a. Bolgar, R.R., ed., *Classical Influences on European Culture A.D. 500–1500.* Cambridge, Eng.: Cambridge Univ. Press, 1971.

Rev. *RenQ*, 25 (1972), 444–445.

Significant essays on classical Renaissance impact, including neoplatonism in its diverse strands, Ausonius, Greek and the vernacular, personification.

614b. Brower, Reuben A., *Hero and Saint: Shakespeare and the Graeco-Roman Tradition.* N.Y., Oxford: Oxford Univ. Press, 1971.

Rev. *RenQ*, 26 (1973), 81–83.

Homeric Achilles in relation to Chapman's and Shakespeare's; Renaissance "heroic" and Virgil's Aeneas; effect of Ovid and Seneca. Classical influences in reading of seven Shakespearean tragedies.

VI.   ICONOGRAPHICAL (see also TOPOI, etc.)

615.   Aurenhammer, Hans, *Lexikon der Christlichen Ikonographie.*
       Wien: Verlag Brüder Hollinek, 1959-1967. Bd. I: "Alpha und
       Omega--Christus und die vierundzwanzig Ältesten."

       Richly documented iconographical lexicon of Christian themes,
       Bible, art, etc.

616.   Bazin, Germain, "Panofsky et la Notion d'Espace," *Gazette des
       Beaux-Arts,* 71 (1968), 265-267.

       On Panofsky's notions of perspective in relation to an age.
       Space as an element of *Weltanschauung* in all the arts.
       Documented.

617.   Boehm, Gottfried, *Studien zur Perspektivität. Philosophie und
       Kunst in der frühen Neuzeit.* (Heidelberger Forschungen, 13.)
       Heidelberg: C. Winter, 1969.

       Includes sections on: "Die Kunst Albrecht Dürers und die Meta-
       physik den frühen Neuzeit," "Der Perspektivismus des Selbst-
       seins bei Montaigne," "Die Perspektivität in der Metaphysik
       der Nicolaus Cusanus," and discussions of Galileo and Descartes.

618.   Bongiorno, Laurine Mack, "The Theme of the Old and the New Law
       in the Arena Chapel," *Art Bulletin,* 50 (1968), 11-20.

       Giotto's use of Roman and Gothic architectural elements in the
       Arena Chapel at Padua to connote, respectively, the Era of
       Law and the Era of Grace.

619.   Brun, Robert, *Le livre français illustré de la Renaissance.*
       Paris: Picard, 1969.

       Rev. *TLS,* 9 April 1970, 392.

       Published previously in 1930, entitled *Le livre illustrée en
       France au XVIe siècle,* this catalogue has been developed from
       almost 500 main headings to almost 700. To cite one literary
       instance, Ovid's various works have risen from 16 to 25. In-
       dexes have also been improved from the original edition; its
       "Table des noms d'artistes" has been split into two--of identi-
       fiable artists and of "chiffres, marques et monogrammes."

620.   Calas, Elena, "Bosch's Garden of Delights: A Theological Re-
       bus," *Art Journal,* 29 (1969/1970), 184-199.

       Aims to examine Bosch's interpretation of certain theological
       texts. Author is particularly concerned with the central panel
       and its representation of Origen's heresy, palingenesis.

621. Callego, Julian, *Vision et symboles dans la peinture espagnole du Siècle d'Or.* Paris: Klincksieck, 1968.

Covers Golden Age of Spanish painting, spanning reigns of three kings and three generations of painters (1598-1700). Part I deals with the culture of symbols, making parallels between allegory and mythology, literature and painting, before examining symbols and allegories in Spanish life and their importance in ceremonies and holidays. Part II discusses symbolic aspects of Spanish painting.

622. *Catalog of the Avery Memorial Architectural Library.* 2nd ed., enlarged. N.Y.: Columbia Univ; Boston: G.K. Hall, 1968. 19 vols. (1st ed., 1895.)

Art as well as architecture. Many subject headings: archaeology, topographical prints, landscape planning, military architecture, sculpture, mosaics, interior design furniture, decorative arts.

623. Chastel, André, *The Crisis of the Renaissance, 1520-1600.* Geneva: Skira (World), 1968. Rev. *Oeil*, 168 (1968), 44.

Emphasis on complexity of 16th-cent. background; lavishly illustrated; includes mannerism.

624. Christensen, Carl C., "Dürer's 'Four Apostles' and the Dedication as a Form of Renaissance Art Patronage," *RenQ*, 20 (1967), 325-334.

Dürer's patronage activities. Renaissance artists had little difficulty in reconciling great achievement with financial gains.

625. Courtauld, Jeanne, et al., eds., *Studies in Renaissance and Baroque Art Presented to Anthony Blunt on His Sixtieth Birthday.* London: Phaidon, 1967. Rev. *Oeil*, 168 (1968), 42.

Thirty-one art historians on 16th- and 17th-cent. French and Italian art and architecture.

626. Dempsey, Charles, "'Mercurius Ver': The Sources of Botticelli's 'Primavera,'" *JWCI*, 31 (1968), 251-273.

Argues for the community of classical literary references shared by Poliziano's *Rusticus* and Botticelli's "Primavera."

627. Edgerton, Samuel Y., Jr., "Alberti's Colour Theory: A Medieval Bottle Without Renaissance Wine," *JWCI*, 32 (1969), 109-134.

By philological analysis of Alberti's discussion of color in Book I of *Della pittura*, author shows why Alberti was unable to come up with a useful color theory. Alberti's ideas were essentially medieval.

628. Ehresmann, D.L., "The Brazen Serpent, A Reformation Motif in the Works of Lucas Cranach the Elder and His Workshop," *Marsyas*, 13 (1966-1967), 32-47.

Close association of Lucas Cranach the Elder (1472-1553) with
Luther, who influenced his art. Brazen serpent was Luther's
symbol, often didactically used to illuminate his idea of justification by faith alone and to clarify his position regarding
images.

629. Evans, Joan, *Monastic Iconography in France from the Renaissance
      to the Revolution.* Cambridge Univ. Press, 1970.

      Rev. *BJA*, 2 (1971), 210; *FR*, 45 (1971), 285-286; *History*, 56
      (1971), 261.

      Iconographical preferences of monastic orders. Provides history
      of each period, bibliography, plates, and some interpretations
      of art in relation to themes.

630. Fleming, John V., *The "Roman de la Rose": A Study in Allegory
      and Iconography.* Princeton U.P., 1969. Rev. *ELN*, 9 (1970),
      134-139.

      Critical interpretation of this successful vernacular poem of
      the late Middle Ages, based partly on iconographic analysis of
      the illuminations found in more than 100 manuscript copies.

631. Gadol, Joan, *Leon Battista Alberti, Universal Man of the Early
      Renaissance.* Chicago: Univ. of Chicago Press, 1969.

      Rev. *Quarterly Journal of Speech*, 56 (1970), 103-104; *Ren. and
      Ref.*, 7 (1970), 17.

      Analysis of the leading role of Alberti (1404-1472) as artist,
      scientist, and humanist.

632. Gombrich, E.H., *Norm and Form: Studies in the Art of the Re-
      naissance.* London: Phaidon, 1966.

      Rev. *Apollo*, n.s., 85 (1967), 361-363.

      Includes: "The Renaissance Conception of Artistic Progress and
      Its Consequences," "Renaissance and Golden Age," "Norm and
      Form: The Stylistic Categories of Art History and Their Ori-
      gins in Renaissance Ideals."

633. Grabar, André, *Christian Iconography. A Study of Its Origins.*
      Princeton U.P., 1968. Rev. *Liturg. Arts*, 38 (1970), 76-77.

      How early Christian images were created and their roles along-
      side other forms of Christian piety in their day. Part III:
      Dogmas expressed by the image. 341 illustrations.

634. Guilman, Maxine Kraut, "Writings on Color in 16th-cent. Italian
      Art Theory." Unpubl. M.A. thesis in Fine Arts, Columbia Univ.,
      1967. (Cf. 635, 1463, 1925.)

      Gives quotations from Italian sources on symbolism of colors,
      with figures providing concordance of color meanings.

635. Harley, Rosamond, "The Interpretation of Colour Names," *Burling-
      ton Mag.*, 110 (1968), 460-461. (Cf. 634, 1463, 1925.)

Useful reminder of changes in meaning of color names between
16th and 17th cents. and our own time; e.g., *pink* in 17th-cent.
painting meant greenish-yellow pigment used for mixing blue to
make greens for landscapes. Another overlooked color of 16th
and 17th cents. is *general*, a yellow pigment.

636. Heckscher, William S., "The Genesis of Iconology," *Stil und
      überlieferung in der Kunst des Abendlandes*. Berlin: Verlag
      Gebr. Mann, 1967. Bd. III, pp. 239-262.

      On modern iconological method in relation to Abby Warburg. De-
      tailed documentation.

637. ———, "Reflections on Seeing Holbein's Portrait of Erasmus at
      Longford Castle," in Douglas Fraser, et al., eds., *Essays in
      the History of Art Presented to Rudolf Wittkower* (London:
      Phaidon, 1967), 128-148.

      Erasmus' values of *tranquillitas* through discarding the four
      passions or *affectus* (*gaudium*, *spes*, *dolor*, and *metus*). De-
      tailed documentation on Stoicism, a word author says (p. 131 n.)
      was not in currency before 1626. Renaissance symbolism of var-
      ious elements of the portrait. Includes, pp. 146-148, useful
      index of terms.

638. Heinzl, Brigitte, *Dürer*. Florence: Sansoni, 1968.

      Analysis of Dürer's most complex works, which were inspired by
      the symbols of Christian hermeneutics. Bibliography.

639. Heinz-Mohn, Gerd, *Lexikon der Symbole: Bilder und Zeichen der
      Christlichen Kunst*. Düsseldorf and Cologne: Eugen Diedrichs
      Verlag, 1971. (Cf. [SYMBOL] under *Topoi*.)

      Condensed volume of useful Christian iconographical material.

640. Hersey, George L., *Alfonso II and the Artistic Renewal of Naples,
      1485-1495*. Yale U.P., 1969. Rev. *Apollo*, n.s. 92 (1970), 498.

      Corrects art-historical views biased in favor of Florence and
      Rome as artistic centers. Rebuilding of Naples under Alfonso
      II and his role as patron of the arts. Full account of paint-
      ing, sculpture, and literature of the age.

641. Johnson, W. McAllister, "Prolegomena to the *Images ou Tableaux
      de Platte Peinture*," *Gazette des Beaux-Arts*, 73 (1969), 277-
      304.

      With the sole exception of Ovid's *Metamorphoses*, Philostrato
      the Elder's *Tableaux de Platte Peinture* was perhaps the most
      important source of images in the Renaissance. Although first
      illustrated edition, translated by Blaise de Vigenère, is
      usually dated 1609, and although it actually appeared in 1614,
      the work belongs to the aesthetics of the Fontainebleau School
      and of the Antoine Caron milieu (1597-1599).

642. Katz, Martin Barry, "Leon Battista Alberti: Art as Moral
      Theory," *DA*, 28 (1968), 4970-A (Syracuse Univ.).

Argues that Alberti, a Petrarchan humanist, largely based his
aesthetic theory on art's public role of moral indoctrination.
Alberti's linking of an aesthetic and humanism created a fusion
which influenced Italian Renaissance.

643. Kennedy, Ruth, "Reports on Scholarship in the Renaissance:
Art," *Ren. News*, 19 (1966), 72-78.

Survey of recent work.

644. Kirschbaum, Engelbert, et al., eds., *Lexikon der christlichen
Ikonographie. I: Allgemeine Ikonographie, A-Ezechiel.* Freiburg i. Br.: Herder, 1968.

Many illustrations, especially for themes of Christ and angels.

645. Krautheimer, Richard, *Studies in Early Christian, Medieval and
Renaissance Art.* N.Y.: N.Y.U. Press; London: Univ. of London
Press, 1969.

Rev. *Choice*, 7 (1970), 1024.

Festschrift includes 21 pieces from past 40 years, especially
seminal essays. Postscript added by author brings his own
views and bibliography up to date.

646. Kurz, Otto, "Four Tapestries after Hieronymus Bosch," *JWCI*, 30
(1967), 150-162.

Iconography of four 16th-cent. tapestries; second tapestry includes pictorial allusion to *topos* in title of Bruegel's drawing, "big fishes eat the small ones" (dated 1556), misattributed
to Bosch (p. 155). Third tapestry, "The Feast of Saint Martin,"
recalls medieval Shrove Tuesday pastime, involving 12 blind men
seeking to kill a hog; author cites *Much Ado*, II.i, in relation
to this.

647. Millar, Oliver, "The Elizabethan and Jacobean Scene," *Burl.
Mag.*, 112 (1970), 170-175.

Review of Roy Strong's *Tudor and Jacobean Portraits, National
Portrait Gallery*, and his *The English Icon*, and an exhibition in
the National Portrait Gallery, London.

648. Mossakowski, Stanislaw, "Raphael's 'St. Cecilia': An Iconographical Study," *Zeitschrift für Kunstgeschichte*, 31 (1968),
1-26.

Contrast between two kinds of music, divine and vulgar; Pytha-
gorean-Platonic theory of proportion and mathematical principle
of harmony.

649. Mühlmann, Heiner, "Über den humanistischen Sinn einiger Kernge-
danken der Kunsttheorie seit Alberti," *AKG*, 33 (1970), 127-142.

Leon Battista Alberti as first to interpret 13th- and 14th-cent.
Italian rediscovery of the Justinian code in aesthetic terms.
As such, he is the founder of later Renaissance artistic theo-
ries; first to define the "beautiful" in ethical-political

rather than pure aesthetic terms. Gave direction to the ideas
of "decorum," "aequum," "inventio," perspective, and historicism in architecture and painting.

650. Panofsky, Erwin, "Erasmus and the Visual Arts," *JWCI*, 32 (1969),
      200-227.

      Like most northern humanists Erasmus was primarily interested
      in the written word and only secondarily in the world accessible
      to the eye. Unless it is a question of the issue of image wor-
      ship, he either moralizes about the visual arts or speaks as an
      interested party. In neither case is Erasmus consistent, ob-
      jective, or original.

651. ————, *Idea: A Concept of Art Theory*, trans. Columbia, S.C.:
      Univ. of So. Carolina Press, 1968. Rev. *Art J.*, 29 (1970), 388.

      Translation of second edition (1960) of 1924 book. Traces his-
      torical destiny of the idea of the beautiful with other major
      ideas: nature of human and divine knowledge, etc.

652. ————, *Problems in Titian, Mostly Iconographic*. Princeton,
      N.J.: Princeton Univ. Press; London: Phaidon, 1969.

      Rev. *TLS*, 26 March 1970, 600.

      On problems of content and meaning rather than on style or
      authenticity; explores Titian's relationship to philosophy and
      literature of his time, his attitude towards the antique.
      Titian thus is revealed to have had a far more complex intel-
      lect than assumed.

653. Praz, Mario, *Mnemosyne*. Princeton, N.J.: Princeton Univ.
      Press, 1970.

      Rev. *BJA*, 2 (1971), 103-104; *JAAC*, 30 (1971), 257-260.

      Structural parallels between visual arts and literature of his-
      torical periods.

654. Rehder, Helmut, "Planetenkinder: Some Problems of Character
      Portrayal in Literature," *Graduate Journal* (Univ. of Texas), 7
      (1968), 69-97.

      Influence of *Planetenkinder*, astrological illustrations, upon
      character portrayal in literature. Such pictures correlated
      character traits, human activities, features of body and mind,
      with influence of planetary deities, determining fates of indi-
      viduals dominated by them. Found in Middle Ages and Renaissance
      in variety of media. Fading from memory, they occupied a sub-
      terranean existence, emerging at times and then identifiable
      through iconographic structure or allegorical content; or
      through cyclical mode of composition or satirical possibili-
      ties. (Illus.)

655. Schiller, Gertrud, *Ikonographie der Christlichen Kunst*.
      Gütersloh: Gütersloher Verlagshaus, Gerd Mohn, 1966, 1968,
      1971. Bd. I. Inkarnation—Kindheit—Taufe—Versuchung—Ver-
      klärung—Werken und Wunder Christi; Bd. II. Die Passion Jesu

Christi. Bd. III. Die Auferstehung und Erhöhung Christi. Detailed and useful volumes, with plates.

656. Secret, F., "Blaise de Vigenère à l'hôtel Bellevue," *BHR*, 31 (1969), 115-127.

Descriptive texts of Vigenère (1523-1596), which affirm the primacy of sight, despite some critics' opinion that, with the exception of Rabelais, 16th-cent. writers did not know how to present a sketch, capture a resemblance, or a flesh and blood character. Also directs attention to Antonius Lullus, Barthelemy de Chasseneu, and C. Gesner, as further proof of writers with descriptive skill.

657. Steadman, John M., "Iconography and Methodology in Renaissance Dramatic Study: Some Caveats," *Shakespearean Research and Opportunities*, nos. 7-8 (1972/1974), 39-52.

Caveats against over-reading in Renaissance iconography. Instances Renaissance use of emblems as tacit *moralitas*. Offers prudent scholarly cautions also regarding non-dramatic emblematic readings. Emblems' chief value as topical, serving ends of rhetoric.

658. Stechow, Wolfgang, *Northern Renaissance Art, 1400-1600: Sources and Documents*. Englewood Cliffs, N.J.: Prentice-Hall, 1966.

Rev. *Art Q*, 30 (1967), 177; *Burl. Mag.*, 109 (1967), 481.

Includes Netherlands, Germany, France, England, and contains excerpts on Nicholas Hilliard (pp. 169-175).

659. ————, *Rubens and the Classical Tradition*. Martin Classical Lectures, 22. N.Y.: Oxford U.P., 1969. Rev. *Burl.*, 112 (1970), 248.

How classical art and mythology permeated Rubens' whole personality and were transferred by him into his paintings; comprehensive footnotes.

660. Steinmann, Ernst, and Rudolf Wittkower, *Michelangelo Bibliographie*, I: *1510-1926*. Hildesheim: Georg Olms, 1967.

Studies of Michelangelo. 2,107 items with indexes and illustrations of his letters.

661. Strong, Roy, *The English Icon. Elizabethan and Jacobean Portraiture*. London: Routledge, 1969; Yale Univ. Press, 1970.

In context of religious, social, and ideological circumstances of the time, discusses factors which produced painting of such distinctive character. Includes all the chief portraits of the period; first attempt to classify and attribute them.

662. ————, *Tudor and Jacobean Portraits, National Portrait Gallery*. H.M.S.O. 2 vols. British Information Services, 1969.

Rev. *Hist. Today*, 19 (1969), 869-871.

Catalogue of all portraits in the National Gallery to 1625;
dovetails with D. Piper's *Catalogue of the Seventeenth Century
Portraits in the National Portrait Gallery* (1963). Entries in
text volume and illustrations in the plate volume arranged alphabetically according to name of sitter. Each work is described, contemporary sources for appearance of the sitter are
given, and a thorough attempt is made to document other representations from this period. All portraits in the National
Gallery as well as many related works from Tudor and Jacobean
eras are illustrated. An annotated index of faces; useful as
reference work for students of English history, literature,
and art.

663. Univ. of London, Warburg Institute Library, *Complete Catalog*
(*Reading Room and Periodicals Catalog* also sold separately).
12 vols. Boston: G.K. Hall, 1967. First supplement, 1971.
1 vol.

Useful catalogue of great iconographical collection, 118,000
cards; second edition, revised and enlarged. Subject index of
accessions up to 1966. Supplement has 16,700 cards.

664. Viglionese, Paschal C., "The Status of the Visual Artist in the
Period of Florentine Humanism," *DA*, 30 (1970), 2982-A (Rutgers
Univ.).

Nature of the artist's status relative to various aspects of
Florentine life and thought. Considers artist's role as a citizen in the light of humanistic ideals of civic life; his education in terms of new liberalized pedagogical thought; his work
of art as a commercial commodity.

665. Weise, Georg, *Il rinnovamento dell'arte religiosa nella Rinas-
cita*. Florence: Sansoni, 1969.

Rev. *Gazette des Beaux-Arts*, 77 (1971), supp. 1226, 24.

Renaissance renovated the formal vocabulary of religious art
used in Middle Ages.

666. Wenneker, Lu Beery, "An Examination of *L'Idea del Theatro* of
Giulio Camillo, including an Annotated Translation, with Special
Attention to His Influence on Emblem Literature and Iconography,"
DA, 31 (1970), 2280-A (Univ. of Pittsburgh).

Camillo's life and his writing of *L'Idea del Theatro*; discusses
memory techniques, development of theater of the period, and
Camillo's influence on other emblemists. Four images from
Camillo as subjects of 16th-cent. paintings or engravings.

667. Wind, Edgar, *Giorgione's Tempesta; with Comments on Giorgione's
Poetic Allegories*. Oxford: Clarendon Press, 1969.

Rev. *BHR*, 32 (1970), 695-699.

Iconographic interpretation of Giorgione's *Tempesta* which
threatens the conventional appreciation of this work as "free
fantasy." Also interprets in succeeding chapters Giorgione's
The Three Philosophers, *Il Bravo*, and fragments of *Fondaco dei
Tedeschi*.

668.   ――――, *Pagan Mysteries in the Renaissance*. New and enlarged
edition. London: Faber and Faber; N.Y.:   Norton, 1969.

Rev. *NQ*, n.s. 16 (1969), 467–469.

Eight of the original 14 chapters are unchanged, as are the
introduction and conclusion.   Remaining chapters include further
references to classical and humanistic sources or entail brief
discussions of new evidence.   Nine new appendices, generally
improved photographical quality, and updated footnotes.

669.   Wundram, Manfred, *Frührenaissance*.   Baden–Baden: Holle, 1970.

Rev. *Bibliographie zur Symbolik, Ikonographie und Mythologie*,
4 (1971), 138–139.

Divided into following thematic sections: Italian Art of the
Trecento, Florence in the Quattrocento, early Florentine art
between Early and High Renaissance, and this last period outside Florence.

670.   Yates, Frances A., "The Allegorical Portraits of Sir John Lut-
trell," in Douglas Fraser, et al., *Essays in the History of Art
Presented to Rudolf Wittkower* (London: Phaidon, 1967), pp.
149–160.

Pagan imagery in a portrait of 1550, reflecting political
anxiety of England during rapprochement with France over the
Treaty of Boulogne and coming of the French embassy.   Emblems
of peace, friendship, shipwreck, etc.

ADDENDA

670a.   Heckscher, William S., "Shakespeare in his Relationship to the
Visual Arts: A study in Paradox," *RORD*, 13–14 (1970–71), 5–71.

Useful suggestive article for research approaches.   Includes,
e.g., "Falstaff's Pillow as a Dramatic Emblem"; Patience
literature; trade-marks; references to works of art, explicit
and oblique; Shakespeare and Ben Jonson in their relationship
to the visual arts; etc.   Plates;   notes, pp. 58–71.

670b.   Steadman, John M., "Iconography and Renaissance Drama: Ethical
and Mythological Themes," *RORD*, 13–14 (1970–71), 73–122.

Renaissance painters and writers inherited same ethical and
mythological traditions.   Fusion of iconographical and poetic
materials in Renaissance manuals.   This suggestive article
usefully examines rewards of iconographical study for Renaissance literary understanding.   Plates;   notes pp. 115–122.

VII.   LEGAL

671.   Abbott, L.W., "Lawyers and Law Reporting in England in the
       Sixteenth Century." (Director, S.T. Bindoff.) London Ph.D.,
       1969.

672.   Berman, Ronald, "Shakespeare and the Law," *SQ*, 18 (1967), 141-
       150.

       Relates Shakespeare's plays, especially *Measure for Measure*,
       to homilies, treatises, codes of law, and to Pauline ethical
       and psychological concepts.   Treats the idea of fallen man in
       Shakespeare.

673.   Bland, D.S., "Arthur Broke, Gerard Legh, and the Inner Temple,"
       NQ, 214 (1969), 453-455.

       Broke's sponsors for admission to Inner Temple were Sackville
       and Norton, lending credence to possibility that this Arthur
       Broke wrote the narrative verse *Romeus and Juliet* on which
       Shakespeare drew.   Vividness of Legh's description of Christ-
       mas revels of 16th-cent. in his book on heraldry, *Accedence*,
       suggests he was member of Inner Temple.

674.   ————, "Inner Temple Revels, 1561," *NQ*, 214 (1969), 464-465.

       Description of Inner Temple revels of Christmas 1561 found in
       Gerard Legh's book on heraldry, *Accedence of Armorie*, 1562.
       [Cf. article by Marie Axton, *Hist. J.*, 13 (1970), 365-378, *s.v.*
       Political.]

675.   Bracton, Henry de, *On the Laws and Customs of England.   De
       Legibus et Consuetudinibus Angliae*, ed. by George E. Woodbine,
       tr. by Samuel E. Thorne.   Cambridge, Mass.:   Harvard Univ.
       Press, 1968.

       First two volumes of projected five-volume work.   First volume
       consists primarily of Woodbine's introduction to his original
       work preceded by a briefer introduction by translator Thorne.
       Second volume contains text and translation, on facing pages,
       of first third of treatise.

676.   Butterfield, Herbert, *Magna Carta in the Historiography of the
       Sixteenth and Seventeenth Centuries*.   The Stenton Lecture 1968.
       Reading (Berks.), Univ. of Reading, 1969.

       English political thinking in the 16th and 17th cents., partic-
       ularly among lawyers and with special reference to their inter-
       pretation of the Great Charter.   To them the Charter was not a

new thing, but a recapitulation of liberties Englishmen were
believed to have had in some imagined primitive time. It was
an unhistorical and anachronistic view, arising from failure to
understand difference in outlook between their own and a former
age, but it lingered on even to 18th cent.

677. Cockburn, J.S., "Seventeenth-Century Clerks of Assize--Some
      Members of the Legal Profession," *Amer. Jour. of Legal Hist.*,
      13 (1969), 315-332.

      Useful biographical records. Includes list of young lawyers
      dropped abruptly from registers of Inns of Court, 16th and
      17th cents. Assize records show formative years of barristers
      who would reach top of their profession and others who reached
      obscurity.

678. Cowie, Leonard W., "Doctor's Commons," *Hist. Today*, 20 (1970),
      419-425.

      A history of the Society of Advocates at Doctor's Commons, a
      voluntary body which gained a monopoly of appointments as
      judges and advocates in ecclesiastical and admiralty courts.
      Founded in 16th cent.

679. Crowe, Michael B., "An Eccentric Seventeenth-Century Witness to
      the Natural Law: John Selden (1584-1654)," *Nat. Law Forum*, 12
      (1967), 184-195.

      Influence of classical Spanish theologians and jurists on John
      Selden and differences in their viewpoints.

680. D'Hommeaux-Sauleau, Jean-Pierre, "Montaigne et sa critique de
      la justice française," *Bull. de la Société des Amis de Mon-
      taigne*, no. 17 (1969), 14-24.

      Montaigne's hatred of cruelty and inanity of justice itself,
      and his condemnation of the profusion of legal texts; his views
      on witchcraft-persecution and torture; and his condemnation of
      colonization.

681. Elton, G.R., "The Law of Treason in the Early Reformation,"
      Historical Journal, 11 (1968), 211-236.

      Drafting of new law of treason under Henry VIII which would
      complete the legal armory of repression.

682. Emmison, F.G., *Elizabethan Life: Disorder*. Chelmsford: Essex
      County Council, 1970.

      Rev. *TLS*, 8 January 1971, 33.

      Summary account of 16th-cent. cases of Essex County, in the
      Assize Courts and Quarter Sessions. Picture of misdeeds of
      high and low, as well as tenor of legal system. Author is
      former archivist of Essex.

683. Finkelpearl, Philip J., *John Marston of the Middle Temple: An
      Elizabethan Dramatist in His Social Setting*. Cambridge, Mass.:
      Harvard University Press, 1969.

Rev. *JEGP*, 69 (1970), 174-177; *RenQ*, 23 (1970), 91-92.

Description of "The Milieu of the Inns of Court," and account of Marston's literary activity, "Playwright at the Inns of Court."

684. Gamble, Giles Yardley, "Institutional Drama: Elizabethan Tragedies of the Inns of Court," *DA*, 30 (1970), 3428-3429-A (Stanford Univ.).

Legal, political, educational, and social interests of the Inns of Court and their effect on the four tragedies--*Gorboduc*, *Jocasta*, *Gismond of Salerne*, and *Misfortunes of Arthur*--which were written under their auspices.

685. Gleason, J.H., *The Justices of the Peace in England 1558 to 1640*. Oxford: Clarendon Press, 1969.

Rev. *AHR*, 75 (1970), 1106; *AmJLH*, 13 (1969), 398-400; *EHR*, 85 (1970), 415-416; *HZ*, 210 (1970), 211-212; *Hist.*, 54 (1969), 422-423.

Based on study of six counties in 1559, 1561, 1584, 1608, 1626, and 1636--made from lists of the justices throughout the country which were prepared from time to time under Elizabeth and the early Stuarts. Analyzes changing size and composition of commissions of the peace.

686. Griffiths, Ralph A., "The Trial of Eleanor Cobham: An Episode in the Fall of Duke Humphrey of Gloucester," *Bull. of the John Rylands Library*, 51 (1969), 381-399.

Story of proceedings against Eleanor Cobham.

687. Hanus, Jerome J., "Certiorari and Policy-Making in English History," *Amer. Jour. of Legal Hist.*, 12 (1968), 63-94.

Discusses royal prerogative in relation to the writ of certiorari, form of royal intervention; from the Conquest, through the Renaissance, to modern times.

688. Hard, Frederick Parham, ed., "William Lambarde's *A Perambulation of Kent*" (Vols. 1 and 2), *DA*, 27 (1967), 4220-4221-A (Indiana Univ.).

This detailed study of Lambarde's work, first published in 1576 and in an expanded version in 1596, useful as evidence of laws, attitudes toward law as a discipline, historiography, and interest in linguistics in the Renaissance.

689. Hassett, J.D., "Some Non-legal Reflections on Suarez' Treatise on Law," *New Scholasticism*, 41 (1967), 79-92.

Views of Suarez (1548-1617) (in *Tractatus de legibus et legislatore Deo*) on communality and law show how man transcends himself in the institutions which are his historical creation.

690. Helmholz, R.H., "Bastardy Litigation in Medieval England," *Amer. Jour. of Legal Hist.*, 13 (1969), 360-383.

English Reformation made no change in practice that questions
of general bastardy were still submitted to the bishops.   Not
till 19th cent. was bastardy jurisdiction taken from church
courts.

691.   Hill, L.M., "The Two-Witness Rule in English Treason Trials:
Some Comments on the Emergence of Procedural Law," *Amer. Jour.
of Legal Hist.*, 12 (1968), 95-111.

Deals with treason acts and the two-witness rule in the late
Middle Ages and Renaissance.

692.   Ives, E.W., "The Common Lawyers in Pre-Reformation England,"
Trans. Royal Historical Society, 18 (1968), 145-173.

Influence of common lawyers in England of Henry VIII on character of business and social life, especially on shaping of law
to fit needs of the state.

693.   ————, "The Genesis of the Statute of Uses," *EHR*, 82 (1967),
673-697.

Statute of Uses (1536) was prompted by royal need to retrieve a
dwindling income supplied through feudal obligations.   When the
Commons failed to pass the measure, the King resorted to the
law; the statute provoked opposition, and the crown later
accepted a compromise measure.

694.   Johansson, Bertil, *Law and Lawyers in Elizabethan England as
Evidenced in the Plays of Ben Jonson and Thomas Middleton.*
Acta Universitatis Stockholmiensis.   Stockholm Studies in English
18; Stockholm: Almqvist and Wiksell, 1967.

Sixty-five-page study of satirical allusions to lawyers, law,
and legal procedure in these playwrights.

695.   Jones, Gareth H., *History of the Law of Charity, 1532-1827.*
Cambridge Univ. Press, 1969.

Rev. *AHR*, 75 (1970), 1105.

Shows how contemporary religious, economic, and social pressures
molded the substantive law and illustrates importance of procedural considerations in defining limits of legal charity.

696.   Jones, W.J., *The Elizabethan Court of Chancery.*   Oxford: Clarendon Press, 1967.

Rev. *AHR*, 74 (1968), 159-160; *Amer. Jour. of Legal Hist.*, 12
(1968), 358-360; *Historical Journal*, 11 (1968), 376-377.

Study of part of the administration of justice in Elizabethan
England.   Discusses work of chancellors or Lord Keepers from
Nicholas Bacon to Egerton (Lord Ellesmere).   Under neither Elizabeth nor James was the central issue that of common law vs.
equity; but in the early years of 17th cent., there is appearance of such a conflict.   Attributing that to Edward Coke,
author holds it untrue that common lawyers hated Chancery.

697. Jones, W.R., "The Two Laws in England: The Later Middle Ages,"
      Journal of Church and State, 11 (1969), 111-131.

      Ecclesiastical vs. political justice. The two laws were capable
      of some degree of cooperation; limited areas of dispute should
      not be exaggerated.

698. Jones, William, "A Note on the Demise of Manorial Jurisdiction:
      The Impact of Chancery," *Amer. Jour. of Legal Hist.*, 10 (1966),
      297-318.

      Discusses means by which, in reign of Elizabeth, the activities
      of Chancery, like the King's Bench or Common Pleas, led to a
      permanent involvement of the central court system in affairs
      previously under manorial jurisdiction. When Chancery recog-
      nized manorial custom, the manorial courts lost initiative and
      went into decline. After 1600 the amount of civil litigation
      in the manorial courts dropped steadily.

699. Keeton, George William, *Shakespeare's Legal and Political Back-
      ground*. N.Y., London: Pitman, 1967.

      Rev. J.E.S. Simon, "Shakespeare's Legal and Political Back-
      ground," *Law Quarterly Rev.*, 74 (1968), 33-47.

      Replaces his earlier book, *Shakespeare and His Legal Philosophy*.
      Survey of legalisms in Shakespeare.

700. Kelley, Donald R., *Foundations of Modern Historical Scholarship:
      Language, Law and History in the French Renaissance*. N.Y. and
      London: Columbia Univ. Press, 1970.

      Rev. *AHR*, 76 (1971), 1152-1154; *AJLH*, 15 (1971), 77-80.

      Contribution to historical scholarship made by legal humanists;
      parallels between development of national European legal sys-
      tems out of Roman law, customary law, and canon law, and devel-
      opment of European vernacular languages, national monarchies,
      and national protestant churches.

701. ————, "Guillaume Budé and the First Historical School of Law,"
      AHR, 72 (1967), 807-834.

      Treats Budé's law-history work; Valla; humanism.

702. ————, "Legal Humanism and the Sense of History," *Studies in
      the Renaissance*, 13 (1966), 184-199.

      Deals with alliance of philology and history: conception of
      legal and linguistic, and hence cultural, change; effect of
      Renaissance philologists, who through their deepened linguistic
      knowledge, demanded a more historical perspective. Discusses
      significance of such figures as Valla, Budé, and other legal
      humanists.

703. ————, "The Rise of Legal History in the Renaissance," *Hist.
      and Theory*, 9 (1970), 174-194.

      Influence of legal scholarship on historiography in 16th-cent.
      Luja's *Observations and Emendations* on Roman law were spring-
      board for Pasquier's creation of new branch of scholarship,
      legal history, in his *Les Recherches de la France* (1560).

704. Kelly, H.A., "Canonical Implications of Richard III's Plan to
      Marry His Niece," *Traditio*, 23 (1967), 269-311.

      Reactions to Richard's proposed marriage in perspective of 15th-
      cent. legal traditions and precedents.

705. Kisch, Guido, *Enea Silvio Piccolomini und die Jurisprudenz.*
      Basel: Helbing & Lichtenhahn, 1967.

      Rev. *AHR*, 73 (1968), 1128; *BHR*, 30 (1968), 416-417; *RenQ*, 21
      (1968), 316-317.

      Concerning the humanist at Basle and his attitude to the law;
      explains his invectives against contemporary jurists.

706. Knafla, Louis A., "The Law Studies of an Elizabethan Student,"
      HLQ, 32 (1969), 221-240.

      Studies marginalia in Sir Thomas Egerton's printed law books.
      Aims to prove that curriculum at Inns of Court was not in decay
      in 16th cent.

707. Kuttner, Stephan, "Select Bibliography, 1969-70, Institute of
      Medieval Canon Law," *Traditio*, 26 (1970), 478-505.

      Manuscripts and microfilms as well as books and articles on
      canon law.

708. Lewis, John Underwood, "Sir Edward Coke (1552-1633):   His
      Theory of 'Artificial Reason' as a Context for Modern Basic
      Legal Theory," *Law Quarterly Rev.*, 84 (1968), 330-342.

      Coke's definition of law as "perfect reason" became a standard
      against which facts of law were measured, constituting the
      core of his theory of precedent and a means of forging an
      aggressive, consistent common law which served as a weapon
      against royal prerogative.

709. Marchant, Ronald A., *The Church Under the Law.*   Cambridge Univ.
      Press, 1969.   Rev. *EHR*, 86 (1971), 842.

      Study of the records of the Ecclesiastical Court in the diocese
      of York from 1560 to 1640.

710. Martines, Lauro, *Lawyers and Statecraft in Renaissance Florence.*
      Princeton, N.J.:   Princeton Univ. Press, 1968.

      Rev. *AHR*, 74 (1968), 654-655.

      Complements his earlier book, *The Social World of the Floren-*
      tine Humanists: 1390-1460 (1963).   Describes the profession of
      lawyers at work, in diplomacy, Church relations, government,
      policymaking, administration, and in struggle for political
      power in Renaissance Florence.

711. McGovern, William M., "Contract in Medieval England: The Neces-
      sity for *Quid pro Quo* and a Certain Sum," *Amer. Jour. of Legal*
      Hist., 13 (1969), 173-201.

The action of debt was the most common remedy for breach of contract only when there had been a receipt of benefits or when a fixed sum was involved. These limitations were avoided in the 16th and 17th cents. by resorting to the action of assumpsit or breach of promise.

712. Richmond, B.J., "The Work of the Justices of the Peace in Hampshire, 1603-42." (Director, A.L. Merson.) Southampton M. Phil., 1969.

713. Rogers, Alan, "Henry IV, the Commons and Taxation," *MS*, 31 (1969), 44-70.

Struggles of king and parliament in the reign of Henry IV were not over minor issues, but over the whole field of royal prerogative and parliamentary power of consent to taxation.

714. Schoeck, R.J., "Recent Scholarship in the History of Law," *Renaissance Quarterly*, 20 (1967), 279-291.

This bibliographic essay covering chiefly the past five years of scholarship in the field (although several primary sources are named) treats Roman Law, Canon Law, laws of individual countries, customary and other laws, history of ideas, and other topics. A guide for further research.

715. ———, "Shakespeare and the Law," *Shakespearean Research and Opportunities*, nos. 7-8 (1972-1974), 61-68.

Areas of research potentials; field largely unworked, yet highly significant for Shakespearean studies.

716. ———, Natalie Z. Davis, and J.K. McConica, "A Finding List of Renaissance Legal Works to 1700," *Ren. and Ref.* (Univ. of Toronto), 4 (1967), 2-28; 4 (1968), 33-85; 4 (1968), 97-126.

Identifies and locates legal works in Toronto, Buffalo, McGill, Queens College (Can.), etc., areas. Annotated. Table of Contents in 4 (1968), 125-126: Roman Civil Law; Canon Law; National and Customary Law (England, France, etc.); Miscellaneous and Comparative Law.

717. Stephanitz, Dieter von, *Exakte Wissenschaft und Recht*. (Beiträge zur Rechts- und Staatswissenschaft, Heft 15, Münster), Berlin: de Gruyter, 1970.

Rev. *Gesnerus*, 28 (1971), 99.

Effect of mathematics and the natural sciences on law and juridical science. Traces empiricism of Renaissance, especially as formulated by Bacon, on law studies of Pufendorf and Thomasius.

718. Walker, N., *Crime and Insanity in England. I. The Historical Perspective*. Edinburgh U.P., 1968. Rev. *TLS*, 3 Oct. 1968, 1100.

First volume of a projected historical introduction to the use of hospital orders and laws for dealing with mentally disordered offenders. Focuses on traditional legal issues since the Saxons and Normans, and includes tables of Statutes and Cases.

VIII. LINGUISTIC-RHETORICAL

719. Alston, R.C., comp., *Rhetoric, Style, Elocution, Prosody, Rhyme, Pronunciation, Spelling Reform*. Bradford, Eng.: Ernest Cummins, 1969.

Rev. *QJS*, 56 (1970), 104.

Volume 6 of his *Bibliography of the English Language from the Invention of Printing to the Year 1800*.

720. ————, and J.L. Rosier, "Rhetoric and Style: A Bibliographical Guide," *Leeds Studies in English*, n.s., 1 (1967), 137-159.

Useful list of primary and secondary works: I. Classical Rhetorical Heritage, II. Medieval Tradition, III. Renaissance Tradition, IV. Teaching of Rhetoric in the Schools of Renaissance England, V. Stylistics.

721. Anderson, Floyd Douglas, "*Dispositio* in the Preaching of Hugh Latimer," *SM*, 35 (1968), 451-461.

Analysis of nine sermons preached between January 1548 and Lent, 1550, showing formal structuring.

722. ————, "The King's Preacher: A Rhetorical Analysis of the Sermons of Hugh Latimer Preached between January, 1548 and Lent, 1550," *DA*, 28 (1968), 3283-3284-A (Univ. of Ill.).

Dominant subject of nine extant sermons: the duties of king, magistrate, preacher, and subject in the divinely ordered Commonwealth. Abuses in its operation are result of two causes: covetousness and failure of preachers to perform their duties. In structure, sermons are adapted from so-called "modern" method, developed by medieval Scholastics: theme, protheme, prayer, introduction of the theme, division, and discussion.

723. Anselment, Raymond A., "Rhetoric and Dramatic Satire of Martin Marprelate," *SEL*, 10 (1970), 103-119.

Stresses Marprelate's debt to rhetoric rather than theater; shows how he adopted rhetorical tradition as both a source of direction and an object of satire—particularly the latter.

724. Bailey, Richard W., and Dolores M. Burton, *English Stylistics: A Bibliography*. Cambridge, Mass.: M.I.T. Press, 1968.

Stylistic studies of English and American texts from 1500 to present.

725. Ball, Bona W., "Rhetoric in the Plays of George Peele," *DA*, 30 (1969), 2011-2012A (Univ. of Kentucky).

Study of Peele's five plays pointing out how Peele relies on and yet modifies traditional rhetoric, analyzing his use of set speeches as structural devices, and exhibiting how the rhetoric of his plays affects plot, characterization, theme, and spectacle.

726. Barker, William, "Three Essays on the Rhetorical Tradition," *DA*, 29 (1969), 2700A (Brandeis Univ.).

Renaissance inherited a rhetorical tradition which contained a tension between faith in words and fear of the power that men employ in aggression and seduction. Sidney's old *Arcadia* and Spenser's "Mutability Cantos" assume a clearer meaning when they are read against this background.

727. Barner, Wilfried, *Barockrhetorik: Untersuchungen zu ihren geschichtlichen Grundlage*. Tübingen: Niemeyer, 1970.

History and social aspects of baroque rhetoric—relation to everyday life as well as to literature and oratory; *theatrum mundi*; man as actor. Rev. *YWML*, 32 (1970), 531-532.

728. Barnes, W.J., "Irony and the English Apprehension of Renewal," *Queens Quarterly*, 73 (1966), 357-376.

Treats irony in England, apart from Erasmian continental influence. Following More, sophisticated Englishmen adopted irony, associated with dialogue and conflict, as a mode for dealing with Renaissance complexities.

729. Baron, Hans, "Leonardo Bruni: 'Professional Rhetorician' or 'Civic Humanist'?," *Past and Present*, no. 36 (1967), 21-37.

Rev. *RLI*, 72 (1968), 130.

Reply to J.E. Seigel, "'Civic Humanism' or Ciceronian Rhetoric? The Culture of Petrarch and Bruni," *Past and Present*, no. 34 (1966), 3-48.

730. Boyd, John D., S.J., *The Function of Mimesis and Its Decline*. Harvard U.P., 1968. Rev. *Thought*, 44 (1969), 295-296.

Traces function of mimesis as critical concept through the cents. to its decline in the moralism of 18th-cent. England.

731. Brake, Robert J., "Michel Montaigne: A Skeptic's Views on Rhetoric," *Southern Speech Journal*, 33 (1967), 29-37.

Montaigne as unsympathetic generally to ancient rhetoric; eloquence; criticism; "schools of talk."

732. Bruns, Gerald L., "Rhetoric, Grammar, and the Conception of Language as a Substantial Medium," *CE*, 31 (1969), 241-262.

Viewing words as objects divorced from referents as attitude rooted in classical antiquity.

733. Bryant, Donald C., ed., *Ancient Greek and Roman Rhetoricians: A Bibliographical Dictionary* (by Robert W. Smith, Peter D. Arnott, F.B. Holtsmark, Galen O. Rowe, et al.). Columbia, Mo.: Artscraft Press, 1968.

Rev. *QJS*, 55 (1969), 84–85.

Articles on ancient rhetoricians, major and minor; three-page bibliography of important works.

734. Cavanaugh, John Richard, "The Use of Proverbs and *Sententiae* for Rhetorical Amplification in the Writings of Saint Thomas More," *DA*, 31 (1970), 2336-2337-A (St. Louis Univ.).

In *Utopia* More's written style retained most characteristics of an oral rhetoric; the proverbial and sententious aspects of *Utopia* and the *History of King Richard III* indicate More's sensitivity to rhetorical decorum. In his last writings, proverbs are effective means for winning his audience.

735. Chambers, Douglas D.C., "Lancelot Andrewes and the Topical Structure of Thought," *DA*, 30 (1969), 314-A (Princeton Univ.).

Chapters on logico-rhetorical theory; ways in which preachers used logical invention; use of topics in exegesis; various collections of topics in Andrewes' sermons.

736. Cooney, James Francis, "*De Ratione Dicendi*: A Treatise on Rhetoric by Juan Luis Vives (Books I-III)," *DA*, 27 (1967), 4218-A (Ohio State Univ.).

English translation, with introduction, of 16th-cent. rhetorical treatise whose influence was widespread and long-lasting.

737. Craigie, William A., and A.J. Aitken, eds., *A Dictionary of the Older Scottish Tongue from the Twelfth Century to the End of the Seventeenth*. Vols. 1-3. Oxford Univ. Press, 1967-.

Literary and spoken vernacular of Scotland from 12th cent. to 1707, covering the Shakespearean period, and, in its analogous detail, unique supplement to *OED*. In progress.

738. Cusick, Bridget, "Shakespeare and the Tune of the Time," *ShS*, 23 (1970), 1-12.

Shakespeare's use of changing linguistic conditions of his time; his manipulation of language to suit particular dramatic and poetic ends.

739. Cytowska, M., "Cyceronianizm Erazma z Rotterdamu" [The Ciceronianism of Erasmus of Rotterdam], *Meander*, 24, no. 1 (1969), 21-29.

Examines effects of enforced Ciceronianism at Italian universities during late 14th and early 15th cent. Points out why Erasmus was against strict imitation of Ciceronian language and its weakness as a literary movement.

740. ———, "*Ciceronianus*—manifest literacki Erazma z Rotterdamu"
      [*De Ciceroniano*—a literary manifesto by Erasmus of Rotterdam],
      Eos, 58 (1969/70), 125-134.

      Analyzes the satirical dialogue (1528) in which Erasmus defends
      an author's right to his own writing style, criticizing the
      rigorous imitation of Ciceronianism as depriving the writer's
      ability. Erasmus on the role of writer in society.

741. Dainville, F. de, "L'évolution de l'enseignement de la rhéto-
      rique au XVIIe siècle," *Dix-Septième Siècle*, 80-81 (1968),
      19-43.

      Seventeenth-cent. rested faithfully on the theories of *Ratio
      studiorum* until about 1660 when rhetoric began to exhibit less
      erudition and oratory.

742. Davies, Horton, "Elizabethan Puritan Preaching I," in *Worship
      and Theology, Vol. I, From Cranmer to Hooker, 1534-1603*.
      Princeton Univ. Press, 1970. Rev. *AHR*, 76 (1971), 1163.

      Part I: analysis of biblical interpretation, sermon structure
      of early English Puritans in contrast with their Catholic pre-
      decessors. Part II: sermon style and topics.

743. Devereux, James A., S.J., "The Collects of the First *Book of
      Common Prayer* as Works of Translation," *SP*, 66 (1969), 719-738.

      Examines translated collects of the first *Book of Common Prayer*
      of 1549. Compares English version with Latin original regarding
      meaning, grammatical structure, and rhetorical elements.

744. Dobson, Eric John, *English Pronunciation 1500-1700*. 2 vols.
      Oxford, 1968. Rev. *NQ*, n.s. 17 (1970), 38-39.

      Revision of first edition published in 1957; changes constitute
      numerous alterations of detail towards more accurate statement
      and more economical expression.

745. Dubois, Claude-Gilbert, *Mythe et langage au seizième siècle*.
      Paris: Editions Ducros, 1970.

      Rev. *FR*, 45 (1971), 749-751.

      French Renaissance myths about supernatural origins and uses of
      language and their search for an archetypal language. Describes
      dissipation of these myths and first steps taken toward es-
      tablishing a scientific method of linguistic analysis.

746. Dyck, Joachim, "Philosoph, Historiker, Orator und Poet:
      Rhetorik als Verständnishorizont der Literaturtheories des
      XVII. Jahrhunderts," *Arcadia*, 4 (1969), 1-15.

      On rhetoric's role in 17th-cent. poetic theory; the Ciceronian
      tradition.

747. Faust, Manfred, "Metaphorische Schimpfwörter," *Indogerman.
      Forsch.*, 74 (1969), 54-125.

      Treatise on insult-terms, with historical references from Plau-
      tus and elsewhere; metaphorical bases of such comparisons. In-
      cludes a lexicon of animal allusions of Shakespearean interest.

748. Fenyo, Jane K., "Grammar and Music in Thomas Campion's *Observations in the Art of English Poesie*," *SRen*, 17 (1970), 46-72.

     Campion adapts classical metrics to English verse following Lily's grammar; *Observations* may have acted as bridge from Latin to English mode.

749. Formigari, Cubeddu L., "Empirismo e critica del linguaggio in Francesco Bacone," *Atti dell'Accademia dei Lincei*, 3-4 (1968), 157-175.

     Examines two aspects of linguistic theory of Bacon: his criticism of traditional arts of discourse and his analysis of semantic correlations.

750. Gibson, C.A., "'Behind the Arras' in Massinger's *The Renegado*," *NQ*, 214 (1969), 296-297.

     "Behind the arras" as it appears in Jacobean and Caroline drama to mean covert sexual activity.

751. Goode, Helen Dill, *La prosa retórica de fray Luis de León en "Los nombres de Cristo."* Madrid: Editorial Gredos, 1969.

     Translation of 1967 doctoral thesis. Thirty-four pages give a list by means of which the reader can refer to the *Nombres* when he seeks rhetorical examples. Analysis based on Quintilian--largely books 8 and 9.

752. Greene, Thomas M., "Roger Ascham: The Perfect End of Shooting," *ELH*, 36 (1969), 609-625.

     Ascham's approach to language and his influence on English prose.

753. Griffin, Robert, *Coronation of the Poet: Joachim du Bellay's Debt to the Trivium.* (Univ. of California Pubs. in Mod. Philology, vol. 96). Berkeley and Los Angeles: Univ. of Calif. Press, 1969.

     Rev. *BHR*, 32 (1970), 704-705.

     Connection between rhetoric and poetry in Renaissance poetic mind as studied in Du Bellay; his conception of grammar, dialectic, and rhetoric related in part to ideas of Ramus. Pléiade's shift not from figured language, but from the ornate to the functional. Glossary of technical terms.

754. ————, "The French Renaissance Commonplace and Literary Context: An Example," *Neophil.*, 54 (1970), 258-261.

     Use of an Erasmian adage in Renaissance poetry; use of commonplaces by humanists expressed their feelings of a shared classical tradition and value of their own contributions to it.

755. Halio, Jay Leon, "Rhetorical Ambiguity as a Stylistic Device in Shakespeare's Problem Comedies," *DA*, 30 (1969), 1135A (Yale Univ.).

     Chapters on the nature of ambiguity; the classification of puns and quibbles; Shakespeare's use of ambiguity as a stylistic device. Included is a glossary of ambiguities.

756. Hall, Vernon, comp., *Literary Criticism: Plato to Johnson.*
      (Goldentree Bibliographies.) N.Y.: Appleton-Century-Crofts,
      Meredith Corp., 1970.

      Selective bibliography of significant classical and medieval
      references; Renaissance criticism, pp. 24-52.

757. Hardin, R.F., "Convention and Design in Drayton's 'Heroicall
      Epistles,'" *PMLA*, 83 (1968), 35-41.

      The *Epistles* approach the *Heroides* of Ovid in the plan of the
      rhetoric and by their moral intention, but their patriotic
      tone is typical of English historical literature of about 1590.

758. Heath, Terence, "Logical Grammar, Grammatical Logic, and
      Humanism in Three German Universities," *SRen*, 18 (1971), 9-64.

      Literary revolutions of humanists in 15th and 16th cents.
      paralleled changes in scholastic education. Rhetorical inno-
      vations in schools subverted the primacy of medieval dialectic.
      Such curricular alterations in the transitional period have not
      been adequately traced. Humanist reform of grammar further
      weakened the main discipline of the trivium, logic.

759. Hirsch, Rudolf, *Printing, Selling, and Reading, 1450-1550.*
      Wiesbaden: Harrassowitz, 1967.

      Rev. *Papers Bibl. Soc. Amer.*, 62 (1968), 139-144.

      Includes cost and selling of books; protection, restraint, and
      politics; printing and reading.

760. Janton, Pierre, *L'éloquence et la rhétorique dans les sermons
      de Hugh Latimer: Étude de l'art et de la technique oratoire.*
      (Publications de la Faculté des Lettres et Sciences Humaines
      de l'Univ. de Clermont-Ferrand, 2e série, fasc. XXVII). P.U.F.,
      1968.

      Rev. *Revue Belge de Philologie et d'Histoire*, 48 (1970), 190-
      193.

      Latimer's 44 sermons reveal an essentially oral technique.
      Six chapters concern his "structure, thèmes, preuves, moeurs,
      passions, style."

761. Kelley, Donald R., "Philology and the Mirror of History," *Jour.
      of Interdisc. Hist.*, fasc. 1 (1970), 125-136.

      On connection between philology and history, as focusing on the
      genesis rather than on the systematic formulations of ideas.
      Shifts attention from formal concepts to questions of epistemo-
      logy.

762. Klinck, Von Roswitha, *Die Lateinische Etymologie des Mittel-
      alters.* Munich: Wilhelm Fink Verlag, 1970.

      Rev. *JEGP*, 69 (1970), 719-723.

      First full-scale work on medieval etymological methods. Three
      parts: theory of etymology, list and discussions of various
      etymologies, uses of etymology as a *genus interpretationis.*

763. Knauf, David M., "George Puttenham's Theory of Natural and Artificial Discourse," *SM*, 34 (1967), 35-42.

     Aims to clarify Puttenham's theory of style; stress on decorum and appropriateness.

764. Kohl, Norbert, "Die Shakespeare-Kritik zum Wortspiel: Ein Beitrag zur historischen Wertung eines Sprachphänomens," *DVLG*, 44 (1970), 530-543.

     Survey of critical attitudes toward word-play in Shakespeare from 18th to 20th cent.

765. Kuhn, Sherman M., and John Reidy, eds., *Middle English Dictionary*, Part H-5 (1967); I-1, I-2 (1968). Ann Arbor: Univ. of Mich. Press, 1968.

     Basic linguistic tool. In progress.

766. Lanham, Richard A., *A Handlist of Rhetorical Terms: A Guide for Students of English Literature*. Berkeley: Univ. of Calif. Press, 1968. Rev. *QJS*, 55 (1969), 85.

     Includes definitions of rhetorical terms, arranged alphabetically; terms by rhetorical divisions to aid in identification of verbal patterns in a text. Alphabetical list of terms especially useful in literary criticism. (Cf. Sonnino below, which also gives quotations from the rhetoricians themselves.)

767. Lentzen, Manfred, "Cristoforo Landinos Antrittsvorlesung im Studio Fiorentina," *RF*, 81 (1969), 60-88.

     Edition of Landino's commentary on Dante delivered in 1458 when former received the chair for Rhetoric and Poetics at the Florentine School. Lecture deals with the function of poetry, the poet's *furor divinus*, and the *Commedia* as hymn in praise of virtue.

768. Leo, Robert Joseph, "Tommaso Campanella: Rhetorician and Utopian," *DA*, 30 (1969), 853A (Univ. of Wash.).

     Investigates the rhetorical and utopian thoughts of Campanella as revealed in *Retorica* and *La Città del Sole*; attempts to present first extended discussion in English of Campanella's rhetorical study.

769. Lynch, Edward Joseph, S.J., "The Origin and Development of Rhetoric in the Plan of Studies of 1599 of the Society of Jesus," *DA*, 29 (1969), 4126-27A (Northwestern Univ.).

     On origins and development of the concept *ad efformandam ad perfectam eloquentiam* of the *Ratio Studiorum* of 1599 of the Jesuits. Includes extensive bibliography on Jesuits and humanists of the time.

770. Mahoney, Patrick, "The *Anniversaries*: Donne's Rhetorical Approach to Evil," *JEGP*, 68 (1969), 407-413.

     Anniversaries as formal examples of deliberative-epideictic rhetoric.

771. Marotti, Arthur F., "The Self-Reflexive Art of Ben Jonson's
      Sejanus," *TSLL*, 12 (1970), 197-220.

      On play's self-reflexiveness in terms of self-conscious rhetoric
      that advertises its own artificiality, and in terms of double
      theme of play-acting and play-making that centers on actions of
      Sejanus and Tiberius.

772. McCall, Marsh H., Jr., *Ancient Rhetorical Theories of Simile
      and Comparison*. Cambridge, Mass.: Harvard Univ. Press, 1969.

      Contains chapter on *Rhetorica ad Herennium*; and chapters on
      Aristotle, Cicero, the Senecas, Quintilian; plus select
      bibliography. Rev. *TLS*, 18 Dec. 1970, 1488.

773. McKay, Margaret Rachel, "Shakespeare's Use of the Apostrophe,
      Popular Rhetorical Device of the Renaissance," *DA*, 30 (1970),
      4459-A (Univ. of Colorado).

      No consistent trend in Shakespearean apostrophe.

774. McLuhan, Marshall, "The Ciceronian Program in Pulpit and in
      Literary Criticism," *Ren. and Ref.* (Univ. of Toronto), 7
      (1970), 3-7.

      Distinguishes the two traditions, patristic and scholastic, in
      medieval church. Donne as practitioner of grammatical exegesis,
      though acquainted with scholastic tradition, is a patristic
      theologian. Entire "Golden Age" of Spanish literature is ex-
      pression of patristic rhetoric and exegesis.

775. McNally, James Richard, "'Prima Pars Dialecticae': The Influ-
      ence of Agricolan Dialectic upon English Accounts of Invention,"
      RenQ, 21 (1968), 166-177.

      Effect of Rudolph Agricola's dialectic on northern humanist
      thought; how his place theory made its way into treatments of
      invention in the major English logics of the early Renaissance.

776. ————, *"Rector et dux Populi*: Italian Humanists and the Re-
      lationship between Rhetoric and Logic," *MP*, 67, no. 2 (1969-
      1970), 168-176.

      Italian humanism on relationship between rhetoric and dialectic,
      the two disciplines competing for pedagogical preeminence in
      15th cent. Petrarch, Valla, Pico, and Ermalao Barbaro show
      that there were as many differences as similarities among
      Renaissance thinkers on the precise question of how rhetoric
      and logic were related.

777. ————, "Rudolph Agricola's *De Inventione Dialectica Libri Tres*:
      A Translation of Selected Chapters," *SM*, 34 (1967), 393-422.

      Agricola's reform of dialectic.

778. Michałowska, T., "Genological Notions in the Renaissance Theory
      of Poetry," *Zagadnienia Rodzajów Literackich*, 12, no. 2 (1970),
      5-20.

Reconstructs principles underlying division and classification of poetic varieties in Renaissance theory of poetry and examines the Horatian, Platonic, and Aristotelian trends in Italian Cinquecento poetics.

779. Morel, J., "Glossaire," *Dix-Septième Siècle*, 80-81 (1968), 143-146.

Typical rhetorical terms are employed in this issue on rhetoric; the definitions proposed are inspired by treatises of 17th and 18th cents.

780. ———, "Rhétorique et tragédie au XVIIe siècle," *Dix-Septième Siècle*, 80-81 (1968), 89-105.

Treats the rhetoric of passion in certain tragedies of 17th cent.

781. Muir, Kenneth, ed., *Shakespeare Survey 23*. Cambridge Univ. Press, 1970.

Rev. *TLS*, 5 March 1971, 276.

Shakespeare's language; his selection between old and new forms of language, principles of word-coinage, representation of common speech.

782. Nattinger, James Ralph, "A Linguistic Study of William Caxton as a Translator," *DA*, 31 (1970), 2351-A (Univ. of Mich.).

Redefines the terms "literal," "free," "improvement," and "error," and applies them to Caxton's translation.

783. Neubert, Fritz, "Die Entstehung der französischen Epistolarliteratur in Zeitalter der Renaissance," *ZRP*, 85 (1969), 56-92.

Publication of Hélisenne de Crennes' *Lettres familieres et invectives* (1539), Estienne du Tronchet's *Lettres missives et familieres* (1569), and *Les Missives de Mesdames des Roches, mère et fille* (1586), paved the way for epistolary literature in the vernacular, which previously had been confined to French verse or Latin.

784. Ong, Walter J., S.J., *The Presence of the Word: Some Prolegomena for Cultural and Religious History*. New Haven/London: Yale Univ. Press, 1967. Rev. *NYRB*, 14 Mar. 1968, 22-26.

Concerned with the "word," spoken, as well as its interior imaginary and intellectual counterparts. Chapter V, especially, deals with Renaissance aspects of rhetoric and language. 19-page list of "readings."

785. ———, "Tudor Writings on Rhetoric," *SRen*, 15 (1968), 39-69.

Survey of Tudor prose literature for projected history of various ancillary areas of Tudor prose (gen. ed., George B. Parks). Ends with F. Bacon.

786. Paris, Jean, "Rabelais et le langage antinomique," *MLN*, 84 (1969), 505-532.

Rabelais' concern with language undermines traditional views of
words as signatures of things. Questioning the link between
language and the divine order, Rabelais discovers contingency;
his linguistic fragmentation corresponds to the external break
between words and things.

787. Rierdan, Richard Cotter, "Sir Thomas Elyot: A Theory and Prac-
      tice of Written Communication in the Early Sixteenth Century,"
      DA, 31 (1970), 1811-A (Univ. of Calif., Los Angeles).

      Elyot's theory of communication and its Platonic roots. His
      Ciceronian view of printed communication. His education, his
      use of the precepts of exempla in Erasmus' *De Copia*; his trans-
      lating technique, and his approach to writing dialogues.

788. Schleiner, Winfried, *The Imagery of John Donne's Sermons*.
      Providence, R.I.: Brown Univ. Press, 1970.

      Rev. *Church Hist.*, 40 (1971), 229-230; *ELN*, 9 (1971), 63-65;
      JEGP, 70 (1971), 541-543.

      Historical framework from which Donne drew his sermon imagery.
      Renaissance theories of rhetoric and certain doctrinal metaphors
      of the biblical and patristic tradition (e.g., sin as sickness,
      life as journey, and salvation as purchase) discussed.

789. Shaffer, William Gaylord, "Rabelais and Language: Studies in
      Communication," *DA*, 30 (1970), 4464-A (Case Western Reserve
      Univ.).

      Rabelais evaluates language in its capacity for communication.
      Seeks the right language amidst threats of persecution for
      heresy and religious controversy of Catholics, Reformists, and
      Evangelists.

790. Sheidley, William Edwards, "The Poetry of Barnabe Googe and
      George Turbervile: A Study," *DA*, 29 (1969), 2228-A (Stanford
      Univ.).

      Relation of their poetry to the Tudor translation movement and
      grammar school practice of writing verse according to prescrip-
      tions of rhetoricians.

791. Slaughter, Mary M., "The Universal Language Movement in Seven-
      teenth-Century England," *DA*, 29 (1969), 3110-A (Univ. of Wisc.).

      On 17th-cent. followers of Bacon's proposal of a universal arti-
      ficial language involving perfect symmetry between symbol and
      thing symbolized.

792. Sloan, Thomas O., "A Renaissance Controversialist on Rhetoric:
      Thomas Wright, *Passions of the Minde in General*," *Speech Mono-
      graphs*, 36 (1969), 38-54.

      In Wright, "minde in general" refers to complex operations in-
      volved in apprehension or response, rather than merely to
      rational soul. His rhetorical theory, with reason at the top,
      is also complexly divided.

793. Snyders, G., "Rhétorique et culture au XVIIe siècle," *Dix-Septième Siècle*, 80-81 (1968), 79-87.

Teachers then felt that strict, rigorous codification of language according to rhetorical rules would help students to achieve the heights of language and of thought.

794. Sonnino, Lee A., *A Handbook to Sixteenth-Century Rhetoric*. London: Routledge & K.P., 1968. Rev. *NQ*, n.s. 16 (1969), 474-475.

Gathers information provided by authorities who helped educate Renaissance authors, including main classical rhetoricians they would probably have read, major Renaissance rhetoricians, and writers of vernacular treatises and major school textbooks. Sections: figures or colours of rhetoric--Latin names; figures--Greek names only; style; genre; bibliography; major systems for dividing material of traditional rhetoric; descriptive index of tropes and schemes. Index: Greek, Latin, Italian terms. Provides quotations from Renaissance rhetoricians to illustrate terms. (Cf. Lanham above.)

795. *Speech Monographs*, "A Bibliography of Rhetoric and Public Address for the Year 1967," *SM*, 35 (1968), 203-254, followed by "Abstracts of Doctoral Dissertations in the Field of Speech," pp. 255-337; "Work in Progress," pp. 338-347; and list of dissertations. (Annual.)

796. Stambough, Ria, "Proverbial Material in Sixteenth-Century German Jestbooks," *Proverbium* (SKS, Halituskatu 1, Helsinki), no. 11 (1968), 257-267.

Toward study of proverbs in context, through reconstruction of the 16th-cent. *Volksmund*.

797. Steadman, John M., "Milton's Rhetoric: Satan and the 'Unjust Discourse,'" *MiltonS*, 1 (1960), 67-92.

Satan evokes Socratic-Aristophanic antithesis of just and unjust discourse. Satan and sophistry of rhetorical skill but false and deceptive eloquence.

798. Stephens, James Willis, "The Origins and Influence of Bacon's Theory of Rhetoric," *DA*, 29 (1968), 914-915 (Univ. of Wisc.).

While Bacon apparently rejects Aristotle, his rhetorical counsel implies Aristotle rather than Cicero or Quintilian: he stresses unobtrusiveness, ethical and pathetic proof, logical modes of argument. Yet Bacon opposes Aristotle on rhetoric--"illustration of discourse," he says, whose purpose is to apply "reason to imagination for the better moving of the will."

799. Stopp, F.J., "*Verbum Domini manet in aeternam*. The Dissemination of a Reformation Slogan," *Essays in Germ. Lang., Cult. and Soc.* ed. S.P. Rawer et al. London: Univ. of London Inst. German Studies, 1969, pp. 123-135.

Rise in significance of this slogan on coins, medals, flags, woodcuts, etc., used in various political and propagandistic contexts.

800. Struever, Nancy S., *The Language of History in the Renaissance: Rhetoric and Historical Consciousness in Florentine Humanism.* Princeton Univ. Press, 1970.

Rev. *AHR*, 76 (1971), 1152-1154; *QJS*, 57 (1971), 360-362.

Historiographic analysis of rhetoric which proposes that traditional rhetoric has functioned in Western thought both as a "meta-language" concerned with discourse about discourse, and as a theory of aesthetics, pragmatics, and psychology.

801. Tans, J.A.G., ed., *Invention et imitation. Études sur la littérature du seizième siècle.* The Hague; Brussels: Van Goor Zonen, 1968.

Rev. *Fr. Studies*, 24 (1970), 282-284.

Includes three lectures: H. Naïs studies literary events of 1555; M.A. Screech examines medical philosophy in Rabelais: the Galen vs. Hippocrates controversy in the *Tiers Livre* enriches it; S. Dresden examines idea of imitation from various points of view, including religious and metaphysical.

802. Thomas, Mary Jean, "The Rhetoric of Juan Luis Vives," *DA*, 28 (1968), 4305-4306-A (Penn. State Univ.).

Aims to bring to light full rhetoric of Juan Luis Vives as it appears in *De Ratione Dicendi* (1533), his rhetoric until now having been left unexamined.

803. Tigerstedt, E.N., "Observations on the Reception of the Aristotelian *Poetics* in the Latin West," *Stud. Ren.*, 15 (1968), 7-24.

Text of the *Poetics*, translations, commentaries, and uses in Middle Ages and Renaissance.

804. Truchet, J., "Pour un inventaire des problèmes posés par l'étude de la rhétorique au XVIIe siècle," *Dix-Septième Siècle*, 80-81 (1968), 5-17.

Description of rhetorical facts and reflections on phenomenon of rhetoric.

805. Van Dorsten, J.A., "The Arts of Memory and Poetry," *ES*, 48 (1967), 419-425.

Relation in Sidney between poetic and mnemonic imagery for rhetorical or didactic ends.

806. Vasoli, Cesare, *La dialettica e la retorica dell' Umanesimo. "Invenzione" e "metodo" nella cultura del XV e XVI secolo.* Milan: Feltrinelli, 1968.

Collection of revised essays under five sections: "Alle origini della dialettica umanistica," "Maestri e testi di dialettica del Quattrocento italiano," "Tre esperienze umanistiche europee [R. Agricola, Lefèvre d'Etaples, Vives]," "Dialettica, retorica e metodo da R. Agricola a Giovanni Sturm," and "Intorno a Pietro Ramo e alle dispute logiche del maturo Cinquecento."

807. Verburg, P.A., "Ennoësis of Language in 17th Century Philosophy," *Lingua*, 21 (1968), 558-572.

     Changing attitudes to language, illustrated with diagrams; e.g., Galileo used mathematics as language; the Book of Nature he viewed as written in an alphabet of squares, triangles, etc.; he aimed at a certitude by rational calculation--his sense of language as noetic.

808. Vickers, Brian, *Classical Rhetoric and English Poetry*. London: Macmillan, 1970.

     Rev. *Choice*, 8 (1971), 231; *Spenser Newsletter*, 2 (1971), 4.

     How emotional and psychological effects are tied to specific figures of rhetoric in English poetry from Chaucer to Wordsworth. Gives history and processes of rhetoric since classical times; defines rhetorical figures; establishes principles of rhetorical analysis.

809. ————, *Francis Bacon and Renaissance Prose*. Cambridge, Eng.: Cambridge Univ. Press, 1968.

     Rev. *QJS*, 55 (1969), 82-83.

     Bacon as master of English prose, with special emphasis on the *Essays* and *Advancement of Learning*. Praises him as masterful thinker of images; his use of rhetorical devices purposeful.

810. Weaver, John Joseph William, "Rhetoric and Tragedy in Thomas Sackville's Contributions to the *Mirror for Magistrates*," *DA*, 29 (1969), 3126A (Ohio State Univ.).

     Assumes Sackville's knowledge of the grammar school rhetoric, the *Progymnasmata* of Aphthonius.

811. Weinstock, Horst, *Die Funktion elisabethanischer Sprichwort und Pseudosprichwörter bei Shakespeare*. Heidelberg: Carl Winter Universitätsverlag, 1966. Rev. *ZAA*, 15 (1967), 183-185.

     Detailed study of proverb use in Shakespeare; sections on Seneca's tragedies and proverbs; survey of scholarship, pp. 49-54.

812. Weiss, Adrian, "The Rhetorical Concept of *Narratio* and Narrative Structure in Elizabethan Prose Fiction," *DA*, 30 (1969), 2503-2504-A (Ohio Univ.).

     Defines concept of *narratio* and related aspects of rhetoric. Shows how that concept influenced narrative structure of Elizabethan prose fiction. Particular emphasis on Sidney's *Arcadia* and Lodge's *Rosalynde* and *The Famous, true and historicall life of Robert second Duke of Normandy*.

813. Whiting, Bartlett Jere et al., *Proverbs, Sentences and Proverbial Phrases from English Writings Mainly before 1500*. Harvard U.P.; Oxford U.P., 1968. Rev. *JEGP*, 68 (1969), 688-689.

     Based on Old and Middle English works, plus certain works post-1500 (e.g., John Heywood). Useful supplement to Tilley.

814. Wilan, Richard Anthony, "The Relation of Logic and Rhetoric to
      Meaning in Shakespeare's *Troilus and Cressida*," *DA*, 31 (1970),
      2359-A (Univ. of Maryland).

      Play dramatizes breakdown of logic and rhetoric. It demon-
      strates inadequacy of formalized modes of expression to a co-
      herent ordering of experience.

IX. MEDICAL

815. Bennassar, Bartolome, *Recherches sur les grandes épidémies dans le Nord de l'Espagne à la fin du XVIᵉ siècle.* Paris: S.E.V. P.E.N., 1970, distrib. by Parkers of Oxford.

Rev. *AHR*, 76 (1971), 1177; *TLS*, 16 July 1970, 776.

Plague viewed from its psychological and economic aspects, based on documents pertaining to plague in Castile in 1598-1599.

816. Brabant, H., *Médicins, malades et maladies de la Renaissance.* Brussels: La Renaissance du Livre, 1966.

Discusses various diseases of the Renaissance and various medical or pseudo-medical modes of treating them.

817. Bylebyl, Jerome Joseph, "Cardiovascular Physiology in the Sixteenth and Early Seventeenth Centuries," *DA*, 31 (1970), 1169-A (Yale Univ.).

Revival by medical humanists of original Greek teachings of Galen on heart and blood vessels. Influence on Harvey's discovery of circulation.

818. Casey, R.L., "Shakespeare and Elizabethan Surgery," *Surgery, Gynecology, and Obstetrics*, 124 (1967), 1324-1328.

Quotes Shakespeare's references to medical authorities, dissection, poisons, illnesses, which reflect surgical knowledge of his time.

819. Castellani, Carlo, "Origini ed evoluzione della teoria della 'aura seminalis' da Fabrici d'Acquapendenta a Marcello Malpighi," *Episteme*, 1 (1967), 173-196.

Medical controversy in 16th and 17th cents. over "aura seminalis" or "aura spermatica" in process of reproduction.

820. Clarke, Edwin, and C.D. O'Malley, *The Human Brain and Spinal Cord. A Historical Study Illustrated by Writings from Antiquity to the Twentieth Century.* Berkeley and Los Angeles: Univ. of Calif. Press, 1968.

Rev. *Annals of Sci.*, 25 (1969), 351-352; *Brit. J. for the Hist. of Sci.*, 4 (1969), 413-414; *Science*, 164 (1969), 164.

Covers main anatomical structures and basic physiological principles, with introductory chapter surveying writings from antiquity. Includes many rare or newly translated selections.

821. Coturri, Enrico, "Il Ritrovamento di antichi testi di Medicina nel primo secolo del Rinascimento," *Episteme*, 2 (1968), 91-110.

Documented study of 13th-16th cents. and retrieval of works by such authors as Galen, Celsus, and Hippocrates.

822. Durling, Richard J., ed., *A Catalogue of Sixteenth-Century Printed Books in the National Library of Medicine*. U.S. Department of Health, Education, Welfare; Public Health Service; Bethesda, Md.: National Library of Medicine, 1967.

Rev. *Ambix*, 15 (1968), 71-72; *BHR*, 30 (1968), 222-223; *Isis*, 59 (1967), 233-234; *Journal of the Hist. of Medicine*, 23 (1968), 298-299; *Scientiarum Historia*, 9 (1967), 149-150.

Describes the 16th-cent. imprints in History of Medicine Division of the National Library of Medicine; some 4,800 items.

823. Edgar, Irving I., *Shakespeare, Medicine and Psychiatry: An Historical Study in Criticism and Interpretation*. N.Y.: Philosophical Library, 1970.

Rev. *JAMA*, 216 (26 April 1971), 683.

Shakespeare's observations on interrelation between emotions and bodily responses, observable and intuitional. Discusses Shakespeare's characters in terms of psychoanalytic theorizing.

824. Ehrlich, G.E., "Shakespeare's Rheumatology," *Ann. Rheumatic Dis.*, 26, no. 6 (1967), 562-563.

Excerpts from work of Shakespeare, concerning rheumatology.

825. Finney, Gretchen, "Vocal Exercise in the Sixteenth Century Related to Theories of Physiology and Disease," *Bull. Hist. of Medicine*, 42 (1968), 422-449.

Useful study of revived Galenic remedy of phonation as specific exercise for the lungs; 16th-cent. advice on speaking and singing had medical background. Vocal exercise recommended by Elyot, Mulcaster, etc. Shakespearean references, pp. 429-443.

826. Fischer-Homberger, E., "Hysterie und Misogynie, ein Aspekt der Hysteriegeschichte," *Gesnerus*, 26, nos. 1-2 (1969), 117-127.

Hysteria from Democritus to Hippocrates, Plato, Middle Ages, to recent times.

827. Grosz, I., "Ophthalmological References in the Works of Shakespeare," Magyar with English abstract, *Communicationes ex Bibliotheca historiae medicae hungarica*, no. 42 (1967), 139-149.

828. Hamby, Wallace B., *Ambroise Paré, Surgeon of the Renaissance*. St. Louis: Warren H. Green, 1967.

Rev. *AHR*, 73 (1967), 1160-1161; *Bull. of the Hist. of Medicine*, 42 (1968), 574-576; *Lancet*, no. 7520 (1967), 812.

Study by a neurosurgeon of the 16th-cent. "father of modern surgery."

829. Herrlinger, Robert, and F. Kudlien, *Frühe Anatomie von Mondino bis Malpighi. Eine Antologie.* Stuttgart: Wissenschaftliche Verlagsgesellschaft, 1967.

    Rev. *Archives Internationales d'Histoire des Sciences*, 21 (1968), 192-193; *Bull. of the Hist. of Medicine*, 42 (1968), 572-573; *Gesnerus*, 24 (1967), 84-85.

    Collection of articles on Renaissance anatomists.

830. Hudson, E.H., "Christopher Columbus and the History of Syphilis," *Acta Tropica*, 25, no. 1 (1968), 1-16.

    Endemic syphilis and venereal syphilis are now considered to be syndromes and epidemiological phases of the same disease. In one form or another, treponematosis had existed on the two continents for thousands of years; thus the attribution to the voyages of Columbus is insignificant in the history of syphilis.

831. Huizinga, E., "Murder Through the Ear," *Nederlands Tijdschrift voor Geneeskunde*, 111 (1967), 1218-1219.

    Suggests relevance to *Hamlet*.

832. Hume, Kathryn, "Leprosy or Syphilis in Robert Henryson's *Testament of Cressid?*," *ELN*, 6 (1968/1969), 242-245.

    Challenges notion in *ELN*, 1 (1964), 175-177, that Cressid had syphilis, not leprosy. Former not diagnosed as a separate disease until 1493 in Spain, 1495 in Naples, and 1497 in Scotland. Henryson's work was completed by 1490.

833. King, Lester S., "Humanism and the Medical Past," *JAMA*, 213 (1970), 580-584.

    "Humanism" applied to certain Renaissance physicians: Thomas Linacre, Rabelais, John Caius, Paracelsus.

834. Koelbing, Huldrych M., *Renaissance der Augenheilkunde, 1540-1630.* Bern: Verlag Hans Huber, 1967.

    Useful study of Renaissance ophthalmology.

835. Krivatsy, Peter, "Metaphysical Symbolism in 16th- and 17th-Century Medicine," *JAMA*, 212 (6 April 1970), 115-120.

    Alchemy, astrology, and medicinal chemistry in terms of the pictorial symbolism of the age.

836. Lavine, B.H., "Elizabethan Toothache: A Case History," *Journal of the American Dental Association*, 74 (1967), 1286-1290.

    Regarding case of toothache experienced by Elizabeth.

837. MacLennan, Hector, "A Gynaecologist Looks at the Tudors," *Medical Hist.*, 11 (1967), 66-74.

    Osler Lecture, 1966. On Henry VIII's wives, and Queen Elizabeth, from this special viewpoint. Dismisses Elizabeth's alleged "virilism" and asserts her normality, while contemplating the effect of physiological tension on history.

838. O'Malley, C.D., "Helkiah Crooke, M.D., F.R.C.P., 1576-1648," *Bull. of the Hist. of Medicine*, 42 (1968), 1-18.

On author of *Microcosmographia*, as reflection of medicine in first half of 17th cent. Shakespeareans may be interested in Brit. Museum manuscript (BM Sloane MS. 640, ff. 192, 266^V), indicating that William Jaggard, publisher of First Folio, suffered from syphilitically induced blindness in 1612, and turned to Dr. Crooke vainly to recover his sight. (The Brit. Museum manuscript is cited also in Edwin E. Willoughby, *A Printer of Shakespeare: The Books and Times of William Jaggard* [London, 1934], p. 103; cf. p. 143.)

839. ————, "The Lure of Padua," *Medical Hist.*, 14 (1970), 1-9.

History of chief center for training English medical students abroad until 1670. When Shakespeare referred to "fair Padua, nursery of arts," he was reflecting general opinion in England that it offered best training in Europe.

840. ————, "Tudor Medicine and Biology," *HLQ*, 32 (1968), 1-27.

Useful survey of Tudor writings on medicine and biology (section on the cooperative history of Tudor prose in contextual areas, such as history, science, religion, politics, sponsored by the MLA discussion group for the Tudor period, chairman and gen. ed., George B. Parks).

841. Pagel, Walter, *William Harvey's Biological Ideas: Selected Aspects and Historical Background*. Basel/N.Y.: S. Karger, Hafner, 1967.

Rev. *Ambix,* 14 (1967), 140-144; *Annals of Science*, 24 (1968), 89-93; *Brit. Journal for the Hist. of Science*, 4 (1968), 68-69; *Episteme*, 1 (1967), 200-203; *Gesnerus*, 24 (1967), 86-89; *Isis*, 59 (1968), 101-102; *Medical Hist.*, 12 (1968), 96-98; *New England Journal of Medicine*, 277 (1967), 54; *Revue d'Histoire des Sciences*, 21 (1968), 275-276; *Science*, 157 (1967), 792-793.

Useful study of Harvey and his predecessors; Harvey and quantification; other intellectual contexts.

842. Paracelsus, "The Begetting of Fools: An Annotated Translation of Parcelsus' *De Generatione Stultorum*," trans. P.F. Cranefield, et al., *Bull. of the Hist. of Medicine*, 41 (1967), 56-74, 161-174.

Hitherto untranslated treatise, written c. 1530, published 1567. On problem of reconciling mental deficiencies with divine creation. Fool is victim of Adam's Fall, but only in physical form is he defective. Last shall be first, etc.

843. Paré, Ambroise, *The apologie and treatise ... Containing the voyages made into divers places with many of his writings upon Surgery*, ed. G. Keynes. N.Y.: Dover Press, 1968.

Reprint of the *Apology and Treatise* followed by general remarks on the nature of surgery and surgical operations, discourses on particular wounds and accidental injuries and their treatment; introduction by G. Keynes.

844. Shrewsbury, J.F.D., *A History of Bubonic Plague in the British Isles*. N.Y. and London: Cambridge Univ. Press, 1970.

Rev. *Brit. Jour. for the Hist. of Sci.*, 5 (1971), 302-303; *Historian*, 33 (1971), 462; *Hist. Jour.*, 14 (1971), 205-215; ., *Isis*, 61 (1970), 533-534; *Med. Hist.*, 15 (1971), 310-311.

Five major outbreaks (1563, 1593, 1603, 1625, 1665). Calls many statistics from parish registrars, bills of mortality, etc., into question, asserting deaths were not due to plague. Claims Great Plague of London (1665) may have been only third largest. Data arranged and correlated with seasonal incidences of death, climatological records, and rate of transmission from sea ports and river towns inland.

845. Silvette, Herbert, *The Doctor on the Stage: Medicine and Medical Men in Seventeenth-Century England*. Knoxville, Tenn.: Univ. of Tenn. Press, 1967.

Rev. *ABC*, 18 (1967), 5-6; *Bull. of the Hist. of Medicine*, 42 (1968), 478-480; *QJS*, 54 (1968), 196; *SCN*, 26 (1968), 13.

Deals with 500 17th-cent. English plays and their use of medical language; references, e.g., to uroscopy, venereal diseases, phlebotomy, and remedies and cures.

846. Stensgaard, Richard, "Shakespeare, Paracelsus, and the Plague of 1603. An Annotated List," *Shakespearean Research and Opportunities*, no. 4 (1968-1969), 73-77.

Topicality of Paracelsus during Plague Years, 1602-1606.

847. Webster, C., "Harvey's *De Generatione*: Its Origins and Relevance to the Theory of Circulation," *Brit. Journal for the Hist. of Science*, 3 (1967), 262-274.

Harvey's failure to substantiate Aristotle's notion of the primacy of the heart in embryology, which led him to doubt other aspects of the heart's primacy, and thus to develop the notion of the primacy of the blood.

848. Wellcome Institute of the History of Medicine, *Current Work in the History of Medicine: An International Bibliography*, 57 (1968).

Quarterly index of arts in history of medicine and allied sciences. Subject-entries followed by index of authors. List of new books by authors appended. Based on wide range of journals indicated by *World List* abbreviations. (Available [1969] to serious scholars gratis from Wellcome Institute of the History of Medicine, The Wellcome Bldg., Euston Rd., London N.W. 1.)

849. Wilshere, Jonathan E.O., "Plague in Leicestershire, 1558-1665," *Leicestershire Archaeol. and Hist. Soc. Trans.*, 44 (1968-1969) [1970], 45-71.

Studies plague in Leicestershire through use of Parish Registers. Discusses plagues year-by-year, reprinting death reports.

X. MILITARY

850. Andrews, K.R., "The Aims of Drake's Expedition of 1577-1580,"
AHR, 73 (1967/1968), 724-741.

Argues that Drake's expedition was to reconnoiter the coast of
South America from the Plate River to the part of the coast
where Spanish occupation ended. The mission of Drake was to
establish contact with the American Indians, and its long-term
purpose was, perhaps, to settle and conquer Spanish Peru.

851. Bovill, E.W., "The *Madre de Dios*," *Mariner's Mirror*, 54 (1968),
129-152.

Account of fight with Portuguese fleet in 1592 of fleet of
English privateers. *Madre de Dios* taken, and English sailors
returned to London laden with spoils from that ship.

852. Boynton, Lindsay, *The Elizabethan Militia, 1558-1638*. London:
Routledge and Kegan Paul; Univ. of Toronto Press, 1967.

Rev. *AHR*, 73 (1968), 809-810.

A study of the organization and arming for defense of Englishmen in this era.

853. Brill, Reginald, "The English Preparations before the Treaty
of Arras: A New Interpretation of Sir John Fastolf's Report;
September, 1435," *Studies in Medieval and Ren. History*, 8
(1970), 213-247.

The Shakespearean conjunction of "Arras" and Sir John Fastolf
is not noted in this study of Fastolf's summary of the manage-
ment of the war.

854. Brockman, Eric, *The Two Sieges of Rhodes, 1480-1522*. London:
J. Murray, 1969. Rev. *Choice*, 8 (1971), 1236.

Hospitallers' victory over the Greek-led armada of Mehmet the
Conqueror in 1480 and their defeat at the hands of Suleiman
the Magnificent in 1522.

855. Brown, William Jackson, "From Persepolis to Cyprus: The Disintegration of the Self-Contained Military Hero in Marlowe and
Shakespeare," *DA*, 27 (1967), 3421-A (Duke Univ.).

Aims to show the apparently self-contained military hero in
process of disintegration, as in *Othello*, one of four plays
studied (others being Marlowe's *1* and *2 Tamburlaine* and
Henry V).

856. Colvin, H.M., "Castles and Government in Tudor England," *EHR*,
      83 (1968), 225-234.

      Despite gunpowder's tendency to make castles militarily obso-
      lete, they were not rapidly abandoned; guns were unwieldy for haul-
      ing about the countryside. Castles continued to be used for
      defense during Tudor period; for most part, however, they were
      left to decay, and by end of 16th cent., their upkeep was no
      longer a concern of Parliament.

857. Cruickshank, C.G., *Army Royal: An Account of Henry VIII's In-
      vasion of France, 1513*. Oxford: Clarendon Press, 1969.

      Rev. *AHR*, 75 (1970), 838; *EHR*, 86 (1971), 168-169; *Historian*,
      33 (1970); *History*, 55 (1970), 107-108.

      Uses 1513 campaign to provide framework for account of charac-
      ter and organization of an English expeditionary force in ear-
      lier Tudor times. Historian of Elizabeth's army describes Henry
      VIII's first invasion of France and his army royal. Included
      are administrative, organizational, operational, and supply
      topics.

858. ———, *Elizabeth's Army*. Oxford, 1966.

      Rev. Henry J. Webb, *Ren. Quar.*, 20 (1967), 53-55.

      A second edition, fully revised, considerably expanded--more
      than twice the length of the earlier version. Includes a new
      chapter on drill, training, tactics, and strategy. Descrip-
      tions of chain of command, giving examples from the 1580's and
      1590's; and a discussion in Chapter I of some of the important
      military campaigns of the late 16th and early 17th cents.

859. ———, "King Henry VIII's Army: Munitions," *Hist. Today*, 19
      (1969), 40-45.

      Surveys the military uses of bows and firearms in the early
      16th cent. Condensed from author's *Army Royal*.

860. Dillon, Harold Arthur [Lee-Dillon], *Armour*. London: Arms and
      Armour Press, 1968. (Reprinted from *Archaeological Journal*,
      52, 60 [1895, 1903.]

      Elucidates the manuscript of Jacobe, the master armourer in
      Elizabeth's reign. Notes include brief biographical sketches
      of owners of the armour, descriptions of various pieces,
      cleaning, manufacture, and etiquette of usage.

861. Dufty, Arthur Richard, *European Armour in the Tower of London*.
      London: H.M.S.O., 1968.

      Rev. *LibJ*, 93 (1968), 4278.

      Photographic illustrations of selected examples of armour,
      shields, Norse furniture, bits and spurs from the armouries of
      the Tower of London, including history of the collection, anno-
      tation of plates, and portraits of persons in armour.

862. Glasgow, Tom, Jr., "The Navy in the First Elizabethan Undeclared War, 1559-1560," *Mariner's Mirror*, 54 (1968), 23-37.

Describes campaigns between 1559 and 1560 which established Royal Navy as permanent institution.

863. ————, "The Navy in the Le Havre Expedition, 1562-1564," *Mariner's Mirror*, 54 (1968), 281-296.

This unsuccessful English expedition accelerated development of naval administration, establishing foundations of mature institution which served well in subsequent war with Spain.

864. Hale, J.R., "Sixteenth Century Explanations of War and Violence," *Past and Present*, no. 51 (1971), 3-26.

Erasmus saw war as inevitable—to avoid it might be impossible.

865. Hamilton, Franklin, *Challenge for a Throne: The Wars of the Roses*. N.Y.: Dial, 1967. Rev. *NYTBR* (11 Feb. 1968), 26.

Personalities and events of the struggles between the Houses of Lancaster and York. Maps, illustrations, genealogical tables, bibliography.

866. La Noue, François de, *Discours politiques et militaires*, ed., introduction, and notes, F.E. Sutcliffe. Geneva: Droz, 1967.

Rev. *BHR*, 30 (1968), 408-412; *FS*, 22 (1968), 154-155; *RenQ*, 21 (1968), 55-58.

First complete edition since 1614 of work by Huguenot captain who hated war.

867. Lewis, Michael, *The Spanish Armada*. N.Y.: T.Y. Crowell, 1968.

Qualifies revisionist view, ca. 1900, which argued weakness of Spain and strength of England. Rev. *Choice*, 5 (1968), 671.

868. Martin, Paul, *Arms and Armour from the 9th to the 17th Century*, trans. R. North. Tokyo: Tuttle, 1968.

Rev. *Choice*, 6 (1969), 564.

Equipment, from swords to breast-plates to spurs, described in detail with comments on reasons for its evolution.

869. Morales Lezcano, Víctor, "La guerra contra España en la filosofía política de Sir Walter Raleigh y Francis Bacon," *Rev. de Indias*, 28, nos. 111-112 (1968), 125-141.

Political speeches of Raleigh and Bacon exemplify importance of war against Spain as fashionable topic in 16th- and 17th-cent. Europe.

870. Mork, Gordon R., "Flint and Steel: A Study in Military Technology and Tactics in 17th-Century Europe," *Smithsonian Journal of History*, 2 (1967), 25-32.

Though in early 17th cent. sword was more convenient than a
musket that required several minutes to load, aim, and fire,
improvement of musket locks caused a revolution in military
tactics that tended toward obsolescence both of pike ("queen of
the battlefield") and sword.

871. Murphy, W.P.D., ed., *The Earl of Hertford's Lieutenancy Papers
      1603-1612*. Devizes: Wiltshire Record Society, 1969; non-
      subscribers from M.J. Lansdown, 37 Hilperton Road, Trowbridge,
      England.

      Papers of Edward Seymour, Earl of Hertford, lord lieutenant of
      Somerset, Bristol, and Wiltshire for about 20 years. Useful
      for history of the militia during the Shakespearean period.

872. Pollitt, R.L., "The Elizabethan Navy Board: A Study in Ad-
      ministrative Evolution," *DA*, 29 (1969), 2192 (Northwestern
      Univ.).

      Evolution of English admiralty during reign of Elizabeth I.

873. Prynne, M.W., "Henry V's *Grace Dieu*," *Mariner's Mirror*, 54
      (1968), 115-128.

      Relics of Henry V's medieval warship (launched in 1418 and
      probably largest built in northern Europe to its time) have
      been found.

874. Richmond, C.F., "English Naval Power in the Fifteenth Century,"
      History, 52 (1967), 1-15.

      Examines resources of Henry V, Edward IV, and Richard III which
      enabled them to carry out policies of sustained vigilance at
      sea, and what those policies achieved.

875. Rogers, Alan, "Maintenance and the Wars of the Roses," *Hist.
      Today*, 17 (1967), 198-203.

      Economic struggles, rather than dynastic or constitutional
      issues, lay behind the 15th-cent. disturbances. Bonds of main-
      tenance and lordship unified a magnate and his retinue; these,
      as they shifted and came into conflict, caused clashes.

876. Shelby, L.R., *John Rogers: Tudor Military Engineer*. Oxford:
      Clarendon Press, 1967.

      Rev. *AHR*, 74 (1968), 594-595.

      Rogers, second only to Richard Lee among military engineers of
      his time, was employed by Henry VIII and responsible for impor-
      tant fortifications. His career reflects a time of transition
      from medieval to more modern styles of military architecture.

877. Soens, Adolph L., "Two Rapier Points: Analysing Elizabethan
      Fighting Methods," *N&Q*, 213 (1968), 127-128.

      1) Although George Silver was wrong in arguing that the English
      cut (movement in arc) in fencing is as quick as the Italian
      thrust, he was correct in reflecting other Elizabethan reali-
      ties. 2) Illustrations of fencing positions in Elizabethan
      works are frequently inaccurate and should, unless supported by
      the text, be disregarded.

878. ———, "Tybalt's Spanish Fencing in *Romeo and Juliet*," *SQ*, 20 (1969), 121-127.

Spanish fencing was admired in 1590's but it was also ridiculed for being foreign. Italian style, unlike the Spanish, did not carry with it implications of pride and cold-blooded efficiency. Mercutio's style is Italian; Tybalt's, Spanish.

879. Tenenti, Alberto, *Piracy and the Decline of Venice, 1580-1615*. Berkeley: Univ. of Calif. Press; London: Longmans, 1967.

Rev. *History*, 53 (1968), 118; *RenQ*, 21 (1968), 314.

New perspective on Venetian decline as international entrepôt. Decline owing to lack of personnel, equipment, ships, and breakdown of responsibility. Role of English raiders stressed. Shift in economic hegemony over Europe in first half of 17th cent. of England and Holland, with extension of influence into Mediterranean at expense of its former masters.

880. Valentine, Eric, *Rapiers: An Illustrated Reference Guide to the Rapiers of the 16th and 17th Centuries, with Their Companions*. London: P. Arms & Armour, 1968.

Rev. *LibJ*, 93 (1968), 2996; *TLS* (13 March 1969), 276.

Illustrated catalogue of items from author's collection; notes on history and collecting of rapiers, authentication, renovation, and appendixes.

881. Wiedemer, Jack Earl, Jr., "Arms and Armor in England, 1450-1471, Their Cost and Distribution," *DA*, 28 (1967), 1362-1363-A (Univ. of Pennsylvania).

Period chosen because England was then greatly troubled by civil wars, general lawlessness, with result that armor played significant part in daily life. Price was major factor, metal armor being so expensive that common soldiers, even many men-at-arms, wore body armor made of fabric. High cost of arms and armor contributed to financial instability, royal government relying on levies of commoners who could not afford expensive weapons, whereas retainers of rebellious Yorkist and Lancastrian magnates could usually acquire good arms from their masters.

882. Wright, L.P., "The Military Orders in Sixteenth and Seventeenth Century Spanish Society; The Institutional Embodiment of a Historical Tradition," *Past and Present*, no. 43 (1969), 34-70.

Study of the military orders after their incorporation into the Crown in 1523. Although the Orders were no longer needed to fight the Moors, they survived because they offered prime source of income, patronage, and prestige.

883. Zitner, S.P., "Hamlet, Duelist," *UTQ*, 39 (1969), 1-18.

Changes in attitudes of the aristocracy represented by fashionable switch in personal weapons from short swords to Italianate rapiers.

XI. MUSICAL

884. Abraham, Gerald, et al., *New Oxford History of Music*, Vol. 4:
      The Age of Humanism, 1540-1630 (gen. ed., J.A. Westrup). Lon-
      don: Oxford Univ. Press, 1968.

      Rev. *BHR*, 30 (1968), 448-449.

      New Oxford History of Music is of unique comprehensiveness; not
      merely a revision of the "old" Oxford. Vol. 4 has contributions
      by leading musicologists, each with a chapter on his own spe-
      cialty, abundant bibliography, full index.

885. Aldrich, Putnam, "An Approach to the Analysis of Renaissance
      Music," *Music Review*, 30 (1969), 1-21.

      Considers overall structure, modal procedure, text, subject,
      melodic structure, harmonic structure, imitation.

886. Ammann, P.J., "The Musical Theory and Philosophy of Robert
      Fludd," *JWCI*, 30 (1967), 198-227.

      Musical theory of Fludd (1574-1637) which formed part of his
      general philosophical structure; controversy with Kepler;
      sources in Ficino, Agrippa, and related figures.

887. Barnett, Howard B., "John Case--An Elizabethan Music Scholar,"
      Music and Letters, 50 (1969), 252-266.

      An Oxford don, Case (c. 1539-c.1599) emerges as a scholar who
      was not wholly connected to any religious doctrine. In oppo-
      sing elimination of complicated music, he was not acting as an
      anti-Puritan but as one who wished to preserve an art form.

888. Berman, Peggy Ruth, "French Names for the Dance to 1588," *DA*,
      29 (1969), 2239-40-A (Univ. of Penn.).

      An etymological, historical, and descriptive study of French
      dances; includes names of dances given by French texts from
      13th cent. *baleries* mentioned by Jacques Bretel in his *Tournoi
      de Chauvency* to sophisticated dances discussed by Jehan Tabou-
      rot in his *Orchesography*, 1588.

889. Bisgrove, Mildred E., "Sacred Choral Music in the Calvinistic
      Tradition of the Protestant Reformation in Switzerland and
      France from 1541-1600," *DA*, 30 (1970), 3489-A (N.Y.U.).

      Calvinist ideas on the relationship between God, man, and art
      influenced translation of Psalms into French metrical texts,
      when they were not actually supervised by Calvin himself.

890.   Blume, Friedrich, *Renaissance and Baroque Music: A Comprehensive Survey*, trans. N.Y.: W.W. Norton & Co., 1967.

Rev. *Music Library Assoc. Notes*, 24 (1968), 488-489.

Justifies the separateness of Renaissance as a musical period, distinguishing it from Baroque. Comprehensive essays cross disciplinary lines, suggesting interrelationships among the arts. Indicates areas where further study by musicologists is needed.

891.   Brown, David, *Thomas Weelkes: A Biographical and Critical Study*. N.Y.: Praeger, 1969.

Rev. *Choice*, 6 (1970), 1758; *Jour. Am. Musicol. Soc.*, 23 (1970), 349-352; *Musical Times*, 110 (1969), 1142-1143.

Demonstrates how Weelkes wedded to the fashionable, Italianate madrigal style of Morley, the older, Flemish-English mastery of polyphonic line and contrapuntal structure characteristic of Byrd; result being, in the madrigal set of 1600 particularly, works of brilliant expressiveness.

892.   Brown, Patricia A., "Influences on the Early Lute Songs of John Dowland," *Musicology* (Australia), 3 (1968-69), 21-33.

The first published examples of the English lute song genre appeared in John Dowland's *The First Booke of Songes or Ayres of foure partes with Tableture for the Lute* ..., London, 1597. These lute songs and their alternative four-part ayre versions are compared with significant English and Continental vocal forms, including English consort song, part song, theatrical song, popular song, and French *air de cour*. Both historical affinities and formal relationships are explored. This examination clarifies the qualities that make the English lute song and ayre unique, and also emphasizes the relationship between Dowland's songs and indigenous English vocal forms.

893.   Charbon, Marie H., *Haags Gemeentemuseum. Catalogus van de muziekbibliotheek. Deel I. Historische en theoretische werken tot 1800*. Amsterdam: Knuf, 1969. Rev. *Notes*, 27 (1971), 494-495.

This first catalog of the rich collection from the Museum of Fine Arts, La Haye, contains an enumeration of theoretical works before 1800.

894.   Coover, James, "Music Theory in Translation: A Bibliography Supplement 1959-1969," *Jour. of Music Theory*, 13 (1969), 230-248.

Listing of significant theoretical translations: Boethius, Bermudo, Descartes, et al., as well as articles on performance.

895.   Doe, Paul, "Tallis's 'Spem in Alium' and the Elizabethan Respond-motet," *Music and Letters*, 51, no. 1 (1970), 1-14.

Generalizations on problem of dating compositions and influence of political and cultural events on compositions.

896. Dostrovsky, Sigalia, "The Origins of Vibration Theory: The Scientific Revolution and the Nature of Music," *DA*, 30 (1970), 4895-A (Princeton).

     Analysis of formation of scientific study of sound in 17th cent. and influence on music theory and practice in Renaissance.

897. Fabry, Frank J., "Sidney's Verse Adaptations to Two Sixteenth-Century Italian Art Songs," *RenQ*, 23 (1970), 237-255.

     Believes to have found Italian *villanelles* used by Sidney as models for 'Certaine Sonnets' 3, 4, and 26. Provides modern song book version of the pieces to show how Sidney adapted his verse to existing polyphonic music. Photographic reproductions of original compositions.

898. Fähnrich, Hermann, "Christopher Marlowes Beitrag zur Bühnenmusik der Elisabethaner," *Musikforschung*, 22 (1969), 274-284.

     Marlowe's use of incidental music to characterize both individuals and the dramatic action and his synthesis of the "music of speech" (blank verse) and incidental music in *Doctor Faustus*.

899. Fellowes, E.H., ed., *English Madrigal Verse, 1588-1632*, 3rd. ed., rev., and enlarged by Frederick W. Sternfeld and David Greer. Oxford: Clarendon Press, 1967; N.Y.: Oxford Univ. Press, 1968.

     Rev. *M&L*, 49 (1968), 164-167.

     Important revision of work which appeared in 1920. Contains poetic texts of most of the madrigal collections and song books printed in England between 1588 and 1632. Includes poems set as both madrigals and lute songs, as well as many song-poems which fall into neither category and are elsewhere unavailable. About 200 new poems are now added, while poems from previous edition have been rechecked against original copies, with insertion of corrections and changes.

900. Ford, Wyn Kelson, *Music in England before 1800: A Select Bibliography*. London: The Library Association, 7 Ridgmount St., 1967. Rev. *TLS*, 24 Aug. 1967, 769.

     Library Assoc. Bibliographies, No. 7, 128 pp.

901. Gerboth, Walter, *An Index to Musical Festschriften and Similar Publications*. N.Y.: W.W. Norton, 1969.

     Rev. *Notes*, 26 (1970), 760-761.

     Three main parts: List of *Festschriften*, Classified List of Articles, and Author-Subject Index to Classified List.

902. Goldron, Romain, *Music of the Renaissance*, ed. A.L. Burkhalter, N.Y.: Doubleday, 1968. Rev. *Music Ed. J.*, 54 (1968), 76.

     Fourth volume in History of Music series discusses music and humanism, 16th-cent. developments in Flanders, Italy, Spain, Germany, France, and England, with discography.

903. Gray, Walter, "Some Aspects of Word Treatment in the Music of
      William Byrd," *Musical Quart.*, 55 (1969), 45-64.

      Discusses word-painting, musical metaphrase, musical imagery,
      musical synonym, and word emphasis.

904. Greer, David, "The Part-Songs of the English Lutenists," *Pro-
      ceedings of the Royal Musical Association*, 94 (1967-68), 97-
      110.

      The part-song versions of several solo songs are considered,
      some of them in the light of their use in masques and other
      court functions.

905. Gregory, Julia, and Hazel Bartlett, *Catalogue of Early Books
      on Music (before 1800)*. N.Y.: Da Capo Press, 1969. (Da Capo
      Press Music Reprint Series.)

      Rev. *Notes*, 26 (1970), 521-524.

      Unabridged republication, in one volume, of 1913 Catalogue
      published in Washington, D.C. and of the 1944 Supplement.
      Entries arranged in dictionary order by author or title (anon-
      ymous works); cross-references.

906. Gruber, Albion, "Evolving Tonal Theory in Seventeenth-Century
      France," *DA*, 30 (1969), 2559-A (Univ. of Rochester, Eastman
      School of Music).

      Traces, in selected French treatises of 17th cent., pertinent
      developments which relate to an evolving theory of tonality.
      Attention is also focused upon relevant ideas formulated by
      Zarlino in 16th cent. Gradual transition from Renaissance
      theoretical thought to early formulation of tonal theory prior
      to Rameau.

907. Hanning, Barbara Russano, "The Influence of Humanist Thought
      and Italian Renaissance Poetry on the Formation of Opera," *DA*,
      30 (1969), 1587-A (Yale Univ.).

      On poetics of dramatic poems and their musical settings that have
      come to be accepted as first operas. Developments in Italian
      humanist thought regarding music and poetry in decades preceding
      formation of the new art-form; manifestation of such thought in
      stylistic interrelationship between libretti and scores of first
      decade of opera composition.

908. Harper, John Martin, "A New Way of Making Ayres? Thomas Cam-
      pion--Towards a Revaluation," *Musical Times*, 110 (1969), 262-
      263.

      Campion as a poet-composer who thus could reconcile poetic and
      musical elements. Examples from the *Two bookes of ayres*
      (ca. 1613).

909. Harran, Don, "'Mannerism' in the Cinquecento Madrigal," *Musical
      Quart.*, 55 (1969), 521-544.

      Mannerism in the Italian madrigal suggested; depends on a num-
      ber of general affinities between music and arts in 16th cent.:
      artificiality, eclecticism, over-preoccupation with detail,
      change as a constant of style and structure.

910. Heartz, Daniel, *Pierre Attaingnant; Royal Printer of Music*.
     Berkeley and Los Angeles: Univ. of Calif. Press, 1970.

     Rev. *BC*, 20 (1971), 261.

     Attaingnant's career as a Paris typographer, amid literary,
     artistic, and political currents of 16th-cent. Europe.

911. Hewitt, Helen, "Supplement (1966) to Doctoral Dissertations in
     Musicology," *Journal of American Musicological Society*, 19
     nos. 3 (1966), 383-397.

     Lists studies by periods (Renaissance, etc.). Gives works in
     progress and studies available from the Society and microfilm
     numbers.

912. Kingsley, Victoria, "Do the Words Matter?" *Consort*, 25 (1968-
     69), 396-404.

     Questions the intelligibility of lute song texts for present-
     day audiences; discusses the emotional content of several songs
     with particular emphasis on the symbolism of the Courts of
     Honor.

913. Knowlton, Jean, "Dating the Masque Dances in British Museum
     Additional MS. 10444," *BMQ*, 32 (1968), 99-102.

     Concordances are given for 40 dance tunes found in music books
     dating from 1614, 1617, and 1621.

914. LaRue, Jan, ed., *Aspects of Medieval and Renaissance Music*.
     N.Y.:   W.W. Norton, 1966. Rev. *Notes*, 23 (1966), 259.

     Fifty-seven essays by American and European scholars relating
     music of the Middle Ages and the Renaissance to liturgy, to
     mathematics, to philosophy, to drama, to social activities,
     to art, and to literature. (Ded. to Gustave Reese.)

915. Le Huray, Peter, *Music and the Reformation in England, 1549-
     1660*. Studies in Church Music; N.Y.:   Oxford Univ. Press;
     London: Jenkins, 1967.

     Rev. *M&L*, 49 (1968), 69-70.

     Traces progress of music from reign of Henry VIII, particularly
     with reference to church music, relating it to religious and
     economic background of the period. Chapters on each of major
     composers, and includes a full list of devotional music of the
     era.

916. Long, John H., "The Ballad Medley and the Fool," *SP*, 67 (1970),
     505-516.

     Traditional association of fool with patches and remnants of
     old songs was regularized by Martin Parker.

917. ————, ed., *Music in Renaissance Drama*. Lexington, Ky.:   Univ.
     of Kentucky Press, 1968. Rev. *RenQ*, 22 (1969), 177-179.

     Wide range of essays on use of music in English Renaissance
     drama, by Ernest Brennecke, Nan C. Carpenter, MacDonald Emslie,
     Willa M. Evans, R.W. Ingram, and Ian Spink. An integral part

of English dramaturgy from medieval mysteries through mid-17th cent., music had functional dramatic role, as in advancing the action or moving the audience. Useful bibliography by Vincent Duckles of primary and secondary sources for music of lyrics in English drama, 1603-1642.

918. Lowbury, Edward, Timothy Salter, and Alison Young, *Thomas Campion: Poet, Composer, Physician*. London: Chatto and Windus, 1970.

Rev. *TLS*, 16 October 1970, 1187.

Interaction in Campion's work between his poetry and his other skills as physician and musician.

919. Lowinsky, Edward E., "The Musical Avant-Garde of the Renaissance or: The Peril and Profit of Foresight," in Charles S. Singleton, ed., *Art, Science and History in the Renaissance* (Baltimore: Johns Hopkins Press, 1967), pp. 111-162.

Renaissance musicians' departure from medieval diatonic tradition and experiments with chromaticism, modulation, harmonies.

920. Mace, Dean T., "Marin Mersenne on Language and Music," *Jour. of Music Theory*, 14 (1970), 2-34.

Works of Mersenne in mid-17th cent. as telescoping and condensing process of music's triumph over poetry; anticipating justification of music as language of feeling, and conviction of music's importance.

921. ———, "Pietro Bembo and the Literary Origins of the Italian Madrigal," *Musical Q.*, 55 (1969), 65-86.

Italian madrigal in the 1530's related to a new aesthetic in poetry developed by Bembo in *Prose della Volgar Lingua*: "Formal" patterns created by rhyme and meter were ignored in favor of the "expressive" function of rhythm and sound.

922. Maniates, Maria Rika, "Musical Treatises in the Renaissance," *Ren. and Ref.* (Univ. of Toronto), 3 (1967), 2-10.

Musical treatises, 15th to 17th cents., in Music Library, Edward Johnson Bldg., Univ. of Toronto. Annotated (biographies; comments on works).

923. Michon, Jacques, *La musique anglaise*. Paris: Armand Colin, 1970.

Rev. *EC1*, 39 (1971), 110.

Includes section on Renaissance, particularly Elizabethan per-period.

924. Miller, Leslie Coombs, "Music and Poetry in Seventeenth Century France," *DA*, 30 (1970), 3950-A-3951-A (Univ. of Rochester).

Allusions to music and poetry in fiction and non-fiction of 17th-cent. France to demonstrate continued close alliance of the two.

925. Monterosso, Raffaello, ed., *Claudio Monteverdi e il suo tempo*.
Verona: Stamperia Valdonega, 1969.

Rev. *Notes*, 26 (1970), 747-748.

Thirty-five scholarly essays and other memorabilia from the
convention in Italy, commemorating fourth centenary of Monteverdi's birth.

926. Newcomb, Anthony Addison, "The *Musica Secreta* of Ferrara in the
1580's," *DA*, 31 (1970), 2424-A (Princeton Univ.).

Cultivation of secular music in the court of Ferrara, particularly with group of singing ladies in the Duke's *Musica Secreta*.
Analyzes material relating to musical practice within the madrigal concerts of 1580's.

927. Paratore, Ettore, "Plaute et la musique," *Maske u. Kothurn*, 15
(1969), 131-160.

World of music has large place in Plautus' theater. Supplements
Günther Wille, ch. 5 of *Musica Romana* (Amsterdam, 1967).

928. Powers, Harold, ed., *Studies in Music History: Essays in Honor
of Oliver Strunk*. Princeton Univ. Press, 1968.

Twenty-three essays divided into: I. Music History; II. Words
and Music in Christian Liturgy; III. Sources, Problems: Ars
Nova and Renaissance. Essays by Pierluigi Petrobelli, Nino
Pirrotta, Charles Hamm, Arthur Mendel, Lewis Lockwood, Edward
E. Lowinsky; IV. Italian Opera; V. Studies of the Great Com-
posers. Index. Rev. *Notes*, 26 (1969), 256.

929. Reese, Gustave, and Robert J. Snow, eds., *Essays in Musicology:
In Honor of Dragan Plamenac on His 70th Birthday*. Pittsburgh,
Pa.: Univ. of Pittsburgh Press, 1969.

Rev. *Choice*, 7 (1970), 238.

Twenty-five articles ranging from the 14th through the 20th
cents.

930. Robbins, Martin Lewis, "Shakespeare's Sweet Music: A Glossary
of Musical Terms in the Work of Shakespeare (with Additional
Examples from the Plays of Lyly, Marston, and Jonson)," *DA*,
30 (1969), 1534-1535-A (Brandeis Univ.).

Considers full scope of music of Shakespeare's period, examining
the actual music, the imagery of music, and particularly the
broader philosophical ideas that underlie and unify these.

931. Ross, Lawrence, "Shakespeare's 'Dull Clown' and Symbolic Music,"
Shakespeare Quarterly, 17, no. 2 (1966), 107-128.

Traditional sounds for irrationality and lust were portrayed by
wind instruments, especially the bagpipe. The music of the
heavens, symbolizing order and virtue, was indicated by stringed
instruments.

932. Ruff, Lillian M., and D. Arnold Wilson, "The Madrigal, the Lute
Song and Elizabethan Politics," *Past and Present*, no. 44 (1969),
3-51.

Relates writing of madrigals and lute songs to rise and fall of
Essex in Elizabeth's court. Most writers of these two forms
were pro-Essex--as he rose in favor (1587-1598), madrigals,
with their exuberant tone, were amply produced by William Byrd
and Thomas Morley. While Essex was imprisoned (1599-1601),
madrigals virtually vanished, while lute songs, meditatively
sad, flourished among lyric writers, especially John Dowland.
Between 1601 and accession of James (1603), government censorship suppressed both types.

933.   Sabol, Andrew J., "Recent Studies in Music and English Renais-
       sance Drama," *Shakespearean Research and Opportunities*, no. 4
       (1968/69), 1-15.

       Surveys recent contributions to relations of music and drama,
       1550-1650. Striking advances, especially since 1950, yet much
       research and criticism still to be done.

934.   Seng, Peter J., *The Vocal Songs in the Plays of Shakespeare: A
       Critical History*. Cambridge, Mass.: Harvard Univ. Press;
       Oxford Univ. Press, 1967.

       Rev. *M&L*, 49 (1968), 171-173; *RenQ*, 21 (1968), 359-361; *TLS*,
       14 December 1967, 1204.

       Useful reference work collects texts of 70 songs from earliest
       authoritative editions of 21 plays, discusses important textual
       variants from earlier and alternate editions, and provides a
       history of critical treatment of songs by editors since 1709.

935.   Shapiro, Michael, "Music and Song in Plays Acted by Children's
       Companies during the English Renaissance," *Current Musicology*,
       no. 7 (1968), 97-110.

       Plays acted by troupes of child actors between 1599 and 1612
       are richer in vocal and instrumental music than those of Shake-
       speare and performed by adult companies. Briefly outlines his-
       tory of children's troupes in England; covers complaints, pas-
       toral, supernatural and religious songs, and instrumental
       music.

936.   Shire, Helena Mennie, *Song, Dance and Poetry of the Court of
       Scotland under King James VI*. Cambridge Univ. Press, 1969.

       Rev. *Forum for Mod. Lang. Studs.*, 6 (1970), 314; *Music and
       Letters*, 51 (1970), 171.

       Complements the musical texts of the author's jointly edited
       Musica Britannica, vol. 15, *Music of Scotland, 1500-1700*.
       Treats aspects of the art song (sacred or secular music in
       several parts, for voice or instruments) at 16th-cent. Scottish
       court. Deals mainly with the period 1579-1590. Indexes, bib-
       liography, documentary appendixes, plates.

937.   Siemens, Reynold, "If Music and Sweet Poetry Agree: Thomas
       Ford's 'Since first I saw your face,'" *RenQ*, 21 (1968), 153-
       161.

       Ford, as both poet and composer, was aware of the subtle possi-
       bilities for enhancing verse through musical expression.

938. Smith, Alan, "Elizabethan Church Music at Ludlow," *M&L*, 49
      (1968), 108–121.

      During reign of Elizabeth, Ludlow, Welsh border castle, was
      residence of Lord President Sir Henry Sidney, father of Sir
      Philip Sidney, and brother-in-law of Earl of Leicester. Remark-
      ably full documentation of parish church of St. Laurence at Lud-
      low exists for latter half of 16th cent; records (now part of
      Ludlow deposit, Shropshire County Record Office, Shrewsbury)
      include: complete set of churchwardens' accounts, large number
      of corporation renters' accounts, corporation minute book, and
      document dated 1581 which exhibits the use of music in services.
      Records show that Ludlow musical establishment was like that of
      a cathedral; these also indicate payments to boy choristers,
      etc. Contents of church music manuscripts (MS. 3 dated ca.
      1597).

939. Stevens, Denis, "Rehearsals in the Renaissance and Baroque,"
      College Music Symposium, 9 (1969), 91–96.

      Glimpses of Renaissance rehearsals; evidence from documents,
      letters, treatises, and prefaces.

940. Waldo, Tommy Ruth, "Music and Musical Terms in Richard Edwards's
      'Damon and Pithias,'" *M&L*, 49 (1968), 29–35.

      Discusses character of the songs, which befit the serious,
      near-tragic theme of the play; stage directions for instrument-
      al music; figurative meaning of music references in the text.

941. Wangermée, Robert, *Flemish Music and Society in the Fifteenth
      and Sixteenth Centuries*, trans. Robert Erich Wolf. N.Y.:
      Praeger, 1968.

      Rev. *Choice*, 6 (1969), 520.

      On contrapuntal music that dominated Europe for nearly 200
      years, from a socio-artistic viewpoint as well as a musical one.
      Compendium of Renaissance musical phenomena, artistic and
      literary allusions to music, and ideas on music's relation to
      Renaissance life.

942. Ward, Tom Robert, "The Polyphonic Office Hymn from the Late
      Fourteenth Century Until the Early Sixteenth Century," *DA*, 30
      (1970), 3979–A (Univ. of Pitts.).

      Polyphonic office hymns in context of liturgy. Presents two
      traditions, Italian and Germanic; criteria for writing hymns.
      Appendix I is thematic index of almost 600 preserved hymns;
      II contains transcriptions of selected examples.

943. Warren, Charles W., "Music at Nonesuch," *Musical Quarterly*, 54
      (1968), 47–57.

      Nonesuch, Surrey country palace begun by Henry VIII (1538),
      was from 1558 to 1609 residence of Lord Lumley. Catalogue of
      Nonesuch library compiled in 1596 records largest Elizabethan
      private collection of books and manuscripts, with special sec-
      tion on music--probably largest library of music in private

Elizabethan house, and one of the largest collections of musical
instruments. Also the finest collection of paintings, as indicated in inventory of household goods made in 1596. A gathering
place for men of letters--Spenser must have been frequent guest
--Nonesuch was outpost of continental Renaissance.

944.   Weiss, Wolfgang, "Die Airs im Stilwandel," *Anglia*, 87 (1969),
       201-216.

       In English poetry of the late 16th and early 17th cent. the
       "ordo naturalis" (logical structure of the lyric statement) was
       superseded by the "ordo artificialis" (a reflection of the frame
       of mind of the speaker). The composers of the airs, however,
       preferred texts that had similar statements in all strophes.
       Includes discussion of the texts of Campion, Morley, Dowland,
       Ferrabosco, R. Jones.

945.   Winternitz, Emanuel, *Musical Instruments and Their Symbolism
       in Western Art*. London: Faber & Faber, 1967.

       Rev. *M&L*, 49 (1968), 155-159.

       Symbolism of musical instruments in Western art. Includes 15
       of his articles published 1942-1964, plus another written for
       the book. Detailed and useful for understanding allusions in
       Renaissance art, literature, and myth.

946.   Woodfill, Walter L., "Patronage and Music in England," in
       Archibald R. Lewis, ed., *Aspects of the Renaissance: A Sym-
       posium*. Austin, Texas: Univ. of Texas Press, 1967, pp. 59-68.

       Examines support that England gave Tudor and early Stuart music
       to suggest factors inhibiting great musical achievement during
       that period. Significant patronage was bound up with the royal
       government, while music held low place in English interests and
       values. Rev. *Choice*, 5 (1968), 390.

947.   Young, Irwin, tr. and ed., *The "Practica musicae" of Franchinus
       Gafurius*. Madison, Wisc.: Univ. of Wisc. Press, 1969.

       Rev. *Mus. Ed. J.*, 56 (1969), 97.

       The *Practica musicae* (Milan, 1496) of Gafurius, one of most emi-
       nent music theorists and composers of the Italian High Renais-
       sance, considered best single source for understanding intricate
       and often enigmatic structure of Renaissance music.

XII. PHILOSOPHICAL

948. Agrippa ab Nettesheym, Henricus Cornelius, *De Occulta Philosophia*, ed. Karl Anton Nowotny. Graz: Akademische Verlagsanstalt,
1967.

Facsimile of 1533 edition with extensive commentary, illustrations, and introduction; essays on historical context and related documents.

949. Alvarez-Gomez, Mariano, *Die verborgene Gegenwart des Unendli-
chen bei Nikolaus von Kues*. Munich: Pustet, 1968.

On symbolical apprehension of the world, the presence of the infinite in the symbol. Multitude and variety enfolded in the
complicatio omnium.

950. Angelelli, Ignacio, "The Techniques of Disputation in the History of Logic," *JP*, 67 (1970), 800-815.

Outlines some aspects of techniques of disputation: argument
method and question method. Medieval *ars obligatoria* related
to the question method, while argument method (not favored by
medieval logicians) is found in literary style of medieval
philosophers and theologians.

951. Anton, John P., ed., *Naturalism and Historical Understanding:
Essays on the Philosophy of John Herman Randall, Jr.* Albany,
N.Y.: State U. P., 1967. Rev. *Choice*, 5 (1968), 496.

Documented papers: e.g., Paul O. Kristeller, "John H. Randall,
Jr., and Renaissance Philosophy," criticizes his partiality to
the Paduan tradition, following Renan line, over-emphasizing
Renaissance Aristotelianism; Neal W. Gilbert, "Renaissance
Aristotelianism and its Fate: Some Observations and Problems,"
also criticizing Randall's Paduanism and the work of Henry
Busson which emphasized it; notes problem of Aristotle for 17th
cent., which rejected his philosophy of nature but retained his
metaphysics, influencing even Newton. (See also William F. Edwards, "Randall on the Development of Scientific Method in the
School of Padua--A Continuing Reappraisal.")

952. Armstrong, Arthur Hilary, ed., *The Cambridge History of Later
Greek and Early Mediaeval Philosophy*. Cambridge/N.Y.: Cambridge Univ. Press, 1967.

Rev. *CJ*, 64 (1968), 88-90; *Latomus*, 27 (1968), 482-483; *PhQ*,
18 (1968), 362-364; *Speculum*, 43 (1968), 686-687; *Thought*, 43
(1968), 630-632.

Composite work by various scholars, of use as background to
Renaissance thought. Contains sections on Greek philosophy
from Plato to Plotinus; Philo and beginnings of Christian
thought; later neoplatonists; Marius Victorinus and Augustine;
Greek Christian tradition to Eriugena; Western Christian thought
from Boethius to Anselm; bibliography and full indexes.

953. Ashworth, E.J., "The Doctrine of Supposition in the Sixteenth
      and Seventeenth Centuries," *Archiv für Geschichte der Philoso-
      phie*, 51 (1969), 260-285.

      Argues that the logic of terms, including supposition theory,
      was not ignored by logicians of 16th and 17th cents. What was
      said about the doctrine of supposition, together with allied
      doctrines, during those centuries.

954. Association Guillaume Budé. *Actes du VIIIe Congrès, 1968*.
      Paris: Société d'Edition "Les Belles Lettres," 1969 [1970].

      Useful discussion of ancient and Renaissance epicurism; in-
      cludes "Etat présent des recherches." Chapters on Greek and
      Latin epicurism, as well as French, and "L'Epicurisme au XVIe
      siècle." Studies by P. Joukovsky; S. Fraisse ("Montaigne et
      les doctrines épicuriennes," pp. 677-685); R. Popkin ("Epicur-
      isme et scepticisme au début du XVIIe siècle," pp. 698-707).

955. (Bacon, Francis, issue): *Studies in the Literary Imagination*,
      issue ed. William A. Sessions, 4 (1971).

      Includes essays by John M. Steadman, "Beyond Hercules: Bacon
      and the Scientist as Hero," pp. 3-47; M.B. McNamee, S.J.,
      "Bacon's Inductive Method and Humanistic Grammar," pp. 81-106;
      and Brian Vickers, "Bacon's Use of Theatrical Imagery," pp.
      189-226.

956. Beck, Lewis White, *Early German Philosophy: Kant and His Pre-
      decessors*. Cambridge, Mass.: Belknap Press of Harvard Univ.
      Press, 1969. Rev. *LJ*, 94 (1969), 3069.

      Part I: German philosophy before the Reformation (Albertus
      Magnus, Eckhart, Cusa, Nominalism), pp. 19-82; II. Luther to
      Leibniz (Luther, Calvin, Agrippa of Nettesheim, Paracelsus),
      pp. 85-240.

957. Beierwaltes, Werner, *Platonismus in der Philosophie des Mittel-
      alters*. (Wege der Forschung, Bd. 197). Darmstadt: Wissen-
      schaftliche Buchgesellschaft, 1969.

      Rev. *Deutsches Archiv für Erforschung des Mitt.*, 26 (1970).

      On the significant influence of Platonism between Augustine and
      Nicholas of Cusa, as well as on so-called Aristotelians such as
      Aquinas. Bibliographical notes; two indexes (*nominum*; *rerum*).

958. Bercovitch, Sacvan, "Empedocles in the English Renaissance,"
      SP, 65 (1968), 67-80.

      Evidence that English Renaissance writers knew Empedoclean
      theories of creation and evolution, of transmigration, flux, and
      cosmic strife. Suggests that Book IV of Spenser's *Faerie
      Queene*, Kyd's *Spanish Tragedy*, and perhaps *R&J* might fruitfully
      be examined for Empedoclean influences.

959. ————, "Love and Strife in Kyd's *Spanish Tragedy*," *SEL*, 9 (1969), 215-230.

Dialectic conflict between love and strife provides structural basis of Kyd's *Spanish Tragedy*. Underlying this structural movement, and lending it a distinctive substantive meaning, is the Empedoclean cosmology, as this was understood and applied in Renaissance English literature.

960. Berger, Harry, Jr., "Pico and Neoplatonist Idealism: Philosophy as Escape," *CentR*, 13 (1969), 38-83.

Developments in perspective and humanist attitudes toward art; limits of particular kind of neoplatonism associated with Florentine Academy.

961. Bonansea, Bernardino M., *Tommaso Campanella. Renaissance Pioneer of Modern Thought*. Washington, D.C.: Catholic Univ. of America Press, 1969. Rev. *LJ*, 95 (1970), 1484.

Emphasis on his theories of knowledge and metaphysics, and his moral and political doctrines.

962. Boon, Jean-Pierre, "Emendations des emprunts dans le texte des essais dits 'stoïciens' de Montaigne," *SP*, 65 (1968), 147-162.

Questions exaggeration of "bookish influences" on Montaigne's "stoic" essays, in favor of an unsuspected measure of originality.

963. Brush, Craig B., *Montaigne and Bayle: Variations on the Theme of Skepticism*. The Hague: Martinus Nijhoff, 1966.

Follows Donald Frame on Montaigne; treats skepticism as a liberating force. Regarding Bayle, opposes Elisabeth Labrousse on the extent to which it is proper to call the 17th-cent. philosopher a skeptic. Rev. *TLS*, 8 Dec. 1966, 1143.

964. Buncombe, Marie Helen, "Fulke Greville's *A Treatie of Humane Learning*: A Critical Analysis," *DA*, 27 (1966), 1026-A (Stanford Univ.).

On Greville's poem as reflecting major intellectual trends of English Renaissance: religious thought, metaphysics, epistemology, and philosophy of education.

965. Caminiti, Francis Norman, "Nicholas of Cusa: *Docta Ignorantia*, A Philosophy of Infinity," *DA*, 29 (1969), 2748-A (Fordham Univ.).

Critique of Cusa's *Docta Ignorantia*, which calls for us synthetically to transcend the either/or disjunctions of rational (finite) logic and to touch, through the *intellectus*, the incomprehensible *coincidentia* guaranteed by Christ.

966. Centre National de la Recherche Scientifique. Sciences Humaines. *Le Néoplatonisme*. Colloques internationaux, Royaumont, 1969. Paris: Editions du Centre National de la Recherche Scientifique, 1971.

Detailed and specialized papers on: I. La préparation du néoplatonisme; II. Plotin; III. Néoplatonisme grec; IV. Néoplatonisme arabe.; V. La tradition néoplatonicienne au moyen age et

dans les temps modernes. Includes Hans Blumenberg, "Neoplato-
nismen und Pseudoplatonismen in der Kosmologie und Mechanik der
Frühen Neuzeit," pp. 447-474.

967. Colish, Marcia L., *The Mirror of Language. A Study in the
       Medieval Theory of Knowledge*. New Haven, Conn.: Yale Univ.
       Press, 1968.

       Rev. *AHR*, 74 (1969), 1260; *Choice*, 6 (1969), 206; M.W. Bloom-
       field, *Spec*., 45 (1970), 119-122.

       Epistemological positions in theology of Augustine, Anselm,
       Aquinas, and Dante. How three parts of trivium of medieval
       schools (rhetoric, grammar, logic) and poetry shaped their
       theologies.

968. Collins, Ardis B., "The Doctrine of Being in the *Theologia
       Platonica* of Marsilio Ficino, With Special Reference to the
       Influence of Thomas Aquinas," *DA*, 29 (1969), 2299-2300-A (Univ.
       of Toronto).

       Ficinian doctrine of being in light of its Thomistic sources,
       limiting attention to Ficino's *Theologia Platonica* and Aquinas'
       Summa Contra Gentiles. Cf. Collins, "Love and Natural Desire
       in Ficino's *Platonic Theology*," *J. Hist. Phil*., 9 (1971), 435-
       442: immortality of the soul, intense desire for God.

969. Cranz, F. Edward, *A Bibliography of Aristotle Editions, 1501-
       1600. With an Introduction and Indices*. (Bibliotheca biblio-
       graphica Aureliana, 38.) Baden-Baden: V. Körner, 1971.

       Aristotle listings of the Index Aureliensis.

970. ———, "Reports on Scholarship in the Renaissance: Philosophy,"
       Ren. News, 19 (1966), 79-90.

       Survey of recent work and problems in the field.

971. Da Crema, Joseph J., "The Neoplatonic Element in John Lyly,"
       DA, 29 (1968), 1204-A (Temple Univ.).

       Lyly's knowledge of, or contact with, Ficino, Pico della Miran-
       dola, Benivieni, as avenue for Platonism and neoplatonism,
       Plotinus and Plato himself.

972. Darst, D.H., "Renaissance Platonism and the Spanish Pastoral
       Novel," *Hispania*, 52, no. 3 (1969), 384-392.

       Attempts to demonstrate that Spanish pastoral novelists tried
       to depict an atmosphere, character development, and theory of
       love which were Platonic in their sharp distinction between the
       sensible and the intelligible world.

973. De Gaetano, Armand L., "Gelli's Eclecticism on the Question of
       Immortality and the Italian Version of Porzio's *De humana
       mente*," *PQ*, 47 (1968), 532-546.

       Sixteenth-cent. Florentine academician, Giambattista Gelli, on
       classical views of immortality, and his own position as a re-
       sult of conflict between faith and reason. Translation of Por-
       zio's work, attributed to Gelli, very close to latter's view.

974. Del Torre, Maria Assunta, *Studi su Cesare Cremonini: Cosmologia e logica nel tardo aristotelismo padovano*. Padova: Antenore, Università di Padova, 1968.

Rev. *Jour. Hist. Phil.*, 9 (1971), 93–94.

Cosmology and logic of Cremonini (1551–1631), professor of Aristotelian philosophy at Padua; at end of tradition of commentators (Alexander of Aphrodisias, Pomponazzi, Zabarella) interpreting Aristotle's physics and psychology naturalistically. Cremonini opposed Aristotelian views, as interpreted by him, as contrary to Christian faith; e.g., human soul is corporeal as informing the body; heavens move by their own nature or soul; God is merely final, not efficient or providential cause of motion. Author rejects views of Cassirer and Randall concerning Cremonini's anticipation of, or influence on, Galileo.

975. Desharnais, R.P., "Scholasticism, Nominalism, and Martin Luther," in *Studies in Philosophy and the History of Philosophy*, vol. 4, ed. John K. Ryan. Washington, D.C.: Catholic Univ. of America, 1969, pp. 207–228.

Various types of "nominalisms" according to scholastics and influence on Luther.

976. Dethier, H., "De 'idolen van de markt en van het theater' in het werk van P. Pomponazzi," *Dialoog*, 9 (1968–69), 1–46.

Uses Foucault's *Les Mot et les Choses* (1966); discusses humanism; Bacon's idols in Pomponazzi.

977. Domandl, Sepp, "Eschatologie und Ideologie bei Paracelsus," *ZPF*, 24 (1970), 126–133.

Paracelsus believed in a non-Christian end of the world which would occur when all human combinations and variations would be completed and no more birth possible.

978. Domański, J., "Glosy do Erazmiańskiej koncepcji filozofii" [A Commentary on Erasmus' Concept of Philosophy], *Archiwum Historii Filozofii i Myśli Społecznej*, 15 (1969), 5–45.

Examines Erasmus's use of term "philosophia" in prefaces to New Testament (1516). Points out that Erasmus never cased to challenge scientific and professional interpretations of philosophy. Rather than being understood as theoretical knowledge, philosophy is identified with ethics since man's life consists in rationalizing his actions.

979. ———, "Scholastyka, Teologia, i Erazmianizm," *Studia Mediewistyczne*, 12 (1970), 167–186.

On several publications concerning the scholastic and theological aspects of Erasmian philosophy, in honor of the 500th anniversary of Erasmus' birth.

980. Doyle, John P., "Suárez on the Analogy of Being, part I," *Modern Schoolman*, 46 (1968/69), 219–249; part II, 46 (1968/69), 323–341.

Suárez's doctrine in passages which refer to analogy of being.

981. ————, "Suárez on the Reality of the Possibles," *Modern Schoolman*, 45 (1967-68), 29-48.

On the doctrine of Being of Suárez (1548-1617). In contrast to other writers on him, Doyle holds that the being which is known and the being it has when known are both prior to God in Suárez's metaphysics. Thus Suárez in this doctrine is more heretical than previously believed.

982. Edwards, Paul, ed., *The Encyclopedia of Philosophy*. 8 vols.; N.Y.: Macmillan Co. and Free Press; London: Collier-Macmillan Ltd., 1967.

Rev. *JHI*, 29 (1968), 616-622; *Mind*, 77 (1968), 602-605; *Theologie und Philosophie*, 43 (1968), 403-406.

First such encyclopedia in English since J.M. Baldwin, ed., *Dictionary of Psychology and Philosophy* (1901). Useful reference work for Renaissance thought. Bibliographies, index, and cross-references.

983. Foucault, Michel, *Les Mots et les Choses: une Archéologie des Sciences Humaines*. Paris: Gallimard, 1966.

Renaissance transformation, especially in chapter III, Représentation, including *Don Quixote*; and VI, Echanger.

984. Garin, Eugenio, *Storia della Filosofia Italiana*. Turin: Einaudi, 1966. 3 vols.

Volumes 1-2: detailed survey of Renaissance philosophy, with bibliographies.

985. Gawlick, Günter, "Die Funktion des Skeptizismus in der frühen Neuzeit," *Archiv für Geschichte der Philosophie*, 49 (1967), 86-97.

Rev. article on R.H. Popkin, *The History of Skepticism from Erasmus to Descartes* (Assen: Van Gorcum, 1960). Useful examination of skepticism via analysis of Popkin's fundamental book.

986. Genz, Henry E., "Montaigne's Concept of 'Non-identity' as a Basis for the Self-Portrait," *Esprit Créateur*, 8 (1968), 194-197.

Form of self-portrait in Montaigne stems from his philosophical concern with "non-identity," i.e., change, movement, instability, variety, and diversity.

987. Gierczyński, Zbigniew, "Le fidéisme apparent de Montaigne et les artifices des 'Essais,'" *Kwart. Neofil.*, 16 (1969), 137-163.

Apparent fideism of Montaigne's "L'Apologie" is camouflage for his attack against all religious beliefs.

988. ————, "Le scepticisme de Montaigne, principe de l'équilibre de l'esprit," *Kwart. Neofil.*, 14 (1967), 111-131.

Despite Montaigne's apparent intellectual mobility, his thought is at bottom permanently skeptical.

989. Give, Michel de, "La pensée philosophique de la Renaissance et de la Réforme," *Revue Philosophique de Louvain*, 65 (1967), 108-114.

Rev. article on M.F. Siacca, ed., *Grande antologia filosofica*, III: *Il pensiero della Rinascenza e della Riforma*. Vols. 6-11. Milan: Marzorati, 1964.

990. Goldsetzer, Lutz, *Philosophengalerie* I: *Bildnisse und Bibliographien von Philosophen aus dem 11. bis 17. Jahrhundert*. Düsseldorf: Philosophia Verlag, 1967.

In volume almost entirely devoted to them, Renaissance philosophers are presented individually, with portraits, brief accounts of their philosophy, lists of their writings, editions, and secondary bibliographies.

991. Grau, Kurt Joachim, *Die Entwicklung des Bewusstseinsbegriffs im 17 und 18 Jht*. Abhandlungen zur Philosophie und ihrer Geschichte, ed. Benno Erdmann, 39; Hildesheim: Olms, 1968.

Useful Halle, 1916, work involving Renaissance epistemology.

992. Grundy, Dominick Edwin, "Sceptical Consistency: Scepticism in Literary Texts of Montaigne, Sir Thomas Browne and Alain Robbe-Grillet," *DA*, 28 (1968), 5015-5016-A (Univ. of Mich.).

Compares Montaigne's third book of the *Essais* to Sextus Empiricus' *Outlines of Pyrrhonism*. Knowing only the moving world of appearances, the skeptic rejects all forms of transcendence into higher realms of intellectual definition and order. Montaigne's *De la Vanité* is unified by a skeptical notion of order which provides an image of the coherence of the literary work, though paradoxically its topic is vanity or inconsistency. Relates skepticism to imaginative structure which is open, fluid, contradictory, and relative, thereby linked to change, self-modification, and subjectivity.

993. Gutsell, James Burnell, "Irony in the Fallen World of George Chapman: A Study of Irony in Chapman's Poems, Comedies, and Tragedies," *DA*, 29 (1969), 2674-A (Univ. of Conn.).

Ambiguities of Neoplatonic mythology offer an ironic perspective. Irony is also present in the Stoic certainty that the wheel of fortune eventually works against ambitious and successful men of the world.

994. Hallie, Philip P., *The Scar of Montaigne: An Essay in Personal Philosophy*. Middletown, Conn.: Wesleyan Univ. Press, 1966.

Montaigne's as a special way of "doing" philosophy, a personal mode, like that of some modern analytical philosophers, involved with language. Rev. *Lib. J.*, 91 (1966), 3956.

995. Harig, G., "From the Critique of Scholasticism to the Critique of Antiquity," *Organon* (Poland), 4 (1967), 19-26.

From Renaissance to beginning of 18th cent. Antipathy to ancient predecessors in Copernicus, Brahe, Galileo. 17th cent. "Querelle des anciens et des modernes."

996.   Hornik H., "Rabelais and Idealism," *Studi Francesi*, 13 (1969), 16-25.

        Schematizes the Rabelaisian pilgrim's progress: first stage--
        Gargantua and *Pantagruel* as intuitive level, based on tradi-
        tional sources; second stage--*Tiers* and *Quart Livres* as the
        rational stage with critical reason; third stage--*Cinquième
        Livre* as the transcendent level which culminates in Platonic
        symbolism.

997.   Horowitz, M.C., "Pierre Charron's View of the Source of Wis-
        dom," *J. of Hist. of Phil.*, 9 (1971), 443-457.

        Moral philosophy's truths contained in natural law, which
        Charron accepts on faith. Stoic influences. Virtue and know-
        ledge as source of wisdom.

998.   Horský, Z., "Le Rôle du Platonisme dans l'origine de la Cos-
        mologie Moderne," *Organon* (Poland), 4 (1967), 47-54.

        Renaissance Platonism in relation to science, especially the
        cosmology of Kepler and Galileo.

999.   Ingegno, A., "Il primo Bruno e l'influenza di Marsilio Ficino,"
        Riv. crit. St. Filos, 23 (1968), 149-170.

        Noe-Platonic influence in the first works of Giordano Bruno,
        through personal thought of Marsilio Ficino and his activity
        in rediscovery of an "art" capable of guaranteeing man perfect
        possession and complete use of his faculties.

1000.   Jacobus, Lee A., "The Problem of Knowledge in *Paradise Lost*,"
        DA, 29 (1969), 2676-A (Claremont Graduate School).

        Background of classical, medieval, and Renaissance epistemolo-
        gies; problem of self-knowledge; knowledge of the physical uni-
        verse; discussion of logic; knowledge of God and ways of know-
        ing Him.

1001.   Jayne, Sears R., "Some Tools for Research in the Intellectual
        History of the English Renaissance," *Shakespearean Research
        and Opportunities*, nos. 5-6 (1970/71), 8-29.

        Useful material on Renaissance platonism; valuable classifica-
        tion of platonic work. Important for subject indexes, cata-
        logues, etc.

1002.   Johnson, Leonard W., "Literary Neo-platonism in Five French
        Treatises of the Early Seventeenth Century," *Rom Rev.*, 60
        (1969), 233-250.

        Rivault's *L'Art d'embellir*; Veyries' *La Geneologie de l'Amour*;
        Anon., *Les Triomphes d'Angelique*; Humière's *La Philosophie
        d'Amour*, and Juliard's *Les Amours de l'Amant Conventy*.

1003.   Joukovsky, F., "Quelques sources épicuriennes au XVIe siècle,"
        BHR, 31 (1969), 7-25.

        Reviews editions and commentaries on prose works which deal
        with epicurism. French Humanism after 1560 may owe more to
        thought of Epicurus than these commentators have been aware.

1004. King, Walter N., "Shakespeare and Parmenides," *SEL*, 8 (1968), 283-306.

Antithesis of appearance and reality in Feste, *TN*; implied criticism of Parmenides' ontological postulates in his poem "Nature," which holds that the difference between "what is" and "what is not" is irreconcilable. Neither logic nor sense perception leads to reliable conclusions about seeming and being, but may help illuminate them.

1005. Kolakowski, L., "Filozoficzna Rola Reformacji" [The Philosophical Role of the Reformation], *Archiwum Historii Filozofii i Myśli Spoŀecznej*, 15 (1969), 159-176.

Interprets Luther's initiative as an evocation of Augustine's dictum: "Deum et animam scire cupio." Man's act of severing all ties represents his opposition to the rest of nature; this leads in two directions—to mystical and existential extremes, the latter of which establishes philosophy of the subjective self.

1006. Korzan, I., "Praski krąg humanistów wokóŀ Giordana Bruna" [The Prague Circle of Humanists Around Giordano Bruno], *Euhemer*, 13 no. 1-2 (1969), 81-93.

Excerpts from larger work; describes reception of Bruno and his philosophy at the conservative Prague Royal Court during a six-month stay in 1588.

1007. Koskimies, Rafael, "The Question of Platonism in Shakespeare's Sonnets," *Neoph. Mitt.*, 71 (1970), 260-270.

Shakespeare's dependence on platonic thought.

1008. Kretzmann, Norman, "Medieval Logicians on the Meaning of the *Propositio*," *JP*, 67 (1970), 767-787.

Propositio as written, spoken, or mental propositional sign; medieval logicians produced theory of reference and theory of sense for propositions—*terminism* and *dictism*.

1009. Kristeller, Paul Oskar, "Erasmus from an Italian Perspective," *RenQ*, 23 (1970), 1-14.

Underscores influence of Italian humanism on Erasmus; Platonism in *Enchiridion* and *Praise of Folly* derived from Florentine Platonism.

1010. ———, *Renaissance Philosophy and the Mediaeval Tradition*. (Wimmer Lecture 15.) Latrobe, Pa.: Archabbey Press, 1966. Rev. *AHR*, 74 (1968), 575-576.

Supplements author's *Renaissance Thought: The Classic, Scholastic, and Humanistic Strains* (1961). Development of knowledge in many fields from medieval times to Renaissance.

1011. ———, *Le Thomisme et la pensée italienne de la Renaissance*. Conférence Albert-le-Grand, 1965; Montreal: Institut d'Etudes Médiévales; Paris: J. Vrin, 1967.

Rev. *BHR*, 30 (1968), 629-630; *JP*, 65 (1968), 490-494; *RenQ*, 21 (1968), 308-310; *RFNS*, 59 (1968), 77-79.

Role of Thomism in intellectual history of the Italian Renaissance; some of the disputes between Renaissance humanists and Thomists still of interest.

1012.   LaGuardia, Eric, *Nature Redeemed: Imitation of Order in Three Renaissance Poets*. London, Hague, Paris: Mouton, 1966.

I. Nature and Spirit. A. Double Law of Nature; B. The Potential of Man; C. Venus and Diana. II. The Imitation of Nature. III. Spenser. IV. *Comus*. V. *All's Well*. Shift from transcendent order to order of nature. Rev. *MLR*, 63 (1968), 676.

1013.   Lange, Ursula, *Untersuchungen zu Bodins Demonomanie*. Frankfurt a.M.: Vittorio Klostermann, 1970.

Rev. *Archiv für das Studium der neueren Sprachen*, 208, no. 1 (1970), 70-71.

Attempts to place this Bodin work in context of his time and his other works. Does not see it as contradictory to his other writings; notes differences between his theories and those of the Neo-Platonists, especially G. Pico della Mirandola.

1014.   Levi, A.H.T., "The Neoplatonist Calculus: The Exploitation of Neoplatonist Themes in French Renaissance Literature," *Humanism in France* ..., ed. A.H.T. Levi. Manchester and N.Y.: Barnes & Noble, 1970, pp. 229-248.

Neoplatonism in French Renaissance: Neoplatonism, evangelical humanism, and emotional love; epistemology, education, and poetic activity.

1015.   Lewis, Clive Staples, *The Discarded Image: An Introduction to Medieval and Renaissance Literature*. Cambridge Univ. Press, 1968.

Rev. *Med. Aev.*, (1968), 1-95; *Tablet* (6 April 1968), 34; *Thought* (1968), 291.

Study of model of the universe discernible in medieval and Renaissance literature.

1016.   Lockwood, William Jeremiah, "The Thoughts and Lyrics of Sir Walter Ralegh," *DA*, 30 (1970), 5414-A (Univ. of Penn.).

Investigation of the lyrical poetry of Ralegh and relationship to his Neo-Platonic leanings.

1017.   Lohmann, J., "Uber die stoische Sprach-philosophie," *Stud. gen.*, 21 (1968), 250-257.

Study emphasizing the central position of the concept of *dicibile*.

1018.   Lohr, Charles H., S.J., "Aristotle in the West," *Traditio*, 25 (1969), 417-431.

Review essay on recent books on Aristotle.

1019. ────, "Medieval Latin Aristotle Commentaries, Authors: Jacobus-Johannes Juff," *Traditio*, 26 (1970), 135-216.

Continues inventory of Aristotle commentaries published in *Traditio*, 23 (1967), 313-413, and 24 (1968), 149-245. This portion contains those of Johannes Canonicus, Johannes Humbleton, Johannes Duns Scotus, and Johannes de Jandun. Brief biobibliographic notes, plus indication of manuscripts and editions.

1020. Lonigan, Paul R., "Montaigne and the Presocratics in the 'Apologie de Raymond Sebond,'" *SFr*, 11 (1967), 24-30.

Notes on pre-Socratic sources of the essay.

1021. Markowski, M., "Problematyka Universaliów w Polskich Piętnastowiecznych Pismach Nominalistycznych" [Problems Concerning Universals in 15th-Cent. ... Nominalist Writings], *Studia Mediewistyczne*, 12 (1970), 73-166.

Aristotle; Buridan. Cf. Falstaff, *1H4*, V.i.131-135.

1022. Masters, G. Mallary, *Rabelaisian Dialectic and the Platonic-Hermetic Tradition*. Albany: State Univ. of N.Y., 1969.

Rev. *FS*, 25 (1971), 68-69.

Traces Platonic and Hermetic sources and usages in Rabelais' work.

1023. Matsen, Herbert Stanley, "Alessandro Achillini (1463-1512) and His Doctrine of 'Universals' and 'Transcendentals,'" *DA*, 31 (1970), 1323-A (Columbia Univ.).

Achillini's importance, not as a seminal thinker, but as an interpreter and transmitter of Aristotelian thought, between 1300 and 1600.

1024. Maxwell, J.C., "Brutus's Philosophy," *NQ*, 215 (1970), 128.

Regarding lines in *JC* (V., i. 101-108), opposes view that the "philosophy" by which Brutus blames Cato for his suicide is Stoicism. No philosophy was more favorably disposed to suicide. Correct reference is Plato.

1025. McCully, George Elliott, Jr., "Juan Luis Vives (1493-1540) and the Problem of Evil in His Time," *DA*, 28 (1967), 1768-A (Columbia Univ.).

Stresses two major hitherto unexplored influences on Vives; Roman Stoicism, via Cicero, Seneca, Epictetus, and Augustine; and Inquisitorial persecution of his Jewish parents, increasing his anguish over general corruptions of power. Difficulty of the Stoic position, that man is part of nature, yet in disagreement with it, modified by Vives' Christian notion of personal God who created nature, and idea of the Fall of Man. Evils seen as discords to be cured by return of concord.

1026. McFarland, Thomas, *Tragic Meanings in Shakespeare*. N.Y.:
       Random House, 1966, 1968.

       Philosophical analyses of *Hamlet*, *Othello*, *Antony and Cleo-
       patra*, *King Lear*; introduction on the meaning of tragedy.
       Existential, Heideggerian readings point as well to some
       Renaissance concerns.

1027. McLaughlin, Elizabeth, "*The Extasie*: Deceptive or Authentic?"
       Bu R, 18 (1970), 55–78.

       Resolution of poem's apparent clashes: views it as a case for
       "Sartrean self-deception." Relevance of Plotinus' philosophy.

1028. Michaud-Quantin, Pierre, *Études sur le Vocabulaire Philoso-
       phique du Moyen Age*. (Lessico Intellectuale Europeo 5.) Rome:
       Ateneo, 1970.

       Rev. *Spec.*, 47 (1972), 784–786.

       Useful essays on medieval and Renaissance philosophical and
       theological terms; e.g., *aestimare* et *aestimatio*; *condicio-
       conditio*; *logica* et *dialectica*; *ordo* et *ordines*; *species*;
       ratio, etc. Evolution of the notion of chance, *casus, fortuna*.

1029. Miethke, Jürgen, *Ockhams Weg zur Sozialphilosophie*. Berlin:
       de Gruyter, 1969.

       Rev. *EHR*, 85 (1970), 792–794.

       An Ockham encyclopedia, with full bibliography. Comprehen-
       sive evaluation of what has been written on Ockham and his
       political, religious, and academic contexts.

1030. Miner, Earl, "Patterns of Stoicism in Thought and Prose Styles,
       1550–1700," *PMLA*, 85 (1970), 1023–1034. (Cf. 2558.)

       See discussion of this article in *PMLA*, 86 (1971), 1028–1030.

1031. Moore, Thomas V., "Donne's Use of Uncertainty as a Vital Force
       in *Satyre III*," *MP*, 67 (1969), 41–49.

       Man cannot depend on anything as a *sure* means of finding Truth.
       The satire directed against mistaken confidence of those who
       believe that there is only one sure way to Truth.

1032. Muñoz Delgado, V., "La lógica en la Universidad de Alcalá
       durante la primera mitad del siglo XVI," *Salmanticensis*, 15,
       no. 1 (1968), 162–218.

       Place of logic in the "arts." *The Summulae*: professors, man-
       uals, treatises. *The Oppositiones*: works of great masters.
       Synthesis.

1033. Myers, J.P., "'This Curious Frame': Chapman's 'Ovid's Banquet
       of Sense,'" *SP*, 65, no. 2 (1968), 192–206.

       Relation between carnal love and divine love, according to
       Renaissance conceptions. Poem illustrates syncretism of Re-
       naissance. Beauty as reflection of the soul.

1034. Napoli, Giovanni di, "La *Metafisica* di Tommaso Campanella,"
Archivio di Filosofia, 13 (1969), 19-35.

Campanella thought his *Metafisica* defended freedom of thinker
while at the same time resolving difficulties of the schools.
It is not anti-Thomistic, but seeks to disassociate Thomas
from Aristotle, who seemed dangerous to Campanella in the form
in which the Renaissance Aristotelians used him.

1035./ Nash, Ronald H., *The Light of the Mind: St. Augustine's*
1036. *Theory of Knowledge*. Lexington, Ky.: Univ. Press of Kentucky,
1969.

Rev. *J. Hist. Phil.*, 9 (1971), 89-90.

Study of Augustine's epistemological theories and central
ideas such as skepticism, truth, faith, and divine light, with
a critique of the Augustinian studies of Gilson and Copleston.
Book is divided into: Chap. 1, The Structure of St. Augustine's Theory of Knowledge; Chap. 2, On Skepticism and Truth;
Chap. 3, The Role of Faith; Chap. 4, Sensation; Chap. 5, Cogi-
tation; Chap. 6, Intellection, Man's Knowledge of the Forms;
Chap. 7, Intellection, Three Interpretations of Illumination;
Chap. 8, Intellection, the Problem of Ontologism. Bibliographical note, and notes.

1037. Noreña, Carlos Garcia, "Juan Luis Vives: A Humanistic Conception of Philosophical Knowledge," *DA*, 28 (1967), 1472-1473-A
(Univ. of Calif., San Diego).

Vives' intellectual biography, including his English career,
connections with Thomas More's circle, Oxford reform. Second
part deals with Vives' theory of knowledge. His theocentric
view of man rejects Averroistic fideism, rationalism, and the
theology of Aristotle. Condemns speculative curiosity and
knowledge as end in itself rather than as God-given instrument
for man's ethical perfection. Sees human knowledge as basically, but limitedly, reliable, and philosophical knowledge not
as (Aristotelian) theoretical contemplation of truth, but as
(more Stoic) prudent choice of morally responsible man.

1038. ———, "Was Juan Luis Vives a Disciple of Erasmus?" *Jour.
Hist. Phil.*, 7 (1969), 263-272.

On Erasmian influence upon Vives and originality of Vives'
thought. Vives' emphasis on a pragmatic observation of nature
led to Telesius and Bacon. His moderate skepticism and prob-
abilistic conception of metaphysics echoed in work of Montaigne. His naturalism was brought to its logical conclusions
by Grotius and Herbert of Cherbury. Nizolius and Ramus learned
from Vives the rhetorical and pedagogical dimensions of Agricola's logic. Roger Ascham, Sturm, and Comenius kept alive
Vives' emphasis on education.

1039. Nowicki, A., "Alchemiczna treść mitow a filozoficzna antropo-
logia Giordana Bruna" [The Alchemystical Content of Myths and

the Philosophical Anthropology of Giordano Bruno], *Euhemer*, 13 no. 3 (1969), 57–67.

Explains sources of Bruno's theory that myths are empty forms which can be filled with philosophical content.

1040. ————, "Bruno w Polsce," *Euhemer*, 13, no. 1–2 (1969), 95–103.

Indicates that the bibliography of Giordano Bruno by V. Salvestrini is not exhaustive. A group of Polish intellectuals who had met Bruno at Oxford (1583) stimulated a great interest among Polish writers (especially Keckermann and Hevelius) to do a large amount of writing between 1599–1668 which has not been included in Bruno's bibliography.

1041. ————, "Giovanni Imperiale (1596–1670), jego 'Muzea i Noce'" [Giovanni Imperiale, His *Musaeum Historicum* and *Physicum, Notti Beriche*], *Archiwum Historii Filozofii i Myśli Społecznej*, 15 (1969), 145–158.

On seldom-studied work of this student of Cremonini, containing philosophically interesting views on man; e.g., Imperiale's fascination with the variety of human intellects, his attempt to classify them on objective grounds, and his broad-minded evaluation of social functions of religion.

1042. ————, "Problem obecności Bernadina Telesia (1508–1588) w kulturze" [The Relevance of Bernadino Telesio's Ideas], *Acta Universitatis Wratislaviensis*, no. 120, *Prace Filozoficzne*, 6 (1970), 37–61.

Discusses anti-Aristotelian metaphysical and physical aspects of Telesio's philosophy, but concludes that the most valuable contribution to modern thought is in Telesio's ideas on man's culture.

1043. Pachet, P., "Précurseurs stoiciens," *Critique*, 24 (1968), 417–422.

Critical review of: 1) B. Mates, *Stoic Logic* (Berkeley and Los Angeles, Univ. of Calif. Press, 1961); 2) V. Goldschmidt, *Le système stoicien et l'idée de temps* (Paris: Vrin, 1953). Discusses Stoic logic and the concepts of "meaning" and "sense."

1044. Partee, Morriss Henry, "Plato and the Elizabethan Defense of Poetry," *DA*, 27 (1967), 459-A – 460-A (Univ. of Texas, 1966). (See 762–3.)

Examines justification that Elizabethan critics were Platonists rather than Neoplatonists or Christian Platonists. Few Elizabethans had direct knowledge of Plato, and Sidney was the only critic who really seemed to understand Plato's thought.

1045. ————, "Sir Thomas Elyot on Plato's Aesthetics," *Viator*, 1 (1970), 327–335.

Elyot's contradictory citation of Plato on poetry and its effects.

1046. Papuli, Giovanni, *Girolamo Balduino: ricerche sulla logica della Scuola di Padova nel Rinascimento*. Manduria: Lacaita Editore, 1967.

Chapters include La natura della logica: La *logica vetus* e il rinnovamento dell'*Organon*; *Logica docens* e *logica utens*.

L'oggetto e la funzione della logica: I *secundo intellecta* e
i presupposti psicologici; Logica e metafisica; le *Categoriae*.
Documentation on materials and history of Renaissance logic.

1047.   Patterson, Annabel M., "Tasso and Neoplatonism: The Growth of
Epic Theory," *SRen*, 18 (1971), 105-133.

Aims to continue rehabilitation of Tasso's neoplatonism; poet
read widely in diverse kinds of neoplatonic work.

1048.   Paterson, Antoinette Mann, *The Infinite Worlds of Giordano Bruno*.
Springfield, Ill.: Thomas, 1970. Rev. *Rev. of Met.*, 24 (1970), 343.

Ethical and epistemological views of Bruno.   Shows how the two
are related and how both develop from his cosmology.

1049.   Pico della Mirandola, Giovanni, *De Dignitate Hominis*. *Latei-
nish und Deutsch*. Introduction, Eugenio Garin. (Respublica
literaria, ed. Joachim Dyck and Gunther List, Bd. 1.) Berlin,
Zurich: Verlag Gehlen, 1968.

Includes Garin's translated 17-page introduction of the
Oratio.

1050.   ————, *Gian Fr. Pico, Opera Omnia*. Hildesheim: Olms, 1969.

Reprint of the publication of Basel, 1557-1573.   Edited, with
foreword by C. Vasoli, Florence.

1051.   Piltch, Charles Neil, "Inspiration and the Claim to Knowledge
in Seventeenth-Century English Poetry," *DA*, 29 (1969), 2722-A
(City Univ. of N.Y.).

Argues that Renaissance verse receives its impetus from an
exalted conception of poetry. This conception allows poet to
claim special knowledge that transcends the limitations of the
human senses and reason and is accessible to him only because
he is inspired by a superior being. With this authority and
sanction his work demands greater respect than that due philosophy or history.

1052.   Pine, Martin, "Pomponazzi and the Problem of 'Double Truth,'"
JHI, 29 (1968), 163-176.

Philosophy was for the initiate, according to Pomponazzi; religion, fables for the masses. His professions of faith were
intended to placate the vigilant church. Doubts Pomponazzi
held belief that two contradictory notions could be legiti-
mately affirmed as long as they pertained to two separate
realms of truth.

1053.   Pouilloux, Jean-Yves, *Lire les "Essais" de Montaigne*. Paris:
Maspero, 1970.

Rev. *TLS*, 7 July 1970, 503.

Critical reading of "Essais" sees disorder as their object;
emphasis on multi-level design in Montaigne.

1054.   ————, "Problèmes de traduction: L. Le Roy et le Xe Livre de
         la *République*," *BHR*, 31 (1969), 47-66.

         Study of Le Roy's translation of Book X of Plato's *Republic*
         and translator's role in spreading Platonic ideas.

1055.   Presson, Robert K., "Wrestling with This World: A View of
         George Chapman," *PMLA*, 84 (1969), 44-50.

         Chapman's choice of material as dictated by his experiences.
         Typically, a good man confronts a corrupt and hostile world.
         Chapman's consolation in Neo-Platonism, Stoicism, and tradi-
         tional Christianity.

1056.   Primack, Maxwell, "Outline of a Reinterpretation of Francis
         Bacon's Philosophy," *Jour. of the Hist. of Phil.*, 5 (1967),
         123-132.

         Aims to correct two mistakes concerning philosophy of Bacon:
         idea that he was not concerned with metaphysical issues, and
         that he can be understood as a precursor of mechanism. Bacon's
         conception of matter was transitional between 16th-cent. ani-
         mism and 17th-cent. mechanism.

1057.   Poppi, A., "Pietro Pompanazzi tra averroismo e galenismo sul
         problema del 'regressus,'" *Riv. Crit. di Storia d. Filos.*, 24
         (1969), 243-266.

         On value of regressive demonstration: from effect to cause,
         then from cause to effect. Opposition to Nicoletto Vernia and
         A. Nifo.

1058.   Reilly, James P., "Ockham Bibliography: 1950-1967," *Francis.
         Stud.* (U.S.A.), 28 (1969), 197-214.

         Complements 1950 bibliography by V. Heynck, "Ockham-Literatur
         1919-1949," *Franzisk. Stud.*, 32 (1950), 164-183.

1059.   Reitman, Renee Leah, "Pierre Charron: The Crisis in Morality
         and Thought at the End of the Sixteenth Century in France,"
         DA, 30 (1970), 3890-A (Univ. of Mich.).

         Charron's *De la sagesse* arose from need for end to chaos after
         religious wars of 1562-1598. Man's major quest seen as that
         for tranquility and peace of mind; Charron derived a reform
         program essentially from ancient stoical teachings.

1060.   Riesco, J., "Führt die Philosophie Senecas zur göttlichen
         Transzendenz?" *Franzisk. Stud.*, 49, no. 1-2 (1967), 80-109.

         Notion of God in Seneca and foundations of his morality (pro-
         vidence; the nature of evil, freedom, death; destiny of the
         soul) reveal an orientation toward a personal and transcendent
         God, which is an advance over Stoicism.

1061.   Risse, Wilhelm, *Logik der Neuzeit, t.1: 1500-1640*. Stuttgart:
         Frommann-Holzboog, 1970.

         Examines principal directions of 16th- and 17th-cent. logic--
         Ciceronian, Aristotelian, Ramistic; influence of religion on
         contemporary logic. Major study.

1062. Rist, J.M., *Stoic Philosophy*. Cambridge Univ. Press, 1969.

Rev. *J. of the Hist. of Phil.*, 9 (1971), 81-86.

Regards Stoic philosophy in its beginnings as an effort to work out problems generated by Aristotle. Finds differences in views of Chrysippus and Posidonius about the human soul indicative of broader distinctions on their philosophies. Chapters on influence of Cynicism on Stoicism and middle and late cents. in the history of the Stoa; on problems of knowing and willing, suicide, the person, and time, dealing with Seneca, Epictetus, Marcus Aurelius.

1063. Rossi, Paolo, *Francis Bacon: From Magic to Science*. London: Routledge and Kegan Paul; Chicago: Univ. of Chicago Press, 1968. (Translation of work first published in 1957 by Editori Laterza, Bari, Italy.)

Rev. *AHR*, 74 (1968), 979-980; *Cambridge Rev.*, 89 (1968), 428-429; *History*, 53 (1968), 426-427.

Sets Bacon in context of Renaissance ideas and concern for rhetoric, alchemy, and magic; Bacon as reformer, not destroyer, of ancient philosophy. Seen as Renaissance philosopher rather than as precursor of Newton, etc.

1064. ————, *Philosophy, Technology and the Arts in the Early Modern Era*. N.Y.: Harper and Row, 1970.

Rev. *Tech. and Cult.*, 12 (1971), 344-345.

Essays translated from Italian on Francis Bacon, emphasizing influence of Prometheus myth on Bacon, Bacon's idea of inseparability of truth and utility, influence of Bacon on subsequent philosophy of science.

1065. Sakharoff, Micheline, "Montchrestien. Le stoïcisme ou la liberté negative. Une demi-efficacité," *Rev. des Sc. humaines*, fasc. 130 (1968), 161-167.

Contrasts view of man in Montchrestien's tragedies with that found in Garnier's.

1066. Sanders, Wilbur, *The Dramatist and the Received Idea: Studies in the Plays of Marlowe and Shakespeare*. Cambridge, Eng.: Cambridge Univ. Press, 1968.

Rev. *MLQ*, 29 (1968), 483-486.

Regard for deeper currents of Elizabethan skepticism and internal tension, rather than for simplistic generalizations about the Elizabethans. Shakespeare's Christianity held to be operative at deeper level than that of theological conformity. Discussion of ideas includes theology of evil and relation between supernature and demonism, and providence and history.

1067. Schmidt, G., "Ist Wissen Macht? Über die Aktualität von Bacons *Instauratio magna*," *Kant-Stud.*, 58 (1967), 481-498.

For Bacon, power is power of man over nature, which he can
master because it is his duty. Finding itself in a direct
relationship to nature, the mind accomplishes its work; a
continuous perception of the natural process by which it knows
serves as its method.

1068. Schmitt, Charles B., *A Critical Survey and Bibliography of
Studies on Renaissance Aristotelianism 1958-1969*. Padua:
Editrice Antenore, 1971.

Rev. *Ren. and Ref.*, 8 (1971), 86.

Useful guide to pervasive intellectual influence; history of
Renaissance Aristotelianism, including unpublished dissertations. Suggests future lines of research.

1069. ———, *Gianfrancesco Pico della Mirandola (1469-1533) and His
Critique of Aristotle*. Archives internationales d'Histoire
des Idées, 23; The Hague: Martinus Nijhoff, 1967.

Rev. *BHR*, 30 (1968), 631.

First detailed account in half-a-century of life and thought
of the nephew of the more famous Giovanni Pico; philosophical
anti-Aristotelianism and rejection of Aristotelian science;
attachment to Scriptures and desire for distance from *fallax
mundus*; influence on later thought of his *Examen vanitatis
doctrinae gentium* (1520).

1070. ———, "Giulio Castellani (1528-1586): A Sixteenth-Century
Opponent of Scepticism," *Jour. of the Hist. of Phil.*, 5 (1967),
15-39.

Castellani's Aristotelianism, though theologically and pla-
tonically tinged, pointed way to 17th-cent. empirical methodology. His attack on skepticism was philosophical rather than
religious; Italian Aristotelianism and skepticism were mutually
exclusive; and skepticism did exert some influence in 16th-
cent. Italy.

1071. ———, "Perennial Philosophy: From Agostino Steuco to Leibniz," *JHI*, 27 (1966), 505-532.

Perennial philosophy is the notion that recognizable through
the history of philosophy are unchanging truths held even by
divergent philosophical schools. Earlier than Leibniz, to
whom the term has often been ascribed, Marsilio Ficino (1433-
1499), Giovanni Pico della Mirandola (1463-1494), and other
syncretistic thinkers provided a background for Agostino
Steuco (1497 or 1498-1548), one of the staunchest defenders of
the tradition of *prisca theologia* and perennial philosophy.

1072. ———, Rev. article on Eugenio Garin, *Italian Humanism*, 1965;
Storia della filosofia italiana, 1966, 3 vols.; *Scienze e vita
civile nel Rinascimento italiana*, Bari, 1965. *International
Philosophical Quarterly*, 8 (1968), 297-303.

Comments on work of a leading student of Italian Renaissance
philosophy.

1073. ————, "An Unknown Seventeenth-Century Translation of Sextus Empiricus," *Jour. of the Hist. of Phil.*, 6 (1968), 69-76.

Discovery of a translation of Sextus Empiricus into vernacular French by Nicolas de la Toison, Baron de Bussy, between 1645-1677. (Manuscript at UCLA.) Sextus' works were available in printed Latin editions after 1569.

1074. Schneider, Gerhardt, *Der Libertin Zur Geistes--und Sozial-geschichte des Burgertums im 16. und 17. Jahrhundert.* Stuttgart: J.B. Metzler, 1970. (Cf. 2242.)

Concept of "free-thinking" in ideological formation of early bourgeoisie in France during development of absolutism; examples from philosophy, theology, and contemporary literature.

1075. Scott, Stan, "Changing Sensibility in the Late Middle Ages," *AJFS*, 5 (1968), 135-154.

Nominalism and beginnings of Humanism; the individual as important.

1076. Seigfried, Hans, *Wahrheit und Metaphysik bei Suárez.* Abhandl. zur Philosophie, Psychologie und Pädagogik, Bd. 32; Bonn: Bouvier, 1967.

Dissertation, Bonn, on Renaissance philosopher (1548-1617).

1077. Sessions, William A., "Bacon and the Negative Instance," *RenP 1970* (Southeastern Ren. Conf., 1971), 1-9.

Bacon necessarily pursues ramifications of the negative on the scientific, the rhetorical and the mythic levels; in order to effect the great renewal of learning, he must deal with man's mind which distorts all reality and reflects that which is not.

1078. Skulsky, Harold, "Paduan Epistemology and the Doctrine of the One Mind," *Jour. of the Hist. of Phil.*, 6 (1968), 341-361.

While Pomponazzi rejected notion of a collective Mind as absurd, Zabarella found consolation in control by a single supreme mentality, providing basis for universal modes of thought and common human logic.

1079. Soellner, Rolf, "Shakespeare, Aristotle, Plato, and the Soul," *SJ(West)*, 1968, 56-71.

On Shakespeare's treatment of the soul and its philosophical background, especially with regard to Lear's "self-discovery."

1080. Soman, Alfred, "Pierre Charron: A Revaluation," *BHR*, 32 (1970), 57-77.

Re-examines biographical, archival, and literary evidence to assess importance of author of *De la Sagesse* (1541-1603). Concludes he put Montaigne into logical order for average reader; was of minor significance as a philosopher, and did not influence Montaigne.

1081. Spitz, Lewis, "Occultism and Despair of Reason in Renaissance
       Thought," *JHI*, 27 (1966), 464-469.

       Review of *Agrippa and the Crisis of Renaissance Thought* by
       Charles G. Nauert (Urbana, Ill.:   Univ. of Illinois Press,
       1965). Spitz suggests relation between Agrippa and German
       humanists needs closer examination and questions some of
       Nauert's views on Luther's anti-rationalism.

1082. Steiger, Renate, "M. Alvarez-Gomez: Die verborgene Gegenwart
       des Unendlichen bei Nikolaus von Kues," *Philosophische Rund-
       schau*, 17 (1970), 28-33.

       Possible applications of philosophy of Cusanus to modern-day
       problems.

1083. Stella, Aldo, "Tradizione razionalistica patavina e radical-
       ismo spiritualistico nel XVI secolo," *Annali della Scuola Nor-
       male Superiore di Pisa*, 38 (1968), 275-302.

       Examines Paduan rationalist tradition and spiritual radicalism
       in the 16th cent. in the light of university and foreign
       influences.

1084. Stough, Charlotte L., *Greek Skepticism: A Study in Episte-
       mology*. Berkeley: Univ. of Calif. Press, 1969.

       Rev. *Choice*, 7 (1970), 852.

       Studies movement of crucial importance for understanding Re-
       naissance and early empiricist and rationalist philosophy.
       Distinguishes among the academic Skeptics (Carneades), Pyrrho-
       nists, Aenesidemus, and Sextus Empiricus and their positions.

1085. Streiter, Aaron, "Against Discord: The Evolution of the Idea
       of Order in Certain Shakespearean Plays," *DA*, 30 (1969), 295-A
       (Brown Univ.).

       Outlines of the idea of order; expression of the idea during
       Elizabethan period in Aristotelian rationalism, and in various
       related traditions. Traces evolution of the idea in *AYL*, *TN*,
       AWW, *Tro.*, and *Tmp*.

1086. Surtz, Edward, S.J., "John Fisher and the Nature of Man,"
       Moreana, no. 21 (1969), 69-84.

       In his most explicit statement on nature of man, Fisher by-
       passes traditional scholastic view, abandons twofold doctrine
       of human nature and propounds a trichotomy of spirit, soul,
       and flesh.

1087. Tarugi, Giovannangiola, ed., *Il Pensiero Italiano del Renas-
       cimento e il Tempo Nostro*. Centro di Studi Umanistici "Angelo
       Poliziano" Fondazione Secchi Tarugi. Atti ... Convegno ...
       1968. Florence: Leo S. Olschki Editore, 1970.

       Collection includes: P.O. Kristeller's essays, "L'influsso
       del primo Umanesimo sul pensiero e sulle scienze"; "La dif-
       fusione europea del platonismo fiorentino"; C.B. Schmitt, "Pris-
       ca Theologia e Philosophia Perennis: Due temi del Rinascimento
       italiano e loro fortuna."

1088. Tatarkiewicz, Wladyslaw, *Estetyka Nowozytna*. Warsaw: Ossolineum, 1967. (Vol. 3 of *History of Aesthetics*, trans. The Hague: Mouton, 1970-74.)

Rev. *BJA*, 8 (1968), 415-416.

Important for Shakespeare students, because it covers 1400-1700, a period neglected by historians of esthetics, etc. (Edgar de Bruyne reaches only Duns Scotus in 14th cent.), while study of later writers begins near start of 18th cent. Contains fresh material.

1089. ————, "L'Esthétique italienne de la Renaissance," *Filosofia*, 18, supp. to no. 4 (1967), 745-760.

Definition of Renaissance and its artistic movements. Lists six theses shared by Italian Renaissance theorists of the *beaux arts*. Also generalizes on Renaissance poetics and theory of music.

1090. ————, "The Romantic Aesthetics of 1600," *The Brit. Jour. of Aesthetics*, 7 (1967), 137-149.

Until 1600 the theory of painting and poetry over two cents. of Renaissance thought had remained relatively unchanged. Classical aesthetic principles were still in vogue. About 1600, however, art began to turn away from classical principles toward romantic ones. Discusses Patrizi, Bruno, Galileo, Shakespeare, and others to show how their theories of art were Romantic. This Romanticism was a brief interlude before the classical aesthetic again came to the fore.

1091. Torrance, T.F., "1469-1969. La Philosophie et la Théologie de Jean Mair ou Major, de Haddington (1469-1550)," *Archives de Phil.*, 32 (1969), 531-547; 33 (1970), 261-293.

Scottish teacher of John Knox and George Buchanan, and his epistemology and logic; influence of his philosophy on his theology; treated under following headings: *notitia* (knowledge), *dialectica*, *theologia*, and *interpretatio*. Through logical analysis and empirical realism, Jean Mair arrived at an intuitive auditive theory of knowledge which paved the way for Calvin.

1092. Vawter, Marvin Lee, "Shakespeare and Jonson: Stoic Ethics and Political Crisis," *DA*, 31 (1970), 2358-A (Univ. of Wisc.).

Evolving anti-stoic tradition which satirizes the stoic wise man by exaggeration of materials of the Stoics; shows how Shakespeare and Jonson seem to be testing Stoicism in midst of political crisis and finding it either ineffective, self-defeating, paralyzing, or deadly to a whole society.

1093. Védrine, Hélène, *Les philosophies de la Renaissance*. Paris: Presse Universitaires, 1971.

Condensed manual: humanism, biblical influence, Bruno, science and philosophy.

1094. Vickers, Brian, ed., *Essential Articles for the Study of Fran-cis Bacon.* Hamden, Conn.: Archon, 1969. Rev. *Choice*, 6 (1969), 660.

Collection of 14 articles, revealing Bacon as scientist, his-torian, political theorist, and psychologist.

1095. Von Leyden, Wolfgang, *Seventeenth-Century Metaphysics: An Examination of Some Main Concepts and Theories.* N.Y.: Barnes and Noble; London: Duckworth, 1968.

Rev. *Choice*, 7 (1970), 240; *J. Hist. Phil.*, 9 (1971), 383-385.

Six parts: main trends, certainty and doubt, substance, essen-ces and individuals, mind-body problem, causality, and space and time. Appraisals of doctrines in terms of contemporary philosophy. Important for perceiving contrasts between Car-tesian universe and pre-Cartesian Shakespearean universe.

1096. Wallace, W.A., "The Concept of Motion in the Sixteenth Century," *Proc. of the Amer. Catholic Phil. Assoc.*, 41 (1967), 184-195.

Nominalists and realists; pre-Galileans.

1097. Walton, Craig, "Ramus and Bacon on Method," *J. Hist. Phil.*, 9 (1971), 289-302.

Dialectic of classical rhetoric. Both distinguish methods for discovery of knowledge.

1098. ———, "Ramus and Socrates," *Proc. Amer. Phil. Soc.*, 114, no. 2 (1970), 119-139.

Questions Ong's charges against Ramus as a philosopher of con-tagious failure. Rejects charge of Ramist depersonalizations. It has already been noted that Northern Renaissance reworking of Italian Humanism included use of spatial analogies in logic. Ramus provided a "Socratic" theory of practice, towards inven-tion. Detailed and documented. Bibliography, pp. 138-139.

1099. Whitaker, Virgil K., "Bacon's Doctrine of Forms: A Study of Seventeenth-Century Eclecticism," *HLQ*, 33 (1970), 209-216.

Ideas about the nature, order, and regularity of the universe inherent in the word "form," as used by Bacon.

1100. Wiley, Margaret L., *Creative Sceptics.* London: G. Allen and Unwin, 1966; N.Y.: Humanities Press, 1967.

Rev. *RenQ*, 21 (1968), 341-344.

"Creative skepticism" as critical instrument to be distin-guished from dogmatic disbelief. Deals *inter alia* with Spen-ser and Bacon.

1101. Wollgast, Siegfried, "Probleme des Pantheismus im 16. Jahrhun-dert," *Wissenshaftliche Zeitschrift* (Friedrich-Schiller-Uni-versität, Jena), 19 (1970), 945-953.

Ancient materialist, medieval, and Renaissance influences. Includes Nicolas of Cusa, Agrippa von Nettesheim, Sebastian Franck, Bruno, in relation to Spinoza.

1102. Wood, James D., "A Touch of Melanchthon in Shakespeare," *NQ*,
       206, n.s. 18 (1971), 150.

       Per. V. i and Melanchthon, *Commentarius de Anima* (Wittenberg,
       1542, sig. L4v).

ADDENDA

1102a. Chang, Joseph S.M.J., "'Of Mighty Opposites': Stoicism and
       Machiavellianism," *RenD*, 9 (1966), 37-57.

       Stoicism and Machiavellianism in the Elizabethan tyrant or the
       villain hero. Contribution of such opposite views to dramatic
       effects of Renaissance tragedy. (Cf. 1030, 1092).

1102b. Façon, Nina, "Su alcune parole-chiave in Giordano Bruno,"
       *Wissenschaftliche Zeitschrift der Humboldt-Universität zu Ber-
       lin*. Ges.-Sprachw., Reihe 18 (1969), 571-577.

       Detailed, documented study of such key-terms as *causa*, *princi-
       pio*, *infinito*.

1102c. Kristeller, Paul O., "The European Significance of Florentine
       Platonism," *Medieval and Renaissance Studies*, ed. John M.
       Headley. Proc. of Southeastern Inst. of Medieval and Renais-
       sance Studies, 1967. Univ. of North Carolina Pr., 1968, pp.
       206-229.

       Ideas and sources which Florentine Platonism, especially
       Ficino, contributed to the sixteenth cent.

1102d. Poppi, Antonino, *Causalità e infinità nella scuola padovana dal
       1480 al 1513*. (Saggi e testi, 5 Coll. del "Centro per la
       storia della tradizione aristotelica nel Veneto." Università
       di Padova.) Padua: Antenore, 1966.

       Rev. *Archiv für Begriffsgeschichte*, 18 (1969), 105-106.

       Ancient, medieval, and Renaissance views of causality; dis-
       placement of Averroism in Paduan naturalism.

1102e. Reilly, John P., *Cajetan's Notion of Existence*. The Hague,
       Paris: Mouton, 1971.

       Cajetan (1468-1534), opponent of Scotism and Averroism; agreed
       with Thomas on being: *esse* is the act of essence--it makes
       being being.

1102f. Ritter, Joachim, ed., *Historisches Wörterbuch der Philosophie*,
       Bd. I. (A-C). Basel, Stuttgart: Schwabe, 1971.

       Based on R. Eisler's *Wörterbuch der philosophischen Begriffe*
       (ed. 4, 1927-1930), this is major tool for the comprehension
       of Renaissance philosophical terminology and ideas. Detailed
       articles by specialists, with bibliographies appended. See
       editor's exposition of the work's plans and premises: "Leit-
       gedanken und Grundsätze des Historisches Wörterbuchs der
       Philosophie," *Archiv für Begriffsgeschichte*, 11 (1967), 75-80.

1103. Anglo, Sydney, *Machiavelli: A Dissection.* London: Victor Gollancz, 1969. Rev. *TLS*, 29 May 1969, 586.

Machiavelli's life in light of history; criticism of his arguments, methods, lack of originality, and other shortcomings; but study accepts established view of his teachings.

1104. Arenilla, L., "Le Calvinisme et le droit de résistance à l'État," *Annales, Economies, Sociétés, Civilisations*, 22 (1967), 350-369.

Calvin allows private subject only right of *passive* resistance, and only in limited cases, as when obedience to man turns one away from obedience to God.

1105. Aronson, Nicole Habatjou, "Les Idées Politiques de Rabelais," *DA*, 30 (1970), 2866-A (City Univ. of N.Y.).

Social and political ideas of Rabelais seen as idealistic, evangelic, cosmopolitan, in direct opposition to an autocratic government.

1106. Axton, Marie, "Robert Dudley and the Inner Temple Revels," *Hist. Jour.*, 13 (1970), 365-378.

Connects Christmas revels at Inner Temple in 1562 celebrating Dudley's reign as Prince Pallaphilos to performance before Queen (in January) of *Gorboduc*. Since its authors, Sackville and Norton, were members of Inner Temple, circumstances of performance are related to Dudley's willingness to support Catherine Grey over Mary Stuart in the succession question. Cites play's lines (V. ii. 165-173) as specifically arising out of advocacy of Catherine.

1107. Badaloni, N., "Natura e società in Machiavelli," *Studi Storica*, 10 (1969), 675-708.

Machiavelli's philosophical interests in political theory as well as practice. Instead of viewing human nature as constant, he saw it as integrated into society and thus mutable as society is mutable.

1108. Baldwin, Anne Wilfong, "Thomas Berthelet and Tudor Propaganda," *DA*, 28 (1968), 5005-5006-A (Univ. of Ill.).

Henry VIII's propagandists, including Berthelet, royal printer, issued contradictory views: King was irreplaceable, a divine minister; and king was "elected," his power coming from

Parliament or people--moreover, if king were supposed to be
beneficent ruler, an evil one might rightfully be deposed.
Contradiction--that God's vicarious throne should not be
usurped, but if someone did so, his place should not be
usurped--was imposed in the interests of order. It may also
have led in law to attempt to reconcile "King's Two Bodies,"
the divine and mortal persons of the ruler. In addition to
influencing Elizabeth's propagandists, the royal contradiction may have left its mark on Elizabethan literature: as in
Daniel's *Civil Wars*, arguing complete obedience to authority
to prevent war; Drayton's *Barons Warres*, showing horrors that
ensue when rulers are unfit to rule; and in Shakespeare. In
R2, he is neutral on elective theory of kingship, but in *H4*,
he shows how civil disorder can be corrected by a "true
prince," who is both divine and mortal, of the flesh and of
the spirit.

1109.   Barish, Jonas A., *"Perkin Warbeck* as Anti-History," *EIC*, 20
        (1970), 151-171.

        Questions historical view of *Perkin Warbeck* as tale of an im-
        postor rebelling against a legitimate monarch. Reasserts
        Eliot's view that the play, as Ford intended, asks us to con-
        sider Perkin's claim.

1110.   Barron, Caroline M., "The Tyranny of Richard II," *Bull. of the
        Institute of Historical Research*, 41 (1968), 1-18.

        Richard II portrayed as a king frightened into tyranny. Con-
        fronted by hostility of his subjects, he avoided conciliatory
        measures and tried to trample them down; thus he increased
        their hostility, while he concealed from himself the fact
        that he was at their mercy. He thus fulfilled the medieval
        (Aristotelian) conception of the tyrant as one who ruled only
        for his own profit, not for his subjects'.

1111.   Battista, Anna Maria, *Alle origini del Pensiero Politico Liber-
        tino: Montaigne e Charron*. (Istituto de Studi Storico-
        Politici, Università di Roma. Facoltà di Scienze Politiche
        no. 11.) Milan: A. Giuffrè, 1966.

        Rev. *AHR*, 73 (1967), 465-466.

        Origins of libertine political thought, stemming from author's
        study of Machiavelli's fortune in France. While the influence
        of his writings there was only slight, a major source of po-
        litical change involved ancient skeptics; Montaigne and Charron
        reflect this influence.

1112.   Bawcutt, N.W., "Machiavelli and Marlowe's *The Jew of Malta*,"
        RenD, 3 (1970), 3-49.

        Which of Machiavelli's ideas were current in Marlowe's time;
        complexity of Elizabethan responses to them. Though not prov-
        ing that Marlowe had first-hand knowledge of Machiavelli, shows
        that many ideas in the play are Machiavellian or relevant to
        Machiavelli in a way that 16th-cent. writers would have con-
        sidered legitimate.

1113.　———, "Some Elizabethan Allusions to Machiavelli," *EM*, 20 (1969), 53-74.

Allusions cited range from hostile to accepting. Believes Englishmen may have been more hostile than French to Machiavelli, and may have known his work less well.

1114. Becker, Marvin B., *Florence in Transition*, Vol. I: *The Decline of the Commune*. Baltimore: Johns Hopkins Press, 1967.

Rev. *BHR*, 30 (1968), 624-627; *Historian*, 30 (1968), 257; *JEH*, 28 (1968), 643-645; *Manuscripta*, 12 (1968), 111-112; *RenQ*, 21 (1968), 312-314; *SCN*, Autumn 1968, 68; *Spec.*, 43 (1968), 689-692.

Emergence of Renaissance in late medieval Florence studied through socioeconomic forces that upset its cultural balance. Communal ideas yielded, in political and economic crises, eventually to despotism, followed by democratized, legalistic, and puritanical regime. Suggests how deficit financing created the Renaissance state; large war-related public debt led to greater concern with state affairs than with private ones; thence, the civic humanism which exalted patriotic virtues of the *bonus civis* of ancient Romans.

1115.　———, *Florence in Transition*, Vol. II: *Studies in the Rise of the Territorial State*. Baltimore: Johns Hopkins Press, 1968.

Rev. *AHR*, 75 (1969), 108; *Choice*, 6 (1969), 694.

Increasing strength of public world of *trecento* Florence, with concomitant depersonalization and repression. Denying the Burckhardtian notion of the state as a work of art, Becker finds it rather a product of deficit financing and socioeconomic mobility.

1116. Beckingsale, B.W., *Burghley: Tudor Statesman 1520-1598*. London: Macmillan; N.Y.: St. Martin's Press, 1967.

Rev. *AHR*, 74 (1968), 158-159.

Biography of William Cecil, who retained his religion while reconciling religion with state policy. Documented study of Elizabeth's adviser in his political, social, and intellectual milieu.

1117. Benert, Richard Roy, "Inferior Magistrates in Sixteenth-Century Political and Legal Thought," *DA*, 28 (1968), 4981-4982-A (Univ. of Minn.).

Analyzes theory of Lutherans and Calvinists of armed political resistance to sovereign authority by inferior magistrates. In 1570's French Huguenots revived the medieval concept of the authority of the community: the French inferior magistrate held his authority from the people and from God. By attributing popular authority to the king and all inferior officials, the Huguenots solved medieval problem of giving constitutional form to community-authority directed against the king. They formed a corporate body uniting royal with popular authority, creating a state in which the governing power limits itself constitutionally.

1118. Bergson, Allen, "The Ironic Tragedies of Marston and Chapman: Notes on Jacobean Tragic Form," *JEGP*, 69 (1970), 613-630.

Tone of ironic tragedies derives from their political nature; involvement in world seen as involvement in corrupting activity.

1119. Berman, Ronald, "Anarchy and Order in *Richard III* and *King John*," *ShS*, 20 (1967), 51-59.

Structural disorder and confusion of political, moral, and religious values emerge under the influence of Machiavelli. The playwright founds himself on paradox but concludes with an apotheosis in which history is subject to law.

1120. Berner, Samuel Joseph, "The Florentine Patriciate in the Transition from Republic to Principato: 1530-1610," *DA*, 31 (1970), 1719-A (Univ. of Calif., Berkeley).

Florence's republic government in an age dominated by monarchical nations; decrease in power of patrician oligarchy. Emphasizes social consequences of emerging principate.

1121. Berry, Lloyd E., ed., *John Stubb's "Gaping Gulf" with Letters and Other Relevant Documents*. Univ. of Virginia Press for the Folger Shakespeare Library; London: Oxford Univ. Press, 1970.

Rev. *TLS*, 4 September 1970, 982.

Besides full text of Stubb's condemnation of Queen's proposed marriage to Duc d'Alençon, contains 24 of his letters; royal proclamation for suppression of the book; reply by Henry Howard, Lord Northampton; and a substantial introduction with relevant historical detail.

1122. Bevington, David, *Tudor Drama and Politics: A Critical Approach to Topical Meaning*. Cambridge, Mass.: Harvard Univ. Press; Toronto: Saunders, 1968.

Rev. *S.St.*, 6 (1972), 335.

Relevance of topical meanings in 16th-cent. English drama to issues, rather than to persons; knowledge of contemporary political viewpoints aids understanding of dramatic forms, characters, and genres.

1123. Bindoff, S.T., *Ket's Rebellion, 1549*. Historical Association General Series, 12. London Historical Association, 1968 (first published 1949).

Account of this event which began as a local riot, developed into a great popular demonstration, and ended in violence and bloodshed. These three phases, separated in time, are differentiated: the first a conflict between landlords and tenants; the second, between governors and governed; the last an interweaving of local and national politics.

1124. Bonadeo, Alfredo, "Machiavelli on Civic Equality and Republican Government," *RomN*, 11 (1969/1970), 160-166.

Machiavelli's notion of two types of republican government:
one, like the Roman republic, based on civic inequality; one
conceived for Florence, based on civic equality. Believes
nobility has to be eliminated from political life for civic
equality to exist.

1125. Bostick, Theodora Pierdos, "English Foreign Policy, 1528-1534:
The Diplomacy of Divorce," *DA*, 28 (1968), 3103-3104-A (Univ.
of Ill.).

Henry VIII had no intention of breaking with Rome until he was
forced to; failure in diplomacy was a leading cause. The divorce from Catherine of Aragon had a preeminent effect on English diplomacy, as well as on English foreign policy. It also
changed an aggressive quest for national prestige into a defensive protection of ecclesiastical innovation.

1126. Boughner, Daniel C., *The Devil's Disciple: Ben Jonson's Debt
to Machiavelli*. N.Y.: Philosophical Library, 1968.

Rev. *Comp. Lit. Studies*, 7 (1970), 113-114.

From a study of Machiavelli's drama and criticism, author develops the relationship beyond the comments in Mario Praz's
The Flaming Heart (1958). Stresses Machiavelli's stature as
dramatist and Renaissance influence.

1127. Bouwsma, William J., *Venice and the Defense of Republican
Liberty: Renaissance Values in the Age of the Counter Reformation*. Berkeley: Univ. of Calif. Press, 1968.

Rev. *AHR*, 75 (1969), 157-159.

Venice was Italy's second great urban republic. Author examines what has been termed the last great creative impulse of
the Italian Renaissance, in its complex political development
from the derivative Quattrocento through the static utopianism
of early 16th cent., to the sophisticated views of the early
17th cent.

1128. Braekman, E.M., "La pensée politique de Guy de Bruès," *Bull.
de la Soc. de l'Hist. de Protest. Français*, 65 (1969), 1-28.

Guy de Bruès reflects Calvin's political ideas: the state
should be served and its laws obeyed, but obedience to God
supersedes the laws of the state. Bruès is silent, however,
about resistance to the state.

1129. Breslow, Martin, *A Mirror of England: English Puritan Views
of Foreign Nations, 1618-1640*. Cambridge, Mass.: Harvard
Univ. Press; London: Oxford Press, 1970.

Rev. *AHR*, 75 (1970), 1720; *EHR*, 86 (1971), 411; *Historian*, 33
(1971), 468-469.

Culls from pamphlets, sermons, parliamentary debates, memoirs,
and literature, political attitudes of English Puritans on
foreign policy. Finds them very close to the emotions of the
inarticulate public in their attitude to Spain, the Palatine,
Gustavus Adolphus, and Elizabethan past.

1130.   Broich, Ulrich, "Machiavelli und das Drama der Shakespeare-
        Zeit," *Anglia*, 89 (1971), 326-348.

        While previous studies of Machiavellian influence dealt with
        his name and reputation, his influence was felt without his
        name--even if he had not been read. Traces *virtù*, *fortuna*,
        and *necessità* in Renaissance drama.

1131.   Brown, A.L., "The King's Councillors in Fifteenth Century Eng-
        land," *Trans. of Royal Hist. Soc.*, 19 (1969), 95-118.

        Attempts to reconstruct the king's council for a period of
        100 years. Council in its role as assistant to king.

1132.   Brucker, Gene, *Renaissance Florence*. N.Y.: John Wiley and
        Sons, 1969.

        Rev. *AHR*, 75 (1970), 1482-1483; *BHR*, 32 (1970), 470-471.

        Includes chapters on the city, its geography, its population;
        on economic and political life; on society; on the Church, and
        relations between Florence and the Papacy; on culture.

1133.   Bush, M.L., "The Tudors and the Royal Race," *History*, 55
        (1970), 37-48.

        On reduction in number of princes of royal blood who could
        assert claims on the throne, in late 15th and early 16th cent.
        Effect of this reduced number of male claimants helped deprive
        crown of its dynastic image; aided stability, and led to de-
        velopment of constitutional rights in later times.

1134.   Calvin, John, *Senecae libri duo de clementia commentarius
        illustrati* (1532), ed., with translation and notes, Ford Lewis
        Battles; introduction, Battles and A.M. Hugo. Leiden: E.J.
        Brill for the Renaissance Society of America, 1969.

        Rev. J. Savignac, *La Rev. Réformée*, 21, no. 84 (1970), 39-46.

        On Seneca's political manual for the young Nero. Calvin's com-
        mentary provides insight into his intellectual development and
        problem of his supposed Stoicism. English translation on fac-
        ing pages; footnotes; bibliography and indexes.

1135.   Catlin, Janet Green, "The Public Non-Parliamentary Speeches of
        Queen Elizabeth I: An Annotated Bibliography and Commentary,"
        DA, 31 (1970), 352-A (Univ. of North Carolina).

        Five speeches of Elizabeth, four in Latin.

1136.   Centouri, Walter, "Francesco Guicciardini's Concept of Govern-
        ment, Part I: His Critics (1862-1950)," *FeL*, 16 (1970), 360-
        372.

        Representative spectrum of opinion on Guicciardini's concept
        of government in *Opere Inedite* is examined.

1137.   Cha, Ha Soon, "The Concept of Equity in Seventeenth-Century
        Political Theory," *DA*, 31 (1970), 334-A (Brandeis Univ.).

Development of Aristotelian proportionate justice and Ciceronian natural equality, leading to dualistic concept of equality, i.e., each man has an equal value, but his equality is
altered by his relationships with other men.

1138. Cherniavsky, Michael, "Ivan the Terrible as Renaissance
Prince," *SlavR*, 27 (1968), 195-211.

Re-examination of personal epithet "terrible" in a Renaissance
context; seen to be more broadly descriptive of the society in
which it meant a certain style of leadership. Ivan the Terrible thus represented two Renaissance trends: cruel ruler
administering justice among weak and evil men, and awe-
inspiring personality free from human and divine law.

1139. Chiappelli, Fredi, *Nuovi studi sul linguaggio del Machiavelli*.
Florence: Le Monnier, 1969.

Rev. *BHR*, 32 (1970), 475-476.

Includes many previously unedited documents from Machiavelli's
days in official capacity in Florence.

1140. Christenson, Richard, "The Political Theory of Persecution:
Augustine and Hobbes," *Midwest J. Pol. Sci.*, 12 (1968), 419-
438.

Analysis of the two varieties of the theory of persecution:
one, medieval, based upon the Church; the other, modern, based
upon the Sovereign State.

1141. Ciliberto, M., "Appunti per una storia della fortuna di Machiavelli in Italia: F. Ercole e L. Russo," *Studi Storici*, 10
(1969), 799-832.

Examines 20th-cent. Italian criticism of Machiavelli in light
of political problems in this century.

1142. Clark, Carol E., "Montaigne and the Imagery of Political Discourse in Sixteenth-Century France," *French Studies*, 24 (1970),
337-355.

Montaigne's imagery, especially from medicine and building
(philosopher as *medicus animi*). But most of Montaigne's
medical images appear in political context: the patient is
the state; state-as-body *topos* developed.

1143. Cohen, Eileen Z., "Poet in the Service of Protestantism: Sir
Philip Sidney as Ambassador," *Historical Magazine of the
Protestant Episcopal Church*, 38 (1969), 167-175.

Presents some evidence that Sidney's credulity in encouraging
the league of Protestant nations made him a "dangerous ambassador" who merited Elizabeth's displeasure.

1144. Colish, Marcia L., "The Idea of Liberty in Machiavelli," *JHI*,
32 (1971), 323-350.

Free state more dynamic, better able to keep its authority.
Appreciation of Roman liberty.

1145.   Cracco, Giorgio, Società e stato nel medioevo veneziano
        (secoli XII-XIV). Civiltà Veneziana, Studi 22; Florence:
        Leo Olschki, 1967.

        Rev. RenQ, 21 (1968), 310-311.

        Attacks Burckhardt's (and other historians') "myth of Venice"
        as instance of harmonious cooperation of social classes. On
        the contrary, Venice's problems paralleled those of other
        states and included a class struggle.

1146.   Cross, Claire, The Royal Supremacy in the Elizabethan Church--
        Historical Problems: Studies and Documents. London and N.Y.:
        Barnes and Noble, 1969.

        Rev. AHR, 76 (1971), 497-498; Church Hist., 39 (1970), 557-558;
        SEL, 10 (1970), 237.

        On political theory of supremacy in relation to a secular head;
        effectiveness in practice of that supremacy. Documents cover
        1558 to 1583, and take up nearly half of book.

1147.   Crowley, Weldon S., "Erastianism in England 1640-1662," DA, 27
        (1967), 2981-A (Univ. of Iowa).

        Erastianism as indigenously English phenomenon with roots in
        medieval political theory and anti-clericalism; it developed
        into a practical plan and system in struggles of the period
        1640-1662.

1148.   Daly, Lowrie J., "Medieval and Renaissance Commentaries on the
        Politics of Aristotle," Duquesne Rev., 13 (1968), 41-55.

        Samples of commentaries; e.g., Michael Piccart (1574-1620).

1149.   D'Andrea, Antonio, "The Last Years of Innocent Gentillet:
        'Princeps Adversariorum Machiavelli,'" RenQ, 15 (1967), 12-16.

        Attempts to dispel the idea that Gentillet, an interpreter of
        Machiavelli, was the sole source of "Elizabethan misunder-
        standing" of Machiavelli. The writings themselves were widely
        available, he points out. He adds, however, the Discours ...
        Contre Machiavel (of Gentillet) did have some importance, and
        the article attempts to reassess circumstances of its writing
        and circulation.

1150.   ————, "The Political and Ideological Context of Innocent
        Gentillet's 'Anti-Machiavel,'" RenQ, 23 (1970), 397-411.

        Political situation in which the Discours were written, inter-
        preting politically the religious wars in France. Gentillet's
        distortion of Machiavelli: he derived main themes of his work
        from Huguenot policies and propaganda.

1151.   Davidson, Clifford, "Coriolanus: A Study in Political Dislo-
        cation," ShS, 4 (1969), 263-274.

        Theme of Coriolanus as the proper relation between individual
        and State. In the civil struggle plebeians are at fault for
        impatience and patricians for greed.

1152.   ————, "*The Phoenix*:   Middleton's Didactic Comedy," *PLL* (Southern Illinois Univ.), 4 (1968), 121-130.

Dramatization of major Renaissance political concern: how prince may distinguish flattery from truth in order to rule well.   Play related to Middleton's pageant, *The Triumphs of Truth* (1613).

1153.   Davies, C.S.L., "Les révoltes populaires en Angleterre (1500-1700), *Annales: Economies, Sociétés, Civilisations*, 24 (1969), 24-60.

Investigation of English class revolts in an attempt to throw new light on 17th-cent. French society.

1154.   Davis, J.C., "More, Morton and the Politics of Accommodation," *JBS*, 9 (1970), 27-49.

On politics of accommodation in thought of More when writing *Utopia*; whether or not he recommended the accommodational approach of the fictional More.   Also studies politics in *The History of King Richard III*.

1155.   Davis, Natalie Zemon, and John A. McClelland, "A Checklist of French Political and Religious Pamphlets, 1560-1635, in the University of Toronto Library," *Ren. and Ref.*, 5, no. 3 (1969), 18-41.

Checklist of 94 pamphlets, intended as the first step toward a union list of such materials in Canada.

1156.   Della Terza, Dante, "The Most Recent Image of Machiavelli: The Contribution of the Linguist and the Historian," *Ital. Q.*, 14 (1970/71), 91-113.

On combined scholarly efforts of historians, literary critics, and linguists; notes defensive position of Italian Machiavellian historiography.

1157.   DeLuna, B.N., *The Queen Declined*.   Oxford Univ. Press, 1969.

Interprets "Willobie His Avisa" (1594) as a cryptic commentary on two of the great questions of the Elizabethan age: why the Queen declined to wed and whether Elizabeth remained *virgo intacta*.   Includes text of original ed.   Rev. *TLS*, 11 June 1970, 645.

1158.   De Mattei, Rodolfo, "Machiavelli e Roma," *Studi Romani*, 18 (1970), 1-21.

Two aspects of Machiavelli's relationships with "Rome":   one practical and direct, "physical" in his functions as Florence state secretary; the other intellectual, cultural, "bookish," his thought on the greatness that once was Rome.

1159.   ————, *Dal Premachiavellismo all'Antimachiavellismo*.   G.C. Sansoni, 1969.

Parte I. Aspetti di premachiavellismo; includes "Il problema della liceità del mandacio." II. Questioni Machiavelliane— relations of *Principe* and *Discorsi*.   III. Confutazioni del

Machiavelli. IV. Aspetti di Antimachiavellismo di Machiavellismo nel Cinque e nel Seicento in Italia. V. Aspetti della Fortuna dell' "Arte della Guerra." Appendice: Machiavelli e Roma.

1160. Dickens, A.G., and Carr, Dorothy, *The Reformation in England to the Accession of Elizabeth I.* Documents of Modern History Series, London: E. Arnold, 1967; N.Y.: St. Martin's Press, 1968. Rev. *TLS*, 11 April 1968, 381.

Significance of state intervention within the context of change and reaction in every aspect of Tudor society.

1161. Draper, John W., "Hero and Theme in *Julius Caesar*," *Riv. di Lett. Mod. e Comp.*, 20 (1967), 30–34.

Play is based on popular Elizabethan theme of usurpation of monarch by divine right; effects national disaster.

1162. ———, "Shakespeare and King James I," *RLMC*, 22 (1969), 5–9.

Discusses aspects of *MM*, *Mac.*, *Lr.*, and *Tmp.* which pertain to rule by Divine Right.

1163. Durand, Georges, *États et Institutions XVIe-XVIIIe siècles.* Paris: A. Colin, 1969.

Rev. *Cahiers d'histoire* ... *Universités de Clermont-Lyon-Grenoble*, 16 (1971), 241–242.

Political evolution of the court in these three centuries. Four chapters on the anatomy, physiology, and pathology of the national basis of monarchy.

1164. Durham, Robert Jay, "In Search of the Council, 1585–1615." *DA*, 30 (1970), 3395-A (Yale Univ.).

On group within the English Privy Council that performed its administrative role 1585–1615.

1165. Ebel, Julia G., "Translation and Cultural Nationalism in the Reign of Elizabeth," *JHI*, 30 (1969), 593–602.

Argues that though there is little of literary value in the "patronage literature" of 1557–1558, the translators did give form to a cultural nationalism without which the achievements of the subsequent period would be unimaginable.

1166. Edwards, Francis, S.J., *The Marvellous Chance. Thomas Howard, Fourth Duke of Norfolk and the Ridolphi Plot, 1570–1572.* London: Rupert Hart-Davis, 1968.

Rev. *EHR*, 85 (1970), 414–415.

On the Ridolphi Plot and execution of Norfolk for treason (1572). Ridolphi was Pope's agent in instigating revolt in England and invasion from Spain; Norfolk communicated with Ridolphi, and violated his promise to cease his intrigue to marry Mary Queen of Scots. Book aims to indict Cecil as manipulating the plot.

1167. Eiter, Richard H., "Ivan IV and Jean Bodin: Reflections on Sovereignty," *Topic*, 17 (1969), 27-38.

Finds that the two contemporaries held similar ideas on nature of sovereignty.

1168. Elliott, J.H., "Revolution and Continuity in Early Modern Europe," *Past and Pres.*, 42 (1969), 35-56.

Challenges view of contemporary historians that mid-16th-cent. political crises were "revolutions." "Revolution" as idealistic 18th-cent. concept does not apply to struggles of social groups to gain supremacy in the 16th cent.

1169. Elton, Geoffrey Rudolph, "*The Body of the Whole Realm*": *Parliament and Representation in Medieval and Tudor England*, published for the Jamestown Foundation by Univ. Press of Virginia, 1969.

Rev. *EHR*, 85 (1970), 841-842.

Essay surveying early parliamentary history: four parts--Origins, Place and Function, Representation and Political Power, Parliament in the 16th cent.

1170. ————, "Reform by Statute: Thomas Starkey's *Dialogue* and Thomas Cromwell's Policy," *Brit. Acad. Proc.*, 54 (1968) [1970], 165-188.

Specific proposals of government and reform voiced by the British humanist Thomas Starkey, and their use by Thomas Cromwell.

1171. ————, "Sir Thomas More and the Opposition to Henry VIII," *Bull. Inst. Hist. Res.*, 41 (1968), 19-34.

On neglected period of More's chancellorship (1529-1532) with emphasis on his attitude toward heresy and relations with the Reformation Parliament.

1172. Elyot, Sir Thomas, *Four Political Treatises* [*The Doctrinal of Princes*, 1533; *Pasquil the Playne*, 1533; *The Banquette of Sapience*, 1534; *The Image of Governance*, 1541], facsimile, ed. Lillian Gottesman. Gainesville, Fla.: Scholars' Facsimiles, 1967.

Not reprinted since 16th cent., these treatises share common concern with qualifications and conduct of kings and royal advisers.

1173. Epstein, Joel J., "Francis Bacon and the Challenge to the Prerogative in 1610," *JHS*, 2 (1969/70), 272-282.

In 1610 Bacon believed that the King should use Parliament as a "junior partner" in government. During the impositions controversy, he felt strongly about supremacy of the prerogative, but was forced to promote a scheme that reduced the King's status.

1174. ——, "Francis Bacon and the Issue of Union, 1603-1608,"
       HLQ, 33 (1970), 121-132.

       James I's plans for union with Scotland--importance to Bacon's
       career of seeing project through Parliament.

1175. ——, "Francis Bacon: Mediator in the Parliament of 1604,"
       Historian, 30 (1968), 219-237.

       Despite common notion of Bacon as royal lackey, his Parliamen-
       tary role in 1604, in addition to neutralizing defiant protests
       against the Crown, was to speak for Parliamentary rights and
       privileges and to harmonize both sides in a balanced system.
       During subsequent blundering on the part of the Crown, he re-
       mained committed to bridging the widening gap with Parliament.

1176. ——, "The Parliamentary Career of Francis Bacon, 1581-1614,"
       DA, 27 (1967), 4190-4191-A (Rutgers State Univ.).

       Qualifies Bacon's usual label of "prerogative man," a position
       he did not hold until final Elizabethan sessions, while not
       until James's reign did he become most articulate royalist
       spokesman in Commons. He professed a tactful prerogative view
       used to promote harmony between ruler and Parliament; he firm-
       ly believed in the latter, though as the junior partner in
       government. After 1604, as Parliamentary opposition grew, the
       task of asserting James's leadership became more difficult.
       Traces Bacon's attitude through various Jacobean parliaments.

1177. Escudero, J.A., *Los secretarios de estado y del despacho
       1474-1724.* 4 vols. Madrid: Instituto de estudios adminis-
       trativos, 1969.

       Rev. *EHR*, 85 (1970), 794-796.

       Study of Spanish bureaucracy, mainly 16th and 17th cents.
       Draws on BM resources for Spanish history of this period, es-
       pecially on Egerton Collection and Additional Manuscripts.
       Stresses Philip II's unique devotion to his bureaucracy.

1178. Eskin, Stanley G., "Politics in Shakespeare's Plays," *BuR*, 15,
       no. 3 (1967), 47-64.

       Examines influence of contemporary politics and political
       theory on Shakespeare's plays.

1179. Esler, Anthony, *The Aspiring Mind of the Elizabethan Younger
       Generation.* Durham, N.C.: Duke Univ. Press, 1966.

       Rev. *AHR*, 73 (1967), 131-132.

       Studies a group of eminent Englishmen born in the 1550's and
       1560's including Shakespeare, Bacon, Raleigh, Cecil, Essex,
       Marlowe. Contrasts their goals and ideals with those of
       their fathers during the generation of Elizabeth I and Lord
       Burleigh.

1180. Fike, Claude E., "A Character Study of Henry VIII," *SoQ*, 8
       (1969/70), 57-74.

       Discusses personality and historical role of Henry VIII.

1181. Fletcher, Anthony, *Tudor Rebellions*. (Seminar Studies in His-
       tory.) London: Longman, 1968.

       Useful compendium: Part I. Background--Ch. I: Tudor Theory
       of Obligation; Ch. II: Rebellion and the Social Structure.
       Part II. Descriptive Analysis: Taxation and Rebellion; The
       Pilgrimage of Grace; The Western Rebellion; Kett's Rebellion;
       Wyatt's Rebellion; The Northern Rebellion. Part III. Assess-
       ment. Part IV. Documents and bibliography; maps.

1182. Forbes, A.H., "Dual Loyalty: The Roman Catholic Dilemma Under
       the Early Stuarts," *Papers Michigan Acad. Sci. Arts Letters*,
       52 (1967), 411-416.

       On oath of allegiance to the crown under James I, condemned by
       Pope Paul V in 1605 and 1606, and fruitless negotiations with
       Roman Curia under Charles I.

1183. Foster, Elizabeth R., "Procedure in the House of Lords during
       the Early Stuart Period," *Jour. of Brit. Studies*, 5, no. 2
       (1966), 56-73.

       Information also on relative sizes of the House under various
       regimes, and training of the Lords for their task.

1184. ------, ed., *Proceedings in Parliament, 1610*. New Haven,
       Conn.: Yale Univ. Press, 1966. 2 vols.

       Rev. *AHR*, 72 (1967), 973-974.

       Introduction sketches historical background and discusses re-
       lation and interaction of the two houses of Parliament of the
       time.

1185. ------, "Speaking in the House of Commons," *Bull. of the Inst.
       of Hist. Res.*, 43 (1970), 35-55.

       William Hakewill sat in parliament in reigns of Elizabeth,
       James I, and Charles I. Several versions of his unpublished
       chapter on procedures for speaking in the House of Commons.
       Private manuscript in British Museum entitled "Orders of
       Speaking in Parliament."

1186. Foster, Frank F., "The Government of London in the Reign of
       Elizabeth I." *DA*, 31 (1971), 4672 (Columbia Univ.).

       Based on original records, this useful and substantial disser-
       tation includes sections on London and the Crown, the City,
       institutions of the ward, parish vestry, the livery companies,
       the rulers of London, rising in City politics.

1187. Franklin, Julian H., ed., *Constitutionalism and Resistance in
       the Sixteenth Century: Three Treatises by Hotman, Beza, and
       Mornay*. N.Y.: Pegasus, 1969.

       Rev. *BHR*, 32 (1970), 231-232.

       French Huguenot political treatises, in abridged translations:
       François Hotman's *Franco-Gallia*, Theodore Beza's *Du Droit des
       magistrats*, and the *Vindiciae contra tyrannos*, attributed to
       Philippe du Plessis-Mornay. Useful introduction on resistance-
       attitudes of the works.

1188.   Fraser, Antonia, "The Murder of Darnley," *Hist. Today*, 17
        (1967), 3-12.

        Events which followed murder of Darnley obscure actual con-
        spirators in the crime. Mary, having discovered Bothwell and
        Moray were among the latter, ceased her active quest for jus-
        tice; sought to achieve strength by marrying Bothwell rather
        than by trying him. Her own innocence in the murder affirmed.

1189.   Friedman, Lawrence Samuel, "Kingship and Politics in Shakes-
        peare's *Richard II*," *DA*, 27 (1967), 3007-A (Univ. of Iowa).

        Rejects Tillyard and the "Tudor myth" approach which stresses
        unswerving obedience to ruler, finding it difficult to square
        divine right in *Homilies* with the theory defined by Figgis in
        his *Divine Right of Kings*. Moreover, pragmatic Tudors inheri-
        ted not only the "Tudor myth" but also respect for natural law
        and rights of subjects. *R2* is politically complex because
        Shakespeare wants us simultaneously to grasp necessity for
        Bolingbroke's usurpation and to sympathize with Richard's
        tragedy. National well-being is ultimate criterion.

1190.   Friesner, Donald N., "William Shakespeare, Conservative," *ShQ*,
        20, no. 2 (1969), 165-178.

        Summarizes biographical and critical information, concluding
        that Shakespeare's political allegiance was not a divided one,
        but that he was always a conservative.

1191.   Fuidge, Norah M., "Some Sixteenth-Century Crown Office Lists
        at the Public Record Office," *Bull. of the Inst. of Hist. Res.*,
        42 (1969), 201-211.

        Collection of lists discussed in this article provides valuable
        source for names of members of House of Commons.

1192.   Giesey, Ralph E., "Hotman, Beza, and Mornay," *BHR*, 32 (1970),
        41-56.

        On extent to which a triumviral bond exists in their concep-
        tions of resistance—of who may resist and why—and in their
        roles as innovators in intellectual history.

1193.   Gilbert, Felix, "Machiavelli in Modern Historical Scholarship,"
        Ital. Q., 14 (1970/71), 9-26.

        Appraisals of Machiavelli and his works through the centuries.
        Sees him as relevant to 20th-cent. problems.

1194.   Gill, Paul Eugene, "Sir John Fortescue: Chief Justice of the
        King's Bench, Polemicist on the Succession Problem, Governmen-
        tal Reformer, and Political Theorist," *DA*, 29 (1969), 3552-A
        (Pennsylvania State Univ.).

        Author examines career and political theories of 15th-cent.
        author of *De Laudibus Legum Angliae*.

1195.   Gillespie, Gerald, "The Rebel in Seventeenth-Century Tragedy,"
        Comparative Literature, 17 (1966), 324-336.

Discusses nature of the rebel in Marlowe, Jonson, Webster, Milton, etc., in light of their historical contexts.

1196.   Goldstein, Leonard, "Alcibiades' Revolt in *Timon of Athens*," *ZAA*, 15 (1967), 256-278.

Explains this episode in light of contradictions emerging from growing strength of bourgeoisie and dissolution of Elizabethan compromise.

1197.   Griffiths, Gordon, *Representative Government in Western Europe in the Sixteenth Century: Commentary and Documents for the Study of Comparative Constitutional History*. International Commission for the History of Representative and Parliamentary Institutions; Oxford: Clarendon Press; N.Y.: Oxford Univ. Press, 1968.

Rev. *History*, 53 (1968), 415-416.

Documents showing working of 16th-cent. representative institutions, and indicating similarities among these bodies.

1198.   Griffiths, Ralph A., "Local Rivalries and National Politics: The Percies, the Nevilles and the Duke of Exeter, 1452-1455," *Speculum*, 43 (1968), 589-632.

Against viewing local outbreaks and national warfare as causally distinct political events. Disintegration of public order and personal enmities displayed in local violence as inevitably resulting in the national event.

1199.   Gunn, John A.W., "'Interest Will Not Lie': A Seventeenth-Century Political Maxim," *JHI*, 29 (1968), 551-564.

"Interest" as a fashionable 17th-cent. political concept: first as mark of Machiavellian ruthlessness, later as necessary tool for description of human designs. In view of the Elizabethan moralist, self-interest upset stable order and organic hierarchy; it destroyed predictable nature of social relations, and thus challenged an order based on transcendental meaning.

1200.   ————, *Politics and the Public Interest in the Seventeenth Century*. Univ. of Toronto Press, 1969.

Rev. *AHR*, 75 (1969), 488-489.

Rise of popular notion of public interest as part of ordinary political language; growth of a social philosophy of individualism which first appeared in 17th cent.

1201.   Hallowell, Robert E., "The Role of French Writers in the Royal Entries of Marie De'Medici in 1600," *SP*, 66 (1969), 182-203.

This study of the entries and of the epithalamia of 1600 reveals important role played by poets and artists as apologists of the King and as creators and perpetuators of dynastic myths; gave aura of divinity to monarchy and royal person.

1202. Hamburger, Michael R., "Besonderheiten der Herzogs-figur in
       Measure for Measure," *SJ (East)*, 105 (1969), 158-167.

       Duke represents James I's weaknesses and faults as transformed
       into virtues and flatteries. Designed to secure James's
       patronage.

1203. Hanft, Sheldon, "Some Aspects of Puritan Opposition in the
       First Parliament of James I (Vol. I and II)," *DA*, 31 (1970),
       1192-A (N.Y. Univ.).

       Puritan opposition to James led to emergence of new leaders
       and rise of freedom of the Commons. Propaganda barrage in-
       creased influence of Puritan movement.

1204. Hanson, Donald W., *From Kingdom to Commonwealth: The Develop-
       ment of Civic Consciousness in English Political Thought.*
       Cambridge, Mass.: Harvard Univ. Press, 1970.

       Rev. *Choice*, 8 (1971), 132; *Hist. Mag. of the Prot. Episc.
       Church*, 40 (1971), 231.

       On emergence of constitutional government in relation to de-
       velopment of a specific consciousness.

1205. Haugaard, William P., "The Coronation of Elizabeth I," *Journal
       of Ecclesiastical Hist.*, 19 (1968), 161-170.

       Elizabeth's changes in liturgical ceremonies at her coronation
       foreshadowed future independence of the English church.

1206. Hexter, J.H., "Claude de Seyssel and Normal Politics in the
       Age of Machiavelli," in Charles S. Singleton, ed., *Art, Science
       and History in the Renaissance*. Baltimore: Johns Hopkins
       Press, 1967, pp. 389-415.

       Political writings of Machiavelli, More, and Seyssel, who
       treated three modern modes of political thought: predatory,
       utopian, and constitutional.

1207. Hinrichs, Ernst, *Fürstenlehre und politisches Handeln im Frank-
       reich Henrichs IV: Untersuchungen über die politischen Denk-
       und Handlungsformen im Späthumanismus.* Veröffentlichungen des
       Max-Planck-Instituts für Geschichte, no. 21. Göttingen:
       Vandenhoeck & Ruprecht, 1969.

       Rev. *AHR*, 75 (1970), 1439-1440.

       Ideas of such "theoreticians" as Bodin and Lipsius and their
       lesser followers: Harault, Le Jay, and Rivault de Fleurance;
       L'Alouette, Dorleans, and Gravelle; Poisson de la Bodiniere,
       Constant, and Duchesne, on such issues as the prince vis-à-vis
       the law (divine and natural, fundamental, civil, etc.), sov-
       ereignty, and the virtues of the ideal ruler. Theoreticians
       followed by series of "practitioners": the king himself and
       his close advisers such as Duplessis-Mornay, Sully, De Thou,
       and Bellièvre.

1208. Hinton, R.W.K., "Husbands, Fathers and Conquerors," *Political
       Studies*, 15 (1967), 291-300.

In 16th and 17th cents., convergence of kings and common-
wealths was explained by analogy of marriage, which did not
always lead to patriarchalism. In contrast to Sir Thomas
Smith's Elizabethan *De Republica Anglorum*, where the analogy
is one of partnership and consent, Sir Robert Filmer in 17th
cent. swerved from traditional analogy.

1209. Holborn, Hajo, "Machtpolitik und lutherische Sozialethik,"
Archiv für Reformationsgeschichte, 57 (1966), 23-32.

Political consequences of Luther's ideas questioned. Calvinism
and Neostoicism, rather, are to be regarded as influential political currents in the transformation of states in modern
times.

1210. Hughes, Peter A.M., "'The Monarch's and the Muse's Seats':
Stuart Kingship and Poetry of the Royal Estate," *DA*, 27 (1966),
180A-181A (Yale Univ.).

Stuart claims of divine right, in the early 17th cent., echoed
through the poetry and politics of the age. The claims even
attracted the quasi-mystical legal concept of the king's two
bodies.

1211. Hurstfield, Joel, "Was There a Tudor Despotism After All?"
Trans. of the Royal Historical Soc., 17 (1967), 83-108.

Questions accepted views on Tudor rule. Finds despotism,
authoritarian rule suppressing dissent, present in first half
of 16th cent.

1212. Hüther, Jochen, *Die monarchische Ideologie in den französischen
Römerdramen des 16. und 17. Jahrhunderts*. (Münchener Univer.-
Schriften. Reihe der Philos. Fak. Band 2.) Munich: Max Hueber
Verlag, 1966.

I. Roman plays of 16th cent.: M.-A. Muret, *Caesar* (1545); J.
Grévin, *César* (1558); R. Garnier. II. Roman plays of first
half of 17th cent.: G. de Scudéry, *La mort de César* (1636);
and plays later in the cent.

1213. Ingersoll, David E., "The Constant Prince: Private Interests
and Public Goals in Machiavelli," *WPQ*, 21 (1968), 588-596.

Machiavelli's political leader in the *Prince* establishes his
power; in the *Discourses*, he seeks glory after death through
longevity of the state. In each of his roles, he is pursuing
selfish goals which also yield positive political results.

1214. Ives, E.W., ed., *The English Revolution 1600-1660*. London:
Edward Arnold, 1968.

Rev. *EHR*, 85 (1970), 417-418.

Includes broadcast talks (1966): political introduction by
Austin Woolrych; relations between central and local affairs
in essays by Ivan Roots, Alan Everitt, D.H. Pennington; on
London, by F.J. Fisher; on Puritans by Woolrych; on lawyers,
by H.F. Kearney; on merchants by Barry Supple; etc.

1215. ——, "Patronage at the Court of Henry VIII: The Case of
       Sir Ralph Egerton of Ridley," *BJRL*, 52 (1970), 346–374.

       Struggles for offices and competition for royal patronage dur-
       ing Henry's first 20 years of kingship; why the gentry were
       drawn to life at court.

1216. James, M.E., "Obedience and Dissent in Henrician England: The
       Lincolnshire Rebellion, 1536," *Past and Pres.*, 48 (1970), 3–78.

       Claims Lincolnshire Rebellion has been unduly characterized
       as bloody and chaotic. It was a controlled popular expression
       of grievances never intended to menace Crown.

1217. Johnson, Jerah, "The Concept of the 'King's Two Bodies' in
       Hamlet," *SQ*, 18 (1967), 430–434.

       Hamlet's "The body is with the king, but the king is not with
       the body" an allusion to concept of "King's Two Bodies"--king
       being both a natural body and the monarchical symbol of the
       body politic.

1218. Jondorf, Gillian, *Robert Garnier and the Themes of Political
       Tragedy in the Sixteenth Century*. Cambridge Univ. Press, 1969.

       Rev. *FR*, 43 (1970), 527–528; *RSH*, 137 (1969), 156.

       Failures of such critical approaches to the theater of Garnier
       (1545-1590) as "the baroque," "the psychological," and stylis-
       tic analyses determined by standards applicable to 17th-cent.
       tragedy. Garnier is a political dramatist who spoke to, and of,
       his contentious times; his dramatic technique can best be under-
       stood in light of this political content.

1219. Jones, G.P., "James I and the Western Border," *Cumberland and
       Westmoreland Antiquarian and Archaeological Soc. Trans.*, 69
       (1969), 129-151.

       Border in relation to its hindrance in uniting the two king-
       doms of King James I; Border Survey of 1604. Discusses pri-
       marily western end of Border.

1220. Jones, J.E., "The Parliamentary Representation of Berkshire
       and its Boroughs during the Reign of Elizabeth I," *Berkshire
       Archeol. Jour.*, 63 (1967-68) [1969], 39–56.

       Country gentry were replacing townsmen as representatives of
       boroughs.

1221. Jones, Richard H., *The Royal Policy of Richard II: Absolutism
       in the Later Middle Ages*. Studies in Medieval History, X.
       Oxford: Basil Blackwell; N.Y.: Barnes and Noble, 1968.

       Aims to explain Richard II in terms that would have been mean-
       ingful to his contemporaries, yet comprehensible to us. Few
       pages alluding to Shakespeare; but see chapter, "Richard II
       and the Historians," pp. 113-124. Rev. *TLS*, 30 May 1968, 554.

1222. Jones, W.R., "Relations of the Two Jurisdictions: Conflict and Cooperation in England during the Thirteenth and Fourteenth Centuries," *Studies in Medieval and Ren. Hist.*, 7 (1970), 77-210.

Tension created between expanding church courts and expanding royal courts. Compromises each was willing to make towards the other.

1223. Kelley, Donald R., "Murd'rous Machiavel in France: A Post Mortem," *Pol. Sci. Quart.*, 85 (1970), 545-559.

Machiavelli's career and reputation in 16th-cent. France. French were frightened and fascinated by his political mask, cynicism, and brutality. This led to image of Machiavelli as demon of power.

1224. Kenny, Robert W., *Elizabeth's Admiral: The Political Career of Charles Howard, Earl of Nottingham, 1536-1624.* Baltimore: Johns Hopkins Press, 1970.

Rev. *AHR*, 76 (1971), 498-499.

His successful career as naval commander under Elizabeth and James. His supervision of the Admiralty and decay of this institution.

1225. ————, "Parliamentary Influence of Charles Howard, Earl of Nottingham, 1536-1624," *Journal of Modern Hist.*, 39 (1967), 215-232.

Tracing a "Howard faction" in Parliament, author examines the career of Lord Charles Howard who led the fleet that turned aside the Armada, and was a ubiquitous influence at court. Diagnoses a career that was a series of missed opportunities owing to a defect of political skill and a failure to attract and discipline an adequate following; e.g., the attack on wine monopolies of 1604 affected him directly, but there was no defense or mitigation by his followers.

1226. Kenyon, J.P., ed., *The Stuart Constitution, 1603-1688. Documents and Commentary.* Cambridge: Cambridge Univ. Press, 1966.

Rev. *AHR*, 72 (1966), 580-581.

Documents are arranged in subject-matter sections, each preceded by editorial comments.

1227. Kinney, Joseph A., Jr., "Dramatization of Fear in Elizabethan Political Plays, 1580-1600," *DA*, 29 (1969), 2265-2266-A (Bryn Mawr Coll.).

Dramatists used specific techniques of structure, character, language, and the supernatural to dramatize fear. Use of these four techniques analyzed in "conqueror" plays, Senecan tragedies, and English histories. Last chapter deals with *Julius Caesar*.

1228. Kluxen, Kurt, "Die necessità als Zentralbegriff im politischen
       Denken Machiavellis," *Zeitschrift für Religions- und Geistes-
       gesch.*, 20 (1968), 14-27.

       Machiavelli a modern, like Marx, in his grasp of practical
       necessity.

1229. ―――, *Politik und menschliche Existenz bei Machiavelli.
       Dargestellt am Begriff der "Necessità."* Stuttgart: Kohlhammer,
       1967. Rev. *Archiv f. Begrif.*, 14 (1970), 123-124.

       Interpretation of Machiavelli based on central meaning of
       necessità as a summary notion. Stoic-Heraclitean sources of
       necessità; various uses of the term; its relations to *Fortuna.*

1230. Knight, J. Richard, "Political Scepticism in Robert Burton's
       Anatomy of Melancholy: Prolegomenon to 'An Utopia of Mine
       Own,'" *DA*, 30 (1970), 2971-72-A (Wash. Univ.).

       Argues that Burton deliberately undercuts his own surface ar-
       guments with his supposedly "supporting" detail. The detail
       makes a consistently skeptical sub-text, which subverts sur-
       face optimism related to English life and the theoretical re-
       formers, especially Botero.

1231. Koerber, Eberhard von, *Die Staatstheorie des Erasmus von
       Rotterdam.* Schriften zur Verfassungsgeschichte, Bd. 4; Berlin:
       Duncker & Humblot, 1967.

       Rev. *BHR*, 30 (1968), 418-419.

       Erasmus' view of justice and law; he favored a mixed state.

1232. Kölmel, Wilhelm, "Machiavelli und der Machiavellismus," *Histori-
       sches Jahr.*, 89 (1969), 372-408.

       The *Principe* is not a practical guide for princes, but an ex-
       pression of Machiavelli's mistrust of power. His political
       theories are to be understood by reading the *Principe* in con-
       junction with the *Discorsi*, which shows his sympathy for a
       republican government of free citizens.

1233. ―――, "Petrarca und das Reich," *Hist. Jahr.*, 90 (1970),
       1-30.

       Role of politics in Petrarch's writings. Political aspects of
       "rediscovery" of classical works also considered.

1234. Krieger, Leonard, and Fritz Stern, eds., *Responsibility of
       Power: Historical Essays in Honor of Hajo Holborn.* N.Y.:
       Doubleday, 1967. Rev. *JMH*, 41 (1969), 517.

       Theme: tension between responsibility and power, from Machia-
       velli to Marcuse. First section covers "formation of sovereign
       power" in 16th and 17th cents. Almost all essays hitherto un-
       published; bibliographic footnotes.

1235. Lamont, W.M., *Godly Rule: Politics and Religion 1603-60.*
       London: Macmillan, 1969.

       Rev. *AHR*, 76 (1970), 145-147; *EHR*, 86 (1971), 171-172.

On Puritan ideas concerning civil power and jurisdiction. Puritans were not necessarily enemies of the Crown; some Puritan acceptance of tradition of the "Christian Emperor" was sustained.

1236. Lawrence, Larry Lee, "Political Pointing as a Dramatic Technique in Shakespeare's Plays," *DA*, 31 (1970), 2349-A (Stanford Univ.).

Operation of political ideas in Shakespeare's plays is a matter of practical dramaturgy and calculated technique; Shakespeare invokes and manipulates political preconceptions of his audience for dramatic purposes.

1237. Lee, Maurice, Jr., "The Jacobean Diplomatic Service," *Amer. Hist. Rev.*, 72 (1967), 1264-1282.

Discusses the duties of the ambassadors under James I (to 1618) and the degree of efficiency they were able to achieve under his rule, considering problems they were forced to face. Questions lucrativeness of such ambassadorial posts and shows them to be mainly stepping stones to better posts at home when their foreign service was terminated.

1238. ————, *James I and Henri IV, an Essay in English Foreign Policy, 1603-1610*. Univ. of Ill. Press, 1970.

Rev. *AHR*, 76 (1971), 147-148; *Choice*, 7 (1970), 1124.

Maintains James had opportunity for solid Anglo-French friendship which could have brought peace in decade after assassination of Henry IV.

1239. Lehmberg, Stanford E., "Early Tudor Parliamentary Procedure: Provisos in the Legislation of the Reformation Parliament," *EHR*, 85 (1970), 1-11.

On manuscript acts passed by the Reformation Parliament (1529-1536) to study process of amending legislation during reign of Henry VIII. Finds over 100 bills out of 222 were subjected to parliamentary revision. Concludes parliament not brow-beaten or entirely subservient to Crown.

1240. ————, *The Reformation Parliament 1529-1536*. Cambridge Univ. Press, 1970. Rev. *AHR*, 75 (1970), 2046.

Central theme is the Henrician Reformation. Principal sources for what happened in Parliament, 1529-1536.

1241. Levack, Brian Paul, "The Politics of the English Civil Lawyers, 1603-1629," *DA*, 31 (1970), 2849-A (Yale Univ.).

Civil lawyers depended on Church and State for their income, hence provided strong support for James I and Charles I. Effects on common and civil law and status of the monarchy resulting from influence of civil lawyers.

1242. Lever, J.W., *The Tragedy of State*. London: Methuen, 1971.

Rev. *Ren. and Ref.*, 9 (1972), 74-75.

Applies politics of early 17th cent. to study of plays; in
contrast to earlier providential English history plays, these
Jacobean works evince, pessimistically, an unalterable
depravity.

1243. Levine, Mortimer, *The Early Elizabethan Succession Question,
1558-1568.* Stanford Univ. Press, 1966.

Rev. Christopher Hill, *Ren. Quar.*, 20 (1967), 260-261.

Gives an account of issues involved in succession, and the
pamphlets which appeared in the question of Elizabeth and Mary
of Scotland. The Parliamentary pamphleteers went back to the
history of Richard II and the usurpation of Henry to gain support for their arguments.

1244. ———, "Henry VIII's Use of His Spiritual and Temporal Jurisdiction in His Great Causes of Matrimony, Legitimacy, and Succession," *Historical Journal*, 10, no. 1 (1967), 3-10.

Illustrates Tudor power and legal background of Elizabeth's
right to the throne.

1245. Lewis, J.U., "Jean Bodin's 'Logic of Sovereignty,'" *Political
Studies*, 16 (1968), 206-222.

Bodin's importance, not as anticipator of Hobbes, but as an-
choring the source of law to demands of justice and reason.
He perceived that a value-free definition of political-legal
sovereignty is inadequate.

1246. Lindsay, Robert Orval, "Antoine Lefèvre de la Boderie's Mission to England: A Study of French-English Relations, 1606-
1611." *DA*, 27 (1966), 652-A (Univ. of Oregon).

Examines the diplomatic missions to England by Antoine Lefèvre
de la Boderie and discusses the relations between France and
England over a five-year period. Concludes that Boderie was
influential in effecting a spirit of "amity" between the two
countries.

1247. ———, and John Neu, comps., *French Political Pamphlets,
1547-1648. A Catalogue of Major Collections in American
Libraries.* Madison: Univ. of Wisc. Press, 1969.

Rev. *BHR*, 32 (1970), 739-740; *Revue Historique*, no. 497 (1971),
216-217.

Collects 6,742 titles, in 15 U.S. libraries, arranged by year
of publication and by alphabetical order.

1248. Loomie, Albert J., S.J., "Bacon and Gondomar: An Unknown Link
in 1618," *RenQ*, 21 (1968), 1-10.

Letter from Bacon to the Spanish ambassador to England, Gondomar, to amend naively optimistic reports sent to Spain by
Gondomar's assistant regarding the state of religious toleration in England.

1249. ————, "Sir Robert Cecil and the Spanish Embassy, *Bull. of Inst. of Hist. Res.*, 42 (1969), 30–57.

During Robert Cecil's influence at James' court, three Spaniards—Don Juan de Tassis, Don Pedro de Zuñiga, and Don Alonso de Velasco—represented the interests of Philip III. From 1603 to 1612 their private correspondence reveals Cecil's varying attitudes to Spain and his confidential opinions.

1250. Machiavelli issue, *Italian Quar.*, 14 (Spring–Summer 1970), no. 53.

Includes Dante Della Terza, cited above; cf. Chiappelli, "Machiavelli as Secretary"; John Geerken, "Homer's Image of the Hero in Machiavelli...."

1251. Machiavelli issue, *Review of National Literatures*, 1, no. 1 (1970).

Has essays by Leo Strauss, "Machiavelli and Classical Literature"; J. Mazzeo, "The Poetry of Power: Machiavelli's Literary Vision"; G.R. Sarolli, "The Unpublished Machiavelli"; R.C. Clark, "Machiavelli: Bibliographical Spectrum," pp. 93–135.

1252. *Machiavellismo e antimachiavellici nel Cinquecento. Il Pensiero Politico*, 2, no. 3 (October 1969), whole issue.

Articles by M. D'Addio; L. Firpo; R. De Mattei; S. Mastellone; J. Malarczyk; by C. Morris, "Machiavelli's Reputation in Tudor England"; and A. Stegmann, "Le Tacitisme: programme pour un nouvel essai de définition." Smaller pieces include: D. Panizza, "Machiavelli e Alberico Gentili" and E. Cochrane, "Machiavelli visto dagli studiosi di scienza politica in America."

1253. Mager, Wolfgang, *Zur Entstehung des modernen Staatsbegriffs*. Akademie der Wissenschaften und der Literatur, Mainz. Abhandlungen der Geistes- und Sozialwissenschaftlichen Klasse, Jhrg., 1968, nr. 9; Wiesbaden: Franz Steiner Verlag, 1968.

Detailed documented account, from Roman times through Middle Ages to second half of 16th cent. of development of the idea of the state. Careful examination of terminology (*status*, etc.). Rev. *Archiv f. Begrif.*, 13 (1969), 97–99.

1254. Major, J. Russell, "Popular Initiative in Renaissance France," in Archibald R. Lewis, ed., *Aspects of the Renaissance: A Symposium*. Austin/London: Univ. of Texas Press, 1967, pp. 27–41.

Popular initiative a prominent factor in Renaissance France and probably other countries, should be stressed, rather than monarchical roles, in creative energy of Renaissance discovery of the world and of man.

1255. ————, "The Renaissance Monarchy as Seen by Erasmus, More, Seyssel, and Machiavelli," in *Action and Conviction in Modern*

Europe: Essays in Memory of E.H. Harbison, ed. T.K. Rabb and
J.E. Seigel. Princeton Univ. Press, 1969, pp. 17-31.

These four figures saw monarchy of the Renaissance as resting
neither on the army nor on the bureaucracy, but on support received from the people. Nationalism was conceived as a negative force directed against the outsider.

1256. Mancini, Dominic, *The Usurpation of Richard the Third*, tr.
with an introduction by C.A.J. Armstrong. 2nd ed. bilingual.
Oxford, 1969. Rev. *Choice* 7 (1970), 447.

New edition, with new introduction and updated notes, of Armstrong's translation of Mancini's work. Considered a source
for *Richard III*.

1257. May, Teresa, "The Cobham Family in the Administration of England, 1200-1400," *Archaeologia Cantiana*, 82 (1968), 1-31.

Family name recalls the Falstaff-Oldcastle topicality problem.

1258. McCann, Timony J., "The Parliamentary Speech of Viscount Montague against the Act of Supremacy, 1559," *Sussex Archaeol.
Colls.*, 108 (1970), 50-57.

Short history of Anthony Brown, 1st Viscount Montague (b.
1526), followed by text of his speech recently discovered in a
recusant manuscript, part of family library at Deere Park,
Northhampton, now at Bodleian Library, Oxford.

1259. McGrath, Patrick, *Papists and Puritans under Elizabeth I*.
Problems of History Series. London: Blandford; N.Y.: Walker
and Co., 1967.

Rev. *Ampleforth Journal*, 73 (1968), 87.

Considers similarities and differences of Puritans and Catholics,
and the reaction of them upon Elizabethan government trying to
establish unity of religion.

1260. McNiven, Peter, "The Cheshire Rising of 1400," *BJRL*, 52 (1970),
375-396.

Evidence for an uprising in Cheshire about January 1400, emphasizing anti-Lancastrian feeling under Richard II, and the importance of Hotspur to this rising, and one in 1403.

1261. Mellano, Maria Franca, "Rappresentanti italiani della corona
inglese a Roma ai primi del Cinquecento," *Studi Romani*, 17
(1969), 438-459.

Although from 1477 onward England was represented continuously
at Rome, after the first envoy the resident ambassador was
usually an Italian.

1262. Metcalfe, William Craig, "The Public Career of Thomas Howard,
First Earl of Suffolk: 1603-1618," *DA*, 28 (1968), 4580-A
(Univ. of Minn.).

Career of Suffolk (1561-1626), successful sea-captain under
Elizabeth, who was promoted into central administration upon
James's accession, 1603. Serving in powerful post of Lord
Chamberlain from 1603 to 1614, he was in similarly powerful
office as Lord Treasurer from 1614 to 1618, when he was dis-
missed for graft and embezzlement. As close friend of Earl of
Salisbury, James's closest adviser until 1612, then of Earl of
Somerset, James's personal favorite for two years thereafter,
Suffolk was consulted on all major policy decisions and con-
trolled enormous power and patronage.

1263. Meyers, Ronald Jay, "The Royal King and Loyal Subject: Chang-
       ing Political Conceptions Reflected in the Drama of Francis
       Beaumont, John Fletcher, and George Chapman," *DA*, 27 (1966),
       750-A (N.Y. Univ.).

       Little attempt has been made to explore the political attitudes
       of Jacobean playwrights other than Shakespeare. Implicit in
       the plays of Francis Beaumont, John Fletcher, and George Chap-
       man is concern for such contemporary issues as the divine
       right of kings and rights of subjects or royalty and loyalty.

1264. Michel, Alain, "À propos de la *Republique*: de Cicéron et
       Tacite à Jean Bodin," *Études latines*, 45 (1967 [1968]), 419-
       436.

       Studies influence of ancients on two 16th-cent. French poli-
       tical writers: La Boétie and Jean Bodin.

1265. Molho, Anthony, "Politics and the Ruling Class in Early Renais-
       sance Florence," *Nuova Rivista Storica*, 52 (1968), 401-420.

       Formulates a working definition from sociological phenomena of
       Florentine ruling class, 1382-1420, using documentation from
       comparative historiographies.

1266. Notestein, Wallace, *The House of Commons 1604-1610*, ed. E.R.
       Foster and B.D. Henning. New Haven and London: Yale Univ.
       Press, 1971.

       Rev. *EHR*, 87 (1972), 363-365.

       Posthumous volume of the historian (d. 1969). Relations of
       Crown and commons, and issues of James's first seven years.
       Compares with Neale's works on Elizabeth's parliaments.

1267. Oakley, Francis, "Jacobean Political Theology: The Absolute
       and Ordinary Powers of the King," *JHI*, 29 (1968), 323-346.

       Traces backgrounds of absolute and ordinary powers of King.
       Discusses Chief Baron Fleming's remarks (1606) about Jacobean
       theories of monarchy; finds inadequate and ill-conceived Mc-
       Ilwain's interpretation of medieval and early modern consti-
       tutionalism. The absolute and ordinary powers discussed by
       17th-cent. English lawyers were not the same as *gubernaculum*
       and *jurisdictio*, or the absolute and ordinary powers in medie-
       val jurists generally.

1268. Occhiogrosso, Frank Victor, "Sovereign and Subject in Caroline
       Tragedy," *DA*, 30 (1969), 2493-2494-A (Johns Hopkins Univ.).

       On two conflicting traditions centering around sovereign-sub-
       ject relationship in 16th and early 17th-cent. political
       thought: 1) tradition of non-resistance leading to doctrine
       of absolutism, traced from Luther, Calvin, and other early
       reformers through Bodin and James I; and 2) tradition of
       natural rights leading to doctrine of resistance, traced from
       Ponet, Knox, and Goodman up to Mariana and the *Vindiciae Con-
       tra Tyrannos*.

1269. Oehling, Richard Alfred, "Late Elizabethan Governmental Treat-
       ment of Religious Non-Conformity, 1589-1603," *DA*, 30 (1970),
       2947-A (Rutgers State Univ.).

       Oppression of Catholic and Protestant dissenters by government;
       its actions, such as censorship of propaganda, raids, torture
       of suspects; stern expectation of obedience to Crown and Es-
       tablished Church.

1270. O'Neill, James N., "Queen Elizabeth I as a Patron of the Arts:
       The Relationship Between Royal Patronage, Society, and Cul-
       ture in Renaissance England," *DA*, 27 (1967), 3405-A - 3406-A
       (Univ. of Virginia).

       Investigates cultural patronage of the Crown during reign of
       Elizabeth. In tracing the Queen's cultural background and her
       support of literature, education, painting, music, and espec-
       ially drama, this work depicts intellectual climate of England
       in the 16th cent. It also demonstrates that patronage was
       widespread during the period.

1271. Ortego, Philip D., "Shakespeare and the Doctrine of Monarchy
       in *King John*," *CLA Jour.*, 13 (1969/70), 392-401.

       Shakespeare's omission of Magna Carta in *Jn* as politically
       expedient.

1272. Parmiter, Geoffrey de C., *The King's Great Matter: A Study in
       Anglo-Papal Relations, 1527-1534*. London: Longmans; N.Y.:
       Barnes and Noble, 1967.

       Rev. *AHR*, 73 (1968), 807; *EHR*, 83 (1968), 832-833.

       On Henry VIII's failure to obtain annulment of marriage to
       Catherine of Aragon, precipitating events which were of crucial
       significance to Englishmen. Its transforming effects on church
       and state and the founding of several modern institutions.
       Major reference work for study of the divorce. Documentation.

1273. ———, "A Note on Some Aspects of the Royal Supremacy of
       Henry VIII," *Recusant Hist.*, 10 (1970), 183-192.

       Sovereignty of Parliament as a result of Henry VIII's role as
       head of Church. Role of lawyers in Parliament; helped esta-
       blish it as flexible law-making body.

1274. Pasquer, André Michel, "La Lutte Contre la Tyrannie au Seizième Siècle (1570-1581): La Boétie, Languet, Hotman," *DA*, 31 (1970), 2396-97-A (Univ. of Colorado).

How 16th cent. considered problem of tyranny: three authors representing different aspects of the problem: humanistic approach of La Boétie; historical approach with the *France-Gaule* of Hotman; and the theological approach with *Vindiciae Contra Tyrannos* of Languet.

1275. Plumb, J.H., "The Growth of the Electorate in England from 1600-1715," *Past and Present*, no. 45 (1969), 90-116.

Discusses origin, development, and political influence of the electorate in those years.

1276. Powell, J. Enoch, and Keith Wallis, *The House of Lords in the Middle Ages: A History of the English House of Lords to 1540*. London: Weidenfeld & Nicolson, 1968.

Rev. *Jour. of Eccl. Hist.*, 20 (1969), 344-345; *New Statesman*, 76 (1968), 112.

Detailed description of fluctuating process by which the Parliament of 1540 had achieved its definite shape, by reference to administration records of the Parliament itself.

1277. Prezzolini, Giuseppe, *Machiavelli*, trans. N.Y.: Farrar, Straus & Giroux, 1967. Rev. *Observer*, 25 Aug. 1968, 22.

Translation of *Machiavelli anticristo*. A reappraisal of his continuing influence in Western affairs.

1278. Pueyo, Jesús, "La teología política del Estado-Nación y el anglicanismo político," *Revista de Estudios políticos*, 157 (1968), 5-29.

Absolute state from 16th to the 17th cents. as product of classic and traditional Christianity and European rationality. Anglican sociopolitical dynamics are based on insularity and religious unity.

1279. Pulman, Michael Barraclough, *The Elizabethan Privy Council in the Fifteen-Seventies*. Berkeley: Univ. of Calif. Press, 1971.

Rev. *AHR*, 77 (1972), 508.

Causes of Council's actions and executive functions.

1280. Rabb, T.K., "Francis Bacon and the Reform of Society," in *Action and Conviction in Modern Europe: Essays in Memory of E.H. Harbison*, ed. T.K. Rabb and J.E. Seigel. Princeton Univ. Press, 1969, pp. 169-193.

Reassesses the S.R. Gardiner, Trevor-Roper, Christopher Hill thesis of Bacon as forerunner and inspiration of revolutionary thought. Stresses Bacon's differences with revolutionaries; he was pro central action and control, pro monarchical power, and anti changes in political structure.

1281.   Rae, Thomas, *The Administration of the Scottish Frontier,*
        1513-1603. Edinburgh Univ. Press, 1966.

        Rev. *AHR,* 72 (1967), 967-968.

        Problems of administration of Scottish-English frontier; pri-
        marily concerned with Scottish side. Part which central
        government played in frontier administration. Treats way in
        which the age regarded the right of the central government to
        act in local affairs.

1282.   Rees, J., *"Richard II* in 1615," *NQ,* n.s. 13 (1966), 130-131.

        Richard II had relevance to political events of 1601. Its
        political explosiveness was also feared in the context of a
        new situation in 1615.

1283.   Roberts, Clayton, *The Growth of Responsible Government in*
        Stuart England. Cambridge Univ. Press, 1966.

        Rev. *AHR,* 72 (1967), 582-583.

        Discusses struggle between the Crown and the minister for con-
        trol of policy formation by means of pamphlets, parliamentary
        debates, and reports of foreign agents. During reign of James
        I and specifically in 1610, a new type of member of Parliament
        arose: ambitious, aggressive, and tired of corruption in
        government.

1284.   Rogers, Alan, "Henry IV, the Commons and Taxation," *MS,* 31
        (1969), 44-70.

        Struggles of king and parliament in reign of Henry IV were not
        over minor issues, but over the whole field of royal preroga-
        tive and parliamentary power of consent to taxation.

1285.   Rose, Paul L., "The Politics of Antony and Cleopatra," *SQ,* 20
        (1969), 379-389.

        Concept of kingship for Antony is romantic, for Cleopatra des-
        potic. Caesar represents the ideal monarch because he can sub-
        ordinate impulse to reason.

1286.   Rosenfield, Manuel C., "Holy Trinity, Aldgate, on the Eve of
        the Dissolution," *Guildhall Misc.,* 3 (1970), 159-173.

        The London church thought to have been used by Henry as test-
        case for dissolution of monasteries. History of the church,
        its civic and religious role in London; its financial status,
        given as reason for its forced surrender.

1287.   Rosenthal, Joel T., "Feuds and Private Peace-Making: A Fif-
        teenth-Century Example," *NMS,* 14 (1970), 84-90.

        Violence in English society in 15th cent.; breakdown of public
        control led to establishment of private methods of controlling
        outbreaks. Document of an argument in 1458 settled by private
        arbitration that avoided a lengthy feud.

1288. Rouse, Richard H. and Mary A., "John of Salisbury and the Doctrine of Tyrannicide," *Speculum*, 42 (1967), 693-709.

Detailed analysis of *Polycraticus* shows his defense of the doctrine to be theoretical and qualified, his aim being to convince Henry II to govern according to law.

1289. Salley, Louise, "A French Humanist's Chef-d'Oeuvre: *The Commentaries on Seneca's 'De Clementia'* by John Calvin," *RenP*, (1967), 41-53.

The *Commentaries* are typical Northern Renaissance study. Calvin's ideal just and humane ruler is similar to the ideal prince of Erasmus' *Institutio Principis Christiani* and Budé's *L'Institution du Prince*.

1290. Sayles, George Osborne, "King Richard II of England: A Fresh Look," *Proc. Amer. Philos. Soc.*, 115, no. 1 (1971), 28-31.

Examines historical views on Richard II's character: 1) his laziness, 2) his absence from Council meetings, 3) his "profoundly conventional mind," 4) his religious orthodoxy. Offers a more charitable, realistic view of King in context.

1291. Schieder, Theodor, "Niccolò Machiavelli," *Hist. Zeit.*, 210 (1970), 265-294.

"Reputation study" of his influence on political thought up to present. Concludes that in all his contradictoriness he is an "image of the modern world."

1292. Schochet, Gordon Joel, "The Patriarchal Content of Stuart Political Thought: The Relation between the Family and Political Obligation in Seventeenth Century England," *DA*, 27 (1967), 1111-A (Univ. of Minn.).

Patriarchalism was major element of political theory of 17th cent., present on all levels of thought and in almost all 17th-cent. ideological controversies; it was the chief alternative to better known contractual and state-of-nature explanations of political obligation. Stuart thinkers who examined the state inevitably had to deal with the family, either to distinguish it from the state or to show how it related to the political order.

1293. ————, "Patriarchalism, Politics and Mass Attitudes in Stuart England," *Hist. Jour.*, 12 (1969), 413-441.

Latent political attitudes of "silent majority" in Stuart England explained in terms of patriarchal theory of obligation rooted in conditions of the family.

1294. Seddon, P.R., "Robert Carr, Earl of Somerset," *Ren. and Mod. Studs.*, 14 (1970), 48-68.

Studies Carr's relationship to factions at court of James to determine his influence as King's favorite. Concentrates on

four important developments in Carr's career: his unsuccessful
attempt with Overbury to recall parliament, his effort to appoint his nominees to vacant place of Secretary, his alliance
with the Howards, and emergence of a powerful opposition group
to him. (Carr came to England in 1603; returned to King's
notice in 1607.)

1295. Senning, Calvin F., "The Visit of Christian IV to England in
1614," *Historian*, 31 (1969), 552-572.

Significance of Christian's visit to be found not as social
affair or as demonstration of brotherly affection but rather
as diplomatic move in power politics of Northern Europe.

1296. Sewell, Ernestine Porcher, "Dictionary of Political References
in English Literature from the Twelfth to the Twentieth Centuries," *DA*, 29 (1969), 3587-A (East Texas State Univ.).

Dictionary of explications of political and historical matters
which have attracted the literary man and his interpreters
from the 12th to the 20th cents.

1297. Slavin, Arthur Joseph, *Politics and Profit: A Study of Sir
Ralph Sadler, 1507-1547*. Cambridge Univ. Press, 1966.

Rev. *AHR*, 72 (1966), 575-576.

Portrait of Henry VIII's principal Secretary of State. Studies of relations with Henry VIII, Thomas Cromwell, etc., as a
vehicle for studying social and political elements of Tudor
society.

1298. Smith, Alan Gordon Rae, *The Government of Elizabethan England*.
London: Edward Arnold, 1967; N.Y.: Norton, 1968.

Rev. *History*, 53 (1968), 424-425.

Introductory brief survey of Elizabethan government. Chapters
on Queen, Privy Council, Parliament, the central administration, the patronage system, government social and economic
policy, local government.

1299. ———, "The Secretariats of the Cecils, circa 1580-1612,"
EHR, 83 (1968), 481-504.

On private secretaries who served the Cecils, and what is
known of their backgrounds, etc. Throws light on inner workings of government machine under Elizabeth and James.

1300. Smith, M.C., "Ronsard and Queen Elizabeth I," *BHR*, 29 (1967),
93-119.

Discusses Ronsard's *Elegies, Mascarades et Bergerie*, dedicated
to Elizabeth. Ronsard also dedicated poems to Robert Dudley
and William Cecil. Shows how he modified texts when political
and religious circumstances changed.

1301. Smith, R.B., *Land and Politics in the England of Henry VIII:
The West Riding of Yorkshire, 1530-1546*. Oxford: Clarendon
Press, 1970.

Rev. *Hist. Jour.*, 14 (1971), 221-223; *Jour. of Mod. Hist.*, 43 (1971), 499-500; *TLS*, 19 March 1971, 327.

Problem of social structure, investigating links between possession of land and exercise of political power; in Tudor age power and control percolated downward through the hierarchy of the landed classes.

1302. Stevens, Richard G., "The New Republic in More's *Utopia*," *Political Sci. Q.*, 84 (1969), 387-411.

More's view of church-state relations; contrary to modern "separatist" notion, More saw connection between piety and magistracy.

1303. Stewart, Pamela D., *Innocent Gentillet e la sua polemica antimachiavellica*. Florence: La Nuova Italia Editrice, 1969.

Rev. *RLC*, 44 (1970), 417-419.

Remarks that a truly documentary study of Gentillet has not been made. Offers: I. Life and work of Gentillet; II. Editions of the *Anti-Mach.*; III. Truth of Machiavelli's doctrine; IV. Anti-Machiavellan polemic in France ...; V. Declaration of 1577; ed. of *Anti-Mach.*, 1585. Conclusion: "La fortuna dell'-*Anti-Mach.*"

1304. Stone, Lawrence, "Office Under Queen Elizabeth: The Case of Lord Hunsdon and the Lord Chamberlainship in 1585," *Historical Journal*, 10 (1967), 279-282.

Denies procurement of an important office under Elizabeth and James was a means to certain wealth.

1305. Storey, R.L., "Lincolnshire and the Wars of the Roses," *NMS*, 14 (1970), 64-83.

Effects of severe political changes wrought on English public by the Wars; examines reasons for inhabitants' commitments to the partisan royal factions, using Lincolnshire as a model.

1306. Tenenti, A., "La religione di Machiavelli," *Studi Storici*, 10 (1969), 709-748.

Machiavelli as possible fideist.

1307. Thompson, William McIlwaine, "The Problem of Political Authority in Calvin's Theory and Practice in the Light of Modern Interpretations," *DA*, 30 (1969), 803-A (Yale Univ.).

Geneva was not a dictatorship, bibliocracy, or clerocracy. Calvin's radical religious monism led to a political pluralism.

1308. Thompson, W.D.J. Cargill, "Martin Luther and the 'Two Kingdoms,'" in David Thomson, ed., *Political Ideas*. N.Y.: Basic Books, 1966, pp. 27-47.

Depicts Luther as political thinker and sheds light on his doctrine of *die zwei Reiche*—the kingdom of God and the kingdom of the Devil—which rationalized the paradox of government

as a necessary evil and the ruler as necessarily divine. As
Luther influenced Anglicanism, he helped promote the fear of
chaos as a means to elicit a people's obedience to their
ruler.

1309.   Thoroughman, Thomas Vernon, "Some Political Aspects of Anglo-
French Relations, 1610-1619," *DA*, 30 (1969), 261-262-A (Univ.
of North Carolina).

Anglo-French diplomatic relations in years leading up to the
break in 1618; based on diplomatic correspondence concerning
the two countries, particularly the Stowe manuscripts in the
British Museum, and State Papers and the Baschet Transcripts
in the Public Record Office.

1310.   Tlili, M., "Méchanceté de l'homme et tyrannie du prince. Essai
sur la théorie machiavelienne du gouvernment," *Rev. Metaphys.
Morale*, 72, no. 2 (1968), 205-222.

On politics as a technique, and the philosophy which underlies
it: a deep-seated pessimism which calls forth a tyrannical
power.

1311.   Trafton, Dain Atwood, "Ideology and Politics in the Second
Tetralogy of Shakespeare's History Plays," *DA*, 30 (1969), 295-
296-A (Univ. of Calif., Berkeley).

Each of the tetralogy's three English kings has a personal
ideology--a set of fundamental ideas about the nature of the
world--which can be discerned through his characteristic patterns of expression and action and by which he guides his political conduct; these personal ideologies differ from each
other in important ways and also from pieties of the Elizabethan world picture.

1312.   Ullmann, Walter, "The Rebirth of the Citizen on the Eve of the
Renaissance Period," in Archibald R. Lewis, *Aspects of the
Renaissance: A Symposium*. Austin/London: Univ. of Texas
Press, 1967, pp. 5-25.

On synchronism between Renaissance humanism and incipient and
growing theory of citizenship. In relation to *civis* and *uni-
versitas civium*, discusses *humanitas*, rebirth, concepts of
fidelis and *sub/ditus*.

1313.   Vahle, Hermann, "Bodins Polenbild. Zur französischen und
polnischen Souveränitätslehre im 16. Jahrhundert," *AKG*, 52
(1970), 4-27.

On the "elected" monarchy in the 16th cent. in Poland and its
effect on the idea of a limited monarchy in Europe, especially
on writings of Bodin.

1314.   Waley, Daniel, "The Primitivist Element in Machiavelli's
Thought," *JHI*, 31 (1970), 91-98.

Primitivist notions of Machiavelli as nostalgia for an age of
simplicity; his views as derived from the classical; his portrait of the German as containing elements of noble savage.

1315. Wernham, Richard Bruce, *Before the Armada: The Emergence of the English Nation*. N.Y.: Harcourt, 1966. Rev. *EHR*, 83 (1968), 122.

An essentially political survey, including information on economics and military hardware as it is politically relevant.

1316. Westfall, Carroll William, "The Two Ideal Cities of the Early Renaissance: Republicanism and Ducal Thought in Quattrocento Architectural Treatises," *DA*, 28 (1967), 2156-A (Columbia Univ.).

Discusses political climate of Renaissance; republican virtues. Ideal city as developed in works of humanists and architectural theorists during early Renaissance, and their view of the city as actual physical center of cultural and political life vs. the medieval view which uneasily regarded city as center of secular life.

1317. White, Howard B., *Copp'd Hills Towards Heaven: Shakespeare and the Classical Polity*. The Hague: M. Nijhoff, 1970.

Argues Shakespeare was political philosopher in platonic tradition (derived from Plato, Plutarch, Montaigne, or himself). *MND, Timon, Pericles, Cymb., Temp.* Rev. *Choice*, 8 (1971), 1331.

1318. ————, *Peace among the Willows. The Political Philosophy of Francis Bacon*. (Archives internationales d'histoire des idées. 24.) The Hague: M. Nijhoff, 1968.

Rev. *J. Hist. Phil.*, 9 (1971), 94-95.

On Bacon's utopian faith in the benevolence of science; he restores final causes in man, i.e., in matters political.

I. Political belief and utopian thought. II. Provisional morals. III. Civil consciousness. IV. The English Solomon. V. Provisional politics. VI. Island Utopias (New Atlantis). VII. The Old and the New Atlantis. VIII. The Bensalem Society. IX. The Feasts of Bensalem. X. Definitive morals. XI. Definitive politics. XII. Imitable thunderbolt.

1319. Whitfield, J.H., "The Charlecote Manuscript of Machiavelli's *Prince*," *IS*, 22 (1967), 6-25.

Provides description, analysis, and parallels.

1320. ————, *Discourses on Machiavelli*. Cambridge: Heffer, 1969.

Rev. *TLS*, 26 March 1970, 331.

Collection of 11 articles and three reviews, all previously published (except the fifth, mainly on Guicciardini); all concerned with Machiavelli.

1321. Wickham, Glynne, "Shakespeare's Investiture Play: The Occasion and Subject of *The Winter's Tale*," *TLS*, 18 December 1969, 1456.

WT may be regarded not only as a figurative compliment to James I but also as Shakespeare's contribution to the investiture of Henry, Prince of Wales and Heir Apparent, in 1610.

Evidence drawn from two pageants by Anthony Munday, two
masques by Ben Jonson, a poem and a masque by Samuel Daniel,
three of James I's own speeches, and two statues sculpted by
Cornelius and William Cure, master-masons to the King.

1322. Williamson, Marilyn, "The Political Context in *Antony and
Cleopatra*," *SQ*, 21 (1970), 241-251.

How Shakespeare develops Plutarch's history and how political
context forms the "extended world" found in all of Shakespeare's mature plays. Divided political context reflects and
amplifies divided characters.

1323. Wilson, Charles, *Queen Elizabeth and the Revolt of the Netherlands*. Berkeley: Univ. of Calif. Press, 1970.

Rev. *AHR*, 76 (1971), 1164-1165; *TLS*, 11 September 1970, 992.

Anglo-Dutch relations during the revolt against the Spanish;
its influence in encouraging ideas of constitutionalism and
rule of law in Queen Elizabeth's England.

1324. Wolf, William D., "'Vigilance, Counsell, Action': Success in
Five of Ben Jonson's Plays," *DA*, 29 (1969), 3114-3115-A
(Univ. of Wisc.).

Jonson favored an authoritarian ruler holding power for the
welfare of the state. Where such a ruler is absent--as *Catiline*, *Sejanus*, *Volpone*, *Alchemist*, and *Barth. Fair* reveal--
fools are continual victims. Relates Jonson's political views
to ideas of human nature and society as debased.

1325. Wolfe, Martin, "Jean Bodin on Taxes: The Sovereignty-Taxes
Paradox," *Political Science Quarterly*, 83 (1968), 268-284.

Bodin provided advice to King to improve his "image" and avoid
blundering in area of taxes; and to his countrymen to stop
disuniting country. Widely quoted by opponents of Stuarts in
England, Bodin was cited for view that "king should live of
his own." Botero followed Bodin on royal revenues and borrowing, but in France Bodin was distorted to defend view that
king must have unlimited right to tax.

1326. Wood, Neal, "Some Common Aspects of the Thought of Seneca and
Machiavelli," *RenQ*, 21 (1968), 11-23.

Machiavelli may have found Seneca a more fertile source than
is usually recognized; cites neglected parallels in their
thought.

1327. ————, "The Value of Asocial Sociability: Contributions of
Machiavelli, Sidney, and Montesquieu," *BuR*, 16 (1968), 1-22.

On the emergence of a new concept of society.

1328. Woodfin, Harold Dobbs, Jr., "James VI and I and the Quest for
Anglo-Scottish Unity: A Study of the Legal and Constitutional
Issues," *DA*, 30 (1970), 4393-A (Tulane Univ.).

House of Commons' rejection of King James's proposal to unite
his two kingdoms revealed its ability to thwart the will of
both the Crown and the House of Lords. Rejection reflected a
deep division in England on fundamental points of law and im-
pending constitutional crisis.

1329. Zagorin, Perez, *The Court and the Country: The Beginnings of
the English Revolution*. N.Y.: Atheneum, 1970.

Rev. *AHR*, 75 (1970), 2047–2049; *Choice*, 7 (1970), 607; *TLS*,
1 July 1970, 747.

Seeds of Puritan Revolution, beginning with reign of Elizabeth
I. Cites many causes; analyzes the Crown and its Country
opposition. Early Stuart society as dominated by concept of
status (not class). Civil War was initially a conflict over a
political and constitutional question between members of the
principal status group, the aristocracy.

1330. Zaller, Robert Michael, "The Parliament of 1621: A Study in
Constitutional Conflict," *DA*, 29 (1968), 1857-A (Washington
Univ.).

Studies the failure of the English constitutional system as
exemplified by Parliament of 1621. By this date, the institutions of Parliament and monarchy had become fundamentally
incompatible. Fresh perspective on character and policy of
James I, modifying conventional view of his ineffectiveness
as ruler.

XIV. PSYCHOLOGICAL

1331. Adams, Charlotte Nelms, "The Role of Anxiety in English Tragedy: 1580-1642," *DA*, 28 (1967), 2198-A (Univ. of So. Carolina).

Relates decline of Jacobean and Caroline drama to rise of cultural anxiety. Stage realism, diminution of heroic stature, defiance or passivity replacing courage and final transcendence, accompanied the death of great tragedy.

1332. Burge, Barbara J., "'Nature Erring from Itself,' Identity in Shakespeare's Tragedies: A Study of the Use of 'I Am Not What I Am' and Its Related Variations in the Delineation of Character," *DA*, 27 (1967), 4216-4217-A (Univ. of Pittsburgh).

Studies Shakespeare's use of latter phrase and variants in *Rom.*, *MM*, *R2*, *Ham.*, *Oth.*, *Mac.*, *Lr.*, and *Ant.* Its function in characterization and in exploring basic questions of identity, e.g., as it alters under pressure from evil or immoral forces.

1333. Clements, Raymond D., "Physiological-Psychological Thought in Juan Luis Vives," *Journal of the Hist. of the Behav. Sciences*, 3 (1967), 219-235.

Possessing little technical knowledge, Vives (1492-1540) nevertheless popularized a biomedical approach to education and psychology, when he relied strongly on humoral physiology rather than on traditional scholastic arguments regarding faculty of the soul. Although Vives (called "father of modern psychology") bases his study of the soul on traditional Aristotelian concept of soul as "entelechy" of matter, his emphasis is on physiological aspects of life processes.

1334. Fandal, Carlos David, "The Concept of 'Self' in the *Essais* of Michel de Montaigne," *DA*, 29 (1968), 567-A (Louisiana State Univ.).

Montaigne's attempts, in *Essais*, to isolate and define the "essential self" of the individual.

1335. Fortenbaugh, W.W., "Recent Scholarship on the Psychology of Aristotle," *Classical World*, 60 (1967), 316-327.

Useful account of relevance to Shakespearean drama.

1336. Greene, Thomas, "The Flexibility of the Self in Renaissance Literature," in *The Disciplines of Criticism*, ed. Peter Demetz et al. New Haven: Yale Univ. Press, 1968, pp. 241-264.

Renaissance speculation on the possibilities, limitations, and
flexibility of the self.

1337. Hadot, Ilsetraut, *Seneca und die griechisch-römische Tradition
der Seelenleitung.* (Quellen und Studien zur Geschichte der
Philosophie, Bd. XIII.) Berlin: de Gruyter, 1969.
Rev. *J. Hist. Philos.*, 9 (1971), 86–87.

Younger Seneca's ideas on psychological guidance in context of
Greek and Roman philosophical traditions. These traditions
merge in Seneca, who transmits them to European cultural history. Ancient psychological guidance (combining philosophy
and psychotherapy) differs from the modern: rather than un-
covering individual patient's psychic structure, it is directed by norms for behavior based on conventional or philosophical concepts.

1338. Higgins, Dennis Vincent, "Intellect–Will in Poetry of the English Renaissance," *DA*, 28 (1968), 4130–4131-A (Claremont Graduate School).

Medieval debate between intellect vs. will as the supreme
power in scholastic faculty psychology, traced as it recurs
in English Renaissance poetry. As in Elyot and Ascham, 16th-
cent. English works of educational theory, psychology, and de-
votion generally leaned to voluntarism, and the same volun-
tarist bias occurs in imaginative works (by N. Breton, Sir
John Davies, S. Bateman, and Spenser). In Book I of *Faerie
Queene*, Una is Intellect and Redcrosse is Will, the book itself revealing their mutual discovery of interdependence and
dependence on divine grace. Discusses later voluntarism in
Phineas Fletcher and Fulke Greville, the 17th-cent. debate
leading to the last major poetic exploration of intellect–will,
Paradise Lost. (Cf. 2680.)

1339. Jorgensen, Paul A., *Lear's Self Discovery.* Berkeley, Calif.:
Univ. of Calif. Press, 1967. Rev. *Yale R.*, 57 (1968), 290.

Examines self-discovery of Lear from several approaches:
Renaissance interpretation of self-knowledge, as well as modern; character interaction and its effects on Lear; Lear as
a representative of mankind. Lear is depicted as expanding
on his self-knowledge from himself as an individual to include
what it means to be a man.

1340. Mora, G., "Paracelsus' Psychiatry: On the Occasion of the
400th Anniversary of His Book *Diseases that Deprive Man of His
Reason* (1567)," *Amer. J. Psychiat.*, 124 (1967), 803–814.

Discusses Paracelsus' controversial views on psychiatry: personality as rooted in passions and will; man's pathetic existential condition between instincts and spirit. Includes biographical data, notes on editions, sources of Paracelsus'
thinking.

1341. Norton, Glyn Peter, "Montaigne and the *Essais*: A Study in In-
trospection," *DA*, 29 (1968), 1231-A (Univ. of Mich.).

Follows recent scholarship in rejecting Villey's notion of
Montaigne's tripartite philosophical evolution. Underlying
views of Stoicism, Pyrrhonism, and Epicureanism is the man,
Montaigne, striving toward one end: the total recognition of
his faculties, the Socratic goal of self-knowledge. Analyzes
Essais as a dynamic approach to individuality, introspective
self-exploration that begins in self-discontent and passes
into practical goals of wisdom and final self-acceptance.

1342. Pruyser, Paul W., "Calvin's View of Man: A Psychological Commentary," *Theology Today*, 26 (1969), 51-68.

Calvin's natural man is close to image of man drawn by contemporary psychology. Man has some freedom in choice and will
but not enough to have "free will": the acquired freedom
which man gains under divine guidance opposes the natural will;
choice is not free but contingent on circumstances.

1343. Riddell, James Allen, "The Evolution of the Humours Character
in Seventeenth Century English Comedy," *DA*, 27 (1966), 1037-
1038-A (Univ. of Southern Calif.).

Provides background for the use of humours as responsible for
human behavior. Discusses variety of 17th-cent. attitudes
towards humours; and traces them in literature until interest
waned in the early 18th cent.

1344. Riese, W., "La théorie des passions à la lumière de la pensée
médicale du XVIIe s.," *J. Hist. Behav. Sci.*, 4, no. 2 (1968),
195-196.

Rev. of Riese (N.Y.: Karger, 1965): passions from a medical
viewpoint, rather than from a philosophical or religious one.
Includes La Chambre's ideas on symptomatology, classification,
etiology of passions as dynamic, etc. Passions as symptoms
vs. ethical view of passions.

1345. Rosen, George, *Madness in Society: Chapters in the Historical
Sociology of Mental Illness*. London: Routledge and Kegan
Paul, 1968.

Rev. *Brit. Jour. of Sociology*, 19 (1968), 233-235; *Gesnerus*,
25 (1968), 121-122.

From antiquity to modern times.

1346. Sarbin, Theodore R., and Joseph B. Juhasz, "The Historical
Background of the Concept of Hallucination," *Journal of the
Hist. of the Behav. Sciences*, 3 (1967), 339-358.

With the Renaissance, control over descriptive terminology
shifted from the medieval church to the physicians. From
value-laden medieval terms, seemingly objective "scientific"
terms were coined, e.g., "hallucination," a word used to apply
to reported perceptions which the new science thought to have
an unreal basis. Thus, "hallucination" is a successor to
terms which churchmen used, in their own way, to describe
negatively valued reported perceptions; e.g., vision, in the
case of mystics; satanic or other mischievous transcendent

manifestations in the case of the scholastics. Along with
this change of judges (churchmen replaced by scientists),
there came a change in the conception of reality. With the
rise of materialism, the "reality" of transcendental "ecology"
came more and more in question; and nearly any utterance that
appeared to refer to beings or events that inhabited that
"ecology" was judged as "unreal."

1347. Schüling, Hermann, *Bibliographie der psychologischen Literatur
       des 16. Jhts.* Studien und Materialen zur Geschichte der
       Philosophie. Bd. 4. Hildesheim: G. Olms, 1967.

       Alphabetical general catalogue of 16th-cent. psychological
       writing supplemented by index of main headings, making the
       literature available according to special themes. Catalogue
       of secondary literature directs the reader to the best new
       treatments of individual psychological writers of the 16th
       cent. Locates items in European libraries. Very useful work.
       Illustrated.

1348. Wallace, Karl R., *Francis Bacon on the Nature of Man: The
       Faculties of Man's Soul.* Urbana: Univ. of Ill. Press, 1967.

       Rev. *J. Hist. Phil.*, 6 (1968), 398-400; *QJS*, 55 (1969), 82-83.

       Analysis of Bacon's psychology as revealed in the *Advancement
       of Learning* and *De dignitate et augmentis scientiarum.* Deals
       with understanding, reason, imagination, memory, will, and
       appetite.

1349. Webber, Joan, *The Eloquent "I": Style and Self in Seventeenth-
       Century Prose.* Madison: Univ. of Wisc. Press, 1968.

       Rev. *QJS*, 54 (1968), 420.

       "Major contrasts in styles of selfhood"--the 17th-cent. wri-
       ter's awareness that he is the subject of his own prose; such
       literary self-consciousness studied in "conservative Angli-
       cans" and "radical Puritans."

1350. Wilden, Anthony, "Montaigne's 'Essays' in the Context of Com-
       munication," *MLN*, 85 (1970), 454-478.

       Discusses the ideology of Montaigne's essays on many different
       levels. Sees the self as a "transcendental ego."

1351. ————, "Par Divers Moyens on Arrive à Pareille Fin: A Read-
       ing of Montaigne," *MLN*, 83 (1968), 577-597.

       Montaigne's open-ended dialectic the path to his essence; dia-
       lectic between "me" and "myself," between becoming and being,
       the relationship between "Que sçais-je?" and "Que suis-je?"

XV. RENAISSANCE

1352. Bakhtin, Mikhail Mikhailovich, *Rabelais and His World*. Cambridge, Mass.: MIT Press, 1968.

Rev. *Choice*, 5 (1969), 1448; *LibJ*, 93 (15 Dec. 1968); *NY Rev. Bks.*, 13 (Sept. 1969), 16; *NYT Bk. Rev.*, (19 January 1969), 36.

Popular humor and folk culture in the Renaissance; focuses on medieval festival cycles. Relates them to Rabelaisian imagery and humor through spirit of license and irreverence which engendered sense of renewal.

1353. Berner, Samuel, "Florentine Society in the Late Sixteenth and Early Seventeenth Centuries," *SRen*, 18 (1971), 203-246.

Florentine society retained its vitality in the late cinquecento. Discusses: Duke Ferdinand I (1537-1609); Tuscan Economy in Late 16th Cent.; "The Other Florence"; the Poor and Hungry; The Law; The Means of Coercion; Decision-making and the Bureaucracy.

1354. Brucker, Gene A., *Renaissance Florence*. N.Y.: Wiley, 1969.

Rev. *AHR*, 75 (1970), 1482-1483; *BHR*, 32 (1970), 470-471; *EHR*, 85 (1970), 835-836.

Essays dealing with topics such as Florentine culture, religious life, politics, society, economy.

1355. Buck, August, ed., *Zu Begriff und Problem der Renaissance*. Darmstadt: Wissenschaftliche Buchgesellschaft, 1969.

Includes essays on: concept of the Dark Ages in Petrarch by T.E. Mommsen, political unity and diversity in the Italian Renaissance by Hans Baron, the question of specific characteristics of the Renaissance by Ernst Cassirer, the role of Classical Humanism in Renaissance science by P.O. Kristeller, of history, by Garin. Rev. *Archiv f. Begrif.*, 18 (1974), 154-155.

1356. Chabod, Federico, *Scritti sul Rinascimento*. Turin: Einaudi, 1967.

Rev. *RLI*, 71 (1967), 252.

Vol. 2 of *Opere*. Collection of his writings on Renaissance: survey of modern interpretations of the Renaissance; on the origin of the modern state; political history, with discussions of Guicciardini, Giovio, Botero, Sarpi.

1357. Chastel, André, *The Myth of the Renaissance, 1420-1520*. Geneva: Ed. d'Art Albert Skira, 1969.

Rev. *BHR*, 32 (1970), 687-688.

Opposes notion that Italy had no Middle Age and that its Renaissance was generated spontaneously without any influence from Northern Europe. Cf. Chastel's companion volume, *The Crisis of the Renaissance, 1520-1600*. Geneva: Skira, 1968. Both are iconographically rich. The *Myth* reflects such Renaissance themes as *renovatio*, *integratio*, *restitutio*, *plenitudo*; the *Crisis* depicts the other side, Renaissance excesses and contradictions.

1358. Clements, Robert J., ed., *Michelangelo: A Self-Portrait*. N.Y. Univ. Press, 1969. Rev. *Apo.*, 93 (1971), 529.

Source book of Michelangelo's thoughts on art, life, politics, love, philosophy, etc., taken from artist's poems, letters, records, and conversations.

1359. Cochrane, Eric, ed., *The Late Italian Renaissance, 1525-1630*. Harper Torchbooks. N.Y.: Harper & Row, 1970.

Collection of essays showing protraction of Italian Renaissance in its vitality and forms beyond customary termination dates. Part I: Problem of Periodization—essays by Croce and Cochrane. Part II: Continuation and Change in Humanistic Disciplines— essays on jurisprudence, historiography, literature, political philosophy (Utopianism), Aristotelian philosophy and popularization of learning. Part III: Reformation and Counter-Reformation—Heresy (by Cantimori), Application of Tridentine Decrees, Submission and Conformity, Flowering and Withering of Speculative Philosophy. Part IV: Political Vitality and Economic Recovery—Rome, Naples, Venice. Part V: Toward a New Age—Sarpi (Bouwsma), Baroque poetry, music—how opera began.

1360. Cronin, Vincent, *The Flowering of the Renaissance*. N.Y.: Dutton, 1969. Rev. *TLS*, 15 Jan. 1970, 52.

Rise and development of Christian humanism were described in the author's *The Florentine Renaissance*. Present book discusses the development of Christian humanism during 16th cent.

1361. Denieul-Cormier, Anne, *The Renaissance in France 1488-1559*. N.Y.: Doubleday, 1968.

Rev. *Choice*, 5 (1968), 396; *History*, 55 (1970), 108-109; *Library J.*, 93 (1968), 1138.

Four parts: first two deal with main political situation and person and court of the king; latter two with social, economic, and intellectual climate. Chapters on "Masters and Workmen of the Renaissance"; "Travellers of the Renaissance"; and "The Gentleman of the Renaissance."

1362. Eisenstein, Elizabeth, "The Advent of Printing and the Problem of the Renaissance," *Past and Present*, no. 45 (1969), 19-89.

The so-called transitional era that lies between 1300 and 1600
may be regarded as a hybrid construct. Problems associated
with this complex period can be clarified by recognizing that
it encompasses two distinctively different cultures shaped by
two distinctively different communications systems.

1363. Elton, W.R., "Professor Tillyard's *Fabula Rasa*," *ShN*, 18
        (1968), 40.

        Criticizes Tillyard's influential *Elizabethan World Picture*
        (1943), which underestimates religious complexities, including
        Reformation impact, skepticism, etc.; reveals unawareness of
        STC materials; perceives Shakespearean and Elizabethan drama
        as uninfluenced by dissolution of moral standards—he delays
        such effects to the Restoration; and, in general, is committed
        to a blandly reductive view of *the* Elizabethans.

1364. Gombrich, Ernst H., "From the Revival of Letters to the Reform
        of the Arts: Niccolò Niccoli and Filippo Brunelleschi," in
        Douglas Fraser, et al., eds., *Essays in the History of Art
        Presented to Rudolf Wittkower*. London: Phaidon, 1967, pp.
        71-82.

        Transformations by the Renaissance exemplified: early humanist
        reform of Latin orthography (Niccolò Niccoli) paralleled by
        reform in invention of scientific perspective (Brunelleschi).

1365. Grendler, Paul F., *Critics of the Italian World, 1530-1560:
        Anton Francesco Doni, Nicolò Franco, and Ortensio Lando*.
        Madison: Univ. of Wisc. Press, 1969.

        Rev. *AHR*, 75 (1970), 1154-1155; *BHR*, 32 (1970), 196-197;
        Church History, 39 (1970), 118-119.

        Popular attitudes in mid-16th-cent. Italy reflecting social and
        and political crisis; Reformation had undermined assurance of
        religious tradition, and antagonism to existing order was wide.
        Poligrafi, a new group of writers centered in Venice, voiced this
        discontent; they attacked the utility of a classical education
        and the ideal of the active life. Scorning theology, they fa-
        vored an Erasmian lack of dogmatism. These writers show the dis-
        tance in values between 1500 and 1600; having mocked the idols,
        they prepared the way for later, more daring formulations.

1366. Haggis, D.R., S. Jones, et al., eds., *The French Renaissance
        and Its Heritage: Essays Presented to Alan M. Boase*. London:
        Methuen, 1968.

        Includes essays by I.D. McFarlane, "Montaigne and the Concept
        of the Imagination," pp. 117-137; J.D. Mackie, "Henri IV and
        James VI and I," pp. 167-188.

1367. Hamilton, A.C., "Recent Studies in the English Renaissance,"
        SEL, 9 (1969), 169-197.

        Covers 42 critical and historical studies in the non-dramatic
        literature of the English Renaissance, including editions which
        appeared in 1968 or late 1967. (See annual rev. by various
        Renaissance scholars.)

1368. Hay, Denys, ed., *The Age of the Renaissance*. London: Thames
        and Hudson, 1967; N.Y.: McGraw-Hill, 1968.

        Rev. *Spectator*, 6 October 1967, 400-402.

Renaissance as it developed in Italy, France, Spain, Germany,
and England. Series of lectures by eminent Renaissance scholars
(e.g., N. Rubinstein) in various fields, such as architecture,
portraiture, etc.

1369. Holmes, George, *The Florentine Enlightenment.* London: Wieden-
feld & Nicolson, 1969.

Rev. *History*, 55 (1970), 105-107; *Hist. Today*, 19 (1969),
361-362.

Florentines were influenced not so much by their classical
learning, of which they were proud, but by the thoughts which
the classics inspired in them that could have contemporary
significance. Discovery of the classical world provided an
impulse, not a framework.

1370. Kermode, Frank, *Shakespeare, Spenser, Donne: Renaissance
Essays.* London: Routledge and Kegan Paul, 1971.

In addition to such pieces as "Spenser and the Allegorists,"
"Cave of Mammon," and "Banquet of Sense," includes essay on
"Shakespeare's Learning"--calling him (p. 199) "man of great
intellectual force." Rev. *Listener*, 86 (1 July 1971), 21.

1371. Kristeller, Paul O., and Philip P. Wiener, eds., *Renaissance
Essays.* N.Y.: Harper Torchbooks, 1968.

Fourteen essays from *JHI* representing cross-section of Renaissance intellectual history: the problem of the Renaissance;
the historical thought of the period; its social, moral, and
religious thought; humanism; philosophy and science; literature; visual arts; and music. Rev. *Nat. R.*, 22 (14 July 1970), 745.

1372. Levi, A.H.T., ed., *Humanism in France at the End of the Middle
Ages and in the Early Renaissance.* Manchester Univ. Press,
1970.

Rev. *TLS*, 15 January 1971, 70.

Fourteen papers delivered at 1969 Warwick symposium. Includes
essays on early thought of Petrarch as Christian and Stoic
moralist, writing in Latin prose; on *dignitas hominis* theme;
and on new sensibility of French Renaissance through the influence of Ficino and Neo-platonism.

1373. Levin, Harry, *Refractions: Essays in Comparative Literature.*
N.Y.: Oxford U.P., 1966. Rev. *Comp. Lit.*, 19 (1967), 274-276.

Contains contextually stimulating essays: e.g., "Shakespeare
in the Light of Comparative Literature," "English Literature
and the Renaissance"--arguing against the simplism of the
"Elizabethan World Picture," and dealing with classical and
medieval modes.

1374. Lewis, Archibald R., ed., *Aspects of the Renaissance: A
Symposium.* Papers presented at a Conference on the Meaning
of the Renaissance. Austin/London: Univ. of Texas Press,
1967.

Rev. *AHR*, 74 (1968), 542-543; *Historian*, 30 (1968), 651.

Conference held in 1964, sponsored by South Central Renaissance Conference and Univ. of Texas. Pt. I: The Political
Scene (Walter Ullmann; J. Russell Major); Pt. II: Old and

New Traditions of Culture (Peter Russell; Walter L. Woodfill);
Pt. III: Arts and Letters (H.W. Janson; Eugénie Droz); Pt. IV:
Renaissance and Reformation (Lewis W. Spitz, Michael G. Hall);
Pt. V: Science and Economic Life (Edward Rosen, Herbert Hea-
ton). (See several of the above under individual entries.)

1375. Lewis, Clive S., *Studies in Medieval and Renaissance Literature*, ed. Walter Hooper (Cambridge Univ. Press, 1966).

Rev. D. Bush, *College English*, 28 (1966), 254-255.

Placing Shakespeare at crossroads of medieval and modern
world, book contextualizes his style, motifs, plot-lines, etc.

1376. Lievsay, John L., ed., *Medieval and Renaissance Studies*.
Durham, N.C.: Duke Univ. Press, 1968.

Eight lectures at Southeastern Institute of Medieval and
Renaissance Studies, 1966: by Arthur Brown; Werner P. Friedrich;
Bruce W. Wardropper; Gustave Reese; Craig R. Thompson on passages in Erasmus's *Convivium Religiosum*; and Urban T. Holmes
on training, habits, repertoire, and technique of medieval
minstrel and his instruments.

1377. Lopez, Robert S., *The Three Ages of the Italian Renaissance*.
Charlottesville: Univ. of Va. Press, 1970.

Rev. *AHR*, 76 (1971), 793; *BHR*, 33, no. 3 (1971), 733-734.

Division of period as follows: (1454-1494)--"Youth"; (1494-
1527)--"Maturity"; (1527-1559)--"Decline."

1378. Malagoli, Luigi, *Le contraddizioni del Rinascimento*. Florence:
La Nuova Italia, 1968.

Cinquecento contradictions noted in this brief study include:
"Il Sannazaro e la dupicità dell'anima rinascimentale," "Gli
ideali morali," "La discordia del Rinascimento," "La nuova
sensibilità."

1379. *Mélanges de Langue et de Littérature du Moyen Age et de la
Renaissance offerts à Jean Frappier par ses collègues et ses
amis*. Geneva: Droz, 1970.

Rev. *ZRP*, 87 (1971), 617-621.

One hundred essays on linguistic and literary subjects of
French Middle Ages and Renaissance. Includes essays on: Old
French Heroic Epic (*Heldenepos*); its relation to courtly novel
(*höfische Romane*); over one-third of the essays dedicated to
"Matière de Bretagne"; allegorical poetry and the epic genre.

1380. Mieck, Ilja, "Periodisierung und Terminologie der Frühen Neuzeit: Zur Diskussion der letzten beiden Jahrzehnte," *Geschichte in Wissenschaft und Unterricht*, 19 (1968), 357-373.

On periodization involving the "Renaissance," with views of
various historians. Distinguishes between "Die erste Phase der
Frühen Neuzeit" connected with the Reformation, and "Die zweite
Phase der Frühen Neuzeit," mid-17th cent.

Renaissance

1381. Molho, Anthony, and John A. Tedeschi, eds., *Renaissance Studies in Honor of Hans Baron.* Florence: G.C. Sansoni, 1971.

Thirty-two articles, including A. Molho, "A Note on Jewish Moneylenders in Tuscany in the Late Trecento and Early Quattrocento"; T.C. Price Zimmermann, "Confession and Autobiography in the Early Renaissance"; N.W. Gilbert, "The Early Italian Humanists and Disputation"; Lewis W. Spitz, "Humanism in the Reformation"; Gerald Strauss, "The Course of German History: The Lutheran Interpretation."

1382. Montano, Rocco, "The Renaissance? What Renaissance?" *Umanesimo*, 1 (1967), 1-10.

Reply to A.E. Neville who suggests that a useful definition is not available. Opposes Burckhardt; Renaissance does not involve diminution of religious interest, and still fosters a Christian life-view. Yet it does involve rejection of former age, a world dividing a poem by Petrarch from the *Divine Comedy*. Brunelleschi represents something new. Humanism is opposed to science and scientific views on religion; it favors the ancient virtues as essential to Christian life.

1383. O'Kelly, Bernard, ed., *The Renaissance Image of Man and the World.* Columbus, Ohio: Ohio State Univ. Press, 1966.

Contains articles by Kristeller on "Philosophy and Humanism in Renaissance Perspective"; D. Bush on "The Renaissance: The Literary Climate," and others.

1384. Panofsky, Erwin, *Renaissance and Renascences in Western Art.* N.Y.: Harper and Row, 1969.

Chapters 1 and 2: the distinctions between the Renaissance which began in the first half of the 14th cent. and the "renascences" of the Middle Ages; Chapter 3: Italian Trecento painting and its influence on the rest of Europe; Chapter 4: 15th-cent. Italian and Dutch painting. Contains 157 plates.

1385. Parkes, Henry Bamford, *The Divine Order: Western Culture in the Middle Ages and the Renaissance.* N.Y.: Alfred A. Knopf, 1969.

Rev. *AHR*, 75 (1969), 465-466.

Sequel to his *Gods and Men: The Origins of Western Culture* (rev. *AHR*, 65 [1960], 581.) Main topic is emergence and decline of an ideology, the "divine order" of the Middle Ages and the Renaissance. From broadest perspective, Renaissance falls within Middle Ages: end of the Middle Ages may be seen in England in 1642.

1386. Prandi, Alfonso, ed., *Interpretazioni del Rinascimento.* Bologna: Società editrice il Mulino, 1971.

Useful collection, mostly translated, of 11 essays, with introduction by editor, and bibliography of recent works. Includes: F. Chabod, "Il Rinascimento nelle recenti interpretazioni" and "Il Rinascimento"; V. Lazarev, "Contro la

falsificazione della storia della cultura rinascimentale";
D. Cantimori, "La periodizzazione dell'età del Rinascimento";
and essays on Renaissance by E.F. Jacob, D. Hay, P.O. Kristeller, G. Mattingly, E. Rosenthal, W.L. Ferguson, Harcourt
Brown.

1387.   Rabb, Theodore K., and Jerrold E. Seigel, eds., *Action and
Conviction in Early Modern Europe: Essays in Memory of E.H.
Harbison.* Princeton Univ. Press, 1969.

Rev. *AHR*, 75 (1970), 836-837; *Church History*, 39 (1970), 254-
255; *Thought*, 44 (1969), 627-629.

Among the 19 essays in this volume are: T.K. Rabb, "Francis
Bacon and the Reform of Society"; L. White, "The Iconography
of *Temperantia* and the Virtuousness of Technology"; G.A.
Brucker, "Florence and Its University 1348-1434"; J.E. Seigel,
"The Teaching of Argyropulos and the Rhetoric of the First
Humanists"; M.P. Gilmore, "Erasmus and Alberto Pio, Prince of
Carpi"; G.H. Williams, "Erasmus and the Reformers on Non-
Christian Religions and *Salus Extra Ecclesiam.*"

1388.   Rowe, J.G., and W.H. Stockdale, eds., *Florilegium Historiale:
Essays Presented to Wallace K. Ferguson.* Univ. of Toronto
Press, 1971.

Fourteen essays plus list of Ferguson's principal writings.
Essays include: Hans Baron, "Petrarch: His inner struggles
and the humanistic discovery of man's nature"; A.B. Ferguson,
"'By little and little': The early Tudor humanists on the
development of man"; M.B. Becker, "An essay on the quest for
identity in the early Italian Renaissance"; J.R. Hale, "In-
citement to violence? English divines on the theme of war,
1578 to 1631."

1389.   Rubinstein, Nicolai, ed., *Florentine Studies: Politics and
Society in Renaissance Florence.* London: Faber and Faber;
Evanston: Northwestern Univ. Press, 1968 [1969].

Rev. *BHR*, 32 (1970), 677-684; *Revue Historique*, no. 496 (1970),
479-483.

Contains 15 essays on Florence by various authorities, from
end of 13th to start of 16th cent. Concerns myth and image of
Florence, its institutional changes during Renaissance, and
its social evolution based on notarial records.

1390.   Schlesinger, Roger, "The Influence of Italian Renaissance
Civilization in Fifteenth Century Spain: A Study in Cultural
Transmission," *DA*, 31 (1970), 2290-2291-A (Univ. of Ill.).

Fifteenth-cent. origins of the "Golden Age" in Spain, through
series of short biographies of several Spaniards and Italians.

1391.   Schoeck, Richard J., "Recent Studies in the English Renaissance," *SEL*, 10 (1970), 215-250.

Survey of over 100 works of scholarship and criticism; stress
on More and Erasmus; contribution of European scholarship; importance of continental literature, history of ideas.

1392. Schweitzer, Frederick M., and Harry E. Wedeck, eds., *Diction-
       ary of the Renaissance*. N.Y.: Philosophical Library; London:
       Vision, 1967. Rev. *Classical Philology*, 63 (1968), 63.

       General, popular, undocumented.

1393. Schwoebel, Robert, ed., *Renaissance Men and Ideas*. N.Y.:
       St. Martin's Press, 1971. Rev. *AHR*, 77 (1972), 1409.

       Essays on Renaissance thought: J.E. Seigel on humanism, R.
       Hirsch on printing and humanism in Germany, George R. Potter
       on Thomas More, Felix Gilbert on Machiavelli, R. Schwoebel on
       the Renaissance papacy, L.W. Spitz on Luther, Edward Rosen on
       Copernicus and Renaissance astronomy, R.B. Henning on Castig-
       lione's *Courtier*, D.M. Frame on Montaigne--the absurdity and
       dignity of man.

1394. Simone, Franco, *The French Renaissance*. London: Macmillan,
       1969; N.Y.: St. Martin's Press, 1970.

       Rev. *TLS*, 11 June 1970, 634.

       Humanist originality of neglected 15th-cent. in France; rela-
       tive independence of Italy and close continuity with French
       Middle Ages. Assimilation of Italian humanism was selective
       and purposeful; what was taken was also changed in accordance
       with national needs. First half of this work is fully trans-
       lated, while the second is replaced by the translation of a
       short essay by Simone on the same theme here presented as an
       "introduction." Latin quotations and footnotes simplified.

1395. ————, "Reflections on the French Renaissance: The Emergence
       of a New Historiographical Framework," *FMLS*, 6 (1970), 342-345.

       On rebirth of research in area of French Renaissance since
       publication of *Il Rinascimento Francese*.

1396. Singleton, Charles S., ed., *Art, Science and History in the
       Renaissance*. Baltimore: Johns Hopkins Press, 1967.

       Rev. *AHR*, 74 (1969), 1276-1278.

       Johns Hopkins Humanities Seminar includes 13 essays in art,
       science, and history, as well as philosophy, political theory,
       and literature. Art: E.H. Gombrich, John White. Science:
       D.W. Waters, George Boas, Marshall Clagett, Stillman Drake,
       Ernan McMullin. History: Felix Gilbert. Political theory:
       J.H. Hexter. Philosophy: Frances A. Yates. Music: Edward
       E. Lowinsky, Walter H. Rubsamen. Literature: Wolfgang Clemen.
       Many of the essays deal with stresses of pre-modern science,
       art, and music. (See also under individual contributors.)

1397. Van Dorsten, J.A., *The Radical Arts: First Decade of an
       Elizabethan Renaissance*. Leiden and Oxford: The Sir Thomas
       Browne Inst.; N.Y.: Oxford Univ. Press, 1970.

       Rev. *AHR*, 76 (1971), 776; *BHR*, 33 (1971), 444-448; *NQ*, June
       1971, 233-236.

       Influence of 1560's (and French and Flemish immigrants) on
       achievements of Elizabethan Age, 1580-1600. In relation to
       strain of Reformation, arts seek to prevent tragic disunion
       of society. Discusses London community of strangers and its
       links to Franco-Flemish intellectual world.

1398. Vasoli, Cesare, *Studi sulla cultura del Rinascimento*. Lacaita: Manduria, 1968.

Contains essays such as: "Immagini e simboli nei primi scritti lulliani e mnemotecnici del Bruno," "Temi mistici e profetici alla fine del '400," "Su alcuni problemi e discussioni logiche del '500."

1399. West, Paul, "Jacob Burckhardt and the Ideal Past," *Of Several Branches: Essays from the "Humanities Association Bulletin,"* ed. Gerald McCaughey et al. Univ. of Toronto Press, 1968, pp. 160–169.

Defense of the accuracy of Burckhardt's insight.

1400. Whitlock, Baird W., "From the Counter-Renaissance to the Baroque," *BuR*, 15 (1967), 46–60.

Development from Counter-Renaissance to Baroque reflects complete change in form and attitude, influencing the arts, political groups, and even military formations. Unresolved formal tensions in static Counter-Renaissance style dissolved in Baroque style. Donne and Herbert shown as exemplars of earlier and later periods.

1401. Williams, Kathleen, "Recent Studies in the English Renaissance," *SEL*, 8 (1968), 151–185.

Useful survey-review of some 40 books in 16th- and 17th-cent. English literature issued in 1967.

1402. Wuttke, Dieter, *Deutsche Germanistik und Renaissance-Forschung: Ein Vortrag zur Forschungslage*. Berlin, Zurich: Verlag Gehlen, 1968.

Forty-six-page lecture of 1967 on the situation of German Renaissance-scholarship. Cites Burdach, Strich, et al.

XVI. SCIENTIFIC (and Pre-Scientific)

1403. Appelbaum, Wilbur, "Kepler in England: The Reception of Kep-
lerian Astronomy in England, 1599–1687," *DA*, 30 (1969), 2440-A
(State Univ. of N.Y. at Buffalo).

How Kepler's laws of planetary motion and his ideas on celestial physics were disseminated; their reception from their
publication early in 17th cent. to their ultimate incorporation in the Newtonian synthesis.

1404. Arrighi, Gino, "Mathématiques italiennes vers la fin du moyen
âge et à l'époque de la Renaissance," *Organon*, 5 (1968), 181-
190.

Urges attention to mathematics from the late Middle Ages to
the Renaissance, in view of the works of Pacioli and the admirable activity of the Bologna school of the 16th cent.
Appendix lists author's principal publications dealing with
the points raised.

1405. Aston, Margaret, "The Fiery Trigon Conjunction: An Elizabethan
Astrological Prediction," *Isis*, 61 (1970), 159–187.

In 1583, the conjunction of Saturn and Jupiter was accompanied
by a change from the watery to the fiery trigon (Aries, Leo,
Sagittarius). Shakespeare's *2 Henry IV*, II.iv.261–265, seen in
light of the controversy and fear created by infrequency of
this phenomenon.

1406. Baron, Margaret E., *The Origins of the Infinitesimal Calculus*.
Oxford: Pergamon Press, 1969.

Rev. *Brit. Journal for the Hist. of Science*, 5 (1970), 89–91.

Chapter 3, on "Some Centre of Gravity Determinations in the
Later Sixteenth Century." 17th-cent. transition from geometri-
cal method of exhaustion to algorithms of the calculus, described in Chapters 4, 5, and 6, constitutes better half of
book. Sets out, in essentially modern notations, procedures
used by at least a dozen precursors, from Kepler and Galileo
on.

1407. Boas, George, "Philosophies of Science in Florentine Platonism," in Charles S. Singleton, *Art, Science and History in the
Renaissance*. Baltimore: Johns Hopkins Press, 1968, pp. 239–
254.

These sought not control, but adequate picture of the world.

1408. Boulind, Richard H., "Drake's Navigational Skills," *Mariner's
Mirr.*, 54 (1968), 349–371.

Drake's concern for the sciences of cartography and navigation
as established from evidence provided by the preparations,
performance, and results of his circumnavigation of the globe.

1409. Brown, Keith, "Hamlet's Place on the Map," *ShS*, 4 (1969),
160–182.

References to geographical concepts available to Elizabethans
through maps of Ortelius, Mercator, and De Jode.

1410. Bullough, Vern L., San Fernando State College, Northridge,
Calif., "Italian Cities and the Development of Modern Science."
Presented at 1968 meeting of the Renaissance Conference of
Southern California.

Useful survey of reasons for Renaissance rise of science, and
for unique dominance of Italy (1450-1650). Cites George Sim-
mel on spread of money economy and its tempo. Alfred von
Martin observed that money economy created ideal of exact
numerical calculation, counterpart of mathematically exact
interpretation of the cosmos. Leonard Olschki connected science with practical activity of urban technicians and artists,
uninterested in humanists' rhetoric. Edgar Zilsel deduced
scientific genesis from union in the city of theoretically
minded upper class with practical workman in the shops. Erwin Panofsky related artist to scientific development and the
discovery of perspective and drawing to scale to growth of descriptive science. Giorgio de Santillana concurred on the
self-transformation of the arts in the development of science.
Hans Baron recognized necessity for science of shift from God-
given immovable universe to evolutionary and dynamic one, a
view which had emerged by end of 15th cent. Alexandre Koyré
found science dependent on mathematization of nature, destruc-
tion of Aristotelian world-view, geometrization of space, and
15th-cent. revival of Platonism with its influence on new
bourgeois in Italian cities. Ernst Cassirer held re-emphasis
on ethical humanity as important preliminary stage. Renewed
emphasis on magic, as means of grasping and controlling workings of the universe, as in Giordano Bruno, would have led to
new interest in science. Concludes with strong possibility
that Italian scientific domination was related to rise of the
Italian city and its institution, the university.

1411. Burmeister, Karl Heinz, *Georg Joachim Rhetikus, 1514-1574.*
Eine Bio-Bibliographie. Bd. I: *Humanist und Wegbereiter der*
Modernen Naturwissenschaften. Wiesbaden: Guido Pressler Ver-
lag, 1967.

Rev. *Isis*, 59 (1968), 231-233.

Study of 16th-cent. scientist, collaborator of Copernicus,
based on fresh sources.

1412. Calder, Richie, *Leonardo and the Age of the Eye.* N.Y.: Simon
and Schuster, 1970.

Rev. *Choice*, 7 (1971), 1500.

Leonardo's activity as scientist-engineer-inventor, seen
against background of the culture of his time.

1413. Castellani, Carlo, "Le Problème de la *Generatio Spontanea* dans
l'oeuvre de Fortunio Liceti," *Revue de Synthèse*, 89 (1968),
323-340.

Renaissance backgrounds of Fortunio Liceti's *De Spontaneo
Viventium* (1618). Includes ancient and Renaissance views attributing to the earth an intrinsic generative capacity. Discusses Ficino's view of three kinds of rational souls, and his
belief in spontaneous generation derived from the influence of
celestial souls; essence of generation resides in the *omne
vivum e vivo*, emphasizing the autonomy of Nature.

1414. Charron, Jean Daniel, "Pierre Charron's Views on Late Renaissance Science," *Renaissance Papers 1966*, ed. George W. Williams
(Durham, N.C., Southeastern Renaissance Conference, 1967),
pp. 11-20.

Charron's Pyrrhonism leads him to systematic doubt of all
theories, and he rejects syllogistic proofs. He tries to reconcile Scripture and a more modern cosmological view.

1415. Cipolla, Carlo M., *Clocks and Culture, 1300-1700*. London:
Collins, 1967.

Rev. *Journal of Econ. Hist.*, 28 (1968), 134.

On technological change in early Renaissance.

1416. Crombie, A.C., J.V. Pepper, D.B. Quinn, J.W. Shirley, and
R.C.H. Tanner, "Thomas Harriot (1560-1621): An Original Prac-
titioner in the Scientific Art," *TLS*, 23 October 1969, 1237-
1238.

Harriot as one of first practitioners of the scientific art.
Details of his life and work. Reports on recent Harriot
scholarship.

1417. Dame, Bernard, *Galilée et l'incorruptibilité des cieux*.
Lille, Université Catholique, Faculté de Théologie, 1967,
Mémoire de licence. Typescript, 170 pp.

Summary in *Archives de Sociologie des Religions*, 12 (1967),
198. First part of this was published: "Galilée et les
taches solaires," *Revue d'Histoire des Sciences*, 19 (1966),
307-370.

Study of shock which scientific innovation brought to church-
recognized theologies and philosophies, and readjustments it
required. Between 1610 and 1613, Galileo affirmed existence
of sun spots, upsetting Aristotelian view of incorruptibility
of the heavens.

1418. Dannenfeldt, Karl H., *Leonhard Rauwolf: Sixteenth-Century
Physician, Botanist, and Traveler*. Harvard Monographs in History of Science; Cambridge, Mass.: Harvard Univ. Press, 1968.

Rev. *AHR*, 74 (1969), 1647.

First modern botanist to work in Near East, and his observations in Renaissance context.

1419.   Davies, Gordon L., *The Earth in Decay. A History of British Geomorphology 1578-1878.* London: Macdonald, 1969.

Rev. *Annals of Sci.*, 25 (1969), 362-363; *Brit. J. for Hist. of Sci.*, 5 (1970), 195-196.

While decay of nature, including human nature, dominated the history of nature and man, power of eroding forces was emphasized. When application of theology to earthly events made stability a desirable feature, the same evidence was employed to minimize the rate of erosion. Introduction on earliest geomorphological ideas; two chapters mainly on 17th cent. Glossary of technical terms.

1420.   Deacon, Richard, *John Dee, Scientist, Geographer, Astrologer and Secret Agent to Elizabeth I.* London: Muller, 1968.

Rev. *TLS*, 12 September 1968, 1033.

Biography which rejects charlatan and conjurer image. Dee, a pioneer of spiritualism as well as efficient intelligence agent, occupied both with state business and undiscovered truths.

1421.   Debus, Allen G., *The Chemical Dream of the Renaissance.* Cambridge: Heffer, 1968.

Lecture on birth of modern science from cosmological viewpoint of Renaissance, i.e., a search for the Creator through his created work by chemical investigation and analogies, with mathematical-logical abstractions often seen as incompatible with new experimental method.

1422.   ————, "Fire Analysis and the Elements in the Sixteenth and Seventeenth Centuries," *Annals of Science*, 23 (1967), 127-147.

Wide range of views regarding validity of fire analysis, greatest analytical concern of 16th- and 17th-cent. theoretical alchemist and iatrochemists. It was associated with search for the Aristotelian elements and Paracelsian principles--on these systems of elementary matter were based the Aristotelian and chemical cosmologies. Recourse was most often had to traditional alchemical method of separation, application of heat through burning, or distillation.

1423.   ————, "Mathematics and Nature in the Chemical Texts of the Renaissance," *Ambix*, 15 (1968), 1-28.

In first half of 17th cent., importance of mathematics in science was limited. It was restricted to quest for divine mathematical harmonies or to reckonings based on experimental measurements of weight. Earlier, Paracelsus had given mathematics a role subservient to chemistry.

1424.   ————, "Renaissance Chemistry and the Work of Robert Fludd," *Ambix*, 14 (1967), 42-59.

Usefully traces transformations in man's view of nature between first and second half of 17th cent. High proportion of books in early 17th cent. dealt with mysticism and occultism, though

its closing decades record names of many founders of modern
science. Pre-Boylean English chemistry was chiefly mystical
alchemy, Paracelsianism. Mystical Renaissance universe, as
interpreted by iatrochemists in the age, had a widespread appeal, from the death of Paracelsus to, e.g., 1670. Fludd
(1574-1630) was an example of the mystic alchemist, as well as
of the general Hermetic-Paracelsian approach to nature. (Cf.
Debus, "Robert Fludd and the Chemical Philosophy of the Renaissance," *Organon* [Poland], 4 [1967], 119-126.)

1425. Dodd, Wayne, "A New Look at Cultural History," *BuR*, 15, no. 2
(1967), 26-40.

Revolutionary movement, from Copernican hypothesis to that of
Galileo, with its effect on 17th-cent. literature.

1426. Drake, Stillman, "Early Science and the Printed Book: The
Spread of Science beyond the Universities," *Ren. and Ref.*
(Univ. of Toronto), 6 (1969/70), 43-52.

Notion of unity of science; sees its break-up as result of passage outside the universities and the advent of inexpensive
printed books; its reunification with Galileo, independent of
institutionalization as in the Middle Ages.

1427. ————, "Galileo's 1604 Fragment on Falling Bodies (Galileo
Gleanings XVIII)," *Brit. Jour. for the Hist. of Science*, 4
(1969), 340-358.

Galileo's first attempted derivation of the law relating space
and time in free fall.

1428. ————, "Renaissance Music and Experimental Science," *JHI*, 31
(1970), 483-500.

Influence of Renaissance music on science and mathematics;
maintains that controversy over musical harmonies was partly
responsible for new approach to the science we know as mathematical physics.

1429. ————, and I.E. Drabkin, eds. and trans., *Mechanics in Sixteenth-Century Italy*. Madison: Univ. of Wisc. Press, 1969.

Rev. *Nature*, 222, no. 5191 (1969), 396.

Attempts to fill gap between Galileo and his medieval precursors with selections from Tartaglia, Benedetti, Ubaldo, and
Baldi, representing two separate schools: practical mechanics
and mathematical mechanics.

1430. Duhem, Pierre, *To Save the Phenomena. An Essay on the Idea of
Physical Theory from Plato to Galileo*, introd. Stanley L. Jaki.
Univ. of Chicago Press, 1969. Rev. *Choice*, 6 (1969), 1036.

Reviews answers given to question of the relations between
physical theory and metaphysics, or between astronomy and physics, by Greek thought, Arabic science, medieval Christian
scholasticism, and the astronomers of the Renaissance.

1431. Düring, Ingemar, "The Impact of Aristotle's Scientific Ideas
       in the Middle Ages and at the Beginning of the Scientific
       Revolution," Archiv für Geschichte der Philosophie, 50 (1968),
       115-133.

       Though he dominated the Middle Ages, Aristotle was misunder-
       stood and reformulated by schoolmen and others, mainly because
       Greek texts were not directly available until 16th cent. In
       16th and 17th cents., his basic scientific ideas were correctly
       understood for the first time, providing stimulus to scholars
       of the period and suggesting long-forgotten types of inquiry.

1432. Edighoffer, R., "Le lion du septentrion," EG, 22 (1967), 161-
       189.

       This prophecy of pseudo-Paracelsus considered as an example re-
       vealing the importance of prophetic and occultist currents
       which influenced numerous 17th-cent. writers.

1433. Eurich, Nell, Science in Utopia: A Mighty Design. Cambridge,
       Mass.: Harvard Univ. Press, 1967.

       Rev. RES, n.s., 19 (1968), 462-463; SCN, 26 (1968), 29-30;
       YR, 57 (1968), 282-285.

       Use of science in 17th-cent. secular utopian views.

1434. Ferguson, Eugene S., Bibliography of the History of Technology.
       Cambridge, Mass.: MIT and the Society for the History of
       Technology, 1968. Rev. Choice, 6 (1969), 992.

       Includes general works and Renaissance materials.

1435. Folaron, S., "Oskarżenie Cesalpina o ateizm" [Accusation
       Against Cesalpinus of Atheism], Euhemer, 13, no. 3 (1969),
       79-92.

       Botanist-philosopher (1519-1603) believed that cosmological
       problems had to be based on accurate knowledge of existing
       reality; beliefs stressed primacy of matter, hinted at self-
       generation, and suggested evolution.

1436. Gille, Bertrand, Engineers of the Renaissance. Cambridge,
       Mass.: Massachusetts Institute of Technology Press, 1966.

       Rev. AHR, 72 (1967), 1341-1342.

       Shows close continuity of technical invention from antiquity
       to 15th-cent. Italians.

1437. Girill, T.R., "Galileo and Platonistic Methodology," JHI, 31
       (1970), 501-520.

       Takes issue with arguments that Galileo's methodology entailed
       a reversion to Platonism. On views of Koyré (on his mathe-
       matics and axiomatics); of Cassirer (on his hypothetico-deduc-
       tive method); and of Crombie (on his use of abstract terms).
       Concludes that Galileo actually led attack on dogmatic ration-
       alism and empiricism, and that he offers example of modern
       pragmatic balance between reason and sense in science.

1438.   Golino, Carlo L., ed., *Galileo Reappraised*. Berkeley, Calif.:
        Univ. of Calif. Press, 1966. Rev. *AHR*, 72 (1967), 634.

        Includes essays by Dante Della Terza, "Galileo, Man of Let-
        ters"; Ernest A. Moore, "Galileo and His Precursors"; Giorgio
        Spini, "The Rationale of Galileo's Religiousness"; etc.

1439.   Greaves, Richard L., "Puritanism and Science: The Anatomy of
        a Controversy," *JHI*, 30 (1969), 345-368.

        Indirect relationship between Puritanism and science. To ex-
        tent that Puritanism participated in the Great Rebellion, it
        was indirectly a factor in development of modern science.

1440.   Grmek, Mirko D., "Réflexions sur des interprétations mécan-
        istes de la vie dans la physiologie du XVIIe siècle," *Episteme*,
        1 (1967), 17-30.

        Change between 16th and 17th cents.; 17th-cent. reduction of
        biological phenomena to mechanical models.

1441.   Guerlac, Henry, "Copernicus and Aristotle's Cosmos," *JHI*, 29
        (1968), 109-113.

        Copernicus' role in transformation from Aristotle's structured
        cosmos--nest of concentric spheres marked off into two con-
        trasting regions, "celestial" above the moon, and below it
        spheres of the four elements. Astronomer's part in shift to
        later view that between earth and celestial bodies there had
        to be some similarity of substance. Refutes charge that Coper-
        nicus clung to Aristotelian view of the universe.

1442.   Heninger, S.K., "Pythagorean Symbola in Erasmus' *Adagia*,"
        RenQ, 21, no. 2 (1968), 162-165.

        Traces through the augmentations and revisions of the *Adagia*
        the importance ascribed by Erasmus to the Pythagorean symbola;
        these were means of emphasizing his syncretic conception of
        similarities between Pythagorean precept and Christianity.

1443.   ————, "Tudor Literature of the Physical Sciences, pt. I,"
        HLQ, 34 (1969), 101-134; pt. II, 34 (1969), 249-270.

        Transition from scholasticism to modern science as reflected
        in Tudor scientific literature. Part I covers Mathematics;
        various fields of Cosmography. Part II treats Physics; Mag-
        netism; and Meteorology, Chemistry, and Divinitory Sciences.

1444.   Hennemann, Gerhard, "Der Fall Galilei: Ein Beitrag zum Ver-
        hältnis von Wissen und Glauben," *ZRG*, 20 (1968), 61-69.

        Case of Galileo as model for 17th-cent. relationship between
        theology and science.

1445.   Hoeniger, F.D., *The Growth of Natural History in Stuart England
        from Gerard to the Royal Society*. (Folger Booklets on Tudor
        and Stuart Civilization.) Charlottesville: Univ. Press of
        Virginia for the Folger Shakespeare Library, 1969.

Rev. *Annals of Sci.*, 26 (1970), 264-266.

This booklet and 1447 trace the study of natural history in Tudor and Stuart England. During the 16th and 17th cents., study of plants and animals progressed from medieval folklore and fantasy to beginning of scientific investigation of actual plants and animals of England.

1446.   ————, and Joel Kaplan, "A Survey of Early Biological Books in Toronto, 1450-1700," *Ren. and Ref.* (Univ. of Toronto), 3 (1967), 2-11.

Locates books: classical works in Renaissance editions, original works printed after 1500, herbals, zoological works, etc.

1447.   ————, and J.F.M., *The Development of Natural History in Tudor England* . (Folger Booklets on Tudor and Stuart Civilization.) Charlottesville: Univ. Press of Virginia for the Folger Shakespeare Library, 1969.

1448.   James, David Gwilym, *The Dream of Prospero*. Oxford Univ. Press, 1967.

Rev. *Cambridge Review*, 89 (1968), 365-366.

Supplements author's *Dream of Learning* (1951), which showed Shakespeare and Bacon as "prophets and makers of the modern world." The new study sees *Tmp.* as another prophetic vision which symbolizes the release of Western civilization from the bonds of magical demonology. In addition to magic, traced from Plotinus to Bruno, author discusses 16th-cent. accounts of America as influencing Shakespeare's vision of the future.

1449.   Jayne, Julian, "The Problem of Animate Motion in the Seventeenth Century," *JHI*, 31 (1970), 219-234.

Concern with motion was a central problem in 17th-cent., sorted out into several of our modern sciences. Motion by machines became important in economics at beginning of cent.

1450.   Kangro, Hans, *Joachim Jungius' Experimente und Gedanken zur Begründung der Chemie als Wissenschaft: Ein Beitrag zur Geistesgeschichte des 17. Jahrhunderts.* (*Boethius*: Texte und Abhandlungen zur Geschichte der exakten Wissenschaften, hrsg. Joseph Ehrenfried Hofmann et al., Bd. 7.) Wiesbaden: Franz Steiner Verlag, 1968.

Jungius (1587-1657), chemical theorist, was first to define elements by accepting experimentally determined constituents only. Study treats contemporary theories of first half of 17th cent. Well documented.

1451.   Kargon, Robert Hugh, *Atomism in England from Hariot to Newton*. Oxford: Clarendon Press, 1966; Oxford Univ. Press, 1967.

Rev. *AHR*, 73 (1968), 811-812.

Describes the influence of two groups of natural philosophers, associated with the Earl of Northumberland and the Duke of Newcastle, whose radical ideas brought atomism into disrepute;

and its revival in England under the influence of Descartes
and Gassendi, culminating in its role in Newton's thinking in
the *Principia*.

1452. ————, "Thomas Hariot, the Northumberland Circle and Early
Atomism in England," *JHI*, 27 (1966), 128-136.

Hariot (1560-1621) left unpublished manuscripts which, still
unstudied at the Sion College Library, are a mine of scientific material. Completion of their assessment will signifi-
cantly alter writing of history of science. Hariot's reluc-
tance to make known his views was related to political and religious controls. Opposition to his atomism by Nathaniel Tor-
perley (1564-1632), who was to edit Hariot's manuscripts, suggests serious divergences among the members of the Northumberland Circle, to which Hariot belonged.

1453. Keller, Alex, "A Renaissance Humanist Look at 'New Inventions':
The Article 'Horologium' in Giovanni Tortelli's *De Orthogra-
phia*," *Tech. and Culture*, 11 (1970), 345-365.

On 25 classical inventions: clock, church bell, compass,
stirrups, watermill, clavichord, tallow candles, spectacles,
blow pipe are some of the items mentioned by Tortelli in his
aside on the Latin word *Horologium*.

1454. Kemsley, Douglas S., "Religious Influences in the Rise of
Modern Science: A Review and Criticism, Particularly of the
'Protestant-Puritan Ethic' Theory," *Annals of Science*, 24
(1968), 199-226.

Conflicting opinions concerning the nature and causes of rise
of modern science. Opposes view that a source of modern
science is theological content of mid-16th-cent. English belief, or that any theological tenet influenced the reformation
of philosophy with which the Royal Society was engaged.

1455. Kepler, Johannes, *Somnium: The Dream, or Posthumous Work on
Lunar Astronomy*, trans. with commentary by Edward Rosen.
Madison/Milwaukee/London: Univ. of Wisc. Press, 1967.

Rev. *Annals of Science*, 23 (1967), 245-246; *Historian*, 30
(1968), 249-250; *Revue d'Histoire des Sciences*, 21 (1968),
180-182; *Science*, 157 (1967), 416.

Dream relates to subject of diss. proposed at Tübingen in
1593: How do celestial phenomena appear to an observer situ-
ated on the moon? *Somnium* (posthumously printed, 1634) of
Kepler, an early 17th-cent. Copernican, is devoted to astronomy of the moon.

1456. Knappich, Wilhelm, *Geschichte der Astrologie*. Frankfurt am
Main: Vittorio Klostermann, 1967.

Discusses Renaissance beliefs, in "Die Blütezeit der Astrologie
1450-1650."

1457. Knight, D.M., "Uniformity and Diversity of Nature in Seventeenth Century Treatises of Plurality of Worlds," *Organon*
(Poland), 4 (1967), 61-68.

Arguments in favor of plurality of worlds, in antiquity and
in 17th cent.: Kepler, Galileo, Wilkins, etc.

1458. Koyré, Alexandre, *Metaphysics and Measurement: Essays in*
Scientific Revolution. Cambridge, Mass.: Harvard Univ.
Press, 1968. Rev. *NYRB*, 11 (11 Aug. 1968), 22.

On foundation of modern (as opposed to contemporary) physics;
six essays of which four are on Galileo: contrary to widespread notion, Galileo was more of theoretician than experi-
menter.

1459. Lagrange, E., "Réflexions sur l'historique de la découverte
de la circulation sanguine," *Episteme*, 1 (1969), 31-44.

Harvey skillfully demonstrated circulation of the blood, but
he had predecessors: A. Cesalpino d'Arezzo (1519), Colombo,
Serveto. Three cents. earlier: Ibn-an-Nafis, who himself
must have been inspired by the Greeks.

1460. Larder, D.F., "The Editions of Cardanus' *De rerum varietate*,"
Isis, 59, no. 1 (1968), 74-77.

Cardanus' *De rerum varietate*, now found in seven editions, reflects the 16th-cent. transition from Aristotelian and
Scholastic to modern chemistry.

1461. Maccagni, Carlo, ed., *Atti del primo convegno internazionale*
di ricognizione delle fonti per la storia della scienza itali-
ana, I. Secoli XIV-XVI (Vol. 1). Pisa: Domus Galilaeana,
1966. *Atti del convegno sui problemi metodologici di storia*
della scienza (Vol. 2). Turin: Centro di Studi Metodologici,
1967. Florence: G. Barbèra, 1967.

Rev. *Tech. and Culture*, 11 (1970), 97-100.

Vol. I includes C. Vasoli, on "La cultura dei secoli XIV-XVI,"
discussing humanists' views of natural problems. Indicates
further areas of research.

1462. MacDonald, Mary Lee, "A Study of the Interrelationships Between the Aristotelian Closed Universe and Renaissance English," *DA*, 30 (1969), 284-285A (Wayne State Univ.).

Aristotle's closed universe and the early physical theories
which it utilized were still commonly accepted in 16th-cent.
England; linguistic parallels.

1463. Maclean, J., "Geschiedenis van de Kleurentheorie in de Zest-
iende Eeuw," *Scientiarum Historia*, 9 (1967), 23-39.

Sixteenth-cent. views on color in relation to four elements,
rainbow prism, etc. Sixteenth-cent. shows that the supposed
opposition between apparent and permanent real colors
continued. (Cf. 634, 635, 1925.)

1464. ———, "Kleurentheorie in de periode 1600-1635," *Scientiarum*
Historia, 9 (1967), 126-147.

Theory and theorists of color in early 17th cent.

1465. Macphail, Ian, ed., *Alchemy and the Occult. A Catalogue of Books and Manuscripts from the Paul and Mary Mellon Collection.* Vol. I: 1472-1623. Vol. II: 1624-1790. New Haven: Yale Univ. Library, 1968. Rev. *TLS*, 17 July 1969, 784.

Catalogue shows bibliographic expertise; excellent illustrations.

1466. Mayr, Otto, *Zur Frühgeschichte der technischen Regelungen.* Munich: R. Oldenbourg, 1969.

Rev. *Tech. and Culture*, 11 (1970), 321-324.

Part I covers Antiquity, Middle Ages, and Renaissance. Mayr presents the early history of automatic controls in mechanical systems.

1467. McMullin, Ernan, "Empiricism and the Scientific Revolution," in Charles S. Singleton, *Art, Science, and History in the Renaissance.* Baltimore: Johns Hopkins Press, 1967, pp. 331-369.

Suggests that scientific revolution was result of change from conceptualist to empiricist view of nature of science.

1468. ———, ed., *Galileo: Man of Science.* N.Y.: Basic Books, 1968 [c. 1967]. Rev. *Choice*, 5 (1968), 806.

Compendious and useful volume, includes: essays presented to Galileo Quatercentenary Congress (1964); addendum to standard bibliographies by Carli-Favaro and Boffito (1564-1940), a Galileo bibliography (1940-1964); and an annotated list of works by Galileo and contemporaries.

1469. Meadows, A.J., *The High Firmament: A Survey of Astronomy in English Literature.* Leicester: Leicester Univ. Press, 1969.

Rev. *Brit. Jour. for the Hist. of Science*, 5 (1970), 90.

Astronomical ideas as reflected in English literature over the past 500 years; technical information for understanding astronomical allusions and metaphors encountered in authors ranging from Chaucer to Wells. Survey covers the medieval universe, time and instruments, astronomy and astrology, Copernican hypothesis, etc.

1470. Mittelstrass, Jürgen, "Remarks on Nominalistic Roots of Modern Science," *Organon* (Poland), 4 (1967), 39-46.

Link between nominalism and late scholasticism, and modern physics; Galileo's scientific attitude.

1471. Morgan, Paul, "George Hartgill: An Elizabethan Parson-Astronomer and His Library," *Annals of Science*, 24 (1968), 295-311.

A list of books owned by Hartgill (made in 1590), and a horoscope made out for his wedding day, reveal more about the life of this little-known Elizabethan astronomer. Manuscript list of books is reproduced.

1472. Multhauf, Robert P., *The Origins of Chemistry.* Oldbourne History of Science Library; London: Oldbourne, 1966; Chicago: Univ. of Chicago Press, 1967.

Rev. *Isis*, 59 (1968), 104-105; *Tech. and Culture*, 9 (1968), 224-226.

Avoids equation of early chemistry with rise of alchemy or mystical pseudo-science; treats earlier figures as serious forerunners, developing a "science of matter."

1473.   Neugebauer, O., "On the Planetary Theory of Copernicus," *Vistas in Astronomy*, 19 (1968), 89-103.

Kinematics of the solar system according to Copernicus as compared with view of Ptolemy; progress made by Copernicus as modest.

1474.   Nichols, R.E., "Sidrak and Bokkus on the Atmospheric and Earth Sciences," *Centaurus*, 12, no. 4 (1968), 215-221.

Encyclopedia (publ. 1530); among the topics dealt with: time, rain, storms, clouds, shape of the earth, sulphur, rocks, precious stones, earthquakes, night and day.

1475.   O'Malley, C.D., ed., *Leonardo's Legacy: An International Symposium*. UCLA Center for Medieval and Renaissance Studies, No. 2; Berkeley: Univ. of Calif. Press, 1968.

Examines aspects of Leonardo: art, literary style, studies in neurophysiology, and his combined scientific and artistic perspective in technology and engineering. In lectures by Sir Kenneth Clark, Carlo Pedretti, E.H. Gombrich, Kenneth Keele, Augusto Marinoni, Ladislao Reti, Bern Dibner, Ludwig Heydenreich, and James Ackerman. Rev. *Choice*, 6 (1969), 1004.

1476.   Pagel, Walter, "Paracelsus: Traditionalism and Medieval Sources," in Lloyd G. Stevenson et al., eds., *Medicine, Science, and Culture: Historical Essays in Honor of Owsei Temkin*. Baltimore: Johns Hopkins Press, 1968, pp. 50-76.

Medieval sources that may have transmitted gnostic and neoplatonic ideas to Paracelsus.

1477.   Peuckert, Will-Erich, *Pansophie*, Part II: *Gabalia. Ein Versuch zur Geschichte der Magia Naturalis im 16. bis 18. Jahrhundert*. Berlin: Erich Schmidt Verlag, 1967.

Documented account of natural magic in the Renaissance. Includes treatment of Agrippa von Nettesheim, alchemy, magic writings, Paracelsus.

1478.   Quan, Stanislaus, "Galileo and the Problem of Infinity: Part I," *Annals of Sci.*, 26 (1970), 115-151.

Analysis and refutation of Galileo's arguments against Aristotelian concept of infinity.

1479.   Quinn, David B., and John W. Shirley, "A Contemporary List of Hariot References," *RenQ*, 22 (1969), 9-26.

Taken from a series of references to books jotted down by Hariot on the back of the final folio of his nearly finished work, *The Doctrine of Nauticall Triangles Compendious*.

References fall into three more or less chronological categories: 1) his activities as an American explorer and the publications which derived from his residence in North America, 1585-1586; 2) those reflecting his scientific (mainly mathematical) interests during this period and concentrating on practical applications, particularly in navigation; and 3) his ideological affiliations, especially his views on religious issues.

1480. Richeson, A.W., *English Land Measuring to 1800: Instruments and Practices*. Cambridge, Mass.: Pub. for the Society for the History of Technology, and M.I.T. Press, 1966.

Describes books on surveying, instruments used, and when they were introduced. Rev. *AHR*, 72 (1967), 967,

1481. Rose, Paul L., and Stillman Drake, "The Pseudo-Aristotelian *Questions in Mechanics* in Renaissance Culture," *SRen*, 18 (1971), 65-104.

To trace the changes in Renaissance science, studies varying Renaissance reactions to this work. See list, pp. 103-104.

1482. Rosen, Edward, "Was Copernicus a Hermetist?" in Roger H. Stuewer, ed., *Historical and Philosophical Perspectives of Science*. Minneapolis: Univ. of Minn. Press, 1970, pp. 163-171. Rev. *Rev. Met.*, 25 (1971), 142.

Questions hermetic ascriptions. Suggests Copernicus feared the opposition of Aristotelians and theologians.

1483. Santillana, Giorgio de, *Reflections on Men and Ideas*. Foreword by Hugh Trevor-Roper. Cambridge, Mass.: M.I.T. Press, 1968.

Rev. *N.Y. Rev. of Books*, 30 January 1969, 27-30.

Articles by Santillana over last 12 years on variety of Renaissance topics: hermetic tradition, Bruno, Platonism, Galileo, Pythagoreanism, etc.

1484. Sarno, Ronald A., S.J., "A Sixteenth-Century War of Ideas: Science Against the Church," *Annals of Science*, 25 (1969), 209-227.

Growth of Aristotelianism from philosophical synthesis to scientific analysis at the University of Padua; "empirical Aristotelians," Copernicus, Kepler, and Brahe. Attitudes of the Church to Galileo.

1485. Schmidt, Albert-Marie, "Haute Science et poésie française au XVIe siècle," *Études sur le XVIe siècle*. Paris: Albin Michel, 1967, pp. 125-171.

Reprint of 1947 essay. Influence on poetry of esoteric doctrines or occultism.

1486. ————, *Paracelse ou la force qui va*. Paris: Plon, 1967.

Rev. *SFr*, 12 (1968), 339.

Discusses Paracelsus (1493-1541), as well as French Renaissance. Includes bibliography.

1487. Schüling, Hermann, *Die Geschichte der Axiomatischen Methode im 16. und Beginnenden 17. Jahrhundert.* (Wandlung der Wissenschaftsauffassung.) Hildesheim and N.Y.: G. Olms, 1969.

Ancient deductive and geometric methods, 16th to 17th cents. Ramist criticism of axiomatic methods. Notes.

1488. Schullian, Dorothy M., "Reports on Scholarship in the Renaissance. Recent Scholarship in the History of Science," *RenQ*, 21 (1968), 239-248.

1489. Secret, François, "Cornelius Gemma, et la prophétie de la 'Sibylle tiburtine,'" *Revue d'histoire ecclésiastique*, 64 (1969), 423-431.

On Guy Le Fèvre de la Boderie (1541-1598), admirer of Cornelius Gemma (1535-1578), in relation to the new star of 1572, which, like many of his contemporaries, he saw as announcing the second coming of Christ.

1490. Shapiro, B.J., "Latitudinarianism and Science in Seventeenth Century England," *Past and Present*, 40 (1968), 16-41.

Relations between religion and science; Puritanism and scientific innovation.

1491. Snare, Gerald, "Satire, Logic, and Rhetoric in Harvey's Earthquake Letter to Spenser," *TSE*, 23 (1970), 17-33.

Harvey's 1580 letters to Spenser as partly a serious literary-scientific discourse on earthquakes and partly a deliberate satire, intended for publication, of methods of investigation inquiring into earthquakes.

1492. Stevenson, Lloyd G., and Robert P. Multhauf, eds., *Medicine, Science and Culture: Historical Essays in Honor of Oswei Temkin.* Baltimore: Johns Hopkins Press, 1968.

Historical essays on science and medicine, ranging from ancient notion of divine madness through Paracelsus and later figures.

1493. Stillwell, Margaret Bingham, *The Awakening Interest in Science during the First Century of Printing 1450-1550.* N.Y.: Bibliographical Society of America, 1970.

Rev. *Ambix*, 18 (1971), 146; *BC*, 20 (1971), 113-117; *PBSA*, 65 (1971), 181-182; *TLS*, 4 December 1970, 1428.

Annotated list of first editions from 1450-1550, with six subject headings: astronomy, mathematics, medicine, natural sciences, physics, and technology. Has general index, two chronologies, and references to authorities in each field. Extension of Arnold C. Klebs, *Incunabula Scientifica et Medica.*

1494. Tanner-Young, R.C.H., "La place de Thomas Harriot dans l'histoire de la médicine et de l'astronomie," *Gesnerus*, 24 (1967),
75-77.

Major Elizabethan mathematician-scientist and his studies on
tumors and ulcers, and effect of tobacco; astronomical views
and influence of Galileo.

1495. ————, "Thomas Harriot as Mathematician," *Physics*, 2 (1967),
235-247.

Harriot's manuscripts show, contrary to recent views of him
as a physicist and astronomer, that he was, above all, a pure
mathematician.

1496. *L'Univers à la Renaissance: Microcosme et Macrocosme* (Université Libre de Bruxelles. Travaux de l'Institut pour l'étude
de la Renaissance et de l'humanisme, IV. Colloque International, 1968.) Brussels: Presses Universitaires de Bruxelles;
Paris: Presses Universitaires de France, 1970.

Useful articles on Renaissance geography and cosmography (A.
de Smet); on Webster-Ward educational debate, 1654, involving
new philosophy (A.G. Debus); "L'infinité du macrocosme et du
microcosme chez Galilée," Boris Kouznetsov; "Un préjuge de la
pensée dite scientifique: microcosme et macrocosme," Jean
Pelseneer; "L'univers de Giordano Bruno et la destinée hu-
maine," Emile Namer. Rev. *BHR*, 33 (1971), 487-488.

1497. Varga, A. Kibédi, "Poésie et Cosmologie au XVIᵉ Siècle," in
Lumières de la Pléiade (Neuvième Stage International d'Études
Humanistes. Tours, 1965.) Paris: Vrin, 1966, pp. 135-155.

Points out that a modern reader does not see the same nature
that a 16th-cent. reader saw. Hence, the need for study of
Renaissance thought and science (e.g., Wightman's book). One
closed world succeeds another. For the previous order, writers, fearful of newly discovered infinite and silent space,
substituted "la belle nature." Effect on literary analogies.

1498. Viarre, Simone, *La Survie d'Ovide dans la littérature scientifique des XIIᵉ et XIIIᵉ siècles*. (Publications du C.E.S.C.M.,
IV. Supplément aux *Cahiers de Civilisation Médiévale*.) Poi-
tiers, 1966.

Rev. *Rom. Phil.*, 24 (1970), 346-349.

Ovid's importance for Shakespeare suggests utility of such
medieval-influence studies. Concerns Ovid on cosmos, animals,
elements, etc.

1499. Wallace, William A., "Mechanics from Bradwardine to Galileo,"
JHI, 32 (1971), 15-28.

Useful survey of development from scholasticism to Galileo.

1500. Waters, D.W., *The Rutters of the Sea: The Sailing Directions
of Pierre Garcie. A Study of the First English and French
Printed Sailing Directions, with Facsimile Reproductions*. New
Haven: Yale Univ. Press, 1967.

Rev. *AHR*, 74 (1968), 148-149.

Rutters were books of sailing directions that guided British
mariners in the 16th and 17th cents. *Rutters of the Sea* (1577)
was of great interest.

1501. ————, "Science and the Technique of Navigation in the Renaissance," in Charles S. Singleton, ed., *Art, Science, and History in the Renaissance*. Baltimore: Johns Hopkins Press, pp.
187-237.

Role of science, especially in Spain and Portugal, in improving
old, and devising new, practical navigational instruments.

1502. White, Lynn, Jr., *Machina ex Deo. Essays in the Dynamism of
Western Culture*. Cambridge, Mass.: M.I.T. Press, 1968.

Rev. *Tech. and Culture*, 11 (1970), 96-97.

Collection of author's essays of 20 years; stress on late
medieval shift from viewing nature as sacred to seeing it as
divine provision for human satisfaction. Breakdown of rever-
ence for nature involved with desire to exploit it, and con-
sequent scientific technology.

1503. Wussing, H.L., "European Mathematics during the Evolutionary
Period of Early Capitalistic Conditions (15th and 16th Centuries)," *Organon* (Poland), 4 (1967), 89-93.

Brief inquiry concerning how mathematical heritage from antiquity was adapted to social conditions of 15th and 16th cents.

1504. Zambelli, P., "Intorno a possibili fonti di Lulio e ad alcuni
sviluppi della sua combinatoria entro la trattatistica astro-
logico-magica dei secoli XIII-XVI," *La filosofia della natura
nel Medioevo*. Milan: Società Editrice Vita e Pensiero, 1966,
pp. 587-593.

Indicates Arab and Jewish sources, as well as the affiliation
not only with Nicolas de Cusa, but also Pico de la Mirandola,
Giordano Bruno, Francis Bacon, and others.

1505. Zubov, V.P., *Leonardo da Vinci*, tr. D.H. Kraus. Cambridge,
Mass.: Harvard Univ. Press, 1968.

Rev. *Brit. Jour. for the Hist. of Sci.*, 5 (1970), 203-204;
Choice, 6 (1969), 349; *LibJ.*, 93 (1968), 3778; *N.Y. Rev. of
Books*, 11 (5 Dec. 1968), 4.

Russian interpretative biography (pub. 1961 in U.S.S.R).
Focuses on social, political, economic, and scientific forces
in Leonardo's background in relation to his humanism.

1506. Zupko, Ronald Edward, *A Dictionary of English Weights and Measures from Anglo-Saxon Times to the Nineteenth Century*. Madison: Univ. of Wisc. Press, 1968.

Rev. *Econ.*, 229 (9 Nov. 1968), 11.

First comprehensive, documented compilation of weights and measures used in Britain during the Shakespearean era (from Anglo-Saxon times until the eve of the Industrial Revolution). Over 3,000 entries; etymologies for metrological units. (Cf. Zupko, "A Dictionary of Medieval Weights and Measures," *DA*, 28 [1967], 1026-A [Univ. of Wisc.])

ADDENDUM

1506a. Rajadurai, Eric B.M., "Shakespeare and the Renaissance Sciences: An Annotated Bibliography," *DA*, 31 (1971), 4178-A (Kent State Univ.).

Includes annotated bibliography of modern works on Shakespeare's use of sciences and pseudo-sciences, including medicine, Elizabethan psychology, etc.; over 1,050 entries.

XVII. THEATRICAL

1507. Anglo, Sydney, *Spectacle, Pageantry, and Early Tudor Policy*.
(Oxford-Warburg Studies.) N.Y.: Oxford Univ. Press, 1969.

Rev. *AHR*, 75 (1970), 2045-2046; *BHR*, 32 (1970), 723-726.

On royal entries, festivals, disguisings, masques, and tourna-
ments from accession of Henry VII to coronation of Elizabeth.

1508. Bacon, Tom Ivey, "Martin Luther and the Drama," *DA*, 31 (1970),
1749-A (Univ. of Texas at Austin).

Traces medieval reactions to drama, drama's secularization,
and Luther's concept of drama as related to his loyalty to
educational reform.

1509. Barker, Walter Lawton, "Three English Pantalones: A Study in
Relations between the *Commedia Dell'Arte* and Elizabethan
Drama," *DA*, 27 (1967), 3419-A (Univ. of Conn.).

Shows the influence of Pantalone, the absurd old man of the
commedia dell'arte, on characterization in *The Jew of Malta*,
The Merchant of Venice, and *Volpone*.

1510. *Le Baroque au théâtre et la théâtralité du Baroque*. Actes de
la deuxième session des Journées Internationales d'Étude du
Baroque; Montaubon: Publs. du C.N.R.S., 1967. (Cf. *Topoi*.)

Rev. *SFr*, 12 (1968), 347-348.

Papers given in September 1966, including: Jean Jacquot, "Rap-
port d'ouverture: drame poétique et fête théâtrale"; R. Le-
bègue, "Origines et caractère du théâtre baroque français";
F. Mathieu-Arth, "Du masque à l'Opéra anglais"; A. Cioranescu,
"Baroque et action dramatique: le dehors et le dedans."
Second part devoted to baroque architecture and music.

1511. Baur-Reinhold, Margarete, *The Baroque Theatre: A Cultural
History of the Seventeenth and Eighteenth Centuries*. N.Y.:
McGraw-Hill, 1967.

Rev. *QJS*, 54 (1968), 299-300.

From the Teatro Olimpico (1580-1584) to the Teatro La Fenice
(1790-1792); describes the privileged classes that supported
the theater.

1512. Berger, Harry, Jr., "Theater, Drama, and the Second World: A
Prologue to Shakespeare," *CompD*, 2 (1968), 3-20.

In change from sacred to secular, "dramatic space-time" split
into fictional and actual plane. Fictional event symbolizes
matters lying "beyond" in a morality play, with actual space-
time less important. Though imaginary space-time characterizes
Elizabethan drama, Shakespeare relates fictional and actual
space-time, describing both the world in which personages live
and the world they project by their language.

1513.   Bergeron, David, "Anthony Munday: Pageant Poet to the City of
         London," *Huntington Library Quarterly*, 30 (1967), 345-368.

         Discusses Elizabethan civic entertainment. Examines contempo-
         rary references to Munday (mostly satirical). Seven lord
         mayor's shows by Munday survive in pamphlets--these are all
         outlined in detail.

1514.   ———, "Charles I's Royal Entries into London," *Guildhall
         Miscellany*, 3 (1970), 91-98.

         Charles I's cancellations of royal entries. How Aldermen,
         Council, and livery companies were involved in civic entertain-
         ment; production problems of civic pageants. Links retreat of
         Crown from public life to replacement of civic pageant by
         court masque as dramatic form, and to replacement of civic
         pageant by Lord Mayor's show as popular spectacle.

1515.   ———, "The Christmas Family: Artificers in English Civic
         Pageantry," *ELH*, 35 (1968), 354-364.

         This family's involvement in production of mayoral shows; re-
         lationship between poet and architect in civic pageantry.
         Rise in artificer's importance.

1516.   ———, "Harrison, Jonson and Dekker: The Magnificent Enter-
         tainment for King James (1604)," *JWCI*, 31 (1968), 445-448.

         Discrepancies between Stephen Harrison's pictorial record and
         the printed texts of Jonson and Dekker.

1517.   ———, "The Elizabethan Lord Mayor's Show," *SEL*, 10 (1970),
         269-285.

         Its development and influence on later pageant writers.

1518.   ———, "Venetian State Papers and English Civic Pageantry,
         1558-1642," *RenQ*, 23 (1970), 37-47.

         Effect of dramatic civic pageantry to honor sovereigns or
         magistrates on evolution of English drama. Utilizes official
         dispatches of Venetian ambassador in London.

1519.   Binger, Norman, *A Bibliography of German Plays on Microcards*.
         Hamden, Conn.: Shoestring, 1970.

         Rev. *Choice*, 8 (1971), 45.

         Bibliography of microcard editions of almost 4,000 German
         plays, dating from 16th to early 20th cent.

1520. Brownstein, Oscar, "The Popularity of Baiting in England be-
       fore 1600: A Study in Social and Theatrical History," *Educ.
       Theatre Jour.*, 21, no. 3 (1969), 237-250.

       Refutes supposed great popularity of baiting in Elizabethan
       London, using historical evidence.

1521. Burch, C.E.C., *Minstrels and Players in Southampton, 1428-
       1635*. Southampton: Southampton Papers, No. 7, 1969.

       Brief survey, with reference to municipal account books of
       the period.

1522. Cirillo, Albert R., "Giulio Camillo's *Idea of the Theater*:
       The Enigma of the Renaissance," *Comparative Drama*, 1 (Spring
       1967), 19-26.

       Giulio's *Theatro* (1550), which reflects religion from each of
       its seven pillars, mirrors the Renaissance, and was soon to
       enlighten Shakespeare's England.

1523. Clubb, Louise George, comp., *Italian Plays (1500-1700) in the
       Folger Library: A Bibliography with an Introduction by Louise
       George Clubb*. Biblioteca di bibliografia Italiana, 52;
       Florence: Leo S. Olschki, 1968. Rev. *PBSA*, 64 (1970), 119.

       Useful bibliography, successor to such works as Beatrice Cor-
       rigan, comp., *Italian Renaissance Plays in the University of
       Toronto Library* (1961); suppl., *RN*, 16 (1963), 298-307; 19
       (1966), 219-228; and to Marvin T. Herrick, comp., *Italian
       Plays, 1500-1700, in the University of Illinois Library* (1966);
       cf. rev. of Herrick, *Library*, 5th ser., 22 (1968), 165-168.

       Present work has 890 items, with helpful annotations; indexes
       of plays by title, and of printers by cities. Cross-referen-
       cing. Folger holdings checked against several other biblio-
       graphies. Scholarly introduction includes "A Chronological
       Guide to Genres Represented in the Folger Collection," fol-
       lowed by list of "Basic Reference Works." Illustrated.

1524. Cope, Jackson I., "The Rediscovery of Anti-Form in Renaissance
       Drama," *Comparative Drama*, 1 (Fall 1967), 155-171.

       Describes the shape of the Renaissance play as a little world
       which refuses to be static, to accept the limitations of mime-
       tic form, which mocks aesthetic objectivity as it incorporates
       the *theatrum mundi* into itself upon its own terms. Examines
       Renaissance drama, not as an objective form, but as a paradox-
       ical "structure" continuously reforming itself in interplay
       with the author and reader, with the society from which it
       comes and into which it flows.

1525. Eccles, Mark, "Recent Studies in Elizabethan and Jacobean
       Drama," *SEL*, 9 (1969), 351-378.

       Survey of books published in 1968.

1526. Erdmann, Louis Otto, "The Printed Festival Book: A Study of
       Northern Continental Festivals in the Late 16th Century," *DA*,
       27 (1967), 3970-A (Ohio State Univ.).

       Dramatic festivals began in the early 12th cent. and lasted
       until the early 17th cent. in the major cities in Europe.
       They had no literary form, but rather had scenic embellish-
       ments and action in its place, as well as allegorical figures.
       Social and political events in the 16th cent. led to the
       printed festival book. Theatrical elements included tourna-
       ments, games of skill, *tableaux vivants*, etc.

1527. Fishman, Burton John, "The Fatal Masque: A Study of Visual
       Metaphor and Dramatic Convention in Renaissance Tragedy," *DA*,
       30 (1970), 728-A (Princeton Univ.).

       History of the "fatal masque" (masque, dumb show, or play-
       within-a-play in which the characters either viewing or parti-
       cipating are killed by the masquers). These "fatal masques"
       functioned as play's visual metaphors.

1528. Fraser, Russell A., "Elizabethan Drama and the Art of Abstrac-
       tion," *CompD*, 2 (1968), 73-82.

       New drama of the Renaissance and its tendency to abstraction
       and generalization; except for Shakespeare, wary of analogy
       and exemplification. Shakespeare produces the elusive, mys-
       terious figure not so amenable to definition or translation,
       whereas Jonson reveals the abstracting impulse.

1529. Galloway, David, ed., *The Elizabethan Theater II*. London:
       Macmillan, 1970.

       Rev. *TLS*, 5 February 1971, 156.

       Papers of the 1969 International Conference on Elizabethan
       Theater: L. Markar on acting theory, T. Lennam on activities
       of Children of St. Paul's between 1551 and 1582, R.A. Foakes
       on acting styles, D.F. Rowan on plans for theater that may be
       missing link between Elizabethan Swan Theater and Caroline
       Cockpit-in-Court.

1530. Gassner, John, and Edward Quinn, eds., *The Reader's Encyclo-
       pedia of World Drama*. N.Y.: Thomas Y. Crowell, 1969.

       Rev. *Educational Theatre Journal*, 22 (1970), 230-232.

       Entries on nations, playwrights, plays, genres, and some
       technical and theoretical terms. Appendix, "Basic Documents
       in Dramatic Theory." Entries for plays are mainly plot sum-
       maries with short paragraphs of critical comment.

1531. *Great Tournament Roll of Westminster. A Collotype Reproduc-
       tion of the Manuscript*. Historical introduction by Sydney
       Anglo. Foreword by Sir Anthony Wagner. Oxford: Clarendon
       Press, 1968.

       Rev. *Medium Aevum*, 38 (1969), 338-341.

Commemorates tournament at Westminster to celebrate birth of a
prince to Henry VIII and Katherine of Aragon on New Year's Day,
1511. Describes (on 36 vellum membranes) a "contest of martial
arts and industries and displays of courtly magnificence."
These included the most popular military pastime, tilting, or
Jousts Royal.

1532. Griffiths, Richard M., *The Dramatic Technique of Antoine de
Montchrestien: Rhetoric and Style in French Renaissance
Tragedy*. London: Oxford, 1970.

Rev. *Choice*, 8 (1971), 234.

Renaissance tragedy evolved from rhetorical training of its
practitioners and from rhetorical tradition. Sixteenth-cent.
tragedy as distinct genre, not as inferior forerunner of 17th-
cent. tragedy. Sees influence of the Progymnasmata.

1533. Gurr, Andrew, *The Shakespearean Stage: 1574-1642*. London:
Cambridge Univ. Press, 1970.

Rev. *Educ. Theat. Jour.*, 23 (1971), 218-219; *TLS*, 5 March
1971, 276.

Summary of information concerning Elizabethan, Jacobean, and
Caroline stage. Sections on acting companies, actors, playhouses, staging, audiences. Appendix contains list of plays
assignable to playhouses and companies. Index, notes,
illustrations.

1534. Hardison, O.B., Jr., "Three Types of Renaissance Catharsis,"
RenD, n.s. 2 (1969), 3-22.

Discusses moral, religious, and literal theories of catharsis,
which were recognized by Elizabethan critics and used by
dramatists.

1535. Hawkins, Harriet B., "'All the World's a Stage.' Some Illustrations of the *Theatrum Mundi*," *SQ*, 17, no. 2 (1966), 174-
178. (Cf. [THEATRUM MUNDI] under *Topoi*.)

Three themes associated with the Renaissance concept of *theatrum mundi*, the idea that the world itself was God's theater:
1) Drama has cosmic importance and is didactic in function;
2) The stage, as a place where men feigned, pretended to be
what they were not, was "an image of the comedy of our life";
3) The logical shape of the theater would be that of the globe
itself.

1536. Hosley, Richard, "The Origins of the So-Called Elizabethan
Multiple Stage," *Drama Rev.* (formerly *Tulane Drama Rev.*), 12,
no. 2 (1968), 28-50.

So-called Elizabethan multiple stage, exemplified in John Cran-
ford Adams' reconstruction, preserves Victorian production
methods, and post-Restoration theatrical elements. Evidence
is lacking for many of the elements of the so-called Elizabethan multiple stage.

1537.   ———, Arthur C. Kirsch, and John W. Velz, eds., *Studies in Shakespeare, Bibliography, and Theater*. N.Y.: Shakespeare Association of America, 1969.

Rev. *South Atlantic Quarterly*, 69 (1970), 296.

Tribute volume to J.G. McManaway, including a brief foreword by the editors; 20 notes and articles by McManaway; the 17 annual analyses of Textual Studies that he prepared for *Shakespeare Survey* from 1948 to 1965; and a bibliography of his writings from 1931 to 1968.

1538.   Jacquot, Jean, ed., *Dramaturgie et société--Rapports entre l'oeuvre théâtrale, son interprétation et son public au XVIe et au XVIIe siècles*. Paris: Editions du Centre National de la Recherche Scientifique, 1968. 2 vols.

Rev. *BHR* , 32 (1970), 649-675.

In collaboration with Elie Konigson and Marcel Oddon, the volumes comprise 910 pages.

1539.   Jeffrey, Brian, *French Renaissance Comedy 1552-1630*. Oxford: Clarendon, 1969.

Rev. *BHR*, 32 (1970), 518-519.

Sources and models available to the Pléiade, and their successors in the comic genre. Examines, from pictorial and internal-textual evidence, nature of the stage and the performances. Third chapter, comprising about half the book, deals with conventions, including dramatic theory, plot, character, unity of time.

1540.   Kernodle, George Riley, "Perspective in the Renaissance Theatre, the Pictorial Sources and the Development of Scenic Forms," *DA*, 28 (1967), 319-A (Yale Univ.).

Evolution of modern scenery and stage, as influenced by painting. Renaissance perspective theater derived from painting not only aims of illusion and great depth, but also the back architectural screen and the side house--both also from ancient theater. Early Renaissance scene was constructed of two long balanced rows of angle wings and curved sections of heavens leading to an unimportant shutter. As means were devised for drawing "depth" on flat surfaces, flat forms took the place of three-dimensional ones.

1541.   Kowzan, Tadeusz, "The Sign in the Theater: An Introduction to the Semiology of the Art of the Spectacle," *Diogenes*, no. 61 (1968), 52-80.

Tendency to reduce all problems of sign to language or linguistic equivalents has led to the semiological ignoring of spectacular arts. Everything constitutes sign in theatrical representation, though seldom in its pure state. Classifications of theatrical signs: 1) word, 2) tone, 3) facial mime, 4) gesture, 5) actor's movements on stage, 6) make-up, 7) hair style, 8) costume, 9) accessory, 10) decor, 11) lighting, 12) music. Illustration from *MND*, III. i, pp. 74-75. Because of its need of confronting varied system of signs, semiology of spectacle may be touchstone of general science of signs.

1542. Krautheimer, Richard, "The Tragic and Comic Scene of the Re-
naissance: The Baltimore and Urbino Panels," *Studies in Early
Christian, Medieval and Renaissance Art*. N.Y.: N.Y. Univ.
Press; London: Univ. of London Press, 1969, pp. 345-359.

In this revision of 1948 essay, finds first representations of
the *scena tragica* and the *scena comica* of the Renaissance in
1470's. Cites Vitruvius and Serlio.

1543. McDonald, Charles Osborne, *The Rhetoric of Tragedy: Form in
Stuart Drama*. Amherst, Mass.: Univ. of Mass. Press, 1966.

Political and social demands helped form a rhetorical education—suited both to drama and to legal profession in 16th-
cent. England. Rev. *JEGP*, 66 (1967), 449.

1544. McGowan, M., "Form and Themes in Henri II's Entry into Rouen,"
RenD, 1 (1968), 199-251.

Description with illustrations of this important royal entry
(1550). Role of such ceremonies, bringing together architects,
painters, sculptors, poets, and engineers. Consideration of
political, religious, and artistic repercussions.

1545. Minor, Andrew Collier and Bonner Mitchell, *A Renaissance Entertainment: Festivities for the Marriage of Cosimo I, Duke
of Florence, in 1539. An Edition of the Music, Comedy and Descriptive Account with Commentary*. Columbia, Mo.: Univ. of
Mo. Press, 1968.

Rev. *Choice*, 6 (1969), 497; *Italica*, 47 (1970), 437-438.

Wedding festivities of Cosimo de'Medici and Eleanor of Toledo;
music, verses, madrigals, comedy by Antonio Landi. (Suppl. to
Nagler, *Theatre Festivals of the Medici 1539-1637*.)

1546. Morgan, Edmund S., "Puritan Hostility to the Theatre," *Proc.
Amer. Phil. Soc.*, 110 (1966), 340-347.

Most intense hostility during Shakespeare's period.

1547. Nagler, A.M., "The Campidoglio Stage of 1513," *Maske und
Kothurn*, 16 (1970), 229-235.

Two types of Renaissance stages: those that point to future
and those that point to past. The Campidoglio of the latter
type based on Badius' idea of Roman stage. Also remarks on
problem of first modern display of *picturatae scaenae*.

1548. Neiiendam, Klaus, "Le théâtre de la Renaissance à Rome," in
Analecta Romana Instituti Danici, pp. 103-197. Copenhagen:
Einar Munskgaard, 1968.

Rev. *BHR*, 32 (1970), 656-658.

Roman theater, 1480-1530.

1549. Niggestich-Kretzmann, Gunhild, *Die Intermezzi des italieni-
schen Renaissance-theaters*. Dissertation zur Erlangung des
Doktorgrades der Philosophischen Fakultät der Georg-August-
Universität zu Göttingen, Göttingen, 1968.

Rev. *BHR*, 32 (1970), 660-661.

On literary music-dance form.

1550. Oreglia, Giacomo, *The Commedia dell'Arte*, trans. N.Y.: Hill
and Wang, 1968. Rev. *TLS*, 16 May 1968, 500.

Italian work first published in 1961; this English translation
based on Swedish edition (1964). Documented, illustrated work
traces origins and history of *commedia dell'arte*. Nine chapters on detailed descriptions of main masks; costumes, repar-
tee, comic business. Includes also texts and rehearsal notes
of several scenarios.

1551. Palmer, Helen H., and Anne J. Dyson, *European Drama Criticism*.
Hamden, Conn.: Shoestring Press, 1968. Rev. *LJ*, 94 (1969), 1583.

Lists criticism of dramatic works by European playwrights in
English and foreign language books and periodicals, 1900–1966.
Emphasis on English language writers.

1552. Peake, Richard Henry, Jr., "The Stage Prostitute in the English Dramatic Tradition from 1558 to 1625," *DA*, 27 (1967),
3847-A – 3848-A (Univ. of Georgia).

Evolution of the stage prostitute from morality figure into
realistic character; various traditions from which she was
drawn. Stock figure in coterie drama (1604-1608). From
1609 to 1613, dramatic emphasis on her lustfulness increased.

1553. Pinciss, Gerald Martin, "The Queen's Men 1583-1592," *DA*, 28
(1967), 1793-A (Columbia Univ.).

Social and political causes of formation of Queen's Men under
patronage of Elizabeth; its history until end of performances
in London; confrontation with increasing antagonism of authorities; appearances in London and provinces and before royalty;
involvement in Marprelate controversy. Repertory of company
and possible publication arrangement with printer, Thomas
Creede; their texts studied to provide basis for determining
company's techniques of staging. Possibility of Shakespeare's
apprenticeship, and relationship of Queen's repertory with his
work.

1554. ————, "Thomas Creede and the Repertory of the Queen's Men
1583-1592," *MP*, 67 (1970), 321.

To establish the repertory of this company; sees Shakespeare's
association with one company atypical of Elizabethan times.

1555. Presley, Horton Edward, "O Showes, Showes, Mighty Showes: A
Study of the Relationship of the Jones-Jonson Controversy to
the Rise of Illusionistic Staging in Seventeenth-Century
British Drama," *DA*, 28 (1967), 1056-A (Univ. of Kansas).

Causes of changes in stages used by dramatists in early and
later 17th cent. as result partly of audience demands for
spectacular staging that can be traced in British drama from
at least last quarter of 15th cent.; conflict in 1631 between
Jonson and Inigo Jones over who was more important in design
of court masque as continuation of traditional conflict between
art and literary theory in 15th-cent. Italy and still alive
in 17th-cent. England; Jones responsible for important changes
in 17th-cent. staging, shift from platform stage to illusionistic stage set behind a proscenium arch.

1556. Radcliff-Umstead, Douglas, *The Birth of Modern Comedy in Renaissance Italy*. Chicago, Ill.: Univ. of Chicago Press, 1969.

Comparative study of Renaissance Italian comedy aims to show that such comedy was not only an imitation of Plautus and Terence, but original drama which expressed Renaissance values and portrayed contemporary customs. Rev. *RQ*, 24 (1971), 528-530.

1557. Raimonde, E., "Il Teatro de Machiavelli," *Studi Storici*, 10 (1969), 949-998.

Machiavelli's comedies are in the "proverbial" style of Terence; moral norm is the simple and affectionate domestic life.

1558. Reibetanz, John H., "The Two Theatres: Dramatic Structure and Convention in English Public and Private Plays, 1599-1613," *DA*, 29 (1969), 4500-A (Princeton Univ.).

Changes in form of English drama from 1599 to 1613, as related to growth and influence of private theater. Many differences which critics have noticed between Elizabethan and Jacobean drama are partially explicable in terms of the way public-theater plays differed from private-theater plays; examination of structure and convention in approximately 120 plays.

1559. *Revue d'Histoire du Théâtre*, 21 (1969), 297-445.

Bibliography for 1968; many 1967 and 1969 items are included. Divisions: bibliographies, catalogs, theaters and troupes, comedy, biographies, history of dramatic literature, etc.

1560. Rhome, Frances Dodson, "Variations of Festive Revel in Four English Comedies, 1595-1605," *DA*, 30 (1970), 5418-A (Indiana Univ.).

Popular festivals and street pageants of the 15th and 16th cents. influenced structure and spirit of Elizabethan comedies. *A Humorous Day's Mirth*; *A Mad World, My Masters*; *The Shoemaker's Holiday*; and *A Tale of a Tub* analyzed separately to determine their adaptation to revel mode.

1561. Richter, B.L., "Recent Studies in Renaissance Scenography," *Renaissance News*, 19 (1966), 344-358.

In the early 1600's, Torelli established new efficiency in scene-changing; fluid state of stage design.

1562. Roston, Murray, *Biblical Drama in England: From the Middle Ages to the Present*. London: Faber and Faber, 1968.

Contains detailed and useful chapters on the biblical elements in medieval stage; the early Renaissance; the later Renaissance. Rev. *Choice* (1969), 1596. (Cf. [BIBLE] under *Topoi*.)

1563. Shapiro, Michael, "Children's Troupes: Dramatic Illusion and Acting Style," *CDR*, 3 (1969), 42-53.

Comic dramatists in Renaissance often exploited "dual consciousness" of child actors as actors and as characters. Focus on the "dual consciousness" in four ways: 1) use of

adult actors; 2) bawdry; 3) self-referential discussions of
actors, plays, etc.; 4) inductions to plays.

1564. ———, "The Plays Acted by the Children of Paul's, 1599-1607,"
DA, 28 (1967), 1795-A (Columbia Univ.).

Studies company, repertory, and audiences of Children of
Paul's; critical of "coterie" description of their audiences;
possibilities in performance (comic incongruity or disparity;
sexual humor) by children, unhampered by post-Romantic notions
of childhood innocence; company's use of prologues, epilogues,
direct and indirect abuse, modes to forestall ridicule by detached audiences. Repertory shows, after revival in 1599,
trend toward increasingly satiric modes of comedy, with ridicule of fathers and other authority figures. Satiric mode of
children's companies almost exclusively occupied with fools
and knaves motivated by lust and greed.

1565. ———, "What We Know about the Children's Troupes and Their
Plays," *SRO*, nos. 5-6 (1970/71), 36-45.

Useful survey of unassembled materials post-Hillebrand, *The
Child Actors* (1926).

1566. Shergold, N.D., *A History of the Spanish Stage: From Medieval
Times until the End of the Seventeenth Century.* N.Y.: Oxford
Univ. Press, 1967.

Rev. *AHR*, 73 (1967), 501.

From tropes through secular drama; important parallels with
Elizabethan and Stuart drama. Major tool for Shakespeareans—
Spanish analogies having been relatively neglected. Documen-
tation.

1567. Slover, George W., "The Elizabethan Playhouse and the Tradition of Liturgical Stage Structure," *DA*, 30 (1969), 435-436-A
(Indiana Univ.).

Deals with symbolic implications of Elizabethan stage structure; considers stage as emblem of the state. Elizabethan
stage in context of classical stage and medieval cycle stage.

1568. Stäuble, Antonio, "Rassegna di testi e studi sul teatro del
Rinascimento," *BHR*, 29 (1967), 227-245.

Survey article on Renaissance theater publications.

1569. Stratman, Carl J., *Bibliography of English Printed Tragedy:
1565-1900.* Carbondale and Edwardsville: Southern Ill. Univ.
Press, 1966. Rev. *PQ*, 46 (1967), 291.

Lists by author 1,483 tragedies written in England, Ireland,
and Scotland and published between 1565 and 1900. Notes various editions of each tragedy and present locations of the
surviving editions. Excludes Shakespeare and literal translations of Latin tragedies and of plays from foreign languages.

1570. Thompson, Lawrence Sidney, *A Bibliography of French Plays on Microcards*. N.Y.: Shoe String Press, 1967.

Nearly 7,000 French plays.

1571. Thomson, Patricia, "World Stage and Stage in Massinger's *Roman Actor*," *Neophil.*, 54 (1970), 409-426. (Cf. [THEATRUM MUNDI] under *Topoi*.)

Massinger's contributions to world-as-stage tradition. Relation of play-within-play to this tradition. Concludes the play is "a tragedy not only of an actor, but of acting."

1572. Tobin, Terence, "Popular Entertainment in Seventeenth-Century Scotland," *TN*, 23 (1968/69), 46-54.

From mid-16th-cent. on, ecclesiastical and civil legislation obstructed nearly all theatrical representation in Scotland. Majority of popular entertainment of the period consisted of quasi-theatrical exhibitions or variety shows used by charlatans to attract crowds.

1573. Weimann, Robert, *Shakespeare und die Tradition des Volkstheaters: Soziologie, Dramaturgie, Gestaltung*. Berlin: Henschelverlag, 1967. Rev. *RES*, n.s. 20 (1969), 220.

Shakespeare and dramatic tradition of the people; use of traditional linguistic patterns, word-play, proverb, "aside," nonsense, and clowning; figures such as Vice and Herod, etc.

1574. West, Herbert Faulkner, Jr., "Unifying Devices in Four Globe Plays," *DA*, 30 (1970), 5424-A (Univ. of Georgia).

Detailed examination of four plays performed at the Globe early in 17th cent.--*The Faire Maide of Bristow*, *Thomas Lord Cromwell*, *The Revenger's Tragedy*, and *The Malcontent*--reveals ten principal unifying devices. Argues against simplistic reductions of unity in English Renaissance drama.

1575. Wickham, Glynne, "Actor and Player in Shakespeare's Theatre," *Maske und Kothurn*, 15 (1969), 1-5.

Playwright during Shakespeare's time was little more than a "play-maker" or "stage-poet"; he was a servant to the players-- thus bondage was fiscal and aesthetic.

1576. Williams, Robert Ileroy, "Skepticism in the Jacobean Comedies of Thomas Middleton, Ben Jonson, and John Fletcher," *DA*, 28 (1967), 207-A (Univ. of Calif., Berkeley).

Each of these playwrights had a skeptical phase, if we measure skepticism by the extent to which a playwright opposes comic values of wit, intelligence, and knowledge to values of honesty, prudence, and nobility. Evidence is lacking that these writers were influenced by philosophical skepticism; they reacted rather through first-hand awareness of the world.

1577. Wren, Robert M., "Ben Jonson as Producer," *Educ. Theat. Jour.*, 22 (1970), 284-290.

Cynthia's Revels as exercise for actors; Jonson's techniques
as producer. Jonson as instructor contrasted to Shakespeare
as actor; his method of instruction is reflected in the instruction that is part of the play's action.

1578. Yates, Frances A., *Theatre of the World*. Univ. of Chicago
       Press, 1969.

       Rev. *N&Q*, 16 (1969), 475–478; *Ren. and Ref.*, 7 (1970), 10–12;
       TLS, 4 September 1969, 980.

       John Dee and Robert Fludd as exemplars of the Renaissance re-
       vival of Vitruvius. Carries the themes of the author's earlier
       Renaissance studies (particularly her study of Dee and Fludd
       as representatives of Hermetic tradition in Tudor and Stuart
       England, *Giordano Bruno and the Hermetic Tradition*) towards
       the English theater and towards Shakespeare.

1579. Young, Steven C.A., "A Check List of Tudor and Stuart Induc-
       tion Plays," *PQ*, 48 (1969), 131–134.

       Induction defined as a dramatic action which precedes a full-
       length play; has at least two speaking roles; exists on a dif-
       ferent narrative plane from that of fuller work. It may stand
       complete in itself, or as beginning of a frame plot. (Cf.
       Thelma N. Greenfield, *The Induction in Elizabethan Drama*.
       Eugene: Univ. of Oregon Books, 1969. Rev. *JEGP*, 70 [1971],
       292–295.)

                              ADDENDUM

1579a. Wickham, Glynne, "The Privy Council Order of 1597 for the De-
       struction of all London's Theatres," in David Galloway, ed.,
       The Elizabethan Theatre. Papers ... International Conference
       on Elizabethan Theatre ... University of Waterloo, Ontario ...
       1968. Hamden, Conn.: Archon Books, 1970, pp. 21–44.

       Why the court order of 1597 to destroy all theaters in and
       about London was never executed. Finds this order a turning
       point between amateur and professional theater. Suggests
       conditions of court performance as rule for production methods
       in public theaters.

XVIII. THEOLOGICAL

1580. Aland, Kurt, *Repetitorium der Kirchengeschichte III. Reformation und Gegenreformation*. Sammlung Töpelmann, 1st ser.,
vol. 10, pt. 3. Berlin: Alfred Töpelmann, 1967.

Rev. *Church Hist.*, 37 (1968), 347-348.

In parallel columns, contains history of church, 1198-1648,
in context of political, economic, and intellectual history.
Special tables of lives of Reformers. Bibliographic handbook.

1581. Alden, John J.W., "An Examination of the Thought of John Colet
(1467?-1519): A Catholic Humanist Reformer at the Eve of Protestant Reformation," *DA*, 31 (1970), 1360-A (Yale Univ.).

Colet as a transitional figure in Erasmianism and formation of
via media of Anglicanism.

1582. Allen, Ward, ed., *Translating for King James: Notes Made by a
Translator of King James's Bible*. Nashville: Vanderbilt Univ.
Press, 1969.

Rev. *Church Hist.*, 39 (1970), 274; *Moreana*, no. 25 (Feb. 1970),
97-99; *SCN*, 28 (1970), 8.

Critical edition and translation with photographic facsimiles
of notes of John Bois on Romans to Revelation for King James
Version, with biography by his contemporary, Anthony Walker.

1583. Allison, C.F., *The Rise of Moralism: The Proclamation of the
Gospel from Hooker to Baxter*. London: SPCK, 1966.

Hooker, Andrewes, Donne, et al., established an Anglican theology vs. the Council of Trent, differing from Roman Catholic
and reformed positions. Synthesis of thought and sensibility
in a doctrine and ethics called "orthodox" or "classical,"
the theology of Jeremy Taylor to Richard Baxter. Appendix has
decrees of Council of Trent. Rev. *TLS*, 9 March 1967, 203.

1584. Althaus, Paul, *The Theology of Martin Luther*. Philadelphia:
Fortress Press, 1966. Rev. *Church Hist.*, 36 (1967), 236.

A translation, this is a detailed documented study.

1585. Anstruther, Godfrey, comp., *The Seminary Priests: A Dictionary of the Secular Clergy of England and Wales, 1558-1850: I
Elizabethan, 1558-1603*. Durham: St. Edmunds College, Ware
and Ushaw College, 1968.

Rev. *EHR*, 86 (1971), 169-170.

Collection of short biographical studies of the Roman Catholic
secular clergy. Includes an appendix of some 270 aliases used
by the priests.

1586.   Armstrong, Brian G., *Calvinism and the Amyraut Heresy: Protes-
        tant Scholasticism and Humanism in Seventeenth-Century
        France.* Madison: Univ. of Wisc. Press, 1969.

        Rev. *AHR*, 75 (1970), 2064-2065; *Jour. of Religious Hist.*, 6
        (1970), 199-201.

        Amyraut, a 17th-cent. heretic against strict Calvinism. Book
        separates rigidly humanist and scholastic elements within French
        Protestantism; holds that French Reformation was product of
        Renaissance humanism. After Calvin's death, continental Cal-
        vinism was altered by stress on deductive reason, by weighing
        reason as heavily as revelation, and by viewing the Bible as con-
        sistent and rational. Distorters of Calvinism included such fig-
        ures as Beza, who defined predestination in supralapsarian terms.

1587.   Asheim, Ivar, ed., *Kirche, Mystik, Heiligung und das Natürliche
        bei Luther.* (Kongress, 1966.) Göttingen: Vandenhoeck &
        Ruprecht, 1967.

        Essays by E.G. Rupp, "Luther: The Contemporary Image"; H.A.
        Oberman; J. Pelikan; W.H. Lazareth, "Luther on Civil Righteous-
        ness and Natural Law."

1588.   Atkinson, James, *The Great Light: Luther and the Reformation.*
        Grand Rapids, Mich.: Wm. B. Eerdmans, 1968.

        Rev. *Church Hist.*, 39 (1970), 119.

        General history of the Reformation; useful for its concise
        statements of the theologies of Luther, Zwingli, Calvin, and
        Cranmer.

1589.   Bainton, Roland H., *Erasmus of Christendom.* N.Y.: Scribner,
        1969.

        Rev. *Jour. of the Amer. Acad. of Rel.*, 39 (1971), 100-104.

        Biography of Erasmus, particularly of his travels in Europe.
        Less a developmental study than an attempt to define "the
        essential Erasmus" as "Christian" and not "Renaissance man."
        Includes thematic discussions of Erasmus' works.

1590.   ――――, "The Paraphrases of Erasmus," *Archiv für Reformations-
        geschichte*, 57 (1966), 67-76.

        The relatively unstudied Paraphrases, containing the "whole"
        of Erasmus, are more important than the Adages for his thought.

1591.   Bangs, Carl, "Dutch Theology, Trade, and War: 1590-1610,"
        Church Hist., 39 (1970), 470-482.

        Signing of truce with Spain and development of the Dutch East
        India Company as factors in theological controversy over pre-
        destination, Arminian debate.

1592.   Baron, Salo W., "Medieval Heritage and Modern Realities in
        Protestant-Jewish Relations," *Diogenes*, no. 61 (1968), 32-51.

        Protestant Revolution of 16th cent. did not deter medieval-type
        folkloristic suspicions of Jews. Though charge of desecration

of the Host, frequent in 14th cent., diminished, alleged
poisonings of Christians or communities and ritual-murder
accusations were widely credited. Luther and Calvin continued
the prejudice. Yet Calvinism and Calvin's legalism helped
undermine major factors responsible for exclusion of Jews.

1593. Basset, Bernard, *The English Jesuits: From Campion to Mar-
tindale*. London: Burns and Oates, 1967; Herder and Herder,
1968 (c. 1967).

Rev. *History*, 53 (1968), 434.

History of Jesuits in mostly anti-Catholic England from mid-
16th to 20th cents.; based on contemporary sources, such as
letters of Jesuits; plentiful footnotes; good index of names.
Suggests Jesuit correspondence as a useful historical source.

1594. Battenhouse, R.W., *Shakespearean Tragedy. Its Art and Its
Christian Premises*. Bloomington, Indiana: Indiana Univ.
Press, 1969.

Rev. *JHI*, 32 (1971), 306-310; *South Atlantic Q.*, 69 (1970),
410-411.

Applies his notions of central tenets of Christian tradition,
derived from Bible, Augustine, and Aquinas, hoping to show, by
pious didacticism, how Shakespearean heroes fall into states
of perverted selfhood. (Some numerological overtones.)

1595. Battles, Ford Lewis, ed. and trans., *The Piety of John Calvin:
An Anthology Illustrative of the Spirituality of the Reformer
of Geneva*. Pittsburgh: Pittsburgh Theological Seminary, 1969.

Collection of texts intended to acquaint Roman Catholic students with spiritual teachings of Calvin; psalms and prayers
as well as excerpts from *Institutes of the Christian Religion*.

1596. Berkowitz, Morris I., and J. Edmund Johnson, *Social Scientific
Studies of Religion: A Bibliography*. Pittsburgh: Univ. of
Pittsburgh Press, 1967. Rev. *Choice*, 4 (1967), 965.

Despite title, bibliography contains material relevant to
Renaissance religion and theology.

1597. Berry, Boyd McCulloch, "The Doctrine of the Remnant 1550-1660:
A Study in the History of English Puritanism and *Paradise
Lost*," *DA*, 27 (1967), 2144-2145-A (Univ. of Michigan).

Changes in Puritan use of term "remnant" (in Bible, a small
group of men). Related to Calvin's interpretation of providential history, which is seen by him, in contrast to Augustine and Luther, as essentially static and timeless; Christ
was not so much the center of human history as an eternal
theological Truth. Thus, Puritan preachers, who systematized
Calvin, understood the patriarchs to be true Christians, and
the "remnant" of Isaiah a good model to reform the church.
Discusses development in such views until Milton.

1598.   "Bibliographia de Historia Societatis Iesu," *Archivum Histori-cum Societatis Iesu*, 38 (1969), 547-610.

        Sections on general history of the Society, Ignatius Loyola, history according to country, cultural history, biographies, etc.

1599.   Blaikie, R.J., "'The Supernatural' in Reformed Theology," *Scottish Journal of Theology*, 20 (1967), 165-182.

        Distinction between nature and super-nature is better marked in England than in Germany; the development of that distinction from the Reformation and its implications.

1600.   Bohlmann, Ralph Arthur, "The Criteria of Biblical Canonicity in Sixteenth-Century Lutheran, Roman Catholic, and Reformed Theology," *DA*, 29 (1969), 4087-A (Yale Univ.).

        Survey of major 16th-cent. treatments of biblical canon; criteria employed in determining status of books included in church's received collection of sacred writings. Important areas of interconfessional agreement and disagreement re: problem of authority in the church.

1601.   Bolam, Charles G., et al., *The English Presbyterians: From Elizabethan Puritanism to Modern Unitarianism*. London: Allen & Unwin, 1968.

        Rev. *Jour. of Eccl. Hist.*, 20 (1969), 359-360.

        Brief section (44 pp.) on period before 1660. Concerned with the Presbyterians who formed basis for modern Unitarianism.

1602.   Booty, J.E., "Preparation for the Lord's Supper in Elizabethan England," *Anglican Theological Review*, 49 (1967), 131-148.

        Importance given to preparation by repentance.

1603.   Bornkamm, Heinrich, *Luther and the Old Testament*. Trans. Eric W. and Ruth C. Gritsch; ed. Victor I. Gruhn. Philadelphia: Fortress Press, 1969.

        On mature Luther: his theological concepts of the Old Testament, beginning with his understanding of Old Testament world.

1604.   Breward, I., "The Significance of William Perkins," *Journal of Religious Hist.*, 4 (1966), 113-128.

        At his death in 1602, Perkins was even more influential than Richard Hooker as a theologian of the Elizabethan Church. He was also the first churchman of the reformed Church of England to earn a reputation outside his own country. Useful as it relates Perkins' role to the larger theological arguments of the Elizabethan Church.

1605.   Brunk, Gerald Robert, "The Bishops in Parliament, 1559-1601," *DA*, 30 (1969), 240-A (Univ. of Virginia).

        Relationship between Elizabeth I and episcopate as seen in latter's role as lords of parliament. Opening of the breach with episcopate at beginning of Elizabeth's reign; closing did not occur until appointment of John Whitgift as Archbishop of Canterbury in 1583.

1606. Burns, Norman Thomas, "The Tradition of Christian Mortalism in England: 1530-1660," *DA*, 28 (1968), 5045-A (Univ. of Mich.).

Controversy concerning soul at death. From beginnings of English Reformation to the Restoration, radical reformers attacked idea that soul is a substance that increases in vitality when freed from the body. Views of most English Protestants, as well as Calvin, that souls of dead men go immediately to heaven or hell were challenged by 1) "annihilationists" (associated with Family of Love), holding that Judgment, resurrection, heaven, and hell were terms for spiritual states in *this* life; and 2) "soul sleepers," more moderate, who believed that human personality would live immortally in the beyond, but that soul would not begin that afterlife except in union with resurrected body on Last Day.

1607. Calvin, Jean, *Three French Treatises* [Traité des Reliques; Traité de la cène; Excuse aux Nicodémites]. Ed. Frances M. Higman. N.Y.: Oxford Univ. Press; London: Athlone Press, 1970.

Three aspects of Calvin: explicit ridicule of Catholic relics; rejection of the Mass as a Sacrament; polemic against the compromisers with the Catholic Church in France. Contains glossary of unfamiliar words.

1608. Calvin, John, and Jacopo Sadoleto, *A Reformation Debate*. N.Y.: Harper and Row, 1966.

Doctrines and beliefs that were the subject of controversy and the battle ground of the Reformer and the Catholic apologists. Letters and documents unfolding these issues: the authority of the Church and Scripture, the justification of man before God. Appendix on Calvin and the Council of Trent on justification.

1609. Cannon, Charles K., "'As in a Theater': *Hamlet* in the Light of Calvin's Doctrine of Predestination," *SEL*, 11 (1971), 203-222.

Stage presentation as metaphor for man predestined to act in a certain way, while still responsible for his acts. Play becomes an image of its own meaning: man's freedom to act is such an illusion as that enacted by the players. Calvin joins these ideas in metaphor of a theater: man stands in double relation to the world and his God as a character in the play to action and to the playwright.

1610. Cantimori, Delio, *Eretici italiani del Cinquecento: Ricerche storiche*. Florence: Sansoni, 1967.

Rev. *RLI*, 71 (1967), 252.

Research on history of heretics and Italian reformers of the Cinquecento by the late historian; based on European archives.

1611. ————, "Le idee religiose del Cinquecento: La Storiografia" in *Il Seicento*, vol. 5 of *Storia della letteratura italiana*, ed. E. Cecchi and N. Sapegno. Milan: Garzanti, 1967, pp. 7-87.

Rev. *RLI*, 72 (1968), 139.

Panorama of Italian religious history of 16th cent.

Theological

1612. Carlson, A.J., "The Puritans and the Convocation of 1563," in
Action and Conviction in Modern Europe: Essays in Memory of
E.H. Harbison, ed. T.K. Rabb and J.E. Seigel. Princeton Univ.
Press, 1969, pp. 133–153.

First important meeting of Elizabethan clergy after the 1559
settlement. (Often misdated 1562, confusing old style with
new style 1563.) It comprised "Fathers of English Puritanism,"
and stressed conscience and liberty, against the conformist-
minded Queen.

1613. Carlson, Leland H., ed., The Writings of Henry Barrow, 1590–
1591. London: Allen and Unwin, 1966.

Fifth volume in the series Elizabethan Nonconformist Texts.
Barrow was a separatist whose writings were suppressed by
authorities; the book throws light on the religious turmoil of
the period. Rev. TLS, 16 Mar. 1967, 225.

1614. Cathcart, Charles Dwight, Jr., "Doubting Conscience: John
Donne and the Tradition of Casuistry," DA, 29 (1969), 3092-A
(Vanderbilt Univ.).

Donne's relation to English Protestant casuistry. Tradition
of casuistry; nature of the casuistical truth posited as basis
for metaphysical style.

1615. Champion, L.S., "Grace versus Merit in 'Sir Gawain and the
Green Knight,'" MLQ, 28, no. 4 (1967), 413–425.

Theological debate on salvation through divine grace or
through human merit. Links between allegory and this theological context.

1616. Chaney, William A., "The Royal Role in the Conversion of
England," Church and State, 9 (1967), 317–331.

On relationship between religious faith and political power;
the crucial figure in conversion in England was the King,
who, as sacral ruler, facilitated path of new religious movement.

1617. Collinson, Patrick, The Elizabethan Puritan Movement. Berkeley, Calif.: Univ. of Calif. Press; London: Cape, 1967.

Rev. AHR, 73 (1967), 474–475; Christopher Hill, Econ. H.R.,
20 (1967), 389–391.

Synthesizes work of historians since M.M. Knappen's Tudor
Puritanism to organize knowledge of English Puritan movement
from mid-16th cent. through reign of James I. Treats religious, political, social, and economic conditions, adding much
new information.

1618. Coolidge, John S., The Pauline Renaissance in England, Puritanism and the Bible. N.Y.: Oxford Univ. Press; Oxford: Clarendon Press, 1970.

Rev. AHR, 76 (1971), 1163–1164; Interpretation: A Journal of
Bible and Theology, 25 (1971), 521–522.

Interprets Puritanism by defining its dependence on the Bible
as a recovery of the Pauline tradition. Puritan critique of
Elizabethan conformity as it was argued by John Whitgift,
Thomas Cartwright, and Richard Hooker.

1619. Cowie, Leonard Wallace, *The Reformation of the Sixteenth Century.* N.Y.: Putnam; London: Weyland, 1970.

Rev. *Choice*, 8 (1971), 1563.

Documentary history with lengthy quotations and profuse illustrations. Index and notes but no bibliography.

1620. Cox, Roger L., "*King Lear* and the Corinthian Letters,"
Thought, 44, no. 172 (1969), 5-28.

Lear uses as its thematic inspiration and creative source the
Christian values and doctrines in St. Paul's Corinthian
Letters.

1621. Cuming, G.J., *A History of Anglican Liturgy.* London: Macmillan, 1969.

Rev. *Church Hist.*, 39 (1970), 257-258; *Journal of Ecclesiastical Hist.*, 21 (1970), 84-85; *Revue d'histoire ecclésiastique*,
65 (1970), 298; *Zeitschrift für Religions und Geistesgeschichte*,
13 (1971), 183-184.

Two-thirds of the study are devoted to development of the Anglican Prayer Book and its contents from 1549 to about 1965.
Last third contains selection of "Documents," many of which,
like Luther's Baptismal Service (1526) and Marriage Service
(1534) and Church Order for Cologne (1545), influenced the
English rite. Bibliography.

1622. Cuming, G.J., ed., *Studies in Church History*, vol. 3. (Papers
... Ecclesiastical History Soc.) Leiden: Brill, 1966.

Rev. *AHR*, 73 (1967), 469.

Twenty-two essays, including P. Collinson, "Episcopacy-Reform
in the Later 16th Cent."; English Church as "mixed polity."
The church might have been involved more closely with English
society, except for episcopal stresses and monarchical directions of church leaders.

1623. Daeley, J.I., "The Episcopal Administration of Matthew Parker,
Archbishop of Canterbury, 1559-75," *Bull. of the Inst. of
Hist. Res.*, 40 (1967), 228-231.

Ways in which Reformation ideas and legislation were implemented during early part of Elizabeth's reign. Because of
shortage of clergymen, Archbishop Parker was forced to appoint
many nonconformists, accounting for the influx of some Puritan
ideas and practices into the Canterbury diocese.

1624. Dannenfeldt, Karl H., *The Church of the Renaissance and Reformation.* St. Louis: Concordia Publishing House, 1970.

Rev. *Church Hist.*, 40 (1971), 220-221.

Surveys European religion from 1400-1700. Stress laid on
16th cent. Appendix with primary sources.

1625. Davies, Horton, *Worship and Theology in England, Vol. 1. From
Cranmer to Hooker, 1534-1603.* Princeton Univ. Press, 1970.

Rev. *AHR*, 76 (1971), 1163; *Interpretation: A Journal of Bible
and Theo.*, 25 (1971), 231-232.

Origins of Anglicanism in Tudor period, especially in relation
to Catholic-Puritan controversy. Special attention to Cranmer
in English Reformation and to ideas of Anglicanism expressed
by Hooker. First of five volumes on English religious life.

1626. Devereux, E.J., "The Publication of the English *Paraphrases*
of Erasmus," *Bull. John Rylands Lib.*, 51 (1969), 348-367.

On publication of English *Paraphrases* of Erasmus, a series of
commentaries on every book of the NT but Revelations. Attempt
to suppress its publication in early 16th cent.

1627. ———, "Sacramental Imagery in *The Tempest*," *HAB*, 19 (1968),
50-62.

Theology behind imagery of *Tmp.* more Catholic than Anglican;
imagery runs from baptism through communion, penance, and
matrimony, through (in its punning final line) indulgence and
prayers for one who can no longer aid himself.

1628. Devereux, James A., S.J., "The Primers and the Prayer Book
Collects," *HLQ*, 32 (1968), 29-44.

Inquiry into the originality of Archbishop Cranmer's prayer,
i.e., whether there existed a tradition of collect translating before 1549, and if so, to what extent Cranmer was in its
debt.

1629. Dickens, A.G., *The Counter Reformation.* N.Y.: Harcourt and
World, 1969.

Rev. *Church Hist.*, 39 (1970), 253-254; *History*, 54 (1969),
425-426.

Deals with the self-reform, self-defense, and counter-attack
of Catholicism; its response to the many protests of the late
15th and early 16th cents. to flowering of the Catholic Reformation. Useful treatments of the Council of Trent, the papacy
after Trent, and the relation of Baroque art to the Catholic
Reformation.

1630. ———, *Martin Luther and the Reformation.* London: English
Universities Press, 1967; N.Y.: Harper and Row, 1969.

Rev. *History*, 53 (1968), 98-99; *Journal of Ecclesiastical
Hist*, 19 (1968), 124-125.

Concise account of Luther's basic theology in context of 16th
cent.

1631. ────, "Recent Books on Reformation and Counter Reformation," *Journal of Ecclesiastical History*, 19 (1968), 219-226.

Lists and describes about a score of books published in 1967 dealing with Reformation.

1632. *Dictionnaire de Spiritualité, Ascétique et Mystique*, ed. Marcel Viller, S.J., continued by A. Rayez, S.J., et al. Paris: Beauschesne, 1967, 1969, 1971.

Tome VI Gabriel to Guzman; tome VII (première partie) Haakman to Hypocrisie; tome VII (deuxième partie) Ibañez to Izquierdo. Major Jesuit theological encyclopedia, in progress (vol. 1, 1937-).

1633. Droz, Eugénie, *Chemins de l'Hérésie*. Vol. 1. Geneva: Slatkine, 1970. Rev. *JMH*, 43 (1971), 135.

Texts of secret Lutheran propaganda suppressed in France during the Reformation. Vol. 1 includes Calvin, Musculus, Landry, and Beza.

1634. Duchrow, Ulrich, *Christenheit und Weltverantwortung. Traditionsgeschichte und systematische Struktur der Zweireichenlehre*. Stuttgart: Ernst Klett Verlag, 1970.

Rev. *DAEM*, 26 (1970), 634-644.

Using idea of the two kingdoms (heavenly and earthly), examines development through Luther of belief in earthly responsibility.

1635. Dugmore, C.W., "Some Recent Aids to Reformation Studies," *Journal of Ecclesiastical Studies*, 18 (1967), 59-64.

Useful bibliographic survey.

1636. *Early Nonconformity, 1556-1800: A Catalogue of Books in Dr. Williams' Library (London)*. Boston, Mass.: G.K. Hall & Co., 5-vol. subject catalogue; 2-vol. chronological catalogue; 5-vol. author catalogue, 1968.

Catalogue of books and pamphlets concerned with early nonconformity in England from Elizabethan Puritanism to end of 18th cent. and printed between 1566 and 1800, together with related works from Scotland, Ireland, Wales, and New England.

1637. Ebeling, Gerhard, "Gewissheit und Zweifel. Die situation des Glaubens im Zeitalter nach Luther und Descartes," *Zeitschrift für Theologie und Kirche*, 64, no. 3 (1967), 282-324.

Confrontation between Luther and Descartes, showing their influence on present thought, characterized as a tension between certainty and doubt.

1638. ────, *Luther: An Introduction to His Thought*. Trans. R.A. Wilson. Philadelphia: Fortress Press, 1970.

Rev. *AHR*, 75 (1970), 2033-2035; *Choice*, 7 (1970), 855-856;
Church Hist., 39 (1970), 549-550; *Interpretation: A Jour. of
Bible and Theo.*, 25 (1971), 230-231; *Jour. of Amer. Acad. of
Rel.*, 24 (1971), 364-368; *Jour. of Ecum. Studies*, 8 (1971),
420-422; *Mennonite Quarterly Rev.*, 45 (1971), 285-286; *Ren.
and Ref.*, 9 (1973), 69-70.

Inner dynamics of Luther's mental processes; tensions between
several sets of key words in his writings. Conflict between
philosophy and theology.

1639.   Elton, W.R., *"King Lear" and the Gods*. San Marino, Calif.:
        Huntington Library Press, 1966, 1968.

        Rev. *RenQ*, 20 (1967), 377-380.

        Changing attitudes to Providence in the Renaissance.

1640.   Emerson, Everett H., *English Puritanism from John Hooper to
        John Milton*. Durham, N.C.: Duke Univ. Press, 1968.

        "This is a useful anthology of twenty Puritan writings, from
        1550 to 1641. The selections are somewhat brief, averaging
        8 pages. There is a helpful general introduction of 44 pages,
        20 brief summaries of the life and writings of the Puritan
        authors, averaging 4 pages, which precede each extract. In
        all, there are 92 pages of material about the authors and 155
        pages of source material. The well-selected bibliography and
        the attractive end-sheet, depicting John Hooper and John Mil-
        ton, deserve special mention."--Leland H. Carlson, *Claremont
        Graduate School*.

1641.   Estes, Vallin Dayton, Jr., "A Luther Glossary. Compiled from
        the First Volume of the Weimar Edition, consisting of the
        German and Foreign Words in the German Writings and All Ger-
        man Words in the Latin Writings which Begin with the Letters *E*
        through *Z*," *DA*, 29 (1969), 2209-2210-A (Univ. of North Caro-
        lina).

        Based on Luther's writings, exclusive of his Bible translation.
        Continuation of author's Master's thesis, which covered let-
        ters *A* through *D*.

1642.   Fischer, J.D.C., *Christian Initiation: The Reformation Period*.
        Alcuin Club Collections, no. 51. London: S.P.C.K., 1970.

        Rev. *Hist. Mag. of the Prot. Episc. Church*, 39 (1970), 327-
        328.

        Texts in English of Reformation rites of Baptism and Confirma-
        tion, including those from 1549 and 1552 Prayer Book, plus re-
        lated statements of Reformers.

1643.   Foss, Michael, *The Founding of the Jesuits*. N.Y.: Weybright
        & Talley, 1970.

        Rev. *Jour. of Church and State*, 13 (1971), 356-358.

        Founding of the Jesuit order and its impact on secular society
        from 1540 to 1770.

1644. Fraenkel, P., and M. Greschat, *Zwanzig Jahre Melanchthonstudium. Sechs Literaturberichte (1945-1965)*. Geneva: Droz, 1967.

Survey of research on Luther's follower and influential 16th-cent. humanist.

1645. Frye, Roland, "Reason and Grace: Christian Epistemology in Dante, Langland, and Milton," in *Action and Conviction in Early Modern Europe*, ed. T.K. Rabb and J.E. Seigel. Princeton Univ. Press, 1969, pp. 404-422.

Rule that Christianity has attempted to preserve a balance between overextending reason and repudiating it provides basis for understanding attitudes toward reason in classical Christianity and Christian humanism. Three poets in the title demonstrate an essential agreement on relation between reason and revelation.

1646. ———, "Theological and Non-Theological Structures in Tragedy," *ShakS*, 4 (1968), 132-148.

Analysis of the use of theological doctrine in building the structure of tragic drama.

1647. ———, "Tragedy and Doctrine: Doctrinal and Non-Doctrinal Structures for Tragedy," *ShN*, 17 (1967), 56.

On extent of theological influence in Shakespeare; argues that he was more interested in structural-rhetorical aspects of drama than in building his plays upon theological doctrine.

1648. Ganoczy, Alexandre, *La Bibliothèque de l'Académie de Calvin. Le Catalogue de 1572 et ses enseignements*. Geneva: Droz, 1969.

Rev. *BHR*, 32 (1970), 519-520.

The *Catalogus Librorum Bibliothecae Genevensis*, preserved in Geneva, gives an inventory of books which constituted Calvin's Academy Library in 1572; biblical sciences, patristic literature, theologians (Evangelic and Catholic authors), humanists, and secular sciences, from the point of view of history of ideas, especially of the teaching of theology.

1649. Gerrish, B.A., ed., *Reformers in Profile*. Philadelphia: Fortress Press, 1967.

Rev. *Journal of the Amer. Academy of Religion*, 36 (1968), 412-413; *Journal of Religion*, 48 (1968), 399-400.

Ten biographical-intellectual essays, including Luther, Calvin, Cranmer, Simmons, Muntzer, Zwingli, Erasmus, Wyclif, Pierre d'Ailly, Loyola.

1650. Ginzburg, Carlo, *Il Nicodemismo: simulazione e dissimulazione religiosa nell' Europe del '500*. Turin: Einaudi, 1970.

Rev. *AHR*, 76 (1971), 1156-1157; *TLS*, 15 January 1971, 76.

Nicodemism is Calvin's term for Protestants who simulated
outward conformity to Catholic ritual while directing their
religiosity inwardly; also for Italian heretics who adopted
practices condemned by Calvin.

1651. Goeser, Robert James, "Word and Sacrament: A Study of Luther's
        Views as Developed in the Controversy with Zwingli and Karl-
        stadt," *DA*, 30 (1969), 380-A (Yale Univ.).

        By the Word of God, Luther means more than Scriptures or the
        preached Word: it is the concept by which Luther deals with
        the relation of divine transcendence and immanence. The Word
        is fully God and yet also the meaning of creation and history
        understood sacramentally.

1652. Greschat, M., "Melanchthonia Nova," *BHR*, 29 (1967), 189-219.

        Surveys new works on the 16th-cent. Reformer.

1653. Hagen, Kenneth, "Changes in the Understanding of Luther: The
        Development of the Young Luther," *Theol. Stud.*, 29, no. 3
        (1968), 472-496.

        Review of the opinions of various schools of historians re
        the "tower experience"--discovery of justification by faith.

1654. Hair, P.E.H., "Protestants as Pirates, Slavers, and Proto-
        Missionaries: 1568 and 1582," *Jour. of Eccl. Hist.*, 21 (1970),
        203-224.

        Rev. Hist. Mag. of the Protestant Episcopal Church, 40 (1971),
        231.

        An account of John Hawkins' expedition to Sierra Leone that
        provides information on religious attitudes and practices of
        English seamen.

1655. Hall, Basil, "The Early Success and Gradual Decline of Luther-
        anism in England," *Concordia Theological Monthly*, 38 (1967),
        576-595.

        Admiration for Luther's anti-papal stand, accompanied by
        Englishmen's reluctance to accept his sacramental theology.
        Yet evidences are found of Luther's influence in Elizabeth's
        reign. Useful, detailed study.

1656. Hall, Charles A.M., *With the Spirit's Sword: The Drama of
        Spiritual Warfare in the Theology of John Calvin*. Richmond,
        Va.: John Knox Press, 1970.

        Calvin as "soldier of Christ," with theology serving as armor;
        personal, modern application.

1657. Hammer, Wilhelm, *Die Melanchthonforschung im Wandel der Jahr-
        hunderte. Ein beschreibendes Verzeichnis*. Bd. I: *1519-1799*.
        Quellen und Forschungen zur Reformationsgeschichte, Verein für
        Reformationsgeschichte, Bd. 35. Gütersloh: Gütersloher Ver-
        lagshaus Gerd Mohn, 1967.

        Contains 1,502 items, to end of 1965.

1658. Hassel, R. Chris, Jr., "Saint Paul and Shakespeare's Romantic Comedies," *Thought*, 46 (1971), 371-388.

Pauline allusions in Shakespearean comedy: *MND*, *LLL*, *TN*, *MV*; role of Christian ritual.

1659. Hassinger, Erich, *Religiöse Toleranz im 16. Jahrhundert: Motive-Argumente-Formen der Verwirklichung*. (Vorträge der Aeneas-Silvius-Stiftung an der Universität Basel, 6.) Basel and Stuttgart: Helbing & Lichtenhahn, 1966.

Lecture with notes, 35 pp. Relation of heresy to risks involved; no indifference in such risks through personal commitment. Power of intolerance in 16th cent.

1660. Haugaard, William P., *Elizabeth and the English Réformation: The Struggle for a Stable Settlement of Religion*. Cambridge Univ. Press, 1968.

Rev. *AHR*, 76 (1971), 497-498; *J. of Eccles. Hist.*, 20 (1969), 350-351.

On first decade of Elizabeth's reign; focuses on convocation of 1563 defining the Puritans as "precisians"; role played by English leaders, clerics, laymen, and the queen in the religious settlement.

1661. ———, "The English Litany from Henry to Elizabeth," *Angl. Theol. Rev.*, 51 (1969), 177-203.

Beginning of a vernacular liturgy in England.

1662. ———, "John Calvin and the *Catechism* of Alexander Nowell," *Arch. for Reformation Hist.*, 61 (1970), 50-66.

Rev. *Hist. Mag. of the Prot. Episc. Church*, 40 (1971), 231.

Nowell's *Catechism* was high watermark of official endorsement of Calvin's theology--an endorsement that never really amounted to more than an authorized manual for instruction of school children.

1663. ———, "Katherine Parr: The Religious Convictions of a Renaissance Queen," *RenQ*, 22 (1969), 346-359.

As revealed in *Lamentations of a Sinner*; her role in the religious formation of Edward and Elizabeth.

1664. Henderson, R.W., "Sixteenth Century Community Benevolence: An Attempt to Resacralize the Secular," *Church Hist.*, 38 (1969), 421-428.

In area of community benevolence, practical programs of 16th-cent. reformers tended toward resacralization of community institutions which had become increasingly secular.

1665. Herbert, James C., "Conceptions of Common Religion: A Study of Developing Alternatives in English Thought 1558-1629," *DA*, 31 (1970), 2845-A (Brandeis Univ.).

Ideas of religious unity in Jacobean England; categories of
Anglican and Puritan inappropriate to the contemporary religious situation.

1666. Hillerbrand, Hans J., *Christendom Divided: The Protestant
       Reformation*. (Theological Resources, gen eds. J.P. Whalen,
       Jaroslav Pelikan). N.Y.: Corpus; Philadelphia: Westminster;
       London: Hutchinson, 1971.

       Divided into the Theological Reformation and the Political Re-
       formation. Latter includes chapter, "The Spread of the Re-
       formation in England," pp. 168-223. Notes and bibliography,
       pp. 307-336.

1667. ———, *A Fellowship of Discontent*. N.Y.: Harper and Row,
       1967.

       Chapters on reformers, schismatics, heretics ...; Thomas
       Müntzer; Sebastian Franck, etc. Bibliography and notes, pp.
       167-176.

1668. ———, *Men and Ideas in the Sixteenth Century*. (Rand McNally
       European History Series.) Chicago: Rand McNally, 1969.

       Compact manual. Chapters include The History of Reformation
       History; The European Dimension (England, pp. 41-50); The
       Nature of the Controversy; The Theological Perspective; The
       Actors (Henry VIII, pp. 106-110). Select bibliography, pp.
       124-127.

1669. ———, ed., *The Protestant Reformation*. Documentary History
       of Western Civilization Series. N.Y.: Walker, 1968.

       Part I. German Reformation (selections from Luther); Part II.
       Huldrych Zwingli; Part III. Anabaptists; Part IV. John Cal-
       vin (selections from Calvin); and Mornay, *A Defence of Liberty
       Against Tyrants* (1579); Part V. English Reformation (selec-
       tions from Tyndale, Jewel, John Field, and Thomas Wilcox;
       Hooker).

1670. ———, "The Spread of the Protestant Reformation of the Six-
       teenth Century: A Historical Case Study in the Transfer of
       Ideas," *SAQ*, 67 (1968), 265-286.

       Examines the extent and means of transmission of Luther's
       ideas and significance of this for an understanding of the
       Reformation.

1671. Hume, Anthea, "Spenser, Puritanism, and the 'Maye' Eclogue,"
       RES, 20 (1969), 115-167.

       Spenser gives Puritan views a force and exactness which cause
       them to emerge as dominant arguments of the ecclesiastical
       eclogues. Spenser in these years was a spokesman for Puritan
       zeal.

1672. *L'Infallibilité*. Son aspect philosophique et théologique.
       Actes du colloque organisé par Le Centre International d'Études
       Humanistes et par l'Institut d'Etudes Philosophiques de Rome.
       Rome, 5-12 janvier, 1970, aux soins de Enrico Castelli. Paris:
       Aubier, 1970.

Rev. *Bibliographie zur Symbolik, Ikonographie und Mythologie*, 4 (1971), 68.

Discusses trials of Galileo and Bruno and of the young Luther.

1673. Iserloh, Erwin, Josef Glazik, and Hubert Jedin, *Reformation, katholische Reform und Gegenreformation*. Vol. 4 of *Handbuch der Kirchengeschichte*, gen. ed., Hubert Jedin. Freiburg im Breisgau: Herder, 1967.

Rev. *BLE*, July-September, 1968, 230.

Covers 1517-1655; Luther, Calvin, and expansion of Reformation; Catholic reformation and Counter-Reformation.

1674. Jobert, Ambroise, "Quelques impies du XVIe siècle: Fauste Socin et les non-adorants," *Cahiers d'Hist.*, 13 (1968), 145-154.

Traces development of 16th-cent. Antitrinitarians, who fled to tolerant Polish territory after persecution by the Protestants, becoming the ancestors of modern Unitarians.

1675. Kaufmann, R.J., "Theodicity, Tragedy and the Psalmist: Tourneur's *Atheist's Tragedy*," *Comp. D.*, 3 (1969/70), 241-262.

Tourneur's *Atheist's Tragedy* is an explicit dramatical projection of themes of 127th Psalm, "Nisi Dominus, nothing can be done without God's grace," and a Calvinist reading at that.

1676. King, Joy Lee Belknap, "A Critical Edition of *A Dialogue Wherein is Plainly Laide Open, the Tyrannicall Dealing of L. Bishopps Against Gods Children*," *DA*, 29 (1969), 2216-A (Rutgers Univ.).

Author of this tract may have been Martin Marprelate. Review of literature of complaint in England from the 14th cent. to the Renaissance; tract is placed in this tradition.

1677. Kittel, Gerhard, ed., *Theological Dictionary of the New Testament*. Vol. 6, ed., Gerhard Friedrich. Grand Rapids, Mich.: Eerdmans, 1969.

Vol. 6 presents among others definitive articles by Cullman on *Petros*, by Bultmann on *pistis*, and by Schweizer on *pneuma*.

1678. Kleinhans, Robert G., "Luther and Erasmus, Another Perspective," *Church Hist.*, 39 (1970), 459-469.

Influence of Luther on Erasmus. Area where Reformation may have exerted influence on 16th-cent. humanism. Erasmus' theme of justification by faith and his concept of baptism, both developed in 1522-1523, may be owed to his reading of Luther.

1679. Kollar, Nathan R., Rev., O. Carm., "The Visitation and Anointing of the Sick in the Church of England. (Studies in Sacred Theology, Second Series No. 184)," *DA*, 28 (1968), 2765-2766-A (Catholic Univ. of America).

Ministry of healing in Church of England, 1549-1662; based on liturgical books, documents, and theological writings of English church. Original Visitation Office, as found in the

Sarum Manual, though life-centered in prayer and structure,
was seen to be death-centered, i.e., looking forward to immi-
nent death. Reformers modified Sarum Office so that its
structure too became death-centered. Anointing was eliminated
because of association with superstitious practices, forgiveness of sins, and charismatic healing. Church's ministry to
the sick was to support sufferer in time of trial and prepare
him for death. Contrast with 20th-cent. views regarding mission of healing.

1680.   Kristeller, Paul O., "The Contribution of Religious Orders to
Renaissance Thought and Learning," *Amer. Benedictine Rev.*, 21
(1970), 1-55. Rev. *BHR*, 73 (1970), 232-234.

Their humanistic studies.

1681.   ————, "The Myth of Renaissance Atheism and the French Tradition of Free Thought," *Journal of the Hist. of Phil.*, 6
(1968), 233-243.

Discredits Renan's work on Paduan Averroism through insistence
that neither Pomponazzi nor Cremonini broke completely with
conventional religious views of their time; though both were
followers of Aristotle, neither philosopher affirmed strictly
atheistic ideas. Pomponazzi's "double truth" was not merely a
protective device. Judgments of Renan and other French historians of Renaissance philosophy have relied too heavily on
charges by Pomponazzi's contemporaries, and provided a distorted view of the thought of Renaissance Italy.

1682.   Krodel, Gottfried G., "Erasmus-Luther: One Theology, One
Method, Two Results," *Concordia Theol. Mon.*, 41 (1970), 648-
667.

Fundamental difference in understanding of theologians: for
Erasmus theology was teaching, descriptive and analytic, in
area of *disputatio*; for Luther it was *assertio* or *affirmatio*
and a confessional task.

1683.   Lamont, William M., "Puritanism as History and Historiography:
Some Further Thoughts," *Past & Present*, 44 (1969), 133-146.

Questions basic premise put forth in an earlier book by C.H.
George (*The Protestant Mind of the English Reformation, 1570-
1640*, Princeton, 1961) that there is no continuity between
pre-revolutionary and revolutionary puritanism.

1684.   Lampe, G.W.J., ed., *The Cambridge History of the Bible. The
West from the Fathers to the Reformation.* Cambridge Univ.
Press, 1969.

Rev. *Church Hist.*, 39 (1970), 403‑404; *Durham Univ. Journal*,
31 (1970), 134-136.

Final chapter on "Erasmus in Relation to the Medieval Biblical
Tradition"; on the extent to which Erasmus's biblical work
was a fresh endeavor; relates his earlier biblical and theological studies to the influence of Valla's *Adnotationes* on
the NT. This is Vol. 2 of three volumes entitled: 1) *From
the Beginnings to Jerome*; 2) *The West, from the Fathers to the*

Reformation; 3) *The West, from the Reformation to the Present Day.* Series of essays which deal with the use, translation, study, influence, and physical form of the Bible in the Western World.

1685. Landeen, William M., *Martin Luther's Religious Thought*. Mountain View, Calif.: Oshawa, Ontario: Omaha, Nebr.: Pacific Press Publ. Assoc., 1971.

Rev. *Ren. and Ref.*, 9 (1973), 67-68.

Dogmatic *topoi* and *loci*, quoted from the range of Luther's work.

1686. Latimer, Hugh, *Selected Sermons*, ed. Allan G. Chester. Published for Folger Library by Univ. Press of Virginia, 1968.

Includes chronological table of Church of England sermons on various occasions.

1687. Lau, Franz, ed., *Luther-Jahrbuch*, 34 (1967). Hamburg: Friedrich Wittig, 1967.

Luther bibliography to 31 May 1966. Volume includes useful bibliographic materials: "Luther und die Welt der Reformation."

1688. ————, ed., *Luther-Jahrbuch*, 35 (1968). Hamburg: Friedrich Wittig, 1968.

Luther bibliography to 31 May 1967. Contains review of books on "Luther und die Welt der Reformation," pp. 108-122. "Luther-Bibliographie, 1968," pp. 123-161. "Bibliographie der marxistischen Literatur in der DDR 1945-1966," pp. 162-172.

1689. La Vallee, Armand Aime, "Calvin's Criticism of Scholastic Theology," Ph.D. diss., Harvard Univ., 1967. (Summarized in *Harvard Theological Review*, 60 [1967], 493.)

Calvin's conception of, and references to, scholastic theology; scholasticism as underlining *foci* in Calvin's theology.

1690. Lecler, Joseph, "Protestantisme et 'Libre Examen,'" *Recherche de Sciences Relig.*, 57 (1969), 231-374.

Notion of a free and personal examination of Christian doctrine appeared in 19th cent. For Luther and Calvin, however, examination was the confrontation of the teaching of Church Fathers with Scripture, the clear word of God.

1691. ————, and Marius-François Valkhoff, eds., *Les Premiers Défenseurs de la Liberté Religieuse*. 2 vols. Paris: Les éditions du Cerf, 1969.

Rev. *BHR*, 32 (1970), 742-743.

Anthology on religious toleration 1560-1650. Vol. 1, historical introduction to theme and selected texts; Vol. 2, texts and commentaries.

1692. Leff, Gordon, *Heresy in the Later Middle Ages: The Relation of Heterodoxy to Dissent c. 1250-1450.* Manchester Univ. Press; N.Y.: Barnes and Noble, 1967. 2 vols.

Rev. *J. Hist. of Phil.*, 8 (1970), 205-211.

1693. Le Goff, Jacques, ed., *Hérésies et sociétés dans l'Europe pré-industrielle 11ᵉ-18 siècles.* Colloque de Royaumont. Paris, La Haye: Mouton, 1968.

Important collection of essays, with discussions; e.g., A. Tenenti, "Libertinisme et hérésie du milieu du 16 s. au début du 17 s.," pp. 303-321, with discussion, pp. 322-325. Extensive "Bibliographie des études récentes"--761 items.

1694. Levin, Harry, "Evangelizing Shakespeare," *JHI*, 32 (1971), 306-310.

Useful review of "Christianizing" excesses in Shakespearean interpretation.

1695. Linder, Robert D., "Pierre Viret and the Sixteenth-Century English Protestants," *ARG*, 58 (1967), 149-170.

Indicative of great interest which England had in continental Reformation, Viret was pre-1558 Calvinist whose works were favorites of English readers for at least three decades after 1558. Ideas of French Calvinists contributed as much to religious turmoil as did those of native English Protestant radicals. Viret's connections with Marian exiles and Protestants in England after 1558. Also affirms Cremeans' findings that Calvinists were on both sides, conformist and nonconformist.

1695a. ——, "Toward a Viret Bibliography: A Proposal," *Foundation for Reformation Research: Bull. of the Lib.*, 2 (1967), 3-6.

Notes toward an annotated bibliography of Swiss reformer Pierre Viret (1530-1571) to update Schetzler and Barnaud's *Notice Bibliographique sur Pierre Viret*, 1905.

1696. Littell, Franklin H., "The Importance of Anabaptist Studies," *ARG*, 58 (1967), 15-28.

On 16th-cent. English currents. Anabaptist non-violence and opposition to oaths, as well as 16th-cent. ruler's claim to religious authority. This claim is contrasted with 17th-cent. idea of government defined so as to check tyranny and seal off any theology of tyranny. James I represented the old order: judges were lions under the throne.

1697. Little, David, *Religion, Order and Law: A Study of Pre-revolutionary England.* N.Y.: Harper & Row, 1970.

Rev. *Choice*, 8 (1971), 132; *Jour. of Ecum. Studies*, 8 (1971), 896-898.

Expands Weber thesis to consider total context of Calvin's theology. Calvin's conception of order was central issue influencing a re-ordering of economic life; relation of Calvin's thought to English Puritanism.

1698. Loades, D.M., *The Oxford Martyrs*. London: Batsford, 1970.

Rev. *History*, 56 (1971), 444-445.

Study of Cranmer, Latimer, and Ridley, and their importance in 16th-cent. development of English Protestant nation. Problem of royal supremacy, of authority in church and state.

1699. Loeschen, John Richard, "Eschatological Themes in Luther's Theology," *DA*, 30 (1969), 797-A (Grad. Theological Union and the Pacific School of Theology).

Primary data derived from *Lectures on Romans, De servo arbitrio*, and the *Lectures on the Galatians*. Eschatological motif, referring to process of divine self-realization in the creation, is a dominant theme.

1700. Logan, F. Donald, *Excommunication and the Secular Arm in Medieval England: A Study in Legal Procedure from the Thirteenth to the Sixteenth Century*. (Studies and Texts, 15.) Toronto: Pontifical Institute of Mediaeval Studies, 1968.

Rev. *Jour. of Eccl. Hist.*, 20 (1969), 341-342.

Excommunication as intended to induce the censured to seek absolution; Church sought secular aid against obdurate excommunicates: writ *de excommunicato capiendo*.

1701. Loomie, Albert J., S.J., "A Jacobean Crypto-Catholic: Lord Wotton," *Catholic Historical Review*, 53 (1967), 328-345.

Career of Lord Wotton in first quarter of 17th cent. successful in part because of his ability to conceal his Catholic conversion in 1610; remained crypto-Catholic for 14 years. Shows versatility of Catholics in dealing with anti-Catholic measures, and the inefficiency of their enforcement.

1702. ———, "King James I's Catholic Consort," *HLQ*, 34 (1971), 303-316.

Problem of religious views of Anne of Denmark, James's wife. Her reticence, but devout reading.

1703. Lyall, R.J., "Alexander Barclay and the Edwardian Reformation, 1548-52," *RLE*, 20 (1969), 455-461.

Barclay was involved in conflict with government over Elizabeth's right to hear Mass and over enforcement of the new Prayer Book.

1704. Manning, Roger B., *Religion and Society in Elizabethan Sussex. A Study of the Enforcement of the Religious Settlement, 1558-1603*. Leicester: Leicester Univ. Press, 1969.

Rev. *AHR*, 75 (1970), 1451; *Revue d'histoire ecclésiastique*, 65 (1970), 296.

Sussex as a microcosm of Elizabethan society—with the diocese of Chichester as the ecclesiastical unit, and Anthony Watson its bishop. Failure of episcopal leadership; resistance of both Puritans and Recusants. Final chapters on enforcement of religious settlement. Establishment process slow.

1705. Martini, Magda, *Fausto Socino et la pensée socinienne: Un maître de la pensée religieuse (1539-1604)*. Paris: Librairie C. Klincksieck, 1967.

On reformer who gave his name, as did his uncle Lelio before him, to Unitarian heresy. 127-pp. study divided into: I. Fausto Socino (life, etc.); II. Fausto Socino et le fait religieux: Textes; III. La Tradition socinienne: Textes, chronologie, bibliographie.

1706. Masinton, Charles Gerald, "Apollo's Laurel Bough: Essays on the Theme of Damnation in Christopher Marlowe," *DA*, 27 (1967), 2133-2134-A (Univ. of Oklahoma).

Marlowe differs from orthodoxy in holding that man brings evil upon himself in this world and does not have to wait for next life to pay for transgression. His world-view presupposes no all-powerful deity; the force behind events is man's own anarchic impulses and passions. No providential pattern rules history, the conflicts of men's wills providing its only visible design.

1707. Mau, Rudolf, *Der Gedanke des Heilsnotwendigkeit bei Luther*. Berlin: Evangelische Verlagsanstalt, 1969.

Luther believed that salvation was to be found in the Gospel rather than through men's actions. The medieval *necessarium ad salutem* was reinterpreted as a recognition of salvation in Christ.

1708. Maurer, Wilhelm, *Der Junge Melanchthon zwischen Humanismus und Reformation. Bd. 2: Der Theologe*. Göttingen: Vandenhoeck & Ruprecht, 1969.

Follows Bd. I (1967): *Der Humanist*. Substantial 617-pp. volume, well indexed. Useful on such concepts as *Gnade*, pp. 336-414.

1709. ————, *Kirche und Geschichte. Gesammelte Aufsätze. Bd. 1: Luther und das evangelische Bekenntnis; Bd. 2: Beiträge zu Grundsatzfragen und zur Frömmigkeitsgeschichte*, hg. von Ernst-Wilhelm Kohls und Gerhard Müller. Göttingen: Vandenhoeck & Ruprecht, 1970.

Rev. *DAEM*, 26 (1970), 566.

Collected essays on Luther and basic questions of church history.

1710. McDonald, William J., et al., eds., *New Catholic Encyclopedia*. 15 vols. N.Y.: McGraw-Hall, 1967.

Rev. *Catholic Historical Review*, 53 (1967), 372-392; *Concordia Theological Monthly*, 39 (1968), 398-402.

Not a revision of *Catholic Encyclopedia* (1907-14), but a completely new work with almost 5,000 international contributors. Takes into account profound changes since the previous work.

1711. McGinn, Donald J., *John Penry and the Marprelate Controversy*.
       New Brunswick, N.J.: Rutgers Univ. Press, 1966.

       Rev. *AHR*, 72 (1966), 579-580; John Carey, *RenQ*, 20 (1967),
       375-377.

       Account of the Marprelate controversy and Penry's role in it.
       Seeks to show that Penry was the writer of the Marprelate
       tracts. Interprets the Martinist controversy in the framework
       of the conformist and non-conformist literature of the day.

1712. McGrade, Arthur S., "The Public and the Religious in Hooker's
       'Polity,'" *Church Hist.*, 37 (1968), 404-422.

       On Bk. V of *Ecclesiastical Polity*, as contributing to whole
       work's structure: as buffer stressing Christianity's role in
       the ordinary world between contrasting intellectual and poli-
       tical methods of making Christianity a "public" religion.
       Discusses 1) search for unity within the church, 2) attempt
       by modern states to establish their individual ideologies in
       the world.

1713. McManaway, James G., "John Shakespeare's 'Spiritual Testa-
       ment,'" *SQ*, 18 (1967), 197-205.

       Gives history of a John Shakespeare's "Spiritual Testament"
       from its reported discovery in 1757, its printing by Malone in
       1790, with first leaf missing, to the present. Summarizes
       evidence linking the work by unknown testator to a Catholic
       formulary, composed by Carlo Borromeo, which, smuggled into
       England by Jesuit missionaries, may have been owned by John
       Shakespeare. Reports English printing (1638) of the formu-
       lary owned by Folger Library as earliest surviving text of
       the Testament, and the only extant English text.

1714. *Mélange d'histoire du XVI siècle offerts à Henri Meylan*.
       Geneva: Droz, 1970. (Travaux d'Humanisme et Renaissance 110.)

       Rev. *Bull. de la Soc. de l'histoire du Protestantisme Français*,
       117e Année (1971), 326-330.

       Collection of essays, mostly on Reformation; e.g., Léon E.
       Halkin, "Erasme de Turin à Rome" situates Erasmus in the his-
       tory of humanism.

1715. Meyer, Carl S., "A John Colet Bibliography," *Found. for Refor-
       mation Res.: Bull. of the Library*, 5, no. 3 (1970), 23-28.

       Comprehensive bibliography; lists major sources.

1716. ————, ed., *Luther for an Ecumenical Age: Essays in Com-
       memoration of the 450th Anniversary of the Reformation*. St.
       Louis: Concordia Publishing House, 1967.

       Rev. *AHR*, 74 (1968), 639.

       Festschrift volume includes U.S. specialists, e.g., Lewis
       Spitz on a Renaissance view of man: double aspect of man's
       dignity and misery, maintained during both Renaissance and
       Reformation. Five of the contributions on related topics.
       (Cf. E.G. Schwiebert on Wittenberg.)

1717. ──────, "Melanchthon's Influence on English Thought in the
       Sixteenth Century," in *Miscellanea Historiae Ecclesiasticae, II*
       (International Congress of Historical Sciences, 12th, Vienna,
       1965.) Louvain: Bibliothèque de l'Université. Publications
       Universitaires de Louvain, 1967, pp. 163-185.

       Melanchthon's influence on Thirty-Nine Articles. Elizabeth
       was a Melanchthonian in theology and political views; her theo-
       logy had been shaped by Ascham, an admirer of Melanchthon,
       while her religious instructions were based on Melanchthon's
       Loci and the Greek N.T. Melanchthon's educational influence
       in England through his textbooks.

1718. Miller, Arlene A., "The Theologies of Luther and Boehme in the
       Light of Their *Genesis* Commentaries," *HTR*, 63 (1970), 261-303.

       The non-Lutheran elements of Boehme's writings, among them
       Platonic, cabalistic and hermetic, are built on a metaphysical-
       theological basis derived from Luther.

1719. Miller, Robert Henry, "A Selected Edition of Sir John Haring-
       ton's *A Supplie or Addicion to the Catalogue of Bishops, to
       the Yeare 1608*," *DA*, 29 (1969), 3104-3105-A (Ohio State Univ.).

       Supplement to Bishop Goodwin's *A Catalogue of the Bishops of
       England*; the *Supplie* gives additional information about a few
       of the bishops under Edward VI and Mary, with brief sketches of
       of most bishops who served under Elizabeth and during early
       period of the reign of James I.

1720. Milner, Benjamin C., *Calvin's Doctrine of the Church*. Leiden:
       E.J. Brill, 1970.

       Rev. *Jour. of Ecum. Studies*, 8 (1971), 644-645; *Church Hist.*,
       40 (1971), 324-325.

       Correlation of spirit and the *ordinatio Dei* in the creation of
       the natural world. Unifying principle of Calvin's theology is
       the correlation of Spirit and Word.

1721. *Miscellanea Historiae Ecclesiasticae* , III, fasc. 50 (Cam-
       bridge, 1968). Louvain: Publications Universitaires, 1970.

       Section B. on "The Recruitment and Training of the Clergy in
       the Sixteenth Century": includes essays by L.E. Halkin, H.
       Meylan, J. van Laarhoven, and communication by R. Peters, "The
       Training of the 'Unlearned' Clergy in England during the
       1580's: A Regional Study."

1722. Mühlenberg, Ekkehard, "Laurentius Valla als Renaissance Theo-
       loge," *Zs. f. Theologie u. Kirche*, 66 (1969), 466-480.

       Valla regards *eloquentia* as the proper form for Christian
       ideas. Language that speaks of man's strongest desire, God's
       love, must move and delight.

1723. Mullany, Peter Francis, "The Dramatic Use of Religious Ma-
       terials in Jacobean and Caroline Plays," *DA*, 28 (1967), 1405-A
       (Fordham Univ.).

Religious associations of such themes as vows, revenge, Divine Right, confrontation of Christian and pagan beliefs, are exploited by Jacobean and Caroline dramatists to suggest an apparent reality and seriousness; plays were planned, however, to thrill audiences through rhetoric and intense conflict. Effects are sought similar to those of Beaumont and Fletcher's tragicomedies, providing emotional fillip for theatrical ends. Other playwrights studied include Massinger, Middleton, Tourneur. Religious materials used to create the emotional excitement of a drama that turns from life to produce an artificial, unreal drama in which theatrical values predominate. Such remoteness and theatricality become standard features of Caroline drama and reappear as characteristics of Restoration heroic drama.

1724. Nugent, Donald, "The Historical Dimension in Reformation Theology," *Journal of Ecumenical Studies*, 5 (1968), 555-571.

Recalling 16th cent. as time of hatred as much as it was of faith, author examines some non-theological factors (e.g., pride, hatred, self-serving arguments from Scripture, historical contingencies) that affected the theology of Luther, Calvin, and the Counter-Reformation.

1725. Nuovo, Victor Lawrence, "Calvin's Theology: A Study of Its Sources in Classical Antiquity," *DA*, 28 (1967), 1893-A (Columbia Univ.).

On Calvin's ambivalence to classical antiquity. His repudiation of natural theology of the ancients was related to his view of it as aiming to demonstrate divine government of the world from the experience of natural and human events; thus for him "natural" is not the opposite of "Supernatural" or "divine," but of contrived, invented, or established by custom. A natural theology of Scripture which he favored is therefore no contradiction when understood in these terms. In addition, Calvin followed a pattern of moral eclecticism (i.e., philosophical doctrine being regarded as meaningful or true irrespective of its systematic context, but according to its practical moral value). His treatment of the doctrines of providence and immortality suggests his dependence on Antiquity (Platonism and Stoicism) for part of their content and the eclecticism of their mode of expression.

1726. Nuttall, G.F., "Calvinism in Free Church History," *Baptist Quarterly*, 22, no. 8 (1968), 418-428.

Calvinist doctrinal influence and its vicissitudes through various English confessions and sects until 19th cent.

1727. Oberman, Heiko A., "The 'Extra' Dimension in the Theology of Calvin," *Jour. of Eccles. Hist.*, 21 (1970), 43-64.

Compares Calvin's view of the "etiam extra ecclesiam" tradition to Luther. Sees God as encompassing not only the sinner's heart, but all of the created order.

1728.   ————, *Forerunners of the Reformation, the Shape of Late Medieval Thought: Illustrated by Key Documents*. London: Lutterworth Press, 1967.

Rev. *Journal of Ecclesiastical Hist.*, 19 (1968), 251-252.

Extracts from thinkers from 14th to early 16th cents., with full introductions, dealing with Reformation controversies on Scripture and tradition, justification and predestination, nature of the church, the Eucharist, exegesis.

1729.   ————, "From Occam to Luther: A Survey of Recent Historical Studies on the Religious Thought of the 14th and 15th Centuries," *Concilium* (Paulist Press, N.Y.), 27 (1967), 135-144.

Concluding section of two-part article, first part of which appeared in *Concilium*, 17. Continuation of Thomism and Scotism as alternative options. Interaction between Scotism and nominalism; G. Biel and Luther. Summarizes advances in late medieval studies: 1) history of exegesis; 2) major doctrinal themes, e.g., justification, eucharist; 3) canon law. Basic survey by a leader in the field.

1730.   Olin, John C., ed., *The Catholic Reformation, Savonarola to Ignatius Loyola*. N.Y.: Harper and Row, 1969.

Rev. *Church Hist.*, 39 (1970), 404-405; *Thought*, 44 (1969), 631-632.

Fifteen documents illustrative of Catholic reform ideas and ideals between Savonarola's theocracy in Florence and papal approval of the Society of Jesus in 1540. Each one is preceded by a brief introduction with bibliographic references.

1731.   ————, et al., eds., *Luther, Erasmus and the Reformation. A Catholic-Protestant Reappraisal*. N.Y.: Fordham Univ. Press, 1969.

Rev. *Church Hist.*, 39 (1970); *Thought*, 45 (1970), 154-155.

Includes essays by R.H. Bainton and Robert E. McNally, S.J. on the problem of authority in the age of the Reformation and the question of Catholic reappraisal of the Reformation; Wilhelm Pauck's "The 'Catholic' Luther" and John T. McDonough's "The Essential Luther"; Margaret M. Phillips' "Some Last Words of Erasmus" and John C. Olin's "Erasmus and St. Ignatius Loyola." Annotated bibliography by Lewis W. Spitz, "Recent Studies of Luther and the Reformation."

1732.   O'Malley, John W., S.J., "Historical Thought and the Reform Crisis of the Early Sixteenth Century," *Theological Studies*, 28 (1967), 531-548.

Disorder of church at beginning of 16th cent.; various factors, social, economic, political, and above all, intellectual, in religious reforms and the Reformation.

1733.   ————, "Recent Studies in Church History, 1300-1600," *Catholic Historical Review*, 55 (1969), 394-437.

Reviews the more important developments in church history for the "Renaissance-Reformation" period since about 1960.

1734. Ozment, Steven E., *Homo Spiritualis: A Comparative Study of the Anthropology of Johannes Tauler, Jean Gerson and Martin Luther (1509-1516) in the Context of Their Theological Thought.* Studies in Medieval and Reformation Thought, Vol. 6. Leiden: E.J. Brill, 1969.

Rev. *Church Hist.*, 39 (1970), 405-407.

Analyzes Tauler's Sermons, Gerson's understanding of mystical theology, and works of Luther from 1509 to 1516, in order to interpret Reformation in context of its systematic dialogue with medieval period.

1735. ————, *"Homo Viator:* Luther and Late Medieval Theology," *HTR,* 62 (1969), 275-288.

Luther differed from the medieval mystics in his resolution of the dichotomy between past and present divine mercy and future judgment. He suspended the Christian's *viator*-status (fear and trembling about a future judgment) without allowing human identification with God, Christ, or the Holy Spirit.

1736. Palmer, David J., "Casting Off the Old Man: History and St. Paul in *Henry IV,*" *Crit Q,* 12 (1970), 267-283.

Prince Hal's speeches in *Henry IV* plays as partially derived from St. Paul.

1737. Parish, John E., "Robert Parsons and the English Counter-Reformation." *Rice University Studies,* 52 (1966). (Monograph in English History.) Houston, Texas.

A member of the Society of Jesus, Parsons provided a basis for the popular image of the scheming Jesuit. Involved in various plots to return England to a Catholic sovereign. Includes also brief history of English treatment of Catholics until Parsons' death.

1738. Parker, T.H.L., ed., *English Reformers.* Philadelphia: Westminster Press, 1966.

Selection of 16th-cent. English Reformers (e.g., Jewel, Foxe, Tyndale).

1739. Pauck, Wilhelm, *The Heritage of the Reformation.* London: Oxford Univ. Press, 1968.

Revision of 1950 edition. Assesses the position of the original ideas of Calvin and Luther in modern Protestantism.

1740. ————, ed., *Melanchthon and Bucer.* Philadelphia: Westminster Press, 1969.

Rev. *Jour. of the Amer. Acad. of Rel.*, 39 (1971), 238-240.

Translations of representative work of each of these two important Reformers. Bucer, virtually untranslated until now,

represented by his "De Regno Christi," a plan to bring about
Reformation of England addressed to Edward VI. Work sheds
light on 16th-cent. ideas of relation of Church and State.

1741. Payne, John B., *Erasmus: His Theology of the Sacraments.*
        Richmond, Va.: John Knox Press, 1970.

        Rev. *Jour. of the Amer. Acad. of Rel.*, 39 (1971), 566-567; *RQ*,
        24 (Summer 1971), 242-244.

        Documented discussion using Erasmus to place the Reformation
        in a medieval perspective. Significance of both Platonic and
        nominalistic thought in Erasmus. Includes his views on mar-
        riage, divorce, eucharist, and baptism.

1742. Pelikan, Jaroslav, ed., *Interpreters of Luther. Essays in
        Honor of Wilhelm Pauck.* Philadelphia: Fortress Press, 1968.

        Rev. *Church Hist.*, 39 (1970), 551-552.

        Festschrift includes pieces on Luther (Robert Barnes, Charles
        Anderson); Calvin (Brian Gerrish); and the Elizabethans
        (William Clebsch).

1743. ————, *Spirit versus Structure: Luther and the Institutions
        of the Church.* N.Y.: Harper & Row, 1968.

        Rev. *Church Hist.*, 39 (1970), 249-250.

        Interaction between innovative ("spirit-directed") and tradi-
        tional aspects of Luther's work. Topics: priesthood and
        ministry, monasticism, infant baptism, canon law, and the
        sacramental system.

1744. Perkins, William, *William Perkins, 1558-1602: English Puri-
        tanist. His Pioneer Works on Casuistry--"A Discourse of Con-
        science" and "The Whole Treatise of Cases of Conscience."*
        Edited with introduction by T.F. Merrill. Nieuwkoop: De
        Graaf, 1966.

1745. Pesch, Otto H., S.J., "Law and Gospel: Luther's Teaching in
        the Light of the Disintegration of Normative Morality," *The
        Thomist*, 34 (1970), 84-113.

        To understand what Christian tradition says on theme of "Law
        and Freedom," investigates meaning of "Law and Gospel" in
        Luther's theology.

1746. Peters, Albrecht, "Sakrament und Ethos nach Luther," *Luther-
        Jahrbuch*, 1969, pp. 41-79.

        Luther based the Christian ethos on baptism, the reminder of
        man's guilt, and on the eucharist, God's gift of grace to
        the community.

1747. Petti, Anthony G., ed., *Recusant Documents from the Ellesmere
        Manuscripts.* London: Catholic Record Society, 1968.

        Texts of manuscripts collected by Baron Ellesmere, Lord Chan-
        cellor of James I, which deal with Catholic recusants in late
        16th and early 17th cents.

1748. Pfaff, R.W., *New Liturgical Feasts in Later Medieval England*. London: Clarendon Press, 1970.

Rev. *TLS*, 18 September 1970, 1060.

Introduction into Church of England of feasts of the Transfiguration, the Visitation, and the Name of Jesus, plus a number of other feasts no longer extant.

1749. Phillips, James E., "Spenser's Syncretistic Religious Imagery," *ELH*, 36, no. 1 (1969), 110-130.

His syncretistic images generally refer to doctrines and beliefs which Neo-Platonic syncreticists of the Renaissance regarded as universal truths found in all of God's revelation of Himself and His will: the truth of an original state of earthly perfection, the truth of a cleansing by water and subsequent renewal, and the truth of sanctification.

1750. Preus, James Samuel, *From Shadow to Promise: Old Testament Interpretation from Augustine to the Young Luther*. Cambridge, Mass.: Belknap Press of Harvard Univ. Press, 1969.

Rev. *Church Hist.*, 39 (1970), 550-551.

Luther as medieval theologian rather than as renegade; his growth in light of medieval placement of OT in the Christian canon and its crucial role in his evolving theology.

1751. ———, "Old Testament *Promissio* and Luther's New Hermeneutic," *Harvard Theological Review*, 60 (1967), 145-161.

Importance of Old Testament for Luther. Cf. author's "Promission: Its Hermeneutical Function in the Middle Ages and the Young Luther," Ph.D. diss., Harvard Univ., 1967, summarized there: examines interpretation of promise in the Old Testament by medieval theologians, who saw OT word as *umbra* of NT *lux*, and describes Luther's rejection of this viewpoint in favor of a recovery of OT *promissio*.

1752. Preus, Robert D., *The Theology of Post-Reformation Lutheranism: A Study of Theological Prolegomena*. St. Louis: Concordia, 1970.

Rev. *Cath. Bib. Quart.*, 33 (1971), 456-458.

First volume of projected three-volume work; surveys Lutheran orthodoxy during three periods: "golden age of orthodoxy" (1580-1618), "high orthodoxy" (1618-1648), and "silver age of orthodoxy" (1648-1710). Portrait of Lutheran orthodoxy as new, distinctive development in history of Christian doctrine.

1753. Rahner, Karl, et al., eds., *Sacramentum Mundi: An Encyclopedia of Theology*, Vol. I: *Absolute and Contingent--Constantinian Era*. Vol. II: *Constantin--Grace and Freedom*. Basle and Montreal: Herder and Herder, I, 1967; II, 1968.

Synthesis of modern religious thought to be published in six volumes; contributions by 600 international experts, treating central topics in theology and related disciplines, including

dogmatics, canon law, moral theology, philosophy, church history, etc.   Each entry cross-indexed and provided with bibliography.   (To appear in English, French, German, Dutch, Spanish, and Italian editions.   Remaining four volumes to appear
at six-month intervals.)

1754. Raines, John Curtis, "The Cosmic Kingdom in the Rise of the
       Christian Interpretation of the State: A Study of the Inter-
       action of Religious and Political Mythology from Hebraic Pro-
       phetism through John Calvin," *DA*, 28 (1967), 1516-A (Union
       Theological Seminary, N.Y.).

       On Luther's complete, and Calvin's more ambivalent, rejection
       of the Catholic dogma of the Cosmic Kingdom as a model and as
       one end of a continuum of hierarchies in which the church is
       the intermediate and intermediary between nature and super-
       nature.

1755. Ratner, Helen M., "The Concept of the Nature of Man in the Ser-
       mons of John Donne," *DA*, 31 (1970), 2352-A (Univ. of Mich.).

       Though Donne falls into school of Peter Lombard in giving the
       Anglican Article Nine the Augustinian interpretation that con-
       cupiscence is "sin in itself," he does not pursue consequences
       of his view of sin; his view of the nature of man not well
       integrated with other areas of his thought.

1756. Reeves, Marjorie, *The Influence of Prophecy in the Later Mid-
       dle Ages. A Study in Joachimism*. Oxford: Clarendon Press,
       1969.

       Influence of Joachim of Fiore's philosophy: his ideas were
       not only the mainspring of various heterodox groups but also
       engaged attention of church leaders, university scholars,
       Protestant thinkers, Protestant theologians, and political
       rulers down to 17th cent. Rev. *EHR*, 86 (1971), 120.

1757. Richards, Michael, "Thomas Stapleton," *Journal of Ecclesiasti-
       cal Hist.*, 18 (1967), 187-199.

       Called by Anthony à Wood "the most learned Roman Catholic of
       all his time," Stapleton (1535-1598) was one of the most dis-
       tinguished of an English school of theologians which flourished
       in the Spanish Netherlands and northern France during Eliza-
       beth's reign.   His main achievement was his investigation of
       theological grounds for careful attention to historical pre-
       cedent in critical study of medieval sources.   Concerned with
       bases of authority of Christian faith.   (Major works of Staple-
       ton still remain untranslated from Latin.)

1758. Richter, M., "Recenti studi calvinani," *Rivista di Storia e
       Letteratura Religiosa*, 3 (1967), 99-130.

       Reviews literature, 1960-1966, on Calvin, his thought and his
       times.

1759. Roberts, John R., ed., *A Critical Anthology of English Recusant
       Devotional Prose 1558-1603*. (Duquesne Studies: Philological
       Ser., 7.)   Pittsburgh: Duquesne Univ. Press, 1966.

1760.   Rohr, John von, "*Extra Ecclesiasm Nulla Salus*: An Early Con-
        gregational Version," *Church Hist.*, 36 (1967), 107-121.

        Discusses the debate in the late 16th and early 17th cents.
        concerning the importance of proper church order for personal
        salvation. Examines the arguments of the separatists and the
        non-separatists concerning the Church of England's ability to
        provide salvation for its members.

1761.   Rolston, Holmes, "Responsible Man in Reformed Theology: Cal-
        vin Versus the 'Westminster Confession,'" *Scottish Jour. of
        Theol.*, 23 (1970), 129-156.

        Responsibility as gift and invitation of God; necessity for
        law-keeping men to become grace-receiving; covenant theology
        as something beyond human power, able to utilize Christian
        faith.

1762.   Rupp, E.G., "Patterns of Salvation in the First Age of the
        Reformation," *Archiv für Reformationsgeschichte*, 57 (1966),
        52-66.

        Discusses the period after Dante and before Calvin. Suggests
        important differences among Protestant reformers. Also briefly
        discusses nominalism.

1763.   ————, and Benjamin Drewery, eds., *Martin Luther*. N.Y.: St.
        Martin's, 1970.

        Rev. *Choice*, 8 (1971), 281.

        Documents of personal, autobiographical, or historic signifi-
        cance. New translations of about one-third of documents in-
        cluded.

1764.   Russell, Conrad, "Arguments for Religious Unity in England,
        1530-1650," *Journal of Ecclesiastical Hist.*, 18 (1967), 201-
        226.

        Examines factors in England which lent force and validity to
        arguments for religious unity. Such arguments were also legal
        and philosophical.

1765.   Scheible, Heinz, "Zeitschriftenschau," *ARG*, 59 (1968), 65-99.

        Useful bibliographic survey of recent articles on the Refor-
        mation, under such headings as: Ausgang des Mittelalters,
        Humanismus und Wissenschaft, Luther, Zwingli, Calvin, Wirt-
        schaftsgeschichte, Landesgeschichte, etc. (See also ibid.,
        58 [1967], 212-248.)

1766.   Schenda, Rudolf, "Die protestantisch-Katholische Legendenpo-
        lemik im 16 Jahrhundert," *AKG*, 52 (1970), 28-48.

        Some of 16th-cent. religious books of legends. Concludes they
        served not only religious-educational needs, but also were
        important as political tracts.

1767.   Schlink, Edmund, *Die Lehre von der Taufe*. Kassel: Stauda,
        1969.

On baptism, historical problems, place of baptism in the Reformation; views of Thomas, Luther, Calvin, Zwingli; theological interpretation of the details of baptism.

1768.   Scott, David Allan, "Egocentrism and the Christian Life: A Study of Thomas Aquinas and Martin Luther and an Attempted Reformulation," *DA*, 29 (1969), 2795-2796-A (Princeton Univ.).

Aquinas and Luther re problem of egocentrism. Aquinas distinguishes between a perverse love of self which loves the self's apparent and private good, from a legitimate self-love which loves the rational operation of desiring God's goodness for its own sake. For Luther the problem of egocentrism is that of sin, viz., incurvature of the will whereby the will seeks the ground of its good in itself and not in God.

1769.   Seaver, Paul S., *The Puritan Lectureships: The Politics of Religious Dissent 1560-1662*. Stanford Univ. Press, 1970.

Rev. *AHR*, 76 (1971), 145-146; *ARG*, 62 (1971), 158-160; *Choice*, 7 (1970), 559; *Church Hist.*, 40 (1971), 229; *Historian*, 33 (1971), 467-468; *History*, 56 (1971), 445-446.

Lectureships as attempt of laity to control pulpit and hear sermons beyond usual church hours. Attempt of church to destroy the institution. Research based on records of London parishes and ecclesiastical authorities.

1770.   Secker, Philip J., "Martin Luther's Views on the State of the Dead," *Concordia Theological Monthly*, 38 (1967), 422-435.

Luther's view of death as "sleep" qualified as not applying to all the dead: they are awakened only at God's pleasure. Luther's views inconsistent. Documented; bibliography, pp. 434-435.

1771.   Secret, François, *L'Esotérisme de Guy Le Fèvre de la Boderie*. Geneva: Droz, 1969.

Rev. *TLS*, 25 September 1969, 1103.

On Guillaume Postel's disciple, Guy Le Fèvre de La Boderie, who, as an adept of the Cabbala and a linguist, succeeded in clothing the millenarist visions of his master in poetic form. Studies La Boderie's career and work to illuminate underworld of erudition, cosmology, and eccentric religion which makes the more familiar aspects of the Renaissance understood.

1772.   Shaw, Duncan, ed., *Reformation and Revolution: Essays Presented to the Very Reverend Principal Emeritus Hugh Watt*. Edinburgh: St. Andrews Press, 1967.

On Scottish and English Reformation: a collection of articles, some of which may bear on James I; e.g., A. Ian Dunlop, "Baptism in Scotland after the Reformation," post-1560; T. Angus Kerr, "John Craig, Minister of Aberdeen, and King's Chaplain," appointed chaplain under James VI (1597); Ian B. Cowan, "The Five Articles of Perth," James I's liturgical changes, with consequences.

1773. Shriver, Frederick, "Orthodoxy and Diplomacy: James I and the Vortius Affair," *Eng. Hist. Rev.*, 85 (1970), 449-474.

James I as "champion of Catholic orthodoxy"; his opposition to Arminius' successor as divinity professor at Leiden; ultimate need for readjustment of England's Dutch policy.

1774. Sieber, Marc, ed., *Discordia Concors. Festgabe für Edgar Bonjour zu seinem 70. Geburtstag am 21. August 1968*. Basel/Stuttgart: Helbing und Lichtenhahn, 1968. 2 vols.

Contains among other essays: George R. Potter, "The Initial Impact of the Swiss Reformers on England"; Marc Sieber on colonization, "Realität oder Utopie?"

1775. Siegel, Paul N., *Shakespeare in His Time and Ours*. Notre Dame, Ind.: Univ. of Notre Dame Press, 1968.

Shakespeare's writings interpreted in the light of Christian humanism and theological views of his time.

1776. Smith, Constance I., "*Descendit ad Infernos*--Again," *JHI*, 28 (1967), 87-88.

On the salvation of the ancient just; ten 16th-cent. theologians and their views on Christ's *descensus*. Classical Protestant theologians interpreted it mystically, while representatives of various sectors of the Radical Reformation favored the literal view through their desire for salvation of the ancients.

1777. Solt, Leo F., "Puritanism, Capitalism, Democracy and the New Science," *Am. Hist. Rev.*, 73, 1 (October 1967), 18-29.

Examines some aspects of Puritanism to ascertain whether Puritan doctrine and discipline led toward the Age of Enlightenment and beyond or backward to medieval times.

1778. Spitz, Lewis, "Current Accents in Luther Study, 1960-1967," *Theological Studies*, 28 (1967), 549-573.

Bibliographic survey; Luther and scholasticism and humanism; Luther's theology and ethic, etc.

1779. Strand, Kenneth A., ed., *Essays on Luther*. Ann Arbor, Mich.: Ann Arbor Publishers, 1969.

1780. ———, *Essays on the Northern Renaissance*. Ann Arbor, Mich.: Ann Arbor Publishers, 1968.

Rev. *Church Hist.*, 39 (1970), 119-120.

These companion volumes reprint selections from the writings of Albert Hyma and essays from his *Festschrift* volume, *The Dawn of Modern Civilization*. Essays on Erasmus, Luther, the Devotio Moderna, and the Brethren of the Common Life are included. Hyma's critical survey, "New Light on Luther," examines strengths and weaknesses of Reformation histories and Luther biographies. Bibliography of Hyma's work, at the end of *Essays on the Northern Renaissance*, by Richard DeMolen.

1781. Süss, Theobald, *Luther*.   Paris: Presses Universitaires de
       France, 1969.

       Rev. *Revue de Théologie et de Philosophie*, 3e S., 20e Ann.
       (1969), 127.

       Subordination of legal justice to justification by faith forms
       core of Luther's thinking; thus removes philosophy from divine
       sphere to the human, since it is based on reason, which is not
       founded in Christ. Existential nature of Luther's thought.

1782. Swanson, Guy E., *Religion and Regime: A Sociological Account
       of the Reformation*. Ann Arbor: Univ. of Mich. Press, 1967.

       Rev. *AHR*, 73 (1968), 1132-1134.

       Relation of success or failure of Reformation to the political
       sociology of particular areas of Europe.

1783. Thomas, Helen, "*Jacob and Esau*--'Rigidly Calvinistic?'" *SEL*,
       9 (1969), 199-214.

       Contends that this 16th-cent. interlude is not "rigidly Cal-
       vinistic" in its view of predestination, as tracing its pro-
       logue and epilogue to the *Institutes* would suggest, but rather
       that it is Erasmian and based on Paul's epistle to the Romans.

1784. Thompson, W.D.J. Cargill, "A Reconsideration of Richard Ban-
       croft's Paul's Cross Sermon of 9 February 1588/9," *Journal of
       Ecclesiastical Hist.*, 20 (1969), 253-266.

       Bancroft's Sermon an important stage in development of doctrine
       of episcopacy. First published Elizabethan work in which in-
       stitution of episcopacy is defended solely on historical
       grounds and in which no mention is made of argument that church
       government is a "thing indifferent."

1785. Tonkin, John, *The Church and the Secular Order in Reformation
       Thought*. N.Y. and London: Columbia Univ. Press, 1971.

       Rev. *LJ*, 96 (1971), 1993.

       Relation of Church to secular state; ecclesiology. Chapters
       include: Medieval Heritage--City of God and the Catholic
       Church; Luther; Calvin; Reformation Heritage.

1786. Volz, Hans, "Die Lutherbibliographie im Licht der Geschichte,"
       Gutenberg-Jahrb., 44 (1969), 313-330.

       Discusses, in chronological order, scholarship on editions of
       Luther's works.

1787. Walker, Williston, *John Calvin*. N.Y.:   Schocken Books, 1969.

       Rev. *Church Hist.*, 39 (1970), 273-274.

       Reprint of standard work in Calvin biography, with new biblio-
       graphic essay by J.T. McNeill divided into two parts: "Thirty
       Years of Calvin Study, 1918-1948" and "1948-1968."

1788. Walty, J.N., "La Réforme au XVIe siècle: Calvin-Bucer-
       Erasme-Zwingli," *Revue des Sciences philosophiques et théolo-
       giques*, 53 (1969), 114-139; 341-367.

       Survey of recent scholarship on these four writers.

1789. Warning, Rainer, "Ritus, Mythos und geistliches Spiel,"
        Poetica, 3 (1970), 83-114.

        Through archetype investigation, provides alternative to
        "secularization" thesis for explanation of events in medieval
        (here esp. French) drama. Suggests that the pure "Christian"
        interpretations of Shakespeare are also inadequate.

1790. Wertz, Dorothy, "The Theology of Nominalism in the English
        Morality Plays," *Harv. Theol. Rev.*, 62 (1969), 371-374.

        Effects of nominalism on popular culture of 15th-cent. *poten-
        tia absoluta*, the complete liberty of God, bypassed the *poten-
        tia ordinata*, which worked through the hierarchy of the
        Church, to the individual directly.

1791. White, B.R., *The English Separatist Tradition: From the Marian
        Martyrs to the Pilgrim Fathers*. Oxford Theological Monographs.
        Oxford Univ. Press, 1971. Rev. *TLS*, 17 Sept. 1971, 1128.

        Chapters on non-conformists include: Seedbed of Separatism;
        Robert Browne and the Covenanted Community; Developments among
        the London Separatists, 1585-1593. (Based on 1961 Oxford
        D.Phil. dissertation.)

1792. Williams, Glanmor, *Reformation Views of History*. Richmond,
        Va.: John Knox Press, 1970.

        Rev. *Jour. of Ecum. Studies*, 8 (1971), 644.

        Concentrates on English reformers William Tyndale, John Ball,
        and John Foxe and deals briefly with the reformers of the Con-
        tinent, Scotland, Ireland, and Wales. These men used scrip-
        tural exegesis and historical argument to prove that the con-
        temporary papal structure had fallen from the early model.

1793. Wilson, Edward M., "Shakespeare and Christian Doctrine: Some
        Qualifications," *ShS*, 23 (1970), 79-89.

        Responds to Roland Mushat Frye's *Shakespeare and Christian
        Doctrine*, with reservations based on 16th and 17th-cent. Span-
        ish drama. Focuses on Frye's interpretation of Father Sankey's
        expurgation of the Valladolid Folio; Frye's generalizations
        about dramatic allegory; and his belief that there is little
        pure New Testament Christianity in Shakespeare.

1794. Wilson, R.A., *Luther: An Introduction to His Thought*. Phila-
        delphia: Fortress Press, 1970.

        Rev. *AHR*, 75 (1970), 2033-2034.

        Emphasizes Luther's heavy reliance on Bible and his discrimina-
        tion between law and gospel in Scriptures.

1795. Wolff, Cynthia Griffin, "Literary Reflections of the Puritan
        Character," *JHI*, 29 (1968), 13-32.

        Diverse characteristics of Puritans, both confident and tor-
        turedly self-condemnatory, as seen in 17th- and early 18th-
        cent. documents which Puritans wrote about themselves.

1796. Wolgast, Eike, "Die Wittenberger Luther-Ausgabe ...," *AGB*, 11
        (1970), 1-335.

        Detailed account of history of publication of corpus of Lu-
        ther's work; its relevance to contemporary history.

1797. Wood, Arthur Skevington, *The Principles of Biblical Interpre-
       tation as Enunciated by Irenaeus, Origen, Augustine, Luther,
       and Calvin.* Grand Rapids, Mich.: Zondervan, 1967.

1798. Ziegler, Donald J., ed., *Great Debates of the Reformation.*
       N.Y.: Random House, 1969.

       Rev. *Quarterly Journal of Speech*, 56 (1970), 100-101.

       Includes Luther and Eck on papal supremacy; Zwingli on the
       mass; Zwingli and Luther on Christ's presence in the Sacrament;
       etc.

                              ADDENDA

1798a. Hudson, Winthrop, and Leonard J. Trinterud, *Theology in Six-
       teenth- and Seventeenth-Century England.* Papers read at a
       Clark Library Seminar, 1971. Los Angeles: William Andrews
       Clark Memorial Library, University of Calif., 1971.

       Hudson's "Fast Days and Civil Religion," pp. 3-24, deals with
       fast days in Elizabethan and Stuart England, and America.
       Trinterud's "A.D. 1689: The End of the Clerical World," pp.
       27-50, finds close of Restoration as endpoint for earlier
       reformation impulses.

1798b. Porter, H.C., *Puritanism in Tudor England.* (History in Depth.)
       London: Macmillan, 1970.

       Rev. *TLS*, 18 June 1971, 717.

       Compact body of documents on 16th-cent. Puritanism; argument
       against seeing it in 17th-cent. terms, as forerunner of later
       dissent and nonconformity. Part I. 1549: Cranmer on the Two
       "Parties" in the Church; Part II. 1525: Robert Barnes versus
       the Prelates; Part III. 1550-1552: Bucer and Calvin Urge Fur-
       ther Reformation in England; Part IV. 1567: The London Separa-
       tist Congregation; Part V. 1583: Autobiography of Robert
       Browne; Part VI. 1572: John Field; Part VII. 1571-1572: The
       Puritans and Parliament; Part VIII. 1576: Peter Wentworth in
       the House of Commons; Part IX. The Puritans and Education;
       Part X. 1589: Marprelate's Anti-Episcopal Rhetoric; Part XI.
       Mid-1580s: Puritan Pleas; Part XII. 1587: Rev. Richard Rogers
       in Essex; Part XIII. 1593: Richard Hooker's Analysis of the
       Sectarian Mind; Part XIV. William Perkins: 1558-1602. Cf.
       Chart of Salvation and Damnation.

1798c. Trinterud, Leonard J., ed., *Elizabethan Puritanism.* N.Y.:
       Oxford Univ. Press, 1971.

       Rev. *Church Hist.*, 41 (1972), 125.

       Major collection of documents on Elizabethan Puritanism, divi-
       ded into Part One: The Original, Anti-Vestment Party (inclu-
       ding John Gough; John Foxe); Part Two: The Passive-Resistance
       Party (including Edward Dering; Peter Wentworth); Part Three:
       The Presbyterian Party (including William Fulke; John Knewstub;
       Eusebius Paget; James Morice). Selected bibliography.

XIX. TOPOI, THEMES, EMBLEMS, ETC.

(cf. Iconography)

1799. [ABRAHAM] Jones, Joseph R., "From Abraham to Andrenio: Observations on the Evolution of the Abraham Legend, its Diffusion
in Spain and its Relation to the Theme of the Self-Taught
Philosopher," *CLS*, 6 (1969), 69-101.

Abraham as self-taught believer--cf. Thomistic "natural light."
In Spain, medieval versions of the Abraham legend and its derivative folk stories appear in the Hebrew poem *Sefer Hayashar*,
in the Arabic novel usually called *El filósofo autodidacto*, and
in the Old Spanish *General estoria*.

1800. [ACHILLES] Cutts, John, "Tamburlaine 'as fierce Achilles was,'"
CompD, 1 (1967), 105-109.

Analogues of Achilles' effeminacy (in Golding's trans. of
Ovid's *Metam.*, XIII. 200, 205), related to Tamburlaine.

1801. [ACHILLES] Steadman, John M., "Achilles and Renaissance Epic:
Moral Criticism and Literary Tradition," in Horst Meller et
al., eds., *Lebende Antike: Symposium für Rudolf Sühnel*. Berlin: Erich Schmidt Verlag, 1967, pp. 139-154.

Transformation of the Homeric *ferus* and *saevus* Achilles into a
"moralized" Renaissance gentleman, by Renaissance poets who
took the *Iliad* as their model.

1802. [ADAM] Hoffeld, Jeffrey M., "Adam's two wives (late 15th-cent.
statue base)," *Metropolitan Mus. of Art Bull.*, 26 (1967/68),
430-440.

References to Scriptural passages and to iconographic and Kabbalistic traditions re 15th-cent statue base which depicts a
Biblical divorce.

1803. [ADAM AND EVE] Röhrich, Lutz, *Adam und Eva. Das erste Mensch-
enpaar in Volkskunst und Volksdichtung*. Stuttgart: Müller
and Schindler, 1968.

Rev. *Germ.-Rom. Monat.*, n.f. 20 (1970), 109-110.

Traces the motif through folk traditions.

1804. [ADAM and EVE] Weiner, Jack, "Adam and Eve Imagery in *La
Celestina*," *PLL*, 5 (1969), 389-396.

291

Rojas used as a literary device elements from Genesis story of
Adam's Fall: perfect example of two basic didactic themes--
importance of obeying God's laws, and effect of each man's
responsibilities and actions on his fellow man.

1805. [ADONIS] Berry, J. Wilkes, "Loss of Adonis and Light in 'Venus
and Adonis,'" *Discourse*, 12 (1969), 72-76.

Shakespeare has mirrored failure of Venus' pleas for winning
Adonis in the day's moving from dawn through sunset to black
night.

1806. [ADVENT] Minott, Charles Ilsley, "The Theme of the Mérode
Altarpiece," *Art Bull.*, 51 (1969), 267-271.

Details of the triptych in terms of the full meaning of the
Advent: the Incarnation, the presence of Christ in our world,
and the Last Judgment.

1807. [*ADYNATA*] Cherchi, Paolo, "Gli 'Adynata' dei Trovatori," *MP*,
68 (1971), 223-259.

On *adynata* (*impossibilia*), later of Shakespearean interest.

1808. [AENEAS] Galinsky, Karl G., *Aeneas, Sicily, and Rome*. Princeton Univ. Press, 1969. (Cf. [DIDO].)

Rev. *Choice*, 7 (1970), 278; *LibJ*, 95 (1970), 1013; *VaQR*, 46
(1970), 1x.

Legend of Aeneas as preserved in art and artifacts of antiquity
and relationship of these to literary accounts, especially
Aeneid of Vergil.

1809. [AENEAS-DIDO] Leube, Eberhard, *Fortuna in Karthago. Die
Aeneas-Dido-Mythe Vergils in den romanischen Literaturen vom
14. bis zum 16. Jahrhundert.* (Studien zum Fortwirken der Antike, Bd. 1.) Heidelberg: C. Winter, 1969.

Rev. *BHR*, 32 (1970), 701-703.

On Vergil's Carthage episode. Influence of extensive and differentiated realm of gods; divine motivation in narrative and
dramatic handling of this subject in French, Spanish, and
Italian literature from 14th to 16th cents., showing similar
adoptions and coherence of Aeneas-reception in Romance literature for over three cents.; permanent presence of idea of Fortuna in all the Aeneas-Dido variations.

1810. [ALEXANDER] Schwarzenberg, Erkinger, "From the 'Alesandro
Morente' to the Alexandre Richelieu. The Portraiture of Alex-
ander the Great in Seventeenth-Century Italy and France,"
JWCI, 32 (1969), 398-405.

Traces presence of the "Alessandro Morente" in 16th and 17th
cent. paintings and sculptures.

1811. [ALIENS] Chitty, C.W., "Aliens in England in the Sixteenth Century," *Race*, 8 (1966), 129-145.

Discusses immigration into England in 16th cent. and subsequent treatment of the aliens by native English.

1812.   [ALIENS] Thrupp, S.L., "Aliens in and around London in the
        15th Century," in A.E.J. Hollaender and W. Kellaway, eds.,
        Studies in London History Presented to Philip Edmund Jones.
        London: Hodder and Stoughton, 1969, pp. 249-272.

1813.   [ALLEGORY] Allen, Don C., *Mysteriously Meant: The Rediscovery
        of Pagan Symbolism and Allegorical Interpretation in the
        Renaissance*. Baltimore and London: Johns Hopkins Press,
        1970.

        Rev. *MLN*, 86 (1971), 946-948.

        Chapters include Pagan Myth and Christian Apologetics; Renais-
        sance Search for Christian Origins: The Philosophers; The
        Sacred History; Undermeanings in Homer ...; Symbolic Wisdom of
        the Ancient Egyptians; Undermeanings in Virgil's *Aeneid*; in
        Ovid's *Metam.*; Allegorical Interpretation of the Renaissance
        Mythographers; Symbolic Interpretations of Renaissance Anti-
        quarians; Rationalization of Myth and the End of Allegory.

1814.   [ALLEGORY] ————, "The Renaissance Antiquarian and Allegorical
        Interpretation," *Medieval and Ren. Studies, 1968*, ed. J.L.
        Lievsay. Durham, N.C.: Duke Univ. Press, 1970, pp. 3-20.

        Sixteenth- and 17th-cent. use of allegory and its symbolic
        Renaissance interpretative methods.

1815.   [ALLEGORY] Collins, Sister Mary Emmanuel, "The Allegorical
        Motifs in the Early English Moral Plays," *DA*, 30 (1969),
        682-A (Yale Univ.).

        Beginnings of allegory; distinctions between allegorical in-
        terpretation and allegory of personification and relations of
        one to the other.

1816.   [ALLEGORY] Dunlap, R., "The Allegorical Interpretation of
        Renaissance Literature," *PMLA*, 82 (1967), 39-43.

        Limits of allegorizing Shakespeare.

1817.   [ALLEGORY] Hartman, Geoffrey H., "'The Nymph Complaining for
        the Death of Her Fawn': A Brief Allegory," *Essays in Crit.*,
        18, no. 2 (1968), 113-135.

        Attempts to find specific allegory and clarify status of Spen-
        serian allegory in Marvell's age.

1818.   [ALLEGORY] Murrin, Michael J., *The Veil of Allegory*. Univ. of
        Chicago Press, 1969. Rev. *Criticism*, 12 (1970), 155.

        "Some Notes Toward a Theory of Allegorical Rhetoric in the
        English Renaissance." On rhetorical dimension of Spenser's
        poems. In a chronological study of uses of allegory in the
        ancient world, the Renaissance, and Romantic period, book
        goes beyond description and definition to a consideration of
        literary and cultural history.

1819.   [ALLEGORY] Saccio, Peter, *The Court Comedies of John Lyly. A
        Study in Allegorical Dramaturgy*. Princeton Univ. Press, 1969.

        Rev. *BHR*, 31 (1969), 682-686; *TLS*, 23 July 1970, 831.

In context of mythographical tradition and Renaissance appe-
tite for allegory, examines plays in terms of "their materials
(mythology), their technique (situational dramaturgy), and
their mode of meaning (allegory)."

1820. [ALLEGORY] ———, "The Curious Frame: A Study of Allegory
and Dramaturgy in Elizabethan Court Comedy of the 1580's,"
DA, 29 (1969), 2684-A (Princeton Univ.).

Many plays studied are distinguished from main body of Elizabethan drama by use of pagan gods as major characters, avoid-
ance of developed plots in favor of exploration of largely
static situations, and organization on an allegorical rather
than a narrative base. Their use of myth, dramaturgy, and
allegory analyzed.

1821. [ALLEGORY] Stahel, Thomas Herbert, "Cristoforo Landino's Alle-
gorization of the *Aeneid*: Books III and IV of the *Camaldolese
Disputations*," *DA*, 29 (1969), 3984-A (Johns Hopkins Univ.).

Summary and critique of contents of the *Disputations*. Summary
history of allegorizations of *Aeneid*. Exposition of Landino's
poetic theory.

1822. [ALLEGORY] Theiss, Winfried, *Exemplarische Allegorik. Untersuchungen zu einem literar-historischen Phänomen bei Hans
Sachs*. Munich: Fink, 1968.

Allegory in poems and dramas of Hans Sachs serves to give
example of decorous behavior.

1823. [ALLEGORY] Tuve, Rosemond, *Allegorical Imagery: Some Mediaeval Books and Their Posterity*. Princeton Univ. Press, 1966.

Rev. *Spec.*, 42 (1967), 196-199.

What 16th cent. meant by allegorical reading and what was enjoyed in it. Includes allegory of virtues and vices.

1824. [ALLEGORY] Zumthor, P., "Charles d'Orléans et le langage de
l'allégorie," *Mélanges offerts à Rita Lejeune*. (Gembloux;
Duculot, 1969), v. 2, 1481-1502.

Allegory in the work of the Duke of Orléans.

1825. [ALLEGORY, Political] Trinquet, Roger, "L'allégorie politique
dans la peinture française au XVIe siècle: les 'Dames au
bain,'" *Bull. Soc. de l'Hist. Art Français*. Année 1967 (1968),
7-25.

Various 16th-cent. French paintings analyzed and shown to be
political allegories.

1826. [AMOR and PSYCHE] Binder, Gerhard, and Reinhold Merkelbach,
Amor und Psyche. Darmstadt: Wissenschaftliche Buchgesellschaft, 1968.

Studies of the myth.

1827. [ANALOGY] Koenigsberger, Dorothy M., "Analogy in Renaissance
       Thought: A Survey of the Role of Analogy in the Development
       of Ideas from the Fifteenth to the Early Seventeenth Century."
       (W.R. Fryer, director.) Nottingham Ph.D., 1969.

1828. [ANALOGY] LaGuardia, Eric, "The Aesthetics of Analogy," _Dio-_
       genes, 62 (1968), 49-61.

       Universal analogy as principle underlying medieval and Renais-
       sance thought, particularly jurisprudence and poetry; "equi-
       parition"--in its legal sense, drawing connections between dif-
       ferent political spheres--can be understood as a poetic pro-
       cedure as well.

1829. [ANGEL] Briggs, K.M., "Heywood's Hierarchie of the Blessed An-
       gells," _Folklore_, 80 (1969), 89-106.

       Traditional angel lore in Heywood's poem.

1830. [ANGEL] Gordan, Paulus, _Boten Gottes. Neun Bildbetrachtungen._
       Beuron: Kunstverlag, 1970.

       Rev. _Bibliographie zur Symbolik, Ikonographie und Mythologie_,
       4 (1971), 57-58.

       Early Christian paintings of angels, under following groupings:
       visibility of the invisible ones, enflamed (_Entflammte_), the
       message (_der Bote_), messenger (_der Gesandte_), bringer of joy
       (_Freudenbringer_), the consoler, Evangelist, the future-teller
       (_Deuter des Zukunftigen_), Herald of Judgment (_Gerichtsherold_).

1831. [ANGEL, Winged] Berefelt, Gunnar, _A Study of the Winged Angel._
       The Origin of a Motif. Stockholm: Almqvist & Wiksell, 1968.

       Follows winged-angel motif from ancient pagan origins through
       Christian centuries.

1832. [ANGEL; DEMON] Rosenberg, Alfons, _Engel und Dämonen._ Munich:
       Prestel, 1967.

       Angels in the religious experience of antiquity; in OT and NT;
       transformations in representation of angels and demons.

1833. [ANGELS] Davidson, G., ed., _A Dictionary of Angels, Including_
       the Fallen Angels. N.Y.: Free Press, 1967. Rev. _TLS_, 14
       Dec. 1967, 1226.

1834. [ANIMALS] Forbes, Thomas R., "Medical Lore in the Bestiaries,"
       Medical Hist., 12 (1968), 245-253.

       Documented study of animal-related ailments and remedies, in
       medieval and later bestiaries (to end of 16th cent.).

1835. [ANIMALS] Himmelhaber, Georg, "Animals as Motifs in Art,"
       Apollo, 92 (1970), 458-463.

       Twelve examples of animals used as symbols in medieval Euro-
       pean paintings and sculpture.

1836. [ANIMALS] Knappe, Karl-Adolf and Ursula, "Zur Tierdarstellung in der Kunst des 15. und 16. Jahrhunderts," *Studium Generale*, 20 (1967), 263-293.

Deals with representation of animals in art during 15th and 16th cents.

1837. [ANIMALS] Lurker, Manfred, "Das Tier in der Bildwelt des Hieronymus Bosch," *Studium Generale*, 20 (1967), 212-220.

To understand Bosch's art, intellectual foundations of waning Middle Ages are indispensable. Represents Bosch's animals in their symbolic garb.

1838. [ANIMALS] Roth, Charles, "Du Bestiaire Divin au Bestiaire d'Amour," *Etudes de Lettres*, 2 (1969), 199-216.

Secular and religious animal symbolism from Rigaut de Barbezieux to Richard de Fournival; importance of knowing religious substrata of secular medieval literature.

1839. [ANIMALS] Schmidtke, Dietrich, *Geistliche Tierinterpretation in der deutschsprachigen Literatur des Mittelalters (1100-1500)*. Part I: Text; Part II: Anmerkungen. 2 vols, 671 pp. (Issued as diss., Freie Universität, Berlin.)

Rev. *Anzeiger f. dt. Altertum*, 82 (1971), 165 ff.

Latin tradition of animal symbolism; German literary use in Middle Ages; pp. 220-248 contain catalogue of animal symbolism; useful research tool.

1840. [ANIMALS] South, Malcolm, "Animal Imagery in Ben Jonson's Plays," *DA*, 29 (1969), 4505-4506-A (Univ. of Georgia).

Ways in which animal references contribute to theme, plot, and characterization.

1841. [ANTEROS] Maurel, Madeleine, "Esquisse d'un Antéros Baroque," *Dix-Septième Siècle*, no. 84/85 (1969), 3-20.

Baroque vision of the antagonism between Eros and Anteros.

1842. [ANTICHRIST] Musper, H.Th., ed., *Der Antichrist und die fünfzehn Zeichen: Faksimile-Ausgabe des einzigen erhaltenen Chiroxylographischen Blockbuches*. 2 vols. Munich: Prestel, 1970. (Cf. [FIFTEEN SIGNS].)

Rev. *TLS*, 29 January 1971, 135.

Fifteenth-cent. popular pictorial treatment of biography of Antichrist. Reproduction of earliest of three existing blockbooks of pictorial treatment of Antichrist. Commentary volume includes iconographical description of pictures.

1843. [APES] Taylor, A.B., "Shakespeare and the Apes," *N&Q*, 214, n.s. 16 (1969), 144-145.

Caliban's fear that he and other conspirators will be transformed into apes (IV. i. 249) recalls fate of Cercopes in *Metamorphoses*, Bk. XIV.

1844. [APHRODITE Armed] Selden, R., "Donne's 'The Dampe,' Lines 22-24," *MLR*, 64 (1969), 726-727.

Lines allude to the *topos* "Aphrodite Armed."

1845. [APOCALYPSE] Fixler, Michael, "The Apocalypse within *Paradise Lost*," *New Essays on Paradise Lost*, ed. Thomas Kranidas (Berkeley and Los Angeles: Univ. of Calif. Press, 1969), pp. 131-178.

Milton's use of the Apocalypse as basic source for his poetic inspiration, his use of poetry as liturgy, and his conception of the structure of the epic.

1846. [APOCALYPSE] Morris, Helen, "Shakespeare and Dürer's 'Apocalypse,'" *ShakS*, 4 (1968), 252-262.

Source of inspiration for various passages in *Ant.* might be series of woodcuts known as Dürer's "Apocalypse."

1847. [ARMINIANISM] Amaru, Betsy Halpern, "Arminianism in England, 1595-1629," *DA*, 30 (1970), 4359-A (Univ. of Mass.).

Roots of English Arminian movement in reactions against Calvinist doctrine of predestination during Elizabeth's reign. During James's, theological controversy shifted to political sphere.

1848. [ARMINIANISM] Tyacke, N.R.N., "Arminianism in England, in Religion and Politics, from 1604 to 1650." (E. Anne Whiteman, director.) Oxford D. Phil., 1969.

1849. [ARMS] Herman, Gerald, "Unconventional Arms as a Comic Device in Some *Chansons de Geste*," *MLQ*, 30 (1969), 319-330.

Unconventional weaponry in the Old French epic may symbolize epic adolescents' state of chivalric immaturity and lack of knightly refinement, or vast distance which separates rustic from the knight; their *raison d'être* is to amuse.

1850. [ARMS vs. LETTERS] Russell, Peter, "Arms versus Letters: Towards a Definition of Spanish Fifteenth-Century Humanism," in Archibald R. Lewis, ed., *Aspects of the Renaissance: A Symposium*. Austin/London: Univ. of Texas Press, 1967, pp. 47-58.

Spanish humanism of 15th cent. as conflict between arms and letters.

1851. [*ARS MORIENDI*] Armstrong, Elizabeth Psakis, "Heinrich Suso in England: An Edition of the *Ars Moriendi* from the *Seven Points of True Love*," *DA*, 28 (1967), 188-A (Indiana Univ.).

On 15th-cent. English abridgement of 14th-cent. Latin work by German mystic Suso.

1852. [*ARS MORIENDI*] Doebler, B.A., "Othello's Angels: The *ars moriendi*," *ELH*, 34 (1967), 156-172.

On V.ii, which evokes the Christian deathbed conflict between good and evil.

1853. [*ARS MORIENDI*] Evans, John X., "The Art of Rhetoric and the
       Art of Dying in Tudor Recusant Prose," *Recusant Hist.*, 10
       (1970), 247-272.

       Education in rhetorical arts at Jesuit schools of Tudor period.
       Theme of "the art of dying well" in exiled Catholic writers.
       Considers commonly used figures of speech and imagery in terms
       of their Counter-Reformation point of view.

1854. [*ARS MORIENDI*] Stewart, Stanley, "Marvell and the *Ars Morien-
       di*," in Earl Miner, ed., *Seventeenth-Century Imagery*. Univ.
       of Calif. Press, 1971, pp. 133-150.

       Concerns "To His Coy Mistress."

1855. [ART and NATURE] Close, A.J., "Commonplace Theories of Art and
       Nature in Classical Antiquity and in the Renaissance," *JHI*,
       30 (1969), 467-486.

       Commonplaces include: art imitates nature, art perfects na-
       ture, art based on study of nature, art has its beginnings in
       nature, art is inferior to nature, etc. Variations, and im-
       portant texts where examples may be found. Footnotes Renais-
       sance contexts where exact parallels to each commonplace occur.

1856. [ART and NATURE] Hatton, Thomas J., "Nature as Poet: Alanus
       de Insulis' *The Complaint of Nature* and the Medieval Concept
       of Artistic Creation," *Language and Style*, 2 (1969), 85-91.

       On medieval concept that process of artistic creation paral-
       lels process of natural creation.

1857. [ART and NATURE] Palmer, D.J., "Art and Nature in *As You Like
       It*," *PQ*, 49 (1970), 30-40.

       On art and nature and Elizabethan fondness for turning these
       ideas inside out. Forest of Arden as representing Nature as
       Art, and the Elizabethan stage as Art holding up the mirror
       to Nature.

1858. [ART and NATURE] Rivers, Elias L., "Nature, Art, and Science
       in Spanish Poetry of the Renaissance," *BHS*, 44 (1967), 255-256.

       On pastoral and neoplatonic traditions; and the dialectic be-
       tween art and nature in the Renaissance.

1859. [ART and NATURE] Salerno, N.A., "Andrew Marvell and the 'Furor
       hortensis,'" *SEL*, 8, no. 1 (1968), 103-120.

       Marvell's poems on gardens belong to 17th-cent. controversy on
       Renaissance concept: Art-Nature. Marvell's happy gardeners
       point towards reordered world after the Fall and link order im-
       posed on external world with that imposed on soul.

1860. [ARTHUR] Turner, Elizabeth J., "The Arthurian Legend as an
       Historical Ideal of Life: Political Theory in Sir Thomas
       Malory's *Le Morte Darthur*," *DA*, 29 (1969), 3590-3591-A (Univ.
       of Pennsylvania).

       Study of Malory centering on phenomenon of literary revival
       and recreation of a cultural model.

1861. [AUBADE] Forster, Leonard, "Conventional Safety Valves: Alba, Pastourelle, and Epithalamium," in Horst Meller et al., eds., *Lebende Antike: Symposion für Rudolf Sühnel*. Berlin: Erich Schmidt Verlag, 1967, pp. 120-138.

Sees all three genres as dealing with intercourse; close assimilation of dawn song with epithalamium, or marriage song.

1862. [BABEL] Anselment, Raymond A., "'Ascensio Mendax, Descensio Crudelis': The Image of Babel in the *Anniversaries*," *ELH*, 38 (1971), 188-205.

On the failure of Babel and need for humility.

1863. [Tower of BABYLON] Foster, David William, "Calderón's *La Torre de Babilonia* and Christian Allegory," *Criticism*, 9 (1967), 142-154.

1864. [BANQUET OF SENSE] Waddington, R.B., "Chapman and Persius: The Epigraph to 'Ovid's Banquet of Sense,'" *RES*, n.s., 19, no. 74 (1968), 158-162.

Epigraph to Chapman's poem, taken from Persius, as an invitation to an ironic reading of the "Banquet" where spiritual ecstasy is attained through the senses, and initiates will see an attack against moral and poetic corruption. (Cf. [EMBLEM].)

1865. [BAROQUE] Bazin, Germain, *The Baroque: Principles, Styles, Modes, Themes*. N.Y.: Graphic Society, 1968. (Cf. THEATRICAL.)

Baroque art from 1580 to 1780, set against background of politics, religion, philosophy, and social conditions.

1866. [BAROQUE] Fietz, Lothar, "Fragestellungen und Tendenzen der anglistischen Barock-Forschung," *DVLG*, 43 (1969), 752-763.

Includes Shakespearean material, p. 755n, as well as useful bibliographic references on baroque. (Cf. THEATRICAL.)

1867. [BAROQUE] Hanak, John Miroslav, "The Emergence of Baroque Mentality and Its Cultural Impact on Western Europe after 1550," *JAAC*, 28 (1970), 315-326. (Cf. THEATRICAL.)

Baroque continues to employ Renaissance forms, but stretches them to the point of explosion of old modes in order to accommodate a new world-view.

1868. [BAROQUE] Rousset, Jean, *L'intérieur et l'extérieur. Essais sur la poésie et sur le théâtre au XVIIe siècle*. Paris: Corti, 1968. (Cf. THEATRICAL.)

Rev. *Fr. Studies*, 25 (1971), 69-70.

Includes critical summary of theories on the baroque especially of the last 15 years, with a chapter "Adieu au Baroque?" Other pages on the Don Juan theme; 17th-cent. attack on analogical metaphor; play-within-the-play.

1869. [Devouring BEAST] Greenberg, Robert David, "The Image of the Devouring Beast: Its Dramatic Use in Selected Works of

Shakespeare," *DA*, 29 (1969), 4487-A (Univ. of California, Berkeley).

Includes *V&A*, *R of L*, *R3*, *TN*, *TC*, *KL*, *Cor.*, *Temp.*

1870. [BELLY, Fable of] Hale, David G., "Intestine Sedition: The Fable of the Belly," *Comparative Literature Studies*, 4 (1968), 377-388.

Political applications during the Renaissance of the fable.

1871. [BIBLE] Avni, Abraham, "The Influence of the Bible on European Literatures: A Review of Research from 1955 to 1965," *Yearbook of Comp. and Gen. Lit.*, no. 19 (1970), 39-57.

Useful survey of research on Bible influence in European literature. Includes pre-Shakespearean and Shakespearean periods. (Cf. 1562).

1872. [BIBLE] Shaheen, Naseeb, "Spenser's Use of Scripture in *The Faerie Queene*," *DA*, 30 (1969), 1535-1536-A (Univ. of Calif., Los Angeles).

Spenser's references to Scripture in *The Faerie Queene*. Contains a list of over 500 allusions which Spenser made to the Bible.

1873. [BIBLE] ————, "The Use of Scripture in *Cymbeline*," *ShakS*, 4 (1968), 294-315.

Biblical allusions and quotations throughout the play.

1874. [BIBLE, GENEVA] Berry, Lloyd E., introd., *The Geneva Bible: A Facsimile of the 1560 Edition*. Madison: Univ. of Wisc. Press, 1969.

Rev. *TLS*, 12 Feb. 1970, 171.

Introduction summarizes influence of *G.B.* on literature of 16th and 17th cents.; on Stubbs, Dekker, Shakespeare, Spenser, Milton, and others. Chapters on its heavy use in Scotland and popularity in early America. Useful bibliography.

1875. [BIBLE, GENEVA] Danner, Dan G., "The Theology of the Geneva Bible of 1560: A Study in English Protestantism," *DA*, 30 (1970), 3085-A (Univ. of Iowa).

Examines the annotations of Geneva Bible of 1560 to uncover basic theological presuppositions of the translators. Special attention given to comparison of Calvin's doctrines with those uncovered in Geneva Bible. Concludes the exiles owed very few of their doctrines to Calvin; most significant contribution translators made to English Protestantism was their view of church and history.

1876. [BIBLE, GENEVA] Lupton, Lewis, *A History of the Geneva Bible. v. 2: Reform*. London: Olive Tree Press, 1969. (Cf. V.I: The Quarrel. London: Fauconberg Press, 1966. 9 vols. in all [1966-1977].)

The circle of Calvin, particularly Beza and Castellio, and the environment of Geneva in which Whittingham's N.T. and the *Geneva Bible* were produced.

1877. [BIBLE: OLD TESTAMENT] Lake, James Hammond, Jr., "The Influence of the Old Testament upon the Early Drama of the English Renaissance," *DA*, 30 (1969), 1530-A (Univ. of Delaware).

Study of six Renaissance OT plays now extant.

1878. [BIRTH, Ruing] Porqueras, Mayo Alberto, "Nuevas Aportaciones al Topos 'No Haber Nacido' en la Literatura Española," *Segismundo*, 3 (1967), 63-73.

Cites instances of a character ruing his birth in Montemayor's *La Diana*, Lope de Vega's *La Dorotea*, Marlowe's *Faustus*, and *Hamlet*.

1879. [BLACKSMITH] Makarius, Laura, "Les Tabous du forgeron. De l'homme du fer à l'homme du sang," *Diogène*, 62 (1968), 23-53.

Taboos surrounding blacksmith in tribal societies as part of greater blood taboo. Ritually violating the latter, blacksmith becomes endowed with magic powers and proper object of taboo himself.

1880. [BLASON] Wilson, D.B., *Descriptive Poetry in France from Blason to Baroque*. Manchester Univ. Press, 1967.

Rev. *FS*, 22 (1968), 243.

1881. [BLIND CUPID] Gilbert, C.D., "Blind Cupid," *JWCI*, 33 (1970), 304.

Origins of concept of Blind Love in classical times, and influences of Middle Ages and Renaissance.

1882. [BLOOD] McCarthy, D.J., "The Symbolism of Blood and Sacrifice," *J. Biblical Lit.*, 88, no. 2 (1969), 166-176.

Mediterranean, Oriental, and Biblical data on religious meaning of sacrificial blood. Apotropaic use and purifying function of blood.

1883. [BLOOD] Sullivan, Lawrence Walter, "Sanguinary Imagery in the Devotional Poetry of Donne, Herbert, Vaughan, Crashaw, and La Ceppède," *DA*, 30 (1969), 1997-A (Univ. of Michigan).

Includes historical discussion of figure of mystical wine press.

1884. [BOAR, Mouth of] Thiébaux, Marcelle, "The Mouth of the Boar as a Symbol in Medieval Literature," *RPh.*, 22 (1969), 281-299.

Traces references to this *V&A* topos through medieval literature.

1885. [BODY] Glatigny, Michel, "Le champ sémantique des parties du corps dans la poésie amoureuse de 1550," *Français Moderne*, 37 (1969), 7-34.

Words designating parts of the human body form a highly struc-
tured semantic field; in Ronsard's *Amours* (1552), J. du Bellay's *L'Olive* (1549), J.A. de Baif's *Amours de Méline* (1552).

1886.   [BODY] Lorgues, Christiane, "Les proportions du corps humain
d'après les Traités du Moyen Âge et de la Renaissance," *Information d'Hist. de l'Art*, 13 (1968), 128-143.

Importance of bodily proportions in medieval and Renaissance
treatises, and their implications.

1887.   [BODY POLITIC] Archambault, P., "The Analogy of the 'Body' in
Renaissance Political Literature," *BHR*, 29 (1967), 21-53.

Traces the use of the "body" as an analogy for the state from
the ancient writers, Plato and Aristotle, through the Renaissance writers, e.g., Elyot and Fortescue. It shows the way in
which the analogy has been used to support both limited monarchy and totalitarianism.

1888.   [BODY POLITIC] Hale, David G., "The Body Politic: A Political
Metaphor in Renaissance English Literature," *DA*, 26 (1966),
4658-4659 (Duke Univ.).

Analogy between human body and the body politic was used to
defend and attack the church, promote order and obedience to
secular rulers, and to criticize political and economic abuses
in Renaissance England. Traced to classical antiquity, it
flourished in the Renaissance and was criticized as invalid in
the early 17th cent.

1889.   [BODY-SOUL] Warr, Nancy Nairn, "The Body-Soul Debate in Seventeenth-Century Poetry," *DA*, 31 (1970), 1243-A (Univ. of New
Mex.).

Its sources and characteristics.

1890.   [BROADSHEETS] Coupe, William A., *The German Illustrated Broadsheet in the Seventeenth Century*. Historical and iconographical studies. I: Text. II: Bibliographical Index with 145
plates. Bibliotheca Bibliographica Aureliana 17, 20. Baden-
Baden: Heitz, 1966/67.

History of ideas and cultural background of themes in illustrated broadsheets: religious themes (*memento mori*, last
judgment); secular themes (misfortune, luck, marriage, power
of money); Thirty Years' War. Chapter on iconography of broadsheets: personification, allegorical coats of arms, allegorical triumphs, *fortuna*, ships, trees; observations on anti-
thetical principle in themes, e.g., right-left, vices-virtues,
etc. Vol. 2: bibliography of 379 broadsheets, location,
secondary literature, and illustrations.

1891.   [Hostile BROTHERS] Mann, Michael, "Die Feindlichen Brüder,"
GRM, n.f., 18 (1968), 225-247.

From 16th to 19th cent.

1892. [BROTHER-SISTER] Craig, Virginia Wallace Robertson, "The Brother-Sister Theme in Lope de Vega's Plays," *DA*, 29 (1969), 3607-A (Univ. of Missouri).

Theme in Greek, Latin, and Italian drama; two main themes in Lope's plays, the honor code and incestuous attraction.

1893. [BROTHER-SISTER] Drabeck, Bernard Anthony, "The Brother-Sister Relationship as a Thematic and Emotive Device in Revenge Tragedy," *DA*, 28 (1968), 3636-A (Univ. of Mass.).

Selfish or political exploitation of a sister by a brother as device in revenge tragedy. Brother's decision to forget or ignore his obligations to his blood bond often begins the pivotal acting; his betrayal of obligations of blood to a sister inspires audience-aversion to him.

1894. [CADUCEUS] Schouten, J., *The Rod and Serpent of Asklepios. Symbol of Medicine.* Amsterdam: Elsevier, 1967.

Traces history of cult and the metamorphoses of Asclepius.

1895. [CAESAR] Bonnell, Robert A., "Salutati--A View of Caesar and Rome," *Annuale Mediaevale*, 8 (1967), 59-69.

1896. [CAESAR] Chang, Joseph S.M.J., "*Julius Caesar* in the Light of Renaissance Historiography," *JEGP*, 69 (1970), 63-71.

Critical perspective of *JC* as demonstrating that truth of character cannot be known is not merely a modern relativistic view. *JC* reflects growing awareness among Renaissance historians that the past is difficult to retrieve and that a man's character cannot be inferred from a record of his actions.

1897. [CAESAR] Koppenfels, Werner von, "Plutarch, Shakespeare, Quevedo und das Drama der Ermordung Caesars," *GRM*, n.f. 20 (1970), 1-23.

How playwrights interpreted the event to illustrate possibilities of comparing literatures without depending on "influences" or "sources" for "scientific" justification.

1898. [CAESAR] Kytzler, Bernhard, "Petrarca, Cicero und Caesar," in Horst Meller et al., eds., *Lebende Antike: Symposion für Rudolf Sühnel.* Berlin: Erich Schmidt, 1967, pp. 111-119.

Both Petrarch and Cicero write "An Caesar." Topos of friend as *alter ego.* Petrarch's relation to Cicero.

1899. [CAESAR] Oppermann, Hans, *Julius Caesar in Selbstzeugnissen und Bilddokumenten.* Rowohlts Monographien, 135; Reinbeck b. Hamburg: Rowohlt, 1968.

1900. [CAESAR] Owen, Trevor Allen, "Julius Caesar in English Literature from Chaucer through the Renaissance," *DA*, 27 (1967), 3847A (Univ. of Minnesota).

Differences in portrayal of Caesar from medieval period through
16th cent.; ambivalent response of 16th cent. to Caesar and
possible reasons for it.

1901.   [CAIN] Braude, Pearl F., "'Cokkel in Oure Clene Corn': Some
        Implications of Cain's Sacrifice," *Gesta*, 7 (1968), 15-28.

        Iconography of Cain's offering, especially in medieval vari-
        ants; Cain as *typus diaboli* and representative of heretic and
        Jew. Discussion of "first fruits." Early Renaissance effected
        a more universalized portrayal of Cain and Abel; and with the
        Reformation, allusions to heresy, tithing, and the Jew in the
        Sacrifice were regarded as extraneous to the Church's counter-
        attack. Documented.

1902.   [CAIN] Enslin, M.S., "Cain and Prometheus," *Jour. of Biblical
        Lit.*, 86 (1967), 88-90.

        Gen. 4: 1-8 and story of Hesiod on Prometheus (*Theog.*, 535-
        560).

1903.   [CAIN] Matthews, Honor, *The Primal Curse: The Myth of Cain
        and Abel in the Theatre*. N.Y.: Schocken; London: Chatto and
        Windus, 1967.

        Rev. *QJS*, 54 (1968), 304.

        From medieval cycles to Ionesco; thematic problems, in drama,
        of murder, guilt, and justice in an earlier God-oriented world
        as contrasted with modern absurdist world.

1904.   [CAIN] Telle, Emile, "Trois contes érasmiques et une note sur
        More," *Moreana*, 15-16 (1967), 63-74.

        Erasmus on Cain.

1905.   [CALENDAR] Dunlop, Alexander, "Calendar Symbolism in the
        Amoretti," *NQ*, 16 (1969), 24-26.

        A few months, not years, confine the "story" with a central
        group of 47 sonnets reflecting days in Lent, 1594. Exact
        structural parallelism involving 21 sonnets before the Lenten
        group and 21 after it suggests symbolic pattern. Sonnets
        linked to Spenser's marriage that year; *Epithalamion* culminates
        the whole. (Cf. [NUMBER SYMBOLISM].)

1906.   [CELEBRANT, Comic] Guthrie, William Bowman, "The Comic Cele-
        brant of Life," *DA*, 29 (1969), 3098-A (Vanderbilt Univ.).

        To exemplify nature of the celebrant: five characters, one
        each from Aristophanes, Rabelais, Chaucer, Shakespeare, and
        Fielding. Falstaff opposes the unnatural and repressive for-
        ces of war, honor, and the state.

1907.   [CENSORSHIP] Devereux, E.J., "Elizabeth Barton and Tudor Cen-
        sorship," *Bull. of the John Rylands Library*, 49 (1966), 91-106.

        Discusses one case of Tudor censorship, intending thereby to
        show the variety of methods of achieving censorship; leading
        up to the passing of the Proclamation of 1538 requiring that

books be examined and licensed before being printed. This
Proclamation was the rule in force during Shakespeare's career.

1908. [CENSORSHIP] Rostenberg, Leona, _The Minority Press & the English Crown: A Study in Repression, 1558-1625._ Nieuwkoop:
B. de Graaf, 1971.

Includes study of the Catholic press, spying and official response, the Archpriest controversy, James I and censorship,
underground Catholic stationers, seminary presses, foreign
circulation of royal texts.

1909. [CENSORSHIP] Thomas, Donald, _A Long Time Burning: The History
of Literary Censorship in England._ N.Y.: Praeger, 1969.

Rev. _Historian_, 32 (1970), 485-486.

Traces history of English literary censorship from William Caxton to Hugh Selby. After surveying era of pre-publication
control, it explores evolution of post-publication suppression,
used in 18th cent. principally against works considered sedi-
tious or blasphemous.

1910. [CHANGELING] Haffter, Carl, "The Changeling: History and Psy-
chodynamics of Attitudes to Handicapped Children in European
Folklore," _Journal of the Hist. of the Behav. Sciences_, 4
(1968), 55-61.

Deformed child or "changeling" studied within framework of
Christian demonology; sins of parents viewed as punished by
child being stolen and "changeling" put in its place, the deformed child bearing stigma, sign of offense against God.

1911. [CHARACTERS, Folk] Malin, Stephen D., "Character Origins in
the English Folk Play," _DA_, 30 (1969), 637-638-A (Univ. of
Florida).

Origins of stock characters of English folk play: the Blackman, the Hobby Horse, the Man-Woman, the Doctor, and the Fool.

1912. [CHARITY] McCreary, Eugene Patrick, "Charity and Related Principles in the Writings of Sir Francis Bacon and Sir Thomas
Browne," _DA_, 30 (1970), 732-A (Univ. of Ill.).

Their concepts of charity as function of their religious
theories.

1913. [CHARITY] Pincus, Debra D., "A Hand by Antonio Rizzo and the
Double Caritas Scheme of the Tron Tomb," _Art Bulletin_, 51
(1969), 247-256.

The two female figures that flank the Doge represent two aspects of charity, _amor proximi_ and _amor Dei_.

1914. [CHASE] Allen, Michael J.B., "The Chase: The Development of a
Renaissance Theme," _CL_, 20 (1968), 301-312. (Cf. [HUNT].)

On related images of the chase, wound, deer, and woman; growing complexity of punning and symbolism.

1915.   [CHASE] Thiébaux, Marcelle, "The Mediaeval Chase," *Speculum*, 42 (1967), 260-274.

Hunting and its special terminology in the Middle Ages, of relevance to Renaissance.

1916.   [CHASER CHASED] Hamer, Douglas, "Shakespeare: Sonnet 143," *NQ*, 16 (1969), 129-130.

Image in Sonnet 143 of the chaser chased derives from English translation of Luigi Pasqualigo's comedy *Il Fedele*, under title *Fedele and Fortunio*.

1917.   [CHASTITY] Pearse, Nancy Cotton, "Mirrors of Modesty: Fletcher's Chastity Plays," *DA*, 30 (1970), 4422-A (Columbia Univ.).

Objections to Fletcher's morality arise from Romantic misconceptions regarding their cultural contexts. Appendix B lists Elizabethan chastity-literature prior to *Faithful Shepherdess*.

1918.   [CHIVALRY] Narkinsky, Johnny McNeil, "Lope de Vega's Chivalric Plays: The Technique of Handling the Chivalric Themes and A Study of the Plays [Portions of the text in Spanish," *DA*, 30 (1970), 5453-A (Florida State Univ.).

Lope's concepts of the chivalric more closely aligned to the Renaissance than to late medieval ideals. He upholds ideals of courtiership while ridiculing conventions of chivalric literature.

1919.   [CHRISTMAS] Kup, Karl, "The Christmas Story in Medieval and Renaissance Manuscripts from the Spencer Collection," *Bull. New York Public Library*, 73 (1969), 625-749.

Selection of illuminated and illustrated medieval and Renaissance manuscripts to illustrate the Christmas story. Commentary on the illustrations.

1920.   [CIRCLE] Greene, Thomas M., "Ben Jonson and the Centered Self," *SEL*, 10 (1970), 325.

Image of the circle and the center (the first representing perfection, the second political or personal center, i.e., king, ruler, or inner self), in plays, masques, and poems.

1921.   [CITY] Mazzolani, Lidia Storoni, *The Idea of the City in Roman Thought: From Walled City to Spiritual Commonwealth*. Trans. from Italian. London: Hollis and Carter, 1970.

Rev. *NQ*, February 1973, 79.

City as related to *civitas*. Roman view of city as both closed and exclusive of strangers; and ecumenical, as in Stoicism and citizenry of world. (Cf. such plays as *Cor.*, etc.)

1922.   [CLEOPATRA] Morris, Helen, "Queen Elizabeth I 'Shadowed' in Cleopatra," *HLQ*, 32 (1969), 271-278.

Attempts to show from contemporary evidence that portrait of Cleopatra in Shakespeare's main source, North's translation of Plutarch's *Lives*, reminded Shakespeare of Queen Elizabeth in many details and that this resemblance was at the back of his mind while he was writing the play.

1923. [CLEOPATRA] Muir, Kenneth, "Elizabeth I, Jodelle, and Cleopatra," *RenD*, n.s. 2 (1969), 197-206.

Points to parallel between Cleopatra's questioning of the messenger about Octavia and Elizabeth I's questioning of James Melville about Mary, Queen of Scots.

1924. [CLOTHES] Debax, J.-P., "Macbeth et la tradition de la Moralité avec référence particulière aux images vestimentaires," *Ann. publ. Fac. Lettres Sci. hum. Toulouse*, 4 no. 1 (1968), 15-29.

Vestimentary images in *Mac.* with reference to morality. How Shakespeare separates himself from medieval tradition of the Fall.

1925. [COLORS] Ostheeren, Klaus, "Toposforschung und Bedeutungslehre: Die Glanzvorstellung im Schönheitskatalog und die mittelenglischen Farbadjective *blak* und *brown*," *Anglia*, 89 (1971), 1-47.

Conventional uses of color in feminine description. Documentation. (Cf. 634, 635, 1463.)

1926. [COMEDY], Brittain, R.L., "A Catalogue of Comic and Satiric Scenes in English Drama--1375-1500," *DA*, 31 (1970), 2334-A (Auburn Univ.).

Development of comic and satiric elements in cycle dramas and interludes as peculiarly English. Structure of English comic and satiric drama as built upon foundation of more than 200 years before Elizabethan drama appeared.

1927. [COMEDY] Hilger, Michael John, "The Rhetoric of Comedy: Comic Theory in the Terentian Commentary of Aelius Donatus," *DA*, 31 (1970), 1759-A (Univ. of Nebraska).

Donatus' rhetorical approach to analysis of comedy, its plot, character, style. Comedy seen as embodiment of universal truth. Comic diction and use of logic, and Donatus' influence on Elizabethan grammar schools.

1928. [COMPLAINT] Dean, Nancy, "Chaucer's *Complaint*: A Genre Descended from the *Heroides*," *Comp. Lit.*, 19 (1967), 1-27.

Planctus tradition; Ovid in French literature, and Chaucer.

1929. [COMPOSITE MISTRESS] Gibson, C.A., "Massinger's Composite Mistress," *AUMLA*, no. 29 (1968), 44-51.

Praise of mistress as having beauties of various goddesses. Continues K.K. Ruthven, *ibid.*, no. 26 (1966), 198-214.

1930.   [CONSCIENCE] Araud, R., "Le Traité de la Conscience chez
        Suarez: Analyse de la Conscience," *Sci. et Esprit*, Pt. 1:
        20, no. 1 (1968), 59-76; Pt. 2:   10, no. 2 (1968), 269-290.

        Analysis of the Suarez text: definition of conscience; its
        main features (rectitude, certainty, obligation).   Suarez's
        contributions; strengths and weaknesses; his influence on
        modern thought.

1931.   [CONSCIENCE] Bergamaschi, Aldo, "Grandeur et limites d'une
        conscience chrétienne: Thomas More," *Études Francis.*, 17,
        no. 48 (1968), 363-375.

        More's Christian conscience: a response to both universal and
        temporal truth.

1932.   [CONSCIENCE] Kelly, Kevin T., *Conscience: Dictator or Guide?
        A Study in Seventeenth-Century English Protestant Moral Theo-
        logy*.   London: Geoffrey Chapman, 1967.

        Rev. *Ampleforth Journal*, 73 (1968), 87-88; *Heythrop Journal*, 9
        (1968), 235; *Journal of Ecclesiastical Hist.*, 19 (1968), 262-
        263.

        Begun as study of Thomistic influences in Anglican theologians,
        then limited to an area of moral discussion in their writings
        and evaluation from the standpoint of Aquinas' "right reason."
        Includes William Perkins, William Ames, Robert Sanderson.   Suc-
        cessor to H.R. McAdoo, *The Structure of Anglican Moral Theo-
        logy* (London, 1959); K.E. Kirk, *Some Principles of Moral Theo-
        logy* (London, 1946).

1933.   [CONSCIENCE] Markham, Coleman Cain, "William Perkins' Under-
        standing of the Function of Conscience," *DA*, 28 (1968), 4256-A
        (Vanderbilt Univ.).

        On the role of William Perkins (1558-1602) in providing a
        Reform theological basis, with aim of demonstrating how faith
        worked itself out in life.   Conscience, the central factor in
        his writings, is the mediator between soteriology and ethics,
        faith and works.   Perkins' interest was more practical than
        theoretical, as shown by his illustration of the role of con-
        science in a wide range of social relationships, public as
        well as private.

1934.   [CONSCIENCE] Nelson, Benjamin, "Scholastic *Rationales* of 'Con-
        science,' Early Modern Crises of Credibility, and the Scienti-
        fic-Technocultural Revolutions of the 17th and 20th Centuries,"
        Jour. for the Sci. Study of Religion, 7 (1968), 157-177.

        Part of series: "The *Protestant Ethic* beyond Weber."   Includes
        "Protestant Reformation and Scientific Revolution: 16th-17th
        Century."   Protestant Reformation and successful challenge to
        the Court of Conscience and other directive agencies of the
        medieval church.

1935.   [CONSCIENCE] Schroeder, Mary C., "The Character of Conscience
        in *Piers Plowman*," *SP*, 67 (1970), 13-30.

Personification of theological concept interacting with other
characters. Blend of scholastic synderesis and conscience.

1936. [CONSCIENCE] Smith, Lacy Baldwin, "A Matter of Conscience," in
_Action and Conviction in Modern Europe: Essays in Memory of
E.H. Harbison_, ed. T.K. Rabb and J.E. Seigel. Princeton Univ.
Press, 1969, pp. 32-51.

On Henry VIII's "conscience," viewed as intense, real, and
tender.

1937. [CONSCIENCE] Woodson, William Charles, "Elizabethan Villains
and the Seared Conscience: The Application of a Theological
Concept to Suggest the Credibility of Barabas, Aaron, Richard
III, and Iago," _DA_, 30 (1969), 1154-1155-A (Univ. of Pennsylvania).

On historical accuracy of assumption that real criminals must
be troubled in their conscience; dramatic credibility of these
four villains. It is unhistorical to expect villains with
"seared consciences" to be bothered by moral guilt.

1938. [CONSCIENCE, CASE OF] Slights, Camille Ann Wells, "The In-
genious Piety of the Anglican Casuists: The Case Divinity of
Robert Sanderson, Thomas Barlow, and Jeremy Taylor," _DA_, 28
(1968), 4145-A (Cornell Univ.).

"Case of conscience" is a prose form which flourished in England between 1600 and 1700; examples here chosen range from
1650 to 1660. A characteristic form of Renaissance English
casuistry, case of conscience attempts to provide the per-
plexed conscience with means of reconciling obligations of
religious faith with demands of particular human problems.
In case of conscience, casuist poses a difficult moral problem
and solves it, with display of ingenuity or erudition.

1939. [_CONSOLATIO_] Christmas, Robert A., "Chaucer's _Tale of Melibe_:
Its Tradition and Its Function in Fragment VII of the _Canter-
bury Tales_," _DA_, 29 (1969), 3093-A (Univ. of Southern Calif.).

Places tale in _consolatio_ tradition; closest analogue is
Boethius's _Consolation of Philosophy_.

1940. [_CONSOLATIO_] Courcelle, Pierre, _La Consolation de Philosophie
dans la tradition littéraire: Antécédents et posterité de
Boèce_. Paris: Études Augustiniennes, 1967.

Rev. P. Dronke, _Spec._, 44 (1969), 123-128.

Boethius did not try to synthesize Christian and neo-platonic;
author stresses neo-platonic character of the _Consolatio_.
Major study of Boethian influence.

1941. [_CONSOLATIO_] West, Michael, "The _Consolatio_ in Milton's
Funeral Elegies," _HLQ_, 34 (1971), 233-249.

Renaissance topos traced--varying a set theme. Renaissance
concept of decorum.

1942. [CONVERSION] Ware, James Montgomery, "The Conversion Theme in
       English Drama to 1575," *DA*, 31 (1970), 1777-A (Claremont Grad.
       School).

       Influence of religious dogma and dramaturgy, especially after
       Reformation. Although Calvinism encouraged and even methodized
       dramatic conversion experience, in its earlier stages it threw
       conversion into disrepute. Reacting against Catholic morality
       plays, it treated rebirth theme ironically, thereby loosening
       the hold of religion on drama, at start of London professional
       theater.

1943. [COSMOS] Carscallen, James, "The Goodly Frame of Temperance:
       The Metaphor of Cosmos in *The Faerie Queene*, Book II," *UTQ*,
       37, no. 2 (1967/68), 136-155.

       Metaphor of harmonious universal proportions reveals the order
       of Spenser's Book II. Adds scheme based on four elements to
       interpretation of this book.

1944. [COURTESY] Culp, Dorothy Woodward, "The Bands of Civility: A
       Study of Spenser's Theory of Courtesy," *DA*, 28 (1967), 1392-A
       (Columbia Univ.).

       Discusses "courtesy" as a moral virtue helping to form founda-
       tion of human society. Especially concerned with Bk. VI of
       Faerie Queene. Chapters on social virtues: justice, charity,
       and courtesy; allegory and romance; discourtesy and the self-
       pleasing mind; the bands of civility.

1945. [COURTESY] Moretti, Walter, *Cortesia e furore nel Rinascimento
       Italiano*. Bologna: Casa Editrice Patron, 1970.

       Includes: La Cortesia nell' "Innamorato" e nel "Furioso"; Il
       Furore nella "Liberata." Parte Terza: Guerra e pace nella
       letteratura italiano del Cinquecento. Ch. I: Magnanimità e
       malinconia. Ch. II: Il "mirabile" e il "patetico."

1946. [COURTIER] Bonadeo, Alfredo, "The Function and Purpose of the
       Courtier in *The Book of the Courtier* by Castiglione," *PQ*, 50
       (1971), 36-46.

       Role of courtier as man of superior abilities; his relation to
       his lord, as moral and political adviser.

1947. [COURTIER, Anti-] Smith, Pauline R., *The Anti-Courtier Trend
       in Sixteenth-Century French Literature*. (Travaux d'Humanisme
       et Ren., 84.) Geneva: Droz, 1966.

1948. [COVENANT] Greaves, Richard L., "The Origins and Early Develop-
       ment of English Covenant Thought," *Historian*, 31 (1968), 21-35.

       On the development and influence of often-neglected Zwingli
       and Tyndale, and their contribution to stream of 17th-cent.
       covenant thought.

1949. [COVENANT] Hillers, Delbert R., *Covenant: The History of a
       Biblical Idea*. Baltimore: Johns Hopkins Press, 1969.

Analyses of biblical and secular documents, and new archaeological discoveries in Near East, toward exposition of complex
OT idea of covenant.

1950.   [COVENANT] Priebe, Victor Lewis, "The Covenant Theology of William Perkins," *DA*, 28 (1967), 1893-A (Drew Univ.).

Two concerns of Perkins (1558-1602), personal nature of salvation and demand for total ethical responsibility, are united
in his concept of the covenant. Affirming salvation by grace
alone, he nevertheless demands that man must always respond
to God's gracious action toward him by radical obedience shown
by his concrete action in the world. Covenant relationship
thus provides basis for man's relation to God and the world,
his radical obedience providing a basic tension to the world
even while fully immersed in it. His worldly position must
therefore be ambivalent, his relationship both relevant and
transecndent. Conscience is not merely moral, but the God-
word stance of the believer as God's servant in the world.
Perkins' popularity held to be based not on his talent for
simplification, but on the contemporary relevance of his
theology.

1951.   [CREATION] Berkowitz, David Sandler, *In Remembrance of Creation: Evolution of Art and Scholarship in the Medieval and
Renaissance Bible.* Waltham, Mass.: Brandeis Univ. Press,
1968.

Rev. *LibJ,* 41 (1968), 1884; *TLS,* 28 November 1968, 1348.

Catalogue: manuscripts, incunabula, 16th-cent. scholarly editions, and 16th- and 17th-cent. translations of Bible. Introduction relates Hebrew and Christian tradition and textual
scholarship; all items described and annotated.

1952.   [CREATION] Ehrhardt, Arnold, *The Beginning: A Study in the
Greek Philosophical Approach to the Concept of Creation from
Anaximander to St. John.* N.Y.: Barnes and Noble, 1968.

Rev. *Choice,* 6 (1969), 378.

On Greek philosophy up to Aristotle; investigates semantic
problems of the concept of creation in comparative texts.

1953.   [CREATION] Feinstein, Blossom Grayer, "Creation and Theories
of Creativity in English Poetry of the Renaissance," *DA*, 28
(1967), 1394-A (City Univ. of N.Y.).

On Renaissance views of creation: orthodox Christian *ex
nihilo*; and heterodox theories of creation from chaos, held
in cosmogonies of Near East, and known to the Renaissance
through numerous channels. Poets interested in this second
view display fascination with grotesque motifs of the "*ex
chaos*" cosmogonies. Great Renaissance writers display conflict between the two views in their work. Implications of *ex
chaos* are affirmed, in part, in *Ant., Tro.,* and *Tmp.*

1954.   [CREATION] ———, "The *Faerie Queene* and Cosmogonies of the
Near East," *JHI*, 29 (1968), 531-550.

Questions general view of English Renaissance, based largely
on Tillyard's world picture, that its heritage is wholly classical and Hebrew-Christian. English poetry in some passages
affirms chaos as source of creation, disorder as value equal
to that of order, and creative principle as double and sexual
in nature. These have affinities to cosmogonies of the Near
East. *Faerie Queene* studied in that light.

1955.   [CREATION] Ghisalberti, A., "La controversia scolastica sulla
creazione 'ab aeterno,'" *Riv. Filos. neo-scolast.*, 60, no. 2-3
(1968), 211-230.

Aquinas' position and that of Franciscan school with respect
to Averroists and Augustinians.

1956.   [CREATION] Lifson, Martha Ronk, "The Theme of Creation in
Paradise Lost," *DA*, 29 (1969), 3976-A (Yale Univ.).

Book VII in regard to poetic and theological works about creation by Plato, Philo, Augustine, Basil, Ambrose, Gregory of
Nyssa, Du Bartas, Calvin, Luther, and Spenser. Milton's presentation is a dramatic account of unfallen golden world.

1957.   [CREATION] Rech, Photina, *Inbild des Kosmos. Eine Symbolik
der Schöpfung.* Salzburg: Müller, 1966.

Creation as prefiguration of Christ; abundance of symbols related to incarnate god as symbol. Discussions of single symbols, lion, eagle, deer, etc. Focus on Biblical-Christian
tradition, but includes Oriental, Indian, Buddhist, and natural
symbolic thinking.

1958.   [CROSS] Brundage, J.A., "'Cruce Signari': The Rite for Taking
the Cross in England," *Traditio*, 22 (1966), 289-310.

Liturgical textual evidence on origin and character of cross-
bestowing ceremony in England. Developed out of ceremony for
blessing insignia of pilgrims; there arose in England variety
of interrelated formulas for this ceremony; traditional English forms for these blessings persisted until end of 15th
cent.

1959.   [CROSS] Ulbert-Schede, Ute, *Das Andachtsbild des kreuztragen-
den Christus in der deutschen Kunst, von den Anfängen bis zum
Beginn des 16. Jahrhunderts.* Munich: Uni-Druck, 1968.

History of the image of Christ bearing the cross.

1960.   [DAPHNE] Giraud, Y.F.-A., *La fable de Daphné. Essai sur un
type de métamorphose végétale dans la littérature et dans les
arts jusqu'à la fin du XVIIe siècle.* Geneva: Droz, 1968.

1961.   [DAPHNE] Rees, Christine, "The Metamorphosis of Daphne in Six-
teenth- and Seventeenth-Century English Poetry," *MLR*, 66
(1971), 251-263.

Renaissance allegorical interpretations of her virtue; use by
Milton in *Comus*. Persuasion-to-love theme and rejection of
metamorphosis. (From Ovid to Marvell.)

1962. [DARKNESS] Bement, Peter, "The Imagery of Darkness and of Light in Chapman's *Bussy d'Ambois*," *SP*, 64 (1967), 187-198.

Bussy (Act I) identified with "true" darkness and values of mental contemplation and mystical knowledge; trades these for daylight corruption of court and physical movement. Play returns to false darkness of moral confusion.

1963. [DARKNESS] Maurin, Margaret S., "The Monster, the Sepulchre, and the Dark: Related Patterns of Imagery in *La Vida es Sueño*," *HR*, 35 (1967), 161-178.

1964. [DEATH] Choron, Jacques, *Der Tod im abendländischen Denken*, trans. with bibliography. Stuttgart: Ernst Klett, 1967.

Rev. *Philosophischer Literaturanzeiger*, 21 (1968), 71-78.

1965. [DEATH] Doebler, B.A., "Donne's Debt to the Great Tradition: Old and New in His Treatment of Death," *Anglia*, 85 (1967), 15-33. (Cf. [ARS MORIENDI].)

Death as man's crowning glory, unity with God; man should prepare for it joyfully.

1966. [DEATH] Friedrich, H., "Montaigne et la mort," *Preuves*, 18, no. 2 (1968), 26-39.

Various aspects of death throughout *Essais*.

1967. [DEATH] Ingham, Muriel Brierly, "Some Fifteenth-Century Images of Death and Their Background," *DA*, 28 (1968), 4132-4133-A (Univ. of Calif., Riverside).

Secularization of themes in 15th-cent. images of death: shift from emphasis on *contemptus mundi* and *memento mori* to ironic comment and raillery, and to this-worldly aspects of death.

1968. [DEATH] Naumann, Walter, "Staub, entbrannt in Liebe: Das Thema von Tod und Liebe bei Properz, Quevedo, und Goethe," *Arcadia*, 3 (1968), 157-172.

1969. [DEATH] Richter, Mario, "Lettura dei 'Sonnets de la Mort' di Jean de Sponde," *BHR*, 30 (1968), 327-345.

Poems on death related to turbulent Calvinist years, 1570-1590.

1970. [DEATH] Robbins, Rossell Hope, "Signs of Death in Middle English," *MS*, 32 (1970), 282-298.

Shows how signs of death found in moralizing religious verse and in medical collections serve two functions: to ascertain whether a sick person will live or die and to warn the dying sinner to repent. Presents texts through 15th-cent. previously unprinted.

1971. [DEATH] Stone, Donald, Jr., "Death in the Third Book of Montaigne's *Essais*," *Esprit Créateur*, 8 (1968), 185-193.

Compares Montaigne's treatment of death in Book Three with that in Book One; concludes that reassessment of attitudes in

the former is already present in the latter; community of
ideas between the periods covered by the two.

1972.   [DEATH] Thon, Peter, "Bruegel's 'The Triumph of Death' Recon-
        sidered," *RenQ*, 21 (1968), 289-297.

        Interpretation of this painting, through a consideration of
        the artist's personal experience and values and the history of
        the Netherlands in the 1560's. Traditional motif and themes
        provide a vehicle for surreptitious political criticism.

1973.   [DEATH, Dance of] Garther, John Maxwell, "La Dança General de
        la Muerte: Symbol of a Declining Age," *DA*, 31 (1970), 2342-A
        (St. Louis Univ.).

        Medieval attitude toward death and probable influences on this
        attitude, e.g., Black Plague, monasticism, and Greek ideas.
        La Dança as the relation of literature to life.

1974.   [DEATH; JUDGMENT] Duvall, Robert Fenton, "The Theater of
        Judgement: The Representation of Death and Judgement in Jaco-
        bean Tragedy," *DA*, 31 (1970), 354-A (Claremont Grad. School).

        These themes in early 17th-cent. drama as reflection of intel-
        lectual and moral milieu.

1975.   [DECORUM] Moore, N.A.N., "Ben Jonson's Concept of Decorum: A
        Study of His Theory and Three Comedies," *DA*, 30 (1969), 286-A
        (Univ. of Ill.).

        Discusses what 16th-cent. theoreticians said about decorum
        and examines Jonson's own theory; he is concerned with suiting
        style to subject, language to speaker, and language to occa-
        sion and tone.

1976.   [Weeping DEER] Uhlig, Claus, "Der weinende Hirsch: *AYL*, II.i.
        21-66, und der historische Kontext," *SJH*, 1968, 141-168. (Ex-
        panded trans. in *Ren. Drama*, n.s. 3 [1970], 79-109.)

        Thematic and emblematic background of First Lord's Speech in
        AYL carefully traced. (For stricken deer in 18th cent.,
        especially Cowper, see J.H. Owen, "The Stricken Deer and the
        Emblem Tradition," *NYPL Bull.*, 75 [1971], 66-78.)

1977.   [*DESENGAÑO*] Schulte, Hansgerd, *El Desengaño. Wort und Thema
        in der spanischen Literatur des Goldenen Zeitalters*. Munich:
        Wilhelm Fink, 1969.

        Historical investigation of the word "desengaño," undeceives;
        focus on the spiritual, moral, and literary coherence of Span-
        ish Golden Age.

1978.   [DESPAIR] Bowe, Elaine Campbell, "Doctrines and Images of Des-
        pair in Christopher Marlowe's *Doctor Faustus* and Edmund Spen-
        ser's *The Faerie Queene*," *DA*, 29 (1969), 2206-A (Univ. of
        Oregon).

        Religious discussions of despair influenced treatment of des-
        pair in tragedy and epic. Review of Christian traditions.
        Images in discourses on despair are classified.

1979. [DESPAIR] Scrimgeour, James, "The 'Ougly Shape': Despair in Early English Drama," *Massachusetts Stud. in English*, 1 (1968), 75-87.

Examines four representative plays; treatment of despair in Elizabethan drama developed out of early morality plays, from an "idealistic" to a more "existential" one.

1980. [DEVIL] Baird, Joseph L., "The Devil in Green," *Neuphil. Mitteil*, 69, no. 4 (1968), 575-578.

Evidence for folk tradition of dressing the devil in green existing at the time of Chaucer's "Friar's Tale." These devils in green furnish evidence of a metaphor out of patristic exegesis influencing folk tradition.

1981. [DEVIL] Kelly, Henry Ansgar, *The Devil, Demonology and Witchcraft: The Development of Christian Beliefs in Evil Spirits.* N.Y.: Doubleday, 1968. (*Towards the Death of Satan: The Growth and Decline of Christian Demonology.* London: Geoffrey Chapman, 1968.)

Rationalist approach to theological question of Christian beliefs in evil spirits, with Scriptural references. On demonology, including Shakespearean; examination of scripture and tradition with a view to the demise of Christian demonology; devil worship, superstition, and witchcraft as deformation of Christian church.

1982. [DEVIL] Patrides, C.A., "The Salvation of Satan," *JHI*, 28 (1967), 467-478.

Renaissance views on belief in Satan's possible salvation or restoration to grace (apocatastasis); Renaissance and Protestant reformers who strictly denied such possible restitution.

1983. [DEVIL] Roos, Keith Leroy, "The Devil-Books of the Sixteenth Century: Their Sources and Their Significance During the Second Half of the Century," *DA*, 29 (1968), 1518-A (Rice Univ.).

Written between 1545 and 1604 were the "Teufelbücher"; 39 devil books were composed which went through over 100 further editions before the end of the 16th cent. Such works attribute every vice to a specialized devil, against which the devil book is directed and after which it is named. This study relates them to other forms and concerns of contemporary moral didactic literature, as well as to the idea of the pact with the Devil.

1984. [DIDO] Lord, Mary Louise, "Dido as an Example of Chastity: The Influence of Example Literature," *Harvard Library Bull.*, 17 (1969), 22-44; 216-231.

Two contrasting roles of Dido: chaste queen who committed suicide rather than marry her African suitor, Iarbas, and tragic victim of love of Aeneas. Despite Dido's passionate love for Aeneas, early Church Fathers gave impetus to Dido as *exemplum virtutis*. Pt. II on persistence in literature of tradition of the chaste Dido.

1985. [DIDO] Schmitz, Alfred, "Quelques Aspects du personnage de Didon chez Virgile," in *Conférences de la Société d'Études Latines de Bruxelles, 1965-1966* (*Latomus: Revue d'Etudes Latines*, 1968), pp. 25-46.

1986. [DIDO] Schramm, Harold B., "William Gager and the Dido Tradition in English Drama of the Renaissance," *DA*, 30 (1970), 3919-A (Univ. of Delaware).

Dido tradition from classical times through Gager and Marlowe, emphsizing Gager's *Dido*. Includes critical edition and translation of this play with textual and explanatory notes.

1987. [DOG; WOLF] Lurker, Manfred, "Hund und Wolf in ihrer Beziehung zum Tode," *Antaios*, 10 (1969), 199-216.

Dog and wolf and the gate to the abyss; harbingers of death and executioner; devouring beast. Ambivalence of dog and wolf.

1988. [DOLPHIN] Johnson, W. McAllister, "A 'Biface' Medal of Henry II?" *JWCI*, 30 (1967), 401-403.

On medal of Henry II dated 1555.

1989. [DON JUAN] Singer, Armand E., "Second Supplement to the 'Don Juan' Theme, Versions, and Criticism: A Bibliography (1965)," *West Va. Univ. Bull. Philol. Papers*, 17 (1970), 102-170, 171-178.

Incorporates first supplement (*ibid.*, 15 [1966], 76-78) with new information.

1990. [DRAGON] Hughes, M.Y., "Satan 'Now Dragon Grown' (*Paradise Lost*, X, 529)," *Et. angl.*, 20, no. 4 (1967), 357-369.

Satan's transformation into a dragon and its neo-platonic, Jungian, etc., interpretations.

1991. [DRAGON] Kaske, Carol V., "The Dragon's Spark and Sting and the Structure of Red Cross's Dragon-fight: *The Faerie Queene*, I. xi-xii," *SP*, 66 (1969), 609-638.

Three-day structure of battle is re-enactment of mankind's struggle for deliverance from "that old dragon" in three states of human nature.

1992. [DREAM] Bloch, Ralph Howard, "A Study of the Dream Motif in the Old French Narrative," *DA*, 31 (1970), 2334-A (Stanford Univ.).

History of theme in classical and patristic literature.

1993. [DREAM] Garber, Marjorie Beth, "The Size of Dreaming: Uses of Dream in Shakespeare," *DA*, 31 (1970), 1227-A (Yale Univ.).

Dreams and their relation to central themes in Shakespeare; illusion vs. reality, transformation and metamorphosis, etc., reflecting an awareness of Renaissance dream tradition.

1994. [DREAM] Hawkins, Harriet, "Jonson's Use of Traditional Dream Theory in *The Vision of Delight*," *MP*, 64 (1967), 285-292.

Kinds of dreams in Jonson's masque seen against background of traditional dream theory. Possible source is Macrobius' *In Somnium Scipionis*, noting that dreams between nightfall and sunrise gradually increase in significance. In final vision before sunrise, the ideal merges with the factual, the king, in Jonson's work, being present both as member of audience and symbol of ideal monarch on stage.

1995. [DREAM] Hieatt, Constance B., *The Realism of Dream Vision: The Poetic Exploitation of the Dream-Experience in Chaucer and His Contemporaries*. De Proprietatibus Litterarum, Series Practica, 2. Hague/Paris: Mouton, 1967.

1996. [DREAM] Presson, Robert K., "Two Types of Dreams in the Elizabethan Drama, and Their Heritage: *Somnium Animale* and the Prick of Conscience," *Studies in English Literature*, 7 (1967), 239-256.

Presson defines the *Somnium Animale* as a dream in which the dreamer repeats the actions of his waking hours. He traces this form of dream through Chaucer, Boccaccio, de Meung, Claudian, and Petronius. These authors all describe catalogues of dreams, and the soldier and lover are characters that occur in all of the catalogues. The prick of conscience dream is one in which the dreamer dreams about matters that he has suppressed during the day. This is a method of revealing a moral conscience in the most depraved characters.

1997. [DREAM] Weidhorn, Manfred, "The Anxiety Dream in Literature from Homer to Milton," *Studies in Philology*, 64 (1967), 65-82.

In the Renaissance, nightmares were thought to be caused by strange demonic beings, involving a direct sexual assault on the dreamer. The paralyzed feeling was due to pressure of the creatures on the chest in committing the assault. The agitated dream was also a manifestation of this imagined experience.

1998. [DREAM] ————, "Eve's Dream and the Literary Tradition," *TSL*, 12 (1967), 39-50.

Traces occurrence of dream-motif through pagan and Christian literature to Milton.

1999. [DRUNKENNESS] Malet, J., "Rotrou: la métaphore de l'ivresse dans *Les Sosies*," *Revue des Sciences Humaines*, 133 (1969), 13-17.

Key to Rotrou's comedy in metaphor of drunkenness, a drunkenness which arises from sentiment of honor and of glory which feeds it, and an inebriation which comes from wine. First is characteristic of mankind; the other, of the gods, both capable of confusing reality and illusion on two apparently independent levels.

2000. [DRUNKENNESS] Telle, Emile V., "Thomas More, *Theotimus* et l'Ivresse," *Moreana*, no. 21 (1969), 15-17.

Reference to More in Gabriel Dupuyherbault's *Theotimus* (1549), concerning the dangers of drunkenness, a vice discussed by

the Church Fathers which, like gluttony, received renewed re-
probation in the 16th cent.

2001. [DRUNKENNESS] Williams, Clyde V., "Taverners, Tapsters, and
Topers: A Study of Drinking and Drunkenness in the Literature
of the English Renaissance," *DA*, 30 (1969), 1539-A (Louisiana
State Univ.).

Drinking references and scenes are practically omnipresent in
literature of the English Renaissance; in overwhelming majority of cases, these references fall into one or more of three
categories--realistic, comic, moral.

2002. [EAST] Goldberg, Jonathan, "Donne's Journey East: Aspects of
a Seventeenth-Century Trope," *SP*, 68 (1971), 470-483.

Christian symbolism of East; relations to Donne's "Goodfriday,
1613. Riding Westward," where a journey west is reunderstood
as an eastward journey.

2003. [EGG] Newall, V., "Easter Eggs," *JAF*, 80 (1967), 3-32.

Symbolism of egg in various cultures and European Christian
tradition.

2004. [EGYPT] Roullet, Anne H.M., "The Survival and Rediscovery of
Egyptian Antiquities in Western Europe from Late Antiquity
until the Close of the Sixteenth Century." (Directors, J.J.
Seznec and J.R. Harris.) Oxford D. Phil., 1969.

2005. [EGYPT] Wortham, John David, "*Uraeus*: A History of British
Interest in the Antiquities of Egypt in the Sixteenth, Seventeenth, Eighteenth, and Nineteenth Centuries," *DA*, 28 (1968),
4075-A (Univ. of Texas).

Account of the development of knowledge of ancient Egypt in
England, 1586-1906.

2006. [ELEPHANTS] Lach, Donald F., "Asian Elephants in Renaissance
Europe," *Journal of Asian History*, 1 (1967), 133-176.

Detailed and documented. Traced from antiquity through
Renaissance.

2007. [ELIZABETH] Northrop, Douglas A., "Spenser's Defence of Elizabeth," *UTQ*, 38 (1969), 277-294.

Praise of Elizabeth's justice and mercy in Book V of *FQ* is not
idle adulation. This praise was meant to meet specific criti-
cisms of Queen; Book V of *FQ* is closely related to the controversial literature of the time. There were two controversies
that involved defence of Elizabeth: right of women to rule,
and justice of her actions as ruler.

2008. [ELIZABETH] Salman, Phillips Cranston, "Spenser's Representation of Queen Elizabeth I," *DA*, 30 (1969), 2498-2499-A (Columbia Univ.).

Principal ways in which Spenser's portrait of the public and
private persons of Queen Elizabeth I may have delighted Elizabeth and her subjects and instructed them in virtue.

2009. [EMBLEM] Bertonasco, Marc F., "Crashaw and the Emblem," *ES*,
49 (1968), 530-534.

Traces a number of Crashaw's key images to specific sources in
emblem books of 17th cent.

2010. [EMBLEM] Goldman, Lloyd, "Samuel Daniel's *Delia* and the Emblem
Tradition," *JEGP*, 67 (1968), 49-63.

Daniel's conscious use of traditional emblems and desire for
controlling emblem governing his conceits.

2011. [EMBLEM] Greschat, Martin, "Die Funktion des Emblems in Johann
Arnds 'Wahrem Christentum,'" *ZRG*, 20 (1968), 154-174.

Illustrated study of use of emblems in 17th-cent. theological
works.

2012. [EMBLEM] Henkel, Arthur, and Albrecht Schöne, *Emblemata*.
Handbuch zur Sinnbildkunst des XVI. und XVII. Jahrhunderts.
Im Auftrage der Göttinger Akademie der Wissenschaften. Stutt-
gart: J.B. Metzlersche Verlagsbuchhandlung, 1967.

Rev. *JEGP*, 67 (1968), 656-672. Useful review article by Henri
Stegemeier appends (pp. 661-672) bibliographic omissions in
the work, under following headings: I. Bibliographische Ver-
zeichnisse der Emblembüchern; II. Zeitgenössische Beiträge zur
Geschichte und Theorie der Emblematik; III. Neuere Arbeiten
zur Vorgeschichte, Geschichte und Theorie der Emblematik;
IV. Kunst- und Kulturhistorische Arbeiten; V. Literarhistori-
sche Arbeiten; VI. Ikonographische Lexika und andere Hilfs-
mittel. In addition, he lists "Some Reprints of Emblem Books"
through 1967. See rev. by W.S. Heckscher et al., *RenQ*, 23
(1970), 59-80.

Monumental illustrated dictionary-index (2,196 cols.) to Renaissance emblems, with useful indexes. (Cf. Albrecht Schöne,
Emblematik und Drama im Zeitalter des Barock [Munich: C.H.
Beck'sche Verlagsbuchhandlung, 1964]; rev. in *MLN*, 83 [1968],
480-481, listing other reviews.)

2013. [EMBLEM] Hill, Elizabeth K., "What Is an Emblem?" *JAAC*, 29
(1970), 261-265.

Emblem is a composite of the *sententia*, the picture and the
poem; it is not any one of these alone.

2014. [EMBLEM] Holtzwart, Mathias, *Emblematum Tyrocinia. Mit einem
Vorwort über Ursprung, Gebrauch und Nutz der Emblematen von
Johann Fischart und 74 Holzschnitten von Tobias Stimmer*.
Stuttgart: Reclam, 1968.

1581 Emblem book, with the oldest introduction to emblems in
German. Appendix includes translation of Latin texts,

chronological table on emblems, literary references, contemporary influence of emblems.

2015.   [EMBLEM] Homann, Holger, "Prolegomena zu einer Geschichte der Emblematik," *Colloquia Germanica*, 3 (1968), 244-257.

Conclusive definition of "emblem" has not been formulated which would obviate redefinition each time the term was discussed; author attempts such definition.

2016.   [EMBLEM] Johnson, L.W., "'Amorum emblemata': Tristan l'Hermite and the Emblematic Tradition," *RenQ*, 21 (1968), 429-441.

Evidence that Tristan worked within emblematic tradition; argues against neglect of emblem literature for 16th- and 17th-cent. French literary history.

2017.   [EMBLEM] Landwehr, John, *Emblem Books in the Low Countries 1554-1949. A Bibliography*. Utrecht: Haentjens Dekker & Gumber, 1970.

Includes general view of Dutch emblem books and indexes of printers, artists, etc.

2018.   [EMBLEM] Mehl, Dieter, "Emblematik im Englischen Drama der Shakespearezeit," *Anglia*, 87 (1969), 126-146.

While emblems and English Renaissance verse have received much attention, the connection of emblems with Renaissnance drama needs further study. Useful survey of materials in the field (including Arthur O. Lewis, "Emblem Books and English Drama: A Preliminary Survey, 1581-1600," unpublished diss., Pennsylvania State College, 1951).

2019.   [EMBLEM] ————, "Emblems in English Renaissance Drama," *RenD*, n.s. 2 (1969), 39-57.

Three ways in which emblems were used in English Renaissance drama: direct borrowing and quotations; allegorical scenes to provide a pictorial commentary on action of play; "as emblematic images in the course of a scene, as a significant construction of verbal and pictorial expression."

2020.   [EMBLEM] Miedema, Hessel, "The Term 'Emblema' in Alciati," *JWCI*, 31 (1968), 234-250.

Queries W.S. Heckscher and K.-A. Wirth's influential article, "Emblem, Emblembuch," *Reallexikon zur deutschen Kunstgeschichte* V, fasc. 49, 50, Stuttgart (1959), col. 85-228, esp. col. 85. Denies that Alciati used term *emblema* in sense in which these and other authors suppose. Suggests a more "*nuancé*" development of the concept of *emblema* even after 1550.

2021.   [EMBLEM] Morgan, Gareth, "The Emblems of *Erotocritos*," *Texas Q.*, 10 (1967), 241-264.

On Cretan song recalling 16th- and 17th-cent. emblems of heart and love.

2022. [EMBLEM] Schuman, Samuel, "The Theater of Fine Devices: Emblems and the Emblematic in the Plays of John Webster," *DA*, 30 (1970), 4425-A (Northwestern Univ.).

Relationship between English emblem books, particularly those published between 1586 and 1620, and the "dark world" of Webster's dramas.

2023. [EMBLEM] Smith, Martin R., "The *Apologia* and Emblems of Ludovico Petrucci," *BLR*, 8 (1967), 40-47.

Apologia (ca. 1619) includes emblems. Work by Italian refugee intended to demonstrate loyalty to England.

2024. [EMBLEM] Stone, Donald, Jr., "Scève's Emblems," *Romanic Review*, 60 (1969), 96-103.

Scève was more interested in the motto than in the emblem's picture; inspirational value of motto lies in its relationship to Petrarchan concepts.

2025. [EMBLEM] South, M.H., "Note on Spenser and Sir Thomas Browne," *MLR*, 62 (1967), 14-16.

Related to figure of glutton Philoxenus, who wished for longer throat to increase his pleasures.

2026. [EMBLEM] Sulzer, Dieter, "Zu einer Geschichte der Emblemtheorien," *Euphorion*, 64 (1970), 23-50.

Changing interpretations of the emblem from the "Imprese" of 16th-cent. Italy, through the "word-picture" of Renaissance culminating in its use as rhetorical device in the Baroque. Differences in Italian, French, and German interpretations through the period.

2027. [EMBLEM, French] Russell, Daniel Stearns, "A Survey of French Emblem Literature," *DA*, 30 (1969), 338-A (N.Y. Univ.).

On background of illustrated literature and pictorial allegory in France; biographical introductions to the emblemists (1536-1570). Form, iconography, and contents of four representative emblem books from this golden age of French *emblemata*. They are *Le Théâtre des bons engins* and *La Morosophie* by Guillaume de la Perrière, Gilles Corrozet's *Hécatomgraphie* and Bartelemy Aneau's *Picta poesis*.

2028. [EMBLEM, Ironical] Cockcroft, Robert, "Emblematic Irony: Some Possible Significance of Tamburlaine's Chariot," *Ren. and Modern Studs.*, 12 (1968), 33-55.

On the "pampered jades" speech. Impact of its imagery on an audience ignorant of its classical, medieval, and Renaissance emblematical and mythological context. Its immediate dramatic antecedents and sources.

2029. [ENDYMION] Colton, Judith, "The Endymion Myth and Poussin's Detroit Painting," *JWCI*, 30 (1967), 426-431.

Endymion-myth attracted Renaissance neo-Platonists. Also discusses Narcissus, Sleep, Night.

2030. [ENVY] Bond, Ronald Bruce, "A Study of *Invidia* in Medieval and
Renaissance English Literature." Unpub. Ph.D. diss. University of Toronto, 1972.

2031. [ENVY] Brenner, Myra, "Shakespeare and Elizabethan Concepts of
Envy," *DA*, 31 (1970), 1263-A (Brandeis Univ.).

Elizabethan understanding of envy as destructive force. Types
of envy, leading to different moral and psychological structures for dramatic characters.

2032. [EPITHALAMIUM] Cirillo, A.R., "Spenser's 'Epithalamion': The
Harmonious Universe of Love," *SEL*, 8, no. 1 (1968), 19-34.

Poem as celebration of harmony on all levels, in verse music
and poetic structure, in instrumental music accompanying the
feast, and in entire universe and human love as symbols of
divine harmony.

2033. [EPITHALAMIUM] McCown, Gary Mason, "The Epithalamium in the
English Renaissance," *DA*, 29 (1969), 2220-A (Univ. of North
Carolina).

Development of the genre from ancient times to Renaissance,
its revival among writers of neo-Latin, French, and Italian,
and its development in the hands of Sidney, Davies, Spenser,
Chapman, and Donne.

2034. [EPITHALAMIUM] Tufte, Virginia, *The Poetry of Marriage. The
Epithalamion in Europe and Its Development in England*. Univ.
of Southern Calif. Studies in Comp. Lit., 2, 1970.

Rev. *RenQ*, 24 (1971), 267-269; *Spenser Newsletter*, 1 (1970).

History of epithalamium; traces prescriptions for nuptial
literature through antique rhetoricians, Erasmus, Scaliger,
and Puttenham. Also a sub-genre, the anti-epithalamium.

2035. [EPYLLION] Rhinehart, Raymond Patrick, "The Elizabethan Ovidian Epyllion: A Definition and Re-evaluation," *DA*, 30 (1969),
2040-A (Princeton Univ.).

Traces the genre from Ovid through Middle Ages to English
Renaissance. Discusses Elizabethan Ovidians and representative works of the Epyllion genre.

2036. [EROS] Marcotte, Paul J., "Eros in *The Comedy of Errors*,"
Rev. de l'Univ. d'Ottawa, 38, no. 4 (1968), 642-667.

"Eros" as an objective correlative which allows Shakespeare's
concept of love to be reflected as a coherent philosophy, in-
ferable from relationships between the couples in this play.

2037. [ESAU] Cohen, Gerson D., "Esau as Symbol in Early Medieval
Thought," in Alexander Altmann, ed., *Jewish Medieval and Renaissance Studies*. Cambridge, Mass.: Harvard Univ. Press,
1967, pp. 19-48.

2038.   [EUCHARIST] De Jong, Johannes Petrus, *Die Eucharistie als Symbolwirklichkeit.* Aus dem Holländischen von Jacques Rommens und Thomas Handgrätinger. Regensburg: Pustet, 1969.

On the eucharist as symbol and as reality.

2039.   [EUCHARIST] Grane, L., "Luthers Kritik an Thomas von Aquin in *De captivitate Babylonica,*" *Zeitschr. f. Kirchengeschichte,* 80, no. 1 (1969), 1-13.

Luther attacks Aquinas on the doctrine of transsubstantiation based on Aristotle's philosophy of nature. For interpretation of the Eucharist, Luther depends on authority of Pierre d'Ailly.

2040.   [EUCHARIST] McCue, James F., "The Doctrine of Transubstantiation from Berengar through Trent: The Point at Issue," *Harvard Theological Review,* 61 (1968), 385-430.

Traces doctrine of assertion of physical presence of Christ in the Eucharist and asserts that there was no such inevitability; that considerable number of medieval theologians for over two cents. prior to Reformation thought it was not necessary consequence of the physical presence. Holds the doctrine was held in place by a mistaken reading of the earlier tradition, especially of Lateran IV (1215).

2041.   [EUCHARIST] McDonnell, Kilian, O.S.B., *John Calvin, the Church, and the Eucharist.* Princeton: Princeton Univ. Press, 1967.

I: The Intellectual Pre-History: Surveys influence of Duns Scotus, Thomas Bradwardine, Gregory of Rimini, William of Occam, on Calvin. Discusses mystical tradition, *devotia moderna,* Erasmus and the Humanists, and Platonism as Calvin was affected by them. II: The Imperatives of the Ascension in Earthly Image and Heavenly Reality. III: Calvin Accuses Rome. IV and V: The Transcendent God and Union with Christ as a Sacramental and Ecclesiological Concern: Calvin's Eucharistic Preoccupations: the transcendent God, the inaccessible light, God's freedom from causes, the elect, Christ and lordship of the church, inwardness; distance from God and necessity for the church; salvation and the Eucharist. VI and VII: The Eucharist in its Christological and Pneumatological Contexts: mystery of the Eucharist, Nestorianism and comingling of spirit and body in Christ; local presence denied, substance an act of Holy Spirit; doctrinal tensions; Christ's sustaining act of creation as spirit and as incarnation, and simultaneity of providence and predestination.

2042.   [EUCHARIST] Meyer, Boniface John, Rev., "John Calvin's Doctrine of the Lord's Supper: An Essay in Historical Development," *DA,* 28 (1967), 287-288-A (Univ. of Iowa).

On question of the modality of Christ's existence in the Lord's Supper. Period between Ambrose and early 16th cent. showed continuity with early emphases upon symbolism and realism, then an accentuation upon modality problem in medieval times.

2043. [EUCHARIST] Pruett, Gordon Earl, "Thomas Cranmer and the Eucharistic Controversy in the Reformation," *DA*, 29 (1969), 2793-A (Princeton Univ.).

Cranmer's position as essentially Calvinist.

2044. [EUCHARIST] Tashiro, Tom T., "English Poets, Egyptian Onions, and the Protestant View of the Eucharist," *JHI*, 30 (1969), 563-578.

Metamorphosis of the onion from "Egyptian barbarism" to "Roman Catholicism" and, finally, to "High Church."

2045. [EUCHARIST] Warnach, Viktor, "Symbolwirklichkeit der Eucharistie," *Concilium*, 4 (1968), 755-765.

On symbolic reality of the eucharist. Typological reference to OT; definition of symbol. Eucharist as real presence, as consecrating act, and as anticipatory eschatology.

2046. [*EXEMPLA*] Tubach, Frederic C., *Index Exemplorum: A Handbook of Medieval Religious Tales*. (FF Communications, no. 204.) Helsinki: Suomalainen Tiedeakatemia Akademia Scientiarum Fennica, 1969.

Rev. *Spec.*, 47 (1972), 557-561.

Provides 5,400 exempla with plot-summaries. Indices, cross-references. Useful with regard to plots.

2047. [EYE] Habicht, Werner, "'With an Auspicious and a Dropping Eye': Antithetische Mimik im Shakespeare's Dramen," *Anglia*, 87 (1969), 147-166.

On the topos of *coincidentia oppositorum* in Shakespeare, including the eye example.

2048. [EYE] Posner, Donald, "The Picture of Painting in Poussin's *Self-Portrait*," in Douglas Fraser et al., eds., *Essays in the History of Art Presented to Rudolf Wittkower*. London: Phaidon, 1967, pp. 200-203.

On Poussin painting (1650), including another painting, with a woman wearing crown with an eye inset. Comparison to Rubens' "Providence" (1635) with similar eye inset. Poussin's figure not Providence, but Painting, an intellectual vision, or Prospect.

2049. [EYES] Arthos, John, "Donne's 'Extasie' and Bruno's 'Candelaio,'" *RES*, n.s. 21 (1970), 63.

Addendum to Graziani's article on Donne's "Extasie" (*RES*, 19 [1968], 121-136) calls attention to passage in Bruno's "Candelaio" (1582) that similarly describes the fascination of lovers in terms of their eye-beams being joined.

2050. [EYES] Maurino, Ferdinando D., "The Theme of the Eyes: Poliziano as a Source of Cetina," *HR*, 38 (1969), 362-369.

Poliziano's *Rispetti Spicciolati* (nos. 9 and 10), among first poems to use the lady's eyes thematically; primary and direct source of Cetina's madrigal "Ojos claros, serenos."

2051. [FACE] Lee, Virgil Jackson, Jr., "The Face in Shakespeare: A Study of Facial Gestures and Attitude as Aspects of Dramatic *Energeia*," *DA*, 30 (1970), 4416-A (Columbia Univ.).

Shakespeare's vocabulary of facial action. Facial gestures rarely appear in the lines of the characters as they speak of what they see in their own or other's face.

2052. [FACE] Wilson, John Delane, "Some Uses of Physiognomy in the Plays of Shakespeare, Jonson, Marlowe and Dekker," *DA*, 26 (1966), 4642 (Mich. State Univ.).

Discusses the place of pseudo-science of physiognomy in Elizabethan England and examines the way in which it was treated by four of the period's dramatists.

2053. [FACE-HEART] Steiger, Klaus P., "May a Man Be Caught with Faces? The Convention of 'Heart' and 'Face' in Fletcher and Rowley's *The Maid in the Mill*," *E&S*, 20 (1967), 47-63.

In Fletcher's subplot, heart-face symbolism, dichotomy between appearance and reality, or outward and inward beauty, appears only in narrow form of eye and face symbolism.

2054. [FAIRY] Blount, Dale Malotte, "Shakespeare's Use of the Folklore of Fairies and Magic in *A Midsummer Night's Dream* and *The Tempest*," *DA*, 30 (1969), 679-680-A (Indiana Univ.).

English popular tradition of fairies, magic, and witchcraft; Shakespeare's use of fairy and magic lore in *MND* and *Tmp*; dramatic functions of folklore in these plays.

2055. [FAIRY] Briggs, K., *The Faeries in Tradition and Literature*. London: Routledge and Kegan Paul, 1967.

Study mentions Shakespeare only briefly. Part III, post-Renaissance.

2056. [FAIRY] Hope, A.D., *A Midsummer Eve's Dream: Variations on a Theme by William Dunbar*. Canberra: Australian National Univ. Press, 1970.

Rev. *Hist. Stud.*, 14 (1970), 638-640.

Fairy world in late medieval Scotland in relation to Dunbar's poem; elements of Celtic religion and its vestiges--including fairy cults--as late as 17th cent. in Scotland.

2057. [FALL OF MAN] Evans, Frank B., "The Concept of the Fall in Sidney's *Apologie*," *RenP*, 1969 (Southeastern Renaissance Conference, 1970), pp. 9-14.

Sidney's use of the Fall as a major concept in his *Apologie*, not in accord with religious notions of the time.

2058. [FAME] Lida de Malkiel, María Rosa, *L'Idée de la gloire dans la tradition occidentale: Antiquité, Moyen-Age, occidental, Castille*, trans. from Spanish. Postface by Yakov Malkiel. (Bibliothèque Française et Romane, Série C.: Études Littéraires, XV.) Paris: C. Klincksieck, 1968.

2059.   [FAME] Ochman, Jerzy, "Pragnienie sławy w twórczości i życiu
        Cardana (1501-1576) [Ambitions for Fame in the Life and Work
        of Jerome Cardan (1501-1576)], *Archiwum Historii Filozofii i
        Myśli Społecznej*, 15 (1969), 47-55.

        On Renaissance aspiration for fame. Cardan conceived it as a
        central category in his philosophy: he defined fame as a
        natural inclination which leads men to do great deeds and in-
        cites them to work.

2060.   [FATE] Newell, Alex, "Fate in Shakespeare's Tragic Art: A
        Critical Study of the Early Development," *DA*, 27 (1967), 4227-
        A - 4228-A (Univ. of Pittsburgh).

        Catalogue and discussion of Elizabethan resources for genera-
        ting the effect of fate: astrology, ghosts, omens, supersti-
        tions, notions concerning the occult, witches, curses, prophe-
        cies, the principle of nemesis, Fortune, folklore, demons,
        natural history, the doctrine of correspondences, and a theory
        of providential history. Treats *Richard II*, *Richard III*,
        Romeo and Juliet, and *Julius Caesar*.

2061.   [FATE] Ringgren, Helmer, ed., *Fatalistic Beliefs in Religion,
        Folklore, and Literature: Papers Read at the Symposium on
        Fatalistic Beliefs ... 1964*. Stockholm: Almqvist & Wiksell,
        1967.

2062.   [FAUSTUS] Kahler, Erich, "Doctor Faustus from Adam to Sartre,"
        CompD, 1 (1967), 75-92.

        Mythical background of Doctor Faustus motif; Renaissance and
        modern uses.

2063.   [FICTION] Nelson, William, "The Boundaries of Fiction in the
        Renaissance: A Treaty Between Truth and Falsehood," *ELH*, 36
        (1969), 30-58.

        In Renaissance, fiction was a story, invented wholly or partly,
        that was not provably false because it could not be demon-
        strated to clash with historical or accepted truth. In con-
        trast to modern view, fiction did not include works of inven-
        tion possessing verisimilitude. Thus, Renaissance fiction
        also involved faraway locations and times, for the lack of
        historical data would allow more freedom of invention and
        limit possibilities of clash between fiction and known truth.

2064.   [FICTION] Trimpi, Wesley, "The Ancient Hypothesis of Fiction:
        An Essay on the Origins of Literary Theory," *Traditio*, 27
        (1971), 1-78.

        First of several major essays on continuity of literary theory,
        ancient, medieval, and modern, relating to idea of fiction.

2065.   [FIFTEEN SIGNS] Grodecki, Louis, "Vitrail. Les quinze signes
        précurseurs de la fin du monde (d'après les éditions de
        l'Ars bene moriendi de Verard et les vitraux de Sainte-Marthe
        de Nuremberg, de l'église de Walbourg et de la cathédrale
        d'Anvers)," *Bull. monumental*, 126 (1968), 388-389.

On works which present theme of 15 signs prefiguring the Last Judgment and end of the world: _Ars bene moriendi_, 15th- and 16th-cent. typographical editions printed in Nuremburg or Strasburg, the stained-glass windows of Saint Martha of Nuremburg before 1400, panes from the northern wing of the Cathedral of Antwerp.

2066. [FIFTEEN SIGNS] Heist, William W., _Sermon Joyeux and Polemic: Two 16th-Century Applications of the Legend of the 15 Signs._ (Univ. of North Carolina Studies in the Romance Languages and Literatures, No. 73.) Chapel Hill: Univ. of North Carolina Press, 1968.

Rev. _FS_, 24 (1970), 284.

Legend of the 15 signs before Last Judgment as an intellectual fixture in 16th-cent. France.

2067. [FIFTEEN SIGNS] Mantou, Reine, "Le thème des 'Quinze signes du Jugement Dernier' dans la tradition française," _RBPH_, 45 (1967), 827-842.

Texts from 12th cent. to 15th cent. on this theme compared.

2068. [FIRE, BLOOD, WATER] Muchembled, R., "Images obsédantes et idées-forces dans le _Printemps_ d'Agrippa d'Aubigné (1552-1630)," _Revue du Nord_, 197 (1968), 213-242.

Fire, blood, and water as obsessive images in _Printemps_. Psychoanalytic interpretation of the themes.

2069. [FLATTERY] Lesnik, H.G., "The Structural Significance of Myth and Flattery in Peele's 'Arraignment of Paris,'" _SP_, 65, no. 2 (1968), 163-170. (Cf. [PRAISE].)

Relation between the myth of Paris and the flattery of Elizabeth; roles in the play's dramatic structure.

2070. [FLOOD] Gombrich, E.H., "Bosch's 'Garden of Earthly Delights': A Progress Report," _JWCI_, 32 (1969), 162-170.

Argues that the theme of the triptych is the Flood.

2071. [FLYTING] Kurz, Jeffery W., "The Flyting," _DA_, 28 (1967), 198-A (Columbia Univ.).

Sixteenth-cent. Scottish and English "insulting" poems; distinctions from satire.

2071a. [FOLKTALE] Briggs, Katherine M., _A Dictionary of British Folktales in the English Language, incorporating the F.J. Norton Collection._ Bloomington, Ind.: Indiana Univ. Press, 1970.

Rev. _Choice_, 8 (1970), 1353.

First volume contains fables and exempla. Second volume contains jocular tales, novelle, and nursery tales. Sources indicated in the footnotes.

2072. [FOLLY] Hawkins, H., "Folly, Incurable Disease, and _Volpone_," _SEL_, 8, no. 2 (1968), 335-348.

Connection between folly and an incurable disease as thematic unity of the action.

2073. [FOLLY] Lefebvre, Joël, "Recherches Récentes sur Brant et la 'Folie,'" *EG*, 24 (1969), 263-272.

Useful survey and criticism of works on Renaissance folly in relation to 16th-cent. humanism.

2074. [FOOL] Bourgy, Victor, *Le Bouffon sur la Scène Anglaise au XVIe Siècle.* Paris: O.C.D.L., 1969. Rev. *RenQ*, 24 (1971), 92-94.

Analyzes role and development of the madman, vice figure, and clown.

2075. [FOOL] Cox, Harvey, *The Feast of Fools: A Theological Essay on Festivity and Fantasy.* Cambridge, Mass.: Harvard Univ. Press, 1969.

Rev. *TLS*, 25 June 1970, 692.

Christianity as closer to comedy than to tragedy. Festivity, fantasy, Utopia; dramatic movement, color, and sound appropriately express emerging religious consciousness.

2076. [FOOL] Ellis, Roger, "The Fool in Shakespeare: A Study in Alienation," *Critical Quart.*, 10, no. 3 (1968), 245-268.

Fool in Shakespeare as savior, pointing way to the unity of existence.

2077. [FOOL] Watts, LeClaire Barnett, "The Clown: A Comparison of the Comic Figures of Lope de Vega and William Shakespeare," *DA*, 27 (1967), 4270-A (Univ. of Conn.).

The tradition of the clown and the gracioso. In Lope, the male lead has a comic servant, creating a contrasting *galán-gracioso* dramatic unit. Shakespeare, on the other hand, set his clown apart from the rest of the cast.

2078. [FOOL] Willeford, William, *The Fool and His Scepter: A Study in Clowns and Jesters and Their Audience.* Evanston, Ill.: Northwestern Univ. Press; London: E. Arnold, 1969.

Primitive ritual clowning, "fool literature" of Middle Ages; jesters of Shakespearean dramas; cartoons, paintings, and farcical films primarily psychological rather than historical, political, or sociological. Includes section on *Lr.*, pp. 208-225. Rev. *ShSt*, 7 (1974), 456-466.

2079. [FOOL and FOLLY] Gavin, J. Austin, and T.M. Walsh, "*The Praise of Folly* in Context: The Commentary of Girardus Listrius," *RenQ*, 24 (1971), 193-209.

On valuable commentary which, after 1515 Basel edition, became standard appendage to Erasmus' piece.

2080. [FOOL and FOLLY] Könneker, Barbara, *Wesen und Wandlung der Narrenidee im Zeitalter des Humanismus: Brant, Murner, Erasmus.* Wiesbaden: Franz Steiner Verlag, 1966.

Rev. *Arcadia*, 2 (1967), 324-325; *Erasmus*, 20 (1968), 604-607; *GR*, 43 (1968), 154-157; *MLR*, 62 (1967), 740-742.

The Fool in these three writers. Introduction on Fool-theme, c. 1500. Well-documented work.

2081. [FOOL and FOLLY] Kraus, Annie, *Der Begriff der Dummheit bei Thomas von Aquin und seine Spiegelung in Sprache und Kultur.* Münster: Aschendorff, 1971.

Contains material which overlaps with the folly-tradition, as it contrasts wisdom and folly, and in relation to Christian conceptions. Divided into sections: 1) Zum ersten Artikel der *quaestio De Stultitia* des Thomas von Aquin; 2) Zum zweiten Artikel; 3) Zum dritten Artikel. Also deals with *luxuria*.

2082. [FOOL and FOLLY] Stenger, Genevieve, "*The Praise of Folly* and Its *Parerga*," in *Medievalia et Humanistica. Studies in Medieval and Ren. Culture*, n.s. 2 (1971), 97-118.

Prefatory material to Erasmus' work and satirical analogues, which help illuminate its significance and reception.

2083. [FOOLS and FOLLY] Gentili, Vanna, *Le figure della pazzia nel teatro elisabettiana.* Lecce: Milella, 1969.

Rev. *RenQ*, 25 (1971), 102-105.

Folly as theme in Elizabethan and Jacobean drama.

2084. [FOOLS and FOLLY] Lefebvre, Joël, *Les Fols et la Folie: Études sur les genres du comique et la création littéraire en Allemagne pendant la Renaissance.* Paris: Klincksieck, 1968.

Rev. *EG*, 26 (1971), 356-363.

Ch. I: Le monde comique du Carnaval; II: *La Nef des Fols* ou la nostalgie de l'Ordo; III: *L'exorcisme des fols* ou le contraste des styles. Naissance de la littérature. IV: *Eloge de la folie* ou la sagesse intempestive; V: Un mythe comique: *Eulenspiegel.* Chronologie sommaire, pp. 359-360. Lists "fool" works, 1444-1534, plus bibliography, pp. 361-387. Documented.

2085. [FOOLS and FOLLY] *L'Umanesimo e "la Follia."* *Scritti di E. Castelli; M. Bonicatti; P. Mesnard; R. Giorgi; I.L. Zupnick; E. Grassi; A. Chastel; F. Secret; R. Klein.* Rome: Editioni Abete, 1971. Rev. *BHR*, 33 (1971), 749-751.

Includes P. Mesnard, "Erasme et la conception dialectique de la Folie"; R. Giorgi, "Un temo della 'Follia': il 'Nessuno,'"; and essays by Zupnick on Bruegel and folly; R. Klein on "Le rire." Useful essays; plates.

2086. [FOOLS and FOLLY] Weimann, Robert, "Antiker Mimus und Shakespeare Theater, Vergleichbare Strukturen ihrer Dramaturgie und Narren-Komik," in Horst Meller et al., eds., *Lebende Antike:*

Symposion für Rudolf Sühnel. Berlin: Erich Schmidt, 1967, pp. 181-196.

Comparison of ancient and Shakespearean theater; mimus in Elizabethan tragedy.

2087.   [FOOLS, SHIP OF] Gaier, U., "Sebastian Brant's *Narrenschiff* and the Humanists," *PMLA*, 83, no. 2 (1968), 266-270.

Brant's friends who were humanists considered *Ship of Fools* a satire in the Roman tradition and compared it to Erasmus's *Praise of Folly*.

2088.   [FOOLS, SHIP OF] Skrine, Peter, "The Destination of the Ship of Fools: Religious Allegory in Brant's *Narrenschiff*," *MLR*, 64 (1969), 576-596.

Brant's poem is a commentary on *Ecclesiastes*, which was the poem's precedent. Aim in *Narrenschiff* was to contribute to divine purpose of redemption by purging some men of their folly through satire.

2089.   [FOREST] Sehrt, E.T., "Der Wald des Irrtums. Zur allegorischen Funktion von Spensers *Faerie Queene*," *Anglia*, 86, no. 4 (1968), 463-491.

Botany in the Renaissance. Shakespeare's forest associated with motifs of unhappiness and labyrinth motif.

2090.   [FORTRESS] Berger, T.L., "The Petrarchan Fortress of *The Changeling*," *Ren. Papers 1969* (Southeastern Ren. Conf., 1970).

Beloved as fortified castle to be besieged.

2091.   [FORTUNA] Kirchner, Gottfried, *Fortuna in Dichtung und Emblematik des Barock. Tradition und Bedeutungswandel eines Motifs*. Stuttgart: J.B. Metzlersche Verlag, 1970.

Fortuna in emblems; good or bad *fortuna*; *occasio*. Many subheadings. Illustrated. Rev. *MLR*, 67 (1972), 210.

2092.   [*FORTUNA* vs. *NATURA*] Bartholomew, Barbara, *Fortuna and Natura: A Reading of Three Chaucer Narratives*. The Hague, London, Paris: Mouton, 1966. Rev. *TLS*, 10 Nov. 1966, 1025.

Goddess Natura vs. Goddess Fortuna. Deals with Physician's, Clerk's, and Knight's Tales.

2093.   [FORTUNE] Aswell, E. Duncan, "The Role of Fortune in *The Testament of Cresseid*," *PQ*, 46 (1967), 471-487.

2094.   [FORTUNE] Casagrande, Gino, "Dio e fortuna nel *Decameron*," in R.W. Baldner, ed., *Proceedings, Pacific Northwest Conference on Foreign Languages ... 1967*, 18. Victoria, B.C., Canada: Univ. of Victoria, 1967, pp. 115-121.

2095.   [FORTUNE] Coogan, Robert, C.F.C., "Petrarch and More's Concept of Fortune," *Italica*, 46 (1969), 167-175.

Investigates More's indebtedness to Petrarch's _De remediis_
utriusque fortunae and attempts to show how this text figures
in More's concept of Fortune.

2096.   [FORTUNE] Kinneavy, Gerald B., "Fortune, Providence and the
Owl," _SP_, 64 (1967), 655-664.

Role of these ideas in relation to Owl in _The Owl and the_
Nightingale (11. 1175-1290).

2097.   [FORTUNE] Pfeiffenberger, Selma, "Notes on the Iconology of
Donatello's _Judgment of Pilate at San Lorenzo_," _RenQ_, 20
(1967), 437-454.

Connects portrait's two-faced servant with two-faced Fortuna.

2098.   [FORTUNE] Quainton, M., "Some Classical References, Sources
and Identities in Ronsard's 'Prière à la Fortune,'" _Fr. Stud._,
21, no. 4 (1967), 293-301.

Sources of themes of Fortune and its caprices, borrowed by
Ronsard for his _Hymnes_ from Pliny the Elder, Horace, Ammianus,
Boccaccio.

2099.   [FORTUNE] Santoro, Mario, _Fortuna, ragione e prudenza nella_
civiltà letteraria del Cinquecento. Collana di testi e di
critica, 7. Naples: Liguori, 1967.

Rev. _Langues néo-latines_, 61 (1967), 93-102.

Essays include: "L'invasione francese e il tema della 'fortuna'"; "Fortuna e prudenza nella lezione del Pontano"; "Il
Galateo"; "L'Ideale della 'prudenza' e la realtà contemporanea
negli scritti di Tristano Caracciolo"; "Fortuna e prudenza nel
De bello italico dal Rucellai"; "Machiavelli e il tema della
'fortuna.'"

2100.   [FORTUNE] Stewart, Douglas J., "Sallust and _Fortuna_," _Hist._
and Theory, 7 (1968), 298-317.

2101.   [FORTUNE] Tarlton, Charles T., "The Symbolism of Redemption
and the Exorcism of Fortune in Machiavelli's _Prince_," _Rev. of_
Politics, 30 (1968), 332-348.

Analysis of the _Prince_ symbolically, as a poetic structure.

2102.   [FORTUNE] Williamson, Marilyn L., "Fortune in _Antony and Cleo-_
patra," _JEGP_, 67 (1968), 423-429.

Play is about love and war, Fortune's special provinces; both
principles have much in common with this force.

2103.   [FORTUNE vs. GOOD GOVERNMENT] Panofsky, Erwin, "'Good Government' or Fortune? The Iconography of a Newly-Discovered Composition by Rubens," _Gazette des Beaux-Arts_, 68 (1966), 305-
326. (See reply by A.-P. de Mirimonde, 69 [1967], 64.)

Renaissance iconography of Fortune as opposed to that of Good
Government. Useful and full documentation.

2104. [FORTUNE vs. *VIRTUS*] Bonicatti, Maurizio, "Dürer nella storia della idee umanistiche fra Quattrocento e Cinquecento" [In Celebration of the Quincentennial of the Birth of Albrecht Dürer], *J. of Med. and Ren. Studs.*, 1 (1971), Whole issue, plus plates.

Includes "La tematica *Virtus-Fortuna*," pp. 143-196; "La tematica *Veritas-Voluptas*," pp. 197-221. Documented.

2105. [FORTUNE vs. *VIRTUS*] Paparelli, Gioacchino, "Virtù e fortuna nel Medioevo, nel Rinascimento e in Machiavelli," *Cultura e Scuola*, 9 (1970), 76-89.

Documented rehearsal of the dualism as typically Renaissance.

2106. [FOUNTAIN] Demers, Edmund Raoul, "The Origin and Development of the Fountain, both as an Artifact and Image, as Shown in Three Works of the Spanish Renaissance," *DA*, 31 (1970), 2278-A (Ohio Univ.).

Pre-Roman culture and ideas concerning the fountain, also Middle Ages. References to fountain in sacred and secular literature.

2107. [FOUNTAIN] Miller, Naomi, "The Form and Meaning of the Fontaine des Innocents," *Art Bulletin*, 50 (1968), 70-77.

Reconstruction of Fontaine des Innocents in Paris, 1549. Renaissance symbolism of its elements: water imagery, nymphs as five senses (cf. Ficino's commentary on Plato's *Symposium*; Ficino on five types of love; five qualities); lion; dolphin. Fontaine des Innocents as a fountain-temple, or nymphaeum. Documented.

2108. [FOUR] George, K.E.M., "*Quatre, quattro, cuatro* ... 'An Approximate or Indeterminate Number,'" *Studia Neophil.*, 41 (1969), 31-38.

Symbolism in Romance, especially French, of popular expressions using "four." (Cf. [NUMBER SYMBOLISM] under *Topoi*.)

2109. [FRANCIS, ST.] Askew, Pamela, "The Angelic Consolation of St. Francis of Assisi in Post-Tridentine Italian Painting," *JWCI*, 32 (1969), 280-306.

After Council of Trent, four Franciscan subjects became especially popular in art: the stigmatization, St. Francis in ecstasy supported by one or more angels, St. Francis adoring the crucifix, and St. Francis' vision of the musical angel.

2110. [FRIENDSHIP] Conley, John, "The Doctrine of Friendship in *Everyman*," *Speculum*, 44 (1969), 374-382.

Essential commonplaces of medieval doctrine of friendship: no man should be accounted a friend whose friendship had not been tested; true friendship is lasting; it is virtuous, indeed supernatural--a gift of God; it is precious; it provides counsel and comfort in this life and next life. These commonplaces adapted to plot in keeping with two articles of faith: 1) necessity of good works for salvation; 2) divine judgment after death.

2111. [FRIENDSHIP] Cook, Robert G., "Chaucer's Pandarus and the Medieval Idea of Friendship," _JEGP_, 69 (1970), 407-424.

Friendship of Troilus and Pandarus, flawed as the love "friendship" is flawed. Moral questions about the nature of friendship.

2112. [FRIENDSHIP] Wimsatt, James I., "The Player King on Friendship," _MLR_, 65 (1970), 1-6.

Player King on friendship, in relation to Hamlet's three schoolfellows and all the major characters.

2113. [FUNERAL POETRY] Maurel, M., "Fastes mortuaires et déploration. Essai sur la signification du baroque funèbre dans la poésie française," _XVIIe Siècle_, no. 82 (1969), 37-54.

On poems written on the deaths of illustrious figures; texts on the death of Henry IV. Role of baroque sensibility.

2114. [GALATEA] Dörrie, Heinrich, _Die schöne Galatea. Eine Gestalt am Rande des griechischen Mythos in antiker und neuzeitlicher Sicht._ Munich: E. Heimeran Verlag, 1968.

Rev. _Revue de litt. comp._, 43 (1969), 427-428.

Traces the Pygmalion-Galatea myth through antiquity and Renaissance; includes appendix on dramatic treatments of the tale since John Lyly. (Cf._MfM_, III.ii.47.)

2115. [GAMES] Antin, David, "Caxton's _The Game and Playe of the Chesse_," _JHI_, 29 (1968), 269-278.

On implications of chess as a game and a form of conflict. Caxton's work and exempla as instances of "riddle transformation," i.e., they involve surprising but (verbally) logical solutions of problems, as in the prophecy in _Mac_.

2116. [GAMES] Bakhtin, M.M., "The Role of Games in Rabelais," _Yale Fr. Stud._, 5 (1968), 124-132.

Games in Rabelais serve to dethrone medieval conception of world and reveal carnivalesque conception of historic process. They also parody legal methods underlying established truth.

2117. [GANYMEDE] Mayo, Penelope C., "_Amor Spiritualis et Carnalis_: The Myth of Ganymede in Art," _DA_, 30 (1970), 4891-A (N.Y. Univ., Inst. of Fine Arts).

Ganymede from 7th cent. B.C. to present: 1) as erotic--Trojan youth as prototype of universal homosexuality; 2) Ganymede's abduction by Zeus: metaphysical symbol of rise of the soul; use in 16th-cent. neo-platonizing emblematists.

2118. [GARDEN] Börsch-Supan, Eva, _Garten-, Landschafts- und Paradiesmotive im Innenraum. Eine ikonographische Untersuchung._ Berlin: Hessling, 1967.

Documented, historical survey. Includes thematic treatments: "Gartenraumdarstellungen im Altertum"; "Gartenraumdarstellungen des Mittelalters und der Neuzeit." (Cf. [PARADISE].)

2119. [GARDEN] Comito, Terry, "Renaissance Gardens and the Discovery of Paradise," *JHI*, 32 (1971), 483-506. (Cf. [PARADISE].)

Garden as symbol of divine promise; relation to Charles VIII of France on visit to Naples, 1495; on Elizabeth's and Burghley's interest.

2120. [GARDEN] Praz, Mario, "Armida's Garden," *CLS*, 5 (1968), 1-20.

Montaigne, Tasso, Webster, in relation to garden.

2121. [GARDEN] Smith, Thomas Norris, "The Garden Image in Medieval Literature," *DA*, 29 (1969), 2685-A (Univ. of Conn.).

Significance of that landscape in the structure of four narratives: spiritual ecstasy in *The Phoenix*, divine love in *Roman de la Rose*, lust in *The Merchant's Tale*, and consolation in *Pearl*.

2122. [GARDEN, ENCLOSED] Stewart, Stanley, *The Enclosed Garden: The Tradition and the Image in Seventeenth-Century Poetry*. Madison, Wisc.: Univ. of Wisc. Press, 1966.

Provides, through iconography of enclosed-garden figure, illumination of Renaissance poetry. Rev. *MP*, 65 (1968), 383.

2123. [GENTLEMAN] Lee, Patricia Ann, "The Ideals of the English Gentleman in the Early Seventeenth Century," *DA*, 28 (1967), 635-A (Columbia Univ.).

Two trends of gentility: the courtly gentleman (divided between courtier and country types) and the Puritan gentleman. Theoretical and practical determinants of claim to be "gentle." Disintegration of courtly gentility under stress of application to daily life and 17th-cent. political and economic change.

2124. [GENTLEMAN] ————, "Play and the English Gentleman in the Early Seventeenth Century," *Historian*, 31 (1969), 364-380.

Significance in the proportion of order, structure, and discipline in the gentlemanly play of the period.

2125. [GENTLEMAN] Newkirk, Glen Alton, "The Public and Private Ideal of the 16th Century Gentleman: A Representative Analysis," *DA*, 27 (1966), 1034-A (Univ. of Denver).

Traces development of classical concept of gentleman trained to serve the state, and growth of the ideal of gentility from philsopher-king, through tradition of the courtier, to 16th-cent. ideal. Illustrates how More, Sidney, Lyly, and Edmund Spenser arrive at final formulation of 16th-cent. ideal. Analyzes several of Shakespeare's plays, contrasting his idea of the perfect man with actual court practices.

2126. [GIANTS] Joukovsky-Micha, F., "La Guerre des dieux et des géants chez les poètes français du XVIe siècle (1500-1585)," *BHR*, 29 (1967), 55-92.

Rev. *SFr*, 12 (1968), 337.

Theme of *titanomachia* in poets of the Pléiade.

2127. [*GLOIRE*] Gerard, Albert S., "Self-love in Lope de Vega's
Fuenteovejuna and Corneille's _Tite et Bérénice_," _AJFS_, 4
(1967), 177-197.

Distinctions among love, "gloire," and self-love in 17th-cent.
tragedy.

2128. [*GLOIRE*] Joukovsky, Françoise, _La gloire dans la poésie française et néolatine du XVIe siècle_. Geneva: Droz, 1969.

Rev. _TLS_, 8 January 1970, 31.

Two parts: how the notion of "gloire" evolved over the hundred years from 1480; various themes of "gloire" and their
evolution in considerable detail.

2129. [*GLOIRE*] ————, "La Notion de 'Vaine Gloire' de Simund de
Freine à Martin le Franc," _Romania_, 89 (1968), 1-30; 210-239.

Distinction between _fama_ (reputation) and true "gloire"
(_gloria_) traced in detail through 15th cent. True "gloire"
based on virtue and justice, and proceeds from the judgment
of conscience, which is more important than another's praise.
Significant Stoic influence, blending well with Christian
thought on idea of "gloire."

2130. [GO-BETWEEN] Ruggerio, Michael J., _The Evolution of the Go-
Between in Spanish Literature through the Sixteenth Century_
(Univ. of Cal. Pubs. in Modern Philology, v. 78). Berkeley:
Univ. of Calif. Press, 1966.

Rev. _Rom. Forsch._, 81 (1969), 274-278.

Deals with image of the go-between in Spanish literature from
Juan Ruiz to imitators of _La Celestina_. Related to witch and
witchcraft.

2131. [GOD, HIDDEN] Weier, Reinhold, _Das Thema von verborgenen Gott
von Nikolaus von Kues zu Martin Luther_. Buchreihe der Cusanus-
Gesellschaft, Bd. 2. Münster in W.: Aschendorff, 1967.

Rev. _Journal of Ecclesiastical Hist._, 19 (1968), 122-124;
Theologie und Philosophie, 43 (1968), 124-127.

Luther's idea of the hidden God; connection between Cusa and
Reformation via early 16th-cent. Jacques Lefèvre; Christian
neo-Platonic tradition and _coincidentia oppositorum_.

2132. [GOLDEN AGE] Armstrong, Elizabeth, _Ronsard and the Age of Gold_.
Cambridge/N.Y.: Cambridge Univ. Press, 1968.

Chapter on "classical, Medieval and Renaissance Concepts of
the Age of Gold." Rev. _TLS_, 12 Sept. 1968, 1007.

2133. [GOLDEN AGE] Cullen, Patrick, "Imitation and Metamorphosis:
The Golden-Age Eclogue in Spenser, Milton, and Marvell,"
PMLA, 84 (1969), 1559-1570.

Each of these writers imitates the messianic eclogue: Spenser
in "April," Milton in his Nativity Ode, and Marvell in "The
Picture of Little T.C.," but each one metamorphoses the conventional generic pattern. Spenser portrays the Orphic order-
ing power of art, the interrelation of the order of art and

the order of the body politic, and the new golden age of poetry. Milton remolds the formulas to praise the true messiah, Christ, and to celebrate the new golden age. Marvell uses the formulas to assert the Renaissance longing for a new golden age of free love.

2134.   [GOLDEN AGE] Gatz, Bodo, *Weltalter, goldene Zeit und sinnverwandte Vorstellungen*. (Spudasmata, Studien zur Klassischen Philologie und ihren Grenzgebieten, Bd. XVI.) Hildesheim: Olms, 1967.

Concepts of paradise and of the golden age (distinct from the myths of ages of the world and ages of metals). Both themes are treated: first, ages of the world; second, myth and history in sequences and eras; finally, paradise. Index.

2135.   [GOLDEN AGE] Levin, Harry, *The Myth of the Golden Age in the Renaissance*. Bloomington, Ind.: Indiana Univ. Press, 1969; London: Faber, 1970. Rev. *Comp. Lit.*, 24 (1972), 88.

Traces myth of the golden age--defined as a nostalgic statement of man's orientation in time--in a spectrum of Renaissance writings: ethics, geography, fictions, pageantry, and historiography.

2136.   [GOLDEN AGE] Milan, Paul B., "The Golden Age and the Political Theory of Jean de Meun: A Myth in *Rose* Scholarship," *Symposium*, 23 (1969), 137-149.

Questions relationship between Jean de Meun's supposed political and social theories and the Golden Age concept in medieval political thought.

2137.   [GOLDEN AGE] O'Malley, John W., "Fulfillment of the Christian Golden Age under Pope Julius II: Text of a Discourse of Giles of Viterbo, 1507," *Traditio*, 25 (1969), 265-338.

Text is reproduced.

2138.   [GOLDEN AGE] Swift, Louis J., "Lactantius and the Golden Age," *Amer. Jour. of Philology*, 89 (1968), 144-156.

Golden Age related by Lactantius to touchstone of Christian faith.

2139.   [GREAT CHAIN of BEING] Wilson, Gayle E., "Jonson's Use of the Bible and the Great Chain of Being in 'To Penshurst,'" *SEL*, 8 (1968), 77-89.

Relationship between "truth" in Bible and great chain of being.

2140.   [GROTESQUE] Dacos, Nicole, *La découverte de la Domus Aurea et la formation des Grotesques à la Renaissance*. Leiden: Brill, 1968; London: Warburg Inst., 1969.

Rev. *Apollo*, 94 (1971), 77-78.

Birth of this genre and its development from ancient models in Quattrocento through "emancipation" of grotesques by Raphael, with chapter on their reception in 16th cent.

2141. [GUILE, CONTEST of] Nelson, Alan Holm, "The Contest of Guile in the English Corpus Christi Plays," *DA*, 28 (1967), 200-A (Univ. of Calif., Berkeley).

Conflict between God and Satan as "contest of guile," God-in-Christ beating Satan with his own weapons of concealed purposes and deceptive appearances. Righteous guile defeating evil guile also visible in individual dramatic episodes.

2142. [GUNPOWDER PLOT] DeLuna, B.N., *Jonson's Romish Plot: A Study of "Catiline" and Its Historical Context.* Oxford: Clarendon Press, 1967.

Rev. *RenQ*, 21 (1968), 232-236.

Jonson's *Catiline* held to allude to the Gunpowder Plot of 1605, written by Jonson to justify his connection with the conspirators prior to plot's discovery and his connection with the government afterward. (Cf. 442.)

2143. [GUNPOWDER PLOT] Durst, Paul, *Intended Treason. What Really Happened in the Gunpowder Plot.* London: W.H. Allen, 1970.

Modern appraisal of Gunpowder Plot with documentation. Challenges many traditional theories. Rev. *TLS*, 8 Jan. 1971, 50.

2144. [GUNPOWDER PLOT] Edwards, Francis, *Guy Fawkes: The Real Story of the Gunpowder Plot.* London: Hart-Davis, 1969.

Rev. *Hist. Today.*, 20 (1970), 140-141; *Revue d'Histoire Ecclésiastique*, 65 (1970), 297-298.

Contends that Salisbury put the idea of the plot into the heads of the leading Roman Catholic conspirators who were thus from the beginning working for the Privy Council. Holds that Tresham, Percy, and Fawkes were double agents.

2145. [GUNPOWDER PLOT] Yaple, Robert D., "Sir Robert Cecil and the Gunpowder Plot," *Univ. of Dayton Rev.*, 5 (1968/69), 3-12.

Cecil must have been aware of the intrigue from its inception and would have used this knowledge to best advantage.

2146. [HEAVEN-HELL] Hughes, Robert, *Heaven and Hell in Western Art.* London: Weidenfeld & Nicolson, 1968.

Rev. *LibJ*, 93 (1968), 4283; *SatR*, 51 (30 Nov. 1968), 45.

General illustrated discussion of heaven-hell themes; expanded to include non-religious aspects (10th to start of 19th cents.) tracing origins of angels, saints, devils, and monsters; metamorphosis of Pan-Dionysus into Lucifer-Satan.

2147. [HEAVENLY SEED] Stewart, Jack F., "Spenser's *Amoretti* LXXIX, 10," *Explicator*, 27 (1969), 74.

The metaphor "heavenly seed" suggests multiple meanings, with Petrarchan, Neoplatonic, Platonic, Catholic, Anglican, and figural implications.

2148. [HECTOR] Loomis, Roger Sherman, "The Heraldry of Hector or Confusion Worse Confounded," *Speculum,* 46 (1967), 32-35.

On Hector and the Nine Worthies in Middle Ages and Renaissance. (Cf. *LLL,* V.ii.)

2149. [HECTOR] Sakharoff, Micheline, "Hector, Conquérant et Acteur. L'Efficacité dans l'Echec," *RSH,* 34 (1969), 189-196.

On Hector in Montchrestien's tragedy by that name (1604); his determination to fight against his destiny, even when condemned to an inevitable defeat. By contesting will of the gods, Hector departs from stoicism and anticipates the Cornelian hero.

2150. [HELEN] Newman-Gordon, Pauline, *Hélène de Sparte, la fortune du mythe en France.* Paris: Nouvelles Editions Debresse, 1968.

Rev. *Fr. Rev.,* 43 (1970), 701-702.

First part includes the myth in Homer and Virgil, and in Middle Ages. Second and third parts on the myth in 19th and 20th cents.

2151. [HERCULES] Hallowell, Robert E., "Matthäus Greuter's *Hercules Tri-Mysticus*: A Study in Renaissance Iconography," *RenP 1966* (Durham, N.C.: Southeastern Ren. Conf., 1967), pp. 75-82.

Frequent use of Hercules as emblem of model prince, in French 16th- and 17th-cent. art. Favorite subject of Greuter (1564-1638), whose work is dense pictorial synthesis of medieval and Renaissance myths of Hercules.

2152. [HERCULES] Herron, Dale Susan, "The 'Triall of True Curtesie': Book VI of the *Faerie Queene,*" *DA,* 30 (1970), 2968-A (Northwestern Univ.).

Spenser's mythological paralleling of Calidore to Hercules in Book VI's depiction of heroic virtue, especially to Hercules' Twelfth Labor. Also deals with Calidore's own weaknesses which lead to violent disruption of social order.

2153. [HERCULES] Jung, Marc-René, *Hercule dans la littérature française du XVI siècle. De l'Hercule Courtois à l'Hercule Baroque.* Geneva: Droz, 1966.

Includes: Souvenir du moyen âge: l'Hercule courtois; l'Hercule de Libye; l'Hercule gaulois; l'Hercule Chrétien; Hercule et l'Amour; les contemporains comparés à Hercule.

2154. [HERCULES] MacKenzie, Margery Walker, "Hercules in the Early Roman Empire, with Particular Reference to Literature," *DA,* 28 (1968), 3163-3164-A (Cornell Univ.).

Hercules' association, as hero-god, with Emperor; role in Stoic literature; identification with protective deity. Later comparisons with Jesus, and of Hercules-Stoic beliefs with Christianity, may reflect impact of Hercules religion on Christianity.

2155. [HERCULES] Panofsky, Erwin, "Hercules Agricola: A Further Com-
plication in the Problem of the Illustrated Hrabanus Manuscripts," in Douglas Fraser et al., eds., *Essays in the History of Art Presented to Rudolf Wittkower*. London: Phaidon,
1967, pp. 20-28.

While Hercules is absent from 7th cent. Isidore's *Etymologiae*
(sometimes cited as *Origines*) section on the pagan gods, his
treatment in 9th-cent. Hrabanus' *De naturis rerum* (usually
cited as *De universo*) is complex and significant.

2156. [HERCULES] Schanzer, Ernest, "Hercules and His Load," *RES*, 19,
no. 73 (1968), 51-53.

On sources credited with description of sign of Globe theater
as bearing figure of Hercules supporting the globe, with motto
beneath.

2157. [HERCULES] Tobin, Ronald W., "A Hero for All Seasons: Hercules
in French Classical Drama," *CompD*, 1 (1967-68), 288-296.

2158. [HERCULES] Tolnay, Charles de, "Une Composition de la Jeunesse
de Michel-Ange: Hercule Etouffant le Lion de Nemée," *Gazette
des Beaux-Arts*, 71 (1968), 205-211.

Recalls Shakespeare's use.

2159. [HERCULES] Vivanti, Corrado, "Henry IV, the Gallic Hercules,"
JWCI, 30 (1967), 176-197.

Henry IV of France, as early as 1592, is related to Hercules,
and most often compared with him, because of the varied meanings of the association.

2160. [HERCULES] Waddington, R.B., "Prometheus and Hercules: The
Dialectic of *Bussy d'Ambois*," *ELH*, 34 (1967), 21-48.

In Chapman's use of myth, Prometheus is liberated by Hercules,
as Christ enfranchises Adam from sin. Mythic heroes symbolize
stages in the transmutation of the human spirit.

2161. [HERMAPHRODITE] Cirillo, A.R., "The Fair Hermaphrodite: Love-
Union in the Poetry of Donne and Spenser," *SEL*, 9 (1969), 81-
95.

Topos includes a metaphysical concept of love as union of two
souls in one.

2162. [HERO] Brombert, Victor, ed., *The Hero in Literature*. Greenwich, Conn.: Fawcett, 1969. Rev. *Choice*, 7 (1970), 227.

Discussions on the hero in literature, from Homer's Ajax to
Sartre's anti-hero; chapters from books by well-known scholars.

2163. [HERO] Homan, Sidney, "Chapman and Marlowe: The Paradoxical
Hero and the Divided Response," *JEGP*, 68 (1969), 391-406.

Defines paradoxical hero as created "with mutually exclusive
qualities, glaring strengths, and demeaning vices, in order

to produce a divided response from his audience." Paradoxical
hero is inseparable part of playwright's tragic vision.

2164.   [HERO] Isler, A.D., "The Allegory of the Hero and Sidney's Two
        Arcadias," *SP,* 65, no. 2 (1968), 171-191.

        Conception of courage in Renaissance: interpretations of
        Iliad, Odyssey, and *Aeneid.* Courage and wisdom as hero's
        basic virtues.

2165.   [HERO] Steadman, John M., *Milton and the Renaissance Hero.*
        Oxford: Clarendon Press, 1967.

        Rev. *RES,* 19 (1968), 319-320; *RQ,* 21 (1968), 491-493; *TLS,*
        8 February 1968, 134.

        Discusses Renaissance ideals relevant to Shakespearean studies:
        amor, sapientia, megalopsychia, etc.

2166.   [HERO] ————, *Milton's Epic Characters: Image and Idol.*
        Chapel Hill, N.C.: Univ. of North Carolina Press, 1968.

        Rev. *ELN,* 7 (1970), 219-222; *MP,* 68 (1970), 201-204; *TLS,* 11
        June 1970, 641.

        Renaissance heroic *ethos* examined in learned detail. Useful
        appendices on Renaissance definitions of the hero; heroes and
        daemons; Mazzoni on nature of the hero.

2167.   [HERO] Sakharoff, Micheline, *Le Héro, sa liberté et son effi-
        cacité de Garnier à Rotrou.* Paris: Nizet, 1967.

        Brief study, suggesting relations to *Hamlet.* Includes Ch. I.
        La situation de l'homme dans le monde; II. Garnier: L'homme
        enchâiné ou l'inefficacité. III. Monchrestien: Le stoïcisme
        ou la liberté négative. Une demi-efficacité. IV. Hector,
        conquérant et acteur. L'efficacité dans l'échec. V. L'action
        pour l'action. Efficacité ou non. VI. Rappel à l'ordre pour
        une methode de l'efficacité....

2168.   [HERO] Truax, Elizabeth, "Preview of the Vanishing Hero: A
        Study of the Protagonists in Jacobean Drama," *DA,* 29 (1969),
        3159-3160-A (Univ. of Southern Calif.).

        Studies the "less than heroic protagonist" in *Antonio's Re-
        venge, Bussy D'Ambois, Revenger's Tragedy, Duchess of Malfi,*
        and *Changeling.*

2169.   [HERO] Turner, Myron, "The Heroic Ideal in Sidney's Revised
        Arcadia," *SEL,* 10 (1970), 63-82.

        Balance of heroic pride and self-sufficiency with Christian
        humility and dependence upon God; deeds of mind of more value
        than deeds of arms.

2170.   [HERO, ANTI-] Schroder, Franz Rolf, "Antiheroica," *GRM,* 20
        (1970), 369-384.

        Thersites in Homer's *Iliad* as original anti-hero; some remarks
        on rediscovery of this character in Renaissance and as source
        of Fool in Shakespeare.

2171. [HERO, Athletic] Fontenrose, Joseph, "The Hero as Athlete," *California Studies in Classical Antiquity,* 1 (1968), 73–104.

Avenging hero type, in widespread type of legend.

2172. [HERO, Journey of] Melczer, Willy, "'The Winged Vessell'-- Variations on the Journey of the Epic Hero in Late Sixteenth-Century Literature," *DA,* 29 (1969), 4462-A (Univ. of Iowa).

Journey of epic hero in late 16th-cent.: Camoens' *Os Lusiadas,* Ercilla's *La Araucana,* d'Aubigné's *Les Tragiques,* Tasso's *Gerusalemme Liberata,* and Spenser's *Faerie Queene.*

2173. [HERO; RITUAL] Riley, Michael Howard, "Ritual and the Hero in English Renaissance Tragedy," *DA,* 31 (1970), 2353-A (Boston Univ.).

Uses materials from social sciences on "primitive" dramatic behavior patterns. *Sejanus* as a "socio-drama" in which Jonson recreates the primitive structure of scapegoat ritual; *Lear* as a "psycho-drama" in which a shaman acts out an asocial and other-worldly "myth."

2174. [HEROD] Weimann, Robert, "Die furchtbare Komik des Herodes: Dramaturgie und Figurenaufbau des vorshakespeareschen Schur-ken," *Archiv,* 204 (1967), 113–123.

Ambivalence of character of Herod in apocrypha and earlier English literature: formidable tyrant, but also grotesque and vulgar; dramatic intermingling of comedy and terror.

2175. [*HEROICUS*] Matuszewski, J., "Potestas Heroica," *Slavia Occidentalis,* 27 (1968), 133–142.

Meaning of "heroicus" (of the lord) and related terms in Polish-Latin documents of 16th–18th cents.

2176. [HEROINE, Persecuted] Johnson, Jean Elizabeth, "The Persecuted Heroine in English Renaissance Tragi-comedy," *DA,* 30 (1969), 1984-A (Columbia Univ.).

Tradition of persecuted heroine, from Greek fertility myths to Renaissance. English tragicomic drama of Renaissance develops as characteristic features heroine's forgiveness of her persecutor and his repentance or reform.

2177. [HIEROGLYPHICS] Haupt, Karl, "Die Renaissance-Hieroglyphik in Kaiser Maximilians Ehrenpforte," *Philobiblon,* 12 (1968), 253–267.

Popularity of enigmatic hieroglyphics among humanists, including German humanist Pirckheimer and artist Dürer. Article discusses involvement of these two men in the representation of Emperor Maximilian.

2178. [HOMER] Broich, Ulrich, "*Batrachomyomachia* und *Margites* als literarische Vorbilder: Einige Bemerkungen zu einem literarkritischen Topos," in Horst Meller et al., eds., *Lebende Antike: Symposion für Rudolf Sühnel.* Berlin: Erich Schmidt, 1967, pp. 250–257.

Renaissance Homeric-attribution of these works and their influence in English literature.

2179. [*HOMO NOVUS*] Truman, R.W., "Lazarillo de Tormes and the 'Homo Novus' Tradition," *MLR*, 64 (1969), 62–67.

Studies *Lazarillo* against literary tradition depicting rise in society of the low-born but worthy man.

2180. [HONESTY] Houser, David John, "The Tradition of Honesty in Elizabethan and Jacobean Drama," *DA*, 31 (1970), 359-A (Univ. of Wisc.).

Theme of ruler disguised in order to purge vice; significance to state and society of corruption.

2181. [HONOR] Council, Norman Briggs, "When Honour's At the Stake," *DA*, 28 (1967), 1047–1048-A (Stanford Univ.).

Renaissance views of honor, one view via Christian humanism, another via Calvinism, Stoicism, and other traditions. Discusses Fulke Greville, *JC*, *Tro.*, *Ham.*, *Oth.*, *Mac.*, *Lr.*

2182. [HONOR] Gagen, Jean, "Hector's Honor," *SQ*, 19 (1968), 129–137.

Hector's honor in Renaissance context of its inner essence as justice and virtue, and its outward form as reputation, which sanctions exercise of these virtues and justifies vengeance; honor and Renaissance ethics of the duel.

2183. [HONOR] Golden, Bruce, "Calderón's Tragedies of Honor: *Topoi*, Emblem and Action in the Popular Theater of the *Siglo de Oro*," *RenD*, 3 (1970), 239–262.

Shows how Calderón used *topoi* from the honor code as constituents of tragic action, as hero follows dictates of that code. Since the hero's identity is determined by his honor, honor becomes the focal point of dramatic action, with the hero living only to regain his honor, though to do so he must lie, dissemble, murder.

2184. [HONOR] Jouanna, A., "Recherches sur la notion d'honneur au XVIe siècle," *Revue d'Histoire Moderne et Contemporaine*, 15 (1968), 597–623.

Classification of meanings of honor. Links which bind aspects of honor to each other and their role in 16th-cent. society. Important impact of concept on French institutions.

2185. [HONOR] Oostendorp, H.Th., "El Sentido del Tema de la Honra Matrimonial en las Tragedias de Honor," *Neophil.*, 53 (1969), 14–29.

On marital honor in Spanish tragedies of honor. Cites Middleton and Rowley, *Fair Quarrel*, and Massinger, *Fatal Dowry*.

2186. [HONOR] Saner, Reginald, "*Antony and Cleopatra*: How Pompey's Honor Struck a Contemporary," *SQ*, 20 (1969), 117–120.

An anonymous pamphlet of 1614 (*A Horrible Cruel and Bloody Murther*) in moralizing the detestability of murder sees Pompey's refusal to murder Antony and Octavius aboard his galley as an example of honor.

2187. [HORSE] Chèvre, Marie, "Quelques éditions d'ouvrages hippiques au XVIe siècle. L'écurie de Frederic Grison," *Gutenberg Jb.* (1968), 160-169.

     The French 16th-cent. editions of Grison's *L'Ecurie* remained faithful to the original, presenting reader with an elegant and practical quarto on equestrian art; Italian editions were constantly being revised, reducing format and illustrations.

2188. [HORSE] Taylor, Arwilla Kerns, "The Manège of Love and Authority: Studies in Sidney and Shakespeare," *DA*, 30 (1970), 3025-3026-A (Univ. of Texas at Austin).

     Studies manège imagery in *Astrophel and Stella* and in *Loves Labours Lost*, *Much Ado*, *Richard II*, *Henry IV*, and *Henry V*. Rider of the manège, in metaphorical terms, was the rational agent who attempted to control the rebellious animal passions.

2189. [HUNT] Rosand, David, "Rubens's Munich 'Lion Hunt': Its Sources and Significance," *Art Bulletin*, 51 (1969), 29-40. (Cf. [CHASE].)

     Intimate relation between hunting and warfare in humanist tract *Il Simoncello o vero della caccia* by Baldovino di Monte Simoncelli and in Rubens's "Lion Hunt."

2190. [IDOLATRY] Brennan, Thomas Augustus, "Idols and Idolatry in the Prose and Early Poetry of John Milton," *DA*, 31 (1970), 2868-A (Tulane Univ.).

     Demonic symbolism in Milton, in opposition to scriptural and classical types of Christ. Satan uses idolatry to confound good and evil: Christian must reestablish Divine Image.

2191. [IDOLATRY] Frankish, C.R., "The Theme of Idolatry in Garnier's *Les Juifves*," *BHR*, 30 (1968), 65-83.

     Play of Robert Garnier (1544?-1590) reflects horror of idolatry among Protestants and Catholics; also deals with question of rebellion against tyrannical ruler.

2192. [IMAGINATION] Halio, Jay L., "The Metaphor of Conception and Elizabethan Theories of the Imagination," *Neophilologus*, 50 (1966), 454-461.

     Elizabethans often thought of imagination as creative and related metaphor of conception to theory of the imagination.

2193. [IMAGINATION] Holyoake, S John, "Further Reflections on Montaigne and the Concept of the Imagination," *BHR*, 31 (1969), 495-523.

     Uses of and attitudes toward the imagination in Montaigne.

2194. [IMAGINATION] Rather, L.J., "Thomas Fienu's (1567-1631) Dialectical Investigation of the Imagination as Cause and Cure of Bodily Disease," *Bull. of the Hist. of Medicine*, 41 (1967), 349-367.

     On *De viribus imaginationibus*, Louvain, 1608.

2195. [IMMORTALITY] Clements, R.D., "A Sixteenth Century Psychologist on the Immortality of the Soul: Juan Luis Vives," *BHR*, 28 (1966), 78-88.

Discusses a chapter in Vives' *On the Soul and Life*, a psychological discussion of immortality. To Vives the question of immortality was not only religious, but was related to the nature of human knowledge and thought. Also discusses earlier treatment of the question of the immortality of the soul, especially the work of Pietro Pomponazzi.

2196. [IMMORTALITY] Pine, Martin, "Pietro Pomponazzi and the Immortality Controversy: 1516-1524," *DA*, 28 (1967), 2183-A (Columbia Univ.).

Pomponazzi's views on immortality studied against background of controversy they provoked, beginning with his *Tractatus de immortalitate animae* (1516), which concluded that Aristotle rejected human immortality. Going much further than Scotus or Averroists, he bases his arguments for mortality on new foundations, reason, and experience, as well as Aristotle. His argument for mortality is also based on his theory of virtue, which is better preserved than by immortality, virtue being weakened if supported by rewards. Although he disclaims his rejection of immortality as a fable, this is regarded as a formal denial to avoid conflict with the church. His opponents drew on Thomist as well as Averroist and eclectic (Augustinian and Neoplatonic) argument, all denying his view that soul was merely a force uniting bodily powers and perishable at death.

2197. [IMMORTALITY] Piper, H.W., "Shakespeare's *Antony and Cleopatra*, V, ii, 279-281," *Explicator*, 26 (1967), Item 10.

Robe and crown as Christian symbols for immortality; juice of the grape suggests Mark 14:25, periphrasis for dying.

2198. [INFANTICIDE] Lyons, Charles R., "Some Variations of *Kindermord* as Dramatic Archetype," *CompD*, 1 (1967), 56-71.

Child-killing in Shakespeare, Racine, and other playwrights.

2198a. [INSCRIPTIONS] Sparrow, John, *Visible Words--A Study of Inscriptions in and as Books and Works of Art*. Cambridge Univ. Press, 1969.

Rev. *RenQ*, 24 (1971), 539-540.

Chapter 2 deals with "The Inscription in Renaissance Works of Art." Renaissance viewers were able to perceive imagery and inscriptions together. Also treats inscriptions on Renaissance tombs.

2199. [ISAAC] Elliott, John R., Jr., "The *Sacrifice of Isaac* as Comedy and Tragedy," *SP*, 66 (1969), 36-59.

Compares Renaissance dramatic treatments with that in English Corpus Christi play.

2200. [ISAAC] Wood, J.E., "Isaac Typology in the New Testament," _New Testament Stud._, 14, no. 4 (1968), 583-589.

Quotations from rabbinic literature and OT show influence of sacrifice of Isaac on writers of NT. Expiatory nature of the sacrifice considered in Jewish tradition as announcement of death of Christ, followed by resurrection.

2201. [ISLAND] Brunner, Horst, _Die poetische Insel_. Stuttgart: Metzler, 1967.

Investigation of island motif in German literature from medieval legends and romances to 20th cent.

2202. [ISLAND, Enchanted] Carey, George G., "Enchanted-Island Traditions of the Sixteenth and Seventeenth Centuries," _Amer. Neptune_, 29 (1969), 275-281.

Enchanted-island tradition in 16th and 17th cents., engendered by mariner's fear of powers of darkness and exemplified by references to islands in Atlantic haunted by spirits and demons.

2203. [ISLES, FORTUNATE] Shapiro, Maurice, "A Renaissance Birthplate," _Art Bull._, 49 (1967), 236-243.

Includes Fortunate Isles motif; suggests intellectual content of minor Renaissance arts has been underestimated.

2204. [ITALY] Baskerville, Edward John, "The English Traveller to Italy, 1547-1560," _DA_, 28 (1968), 4115-A (Columbia Univ.).

Assesses distribution of travellers by social rank or role and apparent motivation; includes biographies of four English visitors to Italy, three of whom went on to the sort of career at home that gave Italy a bad name. Discusses anti-Italian attitudes and Italy as a source of new learning for Englishmen.

2205. [ITALY] Costa-Zalessow, Natalia, "Italy as Victim: A Historical Appraisal of a Literary Theme," _Italica_, 45 (1968), 216-240.

Italian patriotic poetry from the Middle Ages up to 19th cent. portrays Italy as a victim.

2206. [ITALY] Parks, George B., "The Decline and Fall of the English Renaissance Admiration of Italy," _HLQ_, 31 (1968), 341-357.

Traces course of England's praise and dispraise of Italy and Italian society from the early 16th to late 17th cents.

2207. [JACK STRAW] Bergeron, David M., "Jack Straw in Drama and Pageant," _Guildhall Miscellany_, 2 no. 10 (1968), 459-462.

Examination of _The Life and Death of Jack Straw_, a play, plus two Lord Mayor's shows, which incorrectly portray Straw as Walworth's victim in the Peasants' Revolt.

2208. [JEPHTHA'S DAUGHTER] Hoffman, Richard L., "Jephthah's Daughter and Chaucer's Virginia," _ChauR._, 2 (1967), 20-31.

2209. [JEW] Blumenkranz, Bernard, *Le juif médiéval au miroir de l'art chrétien*. Paris: Études Augustiniennes, 1966.

Rev. *Le Moyen Âge*, 75 (1969), 186-189.

Many illustrations and comments in monograph on Jew as seen in medieval Christian art.

2210. [JEW] Rosenberg, Edgar, "The Jew in Western Drama," *BNYPL*, 72 (1968), 442-491.

This is introduction to new edition of *The Jew in English Drama*, which contains checklist, "The Jew in Western Drama," by the author. From *Croxton Play of the Sacrament*; long section on Renaissance English drama to the present.

2211. [JOB] Wirszubski, Chaim, "Giovanni Pico's Book of Job," *JWCI*, 32 (1969), 171-199.

Biblical, philosophical, and Kabbalistic interests meet in Pico's interpretation of the Book of Job. It may yet prove to be more valuable as a document illustrating Pico's encounter with medieval Jewish thought than as specimen of his Hebrew erudition.

2212. [JOSEPH] Schmidt, Josef H.K., *Die Figur des ägyptischen Joseph bei Jakob Bidermann (1578-1639) und Jakob Boehme (1575-1624)*. Zurich: Keller, 1967.

Prefiguration of Joseph as Christ by Bidermann; Joseph also an example of Christian attitudes. Includes 17th-cent. theological contexts.

2213. [JUDGMENT] Holyoake, S. John, "The Idea of 'Jugement' in Montaigne," *MLR*, 63, no. 2 (1968), 340-351.

Montaigne's paradoxical distinction between praise and blame of "jugement" may be clue to sources of his composition.

2214. [JUDGMENT] La Charité, Raymond Camille, "The Concept of Judgment in Montaigne," *DA*, 27 (1967), 3438-A.

A study of Montaigne's usage of the terms *jugement, entendement, sens, raison, discours*, and *conscience*.

2215. [JUDGMENT] ———, "Mental Exaltation and Montaigne's Notion of Judgment," *RomN*, 8 (1967), 278-280.

Montaigne considers that truth may be found, not only through judgment, but also through a certain "élan," indeed through the annihilation or collapse of judgment. E.g., exercise of judgment and appreciation of great poetry are mutually exclusive; moreover, one may know truth intuitively as well as deductively.

2216. [JUDGMENT] ———, "The Relationship of Judgement and Experience in the *Essais* of Montaigne," *SP*, 67 (1970), 31-40.

"De l'expérience" sought not only opposition of experience and reason, but the connections between judgment and experience.

2217. [JUDITH] Reid, Jane Davidson, "The True Judith," *Art Journal*, 28 (1969), 376-387.

Surveys and evaluates various Renaissance representations of Judith.

2218. [JUSTICE] Aptekar, Jane, *Icons of Justice: Iconography and Thematic Imagery in Book V of "The Faerie Queene."* N.Y.: Columbia Univ. Press, 1969.

Rev. *Criticism*, 12 (1970), 156; *RES*, 21 (1970); *Spenser Newletter*, 1 (1970), 2.

Holds that *The Faerie Queene* is too complex for traditional analysis in framework of allegory. By reading of neglected "Legend of Justice," attempts to discover structures of imagery based more soundly in iconography. Iconography of justice in Book V clarifies themes and details. Thematic fields analyzed by iconographical analogues: justice, force and fraud, and the Hercules myth.

2219. [JUSTICE] Dunseath, T.K., *Spenser's Allegory of Justice in Book Five of "The Faerie Queene."* Princeton, N.J.: Princeton Univ. Press, 1968. Rev. *RES*, n.s. 20 (1969), 488.

Chapters on humility and wisdom; desire and love; justice and peace.

2220. [JUSTICE] Phillips, James E., "Renaissance Concepts of Justice and the Structure of *The Faerie Queene*, Book V," *HLQ*, 33 (1969-70), 103-120.

Accepted principles by Renaissance theorists on Justice as organizational method of Book V.

2221. [JUSTICE] Young, John Jacob, "Artegall and Equity: *The Faerie Queene*, Books III-V," *DA*, 29 (1969), 4472-73-A (Case Western Reserve Univ.).

In the Legend of Justice, Artegall, while he does embody characteristics of the virtue of justice as defined by Aristotle in the *Ethics*, is explicitly drawn as a Knight of Equity as interpreted by contemporary political theorists and as practiced in Elizabethan jurisprudence, specifically in Chancery.

2222. [JUSTIFICATION] Bavaud, G., "La doctrine de la justification d'après Calvin et le Concile de Trente," *Verbum Caro*, 22, no. 87 (1968), 83-92.

On question of possibility of doctrinal agreement over justification issue.

2223. [JUSTIFICATION] Forell, George Wolfgang, "Justification and Eschatology in Luther's Thought," *Church Hist.*, 38 (1969), 164-174.

Holds that Luther's justification by faith is an eschatological experience; his view of eschatology makes it the seal of his doctrine of justification. Justification by faith without eschatology is a form of subjectivistic and individualistic self-hypnosis. Eschatology without justification by faith is mere utopianism.

2224. [JUSTIFICATION] Logan, O.M.T., "Grace and Justification: Some
Italian Views of the Sixteenth and Early Seventeenth Centuries," *Journal of Ecclesiastical Hist.*, 20 (1969), 67-78.

In some 16th- and 17th-cent. Italian invocations in which the
testator asks for the forgiveness of his sins there is stress
on his inability to merit salvation, his total dependence upon
divine mercy, and his trust in redeeming power of Christ.
This new ethos was not only a result of impetus of Protestant
Reformation but also of a movement within the Catholic Church.

2225. [KING] Dosher, Harry Randall, "The Concept of the Ideal Prince
in French Political Thought, 800-1760," *DA*, 30 (1970), 3879-A
(Univ. of North Carolina).

Theory of ideal prince traced from Carolingian concept of monarchy, with absolute authority exercised in ethical framework,
through 18th cent. Political thinkers distinguished a just
prince who ruled under law from a tyrant who oppressed the people in defiance of "higher law," even though prince's powers
were limited in theory.

2226. [KING] Greenberg, Jacquelyn J.R., "Tudor and Stuart Theories
of Kingship: The Dispensing Power and the Royal Discretionary
Authority in Sixteenth and Seventeenth Century England (Vols.
1 and 2), *DA*, 31 (1970), 2307-A (Univ. of Michigan).

Position of the king above law was based on the "order model"
of political society, according to the Tudor and early Stuart
tradition of thought, but a rejection of the order model of
society begins in the reign of James I.

2227. [KING] Isaacs, Neil D., "Royal Robes and Regicide: A Preliminary Study of Literary Vestiges of Rule Rituals," *Folklore*, 80
(1969), 199-215.

Parallels between specific details in *Oresteia* of Aeschylus
and OT. Treats examples of one form of a motif, special mark-
ing of a king (maiming, laming, scarring, or robing).

2228. [KING, Sleeping] Jackson, Richard A., "The Sleeping King,"
BHR, 31 (1969), 525-551.

Medieval liturgical origins and knightly antecedents of rituals
of "sleeping king" at Louis XIII's coronation; studies 16th
cent. for further development of the ceremony; re-examines the
ritual and its meaning within the conceptual framework of early
17th-cent. monarchical ideas; looks again at 16th cent. for
examples of solar symbolism.

2229. [KING, Weak] Manheim, Michael, "The Weak King History Plays of
the Early 1590's," *RenD*, n.s. 2 (1969), 71-80.

The anonymous *Woodstock*, Marlowe's *Edward II*, the *King John*
plays, Shakespeare's *H6* plays, and his *R2* involve dilemmas
about the crown which are integral to the construction of the
plays; the ambivalence or violent shift in audience response
to the central characters reflects the contemporary national
fears.

2230. [KING, Weak] Peters, Edward M., *"Rex Inutilis*: Aspects of Royal Inadequacy in Medieval Law and Literature, 751-1400," *DA*, 28 (1968), 4081-A (Yale Univ.).

Studies depositions, of evident relevance to Shakespeare, in regard to royal inadequacy of various kinds. Cf. his book, Yale Univ. Press, 1970.

2231. [KING, Weak] ———, "Roi Fainéant: The Origins of an His- torians' Commonplace," *BHR*, 30 (1967), 537-547.

Roi fainéant, far from being the medieval *rex inutilis*, is figment of 17th-cent. historical fashion; it is vague descrip- tive term, not precise category.

2232. [KISS] Perella, Nicholas J., *The Kiss Sacred and Profane: An Interpretive History of Kiss Symbolism and Related Religio- Erotic Themes*. Berkeley: Univ. of Calif. Press, 1969.

Rev. *Speculum*, 45 (1970), 682-684.

Continues from previous study on soul-kiss (Stephen Gaselee, *Criterion*, 2 [1924], 349-359) which treated influence of clas- sical writers on Renaissance poets. Perella also stresses Patristic and other sources, including the mystics, Ficino, and other neo-platonic writers; he deals also with the death- kiss as sexual metaphor.

2233. [KNIGHT] Honeycutt, Benjamin Lawrence, "The Role of the Knight in the Old French Fabliaux," *DA*, 30 (1970), 4414-A (Ohio State Univ.).

Aided by a computer concordance of the Montaiglon-Raynard edi- tion of the fabliaux. Two distinct types and corresponding attitudes consistently emerge: the honored, poorer tournament knight and his ridiculed, but wealthy and titled counterpart.

2234. [KNIGHT] Moorman, Charles, *A Knyght There Was: The Evolution of the Knight in Literature*. Lexington, Ky.: Univ. of Ken- tucky Press, 1967.

Rev. *Spec.*, 43 (1968), 525-527.

Includes Chaucer, Malory, Spenser, and Shakespeare.

2235. [LABYRINTH] Heller, John L., and S.S. Cairns, "To Draw a Laby- rinth," in *Classical Studies Presented to Ben Edwin Perry* (*Illinois Studies in Language and Literature*, vol. 58). Univ. of Ill. Press, 1969, pp. 236-262.

Includes illustrations of types; typology of variants.

2236. [LAMP] Price, R.M., "The Lamp and the Clock: Quevedo's Reaction to a Commonplace," *MLN*, 82 (1967), 198-209.

Among 17th-cent. illustrations of human transience and vanity, clock illuminated by an oil lamp at night was a commonplace (also mirrors, jewels, skulls, packs of cards, coins, etc.). The flickering lamp represented human frailty, and the clock, passage of time.

2237. [LANDSCAPE] Bergeron, David M., "Symbolic Landscape in English Civic Pageantry," *RenQ*, 22 (1969), 32-37.

Technique of dividing the landscape background into halves of symbolically contrasting character, common to Renaissance art, also found expression in the dramatic form of civic pageantry in late Tudor and early Stuart England.

2238. [LANDSCAPE] Golson, Lucile M., "Landscape Prints and Landscapists of the School of Fontainebleau, c. 1543-c. 1570," *Gazette des Beaux-Arts*, 73 (1969), 95-110.

Study of the vogue of landscape painting at Fontainebleau, center for this type of painting during 16th cent.

2239. [LANDSCAPE] Turner, A. Richard, *The Vision of Landscape in Renaissance Italy*. Princeton Univ. Press, 1966.

Rev. *Art Q.*, 32 (1969), 200-201.

Ten collected essays to introduce non-specialist to landscape in Italian Renaissance painting. (Written at I Tatti.) Chapters include: Leonardo da Vinci, Piero di Cosimo, Giovanni Bellini, Giorgio da Castelfranco, Venetian Landscapes, Northern Vistas, In Ruinous Perfection, Annibale Caracci, The Villa.

2240. [LAST SUPPER] Wulf, Berthold, *Das heilige Mahl--Brot und Wein*. Freiburg i. Br.: Die Kommenden, 1969.

Last Supper traced through wheat and grape as plants of the sun, to miracle of water into wine, to the Last Supper. Its significance as remembrance, transubstantiation, mystery, and sacrament in the church year from Easter week to Pentecost.

2241. [LAUGHTER] Screech, M.A., and Ruth Calder, "Some Renaissance Attitudes to Laughter," in *Humanism in France* ..., ed., A.H.T. Levi. Manchester and N.Y.: Harper & Row, 1970, pp. 216-228.

Interim report on history of theories of laughter and comedy from Plato to Descartes; particular focus on Rabelais and 16th-cent. Calvinistic attitudes toward comic propaganda.

2242. [LIBERTINISM] Rollin, Roger B., "Images of Libertinism in *Every Man in His Humour* and 'To His Coy Mistress,'" *PLL*, 6 (1970), 188-191. (Cf. 1074.)

Possible influence of Jonson's libertine, Prospero, on Marvell's persona: in both, the irresistible sexual force collides with apparently immovable social objects; both begin as stock characters--witty philanderers--but end in transcending their type.

2243. [LIFE, Lease of] Rissanen, Matti, "'Nature's Copy,' 'Great Bond,' and 'Lease of Nature,' in *Macbeth*," *NM*, 70 (1969), 714-723.

In *Mac.* "nature's copy," "great bond," and "lease of nature" form an image of a "lease of life." Man and nature have a contract: nature gives man his copyhold of life until death.

2244. [LIGHT] Frappier, J., "Le thème de la lumière, de la *Chanson de Roland* au *Roman de la rose*," *Cah. Ass. internation. Et. fr.*, 20 (1968), 101-124; cf. discussion, 319-327.

Refers to theologians who offer a graded hierarchy of effects of light. Proceeds from one level of illumination to another, from gold and stones to ideal landscape and human being described in perfection of his beauty, then to his internal life, his aspirations to love and the divine.

2245. [LIGHT] Orlando, F., "La nuit et l'aube dans le IVe acte du *Venceslas* de Rotrou," *Cahiers de l'Association Internationale des Etudes Françaises*, 20 (1968), 137-147; cf. discussion, 319-327.

Religions, baroque metaphors take on poetic depth and give several scenes setting of light and time.

2246. [LION] Rousseau, Michel, "Le Lion dans l'Art," *Histoire de la Médicine*, 18 (1968), 2-25.

2247. [LOT] Kind, Joshua Benjamin, "The Drunken Lot and His Daughters: An Iconographical Study of the Uses of This Theme in the Visual Arts from 1500-1650, and Its Bases in Exegetical and Literary History," *DA*, 28 (1968), 3582-A (Columbia Univ.).

Includes chapters on incest motif, with Lot as exemplar; 16th to 17th-cent. pictorial treatments. Useful catalogue and handlist of theme recurrences.

2248. [LOVE] Absher, Thomas D., "The Metamorphosis of Love in John Lyly's Plays," *DA*, 29 (1969), 2205-A (Univ. of Penn.).

Theme of love in Lyly's plays, and the love-virginity debate. Classical-medieval tradition of metamorphosis and its place in the plays.

2249. [LOVE] Adams, Martha Lou Latimer, "The Origins of the Concept of Romantic Love as it Appears in the Plays of William Shakespeare," *DA*, 29 (1969), 3968-A (Univ. of Mississippi).

Shakespeare's use and transformation of the Greek-Romance formula of romantic love.

2250. [LOVE] Bonadeo, A., "Some Aspects of Love and Nobility in the Society of the *Decameron*," *PQ*, 47 (1968), 513-525.

Takes exception to Auerbach's hypothesis of an ethical code rooted in the right to love; re-examines the roles of love and nobility in light of social and political conflicts of the period.

2251. [LOVE] Braham, Allan, "Veronese's Allegories of Love," *Burl.*, 112 (1970), 205-212.

On this series of four paintings; treats background of symbolism and iconography for the allegory-of-love theme.

2252. [LOVE] Chace, Jo Ann Elizabeth, "Spenser's Celebration of Love:
      Its Background in English Protestant Thought," *DA*, 29 (1968),
      226-A (Univ. of Calif., Berkeley).

      Spenser reveals himself as typical, concurring with English Re-
      formation morality, in holding that lawful erotic love is that
      which leads to matrimony. Context of English Protestant
      thought, 1520-1600; English Protestant commonplaces on mar-
      riage.

2253. [LOVE] Devereux, James A., "The Object of Love in Ficino's
      Philosophy," *JHI*, 30 (1969), 161-170.

      Argues against Nygren's position that Ficino held that all
      love is basically self-love.

2254. [LOVE] Flury, Peter, *Liebe und Liebesprache bei Menander,
      Plautus, und Terenz*. Heidelberg: Carl Winter Universitäts-
      verlag, 1968. Rev. *Class.W.*, 62 (1969), 228.

      Representation of love in these dramatists.

2255. [LOVE] Hazo, Robert G., *The Idea of Love*. N.Y.: Praeger,
      1967. Rev. *N.Y.T.B.R.*, 73 (25 Feb. 1968), 36.

      "Great ideas" approach, citing various Renaissance writers:
      "Natural Human Love" is divided into chapters, "Love as Acqui-
      sitive and as Benevolent Desire" (e.g., Leone Ebreo, Baldesar
      Castiglione); "Love as Acquisitive Desire" (e.g., Marsilio
      Ficino, Giovanni Pico della Mirandola, Pietro Bembo).

2256. [LOVE] Lewalski, B.K., "Love, Appearance and Reality: 'Much
      Ado About Something,'" *SEL*, 8, no. 2 (1968), 235-251.

      Much Ado About Nothing develops neo-Platonic theme of love
      as means of knowing reality.

2257. [LOVE] Memmo, Paul E., Jr., "The Poetry of the *Stilnovisti* and
      Love's Labour's Lost," *Comparative Literature*, 18, no. 1
      (1966), 1-14.

      Studies *LLL* in light of Renaissance philosophy of love, which
      underlies both its lyrical dexterity and dramaturgy.

2258. [LOVE] Moore, John C., "The Origins of Western Ideas: Irving
      Singer's *The Nature of Love: Plato to Luther*," *JHI*, 29
      (1968), 141-151. (Cf. Singer, N.Y.: Random House, 1966.)

      Review of above book, first of several planned volumes which
      will also cover "courtly love," "romantic love," and love in
      the modern world from a historical perspective.

2259. [LOVE] Perry, T. Anthony, "Ideal Love and Human Reality in
      Montemayor's *La Diana*," *PMLA*, 84 (1969), 227-234."

      As abstraction from conditions of real life, pastoral mode per-
      mits both heightened esthetic contemplation and concentrated
      study of human love. Peculiarity of *La Diana* consists in an
      attempt to fuse the neo-aristotelian antithesis between poetry
      (myth) and history.

2260. [LOVE] Pineaux, Jacques, "La femme et la rose: les poètes de
la réforme devant la poésie épicurienne de la Renaissance,"
Rev. des Sci. Hum., 34 (1969), 5-12.

Situation of Protestant poets of 16th cent. who spoke of love
in an environment where "epicurean" and "epicureanism" were
synonymous with "atheist" and "atheism." Distinctive features
of Protestant love poetry compared with the epicurean tendencies of the time were: poetry of duration, seeing in love the
sign of our eternity, praising the woman the poet wishes to
marry, having the living God as a principle as well as an end.

2261. [LOVE, Church of] Jacobson, John Howard, "The Church of Love
in the Works of Chaucer and Gower," *DA*, 31 (1970), 2347-A
(Yale Univ.).

Investigates Christian-pagan mingling represented in the
Church of Love, the poetic "religion" whose deities are Venus
and Cupid, and whose religious forms are those of the Christian
Church.

2262. [LOVE, COURTLY] Newman, F.X., ed., *The Meaning of Courtly
Love*. Albany: SUNY Press, 1968.

Rev. *Choice*, 6 (1970), 1566; *Spec.*, 46 (1971), 747-750.

Five essays, with annotation; varying viewpoints and approaches
to courtly love.

2263. [LOVE, COURTLY] Resnick, Sandra Irene, "Masculine Submission
in Troubadour Lyric," *DA*, 31 (1970), 2398-A (Cath. Univ. of
Amer.).

Theme of masculine submission in poets of southern France during the 12th and 13th cents. Courtly love was not a historical
reality; troubadours did not necessarily practice submission
to one given woman.

2264. [LOVE, COURTLY] Russell, William M., "Courtly Love in Shakespeare's Romantic Comedies," *DA*, 29 (1969), 4502-A (Catholic
Univ. of Amer.).

Identified by characteristic medieval development of carnal
and spiritual values in the same love-relationships, instead of
by list of medieval doctrinal points. There emerges a courtly
spectrum in which some of the love-relationships reveal traditional courtly earnestness and others mock traditional courtly
expectations for sake of comic effect.

2265. [LOVE, FAMILY OF] Ebel, Julia G., "*The Family of Love*: Sources
of Its History in England," *HLQ*, 30 (1967), 331-343.

Concerns play sometimes attributed to Middleton, *The Family of
Love*, performed *ca.* 1602; contains information regarding Anabaptist religious sect and its origins in England.

2266. [LOVE, FAMILY OF] Moss, Jean-Kathleen Dietz, "The Family of
Love in England," *DA*, 30 (1969), 2465-A (West Virginia Univ.).

Little evidence that Familists engaged in licentious behavior.
Many accusations regarding their religious beliefs are shown
to be unsubstantiated. Familist thought had a much greater influence on other religious groups of the period than has previously been supposed.

2267. [LOVE, HEROIC] Rose, Mark, *Heroic Love: Studies in Sidney and
       Spenser.* Cambridge, Mass.: Harvard Univ. Press, 1968.

       Elizabethan attitudes to love and marriage; treatment of love
       in *Arcadia* and *Faerie Queene.* Rev. *TLS*, 3 July 1969, 725.

2268. [LOVE; ILLUSION] Wright, Carol von Pressentin Colin, "The
       Lunatic, the Lover, and the Poet: Themes of Love and Illu-
       sion in Three Renaissance Epics," *DA*, 30 (1970), 3962-A
       (Univ. of Va.).

       Themes of illusion and reality (*maraviglioso* and *verisimile* in
       Tasso's phrase) traced in Ariosto's *Orlando Furioso*, Tasso's
       Gerusalemme Liberata, and Spenser's *The Faerie Queene*, as they
       affect both subject and form of these epic poems.

2269. [LOVE; LUST] Dye, Fred Arthur, "Love and Lust in the Dramatic
       Works of Thomas Middleton," *DA*, 30 (1970), 2964-A (Indiana
       Univ.).

       Middleton's philosophy as naturalistic fatalism; its develop-
       ment from early to late plays in terms of passions of his
       characters.

2270. [LOVE; LUST] Frantz, David Oswin, "Concepts of Concupiscence
       in English Renaissance Literature," *DA*, 30 (1969), 1133-A
       (Univ. of Pennsylvania).

       Difference between the medieval and Renaissance meaning of
       "concupiscentia." Most common Renaissance meaning is "exces-
       sive sexual appetite," which differs from the meaning found in
       Ovid of a passion glorifying physical love. Theological, mo-
       ral, non-dramatic, and dramatic meanings are discussed. Con-
       cludes with a chapter on *Ant.*

2271. [LOVE, PROFANE] Tomory, P.A., "Profane Love in Italian Early
       and High Baroque Painting: The Transmission of Emotive Ex-
       perience," in Douglas Fraser, et al., eds., *Essays in the His-
       History of Art Presented to Rudolf Wittkower.* London: Phai-
       don, 1967, pp. 182-187.

       On depiction of paired lovers, suggesting a sexual, rather than
       platonic, love; depiction reached its highest incidence during
       period spanning early and high baroque. Survey of background
       and psychological changes in debate over the carnality or
       spirituality of love.

2272. [LOVE, UNEVEN] Coupe, William A., "*Ungleiche Liebe*--A Six-
       teenth-Century Topos," *MLR*, 62 (1967), 661-671.

       Sixteenth-cent. German art often depicted *topos* of union of
       old person with young one.

2273. [LOVE POTION] Fedrick, Alan, "The Love Potion in the French Prose *Tristan*," *RPh*, 21 (1967), 23-34.

Effect of love potion weakened by author, influenced by court-ly love and "fine amour."

2274. [MADONNA] Bloch, Peter, *Madonnenbilder Vierzig Denkmäler der Skulpturensammlung*. Berlin: Mann, 1970.

Rev. *Bibliographie zur Symbolik, Ikonographie und Mythologie*, 4 (1971), 25-26.

Changing image of Madonna through the cents., including the individualization of Maria into the Mother-figure during second half of the 15th cent.

2275. [MAGDALEN] Gappa, Richard John, "Robert Southwell's *Marie Magdelens Funeral Teares:* An Edition," *DA*, 30 (1969), 1524-A (St. Louis Univ.).

Traces the "Magdalen" tradition.

2276. [MAGDALEN] Hufstader, Anselm, "Lefèvre d'Etaples and the Magdalen," *SRen*, 16 (1969), 31-60.

Lefèvre's theory of the three Marys.

2277. [MAGDALEN] Malvern, Marjorie M., "The Magdalen: An Exploration of the Shaping of Myths Around the Mary Magdalene of the New Testament Canonical Gospels and an Examination of the Effects of the Myths on the Literary Figure, Particularly on the Heroine of the Fifteenth-Century Digby Play *Mary Magdalene*," *DA*, 30 (1969), 1532-A (Michigan State Univ.).

Tradition of the Magdalen.

2278. [MAGIC] Rosador, Kurt Tetzeli von, *Magie im Elizabethanischen Drama*. Braunschweig: Georg Westermann Verlag, 1970.

Rev. *SJ West* (1971), 214-216.

Ways in which magic occurs in English drama from its first appearance until late drama of Shakespeare.

2278a. [MAGIC] Thomas, Keith, *Religion and the Decline of Magic*. N.Y.: Scribner's, 1971.

Rev. *RenQ*, 26 (1973), 70-72.

Major study of Elizabethan-Stuart religious views as inter-twined with magic and superstition. Witchcraft as a rival belief, among others, to religion.

2279. [MAGIC, White] Woodman, David Roderick, "White Magic in English Renaissance Drama," *DA*, 30 (1969), 699-700-A (Columbia Univ.).

Use of white magic in Shakespeare, Jonson, and Jacobean court masques.

2280. [MAGNANIMITY] Waters, D. Douglas, "Prince Arthur as Christian Magnanimity in Book One of *The Faerie Queene*," *SEL*, 9 (1969), 53-62.

In theological allegory of *The Legende of Holiness* Spenser
uses Prince Arthur as symbol of moral virtue of magnanimity or
greatness of soul, a "Christianized" concept of Aristotle's
megalopsychia appropriated by Thomas Aquinas, Patrizi, Pontano, Cinthio, Piccolomini, Sir Thomas Elyot, La Primaudaye,
Cajetan, and others.

2281. [MAGNIFICENCE] Winser, Leigh, "Skelton's *Magnyfycence* and the
       Morality Tradition," *DA*, 30 (1969), 1154-A (Columbia Univ.).

       Classical and Christian meanings of the term "magnificence."

2282. [MANHOOD] Taylor, Michael, "Ideals of Manhood in *Macbeth*,"
       Etudes anglaises, 21 (1968), 337-348.

       Moral potency of the "naked newborn babe" in a meaningful de-
       finition of manhood.

2283. [MANKIND] Schuchter, Julian David, "Man Redeemable, The Man-
       kind Character in the English Morality Plays: A Study in
       Theatre and Theology," *DA*, 29 (1969), 3156-A (Univ. of Calif.,
       Berkeley).

       Traces Pelagian reaction against Augustinian theology and re-
       currences of this split down to 14th cent., when the morality
       play apparently came into being. Mankind character is fol-
       lowed through 45 plays.

2284. [MANKIND] Wertz, Dorothy, "Mankind as a Type-Figure in the
       Popular Religious Stage: An Analysis of the Fifteenth-Century
       English Morality Plays," *Comp. Studies in Society and Hist.*,
       12 (1970), 83-91.

       Mankind as a character, relates to individualist and voluntar-
       ist emphasis of nominalist thought; also to commercial demand
       for a new form to compete with burghers' mystery plays.

2285. [MANNERISM] Federhofer, Hellmut, "Zum Manierismus: Problem in
       der Musik," *DVLG*, 44 (1970), 393-408.

       Mannerism as a transitional form between Renaissance and Ba-
       roque. Aspects of Renaissance related to later Baroque.

2286. [MARRIAGE] Bernard, Robert William, "Renaissance Attitudes on
       Marriage, Love, and Sexual Mores as Found in the *Heptaméron*,"
       DA, 29 (1969), 3125-A (Univ. of Kansas).

       Marriage question in 16th cent.; marriage and adultery as pre-
       sented in the *Heptaméron*; extra-marital alliances; amatory tac-
       tics of the gallants.

2287. [MARRIAGE] Bullough, G., "Polygamy among the Reformers,"
       *Renaissance and Modern Essays [in honor of] Vivian de Sola
       Pinto*. London: Routledge and Kegan Paul, 1966, pp. 5-23.

       Writings of the 16th and 17th cents. were greatly concerned
       with matrimonial problems, especially that of polygamy. Most
       principal Reformers and Roman Catholics were strongly against
       it. Renaissance theorists recognized that there were four
       kinds of law operating in matrimonial behavior: Divine,

natural, of custom, and of nations. Rationalistic and comparative approaches to such moral and social problems were beginning to enter discussions.

2288. [MARRIAGE] Halkett, John G., _Milton and the Idea of Marriage: A Study of the Divorce Tracts and "Paradise Lost."_ New Haven and London: Yale Univ. Press, 1970.

Rev. _Choice_, 7 (1970), 685; _JEGP_, 70 (1971), 308-310.

How far ideal of matrimony in Milton's divorce tracts is embodied in _Paradise Lost_. Central in Milton is idea that marriage is an end in itself, not a means to propagation.

2289. [MARRIAGE] Johnson, James T., "The Covenant Idea and the Puritan View of Marriage," _JHI_, 32 (1971), 107-118.

Marriage as Puritan covenant between husband and wife to prepare them for salvation. Thus marriage shares aspects of friendship and citizenship, as social involvement.

2290. [MARRIAGE] ———, "English Puritan Thought on the Ends of Marriage," _Church Hist._, 38 (1969), 429-436.

Traces, from William Perkins to Richard Baxter, Puritan idea that the end of marriage was companionship or "mutual meet help."

2291. [MARRIAGE] ———, _A Society Ordained by God: English Puritan Marriage Doctrine in the First Half of the Seventeenth Century._ Nashville: Abingdon Press, 1970. Rev. _Choice_, 8 (1971), 408.

Idea of charity as role in Puritan idea of marriage. Influence of Ramus.

2292. [MARRIAGE] Ringbom, Sixten, "Nuptial Symbolism in Some Fifteenth-Century Reflections of Roman Sepulchrel Portraiture," _Temenos: Studies in Comparative Religion_, 2 (1966), 68-97.

Roman provincial art during late Middle Ages. Includes love-symbolism and illustrations.

2293. [MARRIAGE] Rordorf, Willy, "Marriage in the New Testament and in the Early Church," _Jour. of Eccl. Hist._, 20 (1969), 193-210.

Marriage and eschatology; Augustine on marriage as _sacramentum_ --neither infidelity nor sterility allowed a marital partner to break the _sacramentum_.

2294. [MARRIAGE] Schnucker, Robert Victor, "Views of Selected Puritans, 1560-1630, on Marriage and Human Sexuality," _DA_, 30 (1969), 802-A (Univ. of Iowa).

Puritan attitudes were shaped both by intellectual environment of the time and by Puritan adherence to Scripture as source and norm of their position. Puritans generally did not subscribe to celibate view of life; held that within estate of marriage, it was possible to attain highest and most perfect level of human existence.

2295. [MARRIAGE] Valente, Michael Feeney, "The Sexual Ethics of Martin Le Maistre," *DA*, 30 (1969), 1231-A (Columbia Univ.).

Sex ethic of Martin Le Maistre (1432-1481). Thomistic outline of the Pauline states of chastity and the vices opposed to it. Le Maistre offers critique of the tradition, by breaking down what he calls the Augustinian rule (that intercourse may be undertaken in marriage only for the sake of procreation or the rendering of the debt). Justifies marital intercourse as a remedy against adultery, for reasons of health or pleasure.

2296. [MARS; VENUS; VULCAN] Lord, Carla, "Tintoretto and the *Roman De La Rose*," *JWCI*, 33 (1970), 314.

Artistic representation of the Venus-Mars-Vulcan triangle; its relations to various literary themes.

2297. [MARTYR] Feylock, H.T., "Das Märtyrerdrama im Barock: *Philemon Martyr* von Jacob Bidermann, *Le véritable Saint Genest* von Jean Rotrou, *Théodore, vierge et martyre* von Pierre Corneille, *Catharina von Georgien* von Andreas Gryphius. Ein Vergleich," *DA*, 28 (1967), 1432-A (Univ. of Colorado).

2298. [MARTYR] Szarota, Elida Maria, *Künstler, Grübler un Rebellen: Studien zum europäischen Märtyrerdrama des 17. Jahrhunderts.* Bern: Francke, 1967.

Rev. *KN*, 14 (1967), 313-315; *TLS*, 28 September 1967, 866.

Title references are to protagonists: also has chapters on kings and on secularized martyr-drama. Includes plays by Lope de Vega, Calderón, Rotrou, Massinger, Vondel, Gryphius, etc.

2299. [MELANCHOLY] Engstrom, Alfred Garvin, "The Man Who Thought Himself Made of Glass, and Certain Related Images," *SP*, 67 (1970), 390-405.

Theme in 16th and 17th cent. literary works (including Andreas Laurentius' *Discourse of Melancholike Diseases*, and Burton's *Anatomy of Melancholy*): archetype for man's insecurity about his condition.

2300. [MELANCHOLY] Gellert, Bridget, "The Iconography of Melancholy in the Graveyard Scene of *Hamlet*," *SP*, 67 (1970), 57-66.

Sees scene as an emblem of several major themes: Appearance vs. reality, decay, and disease. Melancholy: its complexity as a Renaissance theme.

2301. [MELANCHOLY] ———, "Three Literary Treatments of Melancholy: Marston, Shakespeare and Burton," *DA*, 28 (1967), 628-629-A (Columbia Univ.).

On usefulness that melancholy had for English writers of late 16th and early 17th cents.; its medical and philosophical background. Chapter on Shakespeare focuses on *Ham.*, arguing that melancholy is central to play's dramaturgy, in mirroring of protagonist's characteristics or actions by lesser characters,

in imagery, in iconographical statements, of which the Grave-
yard Scene is an example. (See: Lyons, Bridget Gellert,
_Voices of Melancholy: Studies in Literary Treatments of
Melancholy in Renaissance England._ London: Routledge and
Kegan Paul, 1971.)

2302. [MELANCHOLY] Heger, Henrik, _Die Melancholie bei den französischen Lyrikern des Spätmittelalters._ Romanistische Versuche
und Vorarbeiten, 21. Romanisches Seminar der Universität
Bonn, 1967.

Rev. _BHR_, 30 (1968), 383-385.

On modes of use of the term _melancholy_ in scientific, moral,
and philosophic literature; its relation to the humors; its
relation to the discovery of the self.

2303. [MELANCHOLY] Madden, J.S., "Melancholy in Medicine and Literature: Some Historical Considerations," _Brit. Jour. of Medical
Psychology_, 39, pt. 2 (1966), 125-130.

Description of Galenical physiological psychology based upon
the four humors, with emphasis on melancholy and its relation
to Elizabethan and later English literature.

2304. [MELANCHOLY] Maier, John Raymond, "Religious Melancholy and
the Imagination in Book One of _The Faerie Queene_,"_DA_ , 31
(1970), 2391-2392-A (Duquesne Univ.).

Spenser's legend of Holiness; ideas of Melancholy and imagination and their meaning for Elizabethan psychology. Classical
and medieval backgrounds and Renaissance transformation of
melancholy and imagination.

2305. [MELANCHOLY] Timken-Zinkann, R.F., "Black Bile. A Review of
Recent Attempts to Trace the Origins of the Teachings on
Melancholia to Medical Observations," _Medical Hist._, 12 (1968),
288-292.

Only recently have scholars begun to seek the connection between physiological phenomena and black bile by empirical methods; limitation of these may have misled the Hippocratics to
hypothesize existence of this humour.

2306. [MELANCHOLY] Veith, Ilza, "Elizabethans on Melancholia," _JAMA_,
212 (6 April 1970), 127-131.

Discussion of Elizabethan melancholy focusing on Burton; also
Thomas Walkington and Timothy Bright.

2307. [MEMORY] Blum, Herwig, _Die antike Mnemotechnik._ Hildesheim:
Georg Olms Verlag, 1969.

Rev. _EIC_, 20 (1970), 353-359.

Based on 1964 Tübingen dissertation, study treats a division
of classical rhetoric, _memoria_; attempts to correct Frances A.
Yates's _The Art of Memory_ (1966), rev. _EIC_, October 1967, pp.
473-478. Summarizes classical aids to orator in improving
memory, as well as classical mnemonic theory.

2308. [MEMORY] Severin, Dorothy Sherman, *Memory in "La Celestina"* (Colección Támesis, Serie A., 19). London: Tamesis, 1970.

Includes Memory: The Tradition, Memory and Character in the *Comedia*, Loss of Memory Through Love, Memory and Time in the *Comedia*. Rev. *MLR*, 67 (1972), 672.

2309. [MEMORY] Van Dorsten, J.A., "The Arts of Memory and Poetry," *English Studies*, 48 (1967), 419-425.

Affinity between poetic and mnemonic uses of imagery in Sidney's *Defense of Poetry*, *Astrophel and Stella*, sonnet xiii, and the *Arcadia*.

2310. [MEMORY] Yates, Frances A., *The Art of Memory*. Chicago, Ill.: Univ. of Chicago Press; London: Routledge and Kegan Paul, 1966.

Rev. Walter J. Ong, *RenQ*, 20 (1967), 253-259.

Traces systems for implementing memory from Greeks through Cicero and Quintilian, Middle Ages, and Renaissance into the Cartesian era. Of particular interest are discussions of *topoi*, of medieval classifications of virtues and vices, of iconography as a memory system, of the connection between memory systems and the Globe Theater, and of the use of "theatre" in many titles of contemporary literature.

2311. [MERCHANT] Donow, Herbert S., "Thomas Deloney and Thomas Heywood: Two Views of the Elizabethan Merchant," *DA*, 27 (1967), 3042-A - 3043-A (Univ. of Iowa).

Deloney, a champion of mercantile endeavor, tried to present the merchant as a secularized modern hero, while Heywood, retaining a Christian asceticism, rejected materialistic values in favor of traditional other-worldly concerns.

2312. [MERCURY] Dempsey, Charles, "*Mercurius Ver*: The Sources of Botticelli's *Primavera*," *JWCI*, 31 (1968), 251-273.

Relation of Botticelli's painting to traditions of Mercury.

2313. [MERCURY] Mirimonde, A.P. de, "Les Allégories de la Musique: Le Retour de Mercure et les Allégories des Beaux-Arts," *Gazette des Beaux-Arts*, 73 (1969), 343-362.

Revival of ancient gods in 15th and 16th cents. considerably influenced the concept of musical allegories. Mercury, in particular, had a marked influence on this iconography. Author traces course of musical allegories from 15th cent. to 19th.

2314. [MESSENGER] Scrimgeour, Gary J., "The Messenger as a Dramatic Device in Shakespeare," *SQ*, 19 (1968), 41-54.

Shakespeare's use of messenger in solving difficulties, from the simplest to the most complex.

2315. [METAPHOR] Allen, Don Cameron, *Image and Meaning: Metaphoric Traditions in Renaissance Poetry*. Baltimore: Johns Hopkins Press, 1968.

New enlarged edition includes four new essays on Shakespeare,
Milton, and Herrick; method of reading a poem by examining
each metaphor and tracing its meaning in a wide context of
Western literature.

2316. [MICHAEL] Küppers, Leonhard, *Michael*. Recklinghausen: Bon-
gers, 1970.

Rev. *Bibliographie zur Symbolik, Ikonographie und Mythologie*,
4 (1971), 80.

Michael as both a warrior against evil and bringer of peace.

2317. [MICHAELMAS] Pace, George B., "Gawain and Michaelmas," *Traditio*, 25 (1969), 404–411.

Primary association of Michaelmas as settling of accounts.

2318. [MICHAELMAS] Taaffe, James G., "Michaelmas, the 'Lawless
Hour' and the Occasion of Milton's *Comus*," *ELN* (1969), 257–
262.

In *Comus* Milton makes use of the Michaelmas day traditions:
1) the hour of misrule and lawlessness, 2) the existence of
guardian angels, and 3) the celebration of the transferral of
temporal power.

2319. [MILL] Rowland, Beryl, "The Mill in Popular Metaphor from
Chaucer to the Present Day," *SFQ*, 33 (1969), 69–79.

Traces history of the mill as popular erotic metaphor.

2320. [MIRROR] Goldin, Frederick, *The Mirror of Narcissus in the
Courtly Love Lyric*. Ithaca: Cornell Univ. Press, 1967.

On courtly mirrors of honor, shame, justice, etc.; ethical
foundations of medieval troubadours. Rev. *Choice*, 5 (1968), 44.

2321. [MIRROR] Mah, Kai-Ho, "The Dramatic Functions of the Mirror in
Selected Elizabethan and Modern French Plays," *DA*, 29 (1968),
232-A (Univ. of Washington).

Use of mirror in eight plays, including Shakespeare's *R2*,
Greene's *Friar Bacon and Friar Bungay*, and Marlowe's *Tamburlaine*.

2322. [MIRROR] Wilson, G.R., Jr., "The Interplay of Perception and
Reflection: Mirror Imagery in Donne's Poetry," *SEL*, 9 (1969),
107–122.

Analysis of 12 occurrences of mirror imagery in Donne's poetry;
use of them in dealing with secular love.

2323. [MISANTHROPE] Pauls, Peter, "Shakespeare's *Timon of Athens*:
An Examination of the Misanthrope Tradition and Shakespeare's
Handling of the Sources," *DA*, 30 (1969), 1146–1147-A (Univ.
of Wisc.).

"Unfinished" state of *Timon* can be attributed largely to source
material at Shakespeare's disposal. Importance of *Life of Alcibiades* and Richard Barckley's *Discourse* as sources. Less
direct sources are also considered.

2324. [MONEY] Rubinstein, E., "*I Henry IV*: The Metaphor of Liability," *SEL*, 10 (1970), 287–295.

References to financial liability, money, and coinage, both literally and figuratively, to show importance of time and cunning to the world of the play. (Cf. 101.)

2325. [MOON] Kratz, Bernd, "*Pulchra ut Luna*," *Arcadia*, 4 (1969), 300–304.

Medieval Arabic-Spanish comparison using the moon as a standard of beauty, as a *topos*.

2326. [MOSES] Lida de Malkiel, María Rosa, "'Las infancias de Moisés' y otros tres estudios," *RPh*, 23 (1970), 412–448.

Josephus' *Jewish Antiquities* is source for medieval and Renaissance histories of the childhood of Moses, the pillars of wisdom (inscribed by the sons of Seth), the bird and the archer (which demonstrate the failure of prognostication), and the woman seduced in a temple by her lover disguised as a god.

2327. [MOSES] Mellinkoff, Ruth, *The Horned Moses in Medieval Art and Thought*. (Calif. Studs. in History of Art, 14.) Univ. of Calif. Press, 1970.

Rev. *JAAC*, 30 (1971), 275–276.

On 600-year gap between the literary and artistic Moses. Although the 4th-cent. Vulgate translation of the OT attributed horns to Moses, they did not appear in art until the 11th cent.

2328. [MUSES] Joukovsky, Françoise, *Poésie et mythologie au XVIe siècle. Quelques mythes de l'inspiration chez des poètes de la Renaissance*. Paris: Nizet, 1970.

Rev. *TLS*, 18 September 1970, 1050.

Treatment of Muses, nymphs, and sibyls. Marot and the Pléiade established use of female figures as symbols of mythic and poetic callings.

2329. [MUSES] Snare, Gerald, "The Muses on Poetry: Spenser's *The Teares of the Muses*," *Tulane Studies in English*, 12 (1969), 31–52.

Muses complain that man rejects harmony of the soul and the perception of the harmony of the world which they were thought to offer; their preference for learned men over the vulgar. Tradition in mythological dictionaries and compendia.

2330. [MUSIC, Emblem of] Scott, William O., "Another 'Heroical Devise' in *Pericles*," *SQ*, 20 (1969), 91–95.

Singing in reunion scene of Pericles and Mariana may owe something to Paradin's *Heroical Devises* (1591), specifically to emblem on the power of music and narrative accompanying it.

2331. [MUSIC OF THE SPHERES] Chamberlain, David, "The Music of the Spheres and 'The Parliament of Foules,'" *Chau R*, 5 (1970), 32–56.

Chaucer shows interest in philosophical aspects of music;
weaves through structure and themes of the poem all four
medieval species of music; the spheres are the cause of almost
all of this music.

2332. [MUSIC OF THE SPHERES] Meyer-Baer, Kathi, *Music of the Spheres
and the Dance of Death: Studies in Musical Iconology*. Princeton Univ. Press, 1970.

Rev. *Choice*, 7 (1970), 1237; *RenQ*, 24 (1971), 239-240; *Spec.*,
46 (1971), 172-174.

First part traces history of the most literal image of *Musica
Mundana*--musical sounds created by the celestial spheres.
Second part presents an association of Orphean subjects from
the musical lore of antiquity with medieval themes of the
dance of death and the musical instrument as an emblem of vice.

2333. [MUSIC OF THE SPHERES] Walker, D.P., "Kepler's Celestial
Music," *JWCI*, 30 (1967), 228-250.

In the long tradition of music of the spheres, the originality
of Kepler's celestial harmonies; e.g., they are real but
soundless; they are polyphonic; they are in just intonation,
i.e., having consonant thirds and sixths, etc.

2334. [MUSICA] Mirimonde, A.P. de, "Les Allégories de la Musique:
I. La Musique parmi les arts libéraux," *Gazette des Beaux-Arts*,
72 (1968), 295-324.

Symbolic representations of Musica; her place and influence
among the liberal and fine arts from the 12th cent. to the
18th cent. Many illustrations; English summary, pp. 320-321.

2335. [MUSICAL INSTRUMENTS] ———, "La Musique dans les allégories
de l'amour," *Gazette des Beaux-Arts*, 68 (1966), 265-290;
"Eros," 69 (1967), 319-346.

Musical instruments as symbols of love and death in paintings
and engravings from the end of the 15th cent. to the 18th
cent. Many illustrations; English summary, pp. 342-343.

2336. [MUTABILITY] Dorn, Alfred, "The Mutability Theme in the Poetry
of Edmund Spenser and John Donne," *DA*, 30 (1970), 4407-A
(N.Y. Univ.).

Donne's natural universe was altered by mutability and chaos
beyond redemption; man could be saved only through supernatural
Grace. Spenser's universe was an interplay of degenerative
and regenerative forces that revealed an immutable cosmic order
beyond the chaos of the world.

2337. [MUTABILITY] Holland, J.F., "The Cantos of Mutabilitie and
the Form of *The Faerie Queene*," *ELH*, 35, no. 1 (1968), 21-31.

Spenser's mythic and metaphoric vision of the course of history from loss to restitution. Conception of time as a set of
cycles within a circle which goes from the Fall to the Apocalypse.

2338.   [MUTABILITY] Mogan, Joseph J., Jr., *Chaucer and the Theme of Mutability*. The Hague: Mouton, 1969. Rev. *Spec.*, 46 (1971), 175.

Survey of ancient and medieval thought and description of themes used to express idea of mutability.

2339.   [MYTH] Borchardt, Frank L., *German Antiquity in Renaissance Myth*. Balt.: Johns Hopkins Pr., 1971. Rev. *Choice*, 9 (1972), 632.

2340.   [MYTH] Bush, D., "Pagan Myth and Christian Tradition in English Poetry," *Mem. Amer. Philos. Soc.*, 72 (1968), 1-112.

Use of mythology and the Christian tradition by principal representatives of English poetry of Renaissance, Romantic period, and modern times.

2341.   [MYTH] Garner, Barbara Carman, "Francis Bacon, Natalis Comes and the Mythological Tradition," *JWCI*, 33 (1970), 264-291.

Bacon's *De Sapienta Veterum*, its relation to Comes's mythography, as a study in Renaissance philosophy and mythography, science, and religion.

2342.   [MYTH] Rush, Mary Minniece, "Bacon's *Wisdom of the Ancients*: The Uses of Mythology," *DA*, 30 (1969), 2498-A (Tulane Univ.).

Bacon's attitude toward pagan myths; his purpose in interpreting their allegorical meaning. Renaissance attitude toward ancient fables, tradition of mythological exegesis, major allegorical treatises by ancient and medieval writers available to Bacon.

2343.   [MYTH] Santillana, Giorgio de, and Hertha von Dechend, *Hamlet's Mill. An Essay on Myth and the Frame of Time*. Boston: Gambit, 1969. Rev. *N.Y.R.B.*, 14 (12 Feb. 1970), 36.

Myths arising from astronomy are seen as sources of science.

2344.   [MYTHS, Ovidian] Lord, Carla Greenhaus, "Some Ovidian Themes in Italian Renaissance Art," *DA*, 29 (1969), 2619-A (Columbia Univ.).

Dozen themes from Ovid's *Metamorphoses* that appear frequently as subjects in Renaissance art. Tales revolve mainly around loves of the gods: abductions of Proserpina and of Europa, Venus and Mars, Venus and Adonis, Apollo and Daphne--or offenses against the gods: stories of Actaeon, Niobe, Marsyas, Midas, Meleager, Phaethon, Narcissus, Perseus, and Andromeda. Related literary sources examined. Also explored are visual precedents: monuments, illuminated manuscripts, and printed editions of *Metamorphoses*.

2345.   [NAMES] Borchardt, Frank L., "Etymology in Tradition and in the Northern Renaissance," *JHI*, 29 (1968), 415-429.

Study of significance of names was important category of thought in English Renaissance. Emphasis of Renaissance etymology shifted from theological concerns to elucidation of the past as a national, secular, and political expression.

2346. [NAMES] Doran, Madeleine, "Good Name in *Othello*," *SEL*, 7
       (1967), 195-217.

       Discusses Roman law concept of *fama* and *mala fama*; "good name"
       is part of legal tradition inherited from Romans as well as
       part of Christian ethical tradition. It is property one is
       born with, but which can be lost or taken away, as by slander
       or envy. Discusses medieval tradition behind slander.

2347. [NAMES] Kytzler, B., "Classical Names in Shakespeare's *Corio-
       lanus*," *Archiv*, 204, no. 2 (1968), 133-137.

       Shakespeare's use of names Cotus, Adrian, and Nicanor to evoke
       situations or fates experienced by their classical counter-
       parts, and of the name Gaius Marcius Coriolanus to connect
       this war-hero with the war-god Mars.

2348. [NAMES] Seaman, William M., "On the Names of Young and Old Men
       in Plautus," in *Classical Studies Presented to Ben Edwin
       Perry.* (Illinois Studies in Language and Literature, vol. 58.)
       Univ. of Ill. Press, 1969, pp. 114-122.

2349. [NAMES] Weidhorn, Manfred, "The Rose and Its Name: On Denomi-
       nation in *Othello, Romeo and Juliet, Julius Caesar*," *TSLL*, 11
       (1969), 671-686.

       Relationship in the three plays between objects and their
       names.

2350. [NARCISSUS] Goldin, Frederick, *The Mirror of Narcissus in the
       Courtly Love Lyric.* Ithaca, N.Y.: Cornell Univ. Press, 1967.

       Rev. *Spec.*, 44 (1969), 181-182.

       Deals with self-awareness in the Narcissus theme in French and
       German lyric.

2351. [NARCISSUS] ————, "The Narcissus Theme in Western European
       Literature (and Some Problems of Thematology)," *RPh*, 23
       (1969), 220-227.

       On Louise Vinge's work below.

2352. [NARCISSUS] Vinge, Louise, *The Narcissus Theme in Western Euro-
       pean Literature up to the Early 19th Century.* Lund: Gleerup,
       1967.

       Rev. *BHS*, 45 (1968), 254-255; *CJ*, 64 (1968), 76-77; *Comp. Lit.
       Studs.*, 7 (1970), 128-131; *JEGP*, 68 (1969), 471-472; *Orbis
       litt.*, 24 (1969), 315-320; *PQ*, 47 (1968), 350; *RF*, 80 (1968),
       444-448; *Spec.*, 44 (1969), 181-182.

       Useful work, from 12th to 19th cent. Bibliography helpful,
       especially for mythological and poetic references.

2353. [NATURA] Economou, George D., "The Goddess Natura in Medieval
       Literature," *DA*, 31 (1970), 1224-A (Columbia Univ.).

       Philosophical origins; Boethius, Jean de Meun, and Chaucer to
       Spenser, with whom long history of goddess Natura is said to
       end.

2354. [NATURA] Raby, F.J.E., "*Nuda Natura* and Twelfth-Century Cosmology," *Speculum*, 43 (1967), 72-77.

Macrobius' *Commentarium in Somnium* as source for opposition to idea that nature, an "infinite book of secrecy," or Goddess Natura, should be stripped and her secrets exposed to the vulgar.

2355. [*NATURAE CURSUS*] Galinsky, Hans, "*Naturae Cursus*: Der Weg einer antiken kosmologischen Metapher von der Alten in die Neue Welt: Ein Beitrag zu einer historischen Metaphorik der Weltliteratur," *Arcadia*, 1 (1966), 277-311; 2 (1967), 11-78, 139-172. Also Heidelberg: Winter, 1968. (Cf. *Archiv. f. Begrif.*, 13 [1969], 86-89.

On the "course of nature" as world-literature metaphor.

2356. [NATURAL LAW] Fellermier, J., "Das Naturrecht in der Scholastik," *Theol. u. Glaube*, 58, nos. 4-5 (1968), 333-369.

Describes essential features of natural law according to the Scholastics and examines thought of Gabriel Vazquez (1549-1604), William of Ockham, Thomas Aquinas, Duns Scotus, Francisco Suarez on this topic.

2357. [NATURAL LAW] Gibbs, Lee W., "The Puritan Natural Law Theory of William Ames," *Harv. Theol. Rev.*, 64 (1971), 37-57.

2358. [NATURAL LAW] Herndl, George C., *The High Design: English Renaissance Tragedy and the Natural Law*. Lexington, Ky.: Univ. Press of Kentucky, 1970. Rev. *MLR*, 67 (1972), 616.

2359. [NATURAL LAW] Kuhre, Walter William, "Natural Law and Prose Works of the English Renaissance," *DA*, 29 (1968), 1514-A (Pennsylvania State Univ.).

Traditional natural law ideas largely accepted by English Renaissance writers (Hooker, Donne, Bacon, Hobbes, Jeremy Taylor, Selden, Herbert of Cherbury, Traherne) as normative and basic. Despite skepticism and doubt that supposedly mark end of Renaissance, moral knowledge in these writers is a certainty; through the integrity of the creation, man can, by nature and grace, recognize his moral responsibilities.

2360. [NATURAL LAW] Sigmund, Paul E., *Natural Law in Political Thought*. Cambridge, Mass.: Winthrop Pubs., 1971.

Summaries and brief selections from Greek thought, Roman thought, Medieval theories. Chapters 4-5: From Medieval to Modern Natural Law: 1) Ockham, Suarez, and Grotius; 2) Hooker, Hobbes, and Locke. Rev. *Choice*, 9 (1972), 133.

2361. [NATURE] Arcoleo, S., "La filosofia della natura nella problematica di Alano di Lilla," *La filosofia della natura nel Medioevo*. Milan: Società Editrice Vita e Pensiero, 1966, pp. 255-259.

Poetic vision of Nature as the gods' daughter, generatrix of all things, *anima mundi*, mistress of man.

2362. [NATURE] Blocian T., "Filozofia Przyrody Cesare Cremoniniego (1550-1631)" [Cesare Cremonini's Philosophy of Nature], *Archiwum Historii Filozofii i Myśli Społecznej*, 15 (1969), 125-143.

Surveys in detail philosophical teachings of this member of Padua's Aristotelian school. Studies Cremonini's definition of "nature" which he understood as encompassing all existing things and possessing a dynamic character.

2363. [NATURE] Davidson, Clifford, "Nature and Judgment in the *Old Arcadia*," *PLL*, 6 (1970), 348-367.

Sidney's paradoxical and ambivalent treatment of Renaissance argument about Nature underlies his analysis of the heroic life as compared with the pastoral.

2364. [NATURE] Margolin, Jean-Claude, *L'Idée de nature dans la pensée d'Erasme*. Vorträge der Aeneas-Silvius-Stiftung an der Universität Basel, 7. Stuttgart: Helbing & Lichtenhahn, 1967.

Rev. *L'Antiquité Classique*, 37 (1968), 385-386; *BHR*, 29 (1967), 747-748; *EP*, no. 1 (1968), 76.

Brief study of significance of "nature" in Erasmus; his thought on nature and human reason; his reconciliation of human nature and Christian grace. (See also Margolin's essay with same title in *Canadian Journal of Hist.*, 3 [1968], 1-33.)

2365. [NATURE] Nobis, H.M., "Frühneuzeitliche Verständnisweisen der Natur und ihr Wandel bis zum 18. Jahrhundert," *Arch. Begriffsgesch.*, 11, no. 1 (1967), 37-58; 13 (1969), 34-57.

Evolution of the concept of nature from early modern times until 18th cent.

2366. [NATURE] Spitz, Leona, "Process and Stasis: Aspects of Nature in Vaughan and Marvell," *HLQ*, 32 (1969), 135-147.

As a source of Vaughan's imagery, nature is in cyclical motion; identification with natural forms and processes is mode of Vaughan's persuasion that he may be a recipient of divine grace. Marvell's intellect takes charge of nature. Bermuda becomes Eden; the Garden, reduced to an abstraction, is made subordinate to the poet's spiritual requirement.

2367. [NATURE] Védrine, Hélène, *La conception de la nature chez Giordano Bruno*. Université de Paris, Faculté des Lettres et Sciences Humaines. Paris: J. Vrin, 1967.

Rev. *EP*, 23 (1968), 187-189.

2368. [NATURE] Wolfe, Cynthia Nash, "The Concept of Nature in Five Religious Poets of the Seventeenth Century, Spee, Vaughan, Silesius, Herbert, and Gryphius," *DA*, 28 (1967), 2272-A (Indiana Univ.).

Seventeenth-cent. views of nature through poets' comments about natural world, time, and death, in period when science had begun revision of attitudes to nature. Rejects generalizations about 17th-cent. views which involve simplistic imposition of *Zeitgeist*.

2369.   [NATURE, STATE OF] Behler, Ernst, "Ideas of the 'State of Nature' and 'Natural Man' in the Arabic Tradition of the Middle Ages and Their Entrance into Western Thought," *Arcadia*, 3 (1968), 1-26.

Includes 17th cent., Hobbes, and Grotius.

2370.   [NEGRO] Hunter, G.K., "Othello and Colour Prejudice," Shakespeare Lecture, 1967, in *Proc. of Brit. Acad.*, 53 (1967), 139-163.

Renaissance views of "blackness" not shared by modern audiences. Economic and theological reactions differed from modern ones. Elizabethan drama and role of Moors.

2371.   [NEGRO] Tokson, Elliot H., "The Image of the Negro in Four Seventeenth-Century Poems," *MLQ*, 30 (1969), 508-522.

Deals with George Herbert, Henry Rainolds, Henry King, and John Cleveland.

2372.   [NEPTUNE] Gerhardt, Mia I., *Old Men of the Sea: From Neptunus to Old French "luiton": Ancestry and Character of a Water-Spirit*. Utrechtse Publikaties voor Algemene Literatuurwetenschap. Amsterdam: Polak & Van Gennep, 1967.

Rev. *RPh*, 22 (1968), 258.

2373.   [NIGHT] Hinman, Martha Mayo, "The Night Motif in German Baroque Poetry," *GR*, 42 (1967), 83-95.

2374.   [NIGHT] Ramnoux, Clémence, "Histoire d'un Symbole--Histoire antique de 'la nuit,'" *Cahiers internationaux de symbolisme*, no. 13 (1967), 57-68.

Discussion of ambivalence of "night" as symbol in ancient Greek uses.

2375.   [NIGHT] Reimbold, Ernst Thomas, *Die Nacht im Mythos, Kultus, Volksglauben und in der transpersonalen Erfahrung*. Cologne: Wison, 1970.

Rev. *Bibliographie zur Symbolik, Ikonographie und Mythologie*, 4 (1971), 109.

Three major sections examine "Nacht" as 1) numinous power, 2) numinous time, and 3) polarity, ambivalence, and unsystematizable phenomenon.

2376.   [NIGHTINGALE] Shippey, Thomas A., "Listening to the Nightingale," *Comp. Lit.*, 22 (1970), 46-60.

Poetic references to the bird seem to emerge suddenly in 12th and 13th cents., poets through Europe using it in similar fashion. Classical impediments (Homer, Virgil, Ovid) to nightingale as bird of love occur in gruesome references (e.g., Philomela and Itys). Detailed study.

2377. [NINE WORTHIES] Crawley, Thomas Francis, "*Love's Labour's Lost* and the Pageant of the Nine Worthies: A Thematic and Structural Analysis," *DA*, 30 (1969), 1522-A (Univ. of Nebraska).

Study of pageant form, thematic patterns of *LLL*, and Nine Worthies tradition reveals that the play is organized around chastening of several human excesses.

2378. [NINE WORTHIES] Schroeder, Horst, *Der Topos der Nine Worthies Literatur und bildender Kunst*. Göttingen, Zurich: Vandenhoeck & Ruprecht, originally diss., 1969, Ratisbon.

2379. [NOBILITY, TRUE] Landino, Cristoforo, *De vera nobilitate*, ed. Manfred Lentzen. Geneva: Droz, 1970.

Landino's contribution to Renaissance views on concept and nature of *nobilitas*; in form of Platonic dialogue; extensive introduction on 14th-cent. *nobilitas* and *dignitas hominis*, as well as components of cardinal virtues.

2380. [NOBILITY, TRUE] Willard, Charity Cannon, "The Concept of True Nobility at the Burgundian Court," *SRen*, 14 (1967), 33-48.

Debates on true nobility, as in Castiglione's *Courtier*, and especially in Bonaccursius de Montemagno (Buonaccurso da Pistoia) whose work was translated into English in mid-15th-cent., and later inspired Henry Medwall's *Fulgens and Lucres*. The debate continues through 16th, 17th, 18th cents.

2381. [*NOSCE TEIPSUM*] Fields, Albert W., "*Nosce Teipsum*: The Study of a Commonplace in English Literature, 1500-1900," *DA*, 30 (1969), 1979-80-A (Univ. of Kentucky).

Common regard for dignity of man and his refusal to despair in face of rapidly changing concepts of reality characterize the English writer's best use of the *nosce teipsum* theme.

2382. [NUMBER SYMBOLISM] Butler, Christopher, *Number Symbolism*. London: Routledge and Kegan Paul; N.Y.: Barnes & Noble, 1970. Rev. *RES*, n.s. 23 (1972), 105.

Chapter 7 on "Renaissance Thought." (Cf. [FOUR].)

2383. [NUMBER SYMBOLISM] Cummings, R.M., "Two Sixteenth-Century Notices of Numerical Composition in Virgil's *Aeneid*," *NQ*, 16 (1969), 26-27.

Re Spenser's use of numerology in the *Faerie Queene*; notes views of Spenser's contemporaries that Virgil used it: Sebastianus Regulus, 1593; Jacobus Pontanus, in 1599.

2384. [NUMBER SYMBOLISM] Friedjung, Walter, *Vom Symbolgehalt der Zahl*. Vienna: Europa, 1968.

From quantitative value of number to its qualitative value, via arithmetic and geometry.

2385. [NUMBER SYMBOLISM] Fowler, Alastair, *Triumphal Forms, Structural Patterns in Elizabethan Poetry*. Cambridge Univ. Press, 1970.

Rev. *SJ West,* (1971), 227; *TLS,* 15 January 1971, 70.

Revision of his book, *Spenser and the Numbers of Time,* to include preceding and subsequent Elizabethan poets, concluding
with Shakespeare. Elaborates on his theory of significance of
numerological structures in poetry.

2386. [NUMBER SYMBOLISM] Shawcross, John T., "Some Literary Uses of
Numerology," *Hartford Studies in Lit.,* 1 (1969), 50-62.

Structuring in terms of mystic qualities of numbers and
structuring by geometric relationship of parts. Jonson's "To
the Holy Trinity" illustrates the first--concept of the Trinity
is related to stanzaic form, including the number of lines and
rhymes and the length of lines.

2387. [NUMBER SYMBOLISM] Tschirch, Fritz, *Spiegelungen. Untersuchungen vom Grenzrain zwischen Germanistik und Theologie.* Berlin: Schmidt, 1966.

Essays on numerological composition in medieval German literature; e.g., numbers 33 and 34 as symbolic numbers relating to
Christ, Mary, and the number 100 in symbolic thinking.

2388. [NYMPH] Wuttke, Dieter, "Zu 'Huius numpha loci,'" *Arcadia,* 3
(1968), 306-307.

On the theme of sleeping nymph of the fountain.

2389. [OATHS] Coppedge, Walter Raleigh, "Shakespeare's Oaths and Im-
precations," *DA,* 28 (1968), 2643-2644-A (Indiana Univ.).

Distinguishes three types of oath: *conventional,* which signi-
fies invocation of a higher power to an act of witness; *ex-
clamatory,* abbreviated form of previous type; and *supplicatory,*
an appeal for higher assistance for purpose of blessing or
cursing. Renaissance England took oaths seriously (cf. Act
of 1606) but censorship of Lord Chamberlain was lax and inconsistent. Double audience of Shakespearean oaths: actors on
stage, and the other seated in the theater observing ironies
implicit in types of oaths; e.g., Richard III's by St. Paul, a
symbol of charity. Analyzes dramatic uses of oaths in 12
Shakespearean plays.

2390. [OATHS] Fontenrose, J., "The Gods Invoked in Epic Oaths:
Aeneid, XII, 175-215." *Amer. J. Philol.,* 89, no. 1 (1968),
20-38.

Evidence for and against various interpretations of the invocation of gods in epic oaths in above passage.

2391. [*OBLIGATIO*] Schramm, H.-P., "Zur Geschichte des Wortes 'obligatio' von der Antike bis Thomas von Aquin," *Archiv für Be-
griffsgeschichte,* 11, no. 2 (1967), 119-147.

History of word "obligatio" from ancient times to Thomas
Aquinas. On changes in its meaning to express sense of duty
and obligations as understood by Scholastic philosophy.

2392. [OLD MAN] Harris, Richard L., "Odin's Old Age: A Study of the Old Man in the _Pardoner's Tale_," _SFQ_, 33 (1969), 24-38.

Character of Odin and its possible relation to the Old Man in the _Pardoner's Tale_; shows how the decline of Odin's cult reduced the god to a less imposing figure.

2393. [OLD MAN] Ross, Lawrence J., "Wingless Victory: Michelangelo, Shakespeare, and the 'Old Man,'" in _Literary Monographs, Volume 2_, ed. Eric Rothstein and Richard N. Ringler. Madison: Univ. of Wisc. Press, 1969.

Rev. _NQ_, 17 (1970), 152-153.

Aims to show how both Michelangelo's "Victory" and Shakespeare's _Henry IV_ fail to accommodate the traditional image of the "Old Man" inherited from medieval morality and art.

2394. [ORPHEUS] Cochrane, Kirsty, "Orpheus Applied: Some Instances of His Importance in the Humanist View of Language," _RES_, n.s. 19, no. 73 (1968), 1-13.

Orpheus myth in 16th-cent. education as the eloquent ideal; subsequent application of Orpheus image when an idea of ethical value was required.

2395. [ORPHEUS] Gros Louis, Kenneth R.R., "Robert Henryson's _Orpheus and Eurydice_ and the Orpheus Traditions of the Middle Ages," _Spec._, 41 (1966), 643-655.

Popular tradition of Orpheus triumphs in the Renaissance. Council of Trent (1563) a turning point.

2396. [ORPHEUS] ————, "The Triumph and Death of Orpheus in the English Renaissance," _SEL_, 9 (1969), 63-80.

Difference between 16th and 17th-cent. allusions to Orpheus as artist-lover and civilizer of mankind. Disappearance of the triumphant Orpheus symptomatic of gradual division between poetry and philosophy or science.

2397. [ORPHEUS] Joukovsky, Françoise, _Orphée et ses disciples dans la poésie française et néolatine du XVIe siècle_. Geneva: Droz, 1970.

Rev. _RSH_, 36 (1971), 315-316; _TLS_, 18 September 1970, 1050.

Traces Orpheus and his disciples Arion and Amphion from literature of antiquity through French, Neo-Latin, and finally, Ronsard, Du Bellay, etc. From being a fixed legendary figure, known for his skills as a musician, poet, and theologian, Orpheus became the mythological embodiment of poetic inspiration itself in the work of the _Pléiade_.

2398. [ORPHEUS] Lee, M. Owen, "Orpheus and Eurydice: Myth, Legend, Folklore," _C&M_, 26 (1967), 402-412.

Supplements Peter Dronke, "The Return of Eurydice," _ibid._, 23 (1962), 198-215.

2399. [ORPHEUS] Penco, G., "Christus-Orpheus. Echi di un tema letterario negli scrittori monastici," *Aevium*, 41, nos. 5-6 (1967), 516-517.

Examples of some Latin authors of the Middle Ages who pick up classic image of Orpheus as redemptor and apply it to Christ or to King David.

2400. [OUROBOROS] Uhlig, Claus, "Ouroboros--Symbolik bei Spenser, *The Faerie Queene*, IV.x.40-41," *Germ.-rom. Monatsschr.*, n.f. 19 (1969), 1-23.

Spenser's mythopoetic activity in terms of his ability to use traditional symbols. Tradition of Ouroboros (snake with tail in its mouth) is traced with reference to *Aion* and the Boethian contrast between endlessness and eternity.

2401. [PAGANISM] Krautheimer, Richard, "A Christian Triumph in 1597," in Douglas Fraser et al., eds., *Essays in the History of Art Presented to Rudolf Wittkower*. London: Phaidon, 1967, pp. 174-178.

Theme of triumph of church over paganism.

2402. [PAN] Merivale, Patricia, *Pan the Goat God: His Myth in Modern Times*. Cambridge, Mass.: Harvard Univ. Press, 1969.

Rev. *MLR*, 66 (1971), 173-174; *PQ*, 48 (1969), 566-567.

Mainly deals with post-Renaissance, but of use for classifying Christian correlations with the Pan motif. Chapter I traces it "From the Arcadian to the Augustan," including Renaissance.

2403. [PAN] Pochat, Gotz, "Luca Signorelli's 'Pan' and the So-Called 'Tarocchi di Mantegna,'" *Konsthistorisk Tijdskrift*, 36 (1967), 92-105.

Iconography of Pan, including neo-platonic and Christian.

2404. [PARADISE] Armstrong, John, *The Paradise Myth*. N.Y.: Oxford Univ. Press, 1969.

Rev. *Choice*, 7 (1970), 379; *LibJ*, 94 (1969), 4526; *Milton Q*, 4 (1970), 44-45.

Explores paradisal potentials of late romances of Shakespeare, Botticelli's "Primavera," paintings of Giorgione, *Paradise Lost*, etc.

2405. [PARADISE] Duncan, Joseph E., "Paradise as the Whole Earth," *JHI*, 30 (1969), 171-186.

Idea of paradise as the whole world, rather than a particular place, reached fullest development in historical exegesis of 16th and 17th cents. and led to emphasis on differences in the entire world before and after the Fall; interpretation of the expulsion as a change in state rather than in location; disputes about the natural phenomena of a paradisal primitive earth and characteristics of the antediluvian era.

2406. [PARADISE] Giamatti, A. Bartlett, *The Earthly Paradise and the Renaissance Epic.* Princeton, N.J.: Princeton Univ. Press, 1966.

Rev. Alan Bullock, *Ren. Quar.,* 20 (1967), 31–35.

On Renaissance concepts of the earthly paradise and Golden Age, and their religious and mythological roots. Six sections of book range from classical gardens and paradises through Dante and Italian Renaissance writings, to England, especially Spenser and Milton. Two kinds of "paradise" in medieval times: secular, in which love of one kind or another is enjoyed in a garden; and religious.

2407. [PARADISE] Grabbe, Mary Louise, "John Salkeld: *Treatise of Paradise,* Edited with Introduction and Commentary," *DA,* 29 (1969), 3137–3138-A (Emory Univ.).

Evolution of tradition of Paradise in the Renaissance; how this unpublished *Treatise* (*S.R.* 1617) reflects the tradition.

2408. [PARADISE] Greenwood, E.B., "Poetry and Paradise: A Study in Thematics," *EIC,* 17 (1967), 6–25.

Includes Golden Age, *locus amoenus,* ideal republic, cosmic harmony, the monad.

2409. [PARADISE] Levin, Harry, "Paradises, Heavenly and Earthly," *HLQ,* 29 (1966), 305–324.

Traces motif in detail from antiquity to the modern age.

2410. [PARADISE] Morgan, Michael N., "Paradise and Lover in the Poetry of Spenser," *DA,* 29 (1969), 3105-A (Univ. of Florida).

Conjunction of Spenser's metaphors of paradise and lover against the Christian background of glory, ruin, and restoration in his work; Spenser's adaptation of the pastoral genre.

2411. [PARADISE] Schade, Herbert, *Das Paradies und die Imago Dei. Eine Studie über die früh-mittelalterlichen Darstellungen von der Erschaffung des Menschen als Beispiele einer sakramentalen Kunst.* (Probleme der Kunstwissenschaft II, hrsg. Hermann Bauer u.a.) Berlin: de Gruyter, 1966.

Iconographical study including Genesis and Christian as well as Judaic symbols.

2412. [PARADISE] Schenk, Gustav, *Am Anfang war das Paradies. Eine Geschichte der Menschheit.* Berlin: Safari, 1967.

General treatments of motifs, including "Die Gärten der Götter und Menschen," "Die vier Säulen der Welt," "Die Sintflut," and "Das Feuer und die Religion."

2413. [PARADISE; UTOPIA] Bauer, Hermann et al., eds., *Wandlungen des Paradiesischen und Utopischen. Studien zum Bild eines Ideals.* Berlin: de Gruyter, 1966.

On problems of representing the "other world," or rendering visible the invisible. Includes essay, "Der Garten des Konigs" after Shakespeare's *R2*, on order in the state seen as a picture of paradise.

2414. [PARADOX] Colie, Rosalie L., *Paradoxia Epidemica: The Renaissance Tradition of Paradox.* Princeton Univ. Press, 1966.

Rev. F. Yates, *N.Y. Rev. Books*, 23 February 1967, 26; *RenQ*, 20 (1967), 271-272.

Examines four types of Renaissance paradox: rhetorical, theological, ontological, and epistemological; studies works in relation to them, e.g., *Ham.*, *Oth.*, *KL*, *Mac.*

2415. [PARADOX] Lefèvre, Eckard, "Die Bedeutung des Paradoxen in der Römischen Literatur der frühen Kaiserzeit," *Poetica*, 3 (1970), 59-82.

Detailed, documented study of Latin use of paradox.

2416. [PARADOX] Michel, A., "Cicéron et les paradoxes stoïciens," *Acta Antiq. Acad. Sci.*, 16 (1968), 223-232.

Explains how Cicero, in his *Paradoxa Stoicorum*, can defend certain important Stoic theses which he has ridiculed in the *Pro Murena* and attacked in *De finibus*.

2417. [PARADOX] Slights, William W.E., "[Ben Jonson's] *Epicoene* and the Prose Paradox," *PQ*, 49 (1970), 178-187.

Renaissance fascination with paradox, as it appears in *Epicoene*. Examines paradoxical speeches on all major themes in the play.

2418. [PARAGONE] Mendelsohn, Leatrice, "Benedetto Varchi's Lezzione and the Letters on the Paragone: Their Sources in Classical Literature and Relation to Cinquecento Theory," M.A. thesis, Institute of Fine Arts, N.Y. Univ., October 1968.

2419. [PARLIAMENT IN HEAVEN] Holaday, Allan, "Shakespeare, Richard Edwards, and the Virtues Reconciled," *JEGP*, 66 (1967), 200-206.

Medieval "Parliament in Heaven" reconciliation occurs in episodes of later drama, e.g., Edwards' *Damon and Pithias*, anticipating trial scene of *MV.*

2420. [PASSION, The] Schiller, Gertrud, *Ikonographie der christlichen Kunst.* II. Gütersloh: Gütersloher Verlagshaus, 1968.

Compendious volume on theme of Christ's Passion. Divided into: theological interpretations and iconographical points of departure, the Passion, the Crucifixion, the Burial. Includes index to literature, iconographical index by key words, index to illustrations, and sources of illustrations.

2421. [PASTORAL] Aziz, Paul Douglas, "The Poet's Poetry: Edmund Spenser's Uses of the Pastoral," *DA*, 30 (1969), 271-272-A (Brown Univ.).

Three main uses: pastoral poetry provided Spenser with a
natural vehicle for philosophic thought; for criticizing contemporary life or discussing problems of contemporary affairs;
for discussing problems of art as he saw them.

2422. [PASTORAL] Cody, Richard, _The Landscape of the Mind: Pastoral-
ism and Platonic Theory in Tasso's 'Aminta' and Shakespeare's
Early Comedies._ Oxford: Clarendon Press, 1969.

Rev. _BHR_, 32 (1970), 488-491; _EIC_, 21 (1971), 390-398; _NQ_, n.s. 17
(1970), 153-154.

Argues that pastoral projects "an aesthetic of the inner life,"
reconciling this-worldliness and other-worldliness. Emphasizes
harmonizing of the warring gods (especially Apollo and Bacchus,
or art and nature) in mystic, Neoplatonic unity.

2423. [PASTORAL] Crupi, Charles William, "Pastoral Elements in Plays
from the Elizabethan Public Theaters of the 1590's," _DA_, 28
(1968), 3175-3176-A (Princeton Univ.).

Pastoral backgrounds, including Elizabethan fiction, to examination of _AYL_.

2424. [PASTORAL] Cullen, Patrick, _Spenser, Marvell and Renaissance
Pastoral._ Cambridge, Mass.: Harvard Univ. Press, 1970.

Rev. _JEGP_, 70 (1971), 535-541.

Classical and continental sources for Renaissance writer of
lyric pastoral; establishes a pastoral mode in which dialectic
is important, and examines pastoralists within this dialectic
frame.

2425. [PASTORAL] Dalle Valle, D., "La pastorale dramatique baroque
et l'influence de l'_Aminta_," _Studi fr._, 35 (1968), 95-108.

Split in the concept of Man, which Tasso proposes by objectify-
ing it in the opposition Nature-Reason, Love-Honor, opens way
to a new sensitivity--that of the Baroque. Use and modifica-
tion of these themes in French dramatic pastoral.

2426. [PASTORAL] Jablon, Barry Peter, "Politics and the Pastoral: A
Study of the Tudor and Stuart Pastoral Eclogue as a Vehicle
for Political Expression," _DA_, 28 (1968), 4133-A (Univ. of
Calif., Berkeley).

Its ambiguity making it an admirable vehicle for religious and
political allegories, the pastoral eclogue was allied from
Elizabeth's accession to the civil war virtually consistently
with the Elizabethan Settlement and conservative authoritarian-
ism. Order and stability dominate all other values in the
pastoral eclogue; despite popular notions, Milton's _Lycidas_
is atypical, the only pastoral eclogue in English and one of
the very few in any language whose political and religious
goals are revolutionary.

2427. [PASTORAL] Lambert, Ellen Zetzel, "The Pastoral Elegy from
Theocritus to Milton: A Critical Study," _DA_, 31 (1970),
1233-A (Yale Univ.).

Study of pastoral elegy, stressing importance of "Lycidas."

2428. [PASTORAL] Neely, Carol Thomas, "Speaking True: Shakespeare's
       Use of the Elements of Pastoral Romance," *DA*, 30 (1970), 3433–
       A (Yale Univ.).

       Renaissance pastoral romance in its search for an adequate
       style, through Sidney, Spenser, and Shakespeare's romantic
       comedies. *WT* understood as culmination of that genre.

2429. [PASTORAL] Nichols, Fred J., "The Development of Neo-Latin
       Theory of the Pastoral in the Sixteenth Century," *Humanistica
       Lovaniensia*, 18 (1969), 95–114.

       Studies treatises on pastoral poetry written in Latin from
       1527 (Vida's *De arte poetica*) to 1561 (Scaliger's *Poetices
       libri septem*). Two polarities emerge: one, represented by
       Vida, makes the pastoral the most appropriate form of poetic
       activity; the other, represented by Minturno and Scaliger,
       denies pastoral the right to deal with any serious subject.

2430. [PASTORAL] Rosenmeyer, Thomas G., *The Green Cabinet: Theocri-
       tus and the European Pastoral Lyric.* Berkeley: Univ. of
       Calif. Press, 1970 [c. 1969].

       Pastoral poetry of Theocritus should be viewed not as a source
       of Virgil's, but as fellow-work with his; book asks to what
       extent the special qualities of Theocritus' poetry are charac-
       teristic of the whole genre.

2431. [PASTORAL] Williams, Raymond, "Pastoral and Counter-Pastoral,"
       Critical Quart., 10, no. 3 (1968), 275–290.

       Study of 16th and 17th-cent. pastoral poetry, focusing on dis-
       placement of traditional images of Golden Age and Paradise by
       images of English countryside. The contrast between pastoral
       and counter-pastoral lyrics reflects that between false and
       true ways of writing.

2432. [PEARL] Dupont, J., "Les paraboles du trésor et de la perle,"
       New Testament Stud., 14, no. 3 (1968), 408–418.

       Opinions of interpreters; essence of the narratives and its
       application to teaching of Jesus. Matthew's vision.

2433. [PEARL] Seaman, J.E., "Othello's Pearl," *ShQ*, 19, no. 1 (1968),
       81–86.

       Play's relation to biblical tradition; function and value of
       Desdemona.

2434. [PEDANT] Lord, Gisela, "Die Figur des Pedanten bei Shakes-
       peare," *SJW*, 1969, pp. 213–244.

       Shakespeare transforms the comic stock figure of the pedant,
       found in the *commedia dell'arte* and the *commedia erudita*,
       into a tragic character.

2435. [PEGASUS] Bland, D.S., "Pegasus at the Inner Temple," *NQ*, 214
       n.s. 16 (1969), 16–18.

Adoption by Inner Temple of Pegasus as its emblem resulted
from 1561 Christmas celebration, when Lord Robert Dudley, an
outsider who had done the Temple a favor, was Master of the
Revels. Dudley was Master of the Queen's Horse; hence appropriateness of Pegasus for him. Emblem "caught on" and has
been retained to this day.

2436. [PENTAGRAM] Schouten, J., *The Pentagram as a Medical Symbol.
An Iconological Study.* Nieuwkoop: DeGraaf, 1968.

On origin and dissemination of this symbol from its use in
Sumerian days as a protective sign, to the Cabbala, 16th- and
17th-cent. medical pharmaceutical texts, and heraldry, showing
its survival for over 5,000 years despite changes in creed and
belief. Illustrations and bibliography.

2437. [*PEREGRINATIO*] Hahn, Juergen S., "The Origins of the Baroque
Concept of *Peregrinatio*," *DA*, 30 (1969), 281-A (Duke Univ.).

Religious and secular evolution of *peregrinatio*: predominant
significance remained Christian (life on earth is an exile,
an estrangement from God).

2438. [PERFECTION] Bloomfield, Morton W., "Some Reflections on the
Medieval Idea of Perfection," in *Essays and Explorations:
Studies in Ideas, Language, and Literature.* Harvard Univ.
Press, 1970, pp. 29-55.

Rev. *Spec.*, 47 (1972), 509-511.

Judaeo-Christian conception united with the Greek.

2439. [PERFECTION] Hafter, Monroe Z., *Gracián and Perfection: Spanish Moralists of the Seventeenth Century.* Harvard Studies in
Romance Languages, 30. Cambridge, Mass.: Harvard Univ. Press,
1966; London: Oxford Univ. Press, 1967.

Rev. *BHS*, 45 (1968), 234-236; *RenQ*, 21 (1968), 70-71.

Includes discussion of varying attitudes in 16th and 17th
cents. concerning extent to which statesman in a wicked world
is justified in using immoral means. Chapter I: Teaching
Morality in a Period of Decline. Chapter IV includes "Absolute
Excellence or Relative Superiority."

2440. [PERFECTION] Milosh, Joseph E., *The Scale of Perfection and
the Mystical Tradition.* Univ. of Wisc. Press, 1966.

Includes Progress of the Soul; Scale of Perfection.

2441. [PERFECTION] Røstvig, M.-S., "Images of Perfection," in Earl
Miner, ed., *Seventeenth-Century Imagery.* Univ. of Calif.
Press, 1971, pp. 1-24.

Failure to pay due attention to Renaissance syncretic tradition
has deprived us of understanding of imagery, especially mathematical images of perfection.

2442. [PERFUME MERCHANT] Mathieu, Michel, "Le personnage du marchand de parfums dans le théâtre médiéval en France. Contribution à l'étude des débuts du théâtre comique," *Le Moyen Age*, 74, no. 1 (1968), 39-71.

Standard character of the perfume seller as it evolved from a liturgical role to a comic role in secular theater, accompanying the evolution of realism.

2443. [PERSPECTIVE] Guillén, Claudio, "On the Concept and Metaphor of Perspective," in *Comparatists at Work*, ed. S.G. Nichols and R.B. Vowles (Waltham, Mass.: Blaisdell Press, 1968), reprinted in Guillén, *Literature as System: Essays toward the Theory of Literary History*. Princeton Univ. Press, 1971, pp. 283-371.

Views of Ortega, Spitzer, and Wellek regarding literary perspectivism, developed into a "secularization of vision."

2444. [PERSPECTIVE] Quintavalle, Arturo Carlo, *Prospettiva e ideologia: Alberti e la cultura del sec. XV*. Parma: Editrice Studium Parmense, 1967.

Perspective in ideological context. Cf. Chapter I: "Storia della prospettiva come storia della cultura." Plates.

2445. [PETRARCHAN] Forster, Leonard, *The Icy Fire: Five Studies in European Petrarchism*. N.Y.: Cambridge Univ. Press, 1969.

Rev. *LibJ*, 95 (1970), 1372; *TLS*, 23 April 1970, 447.

On dispersion of Petrarchan poetic conventions in Europe. Poets working to reform poetic diction in the vernaculars chose the artificial, hence imitable elements of Petrarchism, especially oxymoron and hyperbole, with Latin verse as movement's most important vehicle.

2446. [PETRARCHAN] Mann, Nicholas, "La fortune de Pétrarque en France: Recherches sur le *De remediis*," *Studi Francesi*, 37 (1969), 1-15.

Latin works of Petrarch played a great role in development of humanist movement in 14th cent. *De remediis* seems to have enjoyed most success in 14th and 15th cents. (over 133 manuscripts). Introduced to the French Court before 1378, Latin text met with initial phase of intense diffusion until about 1425. Mainly moral aspect which impresses readers of *De remediis*, its mixture of Stoic and Christian thought. This interest may have slackened in the last quarter of 15th cent.

2447. [PETRARCHAN] Tripet, Arnaud, *Pétrarque ou la connaissance de soi*. Geneva: Droz, 1967.

Rev. *BHR*, 30 (1968), 373-375.

Regarding Petrarch's complexity--his "interior humanism" and his recourse to the powers of literature and language.

2448. [*PHARMAKOS*: Scapegoat] Derrida, J., "La pharmacie de Platon. I," *Tel quel*, 32 (1968), 3-48; Pt. II, 33 (1968), 18-59.

Pharmacy. The father of logos. The sons' inscription: Theuth, Hermes, Thot, Nabu, Nebo. The *pharmakon*. The *pharmakeus*. The *pharmakos*. Heritage of the *pharmakon*: the family scene. Analysis of the *pharmakon* and its ambivalence.

2449. [PHILEMON and BAUCIS] Beller, Manfred, *Philemon und Baucis in der europäischen Literatur: Stoffgeschichte und Analyse*. (Studien zum Fortwirken der Antike, hrs. Walter Marg et al., Bd. 3.) Heidelberg: Carl Winter Universitätsverlag, 1967.

Rev. *L'Antiquité Classique*, 37 (1968), 382-383; *Archiv*, 205 (1968), 296-297; *Arcadia*, 4 (1969), 93-94; *Comp. Lit. Studs.*, 6 (1969), 501-502.

Systematic tracing of Ovid's story through Christian allegory, epicurean, and other variations.

2450. [PHILEMON and BAUCIS] Colton, Robert E., "Philemon and Baucis in Ovid and La Fontaine," *CJ*, 63 (1968), 166-176.

Compares classical and 17th-cent. use of the tale.

2451. [PHOENIX] Schwartz, Elias, "Shakespeare's Dead Phoenix," *ELN*, 7 (1969), 25-32.

Since the phoenix in Shakespeare's poem is not reborn out of its own ashes, Truth and Beauty and Perfect Love perish with the Phoenix and the Turtle.

2452. [PHOENIX] Waida, Edward Joseph, "The Phoenix Legend in Seventeenth-Century English Literature," *DA*, 19 (1968), 1216-1217-A (Arizona State Univ.).

Discusses abstract qualities and metaphorical analogies associated with phoenix in 17th cent.

2453. [PICARESQUE] Alfaro, G.A., "El despertar del Pícaro," *Rom. Forsch.*, 80, no. 1 (1968), 44-52.

How picaresque hero emerges from naiveté to realities of life, an awakening most often dramatic, which changes his view of the world and dictates his rules of conduct.

2454. [PICARESQUE] Guillén, Claudio, "Toward a Definition of the Picaresque," in *Literature as System: Essays Toward the Theory of Literary History*. Princeton Univ. Press, 1971, pp. 71-105. Cf. *ibid.*, pp. 135-158, "Genre and Countergenre: The Discovery of the Picaresque."

Renaissance and modern roguery.

2455. [PICARESQUE] Miller, Stuart, "A Genre Definition of the Picaresque Novel," *DA*, 30 (1969), 1143-1144-A (Yale Univ.).

The genre's norms of form, content, and emotional effect are elicited from eight examples including: *Lazarillo de Tormes* (1554), *The Unfortunate Traveller* (1594), *Guzmán de Alfarache* (1599 and 1605), *El Buscón* (1626).

2456. [PICARESQUE] Parker, Alexander A., *Literature and the Delin-
       quent: The Picaresque Novel in Spain and Europe, 1599-1753*.
       Edinburgh: Edinburgh Univ. Press, 1967.

       Rev. *BHS*, 45 (1968), 227-231; *FS*, 22 (1968), 245-246; *RR*,
       59 (1968), 132-133.

       Survey of whole field of picaresque; shows Spanish pícaro not
       as mere rogue, but as delinquent, offender, short of criminal-
       ity, against moral and civil laws.

2457. [PICARESQUE] Siever, Harry, "Some Recent Books on the Pica-
       resque," *MLN*, 84 (1969), 318-329.

       Review article of Francisco Rico's *La Novela Picaresca es-
       pañola*, I: *Lazarillo de Tormes*; Mateo Alemán's *Guzmán de Al-
       farache*; Stuart Miller's *The Picaresque Novel*; and A.A. Par-
       ker's *Literature and the Delinquent: The Picaresque Novel
       in Spain and Europe 1599-1753*.

2458. [PILGRIMAGE OF GRACE] Davies, C.B.L., "The Pilgrimage of Grace
       Reconsidered," *Past and Present*, 41 (1968), 54-76.

       Religion legitimized rebellion (1536-1537) by providing a
       rallying point for various classes and interests.

2459. [PILGRIMAGE OF GRACE] Haigh, Christopher, *The Last Days of the
       Lancashire Monasteries and the Pilgrimage of Grace*. Manches-
       ter: Chetham Soc., 1969.

       Rev. *EHR*, 86 (1971), 169; *History*, 55 (1970), 110-111.

       Analysis of the monks' reaction to the suppression of the
       monasteries in Lancaster in 1536.

2460. [PLANT SYMBOLISM] Goldhammer, Kurt, "Pflanze und Pflänzliche
       Wachstum als Symbolkomplex bei Paracelsus," *Die ganze Welt
       ein Apotheken. Festschrift für Otto Zekert*, ed. Sepp Domandl.
       (Vienna & Salzburg: Notring der wissenschaftlichen Verbände
       Osterreiches, 1969), pp. 115-131.

       On Paracelsus' abundant use of images of vegetation--growing,
       blossoming, fruit-bearing, and decaying--to represent anthro-
       pological, cosmological, perception-psychological, and reli-
       gious-theological connections.

2461. [PLAY-WITHIN-PLAY] Mroczkowski, P., "Shakespeare's 'as ifs,'"
       Kwartal. Neofilol., 15, no. 1 (1968), 3-29.

       Theme of theater-within-theater is both a motif and a tech-
       nique.

2462. [*PLUS ULTRA* and *NON-*] Rosenthal, Earl, "*Plus Ultra, Non Plus
       Ultra*, and the Columnar Device of Emperor Charles V," *JWCI*, 34
       (1971), 204-228.

       Charles united Herculean proverb and new vision of the world.

2463. [PORTIA] Herschberg, David, "Porcia in Golden Age Literature:
       Echoes of a Classical Theme," *Neophil.*, 54 (1970), 22-25.

Porcia legend in Spanish "Golden Age." Her development into a
figure of "love and self-sacrifice."

2464. [PORTRAIT] Pope-Hennessy, John, _The Portrait in the Renais-
sance_. N.Y.: Bollingen, Pantheon, 1966.

Rev. _Burl. Mag._, 110 (1968), 278-285; _J. Aesth._, 26 (1968),
563-564.

Chapters: I. Cult of Personality, II. Humanism and the Portrait, III. Motions of the Mind, IV. The Court Portrait, V.
Image and Emblem, VI. Donor and Participant. Many plates.
Notes, pp. 303-327, double columns. First Northern painter to
be discussed: Dürer. Treats Renaissance portraiture in terms
of the ideas by which it was formed.

2465. [PRAISE] Cain, T.H., "The Strategy of Praise in Spenser's
'April,'" _SEL_, 8, no. 1 (1968), 45-58.

According to model and themes established by Aphthonius, first
part of panegyric to the Queen presents a static image, sub-
sequently animated into a coronation scene which is transformed into a vision with poet as Orpheus.

2466. [PRAISE] Knoepfle, J.I., "The Use of Renaissance Formulas for
Praise in the Dramas of Christopher Marlowe," _DA_, 28 (1968),
3148-A (St. Louis Univ.).

Elizabethan models for _laus_, as taught in grammar schools, included Erasmus' _De Amatoria Epistola_, on method for soliciting
girl with appeals of flattery and pity; and Aphthonius' _Progym-
nasmata_, 9th exercise, on method of praising a man. In Marlowe's play, Pt. I, Tamburlaine conquers in Erasmian and Aph-
thonian terms; and in Pt. II, he is measured in such terms.
After these, Erasmian mode is of minor importance in Marlowe's
dramas, or not operative at all.

2467. [PRAISE] Lewalski, Barbara K., "Donne's Poetry of Compliment:
The Speaker's Stance and the Topoi of Praise," in Earl Miner,
ed., _Seventeenth-Century Imagery_. Univ. of Calif. Press, 1971,
pp. 45-67.

Donne's praises are, unlike Jonson's, not directed to particular individuals, but to potentialities of the human soul as
divine image.

2468. [PRAISE] Rewa, Michael Peter, Jr., "The Rhetoric of Biography:
Classical Conventions of Praise in Seventeenth-Century English
Biography," _DA_, 28 (1967), 1057-A (Stanford Univ.).

Conventions of rhetorical praise in Isocrates' _Evagoras_, Xeno-
phon's _Agesilaus_, and Tacitus' _Agricola_. Chapter 3 discusses
classical influence in 16th cent.

2469. [PRAYER] Hoffmann, Gerhard, "Wandlungen des Gebets im elisa-
bethanischen Drama," _SJ (West)_, 1966, 173-210.

2470. [PRAYER] Kelly, Faye L., _Prayer in Sixteenth-Century England_.
(Univ. of Florida monographs. Humanities no. 22.) Gainesville: Univ. of Florida Press, 1966.

Her dissertation: "Shakespeare's Use of Prayer in the History Play." Gainesville, 1965.

2471.   [PRAYER-BEADS] Wilkins, Eithne, *The Rose-Garden Game. The Symbolic Background to the European Prayer-Beads.* N.Y.: Herder & Herder, 1969.

Rev. *TLS*, 18 June 1970, 666.

Varied collection of facts and images bearing on beads and roses.

2472.   [PREDESTINATION] Bloomfield, Morton W., "Distance and Predestination in *Troilus and Criseyde*," in *Essays and Explorations: Studies in Ideas, Language, and Literature.* Harvard Univ. Press, 1970, pp. 201-216.

Rev. *Spec.*, 47 (1972), 509-511.

Repr., among other basic studies in history of ideas.

2473.   [PREDESTINATION] Hargrave, O.T., "The Doctrine of Predestination in the English Reformation," *DA*, 27 (1966), 1433-A - 1434-A (Vanderbilt Univ.).

Analyzes treatment of doctrines of predestination--foremost theological issue among English reformers--in treatises, commentaries, and confessions from the middle of the reign of Henry VIII to the middle of reign of Elizabeth. Under Henry VIII moderate trend was followed; under Edward VI, by the first outright repudiation of predestination views in the "Freewill" movement. During the Marian reaction, reformers imprisoned for their Protestant faith split into two views: moderate group led by John Bradford against a group of Freewillers led by John Trewe. Among exiles on continent, earliest genuine expression of Calvinist doctrine among English reformers emerged. In early Elizabethan period, predestinarian thought was channeled into three basic traditions: Major Elizabethan churchmen supported moderate views; wide variety of sources gave ever broadening expression to Calvinist position; and liberal churchmen (Peter Baro, Samuel Harsnett, Hooker) helped shape an anti-Calvinist tradition--in continuity with earlier Freewill movement.

2474.   [PREDESTINATION] Malone, Michael T., "The Doctrine of Predestination in the Thought of William Perkins and Richard Hooker," *Anglican Theol. Rev.*, 52 (1970), 103-117.

Similarities and differences in thought of these two in matters of God and evil, prescience and predestination, and Atonement and perseverance.

2475.   [PRIAM] Menut, A.D., "The Search for 'Priam's Face,'" *Symposium*, 21, no. 2 (1967), 132-140.

The regal beauty of Priam, an example used three times by Nicole Oresme, is the result of an error in the Latin version of Porphyrius' *Isagoge*, because the Greek text does not mention Priam, but rather *proton* (beauty, bearing, above all ...).

2476. [PRIDE] Hempel, Wolfgang, _Übermuot diu Alte_ ... _Der Superbia-_
       Gedanke und seine Rolle in der deutschen Literatur des Mittel-
       alters. (Studien zur Germanistik, Anglistik, u. Komparatistik.
       hrsg. Armin Arnold, Bd. 1.) Bonn: H. Bouvier, 1970.

       Detailed study of _Superbia_ in the Middle Ages. Cf. "Die Sym-
       bolik der Superbia," pp. 187-209.

2477. [PRIDE] Rusche, Harry, "Pride, Humility and Grace in Book I of
       the _Faerie Queene,_" _SEL,_ 7 (1967), 29-39.

       Pride regarded by Spenser as most deadly sin; despair not
       properly to be regarded as having equal status.

2478. [PRIMITIVISM] Mortenson, Peter, "Structure in Spenser's
       Faerie Queene, Book VI: Primitivism, Chivalry, and Greek Ro-
       mance," _DA,_ 27 (1967), 3015-A (Univ. of Oregon).

       Analyzes primitive and chivalric elements in Book VI; former
       are represented by savages, cannibals, and brigands. Primi-
       tivism as vehicle for presenting the source of courtesy in
       human nature, as chivalry is the vehicle for showing the form
       of courtesy in civil society.

2479. [PRIMITIVISM] Weiss, Robert H., "Primitivism and the Satiric
       Mode in English Renaissance Verse and Prose (to Spenser's
       Prosopopoia): The Shaping of a Tradition," _DA,_ 30 (1969),
       2504-A (Temple Univ.).

       Use of primeval Golden Age, _vir bonus,_ the satyr-play and
       other related themes and motifs in Renaissance satire.

2480. [PROCLAMATIONS] Cope, Esther Sidney, "Parliament and Proclama-
       tions, 1604-1629," _DA,_ 30 (1970), 5372-A (Bryn Mawr).

       Parliament, fearing arbitrary government, steadily opposed
       royal proclamations which seemed to violate the subjects'
       rights or embody dangerous policy. Petition from House of
       Commons to James I in 1610 was the major parliamentary protest
       against proclamations between 1604 and 1629.

2481. [PROCLAMATIONS] Heinze, Rudolph W., "The Pricing of Meat: A
       Study in the Use of Royal Proclamations in the Reign of Henry
       VIII," _Historical Journal,_ 12 (1969), 583-595.

       Proclamations on meat price legislation in the reign of Henry
       VIII. Argues that this legislation cannot be used to support
       contention that the Statute of Proclamations was intended to
       introduce a royal despotism; rather suggests that statute was
       motivated by a concern for statutory authority.

2482. [PROCLAMATIONS] Hughes, Paul L., and James F. Larkin, eds.,
       Tudor Royal Proclamations. Vol. 2, _The Later Tudors, 1553-_
       _1587;_ Vol. 3, _1588-1603._ New Haven, Conn.: Yale Univ.
       Press, 1969.

       Rev. _AHR,_ 75 (1970), 1450-1451; _EHR,_ 85 (1970), 842-843;
       TLS, 25 September 1969, 1083.

       These two volumes complete the editors' earlier work, _The_
       Early Tudors, 1485-1553. They include texts of 62

proclamations for Mary I's reign, 377 for Elizabeth's, and 26
newly recovered ones for period covered by Vol. 1.

2483. [PROCLAMATIONS] Youngs, F.A., "The Proclamations of Elizabeth
I." (Director, G.R. Elton.) Cambridge Ph.D., 1969.

Cf. Youngs' book, Cambridge Univ. Press, 1976.

2484. [PRODIGAL SON] Calas, Nicolas, "Hieronymus Bosch and the Prodigal Son," *Harvard Art Review*, 2 (1967), 15-20.

On the riddle of Bosch's "Garden of Delights," and identity of
the Prodigal Son.

2485. [PRODIGAL SON] Domeier, Sister Renée, "The Parable of the Prodigal Son in the Theater of Tirso de Molina," *DA*, 31 (1970),
2381-A (Univ. of Mich.).

Christian motif of redemption and grace as portrayed in Parable
of the Prodigal Son in four of Tirso's plays.

2486. [PRODIGAL SON] Turner, A.M., "The Motif of the Prodigal Son in
French and German Literature to 1910," *DA*, 27 (1967), 3853-
3854-A (Univ. of North Carolina).

Humanist and reformist influences in 16th cent. led to de-
spiritualization of the parable; as it also developed scenes
of rivalry between the two brothers, representing Lutheran
doctrine of faith versus Catholic doctrine of good works.
Stress on return and father's forgiveness showed 17th-cent.
counter-reformist attitude.

2487. [PROMETHEUS] Buck, August, "Über einige Bedeutungen des Pro-
metheus-Mythos in der Literatur der Renaissance," *Die Humanistische Tradition in der Romania*. Bad Hamburg: Verlag Gehlen, 1968.

Re-emergence of classical Prometheus in the Renaissance, ex-
pressing shift from man as creation to man as creator.

2488. [PROMETHEUS] Dempsey, Charles, "Euthanes Redivivus: Rubens'
Prometheus Bound," *JWCI*, 30 (1967), 420-425.

Rubens' work as imitation of classical.

2489. [PROMETHEUS] Goblot, J.-J., "Le mythe de Prométhée dans la
littérature et la pensée modernes," *Pensée*, 132 (1967), 71-82.

Promethean myth in context of other myths, of Greece, as well
as of Plato and church fathers.

2490. [PROPHET] Brady, P.V., "The Ambiguous 'Newer Prophet': A
Sixteenth-Century Stock Figure," *MLR*, 62 (1967), 672-679.

2491. [PROSERPINA] Anton, Herbert, *Der Raub der Proserpina: Literarische Traditionen eines erotischen Sinnbildes und mythi-
schen Symbols*. Heidelberger Forschungen, H. 11. Heidelberg:
Carl Winter, 1967.

From *Ovide Moralisé*, through Renaissance, to Gide.

2492. [PROTEUS] Giammati, A.B., "Proteus Unbound: Some Versions of the Sea God in the Renaissance," in Peter Demetz et al., eds., _The Disciplines of Criticism: Essays in Literary Theory, Interpretation, and History._ New Haven, Conn.: Yale Univ. Press, 1968, pp. 437-475.

On recurrence of Proteus in Renaissance.

2493. [PRUDENCE] Johnson, W. McAllister, "Giulio Romano's _Allegory of Immortality_ Reconsidered," _Art Quarterly_, 33 (1969), 3-22.

Explains meaning of allegory in Jules Romain's work (Detroit Museum) as an allegory of Prudence.

2494. [PSALMS] Jeanneret, Michel, _Poésie et Tradition Biblique au XVIe Siècle._ Paris: Corti, 1969.

Stylistic study of the translations of psalms in France from Marot to Malherbe (1535-1610). Also examines influence of Calvinism and Neoplatonism.

2495. [PYRAMUS and THISBE] Marin, N., "Una fábula inedita de Píramo y Tisbe," _Hispanófila_, 10 (1967), 21-32.

Gives text of 18th-cent. poem, citing differences from Ovidian and Renaissance treatments.

2496. [PYRAMUS and THISBE] Testa, D.P., "An Analysis of Tirso de Molina's 'Fábula de Pýramo y Tisbe,'" _SP_, 64 (1967), 132-146.

Tirso complicates the love experience and provides a form of union superior to Ovid's.

2497. [PYRAMUS and THISBE] Viau, Théophile de, _Les Amours Tragiques de Pyrame et Thisbe._ Critical ed. by G. Saba. Naples: E.S.I., 1967.

2498. [PYTHAGOREAN Symbols] Vonessen, Franz, "Die Pythagoreischen Symbole," _Antaios_, 9 (1968), 284-305.

On Pythagorean symbols, e.g., don't pluck a garland--where garland may be analogous to society, law, etc.

2499. [RAPHAEL] McCutcheon, Elizabeth, "Thomas More, Raphael Hythlodaeus, and the Angel Raphael," _SEL_, 9 (1969), 21-38.

Name of More's traveller-narrator in _Utopia_, Raphael Hythlodaeus, in light of significance of his namesake, Raphael. In Renaissance thought, the angel Raphael is both _medicus salutis_, doctor of health and salvation, and guide.

2500. [RATIOCINATION] Dickey, Harold A., "_Samson Agonistes_: The Dramatic Role of Ratiocination," _DA_, 29 (1969), 2208-09-A (Univ. of Nebraska).

Samson's rise from defeat reveals triumph over the type of reasoning connected with his sin.

2500a. [REALISM] Schober, Rita, _Von der wirklichen Welt in der Dichtung._ Weimar-Berlin: Aufbau-Verlag, 1970.

On theory and practice of realism in French literature:
methods, interpretation, considerations of authors from Marie
de France to Armand Lanoux.

2501. [REASON] Badel, P., "Raison 'Fille de Dieu' et le rationalisme
de Jean de Meun," *Mélanges de lang. et de litt. du m.a. et de
la Ren. offerts à Jean Frappier*. Geneva: Droz, 1970, v. 1,
41-52.

Character of Raison in the *Roman de la Rose*.

2502. [REASON] Brancaforte, Benito, "*La Celestina y la Mandragola*:
la razón como medio de corrupción," *Bull. of Hisp. Studies*,
47 (1970), 201-209.

Both *La Celestina* and Machiavelli's *La Mandragola* reflect mis-
trust in the moral values of their age: reason, rather than
ennobling man and aiding him in the fight against his passions,
is an instrument of corruption.

2503. [REASON] Fox, Kathleen A.C., "Unreason and the Triumph of
Reason in *Twelfth Night*," *DA*, 27 (1967), 3426-A (Univ. of
Nebraska).

Renaissance opinion about moral significance of unreason, in
relation to the play.

2504. [REASON] Marsak, Leonard M., "The Idea of Reason in Seventeenth-
Century France: An Essay in Interpretation," *Jour. World
Hist.*, 11, pt. 3 (1968), 407-416 (*Cahiers d'histoire mondiale*).

Links changes in *reason* to French society, towards a new history of the idea. Three stages of development in the meaning
and role assigned to the word *reason*.

2505. [REJECTION, CRITICAL] Borchardt, Frank L., "The Topos of Critical Rejection in the ·Renaissance," *MLN*, 81 (1966), 476-488.

On the *topos* of *anasceua*, part of a refutation (*refutatio,
reprehensio*) which denies traditions in support of an opposing
opinion (e.g., in a debate over Renaissance inheritors of
Troy).

2506. [REPENTANCE] Mermier, G., "Essai 'Du Repentir' de Montaigne,"
Fr. Rev., 41, no. 4 (1968), 485-492.

Constructive notion of repentance in Montaigne: it should be
a desire for improvement, oriented towards the future and not
a futile regret for the unchangeable past.

2507. [REPENTANCE] Payen, Jean-Charles, *Le motif du repentir dans la
littérature française médiévale (des origines à 1230)*. Publications Romanes et Françaises, 98. Geneva: Droz, 1967.

Substantial book contains useful motifs, e.g., Piramus and
Thisbe, pp. 294-295, under heading, "La Mort d'Amour," of
interest to Renaissance student, in addition to Shakespearean
relevance of repentance theme.

2508. [REPENTANCE] Velie, Alan Rockmore, "Shakespeare's Repentance Plays: The Search for an Adequate Form," *DA*, 30 (1970), 5422-5423-A (Stanford Univ.).

Shakespeare's search for an adequate form in which to explore the nature of sin and repentance culminated in *WT* and *Tmp*.

2509. [REVENGE] Aggeler, Geoffrey Donovan, "The Ethical Problems of Revenge in English Renaissance Tragedy," *DA*, 27 (1967), 3830-A (Univ. of Calif., Davis).

Deals with Renaissance and classical ethical theories concerning revenge. Also studies theories regarding the nature and workings of the human conscience.

2510. [REVENGE] Bevan, Elinor, "Revenge, Forgiveness, and the Gentleman," *Rev. of English Literature*, 8 (1967), 55-69.

Holds that revenge must follow a code, and the man who takes revenge outside of the code loses his stature as a gentleman. Also the cuckold loses his honor, though not through his own fault, and assumes the role of a beast. In a gentleman, moderation and magnanimity serve as antidotes to rage, and these ethical values, rather than a concern with Christian charity, become primary marks of a gentleman. Revenge in Italian literature has a special ferocity to it, whereas English literature is somewhat more subdued.

2511. [REVENGE] Broude, Ronald, "Human and Divine Vengeance in the Tragedy of Revenge," *DA*, 31 (1970), 1752-A (Columbia Univ.).

Controversial issue of Protestant revenge for Catholic conspiracies in England; how dramatists such as Kyd, Webster, Marlowe, and Tourneur popularized this theme.

2512. [REVENGE] Camoin, François André, "The Revenge Convention in Tourneur, Webster, and Middleton," *DA*, 28 (1968), 2643-A (Univ. of Mass.).

With these playwrights, revenge convention serves less as device for character-revelation or plot-unity than as mode of exploration of revenger's relation to his universe. Revenge as device for making metaphysical statements regarding fate, predestination, chance, and divine influence on human life.

2513. [REVENGE] Golden, Bruce, "Elizabethan Revenge and Spanish Honor: Analogues of Action in the Popular Drama of the Renaissance," *DA*, 30 (1969), 1526-A (Columbia Univ.).

Hero's moral obligation to take revenge for honor in response to the demands of the honor code or a rigid ethic of revenge, and his ensuing course of action.

2514. [REVENGE] Prosser, Eleanor, *Hamlet and Revenge*. Stanford: Stanford Univ. Press, 1967.

Rev. *CE*, 29 (1967), 59-60; *ETJ*, 19 (1967), 403-404; *N.Y. Rev. of Books*, 12 October 1967, 14-16; *QJS*, 53 (1967), 387; *RenQ*,

21 (1968), 226-228; *SJH* (1968), pp. 229-230.   See especially
M.C. Andrews rev. art., *RenP, 1974* (Southeastern Ren. Conf.,
1975), pp. 19-29.

Pt. I of controversial study examines Elizabethan attitudes to
revenge and then analyzes revenge conventions in Shakespeare's
plays and those of his contemporaries. Book argues that Hamlet is torn between desire to obey the Ghost and awareness
that to do so would be to dare damnation.

2515.   [REVENGE] Sibly, John, "The Duty of Revenge in Tudor and Stuart
Drama," *A Review of English Literature*, 8 (1967), 46-54.

Discusses the orthodoxy of revenging oneself upon a usurper.
He contends that Elizabethans and Jacobeans distinguished between legitimate kings and "a usurper or usurping regicide."
Moreover, certain statutes and the Bond of Association demanded
that regicides be exterminated.

2516.   [REYNARD, FOX] Pichaske, David Richard, "The Reynardian Tradition in Medieval and Renaissance English Literature," *DA*, 30
(1970), 3953-A (Ohio Univ.).

Medieval fable literature identified; its popularity demonstrated; its use as exempla in sermons and its influence on
Chaucer, Lydgate, Spenser, Ben Jonson.

2517.   [REYNARD, FOX] Varty, Kenneth, *Reynard the Fox: A Study of
the Fox in Medieval English Art*.   Leicester Univ. Press, 1967.

Rev. *Konsthistorisk Tijdskrift*, 37 (1968), 78-79.

Lists 292 items of fox carvings and drawings. Discusses fox
and cock, fox and ape, fox physician, fox's death and resurrection, etc. Bibliography.

2518.   [RIDDLE] Whitman, F.H., "Medieval Riddling," *NM*, 71 (1970),
177-185.

Riddles as evidence of spirit of play, grammatical tradition
and encyclopedic-Christian consciousness.

2519.   [RIGHT REASON] Fernández-Castañeda, Jaime, "Right Reason in
Francis Suarez," *Modern Schoolman*, 45 (1968), 105-122.

Examines right reason's connection with reality, natural law,
and conscience in Suarez (1548-1617); revaluation of Suarez's
supposed voluntarism in light of importance of right reason
to his theory of moral obligation.

2520.   [Marriage of RIVERS] Oruch, Jack B., "Spenser, Camden, and the
Poetic Marriages of Rivers," *SP*, 64 (1967), 606-624.

Marriage of Isis and Tame, with generation of Thamisis, who
sets forth to seek his sire, the Ocean.

2521.   [ROGUES] Taylor, John Alfred, "Rogues in Arden: A Study of
Elizabethan Newgate Pastoral," *DA*, 29 (1969), 3158-A (Univ.
of Calif., Berkeley).

On group of Tudor and Stuart plays about idealized outlaws and
vagabonds, and social customs and non-dramatic literature that
created, or anticipated, that idealization. Included are
chapters on the legend of Robin Hood.

2522. [SAINTS] Keller, Hiltgart L., *Reclams Lexikon der Heiligen und
der biblischen Gestalten. Legende und Darstellung in der
bildenden Kunst.* Stuttgart: Reclam, 1968.

Lexicon of saints and biblical figures in the visual arts.
Vita, followed by article, and references to particular works.

2523. [SAINT'S PLAY] Del Villar, Mary Harmon, "The Saint's Play in
Medieval England," *DA*, 31 (1970), 1221-A (Univ. of Ariz.).

Evaluation of the genre; influence of continental drama on
English plays. Motifs and conventions carried on to Renaissance English drama.

2524. [SALT] Mollat, Michel, ed., *Le Rôle du Sel dans l'Histoire.*
(Publications de la Fac. des Lettres et sciences humaines de
Paris-Sorbonne. Série "Recherches," tome 37.)

Articles on salt in commerce; as well as Jean Palou, "Le sel
et la sorcellerie," pp. 277-285; and J. Toussaert, "Le sel
dans la liturgie," pp. 287-303.

2525. [SALVATION] Tennenhouse, Leonore W., "A Critical Edition of
Three Tudor Interludes: *Impatient Poverty, Lusty Juventus* and
Nice Wanton," *DA*, 31 (1970), 1817-A (Univ. of Rochester).

Critical editions collated from extant editions of plays.
Provides milieu in which to view plays as Tudor dramas of salvation. Treatment of conventional characters. Full notes.

2526. [SAPIENCE] Quitslund, Jon, "Spenser's Image of Sapience,"
SRen, 16 (1969), 181-213.

Rejects argument that Sapience in Spenser is Christ as the
Logos; sees the traditions of Renaissance Platonism, Christian
devotional literature, and Kabbalism influencing Spenser.
These traditions identify this figure as an "entity distinct
from God."

2527. [SATIRE] Alter, Jean V., *Les Origines de la Satire anti-bour-
geoise en France. Moyen Age--XVIe siècle.* Geneva: Droz,
1966.

Première Section: Moyen Age--includes professional satire of
merchants, usurers, trades, jurists; political and social
satire; moral satire; sources. Deuxième Section: XVIe siècle
--deals with medieval themes as above and new themes: "La
satire des financiers; La satire des offices." Sources: literary, spiritual, social.

2528. [SATIRE] Fisk, Viva K., "Court Satire in the Dramas of John
Webster, Thomas Middleton, and John Marston," *DA*, 29 (1969),
4454-A (Univ. of New Mexico).

Dark perspectives of their revenge dramas comprehensible in
light of 17th-cent. political ideals, and the court realities
of tyranny and corruption.

2529.   [SATIRE] Lecocq, Louis, *La Satire en Angleterre de 1588 à
        1603*. Paris: Didier, 1969.

        Rev. *BHR*, 32 (1970), 726–728; *TLS*, 24 July 1970, p. 831.

        Deals extensively with the satirical spirit, targets, and
        techniques of the writers, theory of Elizabethan satire, its
        origins--as much in Piers Plowman and Martin Marprelate as in
        Horace and Juvenal--and above all its reception.

2530.   [SATIRE] Powers, Doris Cooper, "English Formal Satire: Eliza-
        bethan to Augustan," *DA*, 27 (1966), 1036-A (Univ. of Calif.,
        Berkeley).

        Account of the satirical form in the Elizabethan age as it
        shifts to that of the Augustan. Also an account of the shift-
        ing contemporary ideas of human nature and values. Deals with
        period c. 1600-c. 1675.

2531.   [SATIRE] Shaw, D.J., "More about the 'Dramatic Satyre,'" *BHR*,
        30, no. 2 (1968), 301–325.

        On belief by both Latin and vernacular writers of late 15th
        and early 16th cents. that satire was a dramatic genre.

2532.   [*SCURRA*] Corbett, P.B., "The 'scurra' in Plautus," *Eranos*, 66,
        nos. 1–4 (1968), 118–131.

        In Plautus this human type appears as the enemy of the profes-
        sional parasite.

2533.   [SEA] Covo, Jacqueline, "The Lake of Darkness: Marine Imagery
        in Relation to Themes of Disruption in Medieval Poetry," *DA*,
        28 (1967), 2205-A (Brandeis Univ.).

        Relates sea imagery in medieval poetry to Christian and clas-
        sical traditions of sea as an image or emblem of moral aliena-
        tion, disruption, or chaos.

2534.   [SHIP] Gruenter, Rainer, "Das Schiff: Ein Beitrag zur his-
        torischen Metaphorik," in *Tradition und ursprünglichkeit*, ed.
        Werner Kohlschmidt and Herman Meyer. Bern and Munich: Francke,
        1966, pp. 86–101.

        Brant and medieval analogues of a Yeatsian passage.

2535.   [SHIP] Schmidtke, Dietrich, "Geistliche Schiffahrt: Zum Thema
        des Schiffes der Busse im Spätmittelalter," *Beiträge zur Gesch.
        der Deut. Sprache und Lit.* (Tübingen), 91 (1969), 357–385;
        92 (1970), 115–177.

        Detailed, documented study of patristic and medieval Christian
        ship-symbol in the late middle ages (following on Hugo Rahner's
        studies of ship, sea, etc., 1941–1964, in *Zeitschrift für kath.
        Theologie*).

2536. [SHREW; DISGUISED GIRL] Gilbert, Miriam Anne, "The Shrew and the Disguised Girl in Shakespeare's Comedies," _DA_, 30 (1970), 2967-A (Indiana Univ.).

These two conventions as woman's means of escape from social restrictions. Relates them to Elizabethan drama, and then to nine Shakespearean comedies.

2537. [SIBYL] Kinter, W.L., and J.R. Keller, _The Sibyl: Prophetess of Antiquity and Medieval Fay._ Philadelphia: Dorrance, 1967.

Rev. _Spec._, 43 (1968), 355.

2538. [SIGNATURES] Grossinger, Richard, "The Doctrine of Signatures," _IO_, no. 5 (Summer, 1968), issue devoted to doctrine of Signatures: includes Grossinger on the doctrine, pp. 6-14; Michel Foucault, "The Signatures," pp. 15-28; selections in trans. from _Les Mots et les Choses_ (Paris: Gallimard, 1966).

Foucault, along with other contributors, provides Renaissance instances of the mode of knowledge of the world by signatures, or correspondences.

2539. [SILENCE] Waddington, Raymond B., "The Iconography of Silence and Chapman's Hercules," _JWCI_, 112 (1970), 248-263.

Attempting to explain Chapman's phrase "Herculean silence," traces classical association of silence with wisdom, and this to Renaissance mythographers. Also studies mythic figures of silence and eloquence and conflation of these figures.

2540. [SINS] Becker, Reinhard P., "Satirical Types and Methods in the _Epistolae Obscurorum Virorum_," _DA_, 28 (1968), 4116-A (Columbia Univ.).

Renaissance work satirical of New Learning employs Seven Deadly Sins as satirical device, in medieval fashion of anti-clericalism. Thus, fleshly sins, _luxuria_ and _gula_, are more used than other five, to depict _viri obscuri_.

2541. [SINS] Clarke, Dorothy Clotelle, _Allegory, Decalogue, and Deadly Sins in "La Celestina."_ Univ. of Calif. Publ. in Modern Philology, 91. Berkeley: Univ. of Calif. Press, 1968.

Discusses sins of lechery, etc.

2542. [SINS] Fink, Hanno, _Die Sieben Todsünden in der mittelenglischen erbaulichen Literatur._ (Brittanica et Americana. Hrsg. von den Universitäten Hamburg und Marburg/Lahn, Bd. 17.) Hamburg: Cram, de Gruyter & Co., 1969.

Seven deadly sins in 13th and 14th cents.; each sin examined separately, with Biblical background, in sermons and literature.

2543. [SINS] Molinaro, Julius A., "Ariosto and the Seven Deadly Sins," _Forum Italicum_, 3 (1969), 252-269.

In Canto XIV of _Orlando Furioso_ cruelty is substituted for lust as one of the seven sins. Ariosto revises the traditional list because cruelty is harmful to others, while lust is self-punitive.

2544. [SINS] Wenzel, Siegfried, "The Seven Deadly Sins: Some Problems of Research," *Speculum*, 43 (1968), 1-22.

On paucity of work in area since M.W. Bloomfield's major study
(1952); aspects and methods of the problem, and suggestions
for research.

2545. [SKY, Blue] Lillyman, W.J., "A Recurrent Symbol," *CL*, 21
(1969), 116-124.

Blue sky as symbol of isolation; especially effective through
lack of inherent suggestion of enclosure.

2546. [SKY and EARTH] Seidenberg, A., "The Separation of Sky and
Earth," *Folklore*, 80 (1969), 188-196.

Links myth, ritual, and social organization, with special reference to myth of separation of sky and earth at Creation.

2547. [SLANDER] Bohm, Rudolph, "Die Verleumdungsszene bei Shakespeare," *SJH* (1967), 221-233.

Variety of slander-scenes, consummated in *Othello*.

2548. [SLANDER] Hengerer, Joyce H., "The Theme of the Slandered
Woman in Shakespeare," *DA*, 28 (1967), 1078-1079-A (Univ. of
Wisc.).

Studies *Ado*, *Cym.*, and *WT* against background of slandered-
woman theme in Middle Ages and Renaissance.

2549. [SLOTH] Wenzel, Siegfried, *The Sin of Sloth: Acedia in Medieval Thought and Literature.* Chapel Hill, N.C.: Univ. of
North Carolina Press, 1967.

Rev. *Arcadia*, 4 (1969), 91-93.

Follows M.W. Bloomfield's standard work, concentrating on one
of seven deadly sins. Includes scholastic analysis; iconography of the vice; deterioration of *Acedia*. Appendixes include
"Acedia and the Humors." Notes and sources, pp. 204-260;
index of subjects. (Cf. his diss., published, n.p., 1960.)

2550. [*SOCIETAS*] Wegner, Michael, *Untersuchungen zu den lateinischen
Begriffen "socius" und "societas."* Göttingen: Vandenhoek &
Ruprecht, 1969.

Etymology of *socius*; *socius* and *societas* in general usage; and
in area of foreign politics. Bibliography, pp. 108-118.

2551. [Braggart SOLDIER] Huston, J. Dennis, "'Some Stain of Soldier':
Six Braggart Warriors and Their Functions," *DA*, 27 (1967),
2498-2499-A (Yale Univ.).

Deals with tradition of *miles gloriosus*, typified by Lamachos,
Pistol, Braggadochio, Parolles, Bessus, and Falstaff.

2552. [SOUL] Partee, Charles, "The Soul in Plato, Platonism and Cal-vin," _Scottish Jour. of Theology_, 22 (1969), 278-295.

Although Calvin may have been influenced by Plato's _Dialogues_ and Ficino's _Theologia Platonica_, his main sources are scrip-tural.

2553. [SPANIARD] Brown, Louise Stephens, "The Portrayal of Spanish Characters in Selected Plays of the Elizabethan and Jacobean Eras: 1585-1625," _DA_, 27 (1966), 1779-A (Duke Univ.).

Examines Spanish characters in Elizabethan times, when the English and the Spanish were in conflict; and notes the chan-ges made when peace-loving James took throne. Elizabethan playwrights used drama as propaganda to stress Spanish cruelty, pride, lust, and treachery. Under James, no longer could authors attack the Spanish so openly, for the Master of the Revels exercised strong control. Some catered to the royal taste, others such as Middleton, Beaumont, and Fletcher con-tinued to attack the Spanish under various guises. Cites the sympathetic portrayal of Catherine of Aragon in _Henry VIII_.

2554. [SPANIARD] Jorgensen, Paul A., "Foreign Sources for the Eliza-bethan Notion of the Spaniard," _Viator_, 1 (1970), 337-344.

Role of biased translations as propaganda.

2555. [SPANIARD] Maltby, William Saunders, "The Black Legend in Eng-land, 1558-1660," _DA_, 28 (1968), 3610-3611-A (Duke Univ.). (Book: Durham, N.C.: Duke Univ. Press, 1971.)

Anti-Spanish feeling in England, its origins, aggravations, evolution, and consequences. Writers with Puritan leanings seem to have been responsible for bulk of anti-Spanish litera-ture, which depicted Spain as sink of cruelty, treachery, and avarice. By time of accession of James I, "Black Legend" of Spanish wickedness seems to have been widely accepted.

2556. [SPARTA] Rawson, Elizabeth, _The Spartan Tradition in European Thought_. Oxford: Clarendon Press, 1969.

Discusses Sparta in relation to Athens; relates Spartan thought to important periods in European history. Vigorous influence on the political and educational thought of the Renaissance.

2557. [STATUE] Smith, Webster, "Definitions of _Statua_," _Art Bulletin_, 50 (1968), 263-267.

For Alberti, as for Ghiberti, _statua_ meant an ideal, novel, wonderful, and admirable thing. By end of 16th-cent. _statua_ meant again, as in antiquity, nothing more than type of art object, not something remarkable, as in early Renaissance.

2558. [STOIC] Vawter, Marvin Lee, "Shakespeare and Jonson: Stoic Ethics and Political Crisis," _DA_, 31 (1970), 2358-A (Univ. of Wisc.). (Cf. 1030.)

Evolving anti-stoic tradition which satirizes the stoic wise
man by exaggeration of materials of the Stoics; shows how
Shakespeare and Jonson seem to be testing Stoicism in midst of
political crisis and finding it either ineffective, self-defeating, paralyzing, or deadly to a whole society.

2559.   [STORK] Cast, David, "The Stork and the Serpent: A New Interpretation of the 'Madonna of the Meadow' by Bellini," *Art
Quarterly*, 33 (1969), 247-258.

Identifies bird in painting as a stork and investigates possible meanings of the bird in this context. In classical
authors stork is sign of returning spring and symbol of filial
piety.

2560.   [STORK] Datta, Kitty, "Marvell's Stork: The Natural History
of an Emblem," *JWCI*, 31 (1968), 437-438.

Marvell's humorous use of a rare Renaissance iconographical
figure.

2561.   [SUBSTANCE] Hammond, Albert L., *Ideas about Substance*. Baltimore, Md.: Johns Hopkins Univ. Press, 1969.

Rev. *Choice*, 6 (1970), 1760.

Traces views about the concept of substance from pre-Socratics
through Plato, Aristotle, the 17th-cent. rationalists, and
later.

2562.   [SUFFERING HERO] Crompton, Georgia Ronan, "The Protagonist as
Sufferer: A Critical Inquiry into a Topos in Chaucer and
Spenser," *DA*, 28 (1967), 2205-2206-A (Univ. of Oregon).

Traces *topos* of suffering hero to Homer and to Christian and
Stoic literary traditions; relates it, and Chaucer's and Spenser's use of it, to its associated ideas; e.g., that passion
and ignorance or illusion tend to make a man a passive being;
paradox (*vincit qui patitur*) that acceptance transforms suffering into action; relationship of *topos* to issue of free
will and predestination.

2563.   [SUICIDE] Cleary, James J., "Seneca, Suicide and English
Renaissance Tragedy," *DA*, 30 (1969), 1521-1522-A (Temple
Univ.).

No consistent attitude toward suicide in English tragedy;
early adapters of Seneca, Kyd, Marlowe, Chapman, Beaumont and
Fletcher, and Ford waxed and waned in their concern with suicide, both in attitude and technique.

2564.   [SUICIDE] Hicks, Cora Eiland, "Suicide in English Tragedy,
1587-1622," *DA*, 29 (1968), 1868-1869-A (Univ. of Texas).

On discrepancy between rarity (and canonical and legal pro-
scription) of suicide in actual life of the period, and its
frequency and acceptability as an action or theme in stage
tragedy. Various attitudes to, or justification of, suicide
in plays of various dramatists.

2565. [SUN] Eidson, Donald Ray, "The Sun as Symbol and Type of Christ in English Non-Dramatic Poetry from the Anglo-Saxon Period through the Victorian Period," _DA_, 30 (1970), 4407-A (Univ. of Missouri).

Tradition of Christ as the Sun of righteousness from the Old English charms to Browning's "A Death in the Desert."

2566. [SUN] Eigeldinger, Marc, _La Mythologie solaire dans l'oeuvre de Racine_. Geneva: Droz, 1969.

Rev. _French Studies_, 25 (1971), 74-75.

Role of the sun in Racine's poetry. Author assumes that the sun plays similar role in ancient mythology, Greek and Christian symbolism, Jungian archetypes, and images of Racine.

2567. [SUN] Kranz, Walther, "Die Sonne als Titan," _Studien zur Antiken Literatur und ihrem Fortwirken: Kleine Schriften_, ed. Ernst Vogt. Heidelberg: Carl Winter, 1967, pp. 452-456.

Traces origin of the Shakespearean Titan association.

2568. [SUN] Zambelli, P., "Il sole, Il Rinascimento e la ricerca interdisciplinare," _Riv. crit. St. Filos._, 23, no. 4 (1968), 418-434.

Analysis of the _Acta (The sun in the Renaissance. Science and myth)_ of the second international Colloquium held in April 1963 under the auspices of the International Federation of Institutes and Societies for the Study of the Renaissance and of the Ministry of National Education and of Culture of Belgium. (Brussels: Presses Universitaires de Bruxelles; Paris: Presses Universitaires de France, 1965.)

2569. [SYMBOL] Forstner, Dorothea, _Die Welt der Symbole_. 2nd rev. ed. Innsbruck: Tyrolia, 1967.

Reference book of symbols drawn from mythology and theology: 1) signs and writing; 2) numbers and figures; 3) cosmic manifestations; 4) colors; 5) stones and metals; 6) plants; 7) animals; 8) Biblical figures; 9) mythological figures; 10) anatomical parts and physical substances; 11) miscellaneous-- tools, clothing, arms. (Cf. 639.)

2570. [SYMBOL] Kitagawa, Joseph M., and Charles H. Long, eds., _Myths and Symbols. Studies in Honor of Mircea Eliade_. Univ. of Chicago Press, 1969.

Collection includes bibliography of Mircea Eliade's works; contributions by Bareau, Brandon, Dumézil, Widengren, Dimcock, and others, organized into three parts: phenomenological and theoretical, historical, and literary. Essays include R.M. Grant on "Chains of Being in Early Christianity."

2570a. [SYMBOL] Lurker, Manfred, _Bibliographie zur Symbolkunde, Ikonographie und Mythologie: Internationales Referateorgan_. Baden-Baden: Verlag Heitz GmbH, 1968.

Items include more than 11,466 references to writings on symbolism of all kinds. Sections include: Bibliographien; Periodica; Lexica; Begriff, philosophische Grundlegung und Geschichte des Symbols; Auswahl aus der Literatur des 16.-18. Jahrhunderts; Ethnologie--Religionswissenschaft--Mythologie; ... Kunstgeschichte; Literatur ..., Elemente; Pflanzen; Tiere; Kleidung; Handlung; Farben; Zahlen; etc. Concludes with Autorenregister, pp. 577-640; and Sachregister, pp. 641-695. This latter index is especially useful.

2571. [TEMPERANCE] Erskine-Hill, Howard, "Antony and Octavius: The Theme of Temperance in Shakespeare's *Antony and Cleopatra*," *RMS*, 14 (1970), 48-68.

Studies Spenserian theme of Temperance of Bower of Bliss episode in *Ant.*, Antony the hero of intemperance and Octavius the "meane" of Temperance, which Shakespeare shows to be close to policy. Also discusses Temperance in *Cor.*

2572. [TEMPEST] Ijsewijn, Jozef, "Le topos littéraire de l'huile jetée sur les flots pendant la tempête," *Latomus*, 28 (1969), 485-486.

Oil poured on the waves of a stormy sea appears as a mode of rescue in Pliny's *Natural History*, Bk. 2. Also used in Bede's *Historia ecclesiastica gentis Anglorum* and in Erasmus' *Colloquies*.

2573. [TEMPEST] Rougé, J., "*Topos et Realia*: La tempête apaisée de la Vie de saint Germain d'Auxerre," *Latomus*, 27 (1968), 197-202.

Distinction between *topos* and *realia* studied in 5th-cent. miracle of the tempest calmed.

2574. [TEMPEST] Wind, Edgar, *Giorgione's "Tempesta" with Comments on Giorgione's Poetic Allegories*. Oxford: Clarendon Press, 1969.

Shows that in language of the time, *Fortuna* was synonym of *Tempesta*. Relates symbols of broken column and *Fortezza*. Notes and references, pp. 17-43, with useful interpretative materials. Rev. *BHR*, 32 (1970), 695-699.

2575. [TENNIS COURT] Rhodes, Ernest L., "'Me thinks this stage shews like a Tennis Court'" [Discussion of *Lust's Dominion*], *Renaissance Papers 1968* (Southeastern Renaissance Conference, Columbia, S.C., 1970), pp. 21-28.

Examines incidents in the play which likens stage to tennis court with regard to stage for which it was written. Illustrated.

2576. [*THEATRUM MUNDI*] Warnke, Frank J., "The World as Theatre: Baroque Variations on a Traditional Topos," in *Festschrift für E. Mertner*, hrsg. Bernhard Fabian et al. Munich: 1969, pp. 185-200. (Cf. THEATRICAL.)

2577. [THEME] Beller, Manfred, Rev. art. of Elisabeth Frenzel, *Stoff- und Motivgeschichte*. Berlin: Erich Schmidt, 1968; and her *Stoff-, Motiv- und Symbolforschung*, ed. 2. Stuttgart: J.B. Metzlersche Verlagsbuchhandlung, 1966. In *Arcadia*, 2 (1967), 320-323.

Documented comments on research in thematics.

2578. [THEME] Frenzel, Elisabeth, *Stoff- und Motivgeschichte*. Berlin: Erich Schmidt, 1966.

Rev. *Arcadia*, 2 (1967), 320-323; *MLN*, 84 (1969), 846-847.

History of how subjects and motifs arise, develop, are borrowed, and revive.

2579. [THEME] Levin, Harry, "Thematics and Criticism," in Peter Demetz et al., eds., *The Disciplines of Criticism: Essays in Literary Theory, Interpretation, and History*. New Haven/London: Yale Univ. Press, 1968, pp. 125-145.

Useful bibliographic survey, with illuminating comments, of the field of motifs and "thematics."

2580. [THEMES, SPANISH] McCready, Warren T., *Bibliografía Temática de Estudios sobre le Teatro Español Antiguo*. Univ. of Toronto Press, 1966.

Includes *temas* in Parte I: *Período formativo*, 115 items; in Parte II. *Período Aureosecular*, *temas* are numbered 799-1517. In addition, authors have subsections of *temas*; e.g., Calderón's run from pp. 214-238, including, e.g., Fortuna. Useful for analogous Shakespearean work.

2581. [THEORY and PRACTICE] Lobkowicz, Nicholas, *Theory and Practice: History of a Concept from Aristotle to Marx*. Notre Dame, Ind.: Univ. of Notre Dame Press, 1967.

Rev. *Philosophy*, 45 (1970), 75-78.

Opposition between theory and practice from antiquity through Marx. Useful chapters on Middle Ages and Renaissance.

2582. [TIGER] McCullough, Florence, "Le tigre au miroir. La vie d'une image de Pline à Pierre Gringore," *Rev. des Sc. humaines*, fasc. 130 (1968), 149-160.

Historical study of varied and often contradictory meanings represented through the tiger image.

2583. [TIGER] Parsons, Coleman O., "Tygers before Blake," *SEL*, 8, no. 4 (1968), 573-592.

Tigers seen as unnecessarily cruel, more redoubtable than the lion; assimilation of tiger to the Leviathan.

2584. [TIME] Crosby, Virginia, "Agrippa d'Aubigné's *Les Tragiques*: The Conquest of Profaned Time," *DA*, 30 (1970), 5405-5406-A (Univ. of Southern Calif.).

"Carnal metaphysics" distinguish D'Aubigné's poetic reality
from view of the other poets of the Pléiade tradition. By
simultaneously depicting the event and its symbol, he shows
the spiritual reality behind appearances. He reveals the
soteriological reality behind profane time.

2585.   [TIME] Grimal, P., "Place et Rôle du Temps dans la Philosophie
de Sénèque," *Rev. Et. anc.*, 70, nos. 1-2 (1968), 92-109.

Argues that Seneca's thought developed around problem of time
and that he built his ascending dialectic about this concept.

2586.   [TIME] Gross, Laila, "Time in the Towneley Cycle, *King Horn,
Sir Gawain and the Green Knight* and Chaucer's *Troilus and
Criseyde*," *DA*, 29 (1969), 3097.

Mystery cycles present an atemporal reality which depends on a
conscious confusion of temporal connections; Romances ignore
them as much as possible; Chaucer's *T&C* uses temporal connections to the fullest extent.

2587.   [TIME] Jones, Joseph R., "Human Time in *La Diana*," *Romance
Notes*, 10 (1968), 139-146.

Case for *Los siete libros de la Diana* as the first of modern
novels, applying distinction made by Georges Poulet between
the old and new in the novel: discovery of past time as that
which makes the present meaningful.

2588.   [TIME] Lewis, Anthony J., "Description of Time in Shakespeare,"
DA, 29 (1969), 2678-A (Univ. of Wisc.).

Chapter on English rhetorical tradition; Shakespeare's early
development with respect to treatment of time; Shakespeare's
middle and mature periods.

2589.   [TIME] McCutcheon, E., "Lancelot Andrewes' 'Preces Privatae':
A Journey through Time," *SP*, 65, no. 2 (1968), 223-241.

The art in these prose poems as residing in their temporal
effects which are saturated with providential purpose.

2590.   [TIME] Montgomery, Robert L., Jr., "The Dimensions of Time in
Richard II," *ShakS*, 4 (1968), 73-85.

R2 does not work towards illuminating an idea of time; rather
ideas of time help illuminate situations of its characters.

2591.   [TIME] Orr, Robert, "The Time Motif in Machiavelli," *Pol.
Studies*, 17 (1969), 145-159.

Machiavelli's prescriptions on moral and political life in
terms of his perceptions of time. Time rules man and society;
problems stem not from man's deficiencies but from the fact of
his being a temporal creature in a world of temporal events.
Time not composed of measurable intervals but of succession
of events.

2592. [TIME] Quainton, M.D., "Ronsard's Philosophical and Cosmological Conceptions of Time," *French Studies,* 23 (1969), 1-22.

As complement to the article by I. Silver, "Ronsard's Reflections on the Heavens and Time," *PMLA,* 80 (1965), 4, author illustrates diverse meanings of time in Ronsard by reference to allegory and mythology in cosmic, scientific, and philosophic ideas of the poet.

2593. [TIME] Quinones, Ricardo Joseph, "Time in Dante and Shakespeare," *Symposium,* 22 (1968), 261-284.

Theme of time in the three perspectives employed by Dante and Shakespeare: its principles of change, power of human mind and heart to surmount this change, capacity of mind to achieve an overall view of time; emphasizes divergences by showing points of contact.

2594. [TIME] Ter Horst, R., "Time and the Tactics of Suspense in Garcilaso's 'Egloga primera,'" *MLN,* 83, no. 2 (1968), 145-163.

Construction of poem, dedication, and themes (various tactics) form an aside in battle against time the conqueror, seen either as continuous flow or succession of states.

2595. [TIME] Turner, F., "Shakespeare and the Nature of Time." Oxford Univ. B. Litt. diss., 1967. (Cf. book, Oxford, 1971.)

2596. [TIME] Waller, G.F., "Transition in Renaissance Ideas of Time and Place of Giordano Bruno," *Neoph.,* 55 (1971), 3-15.

Bruno's radically immanentist interpretation of eternity; view of change and mutability as bearing the fullness of life.

2597. [TOBACCO] Tanner, Jeri, "The Dramatic and Narrative Influence of Tobacco on Literature of the Renaissance," *DA,* 29 (1969), 2688-A (Texas Technological College).

Influences of tobacco upon literature of the English Renaissance include, in addition to satiric and comic effects, impact upon structural development and characterization.

2598. [*TOPOI*] Beller, Manfred, "Von der Stoffgeschichte zur Thematologie. Ein Beitrag zur komparatistischen Methodenlehre," *Arcadia,* 5 (1970), 1-38.

2599. [*TOPOI*] Dyck, Joachim, "Erfindung und Topik," *Ticht-Kunst. Deutsche Barockpoetik und rhetorische Tradition.* Bad Homburg, Berlin, Zurich: Max Gehlen, 1966, pp. 40-65.

Role of *loci communes* in 17th-cent. poetic.

2600. [*TOPOI*] Emrich, Berthold, "Topik und Topoi," *DU,* 18 (1966), H. 6, 15-46.

Traces the topic from Aristotle and its rhetorical use; includes section on "Die 'Umwertung' der sophistischen Topoi." *Topos* in Latin tradition, etc.

2601. [*TOPOI*] Griffin, Robert, "The French Renaissance Commonplace
       and Literary Context: An Example," *Neophil.*, 54 (1970), 258-
       261.

       Relation of commonplace to text, as in Rabelais's use, *Tiers
       Livre.*

2602. [*TOPOI*] Köttelwesch, Clemens, *Bibliographie der deutschen
       Literaturwissenschaft*, Bd. 7: *1965-1966* (gen. ed., H.W. Eppels-
       heimer). Frankfurt am Main: Vittorio Klostermann, 1967.

       Section on "Stoff- und Motifgeschichte," pp. 65-71, contains
       list of *topoi* for the years covered. Annual.

2603. [*TOPOI*] Uhlig, Claus, *Traditionelle Denkformen in Shakespeares
       tragischer Kunst.* Britannica et Americana (Britannica, neue
       Folge), hrsg. von den Englischen Seminaren der Universitäten
       Hamburg und Marburg/Lahn (Ludwig Borinski et al.), Bd. 15.
       Hamburg: Cram, de Gruyter & Co., 1967.

       Rev. *SJH*, 1968, 234-237.

       Shakespeare's tragic art form understood in the light of con-
       temporary moral views embodied in current patterns of thought
       and commonplaces. Some of these (e.g., topics of conscience,
       love-lust, suffering and consolation) are traced in Renaissance
       literature and helpfully utilized in the interpretation of
       Shakespeare's art, particularly in the great tragedies. Well-
       documented, useful book.

2604. [*TOPOI*] Woods, M.J., "Gracián, Peregrini, and the Theory of
       Topics," *MLR*, 63 (1968), 854-863.

       Acquaintance with classical theory of topics essential for
       full understanding of 17th-cent. treatises on wit.

2605. [*TOPOI*] ———, "Sixteenth-Century Topical Theory: Some Span-
       ish and Italian Views," *MLR*, 63 (1968), 66-73.

       Aristotle and Cicero on the *topoi* were widely read during 16th
       and 17th cents. and conditioned attitudes toward writing of
       poetry. Analytic approach to the writing of poetry resulted
       from poet's attempt to apply the *topoi* in their verse.

2606. [TRAGICOMEDY] Peters, Howard Nevin, "Sixteenth Century Euro-
       pean Tragicomedy: A Critical Survey of the Genre in Italy,
       France, England, and Spain," *DA*, 28 (1967), 240-A (Univ. of
       Colorado).

       Survey stresses *Celestina* as precocious European tragicomic
       example. Tragicomedy as mixture with intention of creating
       new and more modern drama presenting an integrated view of
       life, a practice condoned by classical critics and dramatists
       themselves.

2607. [TREE] Erdman, E. George, Jr., "Arboreal Figures in the Golden
       Age Sonnet," *PMLA*, 84 (1969), 587-595.

       Extent to which stock figures of the tree beset by natural
       forces, the embrace of elm and vine, and the antithesis of

mulberry and almond are revitalized in unique poetic artifacts. These *topoi* highlight shift of emphasis from discursive to pictorial which marks transition from aesthetics of the Renaissance to that of the Baroque.

2608. [TREE] Ormerod, David, "Wyatt and the Execution of Mark Smeaton," *Pubs. on Lang. and Lat.* (Southern Ill. Univ.), 4 (1968), 101-103.

Wyatt's comparison of climbing dangerously high tree, grasping rotten twig, and falling to death; height of tree as hierarchical, rotten twig as extinct branch of genealogical tree.

2609. [TRIAL BY COMBAT] McNeir, Waldo F., "Trial by Combat in Elizabethan Literature," *Die Neueren Sprachen*, 15 (1966), 101-112.

In Elizabethan literature, the trial by combat usually conforms to the precepts of Thomas of Woodstock in his "Ordenaunce." Literary examples occur in Sidney's *Arcadia*, Spenser's *Faerie Queene*, and in Shakespeare's *2 Henry VI*, *RII*, and *Lear*. In *Richard II* the stress is on the remote atmosphere to which the trial contributes, and in *2 Henry VI*, the trial is parodied.

2610. [TRIAL SCENES] Kelly, Michael F., "The Trial Scenes in the Plays of the Beaumont and Fletcher Folio," *DA*, 27 (1967), 4222-4223-A (Univ. of Tenn.).

Trial scenes discussed from five viewpoints: staging, dramatic function, character usage, language, and thematic relevance. Uses of legal terminology, and opposition of justice and mercy discussed.

2611. [TRIAL SCENES] Nagy, N. Cristoph De, "Die Functionen der Gerichtsszene bei Shakespeare und in der Tradition des älteren englischen Dramas," *SJH* (1967), 199-220.

In mysteries, trial and judgment conclude the play; in moralities, trial scenes are detached from main action; in Shakespeare, they are varied, brief, and loosely related to the central action.

2612. [TRIAL SCENES] Oppel, Horst, *Die Gerichtsszene in "King Lear."* Akademie der Wissenschaften und der Literatur, Mainz. Abhandlungen der Geistes-und Sozialwissenschaftlichen Klasse. Jhrg. 1968. Nr. 8. Wiesbaden: Franz Steiner Verlag, 1968.

On trial-scene and justice in *Lr*. Contains chapter on artistic interpretation by Johann Heinrich Füssli (1741-1825). Illustrated.

2613. [TRICKSTER] Slights, William W.E., "The Trickster-Hero and Middleton's *A Mad World My Masters*," *Comparative Drama Review*, 3 (1969), 87-98.

Follywit, the trickster-hero, recalls Roman character types and figure of comic vice in English drama.

2614.   [TRIDENTINE] Casteel, Theodore W., "Calvin and Trent: Cal-
        vin's Reaction to the Council of Trent in the Context of his
        Conciliar Thought," *HTR*, 63 (1970), 91-117.

        Calvin's attack against the Council of Trent does not imply
        his repudiation of a conciliar solution to schism in the
        Church.

2615.   [TRIDENTINE] Cochrane, Eric, "New Light on Post-Tridentine
        Italy: A Note on Recent Counter-Reformation Scholarship,"
        Cath. Hist. Rev., 56 (1970), 291-319.

        Attempts to modify view of Counter-Reformation as a reaction-
        ary period. Discusses political, artistic, and social develop-
        ments, to stress progressive and enlightened achievement.

2616.   [TRIDENTINE] Dickens, A.G., *The Counter Reformation*. N.Y.:
        Harcourt and World, 1969.

        Rev. *Church Hist.*, 39 (1970), 253-254; *History*, 54 (1969),
        425-426.

        Deals with the self-reform, self-defense, and counter-attack
        of Catholicism; its response to the many protests of the late
        15th and early 16th cents. to flowering of the Catholic Refor-
        mation. Useful treatments of the Council of Trent, the papacy
        after Trent, and the relation of Baroque art to the Catholic
        Reformation.

2617.   [TRIDENTINE] Evennett, Henry Outram, *The Spirit of the Counter-
        Reformation*, ed., with postscript, John Bossy. The Birkbeck
        Lectures in Ecclesiastical History given at Univ. of Cambridge,
        1951; Cambridge/N.Y.: Cambridge Univ. Press, 1968.

        Rev. *AHR*, 74 (1968), 579-580.

        Counter-Reformation only in part "counter," since its origins
        precede Protestant Reformation. Main locus: Spain, Italy;
        shifted in 17th cent. to France. Discussion of its spiritual-
        ity; Loyola, etc. Concludes that in 16th cent. Catholic
        church, deprived of its medieval monopoly, adapted itself to
        conditions of postmedieval society and continued religious
        rivalry.

2618.   [TRIDENTINE] Jedin, Hubert, *Crisis and Closure of the Council
        of Trent: A Retrospective View from the Second Vatican Coun-
        cil*. London/Melbourne: Sheed and Ward, 1967.

        Brief survey of Council of Trent and its modern implications.

2619.   [TRIDENTINE] ————, *Geschichte des Konzils von Trient, III*.
        Freiburg i. Br., Basel, Vienna: Herder, 1970.

        Third of eight projected volumes dealing with Council of
        Trent; covers 1545-1547.

2620.   [TRIDENTINE] Lievsay, J.L., "The Council of Trent and Tudor
        England," *Medieval and Ren. Studies* (Southeastern Inst. of
        Medieval and Ren. Studies, 1965). Chapel Hill, N.C.: Univ.
        of North Carolina Press, 1966, pp. 15-39.

Stresses H.J. Hillerbrand's view on Trent's significance. Its
Index Librorum Prohibitorum (1564) banned numerous English
writers. Notes lack of complete survey of English response to
Council of Trent.

2621.   [TRISTAN] Blanch, Robert J., "The History and Progress of the
Tristan Legend: Drust to Malory," _Revue des Langues Vivantes_,
35 (1969), 129-135.

Survey of the legend from 780 to 1485.

2622.   [TRISTAN] Eisner, Sigmund, _The Tristan Legend: A Study in
Sources_. Evanston, Ill.: Northwestern Univ. Press, 1969.

Rev. _Choice_, 6 (1969), 1386; _LibJ_, 94 (1969), 3648.

Sources of original Tristan legend derived from names and traditions of local heroes of author's own past combined with
adventures from Roman and Greek mythology.

2623.   [TROJAN WAR] Schneider, Karin, _Der "Trojanische Krieg" im
späten Mittelalter: Deutsche Trojanromane des 15. Jahrhun-
derts_. Philologische Studien und Quellen, 40. Berlin: Erich
Schmidt, 1968.

Rev. _GQ_, 42 (1969), 430-431.

2624.   [TURK] Bohnstedt, J.W., "The Infidel Scourge of God: The
Turkish Menace as Seen by German Pamphleteers of the Reformation Era," _Trans. Amer. Philos. Soc._, 58, no. 9 (1968), 1-58.

Turk seen as enemy and scourge of God; theological and practical ideas of war against the Turk; appendix of illustrative
materials including two pamphlets in translation and a Lutheran
model sermon; extensive bibliography.

2625.   [TURK] Schwoebel, Robert, _The Shadow of the Crescent: The Renaissance Image of the Turk (1453-1517)_. Nieuwkoop: de
Graaf, 1967.

Rev. _AHR_, 74 (1968), 578-579; _BHR_, 30 (1968), 638-639.

On European concern with Turkish peril, greater than was believed; chapters on Turk as seen by Renaissance humanism, by
Renaissance pilgrims, by Renaissance diplomats.

2626.   [TURK] Setton, Kenneth M., "Pope Leo X and the Turkish Peril,"
Proc. Amer. Phil. Soc., 113, no. 6 (1969), 367-424.

Leo X, Pope 1513-1521, and his European policy against increasing Turkish danger facing Europe.

2627.   [TWINS, Heavenly] Ward, Donald, _The Divine Twins: An Indo-
European Myth in Germanic Tradition_. Berkeley: Univ. of
Calif. Press, 1968.

Resumé and critique of scholarship on "Heavenly Twins" in the
Indo-European culture-language community. Discusses existence
and partial survival of dioskurism in Germanic culture and
religion.

2628. [TYPOLOGY] Davis, Thomas M., "The Traditions of Puritan Typo-
       logy," *DA*, 29 (1969), 3094-A (Univ. of Missouri).

       Development of typological interpretations from NT authors to
       English and Colonial Puritans; shows how typological traditions
       culminate in Puritan literature.

2629. [TYPOLOGY] Reiter, Robert E., "On Biblical Typology and the
       Interpretation of Literature," *CE*, 30 (1969), 562-571.

       Understanding of typology necessary for full appreciation of
       medieval and Renaissance writers--difference among typology,
       prophecy, and allegory.

2630. [TYPOLOGY] Williams, Arnold, "Typology and the Cycle Plays:
       Some Criteria," *Speculum*, 43 (1968), 677-684.

       Critique of quest for typological meanings in studies of medie-
       val drama.

2631. [TYRANNICIDE] Gómez-Moriana, Antonio, *Derecho de resistencia y
       tiranicidio, Estudio de una temática en las comedias de Lope
       de Vega*. Santiago de Compostela: Porto, 1968.

       Attempts to establish a consistent and moderate attitude on
       Lope's part towards tyrannical authority.

2632. [UNICORN] Chatelet-Lange, Liliane, tr. Renate Franciscono,
       "The Grotto of the Unicorn and the Garden of the Villa di Cas-
       tello (belonging to Duke Cosimo I de Medici)," *Art Bulletin*,
       50 (1968), 51-58.

       Grotto theme is seen as an allegory of the unicorn in Earthly
       Paradise. Just as unicorn symbolically purifies waters of the
       Earthly Paradise, so it stands in Castello at source of rivers
       that make Florence fertile, and represents Golden Age brought
       by the Medici.

2633. [USURY] De Roover, Raymond, "The Scholastics, Usury, and For-
       eign Exchange," *Business Hist. Rev.*, 41 (1967), 257-271.

       Usury and its effect on economic growth in the middle ages,
       when it meant any excess above the principal of a *mutuum*, or
       loan. Scholastic interpretations provided escape hatches from
       restrictions against "usury."

2634. [USURY] Ellis, I.P., "The Archbishop and the Usurers," *Jour.
       of Eccles. Hist.*, 21 (1970), 33-42.

       Episcopal investigations of usurers in 16th cent. New economic
       ideas developing as distinction is made between usury and in-
       terest; necessity of interest for commercial enterprise versus
       moral objections to exploitation by usurers.

2635. [USURY] Lunn, M.A.R., "Attitudes to Usury in England in the
       Sixteenth and Seventeenth Centuries." (Director, D.W.J. John-
       son.) Birmingham M.A., 1969.

2636. [USURY] Maloney, Robert P., "Usury in Greek, Roman and Rabbinic Thought," *Traditio*, 27 (1971), 79-109.

Opposition to interest-taking in Talmudic interpretations, even more than in OT.

2637. [USURY] Nelson, Benjamin, *The Idea of Usury: From Tribal Brotherhood to Universal Otherhood*, 2nd. enl. ed. Chicago: U. of Chicago Pr., 1969. Rev. *Choice*, 6 (1970), 1766.

History of Deuteronomic commandment concerning usury in Christendom; particular attention to late medieval and Reformation periods. Observations on transition from particularism of the Hebrew tribe to universalism of modern era.

2638. [USURY] Venard, Marc, "Catholicisme et Usure au XVIᵉ Siècle," *Revue de l'Histoire de l'église de France*, 52 (1966), 59-74.

Brief history of the Catholic Church's policies toward usury and collecting of interest in 16th cent., in regard to rise of materialism and capitalism. It shows Calvin as point of demarcation between forbidding of interest-charging and its encouragement.

2639. [UTOPIA] Bartenschlager, Klaus, "Shakespeares *The Tempest*: Der ideale Traum und Prosperos Magie," *SJ (West)* (1970), 170-187.

The play as example of Renaissance conflict between ideal of perfectibility of life on earth and the reality of life in the crisis years of early-capitalist Europe. Rejection of magic as rejection of an earthly utopia and the hope of a Christian afterlife.

2640. [UTOPIA] Davis, J.C., "Utopia and History," *Hist. St.*, 13 (1968), 165-176.

Refers to the Utopian works of 17th cent. to characterize Utopianism beyond such traditional terms as unrealistic, radical, and unhistorical.

2641. [UTOPIA] Dubois, C.G., "Une utopie politique de la Renaissance française. Rêveries de Guillaume Postel (1510-1581) autour de l'unité européenne," *Information litt.*, 20 (1968), 55-62.

Ideas of Postel link two seemingly contradictory currents, universalism and nationalism, which converge in a dream of world political unity.

2642. [UTOPIA] Fox, Vivian Carol, "Deviance in English Utopias in the 16th, 17th, and 18th Centuries," *DA*, 30 (1969), 1955-A (Boston Univ. Grad. School).

Breaking with apocalpytic other-worldly tradition of past cents., utopists, writers of utopias, concentrated on means with which millennium could be achieved on earth. In two significant ways they can be counted as both initiators and

followers of progress. First, they believed improvement of
mankind on this earth was possible. Second, they maintained
that this improvement was inevitable under conditions of their
utopian society.

2643.   [UTOPIA] Hexter, J.H., "Utopia and Geneva," in *Action and Con-
        viction in Modern Europe. Essays in Memory of E.H. Harbison*,
        ed. T.K. Rabb and J.E. Seigel. Princeton Univ. Press, 1969,
        pp. 77-89.

        Similarities between Utopia and Calvin's Geneva.

2644.   [UTOPIA] Johnson, Robbin S., *More's Utopia: Ideal and Illu-
        sion*. New Haven, Conn.: Yale Univ. Press, 1969.

        Rev. *LJ*, 94 (1969), 4436; *Moreana*, no. 25 (Feb. 1970), 95-97;
        SCN, 27 (1969), 70; *TLS*, 2 October 1970, 1145.

        In *Utopia* More urges that the value of a utopian myth does not
        lie in the ends it espouses, but in the means it discloses by
        which men can introduce true ideals rather than illusory hopes
        into the world.

2645.   [UTOPIA] Khanna, Lee Cullen, "More's *Utopia*: A Literary Per-
        spective on Social Reform," *DA*, 30 (1969), 1530-A (Columbia
        Univ.).

        His two books form a self-contained literary unit whose con-
        sistent theme is the importance of open-mindedness for improve-
        ment of social order. Ability to experiment, learn, and
        change more important to *Utopia* than any particular new insti-
        tution or custom presented.

2646.   [UTOPIA] Nelson, William ed., *Twentieth-Century Interpreta-
        tions of "Utopia." A Collection of Critical Essays*. Engle-
        wood Cliffs, N.J.: Prentice-Hall, 1968.

2647.   [UTOPIA] Steintrager, James, "Plato and More's *Utopia*," *Social
        Research*, 36 (1969), 357-372.

        Prolegomenon to understanding the relationship between *Utopia*
        and the *Republic*.

2648.   [VENUS] Lawrence, Marion, "The *Birth of Venus* in Roman Art,"
        in Douglas Fraser et al., eds., *Essays in the History of Art
        Presented to Rudolf Wittkower*. London: Phaidon, 1967, pp.
        10-16.

        Ancient depictions of Venus compared with Botticelli's.

2649.   [VENUS] McNair, P.M.J., "The Bed of Venus: Key to Poliziano's
        'Stanze,'" *Ital. Studs.*, 25 (1970), 40-48.

        Argues that description of the Realm of Venus is neither a di-
        gression nor independent episode, but central to meaning and
        structure of poem. The sting of war is eased by the act of
        love, rendering the poem an epithalamium on a divine and human
        level.

2650. [VENUS] Schreiber, Earl George, "The Figure of Venus in Late Middle English Poetry," *DA*, 30 (1970), 767-A (Univ. of Ill.).

Investigation of poetic value of Venus in non-Chaucerian poetry of late 14th and 15th cents. Venus as seen by the mythographers and commentators from Bernardus Silvestris to Boccaccio.

2651. [VENUS] Wlosok, Antonie, *Die Göttin Venus in Vergils Aeneis*. (Bibliothek der Klassischen Altertumswissenschaften, Neue Folge, 2 Reihe, Bd. 21.) Heidelberg: Carl Winter, 1967.

Rev. *L'Antiquité Classique*, 37 (1968), 304.

Role of Venus in antiquity and in *Aeneid*; documentation and bibliography.

2652. [VICE] Weimann, Robert, "Rede-Konventionen des Vice von *Mankind* bis *Hamlet*: Zur Herkunft, Dramaturgie und Struktur von 'madness' und 'impertinency,'" *ZAA*, 15 (1967), 117-151.

Speech-conventions of the Vice; continuous development from medieval moralities to Shakespeare in the nonsense speeches of the Vice (e.g., Myscheff in *Mankind*).

2653. [VICE] Wierum, Ann, "'Actors' and 'Play Acting' in the Morality Tradition," *RenD*, 3 (1970), 159-214.

Vice in his two-faced role as "actor," both a comic and an evil figure conspiring against hero for his soul; implications of the deceiver and of his slandering of virtue to show how tragedy and comedy are blended. Play-within-a-play inherent in morality situation, in the deceiver's skillfully "acted" temptation scene.

2654. [VICES] Kiessling, Nicolas, "Antecedents of the Medieval Dragon in Sacred History," *Jour. of Biblical Lit.*, 89 (1970), 167-175.

Shifts in meanings of Hebrew words in OT for various monsters due to mistranslations, etc., resulting in broad, inclusive Satanic symbols or personifications of vices.

2655. [VICES] McGrath, Robert L., "Satan and Bosch, the 'Visio Tundali' and the Monastic Vices," *Gazette des Beaux-Arts*, 71, no. 1188 (1968), 45-50.

Bosch's monster in "The Garden of Delights," connected with the "Visio Tundali," seen to represent specific "monastic vices" of Middle Ages: Lust, Gluttony, and Avarice.

2656. [VILLIAN] Burbridge, Roger T., "The Villain's Role in Shakespearean Tragedy," *DA*, 29 (1969), 2667-A - 2668-A (Univ. of Conn.).

On effects of villainy upon tragic experience in *R3*, *Oth.*, *Ham.*, *Mac.*

2657. [VILLAIN] Beck, Joyce Lorraine Short, "John Webster's Italiante Tragedy," *DA*, 30 (1970), 726-A (Univ. of Mich.).

Transmutation of the Elizabethan and Jacobean myths of Italian villains into tragedy in *White Devil* and *Duchess of Malfi*.

2658. [*VIRTÙ*] Collura, Angelo Joseph, "Machiavelli's Concept of *Virtù* and its Role in His Major Works," *DA*, 30 (1969), 2016-A. (Cath. U.)

Relation between qualitative and quantitative aspects of term *virtù*. Shows that, according to the adjectives of quantity, two systems of measurement can be observed: a system of values and amounts of *virtù* in persons and things; and a system of comparative efficiency in the efforts by an individual, ruler, or institution.

2659. [*VIRTÙ*] Geerken, John Henry, "Heroic Virtue: An Introduction to the Origins and Nature of a Renaissance Concept," *DA*, 29 (1968), 533-534-A (Yale Univ.).

Reconsideration of meaning, origins, and history of Renaissance ideal of *virtù*.

2660. [*VIRTÙ*] Wood, Neal, "Machiavelli's Concept of *Virtù* Reconsidered," *Political Studies*, 15 (1967), 159-172.

Attempts to synthesize the many meanings of this concept into one "special meaning." *Virtù* is that quality which manifests itself in a framework of battle, whether that battle be war or politics.

2661. [VIRTUES AND VICES] Johnson, W. McAllister, "From Favereau's *Tableaux des Vertus et des Vices* to Marolles' *Tableaux du Temple des Muses*: A Conflict between the Franco-Flemish Schools in the Second Quarter of the Seventeenth Century," *Gazette des Beaux-Arts*, 72 (1968), 171-190.

Useful article, citing numerous engravings of *topoi*.

2662. [VIRTUES AND VICES] Schumacher, Paul James, "Virtue and Vice: A Study of the Characters of Hall, the Overburians, and Earle," *DA*, 29 (1968), 1214-A (St. Louis Univ.).

"Character" as device for cataloguing commonplace notions of morals and psychology in the virtue-vice traditions; discusses trend away from rigid virtue-vice mode of conceptualization in the writing of characters.

2663. [VOID] Grant, Edward, "Medieval and Seventeenth-Century Conceptions of an Infinite Void Space beyond the Cosmos," *Isis*, 60 (1969), 39-60.

Changing concepts of cosmos from medieval notion of matter as within finite world, to 17th-cent. conception of void space as three-dimensional, where finite world is located in an infinite space filled with God. Traces Christian views of God in relation to physics and the concept of the void.

2664. [VOID] Schmitt, Charles B., "Experimental Evidence for and Against a Void: The Sixteenth-Century Arguments," *Isis*, 58 (1967), 352-366.

Sixteenth-cent. criticism of Aristotle's dictum, "nature abhors a vacuum," which seems moreover to have been experimentally refuted in 17th cent.; background of the experimental approach.

2665.   [*VOX POPULI*] Boas, George, *Vox Populi: Essays in the History of an Idea.* Baltimore: Johns Hopkins Press, 1969.

Finds that "people's" identity in the arts and philosophy is ambiguous and that their voice lacks authority and often reason.

2666.   [WAGER] Rigg, A.G., "The Wager Story," *Romania*, 88 (1967), 404-417.

Discusses story of knights' wager on wife's fidelity (some influence on *Cym.*).

2667.   [WAR, Just] Flynn, Gerard, "Padre Las Casas, Literature and the Just War," *Rev. de Hist. de América*, 61-62 (1966), 57-72.

Evidence in three authors of Spanish Golden Age (H. de Acuña, Sor Juana Inés de la Cruz, Cervantes) for theme of the "just war," held by Las Casas.

2668.   [WATER] Blume, Bernhard, "Lebendiger Quell und Flut des Todes. Ein Beitrag zu einer Literatur-geschichte des Wassers," *Arcadia*, 1 (1966), 18-30.

Study of water imagery in literature.

2669.   [WATER] Luria, Maxwell S., "Standing Water and Sloth in the *Tempest*," *ES*, 49 (1968), 328-331.

Standing water as symbol of moral obtuseness.

2670.   [WATER] Ninck, Martin, *Die Bedeutung des Wassers im Kult und Leben der Alten. Eine symbolgeschichtliche Untersuchung.* Darmstadt: Wissenschaftliche Buchgesellschaft, 1967.

The chthonic nature of water, water and prophecy, water and darkness (Lethe), water and shape-shifting (Proteus).

2671.   [WEALTH and POVERTY] Hertel, Gerhard, *Die Allegorie von Reichtum und Armut. Ein aristophanisches Motiv und seine Abwandlungen in der abendländischen Literatur.* (Erlanger Beiträge zur Sprach- und Kunstwissenschaft, Bd. 33.) Nürnberg: Verlag Hans Carl, 1969.

Rev. *YWMLS (1969)*, p. 533.

Motif traced through A. Die Antike; B. Das Nachwirken der Antike, including Thomas Heywood, John Fletcher; *Histriomastix*; Richard Barnfield, Ben Jonson, Thomas Carew. Bibliography, pp. 189-200. Renaissance allegorical plates.

2672.   [WELL of Life] Waters, D. Douglas, "Spenser's 'Well of Life' and 'Tree of Life' Once More," *MP*, 66 (1969), 67-68.

Spenser's "well of life" as symbol of continuous washing of
the soul in the word of God prepares Red Crosse to eat of
fruit of "tree of life" as symbol of sacrament of the Lord's
Supper.

2673. [WILD MAN] Cheney, Donald, *Spenser's Image of Nature: Wild
Man and Shepherd in the "Faerie Queene."* Yale Univ. Press,
1966.

Includes also: The Gardens of Adonis; Astraea: The Golden
Age; and Artegall's Savage Injustice; pastoral vision.

2674. [WILD MAN] Jordan, Robert, "Myth and Psychology in *The Changeling*," *RenD*, 3 (1970), 157-165.

Struggle between De Flores and Beatrice as mythic confrontation
of beauty and the beast, or of the wild-man and the lady.
Fairy-tale ending reversed; princess is a beast, the wild man
still wild.

2675. [WILDERNESS] Oleyar, Rita Balkey, "The Biblical Wilderness in
Vaughan, Herbert, and Milton," *DA*, 30 (1969), 287-288-A
(Univ. of Calif., Irvine).

Genesis and development of the metaphor in Christian typological and literary tradition; cultural milieu which makes 17th
cent. appropriate period for evidences of the motif.

2676. [WILL] Hargrave, O.T., "The Freewillers in the English Reformation," *Church Hist.*, 37 (1968), 271-280.

English Freewillers flourished during reigns of Edward VI and
Mary I and were small radical sectarian group, drawing support
primarily from unlearned classes; but stopped short of Ana-
baptism. No necessary link between Freewill movement and
Arminian liberal tendencies toward end of Elizabeth's reign;
these were different groups, yet earlier one provided indigenous precedent for later.

2677. [WILL] *Luther and Erasmus: Free Will and Salvation.* Erasmus:
"De libero arbitrio," trans. and ed. E. Gordon Rupp in collaboration with A.N. Marlow; Luther: "De servo arbitrio," trans.
and ed. Philip S. Watson with B. Drewery. London: S.C.M.
Press, 1969.

Debate between Luther and Erasmus in which the former asserts
the doctrine of predestination and the latter asserts the
freedom of the will.

2678. [WILL] McSorley, H.J., *Luther: Right or Wrong?* Minneapolis:
Augsburg Publishing House, 1969.

Rev. *Church Hist.*, 39 (1970), 250.

English translation of author's Munich dissertation *Luthers
Lehre vom unfreien Willen nach seiner Hauptschrift De Servo
Arbitrio im Lichte der biblischen und kirchlichen Tradition*
(1967). This was reviewed in *Church Hist.*, 37 (1968), 458f.
Bibliography has been expanded as have several sections in the
text, particularly the discussion of Biel's *Canonis Missae* and
the critique of Oberman.

2679. [WILL] ———, *Luthers Lehre vom unfreien Willen.* (Vol. 1: *Beiträge zur ökumenischen Theologie,* ed. Heinrich Fries.) Munich: Max Hueber Verlag, 1967.

Rev. *Church Hist.*, 37 (1968), 458-459.

Question of will as central in Luther's theology, studied by Roman Catholic Lutheran scholar; Luther and nominalism.

2680. [WILL] Schwartz, Paula Judith, "Images of the Will in Jacobean Tragedy: Assertion and Control in the Plays of Webster, Middleton, and Ford," *DA,* 29 (1968), 878-A (Yale Univ.).

Their characters are driven by individualistic demands for personal rights which are present in the political atmosphere of the Stuart period. Jacobean consciousness unites reason and passion to serve a will at once both good and evil; thus individualistic self-expression achieves a complexity that cannot easily be defined. (Cf. 1338.)

2681. [WIND] Hampe, Roland, *Kult der Winde in Athen und Kreta.* Sitzungsberichte der Heidelberger Akademie der Wissenschaften, Phil.-Historische Klasse, Jahrgang 1967, I Abhundlung. Heidelberg: C. Winter, 1967.

2682. [WITCHCRAFT] Currie, Elliot P., "Crimes without Criminals: Witchcraft and Its Control in Renaissance Europe," *Law and Society Review,* 3 (1968), 7-32.

While on the Continent witchcraft was prosecuted as heresy, in England it was viewed as felony and handled by courts with more restraint.

2683. [WITCHCRAFT] Douglas, Mary, ed., *Witchcraft Confessions and Accusations.* London: Tavistock, 1970.

Rev. *TLS,* 30 October 1970, 1237-1241.

Essays on sorcery in late antiquity by Peter Brown, English witchcraft in anthropological terms by Keith Thomas, Essex witchcraft by Alan Macfarlane. Douglas portrays supporters of witchcraft persecutions as insecure intellectuals competing for patronage in corrupt Renaissance courts.

2684. [WITCHCRAFT] Editors, "The Lothian Witches of 1591, and a Link with Burns," *Scot. St.,* 14 (1970), 189-191.

Analyses woodcut depicting Lothian witches of 1591 who sought to drown King James IV and Danish bride at sea. Woodcut taken from broadsheet *Newes from Scotland,* published by Wright in London.

2685. [WITCHCRAFT] Hemphill, R.E., "Historical Witchcraft and Psychiatric Illness in Western Europe," *Proceedings of the Royal Society of Medicine,* 59, no. 9 (1966), 891-901.

Summary of history of witchcraft from Middle Ages through 16th cent. in Western Europe. Also includes discussion of psychiatric and psychological aspects of interactions between the public, the accusers, and the accused.

2686. [WITCHCRAFT] Hitchcock, James, "George Gifford and Puritan Witch Beliefs," *Archiv für Reformationsgeschichte*, 58 (1967), 90-99.

The Puritan Gifford's two works, *A Discourse* in 1587, and *A Dialogue* in 1593, 1603, systematically treated the witch question. He was mainly concerned with the subjective effect of the belief on would-be Christians.

2687. [WITCHCRAFT] Holmes, R., "Shakespeare and Witchcraft," *QR*, 305 (1967), 179-188.

Includes table showing relationship between his plays and witchcraft activities and publications, 1550-1650.

2688. [WITCHCRAFT] Macfarlane, Alan, *Witchcraft in Tudor and Stuart England: A Regional and Comparative Study*. N.Y.: Harper and Row, 1970.

Rev. *AHR*, 76 (1971), 1164; *TLS*, 30 October 1970, 1239.

Using records of Essex quarter-sessions, ecclesiastical courts in Essex and Colchester and of some Essex boroughs, author lists more than 1,200 witchcraft cases, mostly after witchcraft statute of 1563. Little connection between Puritanism and witch-hunting.

2689. [WITCHCRAFT] Midelfort, H.C. Erik, "Recent Witch Hunting Research, or Where Do We Go From Here?" *PBSA*, 62 (1968), 373-420.

Useful bibliography of witch-hunting and related topics. 509 items under headings: I. Selective List of Useful Books Published before 1940; II. European Witchcraft and Ancillary Studies (1940-1967), A. Witchcraft and Witch trials; B. Biographical Studies; C. Legal Studies; D. Interdepartmental ... medical, psychological, and anthropological ...; E. Murray School and the Anti-Sadducees; F. Intellectual Background ...; G. ... Devil and demonology; H. Histories and explanations of the occult; I. Modern European witchcraft-- 1) simple or folk tradition; 2) learned or romantic traditions. III. Republication of Primary Sources since 1940. IV. Witchcraft in Art and Literature: Studies since 1940.

2690. [WITCHCRAFT] Pearson, D'Orsay White, "Shakespeare and the Doctrines of Witchcraft," *DA*, 30 (1970), 4422-A (Kent St. Univ.).

Doctrines of belief concerning witchcraft in Elizabethan England and their use as dramaturgical possibilities in *Oth.*, *Mac.*, and *Tmp.*

2691. [WOMB-TOMB] Parfitt, G.A.E., "Renaissance Wombs, Renaissance Tombs," *Ren. and Mod. Studies* (Nottingham), 15 (1971), 23-33.

Sixteenth- and 17th-cent. English verse rhyme-pair.

2692. [WOMEN] Brustein, Robert, "The Monstrous Regiment of Women ..." *Renaissance and Modern Essays [in honor of] Vivian de Sola Pinto*. London: Routledge and Kegan Paul, 1966, pp. 35-50.

Discusses satiric view of upper-class court lady in Elizabethan literature. This figure is a temptress; she leaves her
male victims the choices of damnation or misogynistic bitter-
ness. Following Bishops' Edict of 1599, there was change in
Elizabethan-Jacobean drama in attitude toward women. Female
independence during Elizabeth's reign was exhibited in wearing
of cosmetics and fashionable clothes, as well as doublets and
jerkins which brought charges of masculinity and vice. A
medieval view of woman as inhuman or demonic, without a rational soul, was common in the drama and in Puritan tracts.

2693. [WOMEN] Cardoza, Minna Ploug, "The Presentation of Women in
Sixteenth-Century Lutheran Biblical Drama," *DA*, 29 (1968),
562-A (Univ. of Calif., Los Angeles).

Lutheran biblical dramatists of Germany, mostly of middle-
class origin, broke with spiritualized idealization of woman
detached from her natural role as wife and mother, traditional
since the *Minnesänger*. Instead, they created heroines and
villainesses characterized by possession, or lack, of wifely
and domestic virtues of contemporary Lutheran preaching and
middle-class life. This characterization was retained often
in disregard of dramatic appropriateness or fidelity to biblical materials.

2694. [WOMEN] Gelber, Norman, "Robert Greene's *Orlando Furioso*: A
Study of Thematic Ambiguity," *MLR*, 64 (1969), 264-266.

Feminine theme (moral quality of the heroine Angelica) reflects
topical controversy, inherited from classical and medieval
polemics, on virtues and vices of womankind.

2695. [WOMEN] Goldberg, Larry Alan, "The Role of the Female in the
Drama of Lyly, Greene, Kyd, and Marlowe," *DA*, 30 (1970), 4410-
A (Northwestern Univ.).

The female, of little importance in the morality plays, as
significant in the synthesis of convention in the new secular
drama between 1583 and 1593.

2696. [WOMEN] Grimal, Pierre, ed., *Histoire Mondiale de La Femme*:
vol. 3, *L'Occident des Celtes à la Renaissance*. Paris: Nou-
velle Librairie de France, 1966.

Includes bibliography, pp. 489-497. In addition to chapters
on women in the Renaissance, including Italy, France, and Germany, is chapter by Richard Marienstras, "L'Anglaise sous le
règne d'Elizabeth."

2697. [WOMEN] Harding, D.W., "Women's Fantasy of Manhood: A Shakespearian Theme," *SQ*, 20 (1969), 245-253.

Deals with Lady Macbeth, Goneril, Cleopatra, and Volumnia and
their concepts of manhood.

2698. [WOMEN] Hirdt, Willi, "*Descriptio superficialis*: Zum Frauen-
porträt in der italienischen Epik," *Arcadia*, 5 (1970), 39-57.

Literary portraits of women.

2699. [WOMEN] Patton, Jon Franklin, "Essays in the Elizabethan She-Tragedies or Female-Complaints," *DA*, 30 (1969), 1534-A (Ohio Univ.).

Survey of female-complaints published in 1590's and study of classical and medieval origins of the genre. Conventions, styles, and structures of three poems of this type published in latter half of 16th cent.: Thomas Churchyard's *Shore's Wife*, Samuel Daniel's *The Complaint of Rosamond*, and Shakespeare's *Rape of Lucrece*.

2700. [WOMEN] Sims, Edna Niecie, "El Antifeminismo en la literatura Española Hasta 1560," *DA*, 31 (1970), 2355-A (Catholic Univ. of Amer.).

Studies misogyny in Spanish literature through 16th cent., finding it not necessarily bitter and sometimes humorous. Traces treatment of women from abstract negative female types of the early "enxiemplos" to criticism of didactic writers who found women to be means of men's fall.

2701. [WOMEN] Valette, Francis Claude, "La Tradition Antiféministe dans la Littérature Française du Moyen Age et sa Continuation dans les Contes du Seizième Siècle," *DA*, 28 (1967), 696-A (Univ. of Ill.).

Stock antifeminist caricatures and plot situations of medieval literature continue into Renaissance French literature of the 16th cent.

2702. [WOMEN] Vecchio, Frank B., "Sempronio y el debate feminista del siglo XV," *Romance Notes*, 9 (1967/68), 320-324.

Some arguments for the pro-feminism of *La Celestina*.

2703. [WOMEN] Wuterich, Joan Gale, "Juan Luis Vives' *The Instruction of Christian Woman*: A Critical Evaluation and Translation," *DA*, 30 (1970), 3752-A (Boston College).

Exegesis of hitherto untranslated proposals (1523) of Juan Luis Vives for the education of women. The first major Christian treatise of its kind; it contains his ideas on woman's nature as well. Includes biographical material, suggestions for further research, and translation of the entire work with exception of certain passages judged parenthetical, which are described in footnotes.

2704. [WONDER] Quinn, Dennis, "Donne and the Wane of Wonder," *ELH*, 36 (1969), 626-647.

The wane of wonder began in the Renaissance, and John Donne stands at the end of the Classical-Christian tradition of wonder which prevailed in the West for centuries. That traditional understanding emerges by observing Donne's explicit statements about wonder, by considering practical effect of theory on his poetic practice, and by noting tradition upon which Donne drew.

2705. [WORLD UPSIDE-DOWN] Donaldson, Ian, *The World Upside-Down: Comedy from Jonson to Fielding.* Oxford: Clarendon Press, 1970.

Rev. *MP*, 70 (1972), 68-70; *TLS*, 9 April 1971, 415.

Festive inversion. Justice as festive; analysis, e.g., of Jonson's *Epicoene* and *Barth. Fair.*

2706. [Y-symbol] Harms, Wolfgang, *Homo Viator in Bivio: Studien zur Bildlichkeit des Weges.* (Medium Aevum: Phil. Studien, Bd. 21.) Munich: W. Fink Verlag, 1970.

Rev. *MLR*, 67 (1972), 207-210.

On Y-symbol in medieval and Renaissance literature and philosophy; Dante. The two roads. Emblem literature, illustrated.

ADDENDA

2706a. [ANIMALS] Lloyd, Joan Barclay, *African Animals in Renaissance Literature and Art.* Oxford Studies in the History of Art and Architecture. Oxford: Clarendon, 1971. Rev. *BHR*, 34 (1972), 571-574.

Based on thesis, University of London.

2706b. [ARDEN] Skipp, V.H.T., "Economic and Social Change in the Forest of Arden, 1530-1649," *Agric. Hist. Rev.*, 18 (1970), Suppt., 84-111. (Cf. 149.)

2706c. [DUTY] Benning, Helmut A., *Die Vorgeschichte von Neuenglisch Duty. Zur Ausformung der Pflichtidee im Substantivwortschatz des Englischen von den Anfängen bis zum Ende des 15. Jahrhunderts.* Habilitationsschrift, Münster, 1966, in *Linguistica et Litteraria*, ed. E. Dickenmann, et al., Bd. 7. Frankfurt a. M.: Athenäum Verlag, 1971. Summary in *Archiv für Begriffsg.*, 12 (1968), 127.

From mid-14th cent. entrance of the word into the language, *duty* becomes an important late medieval term, traced in cultural-linguistic history.

2706d. [EMBLEM] Haaker, Ann, "*Non sine causa*: the Use of Emblematic Structure and Iconology in the Thematic Structure of *Titus Andronicus*," *RORD*, 13-14 (1970-71), 143-168.

Dramatic use of tableaux, etc., as reflective of Renaissance emblems.

2706e. [ENCYCLOPAEDIA] Henningsen, Jürgen, "'Enzyklopädie' zur Sprach- und Bedeutungsgeschichte eines Pädagogischen Begriffs," *Archiv für Begriffsg.*, 10 (1966), 271-362; continued as "Orbis Doctrinae: Encyclopaedia," *ibid.*, 11 (1967), 241-245.

Useful study of, and reference guide to, encyclopaedias in 15th, 16th, 17th cents.

2706f. [FAUST] Henning, Hans, ed., *Faust-Bibliographie*. Teil I. *Das Faust-Thema vom 16. Jahrhundert bis 1790*. Berlin, Weimar: Aufbau-Verlag, 1966.

Vol. I of 5 vols., others dealing with later periods. This part has 3,338 entries.

2706g. [FORTUNE] Pickering, F.P., *Literature & Art in the Middle Ages*. Coral Gables, Fla.: Univ. of Miami Press, 1970 (orig. version: *Literatur und Darstellende Kunst im Mittelalter*, Berlin: Erich Schmidt, 1966).

Despite title, this is a storehouse of materials useful to Renaissance studies, on fortune, the Crucifixion, typology, etc., as well as on iconographic method; Curtius; a lexicon of images, etc. Illustrations include 3b, "Henry VI on Sapientia's throne...."

2706h. [METAPHOR] Heninger, S.K., "Metaphor as Cosmic Correspondence," *Medieval and Renaissance Studies*, ed. John M. Headley. Proc. of the Southeastern Institute of Medieval and Renaissance Studies, 1967. Univ. of North Carolina Pr., 1968, pp. 3-22.

Universal dependencies of metaphor as cosmic analogy--the need for oneness. Illustrations.

2706i. [*OCCASIO*] Specht, Rainer, "Über 'Occasio' und Verwandte Begriffe vor Descartes," *Archiv für Begriffsg.*, 15 (1970), 215-225.

Traces scholastic and Renaissance uses of philosophic *occasio*; its relation to *Gelegenheit*, *causa*, and other terms.

2706j. [PRODIGAL SON] Snyder, Susan, "*King Lear* and the Prodigal Son," *SQ*, 17 (1966), 361-369.

Relation to play of parable of Prodigal Son (Luke xv.11-32); suggestion of faith over works as attractive to Protestants.

2706k. [PROGRESS] Van Doren, Charles, *The Idea of Progress*. (Concepts in Western Thought ... ed. M.J. Adler.) N.Y.: Praeger, 1967.

Includes summaries from antiquity and Renaissance; classifications of ideas of progress.

2706l. [*RATIO*] Mühlen, Karl-Heinz zur, "*Ratio: Ratio, Rationalis, Irrationalis....*" *Archiv für Begriffsg.*, 14 (1970), 192-265.

Detailed semantic study of the idea of *ratio*, and related terms, in scholastic, Reformation, and Renaissance thought, broken down into numerous senses and sub-aspects.

2706m. [RIGHT REASON] De Angelis, Enrico, *L'idea di buon senso. Osservazioni su alcuni scritti comparsi tra il 1584 ed il 1690*. Roma: Edizioni dell' Ateneo, 1967. Rev. *Archiv für Begriffsg.*, 12 (1968), 126.

Examines twenty philosophers on *recta ratio*, in its changes of meaning.

2706n. [SEA] Williams, Kathleen, "Spenser: Some Uses of the Sea and the Storm-tossed Ship," *RORD*, 13-14 (1970-71), 135-142.

Emblematic and allegorical uses of sea and ships.

2706o. [SICKNESS] Goldberg, Jonathan, "The Understanding of Sickness in Donne's *Devotions*," *RenQ*, 24 (1971), 507-517.

Christian symbolism, through paradoxes, in Donne on sickness: e.g., fever burning the "old man," as it thereby creates.

2706p. [*SOPHROSYNE*] North, Helen, *Self-Knowledge and Self-Restraint in Greek Literature* (Cornell Studies in Classical Philology, vol. 35). Ithaca, N.Y.: Cornell U.P., 1966. Rev. *Class. World*, 60 (1967), 254.

On *vis temperata*, restraint polar to Greek heroic principle. Appendix: imagery related to Sophrosyne—used in *topoi* and later emblems.

2706q. [STATE] Weinacht, Paul-Ludwig, *Staat. Studien zur Bedeutungsgeschichte des Wortes von den Anfängen bis ins 19. Jahrhundert* (Beiträge zur Politischen Wissenschaft Bd. 2). Berlin: Duncker & Humblot, 1968. Rev. *Archiv für Begriffsg.*, 13 (1969), 109-112.

Includes Renaissance uses of *state*; change in mid-17th cent.

2706r. [TEMPEST] Luria, Maxwell Sidney, "The Christian Tempest: A Symbolic Motif in Medieval Literature," *DA*, 26 (1966), 5439-A (Princeton University).

Traces classical, medieval, and Christian backgrounds. Storm motifs as intellectually significant. Symbolism in Spenser, Shakespeare, and other post-medieval writers.

2706s. [*VALOR*] Schuchard, Barbara, *"Valor": Zu Seiner Wortgeschichte im Lateinischen und Romanischen des Mittelalters.* Romanisches Seminar der Universität Bonn. Bonn, 1970.

Inaugural dissertation at the University of Bonn, 1967/68, traces the meanings in *valor* through late medieval senses: from strength, courage, etc., through *pretium*, *aestimatio*, *honor*, *gloria*, *virtus*. Relations to *valoir* and *vaillant*; to *pretz*. Appendix on *valor* in Italian and Catalan. Chart fold-out, p. 118, shows relations among uses. Bibliography and index of citations: pp. 179-220.

2706t. [*VIRTUS, VIS*] Nitschke, August, "Wandlungen des Kraftbegriffs in den politischen Theorien des 16 und 17 Jhts.," *Sudhoffs Archiv, Zeitschrift für Wissenschaftsgeschichte*, 55 (1971), 108-206. Rev. *Archiv für Begriffsg.*, 18 (1974), 170-171.

Traces the idea of power (*virtus, vis*) in political theories of 16th and 17th cents.

also:

2706u. [CLEOPATRA] Becher, Ilse, *Das Bild der Kleopatra in der Griechischen und Lateinischen Literatur*. (Deutsche Akademie der Wissenschaften zu Berlin. Schriften der Sektion für Altertumswissenschaft, 51.) Berlin: Akademie-Verlag, 1966. Rev. *AJPh*, 90 (1969), 252-254.

Cleopatra in ancient poets and historians. Ch. VI on "luxuria"; Ch. VII on her love and amorality; Ch. VIII on her death from snake bite.

2706v. [CRISEYDE] Mieszkowski, G.B., "The Reputation of Criseyde: 1155-1500," *DA*, 27 (1966), 459A (Yale Univ.).

Anticipator of Shakespearean heroine as continuous in her reputation.

2706w. [FLOOD] Lewis, Jack P., *A Study of the Interpretation of Noah and the Flood in Jewish and Christian Literature*. Leiden: Brill, 1968.

Useful for symbolic, typological, and allegorical references to the Flood, including exegesis in later Church Fathers.

2706x. [INEFFABLE] Jacomuzzi, A., "Il topos dell'ineffabile nel Paradiso dantesco," in *Da Dante al Novecento. Studi critici offerti ... a Giovanni Getto*. Milano: Mursia, 1970.

Cf. the "ineffable" topos in Shakespeare: e.g., *MV*, III.ii.108-114; *TC*, III.ii.17-20.

2707. Adams, Herbert M., comp., *Catalogue of Books Printed on the Continent of Europe 1501-1600 in Cambridge Libraries*. Vols. 1 and 2. Cambridge Univ. Press, 1967.

Rev. *PBSA*, 62 (1968), 630-632.

Useful guide to non-*STC* 16th-cent. volumes.

2708. Alexander, J.J.G., and Albinia Catherine de la Mare, *The Italian Manuscripts in the Library of Major J.R. Abbey*. London: Faber, 1969.

Rev. *PBSA*, 64 (1970), 121.

Detailed catalogue of Italian manuscripts of the Abbey Collection, most of which are from 15th cent., but range from 12th to 16th. Significance of collection is provenance of a large proportion of manuscripts, going back to such Renaissance patrons of learning and collectors as the Medici, the Visconti, the Aragonese kings of Naples, Matthias Corvinus, Cardinal Bessarion, Duke Francesco Maria della Rovere of Urbino, and various Renaissance popes.

2709. Arnott, James F., and John W. Robinson, *English Theatrical Literature 1559-1900: A Bibliography*. London: Society for Theatre Research, 1970.

Rev. *TLS*, 1 January 1971, 20.

Incorporates and extends Robert W. Lowe's *Bibliographical Account of English Theatrical Literature* (1888). Entries under descriptive headings. Indexes of authors, short titles, places of publication, annotations of major works.

2710. Atkins, Sidney Hubert, *A Select Checklist of Printed Material on Education Published in England to 1800*. Hull: The Univ. of Hull, 1970.

2711. Barroll, J. Leeds, "Significant Articles, Monographs, and Reviews," *ShakS*, 3 (1967), 336-372; 4 (1968), 11-24.

Useful surveys, including some contextual materials.

2712. Bennett, H.S., *English Books and Readers, 1603-1640*. London: Cambridge Univ. Press, 1970.

Rev. *Hist. Today*, 20 (1970), 668; *JEGP*, 70 (1971), 286-288.

Books published during 1603-1640 and their readers. E.g., Shakespeare's first folio, sermons, and polemical tracts, foreign accounts. Kinds of audiences.

2713. *Bibliographie de la Réforme 1450-1648.* Série publiée sur la recommandation du Conseil international de la philosophie et des sciences humaines avec le concours financier de l'UNESCO. *VII: Ecosse/Scotland/Schottland.*, ed. James K. Cameron. Ouvrages parus de 1940 à 1960. Leiden: Brill, 1970.

Rev. *Theol. Zeit.*, 96 (1971), 127.

Bibliography of works appearing in Scotland broadly on the Reformation between 1940-1960. 326 titles included. (Serial.)

2714. Borrie, M.A.F., "Historical Manuscripts," *Bull. of Inst. of Hist. Res.*, 44 (1971), 132-133.

List of historical manuscripts incorporated into collection of British Museum, 1970.

2715. Braet, H., and J. Lambert, *Encyclopédie des Études littéraires Romaines: Répertoire bibliographique.* Gent-Leuven: Wetenschappelijke Uitgeverij en Boekhandel, 1971.

Very selective list dealing with Romance literatures. Histoire des idées, pp. 14-16; thématologie, pp. 16-18; Renaissance, pp. 71-74.

2716. "A Brief Checklist of Left-Wing Reformation Sources and Studies," *Found. for Reformation Research: Bull. of the Library*, 2, no. 2 (1967), 13-14.

Enlargement of selective bibliography for Fifth Institute of Reformation Research by Hans J. Hillerbrand. Contains sources, surveys, works on origins and problems.

2717. British Museum, Department of Printed Books, General *Catalogue of Printed Books. Ten-Year Supplement, 1956-1965.* London: Trustees of the British Museum, 1968-. Vol. I-. In progress.

To be completed in 50 volumes, this first decennial supplement will fill the gap (1956-1962) between the "Photolithographic edition" and the annual volumes of *Additions* (1963-1965), and cumulate the latter.

2718. Brooks, Philip C., *Research in Archives: The Use of Unpublished Primary Sources.* Chicago: Univ. of Chicago Press, 1969.

A highly condensed manual on the use of primary documentation, especially for American history. Selected bibliography; index.

2719. Campbell, Oscar James, and Edward G. Quinn, eds., *The Reader's Encyclopedia of Shakespeare.* N.Y.: Thomas Y. Crowell, 1966; London: Methuen, 1967.

Useful 1,014-p. compendium; articles accompanied by special bibliography; volume appends a selected bibliography. Random reading raises some questions; e.g., Kittredge's *New Lights*

[sic] on *Romeo and Juliet* (1942) is cited (p. 441) as an attempt, in lieu of a Shakespearean work comparable to his *Chaucer and His Poetry*, to preserve some of Kittredge's teachings on Shakespeare. Rather than *New Light*, the 7-pp. essay is a *reductio ad absurdum*, a deliberate spoof on topical-political-allegorical excesses of Shakespearean criticism. While numerous 20th-cent. scholars and critics receive individual articles, there is none for William J. Neidig and his work on falsely dated quartos. In an article on "Ajax," Thersites is identified as "Dekker portrayed by Jonson" (p. 10), a "probability" which has thus far eluded Shakespearean scholarship.

2720. Canney, Margaret, and David Knott, *Catalogue of the Goldsmith's Library of Economic Literature: Vol. 1. Printed Books to 1800*. Cambridge Univ. Press, 1970.

Rev. *Business Hist. Rev.*, 45 (1971), 526-527.

Chronological arrangement of books, pamphlets, and broadsides published from the 15th cent. to 1800. For each year, titles grouped in subject categories, such as agriculture, commerce, and finance.

2721. Chambers, D.D.C., "A Catalogue of the Library of Bishop Lancelot Andrewes (1555-1626)," *Trans. Camb. Bibl. Soc.*, 5 (1970), 99-121.

With bibliographic description: wide range of subjects.

2722. Cioranescu, Alexandre, *Bibliographie de la littérature française du dix-septième siècle*. Tomes II, III, D-M, N-Z, plus index. Paris: Edition de C.N.R.S., 1966.

Detailed and classified. Unannotated. Parallel form to compiler's 18th-cent. bibliography. Rev. *TLS*, 13 July 1967, 628.

2723. Clarke, Derek A., "A Selective Check List of Bibliographical Scholarship for 1967: Incunabula and Early Renaissance," *SB*, 22 (1969), 319-323.

Approximately 100 titles; includes English, French, German, Italian, and Spanish studies. (Annual.)

2724. ———, and Howell J. Heaney, "A Selective Checklist of Bibliographical Scholarship for 1968," *SB*, 23 (1970), 254-273.

Part I: Incunabula and Early Renaissance; Part II: Later Renaissance to the present. (Annual.)

2725. Clough, Eric Allen, *A Short-title Catalogue, Arranged Geographically of Books Printed and Distributed by Printers, Publishers and Book-sellers in the English Provincial Towns and in Scotland and Ireland Up To and Including the Year 1700*. London: Library Association, 1969.

Rev. *Library World*, 71 (1970), 376-377; *Library*, 26 (1971), 175-176.

Index to places in Britain outside London that appear in *STC* and Wing.

2726. Cosenza, Mario Emilio, comp., *Biographical and Bibliographical Dictionary of the Italian Printers and of Foreign Printers in Italy from the Introduction of the Art of Printing into Italy in 1800.* Boston: G.K. Hall, 1968.

Twelve thousand, two hundred cards, 679 pp., 1 volume. In what town a book was published by a printer; lists one publication for each year that the printer produced work.

2727. ————, comp., *Checklist of Non-Italian Humanists, 1300-1800.* Boston: G.K. Hall, 1969.

Ten thousand cards, 312-pp., 1 volume. List includes Latin, English, Scottish, French, German, Polish, Spanish, Portuguese names.

2728. Crum, Margaret, ed., *First-line index of English poetry 1500-1800 in manuscripts of the Bodleian Library Oxford*, 2 vols. Oxford: Clarendon Press, 1969.

Rev. *Library*, 24 (1969), 262-263; *PBSA*, 64 (1970), 477; *TLS*, 3 July 1969, 736.

Indexes more than 20,000 poems, many occurring in more than one manuscript. Each numbered entry gives first and last line of a poem in bold type, followed by a note giving (where possible) author's name, title, and other details, usually from manuscripts. Editorial notes sometimes added, recording printings of poem, etc.; entry notes manuscripts where poem is found and cross-references to variant texts. First and last lines of poems printed in modernized spelling. Vol. 2 has a number of indexes--manuscripts, authors, other persons mentioned, authors of works translated or imitated, and composers of music named or quoted in notes.

2729. Desgraves, L., "Quelques Livres Imprimés à Genève de 1550 à 1600," *BHR*, 32, no. 3 (1970), 645-647.

Twenty books not as yet included in bibliographies of Paul Chaix, Alan Dufour, Gustave Moeckli on this period.

2730. Dr. Williams's Library, *Early Nonconformity, 1566-1800: A Catalogue of Books in Dr. Williams's Library (London).* Boston: G.K. Hall, 1968.

Author catalogue: 10 x 14, 32,200 cards, 4,029 pp., 5 volumes; subject catalogue: 33,500 cards, 4,196 pp., 5 volumes; chronological catalogue: 14,300 cards, 1,797 pp., 2 volumes. Early Nonconformity in England, from Elizabethan Puritanism to the end of the 18th cent., and printed between 1566 and 1800, together with related works from Scotland, Ireland, Wales, and New England.

2731. Domay, Friedrich, *Formenlehre der bibliographischen Ermittlung; eine Einführung in die Praxis der Literaturverschliessung mit einer Beispielensammlung, zahlreichen Einzelbeispielen im Text und dem Modell eines bibliographischen Apparats.* Stuttgart: Hiersemann, 1968.

Rev. *AN&Q*, 7 (1969), 92.

Compares favorably with Winchell's (now Sheehy's) *Guide*.

2732. Donovan, Dennis G., gen. ed., "Literature of the Renaissance in 1968," *SP*, 66 (1969), 225-569.

Bibliographies of general works of Renaissance: English Renaissance, French, German, Italian, Spanish, and Portuguese. Topics under English Renaissance include: history, manners, customs, drama and stage, Shakespeare, non-dramatic literature, Spenser, Donne, and Milton.

2733. Donow, Herbert S., *A Concordance to the Sonnet Sequences of Daniel, Drayton, Shakespeare, Sidney and Spenser*. Southern Ill. Univ. Press; London: Feffer & Simons, 1969.

Rev. *Spenser Newsl.*, 4 (1971), 2; *TLS*, 28 May 1970, 593.

A computerized concordance to these poems.

2734. Ebel, Julia G., "A Numerical Survey of Elizabethan Translations," *Library*, 5th ser., 22 (1967), 104-127.

Provides chart listing (according to year of translation and language of the original) *STC* numbers for translation (1560-1603). From 1560 to 1603, English translation constituted no more than a quarter of books published; theology was most often translated, and prose romances and ballads least; versions of Latin and French exceeded those from other languages.

2735. Emmison, Frederick Gray, ed., *English Local History Handlist: A Select Bibliography and List of Sources for the Study of Local History and Antiquities*, 4th ed. Helps for Students of History, no. 69. London: Historical Association, 1969.

Short lists to guide student in matters of historical and antiquarian interest: topography, prehistory, documents, law and order, industry and trade, transport and travel, religious history, architecture, warfare, entertainment, etc.

2736. ———, *How to Read Local Archives 1550-1700*. London: The Historical Association, 59A Kennington Park Rd., S.E.11, 1967.

Rev. *TLS*, 23 May 1968, 537.

This inexpensive, 21-pp. pamphlet, contains plates of Secretary hand with transcripts. Also shows most common types of local archives; commentaries.

2737. Engel, James E., ed., *Renaissance, Humanismus, Reformation*. (Handbuch der deutschen Literaturgeschichte, zweite Abteilung: Bibliographien, Band 4.) Bern and Munich: Francke Verlag, 1969.

Rev. *Cath. Hist. Rev.*, 57 (1971), 331-332; *MLR*, 66 (1971), 212-213.

Bibliography covers German literary, cultural, religious, and intellectual history, 1450-1600. Select, classified bibliography of books and articles which appeared 1950-1965,

concerning this Renaissance-Reformation period. Useful also
for church history, filling gap between first fascimile of
Bibliographie de la Réforme: Allemagne-Pays Bas (now covering
only up to 1955) and *Bibliographie internationale de l'Humanisme et de la Renaissance* (beginning coverage with 1965).

2738.   Fédération Internationale des Sociétés et Instituts pour
         l'Étude de la Renaissance. *Bibliographie internationale de
         l'humanisme et de la Renaissance.* Vol. 2: Travaux parus en
         1966. Geneva: Droz, 1967; Vol. 3: Travaux parus en 1967
         (1968); Vol. 4: Travaux parus en 1968 (1970); Vol. 5: Tra-
         vaux parus en 1969 (1971); Vol. 6: Travaux parus en 1970
         (1973); Vol. 7: Travaux parus en 1971 (1974). Rev. *BHR*, 32 (1970),
         198-199; 33 (1971), 459.

         Comprehensive listing of works, including articles regarding 15th
         and 16th cent. with subject index. Most extensive such list com-
         pilation. Unannotated; annual. These volumes are produced "sur
         la recommandation du Conseil International de la Philosophie
         et des Sciences Humaines, avec le concours du C.N.R.S. et de
         l'U.N.E.S.C.O."

2739.   Folger Shakespeare Library, *Catalog of Manuscripts of the Fol-
         ger Shakespeare Library* (Washington, D.C.). Boston: G.K.
         Hall, 1970.

         47,500 cards, 2,264 pp., 3 volumes. "History of England and
         English culture in the 16th and 17th cents., and, in the case
         of theater and drama, in the 18th and 19th cents. as well....
         Letters and books pertaining to daily life and government,
         religious and legal matters ... More Family papers in Loseley
         collection, Bacon-Townshend collection, Bagot collection, and
         Newdigate newsletters."

2740.   ————, *Catalog of Printed Books of the Folger Shakespeare
         Library* (Washington, D.C.). Boston: G.K. Hall, 1970.

         387,000 cards, 18,455 pp., 28 volumes. Two hundred years of
         Tudors and Stuarts. "British civilization in the 16th and
         17th cents. [is] represented by both early-printed books
         and modern reference works.... It extends backward to medieval
         and classical materials and forward into the 18th cent."

2741.   Foster, David W., and Virginia Ramos Foster, comps., *Manual
         of Hispanic Bibliography.* Seattle, London: Univ. of Washing-
         ton Press, 1970.

         Rev. *Hisp. Rev.*, 40 (1972), 216.

         Bibliography of Spain and Spanish America in literature; anno-
         tated entries; 796 items.

2742.   Fox-Davies, Arthur Charles, *A Complete Guide to Heraldry*, rev.
         and annot. by J.P. Brooke-Little. N.Y.: Barnes & Noble, 1969.

         Standard reference work updated and annotated by Brooke-Little.
         Shows heraldic thought over past 60 years. Adds many line
         drawings, photographs, and color plates. Rev. *LJ*, 95 (1970), 882.

2743. Franceschetti, Giancarlo, ed., *Studi Francese: Indice Generale del Primo Decennio, 1957-1966*. Turin: Società Editrice Internazionale. Supplemento al n. 31 de *Studi Francese* (gennaio-aprile 1967).

Useful index to 10 years of *Studi Francese*, listing many Renaissance names.

2744. Frye, Roland M., "The New Xerox Library of British Renaissance Books at the University of Pennsylvania," *Univ. of Pennsylvania Library Chronicle*, 34 (1968), 3-6.

Plan of Univ. of Pennsylvania to acquire entire *STC* in xerox. By spring 1968, ca. 85% will have been delivered; the rest will arrive over the next few years.

2745. Gabler, Hans Walter, ed., *English Renaissance Studies in German 1945-1967. A Checklist of German, Austrian, and Swiss Academic Theses, Monographs, and Book Publications on English Language and Literature, c. 1500-1650*. (Schriften der deutschen Shakespeare-Gesellschaft West, n.f. 11.) Heidelberg: Quelle und Meyer, 1971.

Four hundred six items. Author index, and index to Shakespearean topics.

2746. Gelling, Margaret, W.F.H. Nicolaisen, and Melville Richards, *The Names of Towns and Cities in Britain*. London: Batsford, 1970.

Rev. *Scott. Hist. Rev.*, 50 (1971), 79-80.

Guide to history, context, and meaning of names of major centers of population in England, Scotland, Wales, and the Isle of Man.

2747. Giraud, Jeanne, *Manuel de Bibliographie Littéraire pour les XVIe, XVIIe et XVIIIe siècles français, 1946-1955*. Paris: Nizet, 1970.

Rev. *RSH*, 36 (1971), 467.

2748. Giuseppi, M.S., and G.D. Owen, eds., *Calendar of the Manuscripts of the ... Marquess of Salisbury, Presented at Hatfield House, Hertfordshire. Part XX (A.D. 1608)*. (Historical Manuscripts Commission, no. 9.) London: H.M.S.O., 1968 [= August, 1969].

Rev. *AHR*, 76 (1970), 148; *EHR*, 86 (1971), 170-171.

Cecil Papers at Hatfield, major source for Elizabethan-Jacobean history. Reflects Earl of Salisbury, Burleigh's son, at height of his fortunes in 1608.

2749. Goldsmith, V.F., *A Short Title Catalogue of French Books 1601-1700 in the Library of the British Museum*. Folkestone, London: Dawsons of Pall Mall, 1969.

Rev. *PBSA*, 64 (1970), 267.

Basically an author catalogue; order of headings is alphabetical. Final part will contain indexes of printers, publishers and places of publication, translators and editors, dates of publication, alternative forms of author's name, and titles of anonymous books.

2750. Goodwin, Jack, "Current Bibliography in the History of Technology, III: Middle Ages; IV: From the Renaissance through the Seventeenth Century," *Technology and Culture*, 11 (1970), 272–275.

Renaissance and 17th-cent. engineering, transportation, material and processes, mechanical and military technology. (Annual.)

2751. Gray, Richard A., comp., *A Guide to Book Review Citations: A Bibliography of Sources*. Columbus, Ohio: Ohio State University Libraries Publications, 2, 1969. Rev. *LJ*, 94 (1969), 2761.

Annotation of sources that cite reviews found in two or more periodicals. Divided into nine categories (e.g., General, Geography and History, Fine Arts). Contains general and specific subject, personal name, and title indexes, etc.

2752. ———, comp., *Serial Bibliographies in the Humanities and Social Sciences*. Ann Arbor, Mich.: Pierian Press, 1969.

2753. Greg, Walter Wilson, ed., with C.P. Blagden and I.G. Phillip, *A Companion to Arber: Being a Calendar of Documents in Arber's "Transcript of the Register of the Company of Stationers of London 1554-1640," with Text and Calendar of Supplementary Documents*. Oxford: Clarendon Press, 1967.

Rev. *Archives: Journal of the Brit. Record Assoc.*, 8 (1968), 163.

Chronological calendar of documents contained in Arber as illustrative material in his unindexed *Transcript*. Connected survey of materials scattered through Arber's five volumes. Second section calendars documents not in Arber, but in sources he used, concerning Stationers Company, with editor's annotations. Well indexed.

2754. Grendler, Paul, "The Reopening of the National Central Library in Florence, January 8, 1968," *Ren. & Ref.* (Univ. of Toronto), 4 (1968), 91–92.

Describes post-flood conditions: library functioning again, its hours, catalogues, etc.

2755. *Guide to Festschriften. Volume I: The Retrospective Festschriften Collection of The New York Public Library: Materials Cataloged Through 1971*. Boston: G.K. Hall, 1977.

Six thousand one hundred cards. *Festschriften* collected by NYPL over a 50-year period ending in 1971; in alphabetical order by main entry.

2756. Guttman, Selma, *The Foreign Sources of Shakespeare's Works: An Annotated Bibliography of the Commentary Written on this Subject between 1904 and 1940, together with Lists of Certain Translations Available to Shakespeare*. N.Y.: Octagon Books, 1968.

Reprint of 1947 book, based on Columbia Univ. diss. Urgently requires updating and expansion.

2757. Habicht, W., ed., *English and American Studies in German. Summaries of Theses and Monographs*. A Supplement to *Anglia: Zeitschrift für englische Philologie*. Tübingen: Max Niemeyer Verlag, 1969.

First of planned annual supplements containing summaries by the authors themselves of doctoral and inaugural dissertations which have appeared in German-speaking countries in the fields of English and American philology. Aims to inform Anglo-Saxon countries of such contributions. Arranged under headings: Language, English Literature, American Literature.

2758. ————, and Hans Walter Gabler, "Shakespeare Studies in German: 1959-1968," *ShS*, 23 (1970), 113-123.

Critical trends in books and dissertations. Covers general studies; dramatic skills; themes and ideas; text, translation, illustration.

2759. Hatzfeld, Helmut, *A Critical Bibliography of the New Stylistics Applied to the Romance Literatures, 1953-1965*. Chapel Hill, N.C.: Univ. of North Carolina Press, 1966.

Of interest in relation to Shakespearean Romance-language contexts. Rev. *Choice*, 4 (1967), 804.

2760. Heyse, Karl Wilhelm Ludwig, *Bücherschatz der deutschen Nationalliteratur des XVI. and XVII. Jahrhunderts. Systematisch geordnetes Verzeichnis einer reichhaltigen Sammlung deutscher Bücher aus dem Zeitraume von XV. bis um die Mitte des XVIII. Jahrhunderts. Ein bibliographischer Beitrag zur deutschen Literaturgeschichte*. Hildesheim: Olms, 1967.

Reprint of Berlin 1854 edition.

2761. Hinman, Charlton, ed., *The Norton Facsimile: The First Folio of Shakespeare*. N.Y.: W.W. Norton & Co., 1968.

Provides facsimile of finally corrected state of every page, selected from the least imperfect pages of all the 80 Folger First Folios. Has Through Line Numbering; as convenience it also gives Globe act-scene-line numbers for the first and last lines of the page. Introduction on textual relevance of Folio version of each of the plays, as well as on problems of printing First Folio. Appendix A, "Some Variant States of the Folio Text," illustrates before-and-after states of sample pages, including two original proof sheets, with proofreader's marks. Appendix B, "Folger Copies Used," is arranged in columns headed: Norton Facsimile Page, First Folio Page, Signature, Folger Shakespeare Library Copy.

2762. Houck, J. Kemp, comp., *Elizabethan Bibliographies Supplements,*
       XV: Francis Bacon 1926-1966. London: Nether Press, 1968.

       Rev. *SCN,* 28 (1970), 35.

       Arranged in 11 sections (such as Historiography, Law and Poli-
       tics, Science, Translations, Utopia and Political Theory),
       each in chronological order; 873 entries.

2763. Howard-Hill, T.H., *Bibliography of British Literary Biblio-*
       graphies. Oxford: Clarendon Pr., 1969. Rev. *LJ,* 94 (1969), 2907.

       First of a projected three-volume index to British Literary
       Bibliography; it records enumerative and descriptive biblio-
       graphies of the printed works on various subjects. Covers
       books, substantial parts of books, periodical articles written
       in English and published in the English-speaking Commonwealth
       and the U.S. *after 1890.* Topics include printed works of
       British authors, printing and publishing, literary forms and
       genres, and a great variety of subjects (from Accounting
       through Witchcraft). Main sections: General, and Biblio-
       graphies of, and Guides to, British Literature; General and
       Period Bibliographies; Regional Bibliographies; Presses and
       Printing; Forms and Genres (from Almanacs and Prognostications
       to Unfinished Books); Subject; Authors. Index, pp. 509-570.

2764. ————, "The Oxford Old-Spelling Shakespeare Concordances,"
       Studies in Bibliography, 22 (1969), 143-164.

       Series of individual old-spelling concordances to Shakespeare's
       plays, based on the "best early texts" (but not including
       press variants), is being prepared (by means of a computer pro-
       gram) in connection with the Oxford Old-Spelling Shakespeare.
       These concordances will "present all the spelling evidence
       necessary to settle compositor attribution," and the results
       of such analysis will be incorporated into the edition; hopes
       to prepare a definitive single-volume concordance to Shakes-
       peare's plays, in both old- and modern-spelling, from this
       edition.

2765. ————, ed., *Oxford Shakespeare Concordances. The Merry*
       Wives of Windsor. The Two Gentlemen of Verona. The Comedy of
       Errors. The Tempest. Measure for Measure. Clarendon Press;
       Oxford Univ. Press, 1969.

       Rev. *TLS,* 14 August 1969, 903.

       To consist of 37 volumes, not counting the non-dramatic poetry.
       The first five volumes are devoted to first five plays in the
       First Folio. Each volume is based on copy-text in the Oxford
       old-spelling Shakespeare. Words are given in their contexts,
       the spelling of the copy-text is retained, stage-directions
       are included, and the compositor responsible for each page is
       indicated. Some 80 misprints have been corrected in the first
       five volumes.

2766. ————, *Shakespearian Bibliography and Textual Criticism: A*
       Bibliography. Oxford: Clarendon Press, 1971.

Comprises Shakespearean bibliographies and checklists, excluded from compiler's first volume of *Index to British Literary Bibliography*, i.e., the *Bibliography of British Literary Bibliographies* (1969). Includes material published 1890-1969 on bibliography and text of Shakespeare. In addition, it contains Supplement to volume 1 (*Bibliography of British Literary Bibliographies*) of c. 1,000 additions to end of 1969, plus note of corrections. Rev. *Library*, 5th ser., 27 (1972), 155.

2767. Hunger, Herbert, *Lexikon der griechischen und römischen Mythologie mit Hinweisen auf das Fortwirken antiker Stoffe und Motive in der bildenden Kunst, Literatur und Musik des Abendlandes bis zur Gegenwart*. 6 erw. und erg. Augl. Wien: Hollinek, 1969.

Useful handbook for recurrence of mythological motifs in art, music, and literature. In this revised edition, 444 pp.

2768. *Index Aureliensis. Catalogus Librorum Sedecimo Saeculo Impressorum*. Prima Pars: Tomus I-IV (fascicles A1-A14), 1965-1970. Tertia Pars: Tomus I: Indices ad Tomos I & II, 1967. Published by the Foundation Index Aureliensis, Geneva. Distributed by B. de Graaf, Nieuwkoop, Netherlands.

This is planned to be the most comprehensive bibliography of 16th cent.-books and pamphlets (1501-1600 incl.), excluding only broadsides and books printed in oriental, Greek, and cyrillic characters. Alphabetical arrangement. Materials gathered from 500 world libraries. Descriptions include: 1) author's full name (with birth and death years); 2) anonymous entries; 3) short-title forms; 4) imprint; 5) collation; 6) census; 7) literature—references to standard bibliographies or catalogues.

Index Aureliensis is to appear in three series: Prima Pars (A), alphabetical catalogue by authors or anonymous entries; Altera Pars (B), supplement, to appear at later date after completion of Prima Pars; Tertia Pars (C), index volumes, which are cumulative and contain: Registrum bibliothecarum; Fontes citati, Index typographorum et librariorum (secundum urbium & alphabeticus), Index personarum, Index geographicus.

2769. Jauss, Hans Robert, and Jürgen Beyer, eds., *Grundriss der Romanischen Literaturen des Mittelalters*. Vol. 6: *La littérature didactique, allégorique, et satirique*, ed. Jürgen Beyer and Franz Koppe, 2 vols. Heidelberg, Winter, I, 1968; II, 1970. 1: Partie historique; 2: Partie documentaire.

Rev. *Spec.*, 45 (1970), 478-479; 47 (1972), 777.

Useful, basic tool; on Romance literature, e.g., medieval love treatises, etc. Section D: "Die moralische und literarische Satire," Fritz Schalk; E: "Die politische Satire," A. Adler.

2770. Johnson, Arthur M., "Hinman Collators: Present Locations," *PBSA*, 63 (1969), 119-120.

List of the locations of 29 Hinman Collators.

2771. Klapp, Otto, ed., *Bibliographie der Französischen Literatur-
       wissenschaft*, Bd. V: *1965-66.* . Frankfurt am Main: Vittorio
       Klostermann, 1967.

       Contains useful bibliography of Renaissance period.

2772. Knower, F.H., "Graduate theses. An index of graduate work in
       speech. XXXIV," *SM*, 34, no. 3 (1967), 321-376.

       Report on 2,342 graduate degrees; includes a table of statis-
       tics on the institutions and the types of degrees, a section
       listing the titles of theses, and a section indexing the sub-
       ject matter of the theses.

2773. Kristeller, Paul Oskar, *Catalogus translationum et commentar-
       iorum: Mediaeval and Renaissance Latin Translations and Com-
       mentaries*, vol. 2. Associate editor, F. Edward Cranz. Wash-
       ington, D.C.: Catholic Univ. of Amer. Press, 1971.

       Rev. *Gnomon*, 45 (1973), 185-195.

       Continues project (1945-) of cataloguing Latin translations
       and commentaries on ancient literature. Vol. 1, 1960. Issued
       under auspices of the Union Académique Internationale. Impor-
       tant for reception and influence of Greek and Latin works in
       medieval and Renaissance periods.

2774. ———, *Iter Italicum: A Finding List of Uncatalogued or In-
       completely Catalogued Humanistic Manuscripts of the Renais-
       sance in Italian and Other Libraries.* Vol. 2: *Italy, Orvieto
       to Volterra, Vatican City.* London: Warburg Institute; Leiden:
       E.J. Brill, 1967. Rev. *Spec.*, 43 (1968), 515.

       Monumental compilation which will furnish materials and loca-
       tions for centuries of Renaissance research.

2775. Lange, Victor, ed., *Modern Literature.* Princeton Studies Ser-
       ies, Vol. 2; Englewood Cliffs, N.J.: Prentice-Hall, Inc.,
       1968. Rev. *MLJ*, 54 (1970), 68.

       Useful survey of American scholarship (including studies of
       Renaissance and 17th cent.); in Italian (by Thomas G. Bergin);
       in Spanish (by Bruce W. Wardropper); in German (by John R.
       Frey) literatures. (Also includes Russian and Oriental litera-
       tures.)

2776. Lewanski, Richard C., *European Library Directory: A Geo-
       graphical and Bibliographical Guide. Répertoire des Biblio-
       thèques Européennes.* Florence: L.S. Olschki, 1968.

       Companion to compilation, *Subject Collections in European
       Libraries* (N.Y.: R.R. Bowker, 1965). Rearranges materials in
       earlier volumes. Lists about 7,000 European libraries, plus
       special collections, strengths, restrictions, photocopy and
       microfilm facilities, interlibrary loan policies.

2777. Lievsay, John L., *The Englishman's Italian Books, 1550-1700.*
       Philadelphia: Univ. of Pennsylvania Press, 1969.

       Rev. *JEGP*, 71 (1972), 118-119.

A.S.W. Rosenbach Lectures in Bibliography, 1969, dealing with
the efforts of Renaissance English printers to import Italian
books into England. Chapters: I. English Printers, Italian
Books; II. Italian Books on English Shelves; III. Horner's
Plum: Tomaso Garzoni.

2778. ———, ed., *The Sixteenth Century: Skelton Through Hooker*.
Goldentree bibliographies. N.Y.: Appleton-Century-Crofts,
1968.

Useful selected list.

2779. Lipenius, Martin, *Bibliotheca Realis Philosophica*, 2 vols.
Hildesheim: Georg Olms Verlagsbuchhandlung, 1967.

Rev. *EP*, no. 4 (1967), 483.

Photographic reprint of Frankfurt a.M., 1682, ed. (mispagina-
tion of original retained). This valuable subject-index to
numerous topics of importance to Shakespeareans covers materials of 16th and 17th cents.("philosophy" used broadly, to
cover literary areas). Although its earlier reviewers criticized it harshly for its imperfections, it is one of few reprinted subject-guides to Renaissance books; despite its errors, a treasure-house of research opportunities in many
directions. It is to be hoped that all the subject-indexes
listed in Archer Taylor's *General Subject-Indexes since 1548*
(Univ. of Penn. Press, 1966) will similarly be made available.

2780. Litto, Fredric M., *American Dissertations on the Drama and the
Theatre: A Bibliography*. Kent, Ohio: Kent State Univ.
Press, 1969. Rev. *QJS*, 56 (1970), 319.

Brings together references to all doctoral dissertations on
subjects related to theater and drama completed in *all* academic departments of American (and Canadian) universities. Divided into: Bibliography, pp. 15-103; Author Index, pp. 105-
117; Key-Word-in-Context Index, pp. 119-345; Subject Index,
pp. 347-519.

(Raw data and computer programs which entered this work are on
magnetic tapes and available for use on application to the
author at The International Theatre Studies Center, The University of Kansas, Lawrence, Kansas 66044.)

2781. London, University of, *The Palaeography Collection in the University of London Library: An Author and Subject Catalogue*.
Boston, Mass.: G.K. Hall & Co., 1968. 2 vols.

Printed materials concerning manuscripts, both literary and
archival, in classical and western European languages. In two
alphabetical sequences; author catalogue has ca. 10,000 cards
reproduced in 1 volume; subject catalogue has ca. 13,000
cards reproduced in 1 volume.

2782. Lucas, Robert H., "Medieval French Translations of the Latin
Classics to 1500," *Speculum*, 45 (1970), 225-253.

To list of known translations adds Sallust's *Catilina and Jugurtha*, Cicero's *Pro Marcello*, Ovid's *Heroides*, and Publilius Syrus's *Sententiae*. Contains inventory of catalogues of French manuscript collections outside France.

2783. Marder, Louis, "Shakespeare's Glossaries, 1710-1948," *ShN*, 18 (1968), 22-23.

Annotated bibliography. Cites topic of each glossary and number of entries. Reviews quality of entries and definitions.

2784. Marshall, Robert G., ed., *Short-Title Catalog of Books Printed in Italy and of Books in Italian Printed Abroad, 1501-1600, Held in Selected North American Libraries.* Boston: G.K. Hall, 1970.

15,600 slips, 1,954 pp., 3 volumes. "Books printed in Italy and Italian books printed abroad during the 16th cent. In general, the volume follows the lines of the *Short-Title Catalogue of Italian Books, 1465-1600, of the British Museum* (London, 1958)."

2785. Martin, Henri-Jean, *Livre, Pouvoirs et Société à Paris au XVII siècle (1598-1701).* Geneva: Droz, 1969.

Rev. *RSH*, 36 (1971), 127-134.

Published matter and manuscript and archive sources statistically analyzed to document economics and attitudes of the period. Documents intellectual and literary history, sociology of reading, and legislation affecting intellectual production.

2786. McAvoy, William C., "A Review of 1968's Contributions to English Renaissance Textual Studies," *Manuscripta*, 14 (1970), 113-160.

Survey of studies on texts from 1475 to 1642, excluding Shakespeare.

2787. ―――――, "The Year's Contribution to English Renaissance Textual Study," *Manuscripta*, 13 (1969), 12-31.

Survey of textual studies of works dating from 1475-1642 which appeared in 1966-1967. Studies of Shakespeare's texts are omitted.

2788. McGill, W.J., "The *Catholic Historical Review*: A Note," 54 (1968), 311-314.

Results of a systematic study of abstracts in the *CHR* since its origin (1915), with a view to selecting the articles (about 30) relating to the history of the Renaissance and the Reformation.

2789. McKenzie, D.F., "Printers of the Mind: Some Notes on Bibliographical Theories and Printing-House Practices," *SB*, 22 (1969), 1-75.

Inconsistencies with actual practices of printing houses seen in theories of analytical bibliographers (especially in regard to cast-off copy, skeleton forms, proof-correction, and press figures), based on physical evidence found in extant copies of books. Bibliographers have assumed that all the energies of a shop were directed toward one book at one time; but concurrent printing was the rule, not the exception. Calls for the publication of more primary documentation.

2790. McNamee, Lawrence F., *Dissertations in English and American Literature: Supplement One: Theses Accepted by American, British, and German Universities, 1964-1968.* N.Y.: Bowker, 1969.

Rev. *SCN*, 28 (1970), 12.

List of 4,382 dissertations, including not only American, British, and German, but also those from New Zealand, Australian, and Canadian (pre-1964 as well) universities. This supplements the first volume (1968), which included 14,521 dissertations written 1865-1963 and was limited to American, British, and German universities.

2791. Michel, S.P., "Dans la forêt obscure des livres du 'Seicento,'" *Studi fr.*, 35 (1968), 21-29.

Discusses the *Répertoire des ouvrages imprimés en langue italienne au XVIIe siècle* ..., union list of 17th-cent. Italian imprints in French libraries. (Cf. below.)

2792. ————, and Paul Henri Michel, *Répertoire des ouvrages imprimés en langue italienne au XVIIe siècle conservés dans les bibliothèques de France.* Paris: Editions de Centre National de la Recherche Scientifique, 1967-. Vol. 1- (A-B).

Seventeenth-cent. bibliography and union list, this work provides locations of Italian imprints in over 50 French libraries (including Bibliothèque Nationale). Includes only books, predominantly literary (especially dramatic) and religious. Arrangement by author; anonymous works will appear after completion of main author list. Provides brief note on author, followed by his titles; includes collation and further notes where relevant.

2793. Mish, Charles C., "English Short Fiction in the Seventeenth Century," *Studs. in Short Fiction*, 6 (1969), 233-320.

Pt. I covers 1600-1660; 1. Tales of Sentiment; 2. Collections of Tales; 3. Popular Short Fiction; 4. Picaresque and Miscellaneous Fiction.

2794. Molinaro, Julius A., comp., *A Bibliography of Sixteenth-Century Italian Verse Collections in the University of Toronto Library.* Univ. of Toronto Press, 1969.

Rev. *BHR*, 32 (1970), 507-508.

Analytic bibliography of 115 items representing verse collections by individual poets, anthologies, and two separately printed *canzoni* by Anguilara and Guarnello. Also contains 13 16th-cent. editions of Petrarch. Includes Bibliography,

Index of Editors and Works Edited; Index of Printers and
Works; Works Published by Unidentified Printers; Index of
Dedicatees; List of Portraits of Poets; First Editions; First
Lines of Anonymous Poems; Index to the volume.

2795.   Muir, Kenneth, and S. Schoenbaum, eds., *A New Companion to
        Shakespeare Studies*. Cambridge Univ. Press, 1971.

        Includes articles on Shakespeare's reading (G.K. Hunter); on
        Shakespeare's use of rhetoric (Brian Vickers); on Shakespeare
        and music (F.W. Sternfeld); on the historical and social back-
        ground (Joel Hurstfield); on Shakespeare and the thought of
        his age (W.R. Elton). Rev. *RES*, n.s. 23 (1972), 485.

2796.   National Maritime Museum at Greenwich, *National Maritime Mu-
        seum Catalogue of the Library, Vol. II, Biography (Two Parts)*.
        Greenwich, Eng.: National Maritime Museum, 1970.

        Rev. *Scott. Hist. Rev.*, 50 (1971), 82-83.

        Annotated and chronologically arranged volume. Includes a
        reference index of biographies for 15,000 maritime figures.

2797.   Neu, John, ed., "Ninety-third Critical Bibliography of the
        History of Science and its Cultural Influences (to Jan. 1968),"
        Isis, 59 (1968), 1-241.

        Classification both by chronology and subject. Cites book re-
        views; includes index. Includes Renaissance and Reformation,
        1450-1600: general histories of science; exact sciences;
        natural history; pseudo-science and experiments; technology;
        exploration; medicine. Annual.

2798.   Osburn, Charles B., *Research and Reference Guide to French
        Studies*. Metuchen, N.J.: Scarecrow Press, 1968.

        Guide to bibliographic entries; especially useful for its bib-
        liographies of genres and individual authors, and for its in-
        clusion of chapters on dissertations, scholars and critics,
        Romance philology, French language and literature abroad, Pro-
        vençal, medieval and later Latin, comparative literature.

2799.   *Oxford Latin Dictionary*, ed. P.G.W. Glare et al., Fascicle 1.
        A-Cal. Oxford Univ. Press, 1968; Fascicle 2. *Calcitro-
        Demitro*. Oxford Univ. Press, 1969.

        First such dictionary to be based on thorough reading of all
        available literary and epigraphical sources in contexts, to
        c. 200 A.D.; 35 years in preparation; analogous to *OED*. Eight
        fascicles are to appear at two-year intervals.

2800.   Pantzer, Katharine F., "The Serpentine Progress of the *STC*
        Revision," *Papers Bibl. Soc. Am.*, 62 (1968), 297-311.

        Comments by its present editor on its progress and problems.

2801.   Parker, Alexander A., "Recent Scholarship in Spanish Litera-
        ture," *RenQ*, 21 (1968), 118-124.

Leading arguments in current Spanish literary scholarship,
focusing on Américo Castro and his disciples; critical of
sociological use and interpretations of literature.

2802. Parks, George B., and Ruth Z. Temple, comps., *The Greek and
Latin Literatures: A Bibliography.* The Literatures of the
World in English Translations, Vol. 1. N.Y.: Ungar, 1968.

2803. Plezia, Marian et al., eds., *Lexicon Mediae et Infimae Latini-
tatis Polonorum: Vol. II, Fasc. 4-8; Vol. III, Fasc. I,
Fasciculus Extra Ordinem Editus.* Warsaw: Polska Akademia
Nauk, 1961-1969.

Rev. *RenQ,* 23 (1970), 170-172.

Glosses large number of words unattested in modern Latin lexi-
cons and used by 16th-cent. Latin writers in Poland. Terminal
dates 1000 and 1506 (neither, however, strictly observed);
lists a large number of Latin words unattested in modern lexi-
cons and employed by Polish writers in the 15th cent. Thus it
makes available to students of Renaissance Latin (1400-1600)
the only present modern lexical aid to post-medieval Latin
vocabulary.

2804. [Public Record Office, London], *A List of Wills, Administra-
tions, etc., in the Public Record Office, London, England,
12th-19th Century.* Baltimore: Magna Carta Book Co., 1968.

Reproduction from typewritten copy in reference collection of
the P.R.O.

2805. Rancoeur, René, *Bibliographie de la littérature française du
Moyen Age à nos jours: Année 1966.* Paris: Colin, 1967.

Useful work; pp. 38-75 deal with 16th and 17th cents.; first
section includes bibliography, etc.; themes covered in pp.
6-25. Annual.

2806. Raven, Anton A., *"Hamlet" Bibliography and Reference Guide.*
N.Y.: Russell & Russell, 1968.

Reprint of 1936 edition of useful, annotated bibliography,
model of its kind. Urgently requires updating.

2807. Ritcheson, Charles R., and O.T. Hargrave, *Current Research in
British Studies by American and Canadian Scholars--1968.* Dal-
las: Southern Methodist Univ. Press, 1969.

Published quadrennially for the Conference on British Studies;
includes approximately 850 contributors.

2808. Robbins, Rossell Hope, "Middle English Research in Progress,
1969-1970," *NM,* 71 (1970), 501-504.

Contains books, articles, textbooks, reviews in proof and
print. Excludes Old English, Chaucer, and late Tudor studies.
Annual.

2809.   Rollins, Hyder E., comp., *An Analytical Index to the Ballad-Entries (1557-1709) in the Registers of the Company of Stationers of London.* Hatboro, Pa.: Tradition Press, 1967. Reprint of useful index.

2810.   Rosenbach, A.S.W., *The Rosenbach Catalogues*, 10 vols. N.Y.: McGraw-Hill, 1968.

Collects in facsimile 74 catalogues of rare books and manuscripts issued by Rosenbach; useful reference guide, with annotations to individual entries. Separate volume of essays, *To Dr. R.*, also contains complete index.

2811.   Rouse, Richard H., *Serial Bibliographies for Medieval Studies.* Berkeley: Univ. of Calif. Press, 1969. Rev. *Spec.*, 45 (1970), 343.

Includes: General Bibliographies; National and Regional Bibliographies; Byzantine, Islamic, etc.; Auxiliary Studies; Art and Archaeology; Ecclesiastical History; Economic, Social, etc.; Intellectual History; Literature and Linguistics; Music; Science, Technology, etc.

2812.   Rijksbureau voor Kunsthistorische Documentatie, *Decimal Index of Art in the Low Countries.* Netherlands Institute for Art History, Univ. of Leiden; Korte Vijverberg 7, The Hague.

Paralleling the Index of Christian Art (at Princeton; copy at UCLA) which covers religious works to 1400, the *D.I.A.L.* covers religious and secular subjects (in paintings, engravings, and drawings) in the Low Countries, ca. 1400-1800. Includes cards with photographs (ca. 9,000 in 1967), 500 being added yearly; each card has subject designation, attribute, date, source of reproduction. Cards contain serial number relating to master negative at the Rijksbureau, from which glossy reproductions can be ordered at low cost. (Decimal index by general topics, e.g., 1. Supernatural, God, religion; 2. Nature; 3. Man; 4. Society; 5. Abstract Ideas; 6. History; 7. Bible; 8. Myths, legends not of biblical or classical origin; 9. Myths, etc., of classical origin; each number followed by letter for progressive subdivision.) Price of one series (in 1967) of 500 cards: Dutch fl. 150, plus a small charge for postage (one card therefore costing then less than 10 American cents). Subscribers to the index receive, with the cards, a survey of the *D.I.A.L.* iconographic system, the alphabetical index of the subject headings of the published cards, and periodical lists with corrections.

2813.   Schulz, H.C., "English Literary Manuscripts in the Huntington Library," *HLQ*, 31, no. 3 (1968), 251-302.

Significant list of approximately 33,400 manuscripts written by 495 authors.

2814.   *Shakespeare-Literatur in Bochum.* Aus den Bestanden des Englischen Seminars, des Germanistischen Instituts und der Universitätsbibliothek der Ruhr-Universität Bochum, der Deutschen Shakespeare Gesellschaft West und der Stadtbücherei Bochum. Stadtbücherei Bochum, 1968.

Rev. *ES*, 49 (1968), 476.

Contains 236-page catalogue of Shakespearean library.

2815. Sinclair, K.V., *Descriptive Catalogue of Medieval and Renaissance Western Manuscripts in Australia*. Sydney Univ. Press: London: Methuen, 1969.

Rev. *TLS*, 9 April 1970, p. 392.

Describes about two dozen institutional and as many private collections. Only one manuscript dating from after 1550 is, exceptionally, included. Books of Hours and other liturgical manuscripts are by far the most common. Among English manuscripts Bracton, Britton and the *Brut* appear, with some volumes of the statutes. There are some humanist manuscripts of classical texts, a fair amount of canon law, and some archival material such as quitclaims, letters patent, and conveyances.

2816. Smith, Charles G., *Spenser's Proverb Lore, with Special Reference to His Use of the "Sententiae" of Leonard Culman and Publilius Syrus*. Cambridge, Mass.: Harvard Univ. Press, 1970.

Rev. *Choice*, 7 (1970), 1223.

Contains brief introduction, a list of proverbs with references and annotations, followed by a brief bibliography and Latin word, English word, and distribution indexes.

2817. Smith, William G., ed., *Oxford Dictionary of English Proverbs*, 3rd rev. ed., by F.P. Wilson. London: Oxford Univ. Press, 1970.

Rev. *Choice*, 8 (1971), 48, 50.

Revised and modernized guide to literary sources of 10,000 proverbial phrases; contains new material in form of both additional proverbs and earlier references to proverbs included in previous editions.

2818. Spevack, Marvin, *A Complete and Systemic Concordance to the Works of Shakespeare*. Vol. I: Drama and Character Concordances to the Folio Comedies. Vol. II: Drama and Character Concordances to the Folio Histories, Concordances to the Non-Dramatic Works. Vol. III: Drama and Character Concordances to the Folio Tragedies and *Pericles, The Two Noble Kinsmen, Sir Thomas More*. Hildesheim: Georg Olms, 1969.

Rev. *TLS*, 14 August 1969, 903.

First three volumes include individual concordances for each of the plays and poems, individual concordances for each of the characters in each of the plays, concordances of the *Two Noble Kinsmen*, and the "Sh'n" scenes of *Sir Thomas More*, and a composite concordance of all the non-dramatic poems. Frequency of each word is recorded, and relative frequency (expressed as a percentage) of each word in the play and in the speeches of each character.

2819. Steel, Donald John, ed., *National Index of Parish Registers*, Vol. V: *A Guide to Anglican, Roman Catholic, and Nonconformist*

Registers Before 1837, Together with Information on Marriage
Licenses, Bishop's Transcripts, and Modern Copies; South Mid-
lands and Welsh Border comprising the Counties of Gloucester-
shire, Herefordshire, Shropshire, Warwickshire, and Worcester-
shire. London Society of Genealogists; Baltimore: Magna Carta
Book Co., 1967-[1968].

2820. Stubbings, Hilda U., *Renaissance Spain in Its Literary Relations with England and France: A Critical Bibliography*.
Nashville, Tenn.: Vanderbilt Univ. Press, 1969.

Rev. *BHS*, 47 (1970), 154; *PSBA*, 64 (1970), 251-252; *SCN*, 18
(1970), 33-34.

Annotated bibliography listing over 360 works. On phases of
Renaissance Spanish influence, in literature or culture, on
the literature and/or culture of England and France during the
16th, 17th, and 18th cents. Listed on this subject if in
Spanish, English, or French.

2821. ——————, "A Selective and Annotated Bibliography of Articles,
Monographs, and Books Dealing with the Influence of Peninsular
Spanish Literature of the Golden Age (c. 1560 to 1681) on the
Literatures of England and France During the Sixteenth, Seven-
teenth, and Eighteenth Centuries," *DA*, 29 (1969), 2230-2231-A
(Vanderbilt Univ.).

Compiled with attention to needs of students of these literatures in the United States; items include only books, monographs, and articles which can be found in at least the larger
American libraries.

2822. Sugden, Edward H., *A Topographical Dictionary to the Works of
Shakespeare and His Fellow-Dramatists*. London and N.Y.: Manchester Univ. Press, 1925; N.Y.: Adler, 1969.

Important tool, now available in reprint. Brief accounts of
places cited in Shakespeare's plays and those of his fellow
dramatists.

2823. Sugeno, Frank E., "Episcopal and Anglican History, 1969: An
Annotated Bibliography," *Hist. Mag. of the Prot. Episc. Church*,
39 (1970), 199-241.

Annual bibliography of church history.

2824. Taylor, Archer, *General Subject-Indexes Since 1548*. Philadelphia: Univ. of Pennsylvania Press, 1966; London: Oxford Univ.
Press, 1967.

Rev. *Library*, 5th ser., 23 (1968), 260-261.

Useful account of subject-indexes, still of much importance;
reprinting all such subject-indexes would be a service to
Renaissance studies.

2825. Thompson, Lawrence Sidney, *A Bibliography of American Doctoral
Dissertations in Classical Studies and Related Fields*. Hamden,
Conn.: Shoe String Press, 1968. Rev. *Coll. Res.*, 30 (1969),
77.

2826. Tonelli, Giorgio, *A Short-Title List of Subject Dictionaries of the Sixteenth, Seventeenth and Eighteenth Centuries as Aids to the History of Ideas.* (Warburg Institute Surveys, ed. E.H. Gombrich and J.B. Trapp, Vol. 4.) London: The Warburg Institute, 1971.

Rev. *JHI*, 33 (1971), 177-178.

Useful, if incomplete, list of Renaissance dictionaries and encyclopedias valuable for history of ideas. Copies located in libraries. Emphasis on terms and concepts, excluding onomastic dictionaries. Important subject listing, among other indexes. This is a barely exploited area of materials, and the work is but a start towards making fuller use of such research tools. As with early subject indexes (cf. Lipenius above), these early works could profitably be reprinted.

2827. Velz, John W., *Shakespeare and the Classical Tradition: A Critical Guide to Commentary, 1660-1960.* Minneapolis: Univ. of Minn. Press; Toronto: Copp Clark, 1968.

Annotated critical bibliography, with 2,487 references to books, articles, and other materials related to Shakespeare's use of the Greek and Roman past. Useful reference tool arranged by: General Works, Comedies; Histories, Plays on Classical Themes, Tragedies, Last Plays, Poems and Sonnets, Shakespeare's Classics. Full index. Rev. *TLS*, 15 May 1969, 532.

2828. Walther, Hans, ed., *Proverbia sententiaeque latinitatis medii aevi. Lateinische Sprichwörter und Sentenzen des Mittelalters in alphabetischer Anordnung,* Vol. 5. Göttingen: Vandenhoeck & Ruprecht, 1967.

Rev. of earlier volumes in *Historische Zeitschrift*, 204 (1967), 627-629. Collection of Latin proverbs of the Middle Ages, useful adjunct to Tilley and B.J. Whiting.

2829. Wells, James M., "Reports on Scholarship in the Renaissance: Palaeography, Bibliography, and Printing," *Ren. News*, 19 (1966), 169-173.

Discusses recent work.

2830. Whalley, Joyce Irene, *English Handwriting 1540-1853: An Historical Survey Based on Material in the National Art Library.* Victoria and Albert Museum. London: H.M.S.O., 1969.

An illustrated survey of English handwriting with an historical introduction.

2831. Wheatley, Henry Benjamin, *London, Past and Present: A Dictionary of Its History ... Based on "Handbook of London," by Peter Cunningham.* Reprint of 1891 edition; 3 volumes; Detroit: Singing Press, 1968.

Rev. *SCN*, 26 (1968), 59-60.

2832. White, R.C., "Early Geographical Dictionaries," *Geogr. Rev.*, 58, no. 4 (1968), 652-659.

Classical period; Arab world; Renaissance, 17th cent.

2833. Williams, Franklin B., Jr., "Photofacsimiles of 'STC' Books:
       A Sequel," *SB*, 23 (1970), 252-253. (Cf. *SB*, 21 [1968], 109-
       130.)

       A few addenda and some comments by the compiler of "Photo-
       facsimiles of STC Books: A Cautionary Check List."

2834. Ziegler, Konrat, ed., *Supplementband XI* to *Paulys Realencyclo-
       pädie der Classischen Altertumswissenschaft*. Stuttgart:
       Alfred Druckenmüller Verlag, 1968.

       Covers Abragila to Zengisai. 1,378 columns of recent mater-
       ials, additions to various articles.

2835. ————, and Walther Sontheimer, eds., *Der Kleine Pauly, Lexi-
       kon der Antike auf der Grundlage von Paulys Realencyclopädie
       der Classischen Altertumswissenschaft*, Vol. II: *Dicta Catonis
       bis Juno*. Stuttgart: Alfred Druckenmüller Verlag, 1967.

       Rev. *Rivista di Studi Classici*, 18 (1970), 158-159.

       Useful up-to-date abridgement with recent bibliography of the
       great encyclopedia of classical knowledge.

Index of Authors 451